Educational
Psychology

Third Edition

Educational Psychology

Theory into Practice

Robert E. Slavin

Johns Hopkins University

ALLYN AND BACON
Boston   London   Toronto   Sydney   Tokyo   Singapore

Library of Congress Cataloging-in-Publication Data

Slavin, Robert E.
    Educational psychology : theory into practice / Robert E. Slavin.
 -- 3rd ed.
        p.   cm.
    Includes bibliographical references (p.).
    ISBN 0-13-237751-9
    1. Educational psychology.   I. Title.
LB1051.S615 1991
370.15--dc20   90-31310
                                                   CIP

For Jacob, Benjamin, and Rebecca, and their teachers.

Cover Photo: "Tepepul el Adivino," Carlos Merida. Photo from Three Lions.

 Copyright © 1991, 1988, 1986 by Allyn and Bacon
A Division of Simon & Schuster, Inc.
160 Gould Street
Needham Heights, MA 02194

ISBN 0-13-237751-9

Printed in the United States of America

10 9 8 7 6 5 4 3 2   95 94 93 92 91

(Acknowledgments appear on page 597, which constitutes a continuation of the copyright page.)

Contents

Chapter 1

Educational Psychology: A Tool for Teachers 1

Part 1   Development

Chapter 2

Theories of Development 23

Part 2 Learning

Chapter 5

Information Processing and Memory   129

Chapter 6

Meaningful Learning: The Cognitive Perspective   161

Part 3   Instruction

Chapter 9   Accommodating Student Differences   275

Chapter 10   Motivation   317

Chapter 11 Classroom Management 361

Part 4 Individual Differences

Chapter 12 Exceptional Students 403

Chapter 15   Testing and Interpreting Standardized Tests   509

Preface

When I first set out to write *Educational Psychology: Theory into Practice,* I had a very clear objective in mind. What I wanted to do was to give tomorrow's teachers the intellectual grounding and practical strategies needed to be effective as instructors. In looking at the texts that existed then, I felt that most fell into two categories: stuffy and lightweight. The stuffy books were full of research but ponderously written, losing the flavor of the classroom and containing few guides to practice. The lightweight texts were breezy and easy to read, but lacking in research and the dilemmas and intellectual issues brought out by research. They contained suggestions for practice of the "Try This!" variety, without considering evidence about the effectiveness of the strategies suggested.

What I wanted to do was to see if it was possible to write a text that was as complete and up-to-date as the most research-focused texts, but was readable, practical, and loaded with examples and illustrations of key ideas. I wanted to include suggestions for practice based directly on classroom research (tempered by common sense), so that I could have confidence that if teachers actually tried what I suggested, it would be likely to work. I wanted to write the kind of book that I would like to read myself—even though I have been doing educational research for two decades, I find that I never really understand theory or concepts in education until someone writes me a compelling classroom example, and I'm willing to bet that most of my colleagues (and certainly students) feel the same way. As a result, the words "for example" or their equivalent must appear hundreds of times in this text. I have tried to write this book in such a way that the reader will almost hear children's voices and smell the lunch cooking in the school cafeteria. I believe that if there is any chance that students will transfer what they learn in educational psychology to their own teaching, texts (and instructors) must make the connection between theory and practice explicit by the use of many realistic examples.

I can't say whether or not I have succeeded in what I set out to do; that is for the reader to judge. But in this third edition, I have tried to continue to achieve the objectives I had in the first and second editions. I have made changes throughout the text, adding examples, refining language, deleting dated or unessential material. I am a fanatic about keeping the text up-to-date. The text now has about thirteen hundred citations, and about half are from the 1980s. I know that students usually don't care much about citations, but I want them and their professors to know what support exists for any statements I've made and where to find additional information.

The field of educational psychology and the practice of education have changed a great deal in the past three years, and I have tried to reflect this in the text. Only three years ago, direct instruction and related teacher effectiveness research were dominant in educational psychology. Today, discovery learning, constructivist theories of learning, authentic assessment, and other humanistic strategies are once again coming to the fore. In the first and second editions of this test I had a statement (in Chapter 8) to the effect that we shouldn't discard discovery learning and humanistic methods entirely, despite the (then) current popularity of direct instruction. In revising the text this statement seemed oddly anachronistic (even though it is only three years old!).

This edition presents new research and practical applications of these and many other topics. It has new sections on recent conceptions of intelligence and learning styles, continues to update research in the rapidly developing "cognitive revolution" in educational psychology, presents new developments relating to ability grouping, cooperative learning, compensatory and special education, new methods of assessment, and treatments for test anxiety.

Given the developments of the past two decades, no one can deny that teachers matter, that their behaviors have a profound impact on student achievement. To have a positive impact, teachers must have both a deep understanding of the powerful principles of psychology as they apply to education and a clear sense of how these principles can be applied. Effective teaching is neither a bag of tricks nor a set of abstract principles; rather, it is intelligent application of well-understood principles to solve practical problems. I hope this third edition will help give teachers the intellectual and practical skills needed to do the most important job in the world.

HOW THIS BOOK IS ORGANIZED

This book is divided into five principal sections—Development, Learning, Instruction, Individual Differences, and Measurement and Evaluation. Each section has several chapters. Within each chapter is a discussion of important theories, with many examples of how these theories apply to classroom teaching.

This book emphasizes the intelligent use of theory and research to improve instruction. The Instruction section, though only one of the five sections, occupies about one-third of the total pages in the book, and the other chapters all contain references to the meaning of theories and research findings for practice. Whenever possible, the guides for practice in this book are specific programs or strategies that have been evaluated and found to be effective, not just suggestions for things to try. Surgeons are not just given an anatomy course, a scapel, and some hints for practice; rather, they are given specific procedures that are known to work. This book takes a similar approach to teaching. This edition has been revised to place a greater emphasis on "critical thinking," engaging the reader with dilemmas, controversial issues, and research puzzles to present them with the ideas of educational psychology in a way that cannot be accomplished when the subject is presented as a set of well-established, noncontroversial facts.

FEATURES

The goal of giving teachers the tools they need to do their job better is addressed by this book's major feature, the **Theory into Practice** sections that are presented throughout the text. All chapters but the first have at least one Theory into Practice section and many have two or three such sections. These sections present strategies for instructional activities ranging from planning courses to presenting lessons to adapting instruction to meet the needs of students with academic handicaps.

The book's **Teachers on Teaching** sections, presented in all chapters, also contribute to the goal of making this a practical, useful book. In these sections, over 100 teachers offer their ideas on topics such as how to reinforce the desirable behavior of students, how to help students transfer school learning to situations outside the classroom, and how to present instructional objectives to students.

There are two features new to this edition. One is called **Case to Consider.** These are vignettes of classroom life or conversations among teachers designed to create controversy about controversial issues. In line with this edition's focus on critical thinking, the purpose of the **Case to Consider** is to place the reader in the position of a teacher facing a difficult decision or problem. For example, this feature includes vignettes relating to the moral development of elementary students (a class setting class rules), mainstreaming (a teacher frustrated with a mainstreamed child), and standardized testing (two teachers arguing about the ethics and practicality of "teaching to the test"). These cases are meant to avoid pat or simple answers, and to create a conversation in which students can air their own views and sharpen their understanding in discourse with others. Most of these cases were written by Gordon Greenwood of the University of Florida.

A second new feature is called **Focus On.** These sections present issues in the news that relate to education, from concerns about grade repetition and ability grouping to items on "flashbulb memories" and the "Lake Wobegon" effect in standardized testing. Each **Focus On** box shows how material in the text is related to issues brought up every day in the media, and helps students see the place that education and educational psychology have in the broader world.

Other features in *Educational Psychology: Theory into Practice* are designed to help the reader grasp the book's content. It is only fitting that a book that describes effective methods of teaching should itself put these principles to work. This book tries to do just that.

For example, research on how people learn suggests that students should be introduced to a topic before studying it in depth. Two features at the beginning of each chapter serve this purpose. They are

- A **chapter outline** that acquaints the reader with the organization and content of each chapter
- Chapter **learning objectives** that state what the reader should be able to do after reading the chapter

Inserted throughout each chapter (new to this edition) are **Stop and Think** questions that give students an opportunity to pause and reflect on what they have read and to relate it to their own experience and background knowledge.

Features at the end of each chapter are designed to encourage readers to think about and remember the chapter's content. These features are

- A **summary** that recaps main points
- **Study questions** that focus on important facts and concepts
- **Suggested readings** that direct the student to important supplementary materials

In addition, within each chapter important **glossary terms** are printed in boldface type the first time they are used in a significant way. Definitions of the terms are given in the margin of the page. An end-of-book glossary provides an additional reference for students and teachers, as do the book's name index, subject index, and list of references.

SUPPLEMENTS

The **Annotated Instructor's Edition (AIE)** coordinates all the instructor and student supplements so you fully benefit from these resources. It provides a wide range of useful information in the margins, such as examples, abstracts, demonstrations, activities, discussion questions, teaching ideas, and additional research citations. All annotations are keyed into the Instructor's Manual, the Video Teaching Package, the Educational Psychology Computer Disk, and the Transparency Masters.

Instructor's Manual (IM), a rich resource for teaching ideas, includes an outline of each text chapter, chapter overviews and objectives, lecture notes, class activities, essay and discussion questions, and a list of related video, audio, and print sources to draw upon. This manual is authored by James Neal of California State University at Sacramento.

Over 1,100 questions in multiple choice, true-false, and essay formats are available in the **Test Item File.** The multiple choice questions are divided into two categories: general questions and more challenging scholar's questions—helping you prepare tests of varying degrees of difficulty. The answer key to the Test Item File is page-referenced to the text. This supplement is authored by Steve Ross of Memphis State University.

Critical Thinking Video is a professionally-produced video designed to coordinate and enhance *Educational Psychology, 3E,* and your course. The video explores a variety of issues in educational psychology today that correspond to issues found in *Educational Psychology, 3E,* and your course. It is composed of classroom scenes that will help your students better understand how to apply educational psychology to their teaching.

The **Video Teaching Package** is composed of brief (5-10 minute) segments taken from actual classrooms. Totally 60-minutes long, this video illustrates classroom applications and "critical thinking" incidents through such selected topics from the text as behavioral principles, reciprocal teaching, cooperative learning, classroom management, and the lesson.

"Catch 'Em Being Good" Video is a 30-minute video which demonstrates research-based methods for dealing with students who have academic or social difficulties.

The **Transparency Masters** can involve your students and stimulate classroom discussion as well as enhance your lectures with visual amplification of key theories, studies, and topics. All represent charts and illustrations from the book as well as other appropriate activities. And to integrate them more effectively in your lectures, we reference them in the **Instructor's Manual.** The package contains over 50 masters that are keyed to the text and referenced to the AIE.

Prentice Hall offers many ways to help you make up your tests. The **Prentice Hall DataManager** is a state-of-the-art classroom management system that contains three components: **Test Manager**—the test generating system, **Grade Manager**—the grading program, and **Study Manager** a study guide program that has computer network features—all of which are easy to learn and use with IBM and compatible computers.

Apple Testing and MicroTest III, Macintosh Version, are computerized test generators that allows you to create, refine, update, store, and print a variety of tests utilizing your own questions or questions from the test item file.

Telephone Test Preparation allows you to select up to 200 questions from the Test Item File and call us toll free. Prentice Hall will prepare the test (and alternate version if requested) on bond paper or ditto master and mail it together with a separate answer key directly to you within 48 hours.

Educational Psychology on a Disk is a wealth of interactive activities and simulations that allow students to apply textbook principles to classroom experience. Available exclusively for Apple Computers.

For the Student

The **Study Guide and Workbook** help students apply concepts introduced in *Educational Psychology* through study questions, chapter outlines, objectives, key terms, essay and discussion questions, as well as activities.

The **Critical Thinking Audio Study Cassette** is a 60-minute cassette that shows students how developing their critical thinking and study skills will help improve reading, listening, writing, note taking, test performance, job preparation, and job performance. The first 50 minutes of the tape concentrates on critical-thinking skills; the final 10 minutes offers helpful tips on how to study, take notes, and be a more active, effective learner.

ACKNOWLEDGMENTS

The field of educational psychology is so large, and is growing so rapidly, that no one person can possibly know everything about it. For this reason, I relied on other colleagues for draft material for the first edition that provided background and references relating to specific topics outside my own areas of expertise. These colleagues and the chapters (or sections of chapters) of the book to which they contributed are: Jeffrey W. Fagen of St. John's University, Chapter 2, Theories of Development; Stacie G. Goffin of the University of Missouri—Kansas City, Chapter 3, Development During Early Childhood; Gerald W. Green and Craig Jones of the West Virginia College of Graduate Studies, Chapter 3, Development During Middle Childhood; Larry Shelton of the University of Vermont, Chapter 3, Development During Adolescence; William M. Zangwill, New York City, Chapter 4, Behavioral Theories of Learning; Thomas Andre of Iowa State University, Chapter 5, Information Processing and Memory, and Chapter 6, Meaningful Learning; Ralph E. Reynolds of the University of Utah, Chapter 6, Meaningful Learning: The Cognitive Perspective; Ronald L. Taylor of Florida Atlantic University and Frances L. Clark of the University of Louisville, Chapter 12, Exceptional Students; Sandra B. Damico of the University of Florida, Chapter 13, Social Class, Ethnicity and Gender; Thom B. Clark of the University of North Carolina, Chapter 14, Student Evaluation: Tests and Grades; and Philip L. Smith of the University of Wisconsin—Milwaukee, Chapter 15, Using and Interpreting Standardized Tests. Douglas H. Clements, Kent State University, contributed information on the use of computers in education. A special thank you to Gordon Greenwood of the University of Florida who authored the **Case to Consider** boxes.

I also wish to thank my many colleagues who served as reviewers for various sections of the book. Their comments provided valuable information that helped me present a more accurate and useful account of the principles and research in the field of educational psychology. These reviewers include

Linda M. Anderson, Michigan State University

Bonnie B. Armbruster, University of Illinois

Frederick T. Bail, University of Hawaii

Rebecca Barr, National College of Education

Phyllis C. Blumenfeld, University of Michigan

Henry T. Clark, Pennsylvania State University

Margaret W. Cohen, University of Missouri at St. Louis

John Llewellyn David, St. Thomas Aquinas College

Richard Duran, University of California, Santa Barbara

Stephen N. Elliott, Louisiana State University

Richard M. Gargiulo, University of Alabama at Birmingham

Russell Gersten, University of Oregon

Ajaipal S. Gill, Anne Arundel Community College

Bruce R. Hare, State University of New York at Stony Brook

Shelley Hymel, University of Waterloo

Luther M. Kindall, University of Tennessee

Gary Ladd, Purdue University

Tom McFariano, Lewis Clark State College

Cecil D. Mercer, University of Florida at Gainesville

Joel Milgram, University of Cincinnati

Gary Natriello, Teachers College Columbia University

Scott Paris, University of Michigan

Jeanette Roberds, Miami University

Judith M. Roegge, University of Texas at Austin

Barak Rosenshine, University of Illinois

Steven M. Ross, Memphis State University

Charol Shakeshaft, Hofstra University

Barry Wadsworth, Mount Holyoke College

I would also like to thank the many people at Prentice Hall who helped bring this project to fruition, including Susan Willig, executive editor for the first two editions and Carol Wada, editor for the third; Shelly Kupperman, production editor, Florence Dara Silverman, design director; Lorinda Morris-Nantz, photo editor; Debra Kesar, prepress buyer; Mary Ann Gloriande, manufacturing buyer, Roland Hernandez and Tracey Masella, marketing managers; Sharon Chambliss, supplemental books editor and, most particularly, Jane Ritter, the book's development editor. In addition to reading and editing everything I wrote, coordinating the efforts of the many contributors and reviewers, reminding me ever so gently but persistently of deadlines, and about a thousand other tasks, Jane Ritter drafted boxed features, chapter objectives, and questions.

I also want to thank the many teachers who responded to questionnaires and thereby offered the lessons of their experience to future teachers through the **Teachers on Teaching** sections in this book. These teachers are Laura Adkins, Worthington, Ohio; Charlotte Alexander, Orceola, Ark.; Randall Amour, Columbus, Tex.; Margaret Ball, Stratford, Wisc.; Valerie Bang-Jensen, Ithaca, N.Y.; Sharon Beauregard, Glastonbury, Conn., Todd Beese, Rockford, Wash.; Linda Bendorf, Iowa City, Iowa; Paula Ann Berneking, Louisville, Ky.; Jean Bloomquist, Dallas, Tex.; Myrna Bohman, Wausau, Wisc.; Carol Brennan, Trumbull, Conn.; Nadine Brock, Galloway, Ohio; Lavelle Bronniman, Friona, Tex.; Peggy Broxterman, Henderson, Nev.; Mary Bruskotter, Fort Jennings, Ohio; Dyanne Buckelew, Puryear, Tenn.; J. Burrow, Frisco, Tex.; Camille Caldemeyer, Princeton, Ind.; Frank Chambers, Albuquerque, N.M.; Carol Higgins Chasteen, Glasford, Ill.; Jack Clendaniel, Wilmington, Del.;

Sharon Cook, Columbia, Tenn.; Lucille Cramer, Hamtramck, Mich.; Kaye Cutchen, Eufaula, Ala.; Grace Dady, Herkimer, N.Y.; Phaedra Damianakos, New York, N.Y.; Jimmie Dean, Louisville, Ala.; Kevin Dennis, Mingo Junction, Ohio; Dan DiGuglielmo, North Arlington, N.J.; Sandra Dougherty, Shenandoah Junction, W.V.; Mary Dow, Columbus, Ohio; Leroy Durand, Tolono, Ill.; Helen Fields, Tornillo, Tex.; Curt Fulton, Wallkill, N.Y.; Myrta Gerren, Hartville, Ohio; Tom Glover, Belt, Mont.; Anna Grauer, Leesport, Pa.; Gilbert Green, Wilmington, Del.; Cheryl Groninger, Annandale, N.J.; Linda Haddock, Duncanville, Tex.; Carol Hamann, Wisconsin Rapids, Wisc.; Sandra Harrach, Scottsbluff, Neb.; Beverly Harrison, Omaha, Neb.; Gail Hartman, Hobbs, N.M.; Paul Hashem, Lackawanna, N.Y.; Elonda Hogue, Linwood, Kan.; Pat Holman, Marlton, N.J.; William Hug, Pioneer, Ohio; Carol Hyneman, Princeton, Ind.; Linda Jaques, Bellwood, Ill.; Patricia James, Elizabeth City, N.C.; Linda Johnson, Ringsted, Iowa; Shirley King, Dallas, Tex.; John Kobza, Merrillville, Ind.; Margaret LaDue, Lodgepole, S.D.; Betty Lavallee, Dallas, Tex.; Nancy Letts, White Plains, N.Y.; Barbara Levin, Berkeley, Cal.; Donna Lloyd, Maybrook, N.Y.; Marta Lustgraaf, Council Bluffs, Iowa; Debra Criss McFadden, Louisville, Ky.; Marie McIntosh, Newark, Del.; Mike Michelson, New York, N.Y.; Sherm Milcowitz, Hartford, Conn.; Thomas Moyer, Allentown, Penn.; Georganna O'Grady, San Fernando, Cal.; Beth Ohlsson, Frederick, Md.; Terry Olive, Elyria, Ohio; Judy Osburn, Rapid City, S.D.; Patricia Padgett, Pleasanton, Cal.; Dorothy Paulsen, Wausau, Wisc.; Donald Peterson, Ishpeming, Mich.; Charles Petkanas, Long Island City, N.Y.; Glenn Ploegstra, Westlake, Ohio; Krissy Potusna, Ransom, Ill.; Gretchen L. Powers, Lynville, Ind.; Sharon Reed, Bozeman, Mont.; Patricia Rentscher, Terre Haute, Ind.; Walter Roberts, Jr., Gentry, Ark.; Cecilia Ruhnke, Skidmore, Tex.; Lana Sammons, Salem, W.V.; Jean Sancken, Bourbonnais, Ill.; Suzanne Santarelli, Hershey, Pa.; Karen Schilling, Platteville, Wisc.; Deanna Seed, Placerville, Cal.; Audrey Seguin, Alpena, Mich.; Benetta Skrundz, East Chicago, Ind.; Elinor Sorenson, Wilmette, Ill.; Lloyd Stableford, Westport, Conn.; Carol Steele, Gentry, Ark.; Ed Stowell, Newark, Del.; Susan Stoya, Glen Falls, N.Y.; Joseph Sugamele, East Syracuse, N.Y.; Roseanne Swinburne-Sanderfoot, Manawa, Wisc.; Ann Taylor, Dallas, Tex.; Lorraine Thompson, Statesville, N.C.; Richard Thorne, Jr., Stoughton, Mass.; Arlene Vander Geest, Pellston, Mich.; Mary Van Dyke, Atchison, Kan.; Joseph Venuto, West Chester, Pa.; Cheryl Vigue, Pittsfield, Maine; Albertine Warren, Corinth, Miss.; Judy Weeks, Dyersburg, Tenn.; Pamela Weiss, Shawnee Mission, Kan.; Ralph Westenberger, Louisville, Ala.; Peggy Woosley, Stuttgart, Ark.; Pam Woolsey, Knoxville, Ill.

Finally, it is customary to acknowledge the long-suffering patience of one's spouse and children. In my case, this acknowledgment is especially appropriate. My wife, Nancy Madden, not only read and commented on every word, but also as my co-worker kept our classroom research going while I was in the throes of writing. Our children, Jacob, Benjamin, and Rebecca (who were not particularly patient or long-suffering) did, however, contribute to this work by providing cute examples for sections of Chapter 3. They also provided me with a sense of purpose for writing; I had to keep thinking about the kind of school experience I want for them, as a way of making concrete my concern for the school experiences for all children.

This book was written while I was supported in part by grants from the Office of Educational Research and Improvement, U.S. Department of Education (Nos. OERI-G-86-0006 and OERI-R-117-R90002). However, any opinions I have expressed are mine alone, and do not represent OERI positions or policy.

R.E.S.

THE NEW YORK TIMES and PRENTICE HALL are sponsoring A CONTEMPORARY VIEW: a program designed to enhance student access to current information of relevance in the classroom.

Through this program, the core subject matter provided in the text is supplemented by a collection of time-sensitive articles from one of the world's most distinguished newspapers, THE NEW YORK TIMES. These articles demonstrate the vital, ongoing connection between what is learned in the classroom and what is happening in the world around us.

To enjoy the wealth of information of THE NEW YORK TIMES daily, a reduced subscription rate is available. For information, call toll-free: 1-800-631-1222.

PRENTICE HALL and THE NEW YORK TIMES are proud to co-sponsor A CONTEMPORARY VIEW. We hope it will make the reading of both textbooks and newspapers a more dynamic, involving process.

Robert Slavin is currently the director of the Elementary School Program of the Center for Research on Elementary and Middle Schools, and co-director of the Early and Elementary School Program of the Center for Research on Effective Schooling for Disadvantaged Students, Johns Hopkins University. He received his Ph.D. in Social Relations from Johns Hopkins in 1975, and since that time has authored more than 120 articles and book chapters on such topics as cooperative learning, ability grouping, school and classroom organization, desegregation, mainstreaming, and research review. Dr. Slavin is the author or co-author of ten books, including *Cooperative Learning, Educational Psychology: Theory into Practice, School and Classroom Organization,* and *Effective Programs for Students at Risk.* In 1985, Dr. Slavin received the Raymond Cattell Early Career Award for Programmatic Research from the American Educational Research Association, and in 1988 he received the Palmer O. Johnson Award for the best article in an AERA journal in 1986.

Educational Psychology: A Tool for Teachers

Chapter Outline

What Makes a Good Teacher?
Can Good Teaching Be Taught?

Educational Psychology: A Problem-Solving Approach
Teaching as Critical Thinking
Why Is Research in Educational Psychology Important?
What Good Is Educational Psychology to the Teacher?

Research Methods in Educational Psychology
Experiments
Correlational Studies
Descriptive Research

Why Teaching Is the Hardest Job in the World, and Why Teachers Secretly Love It—A Dedication

Chapter Objectives

This chapter tells you about educational psychology and how it can help teachers do their job better. After reading the chapter you should be able to:

- List the major questions that educational psychologists try to answer.

- Describe several types of experiments used to understand learning.

- Describe the difference between a correlational relationship and a causal relationship.

WHAT MAKES A GOOD TEACHER?

What makes a good teacher? Is it warmth, humor, and caring about people? Is it planning, hard work, and self-discipline? What about leadership, enthusiasm, a contagious love of learning, and speaking ability? Most people would agree that all of these qualities are needed to make someone a good teacher, and they would certainly be correct. But these qualities are not enough.

Knowing the Subject Matter Matters. There is an old joke that goes something like this:

Q. What do you need to know to be able to teach a horse?

A. More than the horse!

This joke makes the obvious point that the first thing a teacher must have is some knowledge or skills that the learner does not have; teachers must know the subject matter they expect to teach. But if you think about teaching horses (or children), you will soon realize that while subject matter knowledge is necessary, it is not enough. A cowboy might have a good idea of how a horse is supposed to act and what a horse is supposed to be able to do, but if he doesn't have the skills to make an untrained, scared, and unfriendly animal into a good saddle horse, he's going to end up with nothing but broken ribs and teeth marks for his troubles. Children are a little more forgiving than horses, but teaching them has this in common with teaching horses: knowledge of how to transmit information and skills is at least as important as knowledge of the information and skills themselves. We have all had teachers (most often college professors, unfortunately) who were brilliant and thoroughly knowledgeable in their fields, but who could not teach.

For effective teaching, subject matter knowledge is not a question of being a walking encyclopedia. Effective teachers not only know their subjects, they can also communicate their knowledge to students. In the movie *Stand and Deliver,* math teacher Jaime Escalante is teaching the concept of positive and negative numbers to students in a high school in a Los Angeles barrio. He explains that when you dig a hole, you might call the pile of dirt + 1, the hole − 1. What do you get when you put the dirt back in the hole? Zero. Escalante's ability to relate the abstract concept of positive and negative numbers to the experiences of his students is one example in which the ability to communicate knowledge goes far beyond simply knowing it.

Mastering the Skills of Teaching. The link between what the teacher wants students to learn and students' actual learning is called instruction, or **pedagogy.** Effective instruction is not a simple matter of one person with more knowledge transmitting that knowledge to another. If telling were teaching, this book would be unnecessary. Rather, effective instruction demands the use of many strategies. For example, to teach a lesson on long division to a diverse class of fourth-graders, teachers must accomplish many things. They must make sure that the class is orderly and that students know what behavior is expected of them. They must find out whether students have the multiplication and subtraction skills needed to learn long division, and if any do not, they must find a way to teach students these skills. They must present lessons on long division in a way that makes sense to students, using teaching strategies that help students remember what they have been taught. The lessons should also take into account the intellectual and social characteristics of students in the fourth grade. Teachers must make sure that students are interested in the lesson

Good teaching demands more than having great knowledge. It also requires the ability to present information clearly, to motivate students, and to evaluate their learning.

Chapter 1: Educational Psychology: A Tool for Teachers

and are motivated to learn long division. They may ask questions or use quizzes or other assessments to see if students are learning what is being taught, and they must respond appropriately if these assessments show that students are having problems. After the series of lessons on long division ends, teachers should review this skill from time to time to ensure that it is remembered. These tasks—motivating students, managing the classroom, assessing prior knowledge, communicating ideas effectively, taking into account the characteristics of the learners, assessing learning outcomes, and reviewing information—must be attended to at all levels of education, in or out of schools. They apply as much to the training of astronauts as to the teaching of reading. *How* these tasks are accomplished, however, differs widely according to the ages of the students, the objectives of instruction, and other factors.

What makes a good teacher is the ability to accomplish all the tasks involved in effective instruction. Warmth, enthusiasm, and caring are essential, as is subject matter knowledge; but it is the successful accomplishment of *all* the tasks of teaching that makes for instructional effectiveness.

Can Good Teaching Be Taught?

Some people think that good teachers are born that way. Outstanding teachers sometimes seem to have a magic, a charisma, that mere mortals could never hope to achieve. Yet research over the past fifteen years or so has begun to identify the specific behaviors and skills that make up the "magic" teacher. There is nothing an outstanding teacher does that any other teacher can't also do—it's just a question of knowing the principles of effective teaching and how to apply them. Take one small example. In a high school history class, two students in the back of the class are whispering to each other—and they are *not* whispering about the Treaty of Paris! The teacher slowly walks toward them without looking at them, continuing his lesson as he walks. The students stop whispering and pay attention. If you didn't know what to look for, you might miss this brief but critical interchange, and believe that the teacher just has a way with students, keeping their attention. But the teacher is simply applying principles of classroom management that anyone could learn: maintain momentum in the lesson, deal with behavior problems using the mildest intervention that will work, and resolve minor problems before they become major ones (see Chapter 11). When the movie character Jaime Escalante gave the example of digging a hole to illustrate the concept of positive and negative numbers, he was also applying several important principles of educational psychology: make abstract ideas concrete by using many examples, relate the content of instruction to the students' background, state rules, give examples, and then restate rules (see Chapter 8).

Can good teaching be taught? The answer is definitely yes. Good teaching has to be observed and practiced, but there are principles of good teaching that teachers need to know, which can then be applied in the classroom.

EDUCATIONAL PSYCHOLOGY: A PROBLEM-SOLVING APPROACH

Educational psychology is the study of learners, learning, and teaching. Its principal focus is on the processes by which information, skills, values, and attitudes are transmitted from teachers to students in the classroom, and on applications of principles of psychology to the practice of instruction. All educational psychology texts discuss characteristics of learners and principles of learning and instruction, and

most suggest how to apply these principles. This book is no exception. However, this book is significantly different in one respect. Because of recent developments in the study of instructional practice, it is now possible to present specific strategies that teachers can use to succeed at the tasks they must accomplish. For example, strategies for delivering lessons to the whole class and to groups within the class, for motivating students, for tailoring instruction to meet different students' needs, and for classroom management and discipline have been developed and tested over the past decade. In many cases, use of these strategies can dramatically improve student achievement and attitudes. This book presents such strategies along with the principles on which they are based and the research done to test them.

This book was written to put effective tools into the hands of tomorrow's teachers. These tools are of two kinds. First, teachers should understand the psychology of learners at different ages and the psychological principles of learning and motivation. This is the traditional focus of educational psychology. But second, teachers must know specific procedures to increase their classroom effectiveness. Surgeons must know biology, chemistry, anatomy, and physiology, but they must also know how and where to cut. By the same token, teachers must know developmental, cognitive, motivational, and social psychology, but they must also know how to teach a lesson and how to motivate and manage students. Also, just as a surgeon needs to know a variety of procedures to solve a particular problem, so must a teacher know many ways of solving classroom problems, as well as the consequences of each for student learning, motivation, and other aspects of instruction (Kagan, 1988). A teacher must be an intelligent craftsperson, applying trustworthy tools and procedures along with skill and creativity to the job of teaching.

Teaching as Critical Thinking

There is no formula for good teaching, no seven steps to Teacher of the Year. Teaching involves dozens of decisions each hour. Effective teaching requires critical thinking: seeing situations clearly, identifying problems, and exploring possible solutions. A primary goal of this book is to develop critical thinking skills in tomorrow's teachers. This goal is addressed both by the text itself and by other features. The text highlights the ideas that are central to educational psychology and the research related to these ideas. It also presents many examples of how these ideas apply in practice. The emphasis is on teaching methods that have been evaluated and found to be effective, not just theory or suggestions. The text is designed to develop critical thinking skills for teaching by engaging the reader with discussions of the many dilemmas found in practice and research. No text can provide all the right answers for teaching, but this one tries to pose the right questions and to engage the reader by presenting realistic alternatives and the concepts and research behind them.

Several features support the critical thinking theme. Throughout the text, "Theory into Practice" sections present strategies for instructional activities ranging from planning courses to presenting lessons to adapting instruction for the needs of students with academic handicaps. In sections called "Teachers on Teaching," over 100 experienced teachers describe how they apply the ideas and research presented in the text to their own teaching, from managing classrooms to designing tests and quizzes to helping students use what they learn in situations outside of school. These sections show how the real experts, practicing teachers, use critical thinking to solve typical classroom problems.

New to this edition is a series of sections called "Case to Consider." These are descriptions of classroom events or situations designed to elicit discussion and debate around questions and issues faced every day by practicing teachers. Also new to this edition are the sections called "Focus On . . . ," each of which discusses a current issue bearing on the teaching profession, ranging from the appropriateness of academic instruction in preschool and kindergarten to the need for major restructuring of middle and high schools. Again, the "Case to Consider" and "Focus On" sections provide no easy answers, only an opportunity for readers to apply their own experience and knowledge to questions that are central to the teaching profession.

Other features in *Educational Psychology: Theory into Practice* are designed to help the reader grasp the book's content. It is only fitting that a book that describes effective methods of teaching should itself put these principles to work. This book tries to do just that.

For example, research on how people learn suggests that students should be introduced to a topic before studying it in depth. Two features at the beginning of each chapter serve this purpose. They are

- A **chapter outline** that acquaints the reader with the organization and content of each chapter
- Chapter **learning objectives** that state what the reader should be able to do after reading the chapter

Features at the end of each chapter are designed to encourage readers to think about and remember the chapter's content. These features are

- A **summary** that recaps main points and reviews the learning objectives.
- **Study questions** that focus on important facts and concepts
- **Suggested readings** that direct the student to important supplementary materials

In addition, within each chapter important **glossary terms** are printed in boldface type the first time they are used in a significant way. Definitions of each term are given

Principle
Explanation of the relationship between factors

Theory
A set of principles that explains and relates certain phenomena

in the margin of the page. Each chapter also contains one or more sets of review questions at major junctures in the text. These are designed to encourage the reader to pause and reflect on the topics that have been covered, and to relate the material just read to that covered in other chapters or to actual teaching experiences.

Why Is Research in Educational Psychology Important?

One problem educational psychologists face is that almost everyone is already an expert on their subject. Most adults have spent many years in schools watching what teachers do. Add to that a certain amount of knowledge of human nature, and *voila!* everyone is an amateur educational psychologist. For this reason, professional educational psychologists are often accused of studying the obvious.

However, as we have painfully learned in recent years, the obvious isn't always true. For example, it was considered obvious that schools that spent more per pupil would produce greater student achievement than other schools, until Coleman et al. (1966) found this was not so. It was considered obvious that students would learn more in classes of twenty than in classes of thirty, but decades of research on this topic failed to find much support for this supposition (see Educational Research Service, 1978; Slavin, 1989a). Most people assume that if students are assigned to classes according to their ability, the resulting narrower range of abilities in a class will let the teacher adapt the instruction to the specific needs of the students, and, thereby, increase student achievement. This also turns out to be false (see Chapter 9). Many teachers believe that scolding students for misbehavior will improve student behavior. This is true for many students, but for others, scolding may be a *reward* for misbehavior and will actually increase it (see Chapters 4 and 11).

Some "obvious" truths even conflict with one another. For example, most people would agree that students learn better from a teacher's instruction than by working alone. This belief supports teacher-centered direct instructional strategies, in which a teacher actively works with the class as a whole. On the other hand, most people would also agree that students often need instruction tailored to their individual needs. This belief, also correct, would demand that teachers divide their time among individuals, or at least among groups of students with differing needs—which results in some students working independently, while others receive the teacher's attention. Now, if schools could provide tutors for every student, there would be no conflict; direct instruction and individualization could coexist. In practice, however, classrooms typically have twenty or more students and, as a result, more direct instruction (the first goal) almost always means less individualization (the second goal). For more on this dilemma, see Chapter 9.

The goal of research in educational psychology is to carefully examine obvious as well as less than obvious questions using objective methods to test ideas about the factors that contribute to learning. The products of this research are principles, laws, and theories. **Principles** explain relationships between factors, such as the effects of alternative grading systems on student motivation. Laws are simply principles that have been thoroughly tested and found to apply in a wide variety of situations. **Theories** are sets of related principles and laws that explain broad aspects of learning, behavior, or other areas of interest. Without theories, the facts and principles discovered would be like disorganized specks on a canvas. Theories tie together these facts and principles to give us the big picture. However, the same facts and principles may be interpreted in different ways by different theorists. As in any science, progress in educational psychology is slow and uneven. A single study is rarely a breakthrough,

America's schools have caught the national spotlight.

President George Bush has labeled himself "the education President." State governors unanimously approved an ambitious set of educational goals to be achieved by the year 2000. Businesses are crying out for better-skilled workers, and are contributing expertise and money to improve the nation's schools.

Why all the grandstanding? The U.S. economy is at stake. No longer does the economy reward unskilled labor in mines and factories; the next generation of workers must be well-educated, computer-literate, and able to manage information. Many people fear that public schools are not preparing children for the challenge. Critics say schools must be changed if the United States is to remain competitive in a global, information-based economic society.

Research and statistics support the charge that some schools are failing to hold onto and teach their students. For example, in some big-city high schools, four out of ten students drop out before graduation. American schoolchildren periodically show an embarrassing lack of knowledge about history and geography. And, reading and writing scores have improved little since the early 1970s.

The nation's governors took a step toward solving these problems by setting ambitious 10-year goals, which include the following:

- improving preschool programs so that every child will "start school ready to learn,"
- strengthening math and science achievement so that U.S. students rank first in the world,

- increasing high school graduation rates to 90 percent, and
- freeing schools of drugs and violence.

How these goals will be attained during a time of tight government budgets and escalating social problems is unclear. While national leaders can throw the spotlight on education, they cannot solve problems alone. The U.S. education system is highly decentralized, and decisions about proposed changes will come largely from local and state officials.

Nor are the best solutions readily apparent. Some reformers advocate emphasizing basic skills and toughening graduation requirements within the present educational structure. Other reformers say more radical steps are needed, stating that the system itself must be changed to meet changing needs.

For the good of the schools, this debate should remain in the spotlight. Pay attention to the rhetoric. Analyze what the politicians and educators are proposing. Ask yourself about the importance of the problems being cited and the relevance of the solutions being offered. Most important, ask yourself whether the children will be the real winners when all the changes are made.

Susan Chira, "Governors and Experts Are Divided on Setting Nation's Education Goals," *New York Times*, December 6, 1989.

Edward B. Fiske, "Governors and White House Plan Vast Schooling Reform," *New York Times*, February 26, 1990, p. A12.

Fred M. Hechinger, "About Education," *New York Times*, December 20, 1989, p. B9.

but over time evidence accumulates on a subject and allows theorists to refine and extend their theories.

What Good Is Research in Educational Psychology to the Teacher?

It is probably true that the most important things teachers learn they learn on the job—in student teaching or during their first years in the classroom. However, teachers make hundreds of decisions every day and each decision has a theory behind it, whether or not the teacher is aware of it. The quality, accuracy, and usefulness of those theories are what determines, ultimately, the teacher's success. For example, one teacher may offer a prize to the student with best attendance, on the theory that rewarding attendance will increase it. Another may reward the student whose attendance is most *improved*, on the theory that it is poor attenders who most need incentives to come to class. Which teacher's plan is most likely to succeed? This depends in large part on the ability of each teacher to understand the unique combination of factors that shape the character of their classroom and, therefore, to apply the most appropriate theory.

The aim of educational psychology is to test the various theories that guide the actions of teachers and others involved in education. Here is another example of how this might work.

Mr. Harris teaches a sixth-grade social studies class. He has a problem with Tom, who frequently misbehaves. Today Tom makes a paper airplane and flies it across the room when Mr. Harris turns his back, to the delight of the entire class. What should Mr. Harris do?

Some actions Mr. Harris might take, and the theories on which are based, are as follows:

Whether teachers are called upon to comfort upset children, present complex information, or handle discipline problems, they always base their actions on theories about human behavior and teaching.

Action	Theory
1. Scold Tom.	1. Scolding is a form of punishment. Tom will behave to avoid punishment.
2. Ignore Tom.	2. Yelling may be rewarding to Tom. Ignoring him would deprive him of this reward.
3. Send Tom to the office.	3. Being sent to the office is punishing. It also deprives Tom of the (apparent) support of his classmates.
4. Tell the class that it is everyone's responsibility to maintain a good learning environment, and if any student misbehaves, five minutes will be subtracted from recess.	4. Tom is misbehaving to get his classmates' attention. If the whole class loses out when he misbehaves, the class will keep him in line.
5. Explain to the class that Tom's behavior is interfering with lessons that all students need to know, and that his behavior goes against the rules the class set for itself at the beginning of the year.	5. The class holds standards of behavior that conflict with both Tom's behavior in class and the class's reaction to it. By reminding the class of its own needs (to learn the lesson) and its own rules set at the beginning of the year, the teacher may make Tom see that his behavior is not really supported by the class.

Each of these actions is a common response to misbehavior. But which theory (and, therefore, which action) is correct?

The key may be in the fact that his classmates laugh when Tom misbehaves. This is a clue that Tom is seeking their attention. If Mr. Harris scolds Tom, this may increase his status in the eyes of his peers, and may reward his behavior. Ignoring misbehavior might be a good idea if a student is acting up to get the teacher's attention, but in this case it is the class's attention that Tom is apparently seeking.

Sending Tom to the office does deprive him of his classmates' attention, and thus might be effective. But what if Tom is looking for a way to get out of class to avoid work? What if he struts out with a chip on his shoulder, to the obvious approval of his classmates? Making the entire class responsible for each student's behavior is likely to deprive Tom of his support, and to improve his behavior. But some students may feel it is unfair to punish them for another student's misbehavior. Finally, reminding the class (and Tom) of its own interest in learning and its usual standards of behavior might work if the class does in fact value academic achievement and good behavior.

Research in education and psychology bears directly on the decision Mr. Harris must make. Developmental research (which is described in Chapters 2 and 3) indicates that as students enter adolescence, the peer group becomes all-important to them and they try to establish their independence from adult control, often by flouting or ignoring rules. Basic research on behavioral learning theories (Chapter 4) shows that when a behavior is repeated many times, there must be some reward that is encouraging the behavior, and that to eliminate a behavior, the reward must first be identified and eliminated. This research would also suggest that Mr. Harris consider certain problems concerning the use of punishment to stop undesirable behavior. Research on specific classroom management strategies has identified effective methods to use both to prevent a student like Tom from misbehaving in the first place and to deal with his misbehavior when it does occur (Chapter 11). Finally, research on rule setting and classroom standards indicates that student participation in setting rules can help convince each student that the class as a whole values academic achievement and appropriate behavior, and this can help keep individual students in line (see Chapter 11).

Armed with this information, Mr. Harris can choose an effective response to Tom's behavior that is based on an understanding of why Tom is doing what he is doing and what strategies are available to deal with the situation. Research does not give Mr. Harris a specific solution; that requires his own experience and judgment. But research does give Mr. Harris basic concepts of human behavior to help him understand Tom's motivations, and an array of proven methods that might solve the problem.

Research + Common Sense = Effective Teaching. As the case of Mr. Harris illustrates, no theory, no research, no book can tell teachers what to do in a given situation. Making the right decisions depends on the context within which the

Teachers rely on educational research, knowledge about their students, and common sense to choose the best instructional strategy for a particular situation.

Treatment
A special program that is the subject of an experiment

Variable
Something that can have more than one value

Experiment
Procedure used to test the effects of a treatment

Random Assignment
Selection by chance in the different treatment groups to try to ensure equality of the groups

problem arises, the objectives the teacher has in mind, and many other factors, all of which must be assessed in the light of educated common sense. For example, research in mathematics instruction usually finds that a rapid pace of instruction increases achievement (Good, Grouws, & Ebmeier, 1983). Yet a teacher may quite legitimately slow down and spend a lot of time on a concept that is particularly critical, or may even let students take time to discover a mathematical principle on their own. It is usually much more efficient to directly teach students skills or information than to let them make discoveries for themselves, but if the teacher wants students to know how to find information or to figure things out for themselves, then the research findings about pace can be temporarily shelved.

The point is that while research in educational psychology can sometimes be translated directly to the classroom, it is best to apply the principles with a hefty dose of common sense and a clear view of what is being taught to whom for what purpose.

■ **Stop and Think**
Now that you know a little about the field of educational psychology, recall the content of any other education courses you may already have taken. How does the content and approach of this course differ from those? Recall also any psychology courses you have taken. In what respects does general psychology differ from educational psychology?

RESEARCH METHODS IN EDUCATIONAL PSYCHOLOGY

How do we know what we know in educational psychology? As in any scientific field, knowledge comes from many sources. Sometimes researchers study schools, teachers, or students as they are, and sometimes they create special programs, or **treatments,** and study their effects on one or more variables (a **variable** is anything that can take on more than one value, such as age, sex, achievement level, or attitudes). The following sections discuss the principal methods used by educational researchers to learn about schools, teachers, students, and instruction.

Experiments

In an **experiment,** researchers create special treatments and analyze their effects. For example, Lepper et al. (1973) set up an experimental situation in which children used felt-tipped markers to draw pictures. Some children were given a prize (a "good player award") for drawing pictures, and others were not. At the end of the experiment, all students were allowed to choose among a number of activities, including drawing with felt-tipped markers. The children who had received the prizes chose to continue drawing with felt-tipped markers about half as frequently as did those who had not received prizes. This was interpreted as showing that rewarding individuals for doing a task they already liked could reduce their interest in doing the task when they were no long rewarded. (See Chapter 10 for a more complete description of this study).

Several important aspects of experiments are illustrated by the Lepper study. First, the children were randomly assigned to receive prizes or not. For example, the children's names might have been put on slips of paper that were dropped into a hat and then drawn at random for assignment to a "prize" or "no-prize" group. **Random assignment** ensured that the two groups were essentially equivalent before the experiment began. This is critical, because if we were not sure that the two groups were equal before the experiment, we would not be able to tell if it was the prizes that made the difference in their subsequent behavior.

A second feature of this study that is characteristic of experiments is that everything other than the treatment itself (the prizes) was kept the same for the "prize" and "no-prize" groups. The children played in the same rooms with the same materials and with the same adults present. The researcher who gave the prize spent the same amount of time watching the non-prize children draw. Only the prize itself was different for the two groups. The goal was to be sure that it was the treatment, and not some other factor, that explained the difference between the two groups.

Laboratory Experiments. The Lepper et al. (1973) study is an example of a **laboratory experiment.** Even though it took place in a school building, a highly artificial, structured setting was created that existed for a very brief period of time. The advantage of laboratory experiments is that they permit researchers to exert a very high degree of control over all the factors involved in the study. Such studies are high in **internal validity,** which is to say that any differences they find can, with confidence, be attributed to the treatments themselves (rather than other factors). The primary limitation of laboratory experiments is that they are typically so artificial and so brief that their results may have little relevance to real-life situations. For example, the Lepper et al. (1973) study, which was later repeated several times, was used to support a theory that rewards can diminish individuals' interest in an activity when the rewards are withdrawn. This theory served as the basis for attacks on the use of classroom rewards, such as grades and stars. However, later research in real classrooms using real rewards has generally failed to find such effects (see Chapter 10). This does not discredit the Lepper et al. (1973) study itself, but does show that theories based on artificial laboratory experiments cannot be assumed to apply to all situations in real life, but must be tested in the real settings.

Randomized Field Experiments. Another kind of experiment often used in educational research is the **randomized field experiment,** in which instructional programs or other practical treatments are evaluated over relatively long periods in real classes under realistic conditions. For example, Good and Grouws (1979) used a randomized field experiment to test their Missouri Mathematics Program, or MMP (discussed in Chapter 8). Forty fourth-grade teachers volunteered to participate. These teachers were randomly assigned to receive training in the MMP or to continue teaching as before. In experiments, the group that receives a treatment is called the **experimental group,** while the one that receives no treatment is called the **control group.**

In the Good and Grouws (1979) study, all teachers' classes took a mathematics pretest. Sixteen weeks later, they took the same test again. Experimental classes, whose teachers had received the MMP training, gained more on the second tests than did the control classes, so the experimenters concluded that the MMP was more effective than traditional methods of teaching mathematics.

Note the similarities and differences between the Good and Grouws (1979) randomized field experiment and the Lepper et al. (1973) laboratory experiment. Both used random assignment to make sure that the experimental and control groups were essentially equal at the start of the study. Both tried to make all factors except the treatment equal for the experimental and control groups, but the Good and Grouws study was (by its very nature as a field experiment) less able to do this. For example, experimental and control teachers taught in different schools with different principals and students. Random assignment made it likely that these factors would balance out, but the fact remains that in a field setting control is never as great as in a laboratory

Laboratory Experiment
Experiment in which conditions are highly controlled

Internal Validity
The degree to which an experiment's results can be attributed to the treatment in question, not to other factors

Randomized Field Experiment
Experiment conducted under realistic conditions in which individuals are assigned by chance to receive different practical treatments or programs

Experimental Group
Group that receives treatment during an experiment

Control Group
Group that receives no special treatment during an experiment

External Validity
Degree to which results of an
experiment can be applied to real-life
situations

situation. On the other hand, the fact that the Good and Grouws study took place over a long period of time in real classrooms means that its **external validity** is far greater than that of the Lepper et al. study. That is, the results of the Good and Grouws study have direct relevance to instruction in fourth-grade mathematics, and probably to mathematics instruction at other grade levels as well.

Both laboratory experiments and randomized field experiments make important contributions to the science of educational psychology. Laboratory experiments are primarily important in building and testing theories, while randomized field experiments are the "acid test" for evaluating practical programs or improvements in instruction.

TEACHERS ON TEACHING
Learning to Teach

Teachers learn their craft from education courses, their own experience, and from observations and reading. Here are the comments of a few teachers on the factors that influenced their teaching.

1. We have all been influenced—maybe even inspired— by a few of our teachers. Describe your most unforgettable teacher and the influence that person has had on your career.

Roseanne Swinburne-Sanderfoot, who teaches children with learning disabilities in Manawa, Wisc., writes:

One high school teacher stands out in my mind. Ms. Wittman was my teacher for various English classes, including literature and college prep.

After I had moved to a new high school during those tumultuous teen years, she became a beacon in my life. She made me believe that I was creative, a talented writer, and surely one of the smartest kids in the class. She helped hold my self-esteem together when the adjustment road was rough.

Her excitement for literature and creative writing rubbed off on me. I had always enjoyed reading, but she helped me develop a real love for it—and not just for easy, entertaining material. She made me willing to take a challenge and read deeper, thought-provoking works. She seemed so excited about what she was teaching that it was hard not to feel that enthusiasm.

She had very high expectations for me. I believe I attained the goals she set for me because she inspired me to do no less than that. Ms. Wittman positively influenced my life and my career. Her encouragement allowed me to believe enough in myself to take a challenge and reach towards the highest standard. The good things she gave me still assist me in the day-to-day job of being a teacher.

2. Describe other factors that have influenced your style and methods of teaching.

Sandra Dougherty, a high school teacher in Shenandoah Junction, W. Va., writes:

When I first entered teaching, teachers that I had *and* admired influenced me tremendously. However, the longer I am in the field, the more my own students influence me. What used to work no longer always does. If I do not keep up with the changing needs of my students, I am indeed a failure.

Jack Clendaniel, who teaches at the secondary level in Wilmington, Del., writes:

Those people teaching around me have most influenced my style. I see myself observing, trying new things, using those which I feel comfortable with and discarding those that don't work out.

3. Why should future teachers study educational psychology?

Terry Olive, a teacher of developmentally handicapped children in Elyria, Ohio, writes:

Knowledge of psychology can be helpful in many areas of education. It helps the teacher understand the basic behavior and motivation of students, colleagues, and administrators, and it provides insight into the learning process. This information can supply practical methods of dealing with classroom problems. Psychological training can help a teacher . . . select motivating methods such as a game format, measure words to be more tactful with a parent or administrator, and even improve his or her attitude so as to be more positive with students or co-workers.

Single-Case Experiments.   One type of experiment often used in educational research is the **single-case experiment** (Hersen and Barlow, 1976). In one typical form of this type of experiment, a single student's behavior might be observed for several days. Then a special program is begun and the student's behavior under the new program is observed. Finally, the new program is withdrawn. If the student's behavior improved under the special program, but the improvement disappeared when the program was withdrawn, it suggests that the program affected the student's behavior. Sometimes the "single case" can be several students, an entire class, or a school that is given the same treatment.

An example of a single-case experiment is a study by Barrish et al. (1969), discussed in Chapter 11. In this study, a fourth-grade class was the single case. Observers recorded the percent of time that at least one student in the class was "talking out" (talking without permission) during reading and math periods. After ten days, a special program was introduced. The class was divided into two large teams, and whenever any student on a team misbehaved, the team was given a check mark. At the end of each day, the team with the fewest check marks (or both teams if both received fewer than five marks) could take part in a thirty-minute free period.

The results of this study are illustrated in Figure 1.1. Before the "Good Behavior Game" began (Baseline), at least one student in the math class was talking out 96 percent of the time, and at least one student was out-of-seat without permission 82 percent of the time. When the game was begun in math, the class's behavior improved dramatically. When the game was withdrawn, the class's behavior got worse again, but improved once more when it was reintroduced. Note that when the game was introduced in reading class, the students' behaviors also improved. The fact that the program also made a difference in reading gives us even greater confidence that the "Good Behavior Game" is effective.

The graphs themselves are usually the test of the effects in a single-case experiment. Researchers generally rely on what is called the "interocular trauma" test, which is to say the effect has to hit you between the eyes (figuratively, of course) or it is not worth talking about. When one looks at Figure 1.1, the effects of the "Good Behavior Game" are perfectly clear: when the game is introduced, behavior improves.

One important limitation of the single-case experiment is that it can only be used to study outcomes that can be frequently measured. For this reason, most single-case studies involve observable behaviors, such as talking out and being out-of-seat, which can be measured every day or many times per day.

Correlational Studies

Perhaps the most frequently used research method in educational psychology is the **correlational study.** In contrast to an experiment, where the researcher deliberately changes one variable to see how this change will affect other variables, in correlational research the researcher studies variables *as they are* to see whether they are related. Variables can be positively correlated, negatively correlated, or uncorrelated. An example of a **positive correlation** is the relationship between reading achievement and mathematics achievement. This means that, in general, someone who is better than average in reading will also be better than average in math. Of course, there are students who are good readers but not good in math, and vice versa, but *on the average,* skills in one academic area are positively correlated with skills in other academic areas; when one variable is high, the other tends also to be high. An example

Single-case Experiment
Study of a treatment's effect on one person or one group by contrasting behavior before, during, and after the treatment is applied

Correlational Study
Research into the relationships between variables as they naturally occur

Positive Correlation
Relationship in which high scores on one variable correspond to high scores on another

Negative Correlation
Relationship in which high scores on one variable correspond to low scores on another.

Uncorrelated Variables
Lack of relationship between two variables

of a **negative correlation** is days absent and grades. The more days a student is absent, the lower his or her grades are likely to be; when one variable is high, the other tends to be low. When two variables are **uncorrelated,** there is no correspondence between them. For example, student achievement in Poughkeepsie, N.Y., is probably completely unrelated to the level of student motivation in Portland, Ore.

One example of correlational research is a study by Lahaderne (1968), who investigated the relationship between students' attentiveness in class and their

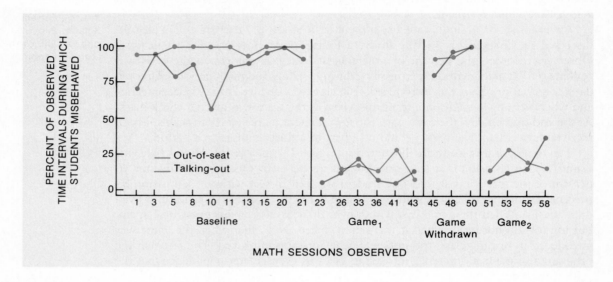

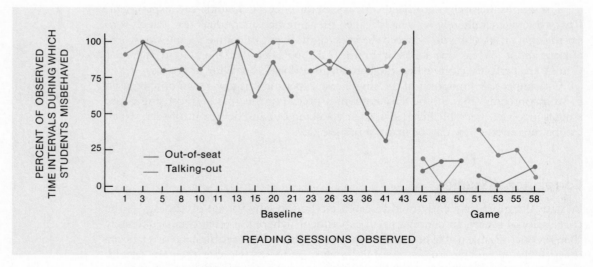

FIGURE 1.1

Results of Successful Single-case Experiments

The effect of rewarding good behavior in fourth-grade math and reading classes is clear from these graphs. They show that misbehavior was high during the baseline period (before the "Good Behavior Game" was introduced), but fell during the game. In single-case experiments on treatments affecting behaviors that can be frequently measured, graphs like these can prove a treatment's effectiveness.

Adapted from Barrish et al., 1969.

Education researchers use correlational studies to assess relationships between variables. A researcher might, for example, want to test the relationship between the use of audio equipment and computers, and levels of reading achievement.

achievement and IQ. She observed 125 students in four sixth-grade classes to see how much of the time students were paying attention (for example, listening to the teacher and doing assigned work). She then correlated attentiveness with achievement in reading, arithmetic, and language, and with students' IQs and attitudes toward school. A brief summary of the results for boys in Lahaderne's study appears in Table 1.1.

The numbers in Table 1.1 are **correlation coefficients,** which can range from −1.0 (perfect negative correlation) to +1.0 (perfect positive correlation). A correlation coefficient of 0.0 indicates no relationship. Table 1.1 indicates strong positive correlations between attentiveness and achievement and between attentiveness and IQ, and (as would be expected) strong negative correlations between inattentiveness and both achievement and IQ.

TABLE 1.1

EXAMPLE OF A CORRELATIONAL STUDY

Sixth-grade boys who paid attention in class also tended to earn high scores on achievement and IQ tests, according to the results of this correlational study. In such studies, positive numbers indicate that strength in one variable predicts strength in a second variable. Negative numbers, on the other hand, indicate that when one variable is low, the other will be high.

	Achievement			IQ
	Reading	Arithmetic	Language	
Attentiveness	.46	.53	.48	.48
Inattentiveness	−.42	−.52	−.47	−.35

SOURCE: Adapted from Lahaderne, 1968, p. 322.

The advantage of correlational studies is that they allow the researcher to study variables as they are, without creating artificial situations. Many important research questions can only be studied in correlational studies. For example, if we wanted to study the relationship between gender and math achievement, we could hardly randomly assign students to be boys or girls! Also, correlational studies let researchers study the interrelationships of many variables at the same time.

The principal disadvantage of correlational methods is that while they may tell us that two variables are related, they do not tell us what *causes* what. The Lahaderne study of attentiveness, achievement, and IQ raised the question: Does student attentiveness *cause* high achievement, or are high-ability, high-achieving students simply more attentive than other students? A correlational study cannot answer this question completely. However, correlational researchers do typically use statistical methods to try to determine what causes what. In Lahaderne's study, it would have been possible to find out whether among students with the same IQ, attentiveness is related to achievement. For example, given two students of average intelligence, would the one who is more attentive tend to achieve more? If not, then we might conclude that the relationship between attentiveness and achievement is simply the result of high-IQ students being more attentive and higher-achieving than other students, not to any effect of attention on achievement.

Figure 1.2 illustrates two possible explanations for the correlation between attentiveness, achievement, and IQ. In Explanation A, attentiveness causes achievement. In Explanation B, both attentiveness and achievement are assumed to be caused by a third variable, IQ. Which is correct? Evidence from other research on this relationship suggests that both explanations are partially correct, that even when the effect of IQ is removed, student attentiveness is related to achievement.

Descriptive Research

Experimental and correlational research looks for relationships between variables. However, some research in educational psychology simply seeks to describe something of interest. One example of **descriptive research** is a survey or interview. Another, called ethnography (Taft, 1987; Wilson, 1977), involves observation of a social setting (such as a classroom or school) over an extended period. An example of descriptive research that combined observation with interviews is a study by Metz

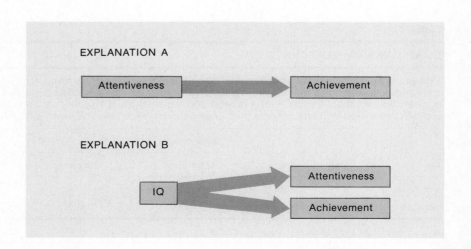

(1978) of three newly desegregated junior high schools. The author observed students and teachers in and out of class; interviewed students, teachers, principals, counselors, and others; attended assemblies and faculty meetings; and obtained and analyzed handbooks, yearbooks, and other written materials. In this way, she was able to describe the meaning and consequences of desegregation in extraordinary detail. Descriptive research is extensively used in developmental psychology (see Chapters 2 and 3) to identify characteristics of children at different ages. The most important research in developmental psychology was done by the Swiss psychologist Jean Piaget (1952b), who began by carefully observing his own children. As a result of his observations, he developed a theory that describes the cognitive development of children from infancy through adolescence.

■ **Stop and Think**

Let's try to apply what you've just read about research methods. Evaluate the validity of the following assertion that might be made by a teacher:

"I did an experiment this semester involving two of my math classes. For one group of students, I gave quizzes every other day. In the other class, the kids took tests every other week. The first class scored terribly on the final, so I've learned that frequent quizzes just waste time."

Is this teacher's conclusion valid?

WHY TEACHING IS THE HARDEST JOB IN THE WORLD, AND WHY TEACHERS SECRETLY LOVE IT—A DEDICATION

This book was written to communicate what we know about students, about the learning process, and, most importantly, about classroom instruction to people who are now or will soon be doing one of the most important jobs in the world—teaching

How do teachers present information to students? How do students respond? To answer such questions, educational psychologists might use descriptive research to study classroom situations.

Fred Knight has taught music at Lincoln Junior High School for five years. He enjoys the challenge of trying to share with students his love of music, but his success as a music teacher is hard to measure. A few of his orchestra and band members have certainly performed well during all-school concerts, but most of his students come to class only because they have to. For them, Fred just has to be satisfied that he is exposing them to music and musicians who they can enjoy throughout their lives.

Each of Fred's days is a mix of whole-class lessons, group-performance classes, and individual instruction. A mid-winter Friday morning finds him giving beginning violin lessons to eight sixth-graders. The students are at a dangerous stage; they know how to make noise but not music.

Today Fred wants to teach the students a tune that involves playing notes on all four violin strings. Instead of working with the students all together, he splits them into two groups of three and one group of two. Each group goes to a corner of the practice room and starts to play. Fred circulates among the groups, helping and praising their efforts. After about 20 minutes, he brings the eight students back together to play the tune all at once. Their rhythm is a bit shaky and a few wrong notes slip in, but the students are pleased at their combined sound. Fred is delighted with the success of his strategy and thinks that the students had more fun with this method than if he had taught them all together as a large group.

The period after lunch is music appreciation class with Mrs. Walton's eighth graders. Most students show up on time, but they are full of chatter about boyfriends, girlfriends, rock stars, and the upcoming baseball season. Four girls slip in several minutes late, saying they were in the restroom.

FRED: Good afternoon, students. Please be seated. Today we'll talk about musical instruments, and I want to start with a quiz. [Fred points to the board where he has written the following list: cello, comb, drum, fluegelhorn, saw, bagpipes, washboard, spoons, banjo, mandolin, and triangle.] Can anyone tell me which of these are musical instruments?

Various members of the class raise hands and note the obvious answers. As the discussion progresses, they are surprised to learn that all the listed items can be used to make music. They are more surprised when Fred shows them how to tap out a rhythm with a pair of spoons and how to make a kazoo out of a comb and tissue paper.

That leads to a discussion of the definition of the term musical instrument, and the varieties that exist outside the typical symphony orchestra or brass band. One girl asks Fred about an old triangle-shaped guitar that hangs in the apartment of her immigrant grandmother. Another student describes hearing a group of men play beautiful songs on steel drums during a Caribbean festival. By the end of class Fred is confident that the students have a broader concept of music and musical instruments. The discussion was a success.

For the final class of the day, Fred has opted to take it easy and show a short movie on Beethoven's life and the next generation. Teaching is one of the toughest jobs there is because a teacher must do so many things well. A teacher must be a leader, an effective speaker, a quick diagnostician, a tactful diplomat, and a firm but fair disciplinarian. Teachers must know their subject and, even more importantly, know their craft. Teachers have to be "on" all the time and they do not leave their jobs behind when they go home at the end of the day.

Yet most teachers love what they do. Society may not always give them the respect they deserve, nor pay them adequately, nor provide them with the facilities they need to do their job well. But it always gives teachers its children. Let's face it, children are fun. Their changes, their challenges, their successes, are fascinating to watch and to participate in. Teachers matter, and they know they matter.

It is a humbling experience to write a book for people who will make such an important difference to our future. This book is dedicated to teachers, in the hope that music. He even leaves the room for a few minutes during the film to organize some paperwork to carry home. All seems to have gone fine until the movie ends and he flips the lights back on. Small pools of water on a couple of desks and the surrounding floor lead him to suspect he missed a squirt-gun fight. The end-of-class bell rings.

FRED: Everyone please remain seated. [He walks over to the water puddles and speaks to the nearest students.] Chris, can you tell me anything about this?

CHRIS: Yes, Mr. Knight.

FRED: Jeremy, were you involved, too?

JEREMY: Yes, Mr. Knight.

FRED: Is there anyone else I should talk with about this?

PATTY: Me, too, I guess, Mr. Knight.

FRED: Anyone else? [waiting a few moments.] All right. Everyone else can go. I'd like to talk with you three for a few minutes.

Fred talks with the students and confiscates the squirt guns. Then he escorts them back to their homeroom and tells their teacher what happened.

A few days later Fred runs into a fellow teacher with whom he attended college. The conversation turns to the courses both are taking to keep their teaching certificates current.

FRED: You know, some of the topics in my Tuesday-night class remind me of Mr. Malone's ed. psych. course.

Remember that old guy? The way he used to talk about how educational psychology contributes to teaching, and how it makes us better decision makers? That still seems like a lot of ivory-tower talk to me.

MADELINE: I'm not so sure. Every once in a while I find myself analyzing classroom situations at the end of the day just the way Mr. Malone used to take apart those teaching situations in class. It kind of helps me understand what's going on with my kids.

FRED: Yeah, those were interesting dilemmas, but didn't the solutions all seem like common sense to you? I still think that common sense is my best tool in the classroom.

QUESTIONS

1. Look back over some of the situations from Fred's day in the class. Which of his decisions might have been informed (whether he chose to realize it or not) by principles and theories from educational psychology?

2. Fred used a different method of lesson presentation for each of his three classes. Think of other ways he might have taught the same material.

3. Describe some of the research methods of educational psychology. How might a teacher use some of these methods informally in the classroom? Of what should the teacher be aware concerning the validity of any conclusions derived from such small-scale experiments?

the information and tools it contains will help the next generation of teachers do the best possible job with the next generation of students.

SUMMARY AND REVIEW OF OBJECTIVES

The Focus of Educational Psychology. Educational psychology is the study of learners, learning, and teaching. It focuses on the processes by which information, skills, values, and attitudes are transmitted from teachers to students in the classroom and on applications of the principles of psychology to the practice of instruction.

The Experimental Process. Educational researchers learn about teachers, students, and instruction through experiments in which they test special programs or treatments. Before such experiments, random assignment of experimental subjects into groups helps to ensure that the groups are equivalent. The group that receives treatment is called the experimental group, while the group receiving no treatment is the control group. High internal validity means that differences found between the groups can be more confidently attributed to the treatments being tested. High external validity means that results can be generalized to applied situations.

Laboratory experiments employ highly structured, short-term conditions, in which a high degree of control is exerted over the factors involved. Randomized field experiments evaluate instructional programs or other treatments over a long period of time under realistic conditions.

A single-case experiment is the observation of one student's (or one group's) behavior over a certain time period. After initial observation, a special program is introduced, and then the student (or group) is observed again.

Descriptive research seeks to describe something of interest, using interviews and observation.

Correlational versus Causal Relationships. Correlational studies examine variables to see whether they are related. Variables can be positively correlated, negatively correlated, or uncorrelated. Correlation coefficients range from -1.0 (perfect negative correlation) to $+1.0$ (perfect positive correlation). Correlational studies provide information about variables as they are, without creating artificial situations. They do not indicate, however, the causes of relationships between variables.

STUDY QUESTIONS

1. Which of the following statements about educational psychology is true?
   a. Its current emphases today make it virtually the same as school psychology.
   b. One of its main purposes is to eliminate the infiltration of pedagogy in the schools.
   c. Over the years it has become more oriented toward real-life classroom applications.
   d. Its developmental orientation makes it generally more useful for preschool teachers than for secondary school teachers.

2. Which of the following products of educational research precedes the other two?
   a. Theory
   b. Law
   c. Principle

3. Which of the following correctly matches a type of research to an advantage that it offers?
   a. Laboratory experiment: has high internal validity
   b. Randomized field experiment: exercises rigorous control
   c. Descriptive study: shows relationships between variables
   d. Correlational: shows cause-effect relationship
   e. Single-case experiment: involves infrequent assessments

4. Match the following types of experiments with the situations that illustrate each (a situation may be used more than once or not at all).

____ randomized field experiment
____ descriptive research
____ laboratory experiment
____ correlational study

   a. Observing and noting how preschoolers play
   b. Recording the number of times a student misbehaves before, during, and after the administration of a special reinforcement program
   c. Determining the relationship between reading ability and math achievement
   d. Evaluating a new teaching technique relative to conventional instruction for several months under typical classroom conditions
   e. Evaluating a new teaching technique relative to conventional instruction for a short period of time under highly controlled conditions

5. Students in Ms. Jameson's class receive a check mark for each day they *fail* to turn in homework. How is the number of check marks received at midterm time likely to correlate with midterm exam scores in that class?
   a. Positively
   b. Negatively
   c. No correlation

Answers: 1. c 2. c 3. a 4. d, a, e, c 5. b (Note: the more checks the lower the score.)

SUGGESTED READINGS

BORG, W. R. (1981). *Applying educational research: A practical guide for teachers*. New York: Longman.

BORG, W. R., and GALL, M. D. (1983). *Educational research: An introduction* (4th ed.). New York: Longman.

CAMPBELL, D. T., and STANLEY, J. C. (1966). *Experimental and quasi-experimental designs for research*. Chicago: Rand McNally.

COOK, T. D., and CAMPBELL, D. T. (1979). *Quasi-experimentation: Design and analysis issues for field settings*. Chicago: Rand McNally.

HERSEN, M., and BARLOW, D. (1976). *Single-case experimental designs*. Elmsford, N.Y.: Pergamon Press.

SLAVIN, R. E. (1984). *Research methods in education: A practical guide*. Englewood Cliffs, N.J.: Prentice-Hall.

Chapter 2

Theories of Development

Chapter Outline

Aspects of Development
Continuous and Discontinuous Theories

Piaget's Theory of Cognitive Development
Principal Concepts in Piaget's Theory
The Stages
Criticisms and Revisions of Piaget's Theory
Theory into Practice: Piaget's Theory of Cognitive
   Development

**Erikson's Theory of Personal and Social
   Development**
The Stages
Theory into Practice: Personal and Social
   Development

Moral Reasoning
Piaget's Theory of Moral Development
Kohlberg's Stages of Moral Reasoning
Limitations of Kohlberg's Theory

Chapter Objectives

This chapter outlines major theories of human
development. After reading it you should be
able to:

- List ways in which elementary school children
  differ in intellectual ability from secondary school
  students.

- Describe the personality crises faced by (1)
  preschoolers and kindergartners, (2) elementary
  school children, and (3) high school students.

- Describe how people progress in their moral
  reasoning abilities from simple compliance with
  authority to development of personal principles.

Theories of development contribute directly to good
teaching. Understanding these theories will allow
you as a teacher to:

- Describe the important cognitive characteristics
  of children who are in the grade you would like
  to teach.

- Specify the attitudes it is hoped children will
  retain after undergoing the social and emotional
  crises that occur during the school years.

- Help children develop a healthy, balanced
  outlook on life.

In the first week of school Mr. Jones tried to teach his first-graders how to behave in class. He said, "When I ask a question, I want you to raise your *right* hand, and I'll call on you. Can you all raise your right hands, as I am doing?"

Thirty hands went up. They were all *left* hands.

*　　*　　*

Ms. Quintera started her eight-grade English class one day with an excited announcement:

"Class, I wanted to tell you all that we have a poet in our midst. Frank wrote such a wonderful poem that I thought I'd read it to you all."

Ms. Quintera read Frank's poem, which was indeed very good. However, she noticed that Frank was turning bright red and looking distinctly uncomfortable. A few of the other students in the class snickered.

Later Ms. Quintera asked Frank if he would like to write another poem for a citywide poetry contest. He said he'd rather not because he really didn't think he was that good, and besides, he didn't have the time.

*　　*　　*

Because her students were getting careless about handing in their homework, Ms. Lewis decided to lay down the law to her fourth-grade class.

"Anyone who does not hand in all his or her homework this week will not be allowed to go on the field trip."

It so happened that one girl's mother became ill and was taken to the hospital that week. As a result of her family's confusion and concern, the girl failed to hand in one of her homework assignments. Ms. Lewis explained to the class that she would make an exception in this case because of the girl's mother's illness, but the class wouldn't hear of it. "Rules are rules," they said. "She didn't hand in her homework, so she can't go!"

ASPECTS OF DEVELOPMENT

Children are not miniature adults. They think differently, they see the world differently, and they live by different moral and ethical principles than adults do.

The three vignettes just presented illustrate a few of the many aspects of children's thinking that differ from those of adults. When Mr. Jones raised his right hand, his first-graders imitated his action *as they perceived it*; they were unable to see that since he was facing them, his right hand would be to their left. Ms. Quintera was surprised that her praise of Frank's poem had an effect opposite to what she intended. Had she paused to consider the situation, she might have realized that highlighting Frank's achievement could cast him in the role of "teacher's pet," a dependent role that students in early adolescence strongly resist. The situation in Ms. Lewis's class illustrates a stage in children's moral development when rules are rules and extenuating circumstances don't count.

One of the first requirements of effective teaching is that the teacher understand how students think and how they view the world. There are ages at which children simply do not have the maturity to learn certain concepts no matter how well or how long the concepts are taught. Effective teaching strategies must take into account students' ages and stages of development. For example, Ms. Quintera's public recognition of Frank's poetry might have been quite appropriate if Frank had been three years younger or three years older. A bright fourth-grader might appear to be able to learn any kind of mathematics, but, in fact, might not have the developmental readiness to do the abstract thinking required for algebra.

This chapter presents three major theories of human development that are widely accepted: Jean Piaget's theory of cognitive development, Erik Erikson's theory of personal and social development, and Lawrence Kohlberg's theory of moral development. Each of these theories describes a set of stages through which children and adolescents go as they grow and develop. Chapter 3 discusses human development from a different perspective, describing the physical, social, cognitive, and other aspects of people in early childhood, middle childhood, and adolescence.

Continuous and Discontinuous Theories

Long ago human development was assumed to follow a smooth progression from infancy to adulthood. By the age of six or seven children were believed to think in much the same way as adults, and it was assumed that all they lacked was experience and education. This belief in a smooth progression is called a continuous theory of development.

In this century, however, developmental psychologists discovered that children do not develop gradually, but rather go through a series of stages of development. The abilities that children gain in each subsequent stage are not simply "more of the same"; at each stage children develop qualitatively different understandings, abilities, and beliefs. Skipping stages is impossible, although at any given point the same child may exhibit behaviors characteristic of more than one stage.

Views of development that emphasize these steps are called discontinuous or **stage theories**. Piaget, Erikson, and Kohlberg each focus on a different aspect of development. Nevertheless, all are stage theorists because they share the belief that distinct stages of development can be identified and described. This agreement does not extend, however, to the particulars of their theories, which differ significantly in the numbers of stages and in their details.

■ **Stop and Think**

1. Three aspects of development are addressed by theories discussed in this chapter; list them.

2. These theories seek to explain the development of people in widely differing cultures. What environmental or social factors could influence child development?

3. These theories explain much about human development, but not everything. In what ways do you think a child's progress in school might be affected by language development and physical development?

4. Aspects of development that can be separated in a textbook are less distinct in reality. List ways that the various aspects of development influence one another.

PIAGET'S THEORY OF COGNITIVE DEVELOPMENT

Jean Piaget is probably the best known child psychologist who ever lived. He was born in Switzerland in 1896, and by age eleven had already published his first scientific paper, about birds. His education was as a biologist, and he became an expert on shellfish. Only after receiving his doctorate in biology did he become

Stage Theories of Development
Explanations of various aspects of development that stress the existence of series of steps or phases of growth

Jean Piaget proposed a theory that suggests people progress through four stages of cognitive development. He arrived at his theory after observing his own and other children.

Schemes
Mental patterns that guide behavior

Assimilation
Interpreting new experiences in relation to existing schemes

interested in psychology, basing his earliest theories on careful observation of his own three children. Piaget thought of himself as applying biological principles and methods to the study of human development, and many of the terms he introduced to psychology were drawn directly from biology.

Principal Concepts in Piaget's Theory

Piaget saw the development of a child's intellectual, or cognitive, abilities as progressing through four distinct stages. Each stage is characterized by the emergence of new abilities, which allows for a major reorganization in the child's thinking. For Piaget, development depends in large part on the child's manipulation of and active interaction with the environment. In Piaget's view, knowledge comes from action (see Wadsworth, 1989).

Schemes. The building blocks of Piaget's theories are his ideas about how children and adolescents organize their thinking and behavior and how they change their thinking as they grow. The patterns of behavior or thinking that children and adults use in dealing with objects in the world are called **schemes.** Schemes can be simple, as when a baby knows how to grasp an object within reach, or complex, as when a high school student learns how to attack mathematical problems. Schemes can also be classified as behavioral (grasping, driving a car) or cognitive (solving problems, categorizing concepts). A scheme is something like a computer program that people construct for dealing with the world. Like a computer program, each scheme treats all objects and events in the same way. For example, most young infants will discover that one thing you can do with objects is bang them. When you do this, the object makes a noise and you see the object hitting a surface. This tells you something about the object. Babies also learn about objects by biting them, sucking on them, and throwing them. Each of these behaviors is a scheme. When babies encounter a new object, how are they to know what this object is all about? According to Piaget, they will use the schemes they have developed and will find out if the object makes a loud or soft sound when banged, what it tastes like, whether it gives milk, and maybe whether it rolls or just goes "thud" (see Figure 2.1a).

Assimilation. **Assimilation** occurs when the baby uses a scheme (such as banging or biting) on a new object. Assimilation is basically the process of incorporating a new object or event into an existing scheme. It's similar to putting new data into a computer. But just as data must be correctly coded before being entered into the computer, the object or event to be assimilated must fit an existing scheme. Therefore assimilation involves more than simply taking in new information. It also involves the "filtering or modification of input" (Piaget and Inhelder, 1973) so that the input fits. Give young infants small objects that they have never seen before but that resemble familiar objects and they are likely to grasp them, bite them, and bang them—in other words, they will try to use existing schemes on these unknown things (see Figure 2.1b).

Accommodation. Sometimes, however, old ways of dealing with the world simply don't work. For example, give an egg to a baby who has a banging scheme for small objects and it's obvious what will happen to the egg (Figure 2.1c). Less obvious, however, is what will happen to the baby's banging scheme. Because of the unexpected consequences of banging the egg, the baby might change the scheme. In

Banging is a favorite **scheme** used by babies to explore their world . . .

. . . And **assimilation** occurs when they incorporate new objects into the scheme.

Accomodation occurs when the new object doesn't fit the existing scheme.

Accommodation
Modifying existing schemes to fit new situations

Equilibration
The process of restoring balance between present understanding and new experiences

FIGURE 2.1

Schemes

Babies use patterns of behavior called schemes to learn about their world.

the future the baby may bang some objects hard and others softly. Piaget used the term **accommodation** to describe this changing of an existing scheme to fit new objects. Another example of accommodation would be the actions of a high school freshman who has always breezed through assigned homework, but then encounters more complex assignments from demanding teachers. Accommodation of the existing "homework scheme" must occur for the freshman to achieve a passing grade.

Equilibration. The baby who banged the egg and the freshman faced with piles of homework had to deal with situations that could not be fully handled by existing schemes. This, in Piaget's theory, creates a state of disequilibrium, or an imbalance between what is understood and what is encountered. People naturally try to reduce such imbalances by focusing on the stimuli that cause the disequilibrium and developing new schemes or adapting old ones until equilibrium is restored. This process of restoring balance is called **equilibration**. According to Piaget, learning depends on this process. When equilibrium is upset, children have the opportunity to grow and develop.

Teachers can take advantage of equilibration by creating situations that cause disequilibrium and therefore spark students' curiosity. Science teachers who introduce new concepts by presenting startling experiments use this technique. Social studies teachers use it when they introduce students to provocative ideas. For example, a teacher who asked American students to defend the position of loyalists in the American Revolution might be introducing a state of disequilibrium in students' minds (see Chapter 8). To resolve this disequilibrium, students must accommodate a new perspective and grow in understanding.

However, not all students can detect the discrepancies in new words, images, or ideas that might create disequilibrium. This is a skill that improves as a person's cognitive abilities develop. For example, Inhelder and Piaget (1958, p. 22) describe a five-year-old who stated the belief that small objects float and large ones sink. When shown a large piece of wood floating, he pushed it under the water with all his strength, saying, "You want to stay down, silly!" The child resisted experiencing disequilibrium by denying it, because he was not yet ready to form a more abstract and sophisticated explanation of why things float.

Sensorimotor Stage
Stage during which infants learn about their surroundings by using their senses and motor skills

Reflexes
Natural responses that people are born with

Object Permanence
Knowing an object exists when it is out of sight

The Stages

Piaget divided the cognitive development of children and adolescents into four stages: sensorimotor, preoperational, concrete operational, and formal operational. He believed that all children pass through these stages *in order*, and no child can skip a stage, although different children pass through the stages at somewhat different rates. It is also important to note that individuals may perform at different stages at different times, particularly at points of transition into a new stage (Crain, 1985). Table 2.1 summarizes the approximate ages at which children and adolescents pass through Piaget's four stages. It also shows the major accomplishments of each stage.

Sensorimotor Stage (Birth to Two Years). This stage is called **sensorimotor** because during it babies and young children explore their world by using their senses and their motor skills.

All infants have inborn behaviors, which are often called **reflexes**. Touch a newborn's lips and the baby will begin to suck; place your finger in the palm of an infant's hand and the infant will grasp it. These and other behaviors are innate and are the building blocks from which the infant's first schemes form.

The earliest schemes that children develop help them explore their own bodies. Soon, however, they turn to external objects like rattles and cups, which they grasp, hit and suck—discovering by accident that these actions have interesting results.

Intentional behavior emerges next. No longer will infants only repeat behaviors that make interesting things happen; now they will try to solve very simple problems, such as searching for things that are out of sight. This shows that they now understand that objects continue to exist even if they cannot be seen. When children develop this notion of **object permanence,** they have taken a step toward somewhat more advanced thinking. Once they realize that things exist out of sight, they can start using symbols to represent these things in their minds so that they can think about them.

TABLE 2.1

PIAGET'S STAGES OF COGNITIVE DEVELOPMENT

People progress through four stages of cognitive development between birth and adulthood, according to Jean Piaget. Each stage is marked by the emergence of new intellectual abilities that allow people to understand the world in increasingly complex ways.

Stages	Approximate Ages	Major Accomplishments
Sensorimotor	Birth to 2 years	Formation of concept of "object permanence" and gradual progression from reflexive behavior to goal-directed behavior.
Preoperational	2 to 7 years	Development of the ability to use symbols to represent objects in the world. Thinking remains egocentric and centered.
Concrete operational	7 to 11 years	Improvement in ability to think logically. New abilities include the use of operations that are reversible. Thinking is decentered and problem solving is less restricted by egocentrism. Abstract thinking is not possible.
Formal operational	11 years to adulthood	Abstract and purely symbolic thinking possible. Problems can be solved through the use of systematic experimentation.

Another hallmark of the sensorimotor stage is the emergence of trial-and-error learning. Suppose a desired object is placed out of the infant's reach but on top of a blanket that can be reached. Very young infants might try a few times to reach for the object, but would soon give up. Older infants, however, having failed to reach the object directly, would try to get it in other ways. They would probably discover eventually that the object can be gotten by pulling on the blanket.

Toward the end of the sensorimotor stage, children progress from their earlier trial-and-error approach to problem solving to a more planned approach. For the first time they can mentally represent objects and events. It is now that what most of us would call "thinking" appears. This is a major advance because it means that the child can think through and plan behavior. For example, suppose a two-year-old is in the kitchen watching Mom prepare dinner. If the child knows where the step stool is kept, he or she may ask to have it set up—to afford a better view of the counter and a better chance for a nibble. The child did not stumble onto this solution accidentally. Instead, he or she thought about the problem, figured out a possible solution that used the step stool, tried out the solution mentally, and only then tried the solution in practice.

Preoperational Stage (Two to Seven Years). While infants can learn about and understand the world only by physically manipulating objects, the preschooler has greater ability to think about things, and can use symbols to mentally represent objects. For example, the letter "a" can stand for "apple" or for the *a* sound. During the **preoperational stage** children's language and concepts develop at an incredible rate. Yet much of their thinking remains surprisingly primitive. One of Piaget's earliest and most important discoveries was that young children lacked the principle of **conservation**. For example, if you pour milk from a tall, narrow beaker into a short, wide one in the presence of a preoperational child, the child will firmly believe that the tall glass has more milk (see Figure 2.2). The child focuses on only one aspect (the height of the milk), ignoring all others, and cannot be convinced that the amount of milk is the same. Similarly, a preoperational child is likely to believe that a sandwich cut in four pieces is more sandwich, or that a line of blocks that is spread out contains more blocks than a line that is compressed, even after being shown that the number of blocks is identical. Wadsworth (1978) presents the following interview with a preoperational child to illustrate this point.

The examiner arranges a row of nine blue blocks, each about an inch apart, between himself and the child.

Preoperational Stage
Stage at which children learn to mentally represent things

Conservation
The concept that certain properties of an object (such as weight) remain the same regardless of changes in other properties (such as length)

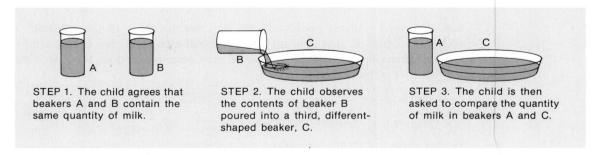

STEP 1. The child agrees that beakers A and B contain the same quantity of milk.

STEP 2. The child observes the contents of beaker B poured into a third, different-shaped beaker, C.

STEP 3. The child is then asked to compare the quantity of milk in beakers A and C.

FIGURE 2.2

The Task of Conservation
A typical procedure for studying conservation of liquid quantity.
(From Liebert et al., 1986)

FIGURE 2.3

Centration

Centration, or focusing on only one aspect of a situation, helps explain some errors in perception made by young children

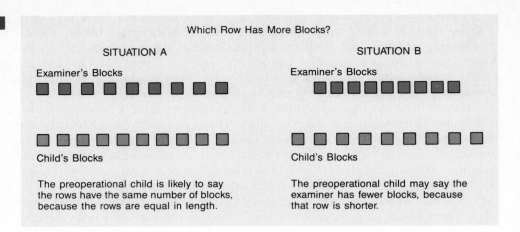

EXAMINER: Will you make a row of blocks using the red ones just like my row, and right in front of you? (The child makes a row below the examiner's row by first placing two end blocks in position, then placing eight blocks between those two without any careful comparison. See Figure 2.3.)

EXAMINER: Does one row of blocks have more blocks than the other, or do they both have the same number?

CHILD: They're the same.

E: Are you sure?

C: Yes.

E: How do you know they're the same number of blocks? (request for reasoning)

C: I can count them. (Child proceeds to count the blocks. He counts nine for the blue row and ten for the red row.) They're different. There are more reds.

E: Can you make them so they have the same number? (Child removes one of the red blocks from the middle of the row and lines the other red ones up corresponding to the blue ones.)

E: Now both rows have the same number of blocks?

C: Yes.

E: Okay, I'm going to move my blue blocks together like this. (The row of blue blocks is collapsed so that they are about one-half inch apart. See Figure 2.3b.) Now, are there more blocks in my row or in your row, or do we both have the same number of blocks?

C: I have more.

E: How can you tell? (request for reasoning)

C: My row sticks out more. (preoperational reasoning)

E: Okay, I'm going to make my row just like your row again. Who has more blocks now, or do we have the same number of blocks? (Examiner makes his row of blocks as long as Child's.)

C: Same.

E: How do you know? (request for reasoning)

C: They both come out to here and here. (The child points to the ends of each row.)

E: Now if I move your blocks closer together (Child's row of blocks is collapsed the way Examiner's row was previously), do we both have the same number of blocks or does one of us have more blocks than the other?

C: You have more.

E: How do you know I have more? (request for reasoning)

C: Same as before; your row is bigger.

(Adapted from Wadsworth, 1978, p. 225)

One characteristic of preschoolers' thought that helps explain the error on conservation tasks is **centration.** In the example illustrated in Figure 2.2, children might have claimed that there was less milk after pouring because they *centered* on the height of the milk, ignoring its width. Similarly, in the block example just quoted, the child is focusing on one aspect of the problem (the lengths of the rows) and ignoring another, equally important one (their density).

Preschoolers' thinking can also be characterized as being irreversible. **Reversibility** is a very important aspect of thinking, according to Piaget, and simply means the ability to change direction in one's thinking so that one can return to a starting point. As adults, for example, we know that if $7 + 5 = 12$, then $12 - 5 = 7$. If we add five things to seven things and then take the five things away (reverse what we've done), we're left with seven things. If preoperational children could think this way, then they could mentally reverse the process of pouring the milk and realize that if the milk were poured back into the tall beaker, its quantity would not change. Likewise, they would understand that four pieces of a sandwich could be put back together to form the original one, or that the blocks could be put back to a one-to-one correspondence between the rows. Such reversible mental routines are called **operations.**

Another characteristic of the preoperational child's thinking is its focus on states. In the milk problem the milk was poured from one beaker to another. Preschoolers ignore this pouring process and focus only on the beginning state (milk in a tall beaker) and end state (milk in a wide beaker). "It is as though [the child] were viewing a series of still pictures instead of the movie that the adult sees" (Phillips, 1975). You can understand how a preoccupation with states can interfere with a child's thinking if you imagine yourself presented with the milk problem and being asked to close your eyes while the milk is poured. Lacking the knowledge of what took place, you would be left with only your perception of the milk in the wide beaker and your memory of the milk in the tall beaker.

Unlike adults, the young preschooler forms "concepts" that vary in definition from situation to situation and are not always logical. How else can we explain the two-year-old's ability to treat a stuffed animal as an inanimate object one minute and an animate object the next? Eventually, though, the child's concepts become more consistent and less private. Children become increasingly concerned that their definitions of things match other people's. But they still lack the ability to coordinate one concept with another. Consider the following problem:

ADULT: Sally, how many boys are in your play group?

SALLY: Eight.

ADULT: How many girls are in your play group?

Centration
Paying attention to only one aspect of an object or a situation

Reversibility
The ability to perform a mental operation and then reverse one's thinking to return to the starting point

Operations
Actions carried out through logical mental processes

If liquid is poured from a wide beaker into a thin one, does the amount of liquid change? Children who do not understand the principle of conservation would probably say yes.

SALLY: Five.

ADULT: Are there more boys or girls in your play group?

SALLY: More boys.

ADULT: Are boys children?

SALLY: Yes.

ADULT: Are girls children?

SALLY: Yes.

ADULT: Are there more boys or children in your play group?

SALLY: More boys.

ADULT: How do you know?

SALLY: I just do!

Sally clearly understands the concepts of "boy," "girl," and even "more." She also knows what children are. However, she lacks the ability to put these separate pieces of knowledge together to correctly answer the question comparing boys and children. She also cannot explain her answer, which is why Piaget used the term "intuitive" to describe her thinking.

Another aspect of preschoolers' thought is that it is **egocentric.** These children believe that everyone sees the world exactly as they do. For example, Piaget and Inhelder (1956) seated children on one side of a display of three mountains, and asked them to describe how the scene looked to a doll seated on the other side. Children below the age of six or seven described the doll's view as being identical to their own, even though it was apparent (to adults) that this could not be so. Preoperational children also interpret events entirely in reference to themselves. Owen et al. (1981) cite a passage from A. A. Milne's *Winnie the Pooh* to illustrate the young child's egocentrism. Winnie the Pooh is sitting in the forest, and hears a buzzing sound.

> That buzzing-noise means something. You don't get a buzzing-noise like that just buzzing and buzzing, without its meaning something. If there is a buzzing-noise, somebody's making a buzzing-noise, and the only reason for making a buzzing-noise that *I* know of is because you're a bee . . . and the only reason for being a bee that *I* know of is for making honey . . . and the only reason for making honey is so as *I* can eat it.

Of course, egocentrism does diminish gradually over time. Two-year-old Benjamin and his four-year-old brother Jacob were driving with their father through dairy country and admiring the cows. "Why do you think farmers keep cows?" said their father. "So my [I] can look at them!" said Benjamin. "No," said his older and wiser brother. "The farmer likes to play with them." Benjamin's egocentrism is extreme; he believes that everything that happens in the world relates to him. Jacob, at four, realizes that the farmer has his own needs, but assumes that they are the same as his.

Preoperational children also take unconventional steps in reasoning rather than using the more logical reasoning that comes later (Phillips, 1975). Consider the following description by Piaget of his daughter Jacqueline, who at the time was two years old:

> J. wanted to go and see a little hunchbacked neighbor whom she used to meet on her walks. A few days earlier she had asked why he had a hump, and after I had explained

she said: "Poor boy, he's ill, he has a hump." The day before J. had also wanted to go and see him but he had influenza, which J. called being "ill in bed." We started out for our walk and on the way J. said: "Is he still in bed?" "No. I saw him this morning, he isn't in bed now." [J. replied:] "He hasn't a big hump now!" (Piaget, 1962, p. 231)

How did Jacqueline reason that the boy's recovery from influenza also meant that he had recovered from his hunchback condition? Instead of distinguishing between two *general* classes of illness, Jacqueline reasoned from one *particular* illness to another, treating both as equivalent. Thus, when cured of one, the boy was cured of the other. In effect, she created a link between two particular events where none existed. As another example, Lucienne, another of Piaget's daughters, said at four years of age, "I haven't had my nap so it isn't afternoon" (Piaget, 1962, p. 232). Here the child reasoned that one particular event (the afternoon) depended upon another particular event (the nap), and if one hadn't occurred, neither could the other.

Concrete Operational Stage (Seven to Eleven Years).   During the elementary school years the cognitive abilities of children undergo dramatic changes. The thinking of an elementary student is therefore quite different from that of a preschooler. Elementary school children no longer have difficulties with conservation problems (such as the milk and block problems) because they have acquired the concept of reversibility. For example, they can now see that the amount of milk in the short, wide beaker must be

Concrete Operational Stage
Stage at which children develop skills of logical reasoning and conservation but can use these skills only when dealing with familiar situations

Perceived Appearance
How something appears to the eye

Inferred Reality
The meaning of stimuli in the context of relevant information

Learning to compare and sort objects according to a particular attribute is an important skill for school-age children.

the same as that in the tall beaker because if the milk were poured back in the tall beaker, it would be at the same level as before. This means that the child is able to imagine the milk being poured back and can recognize the consequences of this—mental skills that are beyond the abilities of the preoperational child.

One fundamental difference between preoperational and **concrete operational** children is that the younger child, who is in the preoperational stage, responds to **perceived appearances,** while the older, concrete operational child responds to **inferred reality.** Flavell (1986) demonstrated this by showing children a red car and then covering it with a filter that made it look black. When asked what color the car is, three-year-olds responded "black," six-year-olds "red." The older, concrete operational child is able to respond to *inferred reality,* seeing things in the context of other meanings; preschoolers see what they see, with little ability to infer the meaning behind what they see.

It is no coincidence that throughout the world children start formal schooling at an age close to the beginning of the concrete operational stage. Most of what children are taught in school requires the skills that appear in this stage. For example, school-aged children who have entered the concrete operational stage can make sense of the question, "If I had three candy bars and you had two, how many would we have all together?" They can visualize the situation without actually seeing the candy bars or being distracted by irrelevant aspects of the situation. They can form concepts and see relationships between things. They are no longer quite so egocentric, but are beginning to see things from another's perspective.

One important task that children learn during the concrete operational stage is to arrange things in order according to one attribute, such as size or weight—for example, lining up sticks from smallest to largest. To do this, they must be able to compare separate but related bits of information along a scale, in this case length. Once this ability is acquired, children can master a related skill known as "transitivity," which requires the mental arrangement and comparison of objects. For example, if you tell preoperational preschoolers that Tom is taller than Becky and Becky is taller than Fred, they won't see that Tom is taller than Fred. Logical inferences such as this are not possible until the stage of concrete operations, during which school-aged children develop the ability to make two mental transformations that require reversible thinking. The first of these is inversion (+A is reversed by −A), and the second is reciprocity (A < B is reciprocated by B > A). Since these kinds of logical inferences are important in such subjects as mathematics and science, lessons for elementary school students in these subjects must take into account the children's newly developing skills of logic.

A final ability that children acquire during the concrete operational stage is class inclusion. Recall the example of Sally, who was in the preoperational stage and believed that there were more boys than children in her play group. What Sally lacked was the ability to think simultaneously about the whole class (children) and the subordinate class (boys, girls). She could make comparisons *within* a class, as shown by her ability to compare one part (the boys) with another part (the girls). She also knew that boys and girls are both members of the larger class called children. What she could not do, however, was make comparisons *between* classes. Concrete operational children, on the other hand, have no trouble with this type of problem because they have additional tools of thinking. They no longer suffer from irreversibility of thinking and can now re-create a relationship between a part and the whole. Second, concrete operational thought is decentered, so that the child can now focus on two classes simultaneously. Third, the concrete operational child's thinking is no longer limited to reasoning about part-to-part relationships. Now part-to-whole relationships can be dealt with as well. It is important to note that these changes do not happen all at the same time. Rather, they occur gradually during the concrete operational stage.

While the differences between the mental abilities of preoperational preschoolers and concrete operational elementary school students are dramatic, concrete operational children still do not think like adults. They are very much rooted in the world as it is, and have difficulty with abstract thought. Flavell describes the concrete operational child as taking "an earthbound, concrete, practical-minded sort of problem-solving approach, one that persistently fixates on the perceptible and inferable reality right there in front of him. A theorist the elementary-school child is not" (1985, p. 103). This is where the term "concrete operational" comes from. The child can form concepts, see relationships, and solve problems, but only so long as they involve objects and situations that are familiar.

Formal Operational Stage (Eleven Years to Adulthood).   Sometime around the onset of puberty children's thinking begins to develop into the form characteristic of adults. The preadolescent begins to be able to think abstractly and to see possibilities beyond the here-and-now. These abilities continue to develop into adulthood.

With the stage of **formal operational thought** comes the ability to deal with potential or hypothetical situations so that the "form" is now separate from the "content." Consider the following problem: A three-foot-tall man jogged ten miles today and five miles yesterday. How many miles did the man jog? Elementary school children in the concrete operational stage might not answer, not because they cannot add ten and five, but because they cannot imagine a three-foot-tall man. Since their thought is concrete, they are unable to draw conclusions from situations that may be possible but are unfamiliar. Another example, the transitivity problem, illustrates the advances brought about by formal thought. Recall the concrete operational child who, when told that Tom was taller than Becky and Becky was taller than Fred, understood that Tom was taller than Fred. If, however, the problem had been phrased the following way, only an older child who had entered the formal operational stage would have solved it: Becky is shorter than Tom, and Becky is taller than Fred: who is the tallest of the three? Here the younger concrete operational child, lost in the combinations of greater-than and less-than relationships, would reason that Becky and Tom are "short," Becky and Fred are "tall," and therefore Fred is the tallest, followed by Becky, and then Tom, who is the shortest. Adolescents in the formal operational stage may also get confused by the differing relationships in this problem, but they can imagine several different relationships between the heights of Becky, Tom, and Fred, and can figure out the accuracy of each until they hit on the correct one. This example shows another ability of preadolescents and adolescents who have reached the formal operational stage, namely, they can monitor or "think about" their own thinking.

Inhelder and Piaget (1958) described one task that will be approached differently by elementary school students in the concrete operational stage and by adolescents in the formal operational stage. The children or adolescents were given a pendulum consisting of a string with a weight at the end. They could change the length of the string, the amount of weight, the height from which the pendulum was released, and the force with which the pendulum was pushed. They were asked which of these factors influenced the speed at which the pendulum swings back and forth. Essentially, the task was to discover a principle of physics, which is that only the length of the string makes any difference in the speed of the pendulum (the shorter the string, the faster it swings). This experiment is illustrated in Figure 2.4.

Formal Operations
Stage at which the ability to deal with hypothetical situations and to reason abstractly is acquired

FIGURE 2.4

A Test of Problem-Solving Abilities

The pendulum problem uses a string, which can be shortened or lengthened, and a set of weights. When children in the concrete operational stage are asked what determines the speed of the pendulum's swing, they will tackle the problem less systematically than will adolescents who have entered the stage for formal operations. (The answer is that only the string's length affects the speed of the pendulum's swing.)

(Inhelder and Piaget, 1958, p. 68)

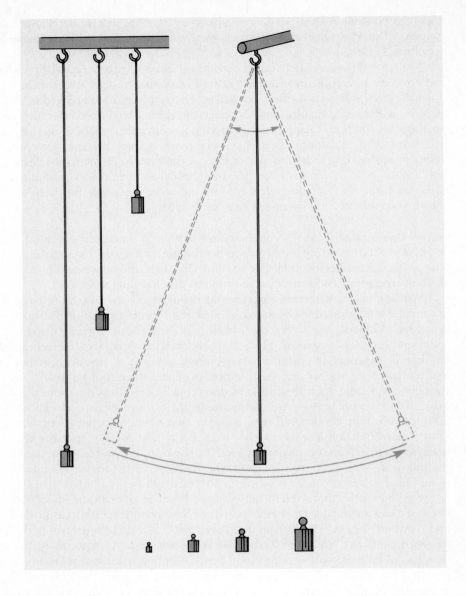

The adolescent who has reached the stage of formal operations is likely to proceed quite systematically, varying one factor at a time (for example, leaving the string the same length and trying different weights). For example, in Inhelder and Piaget's (1958) experiment one fifteen-year-old selected 100 grams with a long string and a medium-length string, then 20 grams with a long and a short string, and finally 200 grams with a long and a short string, and concluded, "It's the length of the string that makes it go faster and slower; the weight doesn't play any role" (p. 75). In contrast, ten-year-olds (who can be assumed to be in the concrete operational stage) proceeded in a chaotic fashion, varying many factors at the same time and hanging on to preconceptions. One boy varied simultaneously the weight and the impetus; then the weight, the impetus, and the length; then the impetus, the weight, and the elevation, etc., and first concludes: *"It's by changing the weight and the push, certainly not the string."*—"How do you know that the string has nothing to do with it?"—*"Because it's*

the same string."—He has not varied its length in the last several trials; previously he had varied it simultaneously with the impetus, thus complicating the account of the experiment. (Adapted from Inhelder and Piaget, 1958, p. 71).

The abilities that make up formal operational thought—thinking abstractly, testing hypotheses, and forming concepts that are independent of physical reality—are critical in the learning of higher-order skills. For example, learning algebra or abstract geometry requires the use of formal operational thought, as does understanding difficult concepts in science, social science, and other subjects.

The formal operational stage brings cognitive development to a close for Piaget. What began as a set of inborn reflexes has developed into a system of cognitive structures that makes human thought what it is. This does not mean, however, that no intellectual growth takes place beyond adolescence. According to Piaget, the foundation has been laid and no new structures need to develop; all that is needed is the addition of knowledge and the development of more complex schemes. However, some researchers (for example, Commons, Richards, and Kuhn, 1982) have taken issue with Piaget's belief that the formal operational stage is the final one.

■ Stop and Think

1. Children in the lower elementary grades have a newly acquired ability to put perceived information into context—to respond to inferred reality rather than perceived appearances. Think of a lesson in which this skill would be important.

2. Young people differ in their ability to formulate and consider hypothetical situations. What effect would this have in the subjects and grade you expect to teach?

Criticisms and Revisions of Piaget's Theory

Piaget's theory revolutionized and still dominates the study of human development. However, some of his central principles have been questioned in more recent research, and modern descriptions of development have revised many of his views.

Teachers must consider their students' levels of cognitive development when planning lessons. This is especially true in science lessons, which often require students to tackle problems systematically and form hypotheses.

Proximal Zone of Development
Level of development immediately
above a person's present level

Psychosocial Theory
A set of principles that relates social
environment to psychological
development

One important Piagetian principle is that *development precedes learning*. That is, Piaget held that developmental stages were largely fixed, and that such concepts as conservation could not be taught. However, research has established some cases in which Piagetian tasks can be taught to children at earlier developmental stages (Gardner, 1982; Price, 1982). Piaget (1964) responded to such demonstrations by arguing that the children must have been on the verge of the next developmental stage already—but the fact remains that some (though not all) of the Piagetian tasks can be taught to children well below the age at which they usually appear without instruction.

Other critics have argued that Piaget underestimated children's abilities by using confusing, abstract language and overly difficult tasks. Several researchers have found that young children can succeed on simpler forms of Piaget's tasks that require the same skills (Donaldson, 1978; Black, 1981). For example, Gelman (1979) found that young children could solve the conservation problem involving the number of blocks in a row when the task was presented in a simpler way with simpler language. Boden (1980) found that the same formal operational task produced passing rates from 19 to 98 percent, depending on the complexities of the instructions (see also Nagy and Griffiths, 1982).

Similar kinds of research have also led to a reassessment of children's egocentricity. In simple, practical contexts children demonstrated their ability to consider the point of view of others (Donaldson, 1978; Black, 1981; Damon, 1983).

The result of this research has been a recognition that children are more competent than Piaget originally thought, especially when their practical knowledge is being assessed. Obviously, older children do succeed at tasks that overwhelm younger children, so differences in their thinking must exist. Gelman (1979) suggests that the cognitive abilities of preschoolers are more fragile than those of older children and therefore are only evident under certain conditions. The skills that preschoolers do display, however, are the roots of later, more complex understandings.

For more on revisions of Piaget's theories, see Miller (1983) and Nagy and Griffiths (1982).

ERIKSON'S THEORY OF PERSONAL AND SOCIAL DEVELOPMENT

As children improve their cognitive skills, they are also developing self-concepts, ways of interacting with others, and attitudes toward the world. Understanding these personal and social developments is critical to the teacher's ability to motivate, teach, and successfully interact with students at various ages.

Like cognitive development, personal and social development proceeds in stages. We speak of the "terrible twos," not the "terrible ones" or "terrible threes," and when someone is acting in an unreasonable, selfish way, we accuse that person of "behaving like a two-year-old." The words "adolescent" and "teenager" are associated in our minds with rebelliousness, identity crises, hero worship, and sexual awakening. These associations are not random, they reflect stages of development that we all go through.

This section focuses on a theory of personal and social development proposed by Erik Erikson, which is an adaptation of the developmental theories of the great psychiatrist Anna Freud. Erikson's work is often called a **psychosocial theory** because it relates principles of psychological and social development. Like Piaget, Erikson had no formal training in psychology, but as a young man he was trained by Freud as a psychoanalyst.

Piaget's theory of cognitive development has many important implications. One is that it makes sense to listen carefully to children and to watch them solve problems to understand how they think and how they perceive their world. Another is that instruction must be adapted to students' developmental levels. It is important to extend students beyond their current level of functioning, but not too far. For example, it is probably pointless to teach first-graders world geography because they have no conception of what a "country," "state," or even "city" is. It would make more sense to teach them local geography—their neighborhood, school, classroom, and so on. Teaching algebra to fourth-graders is also probably a waste of time because the subject requires more ability to deal with abstractions than students at the concrete operational stage are likely to have.

Another implication is that children in preschool and elementary school need to see examples of concepts. With young children you do not say, "Imagine that I had a pie with six slices and I took out two of the slices." Rather, you must show them a picture of a pie and physically remove the slices if you expect them to learn the underlying mathematical concepts. Applying Piaget's insights to instruction means constant use of demonstrations and physical representations of ideas. Students should be allowed to experiment with materials in order to accommodate new understandings, and to discover information for themselves. Discovery learning (Bruner, 1966), discussed in Chapter 6, is one way in which Piaget's principles have been put into action in classroom instruction. Discovery learning emphasizes the active participation of students in learning principles and concepts.

Piagetian principles of instruction are most often applied in preschool and kindergarten programs that emphasize (1) learning through discovery and hands-on experiences, and (2) that the teacher's role is not to instruct children directly but to set up environments in which students can have a wide variety of experiences (see, for example, Lavatelli, 1970; Kamii and DeVries, 1974). Piagetian principles have also been used in elementary school instruction (for example, Weikart et al., 1971).

Joyce and Weil (1980) described a general strategy for applying Piagetian concepts to instruction:

- *Phase 1:* Present a puzzling situation well matched to learners' development stage. For example, ask students for their theories about why things float, and then show examples of floating and sinking objects (such as heavy logs float, light paper sinks) that challenge their current understandings.
- *Phase 2:* Elicit student responses and ask for justifications. Offer counter-suggestions, probe student responses. For example, ask students to give hypotheses to explain why some things float and others sink, and confront them with additional demonstrations to further explore the phenomenon. Create an environment that is accepting of wrong but thoughtful answers. Always ask students to give reasons for their answers.
- *Phase 3:* Present related tasks and probe students' reasoning. Offer counter suggestions. The idea here is to see that the concepts learned previously transfer to new related concepts. For example, if students have acquired the concept of why things float, have them suggest why some balloons rise in the air and others do not, to see if they can generalize to a new situation.

PROXIMAL ZONE OF DEVELOPMENT

One important concept related to the application of Piagetian theory to instruction is Vygotsky's (1978) idea of the proximal zone of development. Vygotsky hypothesized that there are certain skills or understandings that students have mastered completely, others that they are on the verge of mastering, and others that are beyond their present capacity to accommodate. He argued that instruction should focus on those skills that students are "on the verge" of learning, which he called the **proximal zone of development.** That is, the purpose of instruction is to gradually stretch students' understandings into new territory just beyond comfortable concepts. Vygotsky (and Piaget himself) suggested that students be allowed to work and reason together, because if two similar students work together, the one who grasps a concept first is almost certainly operating in the other's proximal zone of development. In fact, researchers have found that by having a student who has mastered conservation work with another student who has not, or even by having two nonconservers work together, students can learn to conserve (Murray, 1982). In practical terms, this means that slightly more advanced students can explain to their classmates how they grasped the concept in terms that directly address the difficulties the slightly less advanced students are experiencing.

TABLE 2.2

ERIKSON'S STAGES OF PERSONAL AND SOCIAL DEVELOPMENT

As people grow, they face a series of psychosocial crises that shape personality, according to Erik Erikson. Each crisis focuses on a particular aspect of personality and each involves the person's relationship with other people.

	Approximate Ages	Psychosocial Crises	Significant Relationships	Psychosocial Emphasis
I	Birth to 18 mo.	Trust vs. mistrust	Maternal person	To get To give in return
II	18 mo. to 3 yr.	Autonomy vs. doubt	Parental persons	To hold on To let go
III	3 to 6 yr.	Initiative vs. guilt	Basic family	To make (= going after) To "make like" (= playing)
IV	6 to 12 yr.	Industry vs. inferiority	Neighborhood, school	To make things To make things together
V	12 to 18 yr.	Identity vs. role confusion	Peer groups and models of leadership	To be oneself (or not to be) To share being oneself
VI	Young Adulthood	Intimacy vs. isolation	Partners in friendship, sex, competition, cooperation	To lose and find oneself in another
VII	Middle Adulthood	Generativity vs. self-absorption	Divided labor and shared household	To take care of
VIII	Late Adulthood	Integrity vs. despair	"Mankind" "My kind"	To be, through having been To face not being

SOURCE: Adapted from Erikson, 1980, p. 178.

Erikson hypothesized that people pass through eight psychosocial stages in their lifetimes. At each stage there are crises or critical issues to be resolved. Most people resolve each crisis satisfactorily and put it behind them to take on new challenges, but some people do not completely resolve these crises and must continue to deal with them later in life (Miller, 1983). For example, many adults have yet to resolve the "identity crisis" of adolescence.

Table 2.2 summarizes the eight stages of life according to Erikson's theory. Each is identified by the central crisis that must be resolved.

The Stages

Stage I: Trust versus Mistrust (Birth to Eighteen Months). The goal of infancy is to develop a basic trust in the world. Erikson (1968, p. 96) defined basic trust as "an essential trustfulness of others as well as a fundamental sense of one's own trustworthiness." This shows the dual nature of this crisis: infants not only have their needs met, but they also help in the meeting of the mother's needs. The mother, or maternal figure, is usually the first important person in the child's world. She is the one who must satisfy the infant's need for food and affection. If the mother is inconsistent or rejecting, she becomes a source of frustration for the infant rather than a source of pleasure. This creates in the infant a sense of mistrust for his or her world that may persist throughout childhood and into adulthood.

Stage II: Autonomy versus Doubt (Eighteen Months to Three Years).   By the age of two, most babies can walk and have learned enough about language to communicate with other people. Children in the "terrible twos" no longer want to depend totally on others. Instead, they strive toward autonomy, or the ability to do things for themselves. The child's desires for power and independence often clash with those of the parent. Erikson believes that children at this stage have the dual desire "to hold on" and "to let go." Nowhere is this more apparent than during toilet training, which usually takes place in this stage. Erikson cautioned parents against strict toilet training because he believed that this led to an unfavorable resolution of the Stage II crisis and caused children to become overcompulsive adults (Thomas, 1979).

Parents who are flexible enough to permit their children to explore freely and do things for themselves, while at the same time providing an everpresent guiding hand, encourage the establishment of a sense of autonomy. Parents who are overly restrictive and harsh give their children a sense of powerlessness and incompetence. This can lead to shame and doubt in one's abilities.

Stage III: Initiative versus Guilt (Three to Six Years).   During this period children's continually maturing motor and language skills permit them to be increasingly aggressive and vigorous in the exploration of both their social and their physical environment. The "troublesome threes" are accompanied by a growing sense of initiative, which can be encouraged by parents and other family members who permit children to run, jump, play, slide, and throw. "Being firmly convinced that he is a person on his own, the child must now find out what kind of person he may become" (Erikson, 1968, p. 115). Parents who severely punish children's attempts at initiative will make them feel guilty about their natural urges both during this stage and later in life.

Stage IV: Industry versus Inferiority (Six to Twelve Years).   One might say that personality at the first stage crystallizes around the conviction "I am what I am given," at the second stage around "I am what I will," and at the third stage around "I am what I can imagine I will be." The fourth stage is characterized by the conviction "I am what I learn" (Erikson, 1980).

Entry into school brings with it a huge expansion in the child's social world. Teachers and peers take on increasing importance for the child, while the influence of parents decreases. Children now want to make things. Success brings with it a sense of industry, a good feeling about oneself and one's abilities. Failure, on the other hand, creates a negative self-image, a sense of inadequacy that may hinder future learning. Failure need not be real; it can be an inability to "measure up to" one's own standards or those of parents, teachers, or brothers and sisters.

Stage V: Identity versus Role Confusion (Twelve to Eighteen Years).   The question "Who am I?" becomes important during adolescence. To answer it, adolescents increasingly turn away from parents and toward peer groups. Erikson believes that during adolescence the individual's rapidly changing physiology, coupled with pressures to make decisions about future education and career, creates the need to question and redefine the psychosocial identity established during the earlier stages.

Success helps young schoolchildren develop healthy self-images.

Adolescence is a time of change. Teenagers experiment with various sexual, occupational, and educational roles as they try to find out who they are and who they can be. This new sense of self, or "ego identity," is not simply the sum of the prior identifications. Rather, it is a reassembly or "an alignment of the individual's *basic drives* (ego) with his endowment (resolutions of the previous crises) and his opportunities (needs, skills, goals, and demands of adolescence and approaching adulthood)" (Erikson, 1980, p. 94).

In Stage I infants try to develop trust in themselves and in their mother or a maternal figure. In a similar manner, adolescents strive to find idols in which to place their trust and faith. At Stage II babies strive to assert autonomy; adolescents seek to choose a direction for the future and, like the "terrible two-year-old," often resist attempts at control. During the third stage preschoolers are free to play and to imagine an unlimited number of roles for themselves. Erikson saw this recurring in adolescence, when teenagers place an almost blind trust in peers and in adults who seem to confirm the teenagers' visions for themselves and their society. Idols are usually chosen because they embody the independence that adolescents seek; they often engage in shocking or even antisocial behavior. (Few teenagers wear an "Albert Einstein" or a "Mother Teresa" T-shirt.) Finally, school-aged children want to make things work and make them work well. In adolescence this becomes the need to choose a career. This last choice, Erikson believed, is the most difficult for teenagers. Role confusion can plague adolescents who have not successfully integrated their psychosocial past, present, and future.

■ **Stop and Think**
Recall from your elementary school years some experiences that gave you confidence in your abilities. Recall situations that made you feel academically inferior to others. How will you encourage your students to feel they have the ability to succeed in school?

Stage VI: Intimacy versus Isolation (Young Adulthood). Once young people know who they are and where they are going, the stage is set for the sharing of their life with another. The theme of this stage is best expressed as "to lose and find oneself in another." The young adult is now ready to form a new relationship of trust and intimacy with another individual, a "partner in friendship, sex, competition, and cooperation." This relationship should enhance the identity of both partners without stifling the growth of either. The young adult who does not seek out such intimacy, or whose repeated tries fail, may retreat into isolation.

Stage VII: Generativity versus Self-absorption (Middle Adulthood). Generativity refers to "the interest in establishing and guiding the next generation" (Erikson, 1980, p. 103). Typically, this comes through raising one's own children. However, the crisis of this stage can also be successfully resolved through other forms of productivity and creativity, such as teaching. During this stage people should continue to grow; if they don't, a sense of "stagnation and interpersonal impoverishment" develops, leading to self-absorption or self-indulgence (Erikson, 1980, p. 103).

Stage VIII: Integrity versus Despair (Late Adulthood). In the final stage of psycho-social development people look back over their lifetime and resolve their final identity crisis. Acceptance of accomplishments, failures, and ultimate limitations brings with it a sense of integrity; a realization that one's life has been one's own responsibility. The finality of death must also be faced and accepted. Despair can occur in those who regret the way they have led their life and how it has turned out.

As with Piaget's stages, it is important to note that not all people experience Erikson's crises to the same degree or at the same time. The age ranges stated here may represent the best times for a crisis to be resolved, but they are not the only possible times. For example, children born into chaotic homes that failed to give them adequate security may develop trust after being adopted or otherwise brought into a more stable environment. People whose negative school experiences gave them a sense of inferiority may find as they enter the work world that they can learn and do have valuable skills, a realization that may help them finally resolve the industry versus inferiority crisis others resolved in their elementary school years.

Erikson's theory emphasizes the role of the environment, both in causing the crises and in determining how they will be resolved. The stages of personal and social development are played out in constant interactions with others and with society as a whole. During the first two stages the interactions are primarily with parents and other family members, but the school begins to play a role for most children in Stage III (initiative versus guilt), and is central in Stage IV (industry versus inferiority) and Stage V (identify versus role confusion).

Figure 2.5 relates the developmental stages described by Erikson to those described by Piaget.

MORAL REASONING

Society could not function without rules that tell people how to communicate with one another, how to avoid hurting others, and how to get along in life generally. If you are around children much, you may have noticed that they are often rigid about rules. Things are either right or wrong, there's no in between. If you remember back to your own years in junior high or high school, you may recall being shocked to find that people sometimes break rules on purpose, and that the rules that apply to some

FIGURE 2.5

Stages in Personal and Cognitive Development

During childhood, adolescence, and adulthood, people face eight crises of personal and social development, and progress through four stages of cognitive development, according to Erikson and Piaget.

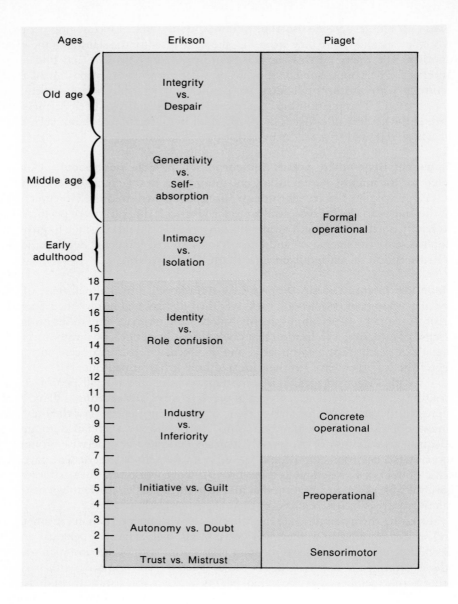

people may not apply to others. These experiences probably changed your concept of rules. Your idea of laws might also have changed when you learned how they are made. People meet and debate and vote; the laws that are made one year can be changed the next. The more complexity you are able to see, the more you find exists.

Just as children differ from adults in cognitive and personal development, they also differ in their moral reasoning. Piaget studied this difference by watching children play games. First we will look at the two stages of moral reasoning described by Piaget, then we will discuss a similar theory developed by Lawrence Kohlberg. There is a relationship between the cognitive stages of development and the ability to reason about moral issues. Kohlberg believed that the development of the logical structures proposed by Piaget are necessary to, although not sufficient for, advances in the area of moral judgment and reasoning.

Piaget's Theory of Moral Development

Piaget spent a great deal of time watching children play marbles and asking them about the rules of the game. He felt that by understanding how children reasoned about rules, he could understand their moral development. The first thing he discovered was that before about the age of six, there were no true rules. Children of about two years old simply played with the marbles. From two to six they expressed an awareness of rules but did not understand their purpose or the need to follow them. The idea of "winning" the game also did not appear, or if it did, it was not by any "rule" that Piaget could understand.

Between the ages of six and ten, Piaget found, children began to acknowledge the existence of rules, though they were inconsistent in following them. Frequently several children supposedly playing the same game were observed to be playing by different sets of rules. Children at this age also had no understanding that game rules are arbitrary and something that a group can decide by itself. Instead, they saw rules as being imposed by some higher authority and unchangeable. It was not until the age of ten or twelve years that Piaget found that children conscientiously used and followed rules. At this age every child playing the game followed the same set of rules. Children understood that the rules existed to give the game direction and to minimize disputes between players. They understood that rules were something that everyone agreed upon, and therefore if everyone agreed to change them, they could be changed.

Because they have no conception of rules, morality does not exist for the infant and preschooler. Piaget's stages of moral development do not begin until around the age of six, when children begin to make the transition from preoperational to concrete operational thinking. Piaget used the changes that take place in understanding and application of rules to propose that there are two stages of moral development (Table 2.3).

TABLE 2.3

PIAGET'S STAGES OF MORAL DEVELOPMENT

As people develop their cognitive abilities, their understanding of moral problems also becomes more sophisticated. Young children, who are in the heteronomous stage of morality, are more rigid in their view of right and wrong than older children and adults tend to be.

Heteronomous Morality	Autonomous Morality
Based on relations of constraint; for example, the complete acceptance by the child of adult prescriptions.	Based on relations of cooperation, mutual recognition of equality among autonomous individuals, as in relations between people who are equals.
Reflected in attitudes of *moral realism:* Rules are seen as inflexible requirements, external in origin and authority, not open to negotiation; and right is a matter of literal obedience to adults and rules.	Reflected in *rational* moral attitudes: Rules are viewed as products of mutual agreement, open to renegotiation, made legitimate by personal acceptance and common consent, and right is a matter of acting in accordance with the requirements of cooperation and mutual respect.
Badness is judged in terms of the objective form and consequences of actions; fairness is equated with the content of adult decisions; arbitrary and severe punishments are seen as fair.	Badness is viewed as relative to the actor's intentions; fairness is defined as equal treatment, or taking account of individual needs; fairness of punishment is defined by appropriateness to the offense.
Punishment is seen as an automatic consequence of the offense, and justice as inherent.	Punishment is seen as affected by human intention.

SOURCE: Adapted from Hogan and Emler, 1978, p. 213.

If you have ever discussed moral or social issues in your classes, please sketch an issue that was examined and describe how the class responded.

In Barbara Levin's computer classes in Mount Horeb, Wisc., the issue of copying computer software was discussed:

> As a computer teacher I have held discussions with children from primary, intermediate, and junior high school levels about computer ethics, especially the issue of copying computer software and the differences between the rules for copyrighted programs versus public domain programs. Children have very different responses and rationales for their beliefs about the issue of illegal copying of software. Very young children say they would never make a copy of a computer program if the law says that it is wrong, but the older the children get, the more relativistic their positions become. Junior high (or middle school) kids begin to say things such as "But I won't get caught," or "No one would know if I did that," or "If I paid for the disk I should be able to do whatever I want to with it," or "I'm not really hurting anyone—they're making so much money anyway that one copy doesn't matter." I see developmental differences in children's thinking about these issues, but I don't always know how to help the older children take the perspective of the person who spent hundreds of hours creating a computer program.

In Deanna Seed's elementary school class in Placerville, Cal., the American flag and its importance as a national symbol were discussed:

> Saluting the flag has been an important part of our classroom routine. One morning the question was posed: What would happen if no one saluted the flag anymore? This question evoked great comment and awareness among my third-graders. It was mentioned that we might be in need of another symbol because the flag would not be serving its purpose. The students attempted to visualize a time twenty or thirty years from now when the flag would be merely a historical fact. They also wrote stories about make-believe countries, and designed symbols to represent each one.

In Newark, Del., Marie McIntosh's high school students discussed racial integration of schools:

> We have forced busing in this state and I have asked my students (both black and white) how they feel about going to a different environment for part of the day. I point out to them how easy it is for people to generalize about members of other races from only one incident. For example, because I am white, if I am robbed by a white person, I don't hate all whites—then how can I turn around and hate all blacks if I am robbed by a black person?

In Westlake, Ohio, Glenn Ploegstra's junior high students examined the problem of garbage disposal in their community:

> We researched the actual population of Westlake, then measured the actual weight of garbage produced by individual class members, and calculated the number of tons of garbage generated in a day, week, and year. We discussed the placement of landfills and the impact on the individual, the community, the metropolitan area, and the environment. The students became more conscious of the problem and of their part in its resolution.

■ **Stop and Think**
What classroom lessons or assignments have helped you develop your thinking about morals or values? What discussion topics could be presented to students in the grade you want to teach to shed light on their ability to sort out moral dilemmas? What book or short story could prompt such a discussion?

Piaget (1964) labeled the first stage of moral development **heteronomous morality;** it has also been called the stage of "moral realism" or "morality of constraint." "Heteronomous" means being subject to rules imposed by others. During this period young children are consistently faced with parents and other adults telling them what to do and what not to do. Violations of rules are believed to bring automatic punishment. Justice is seen as automatic and people who are bad will eventually "get theirs." This reasoning creates in the child the belief that moral rules are fixed and unchangeable.

The second stage is labeled **autonomous morality** or "morality of cooperation." It arises as the child's social world expands to include more and more peers. By continually interacting and cooperating with other children, the child's ideas about rules and therefore morality begin to change. Rules are now what we make them to be. Punishment for transgressions is no longer automatic but must be administered with a consideration of the transgressors' intentions and extenuating circumstances.

Kohlberg's Stages of Moral Reasoning

Kohlberg's (1963, 1969) stage theory of moral reasoning is an elaboration and refinement of Piaget's. Kohlberg's levels and stages are summarized in Table 2.4. Like Piaget, Kohlberg studied how children (and adults) reason about rules that govern their behavior in certain situations. Kohlberg did not study children's game playing, but rather probed for their responses to a series of structured situations or **moral dilemmas.** His most famous one is the following:

TABLE 2.4

KOHLBERG'S STAGES OF MORAL REASONING

When people consider moral dilemmas, it is their reasoning that is important, not their final decision, according to Lawrence Kohlberg. He theorized that people progress through three levels as they develop abilities of moral reasoning.

I. Preconventional Level

Rules are set down by others.
   Stage 1. Punishment and Obedience Orientation
            Physical consequences of action determine its goodness or badness.
   Stage 2. Instrumental Relativist Orientation
            What's right is whatever satisfies one's own needs and occasionally the needs of others. Elements of fairness and reciprocity are present, but they are mostly interpreted in a "you scratch my back, I'll scratch yours" fashion.

II. Conventional Level

Individual adopts rules, and will sometimes subordinate own needs to those of the group. Expectations of family, group, or nation seen as valuable in own right, regardless of immediate and obvious consequences.
   Stage 3. "Good Boy–Good Girl" Orientation
            Good behavior is whatever pleases or helps others and is approved of by them. One earns approval by being "nice."
   Stage 4. "Law and Order" Orientation
            Right is doing one's duty, showing respect for authority, and maintaining the given social order for its own sake.

III. Postconventional Level

People define own values in terms of ethical principles they have chosen to follow.
   Stage 5. Social Contract Orientation
            What's right is defined in terms of general individual rights and in terms of standards that have been agreed upon by the whole society. In contrast to Stage 4, laws are not "frozen"— they can be changed for the good of society.
   Stage 6. Universal Ethical Principle Orientation
            What's right is defined by decision of conscience according to self-chosen ethical principles. These principles are abstract and ethical (such as the Golden Rule), not specific moral prescriptions (such as the Ten Commandments).

Source: Adapted from Kohlberg, 1969.

Applying Erikson's theory to elementary and secondary education requires understanding the characteristics of Stage IV (industry versus inferiority) and Stage V (identity versus role confusion). Stage IV corresponds to the elementary school years (ages six to twelve), and Stage V to the middle and high school years (ages twelve to eighteen).

HELPING STUDENTS WITH THE INDUSTRY VERSUS INFERIORITY CRISIS

In working with elementary school children teachers must be aware that their students are trying very hard to maintain a positive self-concept, a view of themselves as capable, valuable individuals. Almost all children enter kindergarten or first grade believing that they can and will learn. They fully expect to succeed in school (see Entwistle and Hayduk, 1981). However, they soon have to confront reality. Almost from the beginning, they are sorted into high, middle, and low reading groups, and soon afterward they are given grades on a competitive, relative standard. Those students who are put in the lower reading groups and receive poor grades may soon lose their initial expectations that they will succeed. This causes a downward spiral: negative evaluations from teachers lead to poor self-concept as a learner, which leads to low performance (Wattenberg and Clifford, 1964), which in turn leads to more negative evaluations. By third or fourth grade, or even earlier, students know who the winners and losers are. As they approach adolescence, the "losers" are likely to turn to activities outside of school to salvage their self-concept—perhaps sports or social activities, but all too often delinquency, drugs, and other antisocial pursuits.

In Erikson's terms, this downward spiral is a case of poor resolution of the industry versus inferiority crisis of childhood. For the child, the school is the place where success and failure are defined. Erikson (1963) describes the school as providing children with the tools they need to participate in society. If students despair of being able to participate in school society (because they lack the appropriate "tools"), they may reject participation in society as a whole.

Teachers must help students through the industry versus inferiority crisis. Teachers are the source of most student evaluations, and it is these evaluations that largely determine students' self-concepts as learners. The behavior of teachers toward students and the way they structure their classrooms can have important effects on student's self-concepts.

Unidimensional versus Multidimensional Classrooms

As one example of how teachers can help the students maintain a positive self-image, Rosenholtz and Simpson (1984) have described two kinds of classrooms that they hold have different effects on student self-concept. In **unidimensional classrooms** there is one standard of success. Teachers constantly reinforce the idea that some students are smarter than others. For example, they might refer to some reading groups as their "top" groups and others as their "low" groups. They might praise only the "smartest" students

In contrast, in the **multidimensional classroom** teachers make it clear that there are many ways to succeed. They emphasize how much students are learning. For example, many teachers give students pretests before they begin an instructional unit, and then show the class how much everyone gained on a posttest. Multidimensional teachers may stress the idea that different students have different skills; some are good in reading, others in math, still others in art or music. By valuing all of these skills, the teacher can communicate the idea that there are many routes to success, rather than a single path (Cohen 1984).

To maintain positive self-concepts among all students, teachers need not lie and say that all are equally good at reading or math. However, they can avoid unnecessary distinctions among students, recognize progress rather than level of ability, and value all kinds of skills. Also, teachers should focus their praise and evaluation on *effort*, not ability. Even if not every student can get 100 percent on a test, every student *can* give 100 percent effort, and it is this effort that should be recognized and rewarded.

See Chapter 10 for more on rewarding improvement and effort.

HELPING STUDENTS WITH THE IDENTITY VERSUS ROLE CONFUSION CRISIS

We all know that adolescence is a time of turmoil. Erikson points out that because adolescents take on a completely new body image, they must "refight many of the battles of earlier years, even though to do so they must appoint perfectly well-meaning people to play the roles of adversaries" (Erikson, 1963, p. 261). Among these "well-meaning people" are, unfortunately, teachers. Elementary school students often mistakenly call their female teachers "Mom"; the similarity between the teacher's role and the parent's role is helpful in elementary school because at this stage children generally want to please their parents and earn their approval. However, the similarity has the opposite effect in adolescence. The task of adolescents is to break away from their parents' control and establish themselves as independent, self-reliant individuals. This is a normal and desirable process. Thus the similarity between the roles of teacher and parent means that many students will reject their teachers' authority as much as they do their parents'.

There are, however, several ways that teachers can help adolescents through the identity versus role confusion stage. The key point is that adolescents want to be treated as adults, and if they are, they are likely to respond with adultlike behavior.

This principle has many implications. First, students at the middle and senior high school levels should never be referred to or treated as "children." Some high school teachers refer to their students as "ladies and gentlemen," and expect adult behavior in return. Adolescents should never be belittled or humiliated in front of their peers, or anyone else for that matter.

Teachers of adolescents should try not to make judgments of students that appear arbitrary. They should set explicit expectations and rules, with clear consequences for achieving or failing to achieve standards. For example, a teacher might say, "To get an A in this course, you will need to hand in all assignments on time, write five book reports of at least three pages in length, and pass all tests with an average of at least 90 percent." This puts the responsibility for meeting the standards squarely on the

Adolescents should be encouraged to take on adult responsibilities when they are able. Such encouragement can help them through the identity versus role confusion stage.

students themselves, rather than making the teacher the arbitrary giver of good and bad grades.

Adolescents crave resonsiblity. Teachers should take advantage of this and give them as much independent responsibility as they can handle, with clear guidelines for what they are to produce.

Finally, most adolescents are far more concerned about their peer group than they are about school. Teachers can take advantage of this by assigning well-structured group projects and by using cooperative learning strategies (see Chapter 10) in which students work together and succeed as a group.

For more on accommodating instruction to the developmental characteristics of children and adolescents, see Chapter 3.

Unidimensional Classroom
Classroom in which a teacher imposes a single standard by which children's success is measured

Multidimensional Classroom
Classroom in which children are shown many paths to success

Moral Dilemmas
Hypothetical situations that require a person to consider values of right and wrong

In Europe a woman was near death from cancer. One drug might save her, a form of radium that a druggist in the same town had recently discovered. The druggist was charging $2,000, ten times what the drug cost him to make. The sick woman's husband, Heinz, went to everyone he knew to borrow the money, but he could only get together about half of what it cost. He told the druggist that his wife was dying and asked him to sell it cheaper or let him pay later. But the druggist said "No." The husband got desperate and broke into the man's store to steal the drug for his wife. Should the husband have done that? Why? (Kohlberg, 1969, p. 379)

On the basis of the answers he received, Kohlberg proposed that people pass through a series of six stages of moral judgment or reasoning. He grouped these six stages into three levels: preconventional, conventional, and postconventional. These three levels are distinguished by how the child or adult defines what he or she perceives as a correct or moral behavior. As with other stage theories, each stage is more sophisticated and more complex than the preceding one and most individuals proceed through them in the same order (Colby and Kohlberg, 1984). Like Piaget, Kohlberg is not so much concerned with the direction of the child's answer as with the reasoning behind it. The ages at which children and adolescents go through the stages in Table 2.4 may vary considerably; in fact, the same individual may behave according to one stage at some times and according to another at other times. However, most

CASE TO CONSIDER

Case 2

Althea Johnson, a third-grade teacher, is standing in front of her new crop of students on the second day of school. Her goal for the next 20 minutes is to discuss class rules. She hopes that the class can reach a concensus on appropriate rules and behavior, and on the consequences of disobeying the rules.

ALTHEA: OK, class. I want to spend a few minutes talking with you about class rules. Let's start by listing some on the board. Please raise your hands and wait until I call on you before you speak out.

Many students raise their hands, and in a few minutes Althea has noted the following ideas on the board.

- Do not talk in class
- Do not run in the hallways
- Do not put gum under your desk
- Do not throw spitballs (or paper airplanes)
- Do not draw on your desk
- Do not fight
- Do not come late without a note from home
- Do not yell in class
- Do raise your hand to be called on
- Do not bring radios to school
- Do not pass notes to your friends
- Do not write in your books

When the suggestions have slowed, Althea steps back and looks at the list.

ALTHEA: That's a good start. Now let's think about consequences. What happens when you break a rule? [Hands go up] Clare?

CLARE: You go to the principal's office.

ALTHEA: Yes, that's one consequence. Let's list a few more.

As before, Althea lists the students' suggestions. Their ideas are as follows:

- Go to the principal's office
- Sit in the corner for half an hour
- Miss recess
- Stay after school
- Get a letter sent home to your parents

ALTHEA: All right, class. Now let's look again at the rules. Most of them start out by saying "Do not," right? Can we restate them so they tell us what we *should* do? For example, I like the one that says, "Do raise your hand to be called on." Does anyone know what it means to respect the rights of others?

children pass from the preconventional to the conventional level by the age of nine (Kohlberg, 1969).

Stage 1, which is on the preconventional level, is very similar in form and content to Piaget's stage of heteronomous morality. Children simply obey authority figures to avoid being punished. In Stage 2 children's own needs and desires become important, yet they are aware of the interests of other people. In a concrete sense they weigh the interests of all parties when making moral judgments, but they are still "looking out for number one."

The conventional level begins at Stage 3. Here morality is defined in terms of cooperation with peers, just as it was in Piaget's stage of autonomous morality. This is the stage at which children have an unquestioning belief in the Golden Rule (Hogan and Emler, 1978). Because of the decrease in egocentrism that accompanies concrete operations, children are cognitively capable of putting themselves in someone else's shoes. Thus they consider the feelings of others when making moral decisions. No longer do they simply do what will not get them punished (Stage 1) or what makes them feel good (Stage 2).

At Stage 4 society's rules and laws replace those of the peer group. A desire for social approval no longer determines moral judgments. Laws are followed without

Her students offer ideas, and eventually Althea groups several of the rules under a new heading, "Respect the rights of others."

She does the same for the idea of respecting other people's property. Pretty soon the blackboard shows the following five rules, each with several examples underneath:

1. Respect the rights of others
2. Respect other people's property
3. Be courteous to others
4. Be on-task
5. Raise your hand to be called on

The next step is to match rules with consequences. This always seems hard for second graders. When Althea suggests that the circumstances of a rule-breaking situation can sometimes make her decide not to punish a rule-breaker, several hands shoot up.

BOBBY: But Mrs. Johnson, if someone breaks a rule they have to be punished.

MIMI: Yeah, I always get punished when I break a rule, so everyone else should, too.

ALTHEA: OK, let's take an example. What if the person next to you talks during class and you whisper to that person that they should be quiet. If I see only

you whispering, should I punish you? What should the punishment be? Bobby?

BOBBY: I don't know, Mrs. Johnson. Maybe I should have to stay after school?

ALTHEA: Well, how about if I just catch your eye and frown at you? Would that be a consequence?

CLARE: No! That's not a punishment! A punishment is like going to the principal's office or writing something on the blackboard a hundred times!

ALTHEA: OK, let's talk more about consequences tomorrow. For now I want everyone to copy down these rules and think about them. We'll talk more about them tomorrow.

QUESTIONS

1. What statements by the children signal their stage of moral development? Are their concerns about punishment typical of children their age?
2. How well do you think Althea handled this class session? Do you agree that students should be involved in setting class rules?
3. How might a teacher of younger or older children approach the task of setting class rules?

question, and breaking the law can never be justified. Most adults are probably at this stage.

Stage 5 signals entrance into the postconventional level. This level of moral reasoning is probably attained by fewer than 25 percent of adults. Here there is a realization that the laws and values of a society are somewhat arbitrary and particular to that society (Hogan and Emler, 1978). Laws are seen as necessary to preserve the social order and to ensure the basic right of life and liberty. In Stage 6 one's ethical principles are self-chosen and based on abstract concepts such as justice and the equality and value of human rights. Laws that violate these principles can and should be disobeyed because "justice is above the law." More recently, Kohlberg (1978, 1984) speculated that Stage 6 is not really separate from Stage 5, and suggested that the two be combined.

Kohlberg (1969) believed that moral dilemmas can be used to advance a child's level of moral reasoning, but only one stage at a time. He theorized that the way children progress from one stage to the next is by interacting with others whose reasoning is one or, at most, two stages above their own. Thus in dealing with children, teachers must first try to determine their approximate stage of moral reasoning. They can do this by presenting them with the Heinz dilemma discussed earlier. Once a child's level of moral reasoning is established, other moral problems can be discussed and the teacher can challenge the child's reasoning with explanations from the next higher stage. After the child's reasoning advances to this stage, the teacher can advance again. All this must be done over an extended period of time, however. Teachers can help students progress in moral development by weaving discussions of justice and moral issues into their lessons, particularly in response to events that occur in the classroom (see Nucci, 1987).

Kohlberg's levels of moral development roughly parallel Piaget's stages of cognitive development. In general, one should not expect children to go from conventional to postconventional moral reasoning until they have gone from concrete to formal operational thinking.

Limitations of Kohlberg's Theory.   Kohlberg found that his stages of moral reasoning ability occurred in the same order and at about the same ages in the United States, Mexico, Taiwan, and Turkey. Other research throughout the world has generally found the same sequence of stages (Snarey, 1985). However, one limitation of Kohlberg's work is that it mostly involved boys (Aron, 1977). Research on the moral development of girls finds patterns somewhat different from Kohlberg's; while boys' moral development revolves primarily around issues of justice, the girls are more concerned about caring and responsibility (Gilligan, 1982, 1985; Gibbs et al., 1984). Kohlberg (Levine, Kohlberg, and Hewer, 1985) later revised his theory based on these criticisms.

The most important limitation of Kohlberg's theory is that it deals with moral reasoning rather than with actual behavior. Many individuals at different stages behave in the same way, and individuals at the same stages often behave in different ways (Haan et al., 1968; Fodor, 1971). In a classic study of moral behavior Hartshorne and May (1928) presented children of various ages with opportunities to cheat or steal, thinking they would not be caught. Very few children behaved honestly in every case, and very few behaved dishonestly in every case. This study showed that moral behavior does not conform to simple rules, but is far more complex. Similarly, the link between children's moral reasoning and moral behavior may be quite weak (Burton, 1976). Children may have learned to say certain things about moral decisions at various ages, but what they do may be another matter.

SUMMARY AND REVIEW OF OBJECTIVES

Intellectual Abilities of Elementary School and Secondary School Students. The fundamental intellectual ability separating younger students from older ones is the ability to deal with potential or hypothetical situations. Children under about eleven years of age typically have not developed this ability; older children and adults probably have.

This observation about intellectual abilities was made by Jean Piaget, whose stage theory of cognitive development suggests that people progress through a series of four stages, beginning with birth and ending during adolescence. During each stage a young person's thinking is reorganized. He suggested that schemes are patterns of behavior that children and adults use in interpreting events in their words. Assimilation is the mental process of incorporating a new object or event into an existing scheme; accommodation is the changing of an existing scheme to fit new objects.

Piaget divided children's cognitive development into four stages. The first is the sensorimotor stage (birth to two years), during which children explore their world using their senses and motor skills. The second is the preoperational stage (two to seven years), during which children can use symbols to mentally represent objects. Three characteristics of preschoolers' thinking are centration, irreversibility, and egocentrism. The next stage is known as the concrete operational stage (seven to eleven), during which children can perform operations such as reciprocity, inversion, and class inclusion with objects. As a result, the ability to solve conservation tasks is acquired. The fourth stage in Piaget's theory is the formal operational stage (eleven to adulthood), during which young people develop the ability to deal with hypothetical situations. People in the formal operational stage can also monitor their own thinking.

Personality Crises Faced by Various Age Groups. Erik Erikson believed that during each stage of personal and social development people are faced with a psychosocial crisis that results from interaction with the social environment. In his theory, personal and social development is a lifelong process. Stage I (birth to eighteen months) involves trust versus mistrust; the goal is to develop a sense of trust through interaction with the mother or maternal figure. Stage II (eighteen months to three years) is known as autonomy versus doubt; children have a dual desire to "hold on" and to "let go," which is most apparent during toilet training. During Stage III (three to six years), initiative versus guilt, parents who encourage children to explore their social and physical environments can foster initiative, while discouragement can lead to guilt. During Stage IV (six to twelve years), industry versus inferiority, success in school brings with it a sense of industry, while school failure creates a sense of inadequacy. Stage V (twelve to eighteen years), identity versus role confusion, involves increasingly turning away from parents and toward peer groups as adolescents try to develop a sense of identity by striving to find idols and direction for the future, placing trust in certain peers and adults, and searching for a career. In Stage VI (young adulthood), intimacy versus isolation, the goal of young adults is to form a new trust and intimacy with another individual. In Stage VII (middle adulthood), generativity versus self-absorption, productivity and creativity—often in the form of raising children—is the essential conflict. Stage VIII (late adulthood), integrity versus despair, occurs when people look back to resolve the final identity crisis: acceptance of their lives or regret over the way their lives have turned out.

Development of Moral Reasoning Skills. Two theories regarding the development of moral reasoning skills were considered. One was proposed by Piaget, the other by Lawrence Kohlberg. Piaget's stages of moral development begin around age six, when children develop heteronomous mortality or obedience to authority. The second stage is autonomous morality, when rules are no longer seen as automatic but what we want them to be.

Kohlberg's theory of moral development is based on children's responses to moral dilemmas. The three main stages are preconventional, when children simply obey authority figures to avoid being punished; conventional, when children consider the feelings of others in making moral decisions; and postconventional, when people realize that laws and values are somewhat arbitrary and relative to each society.

Adults can help children advance to the next stage of cognitive or moral development by allowing them to freely explore problems, at the same time challenging their reasoning by introducing concepts from the next higher stage.

STUDY QUESTIONS

1. According to Piaget, most elementary school children between the ages of seven and eleven are in the _____ stage of cognitive development.
   a. formal operational
   b. concrete operational
   c. preoperational
   d. sensorimotor

2. Which Eriksonian personality crisis is faced by elementary school students?
   a. Identity vs. inferiority.
   b. Industry vs. isolation.
   c. Industry vs. inferiority.
   d. Identity vs. isolation.

3. The crisis of personality associated with the high school years is
   a. identity vs. role confusion.
   b. industry vs. inferiority.
   c. intimacy vs. isolation.
   d. integrity vs. despair.

4. Which of the following best illustrates the process of assimilation?
   a. A student adopts a new approach to a writing assignment after realizing that an approach learned earlier won't work.
   b. A child learns that she can be noisy when Grandma visits but she must be quiet and polite around Aunt Charlotte.
   c. A student learns how to crack the security code for the school's computer.
   d. A child attempts to ice skate by moving his legs in the same way that he does when he roller skates.

5. An infant searches for a doll that has fallen behind the couch out of view. This behavior suggests the acquisition of
   a. concrete operations.
   b. equilibration.
   c. reversibility.
   d. object permanence.

6. Piaget's principles have been criticized on the basis of findings showing that
   a. many children go through the stages in different orders.
   b. cognitive tasks such as conservation cannot be taught unless the child is in the appropriate stage.
   c. the clarity of task instructions can significantly influence young children's performance on conservation tasks.
   d. children, on the average, are actually less competent than Piaget thought and rarely reach the different stages at the designated age levels.

7. Match the following stages of cognitive development with the brief descriptions identifying each.
   _____ formal operational stage
   _____ concrete operational stage
   _____ preoperational stage
   _____ sensorimotor stage
   a. learning occurs largely through trial-and-error
   b. mental symbols can be used to represent objects
   c. reversible mental operations are developed
   d. abstract thinking is possible and problems can be solved systematically

8. Which of the following strategies should teachers use to help students develop a sense of industry?
   a. Maintain a classroom environment that can be described as "unidimensional."
   b. Use labels on test results, such as "good," "bad," or "above average," "below average," so that students become more aware of their performance levels.
   c. Praise ability more than effort.
   d. Stress the idea that different students have different strengths and weaknesses.
   e. Emphasize to students that there is always one best path to success.

9. Match the following stages of Kohlberg's theory to descriptions of each.
   _____ conventional

_____ postconventional
_____ preconventional
a. "Do what the rule says, regardless of the consequences"
b. "If I get caught, I was bad"
c. "Before judging her, let's consider her situation and motives."

10. Evidence that challenges some of Kohlberg's assumptions has shown that
   a. the various stages tend to occur in different orders in different countries.
   b. girls may display different patterns of moral reasoning than those revealed for boys in earlier studies.

c. once the formal operations stage is reached, progression to the highest moral reasoning stage usually follows fairly rapidly.
d. skipping stages is fairly common, especially when moral training is provided.
e. all of the above.

10. b

Answers: 1. b, 2. c, 3. a, 4. d, 5. d, 6. c, 7. d, 8. b, 9. a, c, b

SUGGESTED READINGS

CRAIN, W. C. (1985). *Theories of development: Concepts and applications.* Englewood Cliffs, N.J.: Prentice-Hall.

ERIKSON, E. H. (1963). *Childhood and society* (2nd ed.). New York: Norton.

ERIKSON, E. H. (1980). *Identity and the life cycle* (2nd ed.). New York: Norton.

FLAVELL, J. H. (1985). *Cognitive development* (2nd ed.). Englewood Cliffs, N.J.: Prentice-Hall.

FURTH, H. G. (1969). *Piaget and knowledge.* Englewood Cliffs, N.J.: Prentice-Hall.

GELMAN, R. (1979). Preschool thought. *American Psychologist, 34,* 900–905.

GILLIGAN, C. (1982). *In a different voice: Sex differences in the expression of moral judgment.* Cambridge, Mass.: Harvard University Press.

GREEN, M. (1989). *Theories of human development: A comparative approach.* Englewood Cliffs, N.J.: Prentice-Hall.

HOGAN, R., and EMLER, N. P. (1978). Moral development. In M. E. Lamb (Ed.), *Social and personality development* (pp. 200–233). New York: Holt, Rinehart & Winston.

INHELDER. B., and PIAGET, J. (1958). *The growth of logical thinking from childhood to adolescence.* New York: Basic Books.

KOHLBERG, L. (1981). *The philosophy of moral development.* New York: Harper & Row.

MILLER, P. H. (1983). *Theories of developmental psychology.* San Francisco: Freeman.

PIAGET, J. (1964). *The moral judgment of the child.* New York: Free Press.

SUND, R. (1976). *Piaget for educators.* Columbus, Ohio: Merrill.

THOMAS, R. M. (1985). *Comparing theories of child development* (2nd ed.). Belmont, Cal.: Wadsworth.

VYGOTSKY, L. S. (1978). *Mind in society* (M. Cole, V. John-Steiner, S. Scribner, and E. Souberman, Eds.). Cambridge, Mass.: Harvard University Press.

WADSWORTH, B. (1978). *Piaget for the classroom teacher.* New York: Longman.

WADSWORTH, B. (1989). *Piaget's theory of cognitive and affective development* (4th ed.). New York: Longman.

Chapter 3

Development During Childhood and Adolescence

Chapter Outline

Development During Early Childhood
Physical Development
Cognitive Abilities
Language
Early Childhood Education
Socioemotional Development
Play
Theory into Practice: Teaching Preschoolers and
   Kindergartners

Development During Middle Childhood,
Physical Development
Cognitive Abilities
Socioemotional Development
Theory into Practice: Teaching Elementary-Age
   Children

Development During Adolescence
Physical Development
Cognitive Abilities
Socioemotional Development
Problems of Adolescence
Theory into Practice: Teaching Junior High and High
   School Students

Chapter Objectives

After reading this chapter you should better
understand the characteristics of children in early
childhood, middle childhood, and adolescence. You
should also be able to:

- Describe how children learn about language.

- Understand the debate over whether early
  childhood education should stress intellectual or
  social development.

- Understand the emotional turmoil that can
  accompany puberty.

- Describe how adolescents learn to share their
  feelings and thoughts with friends of their own
  sex and with members of the opposite sex.

Fine Motor Activity
A physical action of the fine muscles of the hand involving precision and dexterity

Gross Motor Activity
A physical action, such as running or throwing, that involves the limbs and large muscles

All farmers must know general principles of botany, such as photosynthesis, germination, pollination, and how plants use water and minerals. But, in addition, wheat farmers, orchardists, and vegetable farmers must know how these principles apply to their own specific problems. By the same token, all educators must know the principal theories of cognitive, social, and moral development presented in the previous chapter so that they will understand how young people grow over time in each of these domains. However, teachers usually deal with children of a particular age, or in a narrow age range. A preschool teacher needs to know what preschool children are like. Elementary teachers are concerned with middle childhood, and junior and senior high school teachers with adolescence. This chapter presents the physical, social, and cognitive characteristics of students at each phase of development. It discusses how the principles of development presented in Chapter 2 apply to children of various ages, and adds information on physical development, language development, and self-concept.

DEVELOPMENT DURING EARLY CHILDHOOD

Children can be termed "preschoolers" when they are between three and six years of age. This is a time of rapid change in all areas of development. Children master most motor skills by the end of this period and can use their physical skills to achieve goals. Cognitively, they start to develop an understanding of classes and relationships and absorb an enormous amount of information about their social and physical worlds. By the age of six, children use almost completely mature speech, not only to express their wants and needs, but also to share their ideas and experiences. Socially, children learn appropriate behaviors and rules and become increasingly adept at interacting with other children.

As each of these aspects of development is discussed, keep in mind the complexity of development and how all facets of a child's growth are interrelated. Although physical, cognitive, and social development can be put in separate sections in a book, in real life they are not only intertwined but are also affected by the environment within which children grow up.

Physical Development

Physical development describes the changes in the physical appearance of children as well as in their motor skills. During the preschool years the sequence in which all children develop motor skills is generally the same, though some gain skills faster than others.

Children's physical growth is marked by the loss of their characteristic protruding abdomen as their legs and trunk grow faster than their heads. The center of gravity—the point in the body around which weight is evenly distributed—begins to move lower, allowing children to become steadier on their feet and capable of movements that were impossible when they were top-heavy infants and toddlers (Schickedanz et al., 1982). During this time children also develop a preference for one side of their body, which can be observed when they use one hand more frequently than the other. Most children will favor their right hand, but those who show a preference for their left should not be forced to change.

The major physical accomplishment for preschoolers is increased control over gross and fine motor movements. **Fine motor activity** refers to movements requiring precision and dexterity, such as tying a shoe and writing letters of the alphabet. **Gross motor activities** involve such movements as walking and running.

By the end of the preschool period, most children can easily perform self-help tasks such as buckling, buttoning, snapping, and zipping. They can go up and down steps with alternating feet. They can perform fine motor skills such as cutting with scissors and using crayons to color a predefined area. They also begin learning to write letters and words.

After six or seven years of age children gain few completely new basic skills; rather, the quality and complexity of their movements improve (Malina, 1982).

Implications of Physical Development for Preschool Education. Preschool children are natural wigglers. Their activity levels are very high, and they are unable to sit for long periods unless they are engaged in very interesting activities. They need (and actively seek) opportunities to run, jump, climb, slide, and crawl.

Preschoolers' play can be structured by providing engaging equipment such as tires, walking boards, jungle gyms, and large blocks. Children gain in balance, coordination, and strength from a variety of activities, but well-chosen equipment and activities also help encourage social play, as children learn to share and have fun together (see Frost and Klein, 1979; Cratty, 1982).

For most preschoolers (especially boys), gross motor skills far outpace fine motor skills. Children who are quite skilled at climbing or running may be clumsy and awkward at writing, drawing, cutting with scissors, tying shoelaces, and other fine motor activities. With their natural enthusiasm and love of movement, preschoolers can literally run until they drop. For this reason, they need frequent rest periods after periods of intense activity.

In addition, children's visual perception usually lags behind other aspects of their development. Preschoolers need large-print books, and have difficulty with tasks (such as threading needles) that require acute eyesight. Because of their problems with fine motor skills and visual perception, preschoolers should not be forced to master activities requiring manipulation of small objects. They need big brushes, fat crayons and pencils, and large equipment.

Cognitive Abilities

The Preoperational Child. During the sensorimotor stage of development (from birth to about two years of age), infants try to understand their world by using their senses. Their knowledge is based on physical actions, and their understanding is restricted to events in the present or the immediate past. Only when children enter the preoperational stage (at about age two), and begin to talk and to use mental symbols, are they able to use thoughts or concepts to understand their world. During the preoperational stage, however, their thoughts are still tied to physical actions.

Because a preschooler's thinking is tied to action and the ways things appear, it is prelogical. Art Linkletter showed television viewers that kids say the "darnedest things"; having read Piaget's descriptions of preoperational thought in Chapter 2, you can see that children's words reflect their understanding of the world.

Most children remain in the preoperational stage of cognitive development until they are seven or eight years old.

Language

Children normally develop basic language skills before entering school. Language development involves both verbal and written communication. Verbal abilities develop very early, and by age three, children are already skillful talkers. By the end of the preschool years, children can use and understand an almost infinite number of

Transformational Grammar Theory
A theory that emphasizes the quality of language as dependent on its ideas or content rather than its external form

"No, Timmy, not 'I *sawed* the chair.' It's 'I *saw* the chair' or 'I *have seen* the chair.' "

(Glenn Bernhardt. From *Kappan Magazine*, January 1984, p. 355)

sentences, can hold conversations, and know about written language (Gleason, 1981; Menyuk, 1982; Schickedanz et al., 1982).

Verbal Language.   Development of verbal language—or spoken language—requires not only learning words but also learning the rules of word and sentence construction. For example, children learn how to form plurals before they enter kindergarten. Berko (1958) showed preschoolers a picture of a made-up bird, called a "Wug." She then showed them two such pictures, and said, "Now there is another one. There are two of them. There are two _____." The children readily answered, "Wugs," showing that they could apply general rules for forming plurals to a new situation. In a similar fashion, children learn to add "-ed" and "-ing" to verbs. As they learn these rules, they initially overgeneralize them, saying words like "goed" instead of "went," and "mouses" instead of "mice." Interestingly, children often learn the correct forms of irregular verbs (such as "He broke the chair"), and then replace them with incorrect but more logical constructions ("He *breaked* [or broked] the chair"). One four-year-old said, "I flew my kite." He then thought for a moment and emphatically corrected himself, saying, "I *flewed* my kite!" These errors are a normal part of language development and should not be corrected.

Just as they learn rules for forming words, children learn rules for sentences. Their first sentences usually contain just two words ("Want milk," "See birdie," "Jessie outside"), but soon they learn to form more complex sentences and to vary their tone of voice to indicate questions ("Where doggie go?") or to indicate emphasis ("Want *cookie!*"). Three-year-olds can usually express rather complex thoughts even though their sentences may still lack such words as "a," "the," and "did." Later, children continually expand their ability to express and understand complex sentences. However, they still have difficulty with certain aspects of language throughout the preschool and early elementary school years. For example, Carol Chomsky (1969) showed children a doll that was blindfolded and asked, "Is the doll easy to see or hard to see?" Only 22 percent of five-year-olds could respond correctly; not until age nine could all her subjects respond appropriately to the question. Many students confuse such words as "ask" and "tell" and "teach" and "learn" well into the elementary grades.

Preschoolers often play with language, or experiment with its patterns and rules (Schwartz, 1981). Frequently this experimentation involves changing sounds, patterns, and meanings. One three-year-old was told by his exasperated parent, "You're impossible!", to which he replied, "No, I'm impopsicle!" The same child said that his baby brother, Benjamin, was a man because he was a "Benja-man." Children often rearrange word sounds to create new words, rhymes, and funny sentences. The popularity of finger plays, nonsense rhymes, and Dr. Seuss storybooks shows how young children enjoy playing with language.

Transformational Grammar.   One of the most important theories of language development is Noam Chomsky's (1968) **transformational grammar theory.** This theory emphasizes the development of increasingly complex *ideas* in language but deemphasizes the particular forms in which the ideas are expressed. For example, the sentences "John read the book carefully to prepare for the exam" and "To prepare for the exam, John carefully read the book" contain the same ideas, even though they differ in form. Chomsky noted that people recall the meaning of sentences they heard but rarely the particular sentence structure used, which suggests that language is transformed into ideas before it is put into memory, and then reformed into perhaps different forms when it is recalled.

One important implication of transformational grammar theory is that different languages or dialects that can express the same information are linguistically equivalent. For example, although a dialect used within black communities in the United States has its own grammatical rules and conventions, it is equivalent in conceptual quality to standard English. Standard English should still be taught to all students because proficiency in it is important in its own right, but this does not imply that the cognitive level of different languages or dialects differ (Edwards, 1979).

Reading. Learning to read is a process of learning how language works rather than acquiring a series of independent reading skills (McKenzie, 1977; Schickedanz, 1982).

Even before entering school, children begin to build an understanding of written language. Many researchers suggest that this knowledge follows a course of development similar to that of spoken language. From seeing print, children make guesses about how it works. This process works best when children have many books, magazines, and other printed materials available (McKenzie, 1977; Schickedanz, 1982).

If they are read to frequently, children between three and five years of age dramatically increase their understanding of reading (Taylor, 1983). They learn that readers look at the text while reading, that reading involves looking at print rather than at pictures. They learn that sentences go from left to right and from top to bottom on a page. Very young children can identify individual letters and strings of letters that form words. Older preschoolers can distinguish words from letters and know what printed words look like. However, there are very wide variations in children's readiness for reading at any given age.

Writing. Most children begin to grasp the fundamentals of writing during early childhood. Children as young as three years of age recognize differences between print and drawings. They gradually begin to discriminate the distinctive features of print, such as whether lines are straight or curved, open or closed, diagonal, horizontal, or vertical. But through kindergarten, many children continue to reverse letters such as "b" and "d", and "p" and "q," until they learn that the orientation of letters is an important characteristic (Schickedanz et al., 1982).

Children can more quickly learn to read if adults frequently read aloud to them and show them children's books.

FIGURE 3.1

Development of Writing Skills

A young child's attempt at writing "This is carrots, peas" illustrates how children invent spellings according to the sounds of words.

Children's writing follows a developmental sequence. It emerges out of early scribbles and at first is spread randomly across a page. This reflects an incomplete understanding of word boundaries as well as an inability to mentally create a line for placing letters. Children invent spellings by making judgments about English sounds and by relating the sounds they hear to the letters they know. In trying to represent what they hear, they typically use letter names as opposed to letter sounds; short vowels are frequently left out because they are not directly associated with letter names (Downing et al., 1986) (see Figure 3.1). For example, one kindergartner labeled a picture of a dinosaur, "DNSR." In recent years educators have experimented with teaching kindergartners and first-graders to write stories using invented spellings, to help them learn reading as well as writing (Calkins, 1983).

Early Childhood Education

In almost all the countries of the world, children begin their formal schooling at about six years of age, a time when they have typically attained the cognitive and social skills necessary for organized learning activities. However, there is much less agreement on what kind of schooling, if any, children younger than five need. The kindergarten originated in Germany in the 1800s, but it was not until the turn of the century that this innovation gained widespread acceptance. Since World War II nursery schools and day-care programs have mushroomed, as increasing numbers of women with children have entered the work force (Scarr and Weinberg, 1986; White and Buka, 1987). For example, in the late 1980s, more than half of all working women had children under three years of age. By contrast, the proportion of working mothers with young children in 1970 was one in four (U.S. Government, Bureau of Labor Statistics, 1988). Group day-care programs exist for children from infancy on, and organized preschool or nursery school programs sometimes take children as young as two.

Day-Care Programs.   Day-care programs exist primarily to provide child-care services for working parents. They range from a baby-sitting arrangement in which one adult takes care of several children to organized preschool programs that differ little from nursery schools.

Nursery Schools. The primary difference between day-care and nursery school programs is that nursery schools provide a planned program designed to foster the social and cognitive development of young children.

Most nursery schools are half-day programs, with two or three adults supervising a class of fifteen to twenty children. Unlike day-care centers and Head Start programs (which are discussed in the following section), nursery schools most often serve middle-class families (White and Buka, 1987).

A key concept in nursery school education is **readiness:** students learn skills that are supposed to prepare them for formal instruction later, such as how to follow directions, stick to a task, cooperate with others, and display good manners. Children are also encouraged to grow emotionally and develop a positive self-concept, and to gain in gross and fine motor skills. The nursery school day usually consists of a variety of more and less structured activities, ranging from art projects to group discussion (circle time) to unstructured indoor and outdoor play. These activities are often organized around themes. For example, a unit on animals might involve making drawings of animals, acting out animal behavior, hearing stories about animals, and taking a trip to the zoo.

Compensatory Preschool Programs. Perhaps the most important development in early childhood education over the past twenty-five years has been the introduction of **compensatory preschool programs** for children from disadvantaged backgrounds. A wide variety of programs were introduced under the overall federal Head Start program, begun in 1965. Head Start was part of President Lyndon Johnson's war on poverty, an attempt to break the cycle of poverty. The idea was to give disadvantaged children a chance to start their formal schooling with the same preacademic and social skills possessed by middle-class children.

Typically, Head Start includes early childhood education programs designed to increase school readiness. However, the program also includes medical and dental services for children, at least one hot meal per day, and social services for their parents.

Research on Head Start has generally found positive effects on children's readiness skills and on many other outcomes (Karweit, 1989a; McKey et al., 1985; Zigler and Valentine, 1979). The effects on academic readiness skills have been greatest for those Head Start programs that stress academic achievement (Stallings and Stipek, 1986). Research that followed disadvantaged children who participated in several such programs found that these students did better throughout their school years than similar students who did not participate in the programs (Berrueta-Clement et al., 1984). For example, 67 percent of the students in one program, the Perry Preschool, ultimately graduated from high school, as compared with 49 percent of students in a control group who did not attend preschool.

The research on compensatory early childhood education might seem to indicate that preschool programs are crucial for all students. However, many researchers (for example, Nurss and Hodges, 1982) hypothesize that preschool programs are more critical for lower-class than for middle-class children, because many of the experiences provided by preschools are typically present in middle-class homes but lacking in lower-class homes. For example, Morella (1974) found no differences in later academic performance between middle-class children who had attended nursery school and those who had not.

Kindergarten Programs. Most students attend kindergarten the year before they enter first grade. However, a few public school systems still do not offer kindergarten, and only seven states require kindergarten attendance (Karweit, 1989b). The original

Readiness
The state of having the skills and knowledge necessary for a given activity

Compensatory Preschool Programs
Programs designed to prepare disadvantaged children for entry into kindergarten and first grade

Headstart, a federally funded compensatory preschool program can increase children's readiness for school and improve their chances of academic success and of graduating from high school.

purpose of kindergarten was to prepare students for formal instruction by encouraging development of their social skills, but in recent years this function has increasingly been taken on by nursery schools and preschool programs. The kindergarten has increasingly focused on academics, emphasizing prereading and premathematical skills, as well as behaviors that are appropriate in school (such as raising hands, lining up, and taking turns). In some school districts, kindergarten programs are becoming similar to what first grades once were, a trend that is opposed by most child development experts (e.g., Elkind, 1981). One particularly distressing aspect of this trend is that increasing numbers of schools are failing students in kindergarten if they do not meet certain performance standards (see Shepard and Smith, 1986).

Research on kindergarten indicates that attending a full- or half-day kindergarten program is beneficial for academic readiness and increases a child's achievement in the first and second grades, but these effects diminish or disappear by the third or fourth grade (Nurss and Hodges, 1982). Recently research has indicated that lower-class students gain more from well-structured full-day kindergarten programs than from half-day programs (Karweit, 1989b).

The Preschool Years: A Critical Period in Intellectual Development? The 1960s were marked by the introduction of preschool programs such as Head Start, which were based on the belief that the preschool years were critical to a child's cognitive development. These programs emphasized structured learning experiences designed to accelerate development by matching curriculum activities to the cognitive level of children (Weinberg, 1979; Zigler and Seitz, 1982).

Associated with the idea that cognitive development is shaped by early experience is the belief that later development can be predicted from early experiences (Kagan, 1976; Kagan et al., 1979). However, many researchers question the degree to which early experiences determine later development (Clarke and Clarke, 1976; Goldhaber, 1979; Kagan et al., 1979; Thomas, 1981). Their research has shown that young children who are deprived of appropriate early experiences can catch up if given supportive environments later (Clarke and Clarke, 1976). Such findings do not imply that early environments are unimportant, but they do indicate that both early and later experiences affect development.

■ **Stop and Think**

1. A child's social environment can strongly influence school readiness. What attitudes prevail in the community in which you grew up that might have influenced your success in school?

2. Some children come to first grade as graduates of nursery schools, day-care programs, or other forms of preschool education. Others have never before been in a group learning situation. What differences might you expect between these two groups of children? How would this affect your approach to them in the first days of school?

Socioemotional Development

A young child's social life evolves in relatively predictable ways. The social network grows from an intimate relation with parents or other guardians to include other family members, nonrelated adults, and peers. Social interactions extend from home to neighborhood, and from nursery school or other child-care arrangements to formal school.

Psychosocial Development. Erik Erikson's theory of personal and social development suggests that during early childhood children must resolve the personality crisis of initiative versus guilt. The child's successful resolution of this stage results in a sense of initiative and ambition, tempered by a reasonable understanding of the permissible. Early educators can encourage this by giving children opportunities to take initiative, to be challenged, and to succeed.

During the initiative versus guilt stage, children become able to imagine what they themselves can do and can become. If they gain a sense of initiative, their sense of identity will be strengthened by a belief in their unlimited role possibilities; if a sense of guilt prevails, their belief in their own possibilities may be stunted.

Parenting. Parents usually have the earliest and strongest influence on a child. People appear to have a preferred style of interacting with their children, and these parental variations in style affect children's social development. During the last two decades researchers have tried to identify strategies used by effective parents. The best-known studies of **parenting styles** have been done by Diane Baumrind (1973). Her research identified three main styles that varied around the degree of parental control, clarity of parent-child communications, parents' maturity demands, and nurturance.

Authoritarian parents value obedience even at the expense of the child's autonomy. These parents do not encourage verbal give-and-take, believe children should accept parental authority without question, and tend to be harsh. In contrast, **permissive parents** give their children as much freedom as possible and place few expectations on them. **Authoritative parents,** however, attempt to direct their children's behavior in ways that respect children's abilities, but at the same time express their own standards of behavior and expect these standards to be met. Authoritative parents are both warm and demanding (Baumrind, 1973). Note that these two similar words, "authoritarian" and "authoritative," describe very different styles of parenting.

Baumrind (1973, 1980) concluded that the most effective parents more often chose an authoritative style. Authoritative parents tend to have children who are independent, self-assertive, friendly, cooperative with parents, high in self-esteem, and achievement-oriented. On the other hand, parents who are authoritarian or overly permissive tend to have children who lack these traits (Baumrind, 1973). Baumrind's findings emphasize the importance of parental control and warmth, of giving age-appropriate reasons for actions, of giving children responsibility when appropriate, and of expecting children to act in a mature way. These findings suggest strategies that teachers can use with children. Adults most effective in influencing children explain the reasons behind their demands. They also tell children their expectations and express their belief that these standards will be met.

Peer Relationships. It is during early childhood that **peers,** other children who are a child's equals, first strongly influence a child's development. Children's relations with their peers differ from their interactions with adults in several ways. Most importantly, children interact with each other as equals. This relationship lets them assert themselves, present their own views, and argue different viewpoints.

Peer play allows children to interact with other individuals whose level of development is similar to their own. When peers have disputes among themselves, they must make concessions and must cooperate in resolving them if the play is to continue; unlike adult-child disputes, no one can claim to have ultimate authority. Peer relationships also help young children overcome the egocentrism that Piaget described as being a characteristic of preoperational thinking.

Peer conflicts let children see that others have thoughts, feelings, and viewpoints different from their own. Conflicts also heighten children's sensitivity to the effects of their behavior on others.

Parenting Styles
General patterns of behavior used by parents when dealing with their children

Authoritarian Parents
Parents who strictly enforce their authority over their children

Permissive Parents
Parents who give their children great freedom

Authoritative Parents
Parents who mix firm guidance with respect and warmth toward their children

Peers
People who are equal in age or status

The manner in which parents interact with their children strongly influences the children's development.

Successful interactions with peers require communication and specific social skills such as initiating interactions, maintaining relations, and resolving conflicts. Research suggests that unpopular children lack social skills and seem not to know the kinds of behavior that are most appropriate in different social situations (Asher et al., 1977; Asher et al., 1982).

Teachers can help children who are having social difficulties by arranging classroom situations that will help them improve their social skills. Peer interactions can be encouraged by use of small groups, toys and materials involving more than one child, and activities such as puppets or sociodramatic play. In particular, use of cooperative learning or peer tutoring activities can increase peer acceptance and reduce rejections (Slavin, 1983a). Also, students can be taught specific social behaviors that will help them get along with peers (Gresham, 1981).

Friendships. Friendship is the central social relationship between peers during childhood (Damon, 1977), and it undergoes a series of changes before adulthood. Using as their basis the developmental stages of Piaget and children's changing abilities to consider the perspective of others, Selman (1981, Selman and Selman, 1979) has described how children's understanding of friendship changes over the years. Between the ages of three and seven, children usually view friends as momentary playmates. Children of this age might come home from school exclaiming, "I made a new friend today; Jamie shared her doll with me," or "Bill's not my friend anymore 'cause he wouldn't play blocks with me." These comments reveal the child's view of friendship as a temporary relationship based on a certain situation rather than on shared interests or beliefs (Furman and Bierman, 1984). Later, children become more aware of the thoughts and feelings of others, and their image of a friend becomes one of someone who will do what they want. Eventually children realize that good relationships depend upon give-and-take.

Prosocial Behaviors. **Prosocial behaviors** are voluntary actions toward others such as caring, sharing, comforting, and cooperation. Understanding the roots of prosocial behavior has contributed to our knowledge of children's moral development.

Several factors seem to be associated with the development of prosocial behaviors (Caldwell, 1977). These include:

- Parental disciplinary techniques that stress the consequences of the child's behavior for others and that are applied within a warm, responsive parent-child relationship (Baumrind, 1973; Hoffman, 1979).

- Contact with adults who indicate they expect concern for others (Bryan, 1975; Grusec and Arnason, 1982).

- Contact with adults who let children know that aggressive solutions to problems are unacceptable and who provide acceptable alternatives.

Play

Children spend a major portion of their time playing. Play, which contributes to development, can be characterized as follows (Krasnor and Pepler, 1980; Rosenblatt, 1982; Damon, 1983):

- Play is voluntary, pleasurable, spontaneous, and self-initiated.

- Play involves repetition or elaboration of behaviors already acquired, but it also promotes new skills and abilities.

Pretend Play
Creative activity in which children put themselves into imaginary roles or situations

Sociodramatic Play
Activities in which children act out prescribed roles

Play contributes to children's mental and social development. It allows children to be creative, to cooperate with others, and to vent emotions.

- Play is pursued "for its own sake"; it is not goal-directed.
- Play is creative and nonliteral. It contains elements of reality interwoven with fantasy.
- Play changes as children develop.

A form of play that dominates the preschool period is pretend or make-believe play. **Pretend play** involves transforming oneself or objects into other persons, places, or objects. This has been the most researched form of play because it is thought to contribute to cognitive, social, and language development. Its appearance marks the emergence of the ability to use mental symbols and images to stand for the real world of objects and actions.

Pretend play first appears during the second year of life, increases in frequency and complexity during the preschool years, and then declines in middle childhood. At first children play alone, or engage in *parallel play,* in which they play side by side without taking much notice of one another. At around three, children begin to engage in *cooperative play* in which they coordinate their activities, take turns, and work together to achieve a group goal (Guralnick and Weinhouse, 1984). One example of cooperative play is **sociodramatic play,** which includes such activities as playing "house" or "teacher," in which children act out prescribed roles. According to Piaget (1973), pretend play becomes more realistic as logic replaces preoperational thought.

The Contributions of Play to Early Childhood. Play reveals important elements of children's ability to make sense of their environment, of their linguistic, cognitive, and social skills, and of their general personality development.

Children exercise their minds when playing because they think and act as if they were another person. When they make such a transformation, they are taking a step toward abstract thinking in that they are freeing their thoughts from a focus on concrete objects. Play is also associated with creativity, especially the ability to be less literal and more flexible in one's thinking (Fein, 1979; Christie, 1980; Yawkey, 1980).

Play also gives children safe situations in which to express ideas and feelings that would be unacceptable in other settings. In play they can freely express their hostility and anger and relive hurtful events. For example, two four-year-old neighbors had new baby sisters at about the same time. Both children were affectionate toward their new sisters, but they also played a game called "bad baby," in which they scolded and punished a certain doll. This game helped them deal with their natural jealousy toward the new babies. This kind of play can help children come to grips with their feelings and with the often harsh aspects of reality (Damon, 1983).

The Disappearance of Childhood. Despite overwhelming evidence supporting the importance of play to all aspects of development, society is making fewer and fewer play opportunities available to children. Since play is one of the most distinctive characteristics of childhood, its decline is a measure of the disappearance of childhood as a separate and unique phase of human development.

The concept of childhood as a separate stage of development is a cultural invention that has only existed for about four hundred years. The precise marking of a child's birthday in any way is only two hundred years old (Postman, 1982). Prior to the recognition of a stage called childhood, children slept, ate, worked, and played with

THEORY INTO PRACTICE
Teaching Preschoolers and Kindergartners

ENCOURAGING COGNITIVE AND LANGUAGE DEVELOPMENT

The most obvious implication of Piaget's theory of cognitive development is that young children view the world differently from older children and adults. Consequently, Piagetian theory is often used to guide decisions about the readiness of children for specific activities. This has been especially true of the teaching of mathematics and science—subjects in which the mental operations described by Piaget are critical (Price, 1982).

Attempts to apply Piaget's ideas to early education focus on encouraging children to construct more adequate concepts (Goffin and Tull, 1984). Cognitive development consists not of the accumulation of isolated pieces of information, but, rather, of the construction by children of a framework for understanding their environment. Teachers should serve as role models by solving problems with children, and by talking with them about the process of problem solving and about the relationships between actions and outcomes. Teachers should be available as resources, but should not become the authorities who enforce correct answers. Children must be free to construct their own understandings.

Educators should also learn from children. Observing children during their activities and listening carefully to their questions can reveal much about what they are interested in and about their levels of thinking.

Children's solutions to problems and their questions reveal their point of view, and sensitive observations can help teachers be more responsive to children's developmental perspective.

Many of the educational implications derived from research on children's language development transfer findings from two sources: parental behaviors that encourage oral language development, and studies of young children who learn to read without formal instruction. The most frequent recommendations include reading to children, surrounding them with books and other printed materials, making various writing materials available, encouraging reading and writing, and being responsive to children's questions about letters, words, and spellings (McKenzie, 1977; Schickedanz, 1982; Vukelich and Golden, 1984).

There are numerous props teachers can use in the classroom, such as telephone books and "office space" in a dramatic play area. Classrooms can have writing centers with materials such as typewriters, magnetic letters, chalkboards, pencils, crayons, markers, and paper (Tompkins, 1981; Vukelich and Golden, 1984).

Art activities also contribute to children's understanding of print; children's recognition that their images can stand for something else helps develop an understanding of abstractions, which is essential to understanding symbolic language (Eisner, 1982).

Teachers can encourage children's involvement with print by reading in small groups, having tutors read to children individually, and allowing children to choose adults. Their shared lives did not take age differences into consideration (Postman, 1982; Sommerville, 1982).

With the advent of the idea of childhood, the early childhood years came to be treated and studied as a unique period of development. Yet today numerous authors contend that the concept of childhood is disappearing (Elkind, 1981; Postman, 1982; Sommerville, 1982; Suransky, 1982). Elkind (1981, 1986b) argues that children are pushed to achieve and are not allowed to grow up at their own pace. He feels the "hurried child" has no opportunity to nurture developmental capabilities.

For example, kindergarten classrooms and even nursery school programs have become more academically oriented because of the trend throughout the educational system to put more emphasis on basic skills. Arguing that this trend has gone too far, educators who regard play as an essential component of early childhood education (for example, Elkind, 1986) have shown its relationship to success with academic skills.

If childhood is to continue to exist as we know it, we must recognize its uniqueness and allow children the time and opportunity to respond to their

books to read. Intimate reading experiences allow children to turn pages, pause to look at pictures or ask questions, and read along with an adult. These experiences cannot occur as easily if the teacher sits at the front of the room reading to a large group of children (Schickedanz, 1978, 1982).

Predictable books such as *The Three Little Pigs* and *There Was an Old Lady Who Swallowed a Fly* allow beginning readers to rely on what they already know about language while learning sound-letter relationships. Stories are predictable if a child can guess what the author is going to say and how it will be stated. Repetitive structures, rhyme and rhythm, and a match between pictures and text increase predictability (Rhodes, 1977).

Children's understandings about language are enhanced when adults point out the important features of print (Harste and Burke, 1980; Dyson, 1984). Statements such as "We must start at the front, not at the back of the book"; "Move your finger; you're covering the words and I can't see to read them"; and "You have to point to each word as you say it, not to each letter, like this" (Schickedanz, 1982, p. 256), help clarify the reading process. Teachers can indicate features in print that are significant and draw attention to patterns of letters, sounds, or phrases (McKenzie, 1977). These informal experiences also teach children the words that are related to written language, such as "letter," "word," and "a, b, c" (Schickedanz, 1982).

Encouraging Socioemotional Development

Teachers of young children should provide a variety of materials such as puppets, blocks, water, and a dramatic play area that encourage cooperative play. Too many materials, however, can make cooperation unnecessary (Asher et al., 1982). Competition that emphasizes outdoing others should be minimized; instead, you should help children learn to cooperate and should set a good example by trying to understand the perspectives of the children you are teaching.

Group games that let children develop rules and abide by them encourage cooperation and self-governance (Kamii and DeVries, 1980). Because preoperational thinking is still tied to actions, the actions necessary for cooperation should be concrete and observable. For example, three-legged stilts where two children stand next to each other and have their inside leg tied to a shared middle stilt require children to coordinate their physical movements (Goffin and Tull, 1984).

Kamii and DeVries (1978) emphasize the importance of minimizing adult authority. Adult-oriented morality encourages blind obedience, whereas children's cooperative planning, decision making, and resolution of conflict promote compromise. Support for peer interactions, and peer conflict in particular, is the most frequent social application of Piaget's work. Peer play also encourages a peer-oriented morality based on cooperation, which is believed to be a developmental root of morality (Piaget, 1932; Damon, 1983, 1984).

environment as children. This means monitoring their access to television, which takes up time that should be spent in active play. It means recognizing that leisure time is important because children need to initiate activities independent of adult structure. It means supporting and protecting children's right to autonomous play separate from both formal schooling and the extracurricular bombardment of gymnastics, music, and swimming lessons (Klieber and Barnett, 1980; Suransky, 1982, 1983).

DEVELOPMENT DURING MIDDLE CHILDHOOD

Children entering the first grade are in a transitional period from the rapid growth of early childhood to a phase of more gradual development. Shifts in both mental and social development characterize the early school years.

Several years later, when children reach the upper elementary grades, they are nearing the end of childhood and entering preadolescence. These "transescents," as Donald Eichorn (1966) called them, are in transition from childhood to adolescence.

Physical Development

Lower Elementary Children. As children progress through the primary grades, their physical development slows in comparison with earlier childhood. Children change relatively little in size during the primary years.

To picture the "typical" child in the primary grades, we must picture a child in good physical condition. Girls are slightly shorter and lighter than boys until around the age of nine, when height and weight are approximately equal for boys and girls (see Table 3.1).

Muscular development is outdistanced by bone and skeletal development. This may cause the aches commonly known as "growing pains." Also, the growing muscles need much exercise, which may contribute to the primary child's inability to stay still

TABLE 3.1

DEVELOPMENT OF GIRLS AND BOYS

Girls are typically somewhat shorter and lighter than boys during early elementary school and in high school. However, in late elementary school many girls begin a major growth spurt and for a few years are taller and heavier than their male classmates.

	Girls			Boys	
Age (years)	Height (feet-inches)	Weight (pounds)	Age (years)	Height (feet-inches)	Weight (pounds)
7	3-11½	48	7	4-0	50
9	4-4	63	9	4-4	62
11	4-9	82	11	4-8½	78
13	5-2	102	13	5-1½	99
15	5-3¾	118	15	5-6½	125
17	5-4¼	125	17	5-9½	146

SOURCE: Adapted from USDHEW, 1978.

for long. By the time children enter the primary grades, they have developed many of the basic motor skills needed for balance, running, jumping, and throwing. During the primary years gross and fine motor skills are improved through practice. As development progresses, children can switch from using oversized pencils to regular-sized ones, and from activities like finger painting that use awkward whole-arm movements to building intricate models and using delicate finger movements to play the piano and stringed instruments. In addition, the eyesight of children often improves during this period. Many preschoolers tend toward farsightedness, but as the eye changes shape during the early primary grades, this condition improves.

Although this is a period of general good health, not all children fit the description of the "typical" child. Some of the childhood diseases that previous generations of children were expected to suffer through (such as measles and mumps) are now controlled through immunization programs, but not all children are protected. Other diseases now controlled by immunization programs include smallpox, diphtheria, polio, and German measles.

Upper Elementary Children.   As can be seen in Table 3.1, nine-year-old boys and girls are similar in both height and weight. Upper elementary students are, on average, healthier than their younger brothers and sisters. Children who have entered the middle childhood period show more resistance to fatigue and disease. They are better coordinated than seven- or eight-year-olds.

During the latter part of the fourth grade, however, many girls begin a major growth spurt that will not be completed until puberty. This spurt begins with the rapid growth of the arms and legs. At this point there is *not* an accompanying change in trunk size. The result is a "gangly" or "all-arms-and-legs" appearance. Because this bone growth occurs before the development of associated muscles and cartilage, children at this growth stage temporarily lose some coordination and strength.

By the start of the fifth grade, almost all girls have begun this spurt. In addition, muscle and cartilage growth of the limbs resumes in the earlier-maturing females and they regain their strength and coordination. By the end of the fifth grade, girls are typically taller, heavier, and stronger than boys. Since males are twelve to eighteen months behind girls in development, even early-maturing boys do not start their growth spurt until age eleven. By the start of the sixth grade, therefore, most girls will be near the peak of their growth spurt and all but the early-maturing boys will be continuing the slow, steady growth of late childhood. Girls usually will have started their menstrual period by age thirteen. For boys, the end of preadolescence and the onset of early adolescence is measured by the first ejaculation, which occurs between the ages of thirteen and sixteen.

Cognitive Abilities

Between the ages of five and seven, children's thought processes undergo significant changes (Osborn and Osborn, 1983). This is a period of transition from the stage of preoperational thought to the stage of concrete operations. This change allows them to do mentally what previously was done physically, and to mentally reverse the actions involved (see Chapter 2).

All children do not make this transition at the same age, and no individual child changes from one stage to the next quickly (see Table 3.2). Children will often use cognitive behaviors characteristic of two stages of development at the same time. As individuals advance from one stage to the next, the characteristics of the previous stage are maintained as the cognitive behaviors of the higher stage develop.

TABLE 3.2

PERCENT OF STUDENTS AT PIAGETIAN STAGES

People reach the cognitive stages of development described by Piaget at different ages. At age thirteen, for example, a small percentage of children are in the preoperational or formal operational stage, while most are in the concrete operational stage.

Age (years)	Preoperational	Concrete Operational		Formal Operational	
	(%)	Onset (%)	Mature (%)	Onset (%)	Mature (%)
5	85	15			
6	60	35	5		
7	35	55	10		
8	25	55	20		
9	15	55	30		
10	12	52	35	1	
11	6	49	40	5	
12	5	32	51	12	
13	2	34	44	14	6
14	1	32	43	15	9

SOURCE: Adapted from Epstein, 1980.

The third stage of cognitive development is called *concrete* operational because thought is restricted to what children experience in direct, hands-on, face-to-face encounters. Children in, or at least entering, the concrete stage can perform some or all of the following activities:

1. *Conservation:* Concrete operational children realize that altering one aspect of an object does not necessarily alter other aspects. Prior to age nine, most children understand conservation as it relates to substances, number (rearranging objects does not change their number), length (unbending a circle-shaped wire does not change the length of the wire), and area (the area covered by paper cut in half is the same as that covered by the paper when it was whole). At about nine, children also begin to understand conservation of weight (a mashed piece of clay weighs the same as when it was round). (See Sund, 1976).

2. *Classification:* As with conservation, the ability to classify develops in stages. First, children develop the ability to see single characteristics. This is followed by the ability to recognize common properties of objects. The other skills of classification, in sequence, are: multiple classification, or classifying by more than one property; seeing like and unlike qualities; forming subclasses and including them in major classes; grouping by hierarchy; and forming relatively complex classifications systems.

3. *Number:* The ability to mentally ask how many objects there are and to classify them.

4. *Mathematical operations:* By the end of the concrete operational stage, children have the mental abilities to learn how to add, subtract, multiply, divide, and place numbers in order by size.

5. *Forming limited hypotheses:* Children in the concrete operational stage can think what will happen "If . . .," especially if the hypothesis involves conservation and the objects about which the hypothesis is made are in view. Children at this stage are usually limited to one hypothesis and one variable.

6. *Understanding time and space:* Children can now better appreciate historical time and geographic space. They can draw an accurate map of the route from their home to school and can appreciate the relationships of areas they have visited in their city and state. However, concrete operational children can still have difficulty fully appreciating historical time spans such as those between the Pilgrims, the pioneers, and the astronauts.

Children in the upper elementary grades move from what Piaget calls egocentric thought to decentered, or more objective, thought. They understand that events are governed by physical laws (such as gravity), and that different people see things from different perspectives. An example of the ability of children to decenter is their realization that three or four other children can have three or four different interpretations of a single cloud formation in the sky. This ability helps the concrete operational child not only to interpret physical events but also to understand human relationships. The movement from egocentric to decentered thought indicates entrance into the concrete *mature* operational stage.

Although Piaget has indicated that children start moving to the formal operational stage of mental operations around age eleven, as Table 3.2 indicates, the percentage of upper elementary students even just entering the formal operational stage is very small. Formal operational children can begin to hypothesize, to build abstract categories, and see cause-and-effect relationships in the absence of concrete materials. They can also begin to handle more than two variables at the same time. They take symbols in stories and art less literally, and their understanding of social concepts, such as democracy, becomes more sophisticated.

Elementary school children are typically in the concrete operational stage of cognitive development. Their mental skills are most effective when dealing with things they can see and touch and experience.

Self-Concept
A person's perception of his or her own strengths and weaknesses

In addition to entering the concrete operation stage, elementary school-age children are rapidly developing memory and cognitive skills, including the ability to think about their own thinking and to learn how to learn. Cognitive development is discussed in Chapters 5 and 6.

Socioemotional Development

By the time children enter elementary school, they have developed skills for more complex thought, action, and social influence. Up to this point, children have been basically egocentric, and their world has been that of home, family, and possibly a nursery school or day-care center.

The early primary grades will normally be spent working through Erickson's (1963) fourth stage, industry versus inferiority. Assuming that a child has developed trust during infancy, autonomy during the early years, and initiative during the preschool years, that child's experiences in the primary grades can contribute to his or her sense of industry and accomplishment.

During this stage children start trying to prove that they are "grown up"—in fact, this is often described as the "I-can-do-it-myself" stage. Work becomes possible. As children's powers of concentration grow, they can spend more time on chosen tasks and they often take pleasure in completing projects. This stage also includes the growth of independent action, cooperation with groups, performing in socially acceptable ways, and a concern for fair play.

Self-Concept.   An important area of personal and social development for elementary school children is **self-concept,** or self-esteem. This aspect of their development will be strongly influenced by experiences at home, with peers, and at school. Self-concept includes the way we perceive our strengths, weaknesses, abilities, attitudes, and values. Its development begins at birth and is continually shaped by experience. Lack of a positive self-concept can severely damage a child's social development.

When children begin school, they tend to judge themselves on specific accomplishments rather than on a general sense of worth. (Damon and Hart, 1982; Harter, 1982). You can understand this when you see that even the smallest failure can cause a child to feel worthless. It is also important to note that a child's self-concept can be different in different areas. For example, it is possible to have a positive self-image in school or sports but not in peer relations or physical self-image.

The primary grades give many children their first chance to compare themselves with others and to work and play under the guidance of adults outside their family. These adults must provide experiences that let children succeed, feel good about themselves, and maintain their enthusiasm and creativity.

Growing Importance of Peers.   The influence of the child's family, which was the major force during the early childhood years, continues in importance as parents provide role models in terms of attitudes and behaviors. In addition, relationships with brothers and sisters affect relationships with peers, and routines from home are either reinforced or must be overcome in school.

However, the peer group takes on added importance. Speaking on the child's entrance into the world outside the family, Ira Gordon noted the importance of peers:

> If all the world's the stage that Shakespeare claimed, children and adolescents are playing primarily to an audience of their peers. Their peers sit in the front rows and the box seats; parents and teachers are now relegated to the back rows and the balcony. (Gordon, 1975, p. 166)

Child Development

1. Please describe a major social or emotional challenge facing the students you teach.

Elonda Hogue, who teachers first grade in Lawrence, Kan., said:

As a teacher of first-graders, one of the major challenges I see facing my students is the adjustment to the more structured "school-like" atmosphere of first grade, as opposed to the less structured atmosphere of kindergarten.
   Upon entering first grade even the organization of the room changes. Students have individual desks and chairs, meaning they are responsible for their own space and supplies. They will also be asked to sit and attend in the same chairs for a big part of the day. The students are also asked to begin performing as "grade school students" not as kindergartners. This is sometimes a great adjustment for the many "free spirits" coming to us as educators of the young child. It is very important that as teachers we try to make that adjustment as stress free as possible.

2. What aspects of a child's physical, cognitive, and social development do you consider when planning lessons?

Curt Fulton, who teaches fifth grade in Wallkill, N.Y., has suggestions regarding planning classes at the upper elementary level:

A teacher of upper elementary school students needs to remember that students at this age (nine to eleven) are "transitioning" between the early childhood and middle childhood stages of development. In addition to all the rigors of academic life, a child this age is in a never-ending conflict between the joys of simple childhood activities on the one hand, and the pressure to "grow up" or "act your age" on the other. The problem is that these children really don't know how to act their age and become frustrated when teachers keep reminding them how they should act. There is an imaginary line somewhere between these two developmental stages and the children know where it is. What we as teachers need to assure them of is that it is okay to jump back and

forth across this "line" from time to time. Yes, a child should endeavor to "grow up" when it comes to taking responsibility for getting all the week's assignments done on time, but it's also acceptable for that same child to play with matchbox cars or dolls.

Beverly Harrison, a seventh-grade teacher in Omaha, Neb., says teachers must remember the limitations of students' experience and knowledge:

I tended to overestimate the readiness and background of my students, so I taught "over their heads" for many years. I expected them to have heard about the things I knew about as an adult. It wasn't until my own child reached the level that I was teaching that I realized children are limited in their scope of experiences, vocabulary, and conceptual development. Teachers must remember themselves as students at the level at which they are teaching. I became a better teacher when I realized the limitations of my students.

3. Think back to your education training, specifically to the course you took in educational psychology. What did you learn in that course that has proven particularly helpful in your teaching?

Roseanne Swinburne-Sanderfoot, who teaches learning disabled children in Manawa, Wisc., said:

All joking aside, one of the most memorable and helpful things I learned in my educational psychology class was a quotation from my middle-aged psychology professor. What he said probably didn't contain any deep truth, but it stands out in my mind years later. When discussing the development of children and youth, he would always say, perfectly timed, "God made one mistake—thirteen-year-olds." He went on, of course, to discuss the many changes that early teens go through and how challenging they can be at age thirteen.
   Occasionally, when things seem to go crazy while working with middle-schoolers, it's great to remember that being 13 is traumatic and that this, too, will pass. Reminding myself of this helps keep my job in perspective.

Having fun with a peer group can help a child's self-image and provide opportunities for learning about others. Younger children often form single-sex peer groups, while older children have friends of both sexes.

In the lower elementary grades peer groups usually consist of same-sexed children who are around the same age. This preference may be due to the variety of abilities and interests among young children. By the sixth grade, however, students often form groups that include both boys and girls. Whatever the composition of peer groups, they let children compare their abilities and skills to those of others. Members of peer groups also teach one another about their different worlds. Children learn through this sharing of attitudes and values how to sort out and form their own attitudes and values.

Groups composed of boys and those made up of girls seem to value different attitudes and behavior. Boys gain prestige by being physically aggressive, good at sports, daring, attention-getting, and friendly to other males. In female peer groups membership is related more to being attractive, popular (with girls *and* boys), friendly, optimistic, and having a sense of humor about oneself (Rubin, 1980). Boys are expected by their peers to misbehave in class, while among girls being well-behaved and courteous are usually more important.

For both boys and girls in the upper elementary grades, membership in groups tends to promote feelings of self-worth. *Not* being accepted can bring serious emotional problems. Herein lies the major cause of the preadolescent's changing relationship with parents. It is not that preadolescents care less about their parents. It is just that their friends are *more* important than ever. This need for acceptance by peers helps explain why preadolescents often dress alike. Girls' conformity may be neater, but boys are just as likely to copy one another, perhaps in wearing their shirttails out or in wearing special athletic shoes. This phenomenon of conformity among preadolescents is not limited to the United States; in one Israeli elementary school a visitor once noted that every fifth-grader was wearing a blue jogging suit with a white stripe!

Partly as a result of their changing physical and cognitive structures, children in the upper elementary grades seek to be more "grown up." They want their parents to treat them differently, even though many parents are unwilling to see them differently. Nine- to twelve-year-olds still depend heavily on their families and generally report that they love their parents. They also report that though they feel their parents love them, they do not think they *understand* them.

Regarding the changing relationships of preadolescents with their parents, Hershel Thornburg in *The Bubblegum Years* writes:

> Some parents believe that their happiest years as parents were when their children were in these bubblegum years. Nine- to twelve-year-olds do not have the same time-consuming needs they do when they are younger and neither have they matured to the point where they will be active, often unmanageable—their adolescent years. At the risk of discouraging some parents, it may be that this "sense of easy childrearing" is one reason why so many preteens have problems. At the very point in time where parents relax in their childrearing roles, their preteens are going through the most significant changes of their lives. (Thornburg, 1979, p. 57)

Thornburg suggests that parents (and teachers) of preadolescents remember two facts (1979, p. 58):

1. When change is occurring, preteens are breaking up the well-defined, predictable behaviors and attitudes of childhood. They are growing up and changing the ways they do things, ways to which their parents have become accustomed.

2. When change is occurring, preteens need additional guidance. Parents must remember that many of their children's ways of acting are as new and unpredictable to the children as they are to them. Therefore parental direction and reassurance are important to normal growth.

The middle childhood years often also bring changes in the relationship between children and their teachers. Early in primary school, children easily accept and depend on teachers. During the upper elementary years this relationship becomes more complex. Sometimes students will tell teachers personal information they would not tell their parents. Some preadolescents even choose teachers as role models. At the same time, however, some preteens talk back to teachers in ways they would never have considered several years earlier, and some openly challenge teachers.

■ **Stop and Think**
During the elementary school years, children engage in an increasing number of activities outside of the home. What activities are available for young people in your community? Are these activities generally beneficial for children? Or potentially harmful? What influence might these activities have on school success?

Emotional Development.   Emotional problems related to the physical, cognitive, and social development of upper elementary children are common. Though preadolescents are generally happy and optimistic, they also have many fears, such as:

- not being accepted into a peer group
- not having a "best friend"
- being punished by their parents
- having their parents get a divorce
- not doing well in school
- getting hurt

Other emotions of this age group include anger (and fear of being unable to control it), guilt, frustration, and jealousy. Preadolescents need help in realizing that these emotions and fears are a natural part of growing up. Adults must let them talk about these emotions and fears, even if they seem unrealistic to an adult. Feelings of guilt often arise when there is a conflict between children's actions (based on the values of the peer group) and their parents' values.

Anger is another common emotion at this age. It is displayed with more intensity than many of the other emotions. Just as they often tell their preadolescents they shouldn't be afraid, parents often tell them that they should not get angry. Unfortunately, this is an unrealistic expectation, even for adults—including parents!

DEVELOPMENT DURING ADOLESCENCE

The adolescent period of development begins with puberty. The pubertal period, or early adolescence, is a time of rapid physical and intellectual development. Middle adolescence is a more stable period of adjustment to and integration of the changes of

THEORY INTO PRACTICE

Teaching Elementary-Age Children

In many ways middle childhood is the ideal time for teaching. Children have the cognitive and social skills needed to learn most of what is taught in school, but they have not yet reached the "storm and stress" of adolescence. However, instruction must still take into account the developmental characteristics of children of elementary school age.

One important principle is that most children in elementary school are at the concrete operational stage of cognitive development and therefore lack the ability to think in abstractions, an ability that comes with the formal operational stage in adolescence. This means that classroom instruction in the elementary grades should be as concrete and experiential as possible. Science lessons should involve touching, building, manipulating, experimenting, and tasting. Social studies lessons should include field trips, guest speakers, role playing, and debates. Language arts and reading activities should include creating, imagining, acting out, and writing. Mathematics lessons should use concrete objects to show concepts, and allow students to manipulate objects to represent mathematical principles and operations. An emphasis on the use of mathematics to solve real-life problems, as in simulations of buying things and receiving change or running a simulated bank or store, can be important. These activities give students concrete mental representations of the concepts they are learning, and these mental representations are critical in forming a solid basis of concepts on which later instruction will build.

Creative activities help elementary age children understand new concepts. The concrete operational stage of cognitive development limits their understanding to only those things they can experience.

Particularly in the early grades, elementary school children need to be able to relate concepts and information to their own experiences. For example, a "kilometer" has no meaning to students in the abstract, but may be related to the distance students walk to school. "Democracy" is a meaningless abstraction unless students can elect class leaders and live by a set of rules they had a part in developing.

Along with basic skills, the most important things elementary students are learning in school is whether early adolescence. Later adolescence is marked by the transition into the responsibilities, choices, and opportunities of adulthood. In this section we will review the major changes that occur as the child becomes an adolescent and we will examine how adolescent development affects teaching, curriculum, and school structure.

Puberty
Developmental stage at which a person becomes capable of reproduction

Physical Development

Variability in Onset and Rate of Puberty.   **Puberty** is a series of physiological changes that render the immature organism capable of reproduction. Nearly every organ and system of the body is affected by these changes. The prepubertal child and the postpubertal adolescent are different in outward appearance because of changes in stature and proportion and the development of primary and secondary sexual features. Table 3.3 summarizes the typical sequence of physical development in adolescence.

Although the sequence of events at puberty is generally the same for each person, the timing and the rate at which they occur vary widely. The average girl typically begins pubertal changes one and a half to two years before the average boy. In each

they are "smart" or "dumb," "good kids" or "bad kids," popular or unpopular. A person's self-concept is largely formed during middle childhood, and the impact of school on self-concept can be profound.

The key word regarding personal and social development is "acceptance." The fact is, children do differ in their abilities, and no matter what teachers do, students will have figured out who is more able and who is less able by the end of the elementary years (usually earlier). However, teachers can have a substantial impact on how students feel about these differences, and on the value that low-achieving students place on learning even when they know they will never be the class star.

Teachers must accept students as they are and communicate a norm that all students are valuable and all are learners. They may also communicate the idea that there are many valuable skills. Some students are good in reading, others in math, others in sports, others in art. Particularly in the elementary school it is important to avoid setting up competition among students to be the "best" if only the most able students have a chance to win (Cohen, 1984).

If ability grouping within the class is used in reading or in mathematics (see Chapter 9), assignments to such groups should be done flexibly and changed often as students change in performance. This gets away from the idea that there are "high" and "low" students, but maintains the notion that different students need help with different skills at different times.

It goes without saying that teachers should never tell a student that he or she is "dumb," and should avoid implying this by word or action. For example, even if the entire class knows that the "Yellowbirds" are the low reading group, the teacher should never refer to the "Yellowbirds" as such; to do so communicates the idea that those students will *always* be poor readers, which is rarely true and is harmful to the students' self-concepts.

Middle childhood is also a critical time for moral development. Teachers can promote the development of prosocial behaviors by demonstrating fairness, consistency, consideration, politeness, and other appropriate behaviors. Just as authoritative (as opposed to authoritarian or permissive) parenting has the most favorable effect on children (Baumrind, 1973), so does authoritative *teaching* best contribute to prosocial development (Rohrkemper, 1984). For example, teachers should give reasons for their classroom management or disciplinary actions and should let students have some say in setting rules. On the other hand, teachers must consistently and fairly enforce the rules they (and the class) have established, and should follow through on applying consequences when students violate established rules (see Chapter 11).

Moral development in elementary school-age children may also be enhanced by classroom discussions of moral dilemmas. For example, the class might discuss what should be done about copying during tests or how tattling should be handled.

Chapter 3: Development During Childhood and Adolescence

79

TABLE 3.3

THE TYPICAL SEQUENCE OF PHYSICAL DEVELOPMENT IN ADOLESCENCE

Girls	Boys
Initial enlargement of the breasts occurs (breast bud stage).	Growth of the testes and scrotum begins.
Straight, lightly pigmented pubic hair appears.	Straight, lightly pigmented pubic hair appears.
Maximum growth rate is attained.	Growth of the penis begins.
Pubic hair becomes adult in type but covers a smaller area than in adult.	Early changes in the voice occur.
	First ejaculation of semen occurs.
Breast enlargement continues; the nipple and the area around it now project above the level of the breast.	Pubic hair becomes adult in type but covers a smaller area than in adult.
	Maximum growth rate is attained.
Menarche occurs.	Underarm hair appears; the sweat glands under the arms increase in size.
Underarm hair appears; the sweat glands under the arms increase in size.	The voice deepens noticeably.
Breasts and pubic hair reach adult stage.	Growth of mustache and beard hair begins. Pubic hair reaches adult stage.

SOURCE: The Committee on Adolescence, Group for the Advancement of Psychiatry, 1968; Tanner, 1978.

sex, however, the normal range of onset is approximately six years. Like the onset, the rate of changes also varies widely, with some people taking only eighteen to twenty-four months to go through the pubertal changes to reproductive maturity, while others may require six years to pass through the same stage.

These differences mean that some individuals may be completely mature before others the same age have even begun puberty. The age of maximum diversity is thirteen for males and about eleven for females. The comparisons children make among themselves, as well as the tendency to hold maturity in high regard, can be a problem for the less mature. On the other hand, the first to mature are also likely to experience temporary discomfort because they stand out from the less mature majority.

Reactions to Puberty.   One of the most important challenges to adolescents is to accommodate to the changes in their bodies. Coordination and physical activity must be adjusted rapidly as height, weight, and skills change. The new body must be integrated into the existing self-image. New routines of care must be learned and new habits developed. As adolescents become more like adults in appearance, they find themselves expected to behave more like adults, regardless of their emotional, intellectual, or social maturity.

The purpose of puberty is to make people able to reproduce. Thus the adolescent is faced with a new potential that includes increased interest in sexual activity, erotic fantasy, and experimentation. Masturbation becomes a regular activity for many adolescents, and increasing percentages of adolescents engage in intercourse (Hass, 1979). Sexual activity necessitates facing the possibility of sexually transmitted diseases, conflict with parents, and pregnancy.

Early and Late Maturing.   Researchers have long been interested in the possible differences between children who enter puberty early and those who enter it when they are older. Peskin (1967) demonstrated that earlier maturers have a harder time *at* puberty. Youths who mature earlier experience more anxiety and have more temper tantrums, more conflict with their parents, and lower self-esteem at puberty than do those who are older at puberty. But by the time the earlier maturers are in high school, long past puberty and having accommodated its changes, they are more at ease, popular, and mature than are later maturers, who are still experiencing pubertal changes. Problems of late maturation seem to be much greater for boys than for girls (Greif and Ulman, 1982; Steinberg and Hill, 1978). A few studies have found that even in their thirties early-maturing males are more confident and poised than males who matured later (Livson and Peskin, 1980).

Cognitive Abilities

As the rest of the body changes at puberty, the brain and its functions also change. Just as pubertal changes vary widely across individuals, so does the timing of intellectual changes vary. One indication of this is that scores on intelligence tests obtained over several years from the same individual fluctuate most during the period from twelve to fifteen years of age.

Piagetian Theory. In Piaget's theory of cognitive development, adolescence is the stage of transition from the use of concrete operations to the application of formal operations in reasoning. Adolescents begin to be aware of the limitations of their thinking. They wrestle with concepts that are removed from their own experience. Inhelder and Piaget (1958) acknowledge that brain changes at puberty may be necessary for the cognitive advances of adolescence. They assert, however, that experience with complex problems, the demands of formal instruction, and exchange and contradiction of ideas with peers are also necessary for formal operational reasoning to develop.

Although the thinking of the concrete operational child has great power, it also has limitations. These limitations are few but important. The development of formal operational reasoning overcomes these shortcomings. Adolescents who reach this stage (not all do) have attained an adult level of reasoning.

Games like chess that require analytical skills are too hard for most young children but become interesting challenges for the more advanced cognitive skills of high-schoolers.

Examining some of the tasks that Inhelder and Piaget used to measure the cognitive abilities of children will illustrate the changes that take place in adolescence.

Combinational Systems. In this task the subject is presented with four beakers of clear liquids, labeled *1, 2, 3,* and *4,* and a small bottle labeled *g.* The examiner displays a test tube, explaining that it contains liquid taken from one or more of the numbered beakers. The examiner then adds a few drops of liquid from bottle *g,* whereupon the liquid in the test tube changes color from clear to yellow-orange. The subject is asked to find out what liquid was in the test tube and to reproduce the color change. (See Figure 3.2.)

The typical concrete operational child approaches the task by trying each of the chemicals in turn. None of these produces the effect. With or without prompting, the child may try combinations of *1* and *2* and *3* and *4.* Neither of these creates the desired color change. Occasionally *1* and *3* will be tried, which *does* cause the change. The child is then asked to see if any other combinations will work. Concrete operational children try other combinations, more or less randomly, and have difficulty explaining their results.

Adolescents who have developed formal operational reasoning approach the task assuming, or rapidly realizing, that there are a limited number of combinations, that they should try them all, and that they must keep track of what they have tried and of the results. Doing so, they can discover that the color is produced by combinations of *1* and *3* and *1, 2,* and *3.* They can draw from this the conclusion that *1* and *3* are necessary, but *2* is not. They may also observe that adding *4* to either combination works against the desired reaction.

The adolescent's performance is distinguished by

- the assumption that there is a way to find all possible combinations
- a procedure for keeping track of results

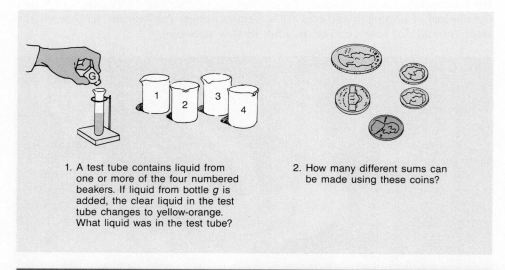

1. A test tube contains liquid from one or more of the four numbered beakers. If liquid from bottle *g* is added, the clear liquid in the test tube changes to yellow-orange. What liquid was in the test tube?

2. How many different sums can be made using these coins?

FIGURE 3.2

Problem Solving

Adolescents who have reached the formal operational stage of cognitive development typically use a systematic approach to solving problems such as those shown here. Younger students will often take a haphazard approach to problem solving.

- the recognition that there may be more than one way to make the color
- the comparison of results to understand the effects of each chemical

An easy test of a student's approach can be based on a familiar puzzle: How many different sums can be made using a quarter, two dimes, a nickel, and two pennies? Try it with children and adolescents. Notice the differences in how they attack the problem. The younger child is likely to try random combinations of coins, while the adolescent is more likely to use a systematic plan to be sure that all possibilities have been covered.

Generating abstract relationships from available information, and then comparing those abstract relationships to each other, is a general skill underlying many tasks in which adolescents' competence leaps forward. Piaget (1952a) described a task in which students in the concrete operational stage were given a set of ten proverbs and a set of statements that meant the same thing as the proverbs. They were asked to match each proverb to the equivalent statement. Again, children can understand the task and choose answers. Their answers, however, are often incorrect because they often do not understand that a proverb describes a general principle. They match statements that have similarities, but they fail to compare the meanings of the statements to find the *best* matches. Adolescents and adults have little difficulty with this task.

Hypothetical Conditions. Another ability Piaget and others recognized in the young adolescent is the ability to reason about situations and conditions that have not been experienced. The adolescent can accept, for the sake of argument or discussion, conditions that are arbitrary, that are not known to exist, or even that are known to be contrary to fact. Adolescents are not bound to their own experiences of reality, so they can apply logic to any given set of conditions.

One illustration of the ability to reason about hypothetical situations is found in formal debate. In structured debate participants must be prepared to defend either side of an issue, regardless of their personal feelings or experience, and their defense is judged on its documentation and logical consistency. For a dramatic illustration of the difference between children and adolescents in the ability to suspend their own opinions, compare the reactions of fourth- and ninth-graders when you ask them to present an argument in favor of the proposition that schools should be in session six days a week, forty-eight weeks a year.

Socioemotional Development

One of the first signs of early adolescence is the appearance of **reflectivity,** or the tendency to think about what is going on in one's own mind and to study oneself. Adolescents begin to look more closely at themselves and to define themselves differently. They start to realize that there are differences between what they think and feel and how they behave. Using the developing intellectual skills that permit them to consider possibilities, adolescents are prone to be dissatisfied with themselves. They critique their personal characteristics, compare themselves to others, and try to change the way they are.

Adolescents may also ponder whether other people see and think about the world in the same way they themselves do. They become more aware of their separateness from other people, and of their uniqueness. They learn that other people cannot know fully what they think and feel. The issue of who and what one "really" is dominates personality development in adolescence.

Reflectivity
The act of analyzing oneself and one's own thoughts

The preoccupation of adolescents with their appearance is typically a step toward finding a more grown-up image and identity.

Chapter 3: Development During Childhood and Adolescence

Identity Diffusion
The adolescent's inability to develop a clear sense of self

Identity Foreclosure
The premature choice of a role, often done to reinforce self-concept

According to Erikson, the stage is set during adolescence for a major concern with who one is—with one's identity.

Identity. The physical and intellectual changes of adolescence disrupt the child's sense of continuity and personal wholeness. The cognitive ability to relate past to present, and to think about the future, presents the young adolescent with the problem of understanding the continuity of experience across time and projecting that continuity into the future. The adolescent's psychosocial task, then, is to create a sense of what Erikson calls ego identity.

To accomplish this, adolescents usually depend on several activities.

1. *They pay great attention to how other people view them:* Young adolescents have sensitive antennas, tuned to receive subtle messages about themselves from other people. They listen carefully to their peers, parents, teachers, and other adults for any information that indicates how those people view them. Information obtained is chewed over, worried about, compared to other views, and inserted into their self-concept, if it can be made compatible with information already there.

2. *They search the past:* Young adolescents often want to know about their ancestors, family trees, their own infant and childhood experiences. Some learn basic genetics, and are concerned about the sources of their physical and psychological characteristics. All these contribute to their understanding of continuity across time and of their potential future.

3. *They experiment with roles:* Their attempts to find out what kind of person they are lead to trying out different ways of being. Healthy adolescents explore who they are by attempting to be different. They adopt the characteristics of other people to see if they fit themselves. They take on, and quickly cast off, the traits of peers, teachers, and other acquaintances. As they try on characters and roles, they test how they feel. They also watch carefully how other people respond to their experiments in order to see if they can fit them into their relationships with others.

4. *They act on feelings and express their beliefs and opinions:* Adolescents place a high value on "being honest" and on behaving in ways that are "true to oneself." Some adolescents become distressed if they think they are not presenting their real feelings or if they are not being consistent in their behavior. Gradually most come to realize that feelings, beliefs, and people can change, and that consistency is less important than accurate representation of oneself.

Erikson calls the experience of not having a sense of one's identity **identity diffusion.** This is the unpleasant awareness of continual change in oneself and of the differences between one's self-concept and how others see one. To escape this troubling situation, some adolescents adopt a role—an identity—prematurely. Such a choice, which Erikson calls **identity foreclosure,** gives a person a self-concept around which to organize feelings and behavior. The choices are usually supported by the reactions of parents and other people, because they find it helpful to know how to relate to the adolescent. Often adolescents choose a role that they know will be socially desirable—the premed scholar, for example. Sometimes, however, as in the choice of sexual promiscuity by a rebellious youth, the behavior may draw disapproval, even though it may have been "forecast" by anxious parents.

Let's face it, adolescence is a challenge.

It's a time when pimply faced preteens and teenagers wallow in anxiety about self-image and social status. For parents, it's a time to pray that children don't stray into the dangers of drugs and alcohol, unprotected sex, and unsafe peer group hijinks. And, for teachers, it's a time to be patient with classrooms full of preoccupied students, and to have a sense of humor about the effects of hormones on young people.

In spite of all this, preteens and teenagers must attend school, and schools must do their best to educate them.

How middle schools go about the job of educating adolescents was the focus of a report by a task force of New York's Carnegie Corporation. In the first major study of public schools to focus on children ten to fifteen years old, the corporation's Task Force on Education of Young Adults concluded that middle schools should be fundamentally restructured to meet the needs of their students.

The report, titled "Turning Points," said middle schools should be kept small (possibly by establishing schools within schools), with 200 to 300 students, so that teachers and administrators would know their students better. Also, teachers should work in multidisciplinary teams, again so that the teachers would work with and become well acquainted with a particular group of students. Finally, middle schools should be integrated with community services, should seek greater involvement by parents, should take advantage of the interest of adolescents in their bodies to convey more health-related information in the curriculum, and should involve students in their communities through community service and volunteer programs.

The Carnegie Corporation's ideas may seem simple, but they are radical. They depart from the "more of the same" approach advocated by reformers in the mid-1980s, who pushed for back-to-basics curriculums, more school days, tougher graduation requirements, and higher teacher pay. Despite the acceptance of many of those ideas, the cracks in the system persisted, and drop-out rates have remained stubbornly high.

The Carnegie Corporation report focuses on students who are at a critical juncture in their lives. It deserves attention because these students have unique needs, and schools need to figure out new ways to meet those needs.

Edward B. Fiske, "Lessons," *New York Times,* June 21, 1989, p. B6.

"What Middle Schools Can Teach," *New York Times,* June 24, 1989, p. 22 (an editorial).

John Rather, "Pupil Advisory Program Looks New in 17th Year," *New York Times,* June 28, 1989, p. B8.

Foreclosed identities may help adolescents cope with the normal identity crisis, but may not be psychologically healthy. Eventually, the hastily chosen identity is found to be a poor fit. Role confusion can also reemerge because a foreclosed identity is less adaptable in later adolescence and adulthood as psychosocial development continues. A new identity crisis will then occur, which may be harder to resolve successfully, particularly if choices and commitments have been made that cannot be easily changed.

Adolescents need to experiment and remain flexible if they are to successfully find their own identity. By trying out ways to be, then testing and modifying them, the adolescent can pick those characteristics that are most comfortable, and drop the others. To do this, the adolescent must have the self-confidence to experiment and to declare an experiment over, to vary behavior, and to drop characteristics that don't fit, even if the characteristics are supported by others. It helps to have a stable and accepting set of parents, teachers, and peers who will respond to one's experimentation.

Adolescents need time and freedom to experiment. Erikson prescribes for adolescents a psychosocial moratorium, a period when the adolescent is not forced to

Interpersonal Theory of Psychiatry
A theory that focuses on a person's
relationships and need for security

make lasting commitments and when adults refrain from settling on lasting expectations for the adolescent's identity.

Autonomy. Another important personality development during the adolescent years is an increase in demands for autonomy, for self-determination. As adolescents' awareness of their increasing similarity to adults grows, and as their ability to analyze and plan improves, it becomes increasingly difficult for them to accept adult direction. Adolescents know that they will have to take responsibility for their actions as adults, and they need to practice that responsibility in more and more important arenas.

Adults who work with adolescents sometimes get caught up in giving more advice than is necessary, or than the adolescent can allow. Sensitivity to the need of adolescents to maintain their autonomy is a valuable characteristic in teachers. Guidance can be given, sometimes even firmly, without stopping adolescents from exercising choices. By allowing choices, schools can help adolescents develop both responsibility and independence. By expecting adolescents to gradually take on more responsibility and to face the consequences of their choices, schools help prepare them for adulthood.

Conformity. At the same time adolescents are seeking autonomy from their parents and other adults, they are often seeking to conform to their peer group. Group pressure to conform is at a maximum among students in the eleven-to-thirteen age range (Costanzo and Shaw, 1966), but remains high throughout adolescence.

One illustration of the dramatic change in peer influence is shown in Figure 3.3 (based on data from Bowerman and Kinch, 1969). More than 80 percent of fourth-graders claimed that their ideas were most like those of their families, while only four years later the peer group played a much more important role.

Interpersonal Development. Peers are the focus of adolescence, much to the consternation of parents and teachers. Friendship, popularity, conflict with peers, dating, and sexual relationships all take a tremendous amount of the adolescent's time and energy. The actions and opinions of peers may loom large as adolescents try to establish their own identity. Teenage gossip spreads quickly. For many, the telephone provides an essential link to peers. Fads are shared, imitated, and rejected. Adolescents with similar interests and values form groups. The friendships made in adolescence may endure through life—if not in reality, at least in nostalgia.

■ **Stop and Think**

1. High schools can be huge, with thousands of students, or small, with only several hundred. What might be the advantages and disadvantages to students of each type of school?

2. High schools also differ by curricula, with some offering vocational training while others emphasize the arts or sciences or college preparation. What might be the advantages and disadvantages of these various approaches?

Intimacy. A powerful interpretation of adolescent interpersonal relationships is provided in the work of Harry Stack Sullivan (1953). In his **Interpersonal Theory of Psychiatry** Sullivan presents a hypothesis to describe the changes in important relationships from infancy to adulthood.

In Sullivan's view, human behavior is shaped by our attempts to maintain comfortable relationships with significant other people. We often act to avoid anxiety, the emotion we feel when one of our significant relationships—and therefore our security—is threatened. As children develop, the number and the variety of their

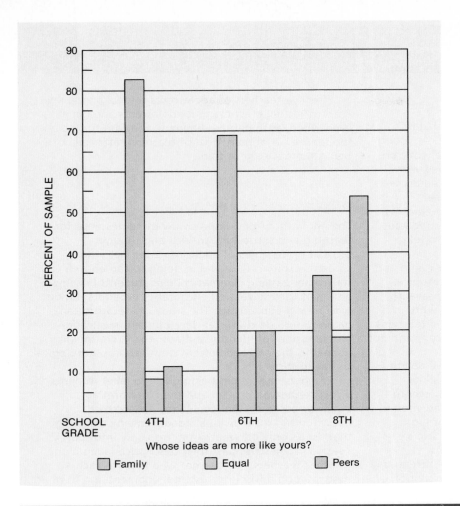

FIGURE 3.3

The Responses of Fourth, Sixth, and Eighth Graders to the Question, "Whose ideas are more like yours: family or friends?"

(Source: Harris and Liebert, 1987. Original data from Bowerman and Kinch, 1969)

significant relationships expand: the newborn's sole relationship is with the mother, but the older child develops relationships with other family members and caretakers. Moving on, playmates are added, then classmates, teachers, and other adults. As the circle of important relationships expands, new social skills are required, and children gradually join the larger society. Security of relationships is the most important human need, and it governs and motivates social behavior and development.

In early adolescence, according to Sullivan, two new needs arise. First is the need for intimacy, for relationships in which a person can share feelings and thoughts with an equal. Second, and less important, is the need for sexual gratification. The tasks of adolescence are to develop the skills of intimacy and to begin developing relationships that will lead to the choice of a partner for sexual gratification.

The skills of intimacy are not easily learned. As adolescents interact, they are constantly practicing and testing these skills. The need for intimacy is first felt by adolescents when they experience the emotion reflecting its absence—loneliness, what

ENCOURAGING COGNITIVE DEVELOPMENT

The cognitive changes of adolescence have major implications for teaching and for curriculum. As young adolescents begin to sense the inadequacy of concrete operational logic, they may become frustrated with learning. They may struggle with tasks that adults see as simple, but that require new and unfamiliar assumptions. Teachers should help young adolescents explore the uses of abstract thinking, but should keep in mind that it takes students several years to fully develop their newfound intellectual skills.

Just as physical puberty occurs at different ages and rates, so do the intellectual changes of adolescence. Since grade assignment is based on age, the seventh through ninth grades typically mix students with different levels of cognitive maturity. It is the teacher's job to accommodate these student differences—and not to punish the slower-maturing pupils.

The curriculum should change as cognitive abilities change. It is no accident that algebra, with all its abstract concepts, is introduced in early adolescence. Science moves from simple content and observational skills toward experimentation and full use of logic. Mathematics is integrated into the study of science as students become able to use the two systems simultaneously. Social studies and literature increasingly emphasize interpretation, synthesis, and exploration of different forms of both creation and criticism.

Effective teachers of adolescents respect and enjoy the intellectual practices that adolescents engage in, even when, as sometimes happens, they are turned on the teacher. A primary goal of teaching, after all, is to help students learn to think.

ENCOURAGING SOCIOEMOTIONAL DEVELOPMENT

The implications of Erikson's view of adolescence for teaching and curriculum are rich and thought-provoking. Teachers of adolescents can help their students explore roles, and in doing so can enliven classroom learning. Dramatics helps students become aware of themselves and encourages experimentation with new characteristics. The study of literature can begin to include character development, motivation, and questions of identity and autonomy, which will appeal to the early adolescent's interest in psychological characteristics.

Teachers must avoid being quick to label students, in effect stereotyping them and then interpreting behavior based on the label. They may restrict opportunities for individual adolescents by assuming that "she's only into math" or "he's only into sports." Teachers sometimes pass their descriptive labels along to other teachers. The teacher who receives such a description is advised to suspend judgment and form an independent impression of the adolescent.

we feel when there is no one with whom we can be intimate. The first peers with whom the young adolescent attempts intimate communication are usually same-sex playmates.

To communicate intimately requires learning to talk about feelings and thoughts in ways that can be understood by another person. In an intimate relationship people try to both express their own ideas and understand the other's. They tolerate the difficulty of putting thoughts into words, and help each other sharpen expression and understanding by exploring meanings and implications. Obviously, such communication requires trust in the partner's goodwill and tolerance.

Learning to develop intimate communication with peers of the other sex is one of the major interpersonal tasks of adolescence. Intimacy with same-sex peers is easier to achieve because they are going through similar changes and are more like oneself. The other sex is less familiar for most adolescents.

Intimacy with peers of the other sex is made more complicated by the fact that such intimacy often involves concern with another need—sexual gratification. How much simpler adolescence would be if the needs for intimacy and for sexual gratification were not first felt at the same time!

Chapter 3: Development During
Childhood and Adolescence

Good schools give adolescents many chances to explore potential futures. Courses that encourage analysis of values, careers, consumer issues, adult relationships, and parenting are of particular interest to adolescents as they begin to be able to set realistic goals. Career and college orientation and guidance help adolescents examine ways to shape their adult lives. Programs that involve adolescents in community activities provide experiences that can clarify their expectations. Adolescents can use such explorations to test, in their imaginations, the appropriateness and the desirability of the variety of adult roles open to them.

PERSONAL AND SOCIAL DEVELOPMENT

Friendships change quickly and constantly during adolescence. Teachers encounter this phenomenon as they intercept notes passed between friends and struggle to keep the attention of young adolescents for whom, at a particular moment, nothing may be as important as telling their best friends the latest and hottest gossip. They will also see groups of friends who must sit together, do projects together, and play on the same teams.

Good teachers have a sense of humor about adolescent relationships. They know that the skills of friendship are necessary throughout life, whereas any particular school lesson is likely to have a slight long-term effect. While teachers must limit the intrusion of social activities into the classroom, they should acknowledge their importance and be respectful of their significance.

If school is to be a place where students are helped to understand the world around them and to interpret their experiences in it, educators have to pay attention to interpersonal skills and relationships. At some point in the curriculum, adolescents' experience as peers, friends, intimates, and potential mates should be addressed, though it is an unusual school that does this in a systematic way. Typically these issues are incorporated into courses on family living or health. Probably more important are spontaneous class discussions or an impromptu discussion with a particularly astute teacher. The teacher who is prepared and willing to talk about the important issues of friendship with young adolescents will be sought out by students and is sure to have challenging and rewarding interactions with them.

Schools, like families, must deal with the pressures placed on adolescents by their peer groups to conform. It is discouraging to a teacher to suspect that a student is holding back in class for fear of risking ridicule or laughter. Teachers should use such incidents to encourage appropriate risk taking and talk to students about acceptance and tolerance. It may take sensitive individual encouragement to convince a student to try an activity or a challenge that is not considered "cool" by that student's peers.

Adolescents who develop relationships with the other sex without major mishap are those who can separate their needs for intimacy and for sexual gratification. They give priority to developing friendships with peers of both sexes. They do not confuse real intimacy, which may or may not include sex, with sexual "intimacy." Wise adolescents seem to know what Sullivan proposed: that mature adult relationships are those in which intimacy is maintained, and that lasting sexual gratification is achieved within an intimate relationship.

Sullivan's approach helps us understand the gradual changes in peer interactions around the time of puberty. The "gang" of playmates, chosen mainly on the basis of proximity, begins to split up into pairs. Friends spend more time talking; action becomes less necessary. Young people seek privacy from adults and peers. Friendships may shift rapidly as adolescents seek others at similar stages of development. Friendships are tested repeatedly. Exclusivity is sought—"We have to be *best* friends"—to protect the adolescent who wants to share inner feelings. But, inevitably, confidences are broken, secrets are shared, and best friends become untrustworthy enemies. Concern, trustworthiness, and loyalty characterize these early efforts at intimacy (Berndt, 1982).

Expressing thoughts and feelings is never easy, especially for adolescent boys and girls. Learning to communicate intimately is a major task of the teenage years.

Dating.   Dating plays an important role in the process of identity formation because the dating "game" lets adolescents try out the male and female roles. The reaction of the partner provides the adolescent with information about how to play the role, and how well he or she is playing it. Although dating may be less formal today than in earlier generations, and may involve more equality between boys and girls, it still includes awkward moments as adolescents use dates to learn more about one another than can be learned in a group.

Seen in this way, dating is a step toward the stage beyond Erikson's identity stage. In his theory, the stage of young adulthood is marked by concern for intimacy, which is the sharing of one's identity with that of another person. Intimacy develops as the two identities come to overlap and to include as a part of each being a member of the intimate pair. As young couples date and move toward "going steady," seeing themselves and being seen by others as a couple, they gain shared experiences on which to base a shared identity.

Problems of Adolescence

Adolescence is the time when a person's identity is largely established (Erikson, 1963). A group of eleven-year-olds is fairly homogeneous. However, six years later some will be delinquents, others star pupils. Some will be math whizzes, others will be interested in art or drama, and still others will be concerned with auto mechanics. High school teen groups have clear demarcations: "jocks," "grinds," "grits," "hoods," "druggies," and so on. Obviously, experiences at home and in school before adolescence play an important role in determining how an individual's adolescence will turn out, but junior and senior high schools play a crucial role in helping students through a period that is quite difficult for most of them (Elkind, 1984).

Most adolescents experience emotional conflicts at some point (Blos, 1979). This is hardly surprising since they are going through rapid and dramatic changes in body image, expected roles, and peer relationships. The transitions from elementary to middle or junior high and then onto high school can also be quite stressful for many students (Simmons et al., 1987; Hirsch and Radkin, 1987). For most adolescents, emotional distress is temporary and is successfully handled, but for some, the stresses lead to delinquency, drug abuse, or suicide attempts.

Emotional Disorders.   Mild to serious emotional disorders frequently arise during adolescence. These range from depression to being overly anxious about health to suicidal thoughts or attempts (Masterson, 1967). Many adolescents who engage in delinquent, bizarre, or self-abusive behavior do so as a call for help during a difficult period. Others use drugs, alcohol, or sex as a response to emotional disorders that could have been detected and resolved.

Secondary educators should be sensitive to the stresses faced by adolescents and should realize that emotional disturbances are common. They should understand that depressed, hopeless, or unaccountably angry behavior can be a clue that the adolescent needs help, and should attempt to put such students in touch with school counselors or other psychologically trained adults. See Chapter 12 for more on emotional disturbance.

Drug and Alcohol Abuse.   Drug and alcohol abuse have increased dramatically in recent years. A majority of high school students have used marijuana at least once, and increasing numbers seriously abuse alcohol (Johnston et al., 1979). It is safe to say that most high school teachers will sooner or later encounter students who come to school drunk or stoned.

Experimentation with marijuana and alcohol is not particularly harmful in itself. However, rates of alcoholism and of daily marijuana use among high school students are at alarming levels, and the rates of cocaine use are increasing (although uses of heroin and hallucinogens are decreasing; National Institute on Drug Abuse, 1985). Not surprisingly, heavy use of alcohol and drugs has a serious impact on students' performance in school (Conger and Peterson, 1984).

Delinquency.   One of the most dangerous problems of adolescence is the beginning of serious delinquency. The problem is far more common among males than females (Dornbusch et al., 1985). Delinquents are usually low achievers who have been given little reason to believe that they can succeed by following the path laid out for them by the school. Delinquency in adolescence is overwhelmingly a group phenomenon; most delinquent acts are done in groups or with the active support of a delinquent subgroup (Hirschi, 1969).

Delinquency (and its prevention) is discussed in Chapter 11.

Pregnancy.   Pregnancy and childbirth are increasing among all groups of female adolescents, but particularly among those from lower-income homes (Morrison, 1985). Just as adolescent boys often engage in delinquent behavior to try to establish their independence from adult control, so adolescent girls often engage in sex, and in many cases have children, to force the world to see them as adults. Since early childbearing makes it difficult for adolescent girls to continue their schooling or get jobs, it is a primary cause of the continuation of the cycle of poverty into which many adolescent mothers were themselves born.

Makita Reynolds, a junior high school teacher with four years experience, talks with Bobby Ryan, a seventh-grader, in her classroom after school.

MAKITA: Bobby, we have to talk about your last report card. I'm worried about your grades.

BOBBY: But, Mrs. Reynolds, I'm going to miss my bus.

MAKITA: Don't worry. I let the driver know you'd be a few minutes late. She promised to wait for you. Bobby, are you doing your homework?

BOBBY: Yes, uh, no—not really. It's always too hard.

MAKITA: Now, Bobby, you're a smart boy. Do you think you might not be spending enough time on the work each evening?

BOBBY: I don't know. I just can't do it.

MAKITA: Bobby, what do you like to do after school?

BOBBY: Mostly I go out with my friends, or watch TV when I'm home.

MAKITA: What do you do with your friends?

BOBBY: I don't know. Sometimes we go downtown, or over to someone's house.

MAKITA: Do you think you and your friends could spend some time doing homework after school?

BOBBY: Nah, I don't think so, Mrs. Reynolds. Todd and Kevin are both in high school like my brother, and none of them ever brings books home.

MAKITA: But they must have homework to do. When do they do theirs?

BOBBY: I don't know. In school, I guess.

MAKITA: In any case, that shouldn't have anything to do with your work. If you're finding the assignments too hard do you think that your mom or dad could help you?

BOBBY: Nah. Last time I showed them some of those math problems you wanted us to do, they said they didn't understand them either.

MAKITA: Isn't there any way we can get you to do more homework?

BOBBY: I don't know, Mrs. Reynolds. I guess I could try a little harder.

MAKITA: OK, and maybe I can give you some help, too. We'll find some extra time to work together.

BOBBY: Can I go now?

MAKITA: I guess so. Go ahead.

A week later after school, Makita visits Ann Macy, the school's guidance counselor.

MAKITA: I talked with Bobby Ryan the other day about his homework but I'm not sure it did much good. He's a good kid, but I can't tell whether he cares about doing better in school. Twice this week I've gone over the homework assignments with him to be sure he understands them, but he still comes in the next day with little or nothing done. And he's not the only one of my boys who is starting to slack off on his work.

ANN: I know what you mean. This is a tough age for these kids. And it's hard for you to know how to respond. If you grade them too hard, they might give up on school, but if you're too easy on them, they'll figure they've outsmarted you.

MAKITA: Yeah, I've been wondering how tough to be with the grades this quarter. But I just don't know any other way to get the attention of these kids.

ANN: And it's a shame in Bobby's case because his test scores and grades have always been good. He could go places if he'd only put his mind to it.

MAKITA: Ann, what can we do to steer Bobby straight? We've got to do something.

QUESTIONS

1. What are the physical and socioemotional characteristics of children Bobby's age? Does Bobby seem typical of children his age in relation to these developmental patterns?
2. What are the various authority figures in Bobby's life and which are apparently exerting the most influence at present? Is this typical of young adolescents?
3. What can Makita do to help Bobby? Can you think of ways a teacher might approach and involve parents in helping a student of this age?

SUMMARY AND REVIEW OF OBJECTIVES

Characteristics of Early Childhood.   Gross motor skills develop earlier than fine motor skills. Therefore, teachers of young children should choose activities and materials that are appropriate for the children's development level.

Peer relationships let young children assert themselves, present their own views, and argue different viewpoints. Conflicts with peers let children recognize others' thoughts, feelings, and viewpoints. Teachers can promote peer interaction by using small groups and by providing toys and activities that involve more than one child.

Teachers and parents must also give children ample time to play. Play is voluntary, pleasurable, and spontaneous; involves repetition or elaboration of behaviors; is not goal-directed; is creative and nonliteral; and changes as children develop.

In research on effective parenting, authoritative parents—those who direct their children's behavior in ways that respect the child's abilities but also set standards—were more effective than either authoritarian or permissive parents.

Language Development.   By age three, children are already skillful talkers. During their preschool and early elementary years they learn rules governing words and sounds, first by overgeneralizing, then by revising their language to include exceptions. The skills of reading develop through a similar process. Children's writing emerges from early random scribbles and invented spellings.

Studies of children's language development frequently recommend that adults and teachers encourage children to read and write, set good examples by modeling reading and writing, and make books, other printed matter, and writing materials available to children.

Early Childhood Education.   With increasing numbers of women joining the work force, the popularity of preschool programs is growing. The major forms are day-care programs, nursery schools, and compensatory preschool programs.

In early childhood, social interactions extend from home to neighborhood and from child-care arrangements to formal school. Early educators can foster the development of initiative by providing appropriate opportunities for it. Some researchers believe that early experiences shape later development; others have shown that young children who are deprived of appropriate early experiences can catch up if given supportive environments later.

Characteristics of Middle Childhood.   Between the ages of five and seven, physical growth slows in comparison to earlier years, but general health and motor skills improve. Children enter the concrete operational stage, during which thought is restricted to what they experience in direct, hands-on, face-to-face encounters. At this stage they develop the skills of conservation, classification, number, mathematical operations, formation of limited hypotheses, and understanding of time and space. Children in the upper elementary grades move from egocentric thought to more decentered thought. Nine- to twelve-year-olds can perform logical, reversible thinking; can reason without having to physically manipulate objects; and are aware of different variables and their relationships.

Three major influences on a child's social development during the primary grades are parents and family; the increasingly important peer group; and school, in which the child develops a public self and social skills. Groups of girls and groups of boys tend to value different attitudes and behavior: among groups of boys, aggressiveness and skill in sports are valued; among groups of girls, attractiveness and popularity are important.

The Emotional Turmoil of Puberty.   Puberty is a series of physiological changes that make people able to reproduce. One of the most important challenges to adolescents during this period is to intellectually and emotionally accommodate the changes in their physical self. Early maturers may need help understanding the changes occurring at the time of puberty. Late maturers, especially boys, may need help in coping with their physical immaturity and gaining confidence in themselves.

Characteristics of Adolescence.   During adolescence young people become aware of the limitations of their thinking. Nevertheless, their problem-solving skills often improve because they begin to look for all possible solutions to problems, keep track of results, recognize that problems may have more than one solution, and compare various solutions. At this age young people also become able to reason about hypothetical situations or those that they have not yet experienced. The cognitive changes of adolescence have major implications for teaching and curriculum. Adolescents can grasp the abstract concepts of mathematics and science, and become better able to examine and interpret issues in social studies and literature. However, teachers should keep in mind that the cognitive abilities of adolescents are still in the process of developing.

Some of the signs of adolescents' socioemotional development are reflectivity and thinking about whether others see the world in the same way they do. To create a sense of identity, adolescents pay a great deal of attention to how others view them, search their past, experiment with roles, act on feelings, and express beliefs and opinions. Identity foreclosure occurs when an adolescent chooses a role prematurely.

Learning About Intimacy.   Interpersonal relationships during this time reflect the adolescent's need for intimacy. In peer relationships exclusivity is sought; concern, trustworthiness, and loyalty shape early efforts at intimacy.

STUDY QUESTIONS

1. Which of the following can children usually do when they enter first grade?
   a. Understand abstract concepts
   b. Understand an almost infinite variety of sentences
   c. Use systematic approaches to solving problems
   d. Concentrate for long periods of time
2. Which of the following statements about play is true?
   a. Psychologists today generally agree that play is overemphasized in kindergarten and detracts from cognitive training.
   b. Parallel play occurs when children interact purposefully with each other to create shared experiences.
   c. Sociodramatic play developmentally precedes pretend play.
   d. Because play is spontaneous and nonreflective, it does not appear to stimulate creativity.
   e. none of the above.
3. According to the transformational grammar theory, dialects of English should be considered equal to standard English if the dialect
   a. follows the same rules of grammar as standard English.
   b. can express the same information as standard English.
   c. uses the same structural form as standard English.
   d. is spoken by people of different cultural backgrounds.
4. Participation in compensatory preschool programs has been found to
   a. benefit middle-class children more than lower-class children.
   b. increase disadvantaged children's readiness for kindergarten and first grade.
   c. have stronger effects on long-term achievement than on initial achievement.
   d. be of little benefit to either disadvantaged or middle-class children.
5. Match the following types of parenting styles with the correct definition of each.

_____ Authoritarian
_____ Permissive
_____ Authoritative

a. Parents respond to children with warmth and respect while also providing firm guidance.
b. Parents expect children to accept parental authority without question.
c. Parents place few expectations on children and give them great freedom.

6. Physical growth patterns in upper elementary school show that
   a. the average girl experiences a growth spurt earlier than the average boy.
   b. children are more susceptible to illness than they were in lower elementary school.
   c. muscles and cartilage develop more rapidly than bones.
   d. the average girl reaches puberty at 11.5 years.
   e. the average boy reaches puberty at 11.5 years.

7. A child's social development during the primary grades is shaped by three major influences. What are they?
8. Which of the following is a recommended strategy for teaching elementary-age children?
   a. Frequently use abstract thinking exercises to help students reach formal operations.
   b. Use competitive exercises in which individuals can win recognition and develop self-esteem as the "best" in those activities.
   c. Use authoritarian teaching styles as much as possible.
   d. When ability groups are used, make group assignments flexible based on performance.
   e. To make classroom rules appear absolute and firm, avoid discussing moral dilemmas in which different decisions are possible.

Answers: 1. b 2. c 3. b 4. b 5. b, c, a 6. a 7. family, peers, and school 8. d.

SUGGESTED READINGS

BAUMRIND, D. (1980). New directions in socialization research. *American Psychologist, 35,* 639–652.

BERRUETA-CLEMENT, J. R., SCHWEINHART, L. J., BARNETT, W. S., EPSTEIN, A. S., and WEIKART, D. P. (1984). *Changed lives.* Ypsilanti, Mich.: High/Scope.

CHOMSKY, N. (1968). *Language and mind.* New York: Harcourt Brace Jovanovich.

COLLINS, W. A. (Ed.) (1984). *Development during middle childhood.* Washington, D.C.: National Academy Press.

CRAIG, G. J. (1989). *Human development* (5th ed.) Englewood Cliffs, N.J.: Prentice-Hall.

CSIKSZENTMIHALYI, M., and LARSON, R. (1984). *Being adolescent.* New York: Basic Books.

DAMON, W. (1983). *Social and personality development: Infancy through adolescence.* New York: Norton.

EDUCATIONAL RESEARCH SERVICE (1983). *Organization of the middle grades: A summary of research.* Arlington, Va.: Educational Research Service.

ELKIND, D. (1981). *The hurried child: Growing up too fast too soon.* Reading, Mass.: Addison-Wesley.

HARRIS, J. R., and LIEBERT, R. M. (1987). *The child: Development from birth through adolescence.* Englewood Cliffs, N.J.: Prentice-Hall.

KAMII, C., and DE VRIES, R. (1978). *Physical knowledge in preschool education: Implications of Piaget's theory.* Englewood Cliffs, N.J.: Prentice-Hall.

LAY, M. Z., and DOPYERA, J. E. (1977). *Becoming a teacher of young children.* Lexington, Mass.: Heath.

NURSS, J. R., and HODGES, W. L. (1982). Early childhood education. In H. E. MITZEL (Ed.), *Encyclopedia of educational research* (4th ed.) (pp. 477–513). New York: Free Press.

OSBORN, J. D., and OSBORN, P. K. (1983). *Cognition in early childhood.* Athens, Ga.: Education Associates.

POSTMAN, N. (1982). *The disappearance of childhood.* New York: Delacorte Press.

SCHICKEDANZ, J. A., SCHICKEDANZ, D. I., and FORSYTH, P. D. (1982). *Toward understanding children.* Boston: Little, Brown.

THORNBURG, H. (1979). *The bubblegum years: Sticking with kids from 9–13.* Tuscon, Ariz.: HELP Books.

ZIGLER, E., and VALENTINE, J. (1979). *Project Head Start: A legacy of the war on poverty.* New York: Free Press.

Chapter 4

Behavioral Theories of Learning

Chapter Objectives

This chapter will introduce you to the behavioral theories of learning. After reading it you should be able to:

- Define learning.

- Describe experiments that led to the theories of classical and operant conditioning, and describe differences between these theories.

- Define and give classroom examples of the consequences of positive reinforcement, negative reinforcement, and punishment.

- Describe how teachers can use shaping to help students learn complex skills.

- Define and give examples of observational learning, or modeling.

Learning
A change in an individual that results from experience

Stimulus
Environmental condition that activates the senses

WHAT IS LEARNING?

What is learning? This seems like a simple question until you begin to think about it. Consider the following examples. Are they instances of learning?

1. A young child takes her first steps.
2. An adolescent boy feels a strong attraction to pretty girls.
3. A child feels anxious when he sees the doctor coming with a needle.
4. Long after learning how to multiply, a girl realizes on her own that another way to multiply by 5 is to divide by 2 and multiply by 10 (for example, 428 × 5 can be figured as follows: 428 ÷ 2 = 214 × 10 = 2140).

Learning is usually defined as a change in an individual caused by experience. Changes caused by development (such as growing taller) are not instances of learning. Neither are characteristics of individuals that are present at birth (such as reflexes and responses to hunger or pain). However, human beings do so much learning from the day of their birth (and some say earlier) that learning and development are inseparably linked. Learning to walk (Example 1) is mostly a developmental progression, but also depends on experience with crawling and other activities. The adolescent sex drive (Example 2) is not learned, but a great deal of learning goes into the adolescent boy's definition of what a "pretty" girl is. Young men of another generation—or of another culture—might be aroused by the sight of girls far paler, darker, skinnier, or fatter than would be considered particularly attractive in the United States today.

A child's anxiety on seeing a doctor with a needle (Example 3) is definitely learned behavior. The child has learned to associate the needle with pain, and his body reacts emotionally when he sees the needle. This reaction may be unconscious or involuntary, but it is learned nonetheless.

The fourth example, the girl's insight into the multiplication shortcut, is an instance of internally generated learning, better known as "thinking." Some theorists would not call this learning because it was not caused by the environment. But it might be considered a case of delayed learning, in which deliberate instruction in multiplication plus years of experience with numbers plus mental effort on the part of the girl produced an insight.

Learning takes place in many ways. Sometimes it is intentional, as when students acquire information presented in a classroom or when they look something up in the encyclopedia. Sometimes it is unintentional, as in the case of the child's reaction to the needle. All sorts of learning are going on all the time. As you (the reader) are reading this chapter, you are learning something about learning. However, you are also learning that educational psychology is interesting or dull, useful or useless. Without knowing it, you are probably learning about where on the page certain pieces of information are to be found. You may be learning to associate the content of this chapter with unimportant aspects of your surroundings as you read it, such as the musty smell of books in a library or the temperature of the room you are reading in. The content of this chapter, the placement of words on the page, and the smells, sounds, and temperature of your surroundings are all **stimuli.** Your senses are usually wide open to all sorts of stimuli, but you are consciously aware of only a fraction of them at any one time.

The problem faced by educators is not how to get students to learn; students are already engaged in learning every waking moment. Rather, it is to help them learn particular information, skills, and concepts that will be useful in adult life. How do we present students with the right stimuli on which to focus their attention and mental effort so that they will acquire important skills? That is the central problem of instruction.

THEORIES OF LEARNING

Psychologists have developed two principal types of learning theories to explain how individuals learn: behavioral and cognitive. **Behavioral learning theories,** discussed in this chapter, tend to emphasize observable behavior, such as classroom behaviors or new skills or knowledge that can be demonstrated. Behavioral learning theorists are particularly interested in the way pleasurable or painful consequences of behavior change the individual's behavior over time. They try to discover principles of learning that apply to all living beings.

In contrast, cognitive learning theorists are concerned almost exclusively with human learning, particularly with the unobservable mental processes individuals use to learn and remember new information or skills. **Cognitive learning theories** are discussed in Chapters 5 and 6. The boundaries between behavioral and cognitive theories of learning have become indistinct in recent years as each school of thought has incorporated findings of the other.

EVOLUTION OF BEHAVIORAL LEARNING THEORIES

The systematic study of learning is relatively new. It was not until the late nineteenth century that learning was studied in a scientific manner. Using techniques borrowed from the physical sciences, researchers began conducting experiments to understand how people and animals learned. Two of the most important of the early researchers were Ivan Pavlov and Edward Thorndike. Among later researchers, B. F. Skinner is important for his studies of the relationship between behavior and consequences.

Ivan Pavlov: Classical Conditioning

In the late 1800s and early 1900s Pavlov and his colleagues studied the digestive process in dogs. During the research the scientists noticed changes in the timing and rate of salivation of these animals.

Pavlov observed that if meat was placed in or near the mouth of a hungry dog, the dog would salivate. Because the meat provoked this response automatically, without any prior training or conditioning, the meat is referred to as an **unconditioned stimulus.** Similarly, because the salivation occurred automatically in the presence of meat, also without the need for any training or experience, this response of salivating is referred to as an **unconditioned response.**

While the meat will produce salivation without any previous experience or training, other stimuli, such as a bell, will not produce salivation. Because other stimuli have no effect on the response in question, they are referred to as **neutral stimuli.** Pavlov's experiments showed that if a previously neutral stimulus is paired with an unconditioned stimulus, the neutral stimulus becomes a conditioned stimulus and gains the power to prompt a response similar to that produced by the unconditioned stimulus. That is, the ringing of the bell alone causes the dog to

Behavioral Learning Theories
Explanations of learning that emphasize observable changes in behavior

Cognitive Learning Theories
Explanations of learning that focus on mental processes

Unconditioned Stimulus
A stimulus that naturally evokes a particular response

Unconditioned Response
A behavior prompted automatically by stimuli

Neutral Stimulus
A stimulus that does not naturally prompt a particular response

Classical Conditioning
Associating a previously neutral stimulus with an unconditioned stimulus to evoke a conditioned response

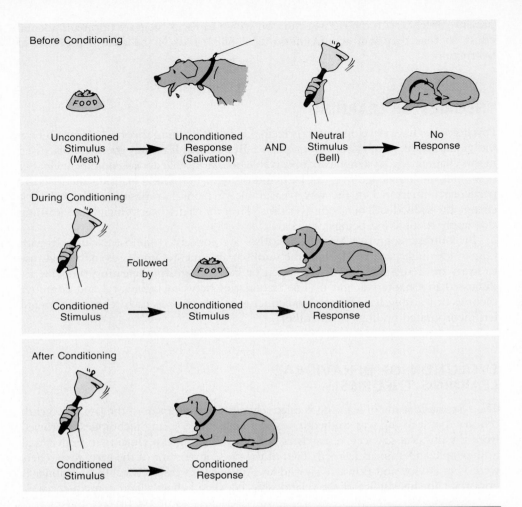

Before Conditioning

Unconditioned Stimulus (Meat) → Unconditioned Response (Salivation) AND Neutral Stimulus (Bell) → No Response

During Conditioning

Conditioned Stimulus → Unconditioned Stimulus → Unconditioned Response

Followed by

After Conditioning

Conditioned Stimulus → Conditioned Response

FIGURE 4.1

Classical Conditioning

In classical conditioning, a neutral stimulus (such as a bell) that at first prompts no response becomes paired with an unconditioned stimulus (such as meat) and gains the power of that stimulus to cause a response (such as salivation).

salivate. This process is referred to as **classical conditioning.** A diagram of Pavlov's theory is shown in Figure 4.1.

1. Prior to training:
    Presenting unconditioned stimulus (meat) produces unconditioned response (salivation).
    Presenting neutral stimulus (bell) does not produce any salivation.

2. During training:
    The bell is rung when the meat is presented. The formerly neutral stimulus (the bell) becomes a conditioned stimulus.

3. After training:
    Presenting conditioned stimulus (ringing the bell) produces conditioned response (salivation).

In experiments such as these, Pavlov and his colleagues showed how learning could affect what were once thought to be involuntary, reflexive behaviors, such as salivating.

The importance of Pavlov's work lies as much in the method as in the results. A look at the apparatus pictured in Figure 4.2 shows how Pavlov and his associates were able to carefully observe and measure their subjects' responses to various experiments. Pavlov's emphasis on observation and careful measurement, and his systematic exploration of a number of aspects of learning, helped advance the scientific study of learning. He also left other behavioral theorists with significant mysteries, such as the process by which "neutral" stimuli take on meaning. Also, what does his work tell teachers? Although his findings have few applications to classroom instruction, they can help a teacher understand such situations as when a child's anxiety about being among strangers gradually develops into a debilitating fear of coming to school.

E. L. Thorndike: The Law of Effect

Pavlov's work inspired researchers in the United States such as E. L. Thorndike (Hilgard and Bower, 1966). Thorndike, like many of the early behavioral learning theorists, linked behavior to physical reflexes. In his early work he also viewed most behavior as a response to stimuli in the environment (notice the parallel to Pavlov). This view that stimuli can prompt responses was the forerunner of what became known as stimulus-response or S-R theory. These learning theorists noted that certain reflexes, such as the knee jerking upward when it is tapped, occur without processing by the brain. It was hypothesized that other behavior was also determined in a reflexive way by stimuli present in the environment rather than by conscious or unconscious thoughts.

Thorndike went beyond Pavlov by showing that stimuli that occurred *after* a

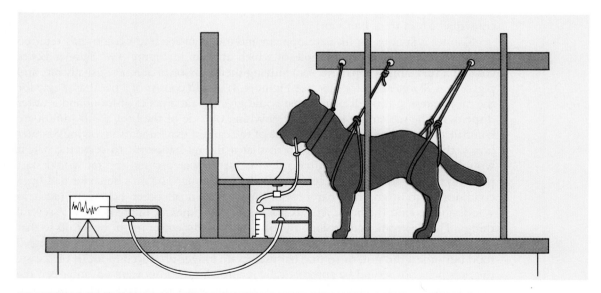

FIGURE 4.2

Apparatus Used in Classical Conditioning Experiments

The apparatus that Pavlov used in his classical conditioning experiments included a harness to hold a dog quiet and a tube attached to the dog's salivary gland to measure salivation.

behavior had an influence on future behaviors. In many of his experiments Thorndike placed cats in boxes from which they had to escape to get food. He observed that over time the cats learned how to get out of the box more and more quickly by repeating the behaviors that led to escape and by not repeating those behaviors that were ineffective. From these experiments, Thorndike developed his Law of Effect.

Thorndike's **Law of Effect** stated that if an act is followed by a satisfying change in the environment, the likelihood that the act will be repeated in similar situations increases. However, if a behavior is followed by an unsatisfying change in the environment, the chances that the behavior will be repeated decrease. Thus the consequences of one's present behavior were shown to play a crucial role in determining one's future behavior.

B. F. Skinner: Operant Conditioning

It is clear that some human behaviors are prompted by specific stimuli. Just like Pavlov's dogs, we, too, salivate when we are hungry and see appetizing food. And, we, too, lend credence to Thorndike's early emphasis on reflexive behavior when we learn things so well, such as how to touch-type, that the brain seems to respond reflexively. However, B. F. Skinner proposed that such behavior accounts for only a small proportion of all actions. He proposed another class of behavior, which he labeled *operant* behaviors because they *operated* on the environment in the apparent absence of any unconditioned stimuli, such as food. Like Thorndike, Skinner's work focused on the relation between behavior and its consequences. For example, if an individual's behavior is immediately followed by pleasurable consequences, the individual will engage in that behavior more frequently. The use of pleasant and unpleasant consequences to change behavior is often referred to as **operant conditioning.**

Skinner's work has focused on placing subjects in controlled situations and observing the changes in their behavior produced by systematically changing the consequences of their behavior.

Skinner is famous for his development and use of an apparatus commonly referred to as the Skinner box, an example of which appears in Figure 4.3. Skinner boxes contain a very simple apparatus for studying the behavior of animals, usually rats and pigeons. A Skinner box for rats (see Figure 4.3) would consist of a bar that is easy for the rat to press, a food dispenser that could give the rat a pellet of food, and a water dispenser. The rat cannot see or hear anything outside of the box, so all stimuli are controlled by the experimenter. In some of the earliest experiments involving Skinner boxes, the apparatus was first set up so that if the rat happened to press the bar, it would receive a food pellet. After a few accidental bar presses, the rat would start pressing the bar frequently, receiving a pellet each time. The rat's behavior had been conditioned to strengthen bar pressing and weaken all other behaviors (such as wandering around the box). At this point, the experimenter might do any of several things. The electronics controlling the bar and food dispenser might be set up so that it now took several bar presses to obtain food, or so that some bar presses produced food but others did not, or so that bar presses no longer produced food. In each case, the rat's behavior would be automatically recorded. One important advantage of the Skinner box is that it allows for careful scientific study of behavior in a controlled environment. Skinner's contribution, like that of Pavlov, consists not only of what he discovered but also of the methods he used. Skinner's experiments can be repeated by anyone with the same equipment.

FIGURE 4.3

Skinner Box

Skinner's operant conditioning experiments used a box that allowed experimenters to control all stimuli reaching the rat. This Skinner box has a bar that the rat can press and a food dispenser linked to the bar.

(Eliot Elisofon/Life Magazine © 1958 Time Inc.)

Skinner's pioneering work with rats and pigeons established a set of principles of behavior that have been supported in hundreds of studies involving humans as well as animals. These principles are discussed in the following section.

■ **Stop and Think**

What aspects of your own learning could be explained by classical conditioning? By the Law of Effect? By operant conditioning? Evaluate the relevance of these theories to classroom instruction.

Consequence
A condition that follows a behavior and affects the frequency of future behavior

Reinforcer
A pleasurable consequence that maintains or increases a behavior

Primary Reinforcer
Food, water, or another consequence that satisfies basic needs

Secondary Reinforcer
A consequence that people learn to value through its association with a primary reinforcer

Positive Reinforcer
Consequence given to strengthen behavior

PRINCIPLES OF BEHAVIORAL LEARNING THEORIES

Consequences: Reinforcers and Punishers

Perhaps the most important principle of behavioral learning theories is that behavior changes according to its immediate **consequences.** Pleasurable consequences "strengthen" behavior, while unpleasant consequences "weaken" it. That is, pleasurable consequences increase the frequency with which an individual engages in a behavior, while unpleasant consequences reduce the frequency of a behavior. If students enjoy reading books, they will probably read more often. If, instead, they find stories boring or are unable to concentrate, they may read less often, choosing other activities instead.

Pleasurable consequences are generally called *reinforcers,* while unpleasant consequences are called *punishers.*

Reinforcers. A **reinforcer** is defined as any consequence that strengthens (that is, increases the frequency of) behaviors. Note that the effectiveness of the reinforcer must be demonstrated. We cannot assume that a particular consequence is in fact a reinforcer until we have evidence that it strengthens behavior for a particular individual. For example, candy might generally be considered a reinforcer for young children, but after a big meal a child might not find candy pleasurable, and some children do not like candy at all. If teachers say, "I reinforced him with praise for staying in his seat during math time, but it didn't work," they may be misusing the term "reinforced," because they have no evidence that praise is in fact a reinforcer for this particular student. No reward can be assumed to be a reinforcer for everyone under all conditions.

Primary and Secondary Reinforcers. Reinforcers fall into two broad categories: primary and secondary. **Primary reinforcers** satisfy basic human needs. Examples include food, water, security, warmth, and sex.

Secondary reinforcers are reinforcers that acquire their value by being associated with primary reinforcers or other well-established secondary reinforcers. For example, money has no value to a young child until the child learns that it can be used to buy things that are themselves primary or secondary reinforcers. Grades have little value to students unless their parents notice and value them, and parents' praise is of value because it is associated with love, warmth, security, and other reinforcers. Money and grades are examples of secondary reinforcers because they have no value in themselves but have been associated with primary reinforcers or with other well-established secondary reinforcers. There are three basic categories of secondary reinforcers: social reinforcers (such as praise, smiles, hugs, or attention), activity reinforcers (such as access to toys, games, or fun activities), and token (or symbolic) reinforcers (such as money, grades, stars, or points that individuals can exchange for other reinforcers).

Chapter 10 discusses reinforcers, rewards, and human needs from a humanistic perspective, and Chapter 11 lists reinforcers teachers can use in the classroom.

Positive and Negative Reinforcers. Most often, reinforcers used in schools are things *given* to students. These are called **positive reinforcers,** and include praise, grades, and stars. However, another way to strengthen a behavior is to have the behavior's consequence be an escape from an unpleasant situation or a way of preventing something unpleasant from occurring. For example, a teacher might release students

Classroom Uses of Reinforcement

The most useful principle of behavioral learning theories for classroom practice is also the simplest: Reinforce behaviors you wish to see repeated. This principle seems obvious, but in practice it is not as easy as it appears. For example, some teachers take the attitude that reinforcement is unnecessary, on the grounds that, "Why should I reinforce them? They're just doing what they are supposed to do!"

The main principles of the use of reinforcement to increase desired behavior in the classroom are as follows:

1. Decide what behaviors you want from students, and reinforce them when they occur. For example, praise or reward good work. Do not praise or reward work that is not up to students' capabilities. (See the upcoming section on Shaping.)
2. Tell students what behaviors you want, and when they do them and you reinforce them, tell them why. (See the upcoming section on Discrimination.)

Many studies have shown that when reinforcement is given to students on the basis of their classroom behavior and schoolwork, their behavior improves. For example, Hall and colleagues (1968) described a highly disruptive third-grader, "Robbie," who engaged in study behavior only 25 percent of the time. They then asked Robbie's teacher to praise him, smile at him, pat him on the back, or otherwise socially reinforce him from time to time when he was studying. Robbie's studying behavior increased to 71 percent of class time. When the teacher stopped reinforcing him, his study behavior dropped off, but when she resumed reinforcement, it increased. Later observations (postchecks) indicated that Robbie's improved study behavior remained several weeks after the reinforcement program was reinstated. These results are illustrated in Figure 4.4

Note that the study of reinforcing Robbie uses a single-case experimental design (see Chapter 1), which is typical of behavioral learning theorists. Robbie's behavior was observed before the reinforcement program was begun (Baseline), after the program was put in place (Reinforcement$_1$), when it was withdrawn (Reinforcement withdrawn), and when it was reinstated (Reinforcement$_2$). The fact that Robbie's behavior clearly changed in accordance with the introduction and removal of the reinforcement program (as is apparent in Figure 4.4) indicates that the reinforcement program was responsible for his improved behavior.

Several additional examples of the use of reinforcement to improve students' behaviors are presented in Chapter 11.

FIGURE 4.4

Effect of Reinforcement on Behavior

Reinforcement for studying improved the study habits of a highly disruptive third-grader called "Robbie." The student studied less than 25 percent of the time when first observed, but when the teacher reinforced his studying behavior, he studied more than 70 percent of the time. When the reinforcement was stopped, his study habits worsened, but improved again when reinforcement resumed.

Adapted from Hall, Lund, and Jackson, 1968, p. 3.

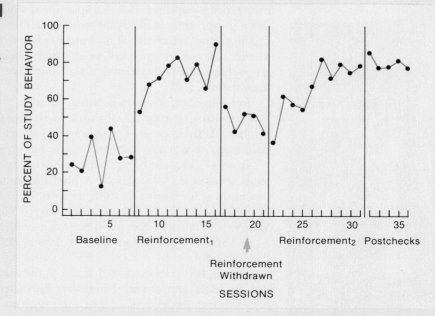

Negative Reinforcer
Release from an unpleasant situation to strengthen behavior

Premack Principle
Using favored activities to reinforce participation in less desired activities

Punishment
Using unpleasant consequences to weaken a behavior

Aversive Stimulus
A condition that a person tries to avoid or escape

Should teachers send students to the hall as punishment for misbehavior? Not necessarily. Some students may consider the release from class a reward. In such cases, the "punishment" may actually increase misbehavior.

from homework if they do a good job in class. If homework is seen as an unpleasant task, release from it will be reinforcing. Reinforcers that are escapes from unpleasant situations are called **negative reinforcers.**

This term is often misinterpreted to mean "punishment," as in "I negatively reinforced him for being late by having him stay in during recess." One way to avoid this error in terminology is to remember that reinforcers (whether positive or negative) *strengthen* behavior, while punishment *weakens* it.

Premack Principle. One important principle of behavior is that less desired ("low-strength") activities can be increased by linking them to more desired activities. In other words, access to something desirable is made contingent on doing something less desirable. For example, a teacher might say, "As soon as you finish your work, you may go outside," or "Clean up your art project and then I will read you a story." These are examples of the Premack Principle (Premack, 1965). The **Premack Principle** is sometimes called "Grandma's Rule" from the age-old statement, "Eat your vegetables and then you may play." Teachers can use the Premack Principle by alternating more enjoyable activities with less enjoyable ones, and making participation in the enjoyable activities depend on successful completion of the less enjoyable ones. For example, it may be a good idea to schedule music (considered an enjoyable activity by most students) after completion of a difficult subject in elementary school, so that students will know that if they fool around in the difficult subject, they will be using up part of their desired music time.

Punishers. Consequences that are not reinforcing—that is, that do not strengthen behavior—are called punishers. Again, note the difference here between negative reinforcement (the *strengthening* of desirable behavior by withdrawing unpleasant consequences) and **punishment,** which is aimed at *reducing* behaviors by imposing unwanted consequences. Note also that there is the same catch in the definition of punishment as in the definition of reinforcement: if an apparently unpleasant consequence does not reduce the frequency of the behavior it follows, it is not necessarily a punisher. For example, some students *like* being sent to the principal's office or out to the hall because it releases them from what they see as an unpleasant situation, the classroom. Some students like to be scolded because it gains them the teacher's attention and perhaps enhances their status among their peers. As with reinforcers, the effectiveness of a punisher cannot be assumed but must be demonstrated.

Punishment can take two primary forms. "Punishment I" is the use of unpleasant consequences, or **aversive stimuli,** as when a student is asked to write "I will not talk in class" 100 times or is scolded or spanked. "Punishment II" is the removal of reinforcers, as when a student must give up recess, stand in the hall, or lose a privilege.

In some cases, use of punishment can improve student behavior. For example, one study (Hall et al., 1971) used a simple punishment procedure to reduce the time that ten emotionally disturbed students spent out of their seats without permission. The researchers simply had the teacher carry a clipboard with students' names on it. Whenever students were out of their seats without permission, the teacher gave them a check mark worth five minutes of after-school detention. The results are illustrated in Figure 4.5.

Figure 4.5 clearly shows that the punishment program was effective in reducing the students' out-of-seat behaviors. However, note that when the punishment program was stopped (Baseline$_2$), the students' behavior worsened again.

The topic of if, when, and how to punish has been a source of considerable

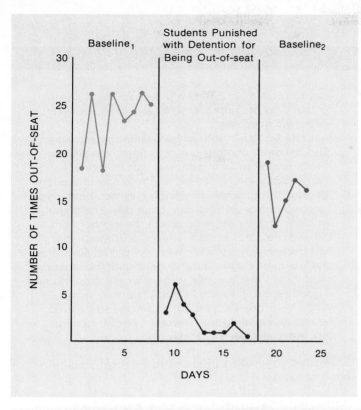

FIGURE 4.5

Punishment

The number of times that students were out of their seats without permission dropped sharply in this experiment when misbehavior led to after-school detention. Each instance of misbehavior recorded by the teacher cost the students five minutes of after-school detention. When misbehavior no longer prompted punishment (Baseline₂), students more often got out of their seats without permission.

Adapted from Hall et al., 1971, p. 25.

controversy among behavioral learning theorists. Some have claimed that the effects of punishment are only temporary, that punishment produces aggression, and that punishment causes individuals to avoid settings in which it is used (Bates, 1987). However, even behavioral learning theorists who do support the use of punishment generally agree that it should be resorted to only when reinforcement for appropriate behavior has been tried and has failed, that when punishment is necessary it should take the mildest possible form, and that punishment should always be used as part of a careful plan, never inconsistently or out of frustration. Physical punishment in schools is almost universally opposed by behavioral learning theorists on ethical as well as scientific grounds (see O'Leary and O'Leary, 1977).

Immediacy of Consequences. One very important principle of behavioral learning theories is that consequences that follow behaviors closely in time affect behavior far more than delayed consequences. If we waited a few minutes to give a rat in a Skinner box its food pellet after it pressed a bar, the rat would take a long time to learn the connection between bar pressing and food, because by the time the food arrived, it might be doing something other than bar pressing. A smaller reinforcer given

1. Behavioral learning theories can be effective only to the extent that teachers correctly identify reinforcers and punishers. Describe a situation in which your response to student behavior might have had unintended results.

Carol Hamann, who teaches third grade in Wisconsin Rapids, Wisc., said:

Several years ago I had a student named Frank, who was both very bright and hyperactive. One morning Frank was down on "all fours" barking, pretending to be a dog. I remarked that this was a classroom for children and that "pets" were not allowed. He raised his head (still on all fours) "barked" once more and said, "Just think how famous you'd be if everybody knew how much you could teach a dog." Caught off guard, I couldn't suppress a half smile. The "dog" appeared in my classroom many more times in the next several weeks.

Benetta Skrundz, who teaches learning disabled children in East Chicago, Ind., said:

One nine-year-old boy in my class was extremely disruptive on a daily basis. After several conferences with his mother, I realized that the home situation was such that I would receive no assistance from there. It was many weeks later, however, that I discovered that the home situation was actually going against all that I was trying to achieve.

Initially, I set up a behavior modification program that rewarded the young student at five-minute intervals for proper school behavior. A pattern quickly emerged in which he would have an extremely good day followed by two days in which I couldn't find a

way to reward him. This would be followed by one or two days of "improvement" and then another extremely good day.

Little by little I noticed he was having more bad days between good days. It was finally decided between myself and our principal that he would have a day suspension. When his mother came the following day to return him to school, I learned how much confusion I was causing the young boy. There was an older brother at home whom the mother admitted she could not control. He was a dropout and had been in some trouble with the police. Since this was the male figure in my student's life, he looked up to him. Whenever my student would bring home a good report, his brother would put him down. When his brother found out about the suspension, he not only praised the "success," but he treated him especially nicely that day.

2. How do you make sure that you frequently praise good behavior?

Roseanne Swinburne-Sanderfoot, a special education teacher in Manawa, Wisc., writes:

While I was student-teaching, I was required to give eight reinforcers per minute. (My supervisor monitored my behavior to make sure that I did so.) Experience has shown me that most kids will do what you want them to do if they are urged into it by verbal praise. You have to "catch them" doing well and let them know when they are. I basically challenge myself to find something good so that I can point it out. Generally, I no longer give eight reinforcers per minute, but sometimes I try it just to make sure that I still can!

immediately generally has a much larger effect than a large reinforcer given later (Kulik and Kulik, 1988). This concept explains much about human behavior. It suggests, for example, why people find it so difficult to give up smoking or overeating. Even though the benefits of giving up smoking or losing weight are substantial and well known, the small but immediate reinforcement of just one cigarette or one doughnut often overcomes the behavioral effect of the large but delayed reinforcers.

In the classroom the principle of immediacy of consequences is also very important. Particularly for younger students, praise for a job well done given immediately can be a stronger reinforcer than a grade given much later. A study by Leach and Graves (1973) clearly demonstrated that immediate feedback can be a more effective reinforcer than delayed feedback. Two girls in a regular seventh-grade language arts class were having trouble completing their assignments. At first, the teacher asked the girls to write ten sentences using correct grammar and punctuation each day. The sentences were scored and returned the following day. Under these conditions, the girls averaged about 58 percent correct sentences. Then the teacher decided to grade and return the papers immediately. When the immediate correction procedure was introduced, the girls' correct sentence writing increased dramatically, to 90 percent for "Betty" and 93 percent for "Jane." When the immediate correction procedure was withdrawn, the girls' performances deteriorated, but improved once more when it was reinstated.

Immediate feedback serves at least two purposes. First, it makes the connection between behavior and consequence clear. Second, it increases the informational value of the feedback. In the Leach and Graves (1973) study, immediate feedback not only increased the girls' motivation to write sentences but also probably made it easier for them to use the information on the correctness of their sentences to improve their sentence writing in the future.

In practice, few classroom teachers can provide individual feedback immediately to all their students (although special education teachers with small classes can and must do so). However, the same results can be obtained by giving students answers right after they complete their work, or by having students exchange papers to correct each other's work. In dealing with misbehavior, the principle of immediacy of consequences can be applied by responding immediately and positively when students are *not* misbehaving, catching them in the act of being good!

■ **Stop and Think**

1. Much of the research supporting the use of behavioral learning theories in the classroom consists of single-case experiments involving children with academic behavior problems. In light of this, what might be the general applicability of behavioral theories to the classroom?

2. What are the possible consequences of using the various forms of punishment in a classroom?

Shaping

Shaping
Using small steps combined with feedback to help learners reach goals

Immediacy of reinforcement is important to teaching, but so is the decision of what to reinforce. Should a kindergarten teacher withhold reinforcement until a child can recite the entire alphabet? Certainly not. It would be better to praise children for saying one letter, then for saying several, and finally for learning all twenty-six letters. Also, should a music teacher withhold reinforcement until a young student has played a piano piece flawlessly? Or should the teacher praise the first halting run-through? Most students need reinforcement along the way. When teachers guide students toward goals by reinforcing the many steps that lead to success, they are using a technique called shaping.

The term **shaping** is used in behavioral learning theories to refer to the teaching of new skills or behaviors by reinforcing learners for approaching the desired final behavior. For example, in teaching children to tie their shoelaces, we would not simply show them how it is done and then wait to reinforce them until they do the whole job themselves. Rather, we would first reinforce them for tying the first knot, then for making the loops, and so on, until they can do the entire task. In this way, we would be shaping the children's behavior by reinforcing all those steps that lead toward the final goal.

Reverse Chaining
Shaping process in which the final
subskills of a complex task are
learned before the first subskills

Shaping is an important tool in classroom instruction. Let's say we want students to be able to write paragraphs with a topic sentence, three supporting details, and a concluding sentence. This task has many parts: being able to recognize and then produce topic sentences, supporting details, and concluding sentences; being able to write complete sentences, using capitalization, punctuation, and grammar correctly; and being able to spell. If a teacher taught a lesson on all these skills, asked students to write paragraphs, and then scored them on content, grammar, punctuation, and spelling, most students would fail, and might learn little from the exercise.

Instead, the teacher might teach the skills step by step, gradually shaping the final skill. Students might first be taught how to write topic sentences, then supporting details, then concluding sentences. Early on, they might be held responsible only for paragraph content. Later, the requirement for reinforcement might be increased to include grammar and punctuation. Finally, spelling might be added as a criterion for success. At each stage, students would have a good chance to be reinforced because the criterion for reinforcement would be within their grasp.

The principle here is that students should be reinforced for behaviors that are within their current capabilities but which also stretch them toward new skills. A student who can do ten math problems in 15 minutes should be reinforced for doing twelve, but not for doing eight. However, a classmate who can do twenty problems should be reinforced for doing twenty-four, not for doing less than twenty.

Shaping is being used effectively when students move rapidly from success to success. This requires breaking down tasks into small steps, a process called chaining (see Task Analysis in Chapter 7 and Programmed Instruction in Chapter 9), and then reinforcing students as they accomplish each step.

Here is a summary of the steps involved in shaping a new behavior:

Steps in Shaping

1. Choose your goal—make it as specific as possible.

2. Find out where the students are now. What are their abilities?

3. Develop a series of steps that will serve as a stairway to take them from where they are now to your goal. For some students, the steps might be too big; for others, too small. Modify according to each student's ability.

4. Give feedback as the students go along. In some ways, learning is like driving a car. The more unfamiliar the area, the more feedback one needs—that is, the more one will consult a map or look for street signs. Similarly, the newer the subject material, the more feedback students require.

Reverse Chaining.   One interesting form of shaping that has educational applications is called **reverse chaining,** a procedure in which a complex skill is taught "backwards." For example, in teaching the lesson on paragraph writing, we might first give students a paragraph missing only a concluding sentence, and ask them to supply that one sentence. The final product of this exercise would be a complete paragraph. Next, students might be given another incomplete paragraph, and asked to complete it by adding both one supporting detail *and* a concluding sentence. Then they might be given only a topic sentence and asked for several supporting details and a concluding sentence. The advantage of this teaching strategy is that the product of each exercise is a good paragraph. Students may be able to see the "big picture" better this way, and may take a shorter route to reinforcement.

Extinction

By definition, reinforcers strengthen behavior. But what happens when reinforcers are withdrawn? Eventually, the behavior will be weakened, and ultimately, it will disappear. This process is called **extinction** of a previously learned behavior.

Extinction is rarely a smooth process. When reinforcers are withdrawn, individuals often *increase* their rate of behavior for a while. For example, when we come to a door that is usually unlocked and find that it will not open, we often push even harder for a while, shake the door, turn the handle both ways, perhaps even kick the door. We are likely to feel frustrated and angry. However, after a short time we will realize that the door is locked and go away. If the door is permanently locked (without our knowing it), we might try it a few times over the next few days, then perhaps once after a month, and only eventually give up on it.

Our behavior when confronted by a locked door is a classic extinction pattern. Our behavior intensifies when the reinforcer is first withdrawn, and then rapidly weakens until it disappears. The behavior may return after much time has passed. For example, we might try the door again a year later to see if it is still locked. If it is, we will leave it alone for a longer time, but probably not forever.

Williams (1959) gives a clear example of the process of extinction. An eighteen-month-old boy had been ill as a young baby and had received constant attention and care. Now that he was well, he was continuing to demand attention and refused to go to bed. When put in bed, he would cry, and if his parents did not come at once, he would have a full-blown tantrum. Then his parents would come and calm him down. However, their attention to his crying and tantrums was reinforcing the child's behavior.

Finally, a therapist suggested that the parents put a stop to this pattern. They were asked to put the child to bed in a pleasant, leisurely way, and not to come back no matter how hard he cried.

The results are illustrated in Figure 4.6. Note that the child cried for nearly an hour the first night of extinction. Then the crying diminished rapidly until the seventh night, at which time it disappeared entirely. The child no longer cried, but played happily in his room until he dropped off to sleep. Later the boy's aunt heard him cry again when he was put to bed. She went to comfort him. This reinforced his crying behavior, and it returned to a high level. The extinction program was then reinstated, and the boy's crying dropped off again. This is seen in the "Second Extinction" graph in Figure 4.6.

Extinction is a key to managing the behavior of students (see Chapter 11). Undesirable behavior can often be extinguished if the reinforcer(s) maintaining the behavior are identified and removed. Chapter 11 discusses a study by Zimmerman and Zimmerman (1962) in which a teacher eliminated a student's tantrums by taking the child to an empty room and letting him scream and kick the floor to his heart's content. Because the child's tantrums no longer brought him the adult attention they once did, they soon ceased.

Note that in these cases the behavior intensified before it diminished. If the parents of the child who refused to sleep had given up after forty-five minutes of his crying the first night and gone to him, if the teacher in the Zimmerman and Zimmerman (1962) study had given up after the boy's tantrums had gotten severe and released him from his solitary confinement, the results might have been disastrous. Giving in would have reinforced the undesirable behaviors—in fact, it would have strengthened them because the children would have learned that "if at first you don't succeed, try, try again."

Extinction
Eliminating or decreasing a behavior by removing reinforcement for it

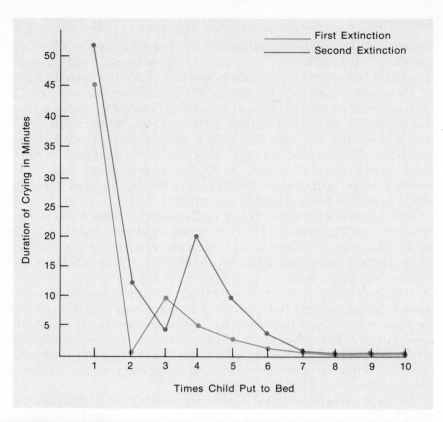

FIRST EXTINCTION

Second Extinction

Duration of Crying in Minutes

Times Child Put to Bed

What young student isn't nervous on the first days of school? The nervousness is likely to fade, however, when over several weeks it is not reinforced.

FIGURE 4.6

Extinction

When parents stopped reinforcing their young son's crying, the crying stopped. At first, the boy cried for almost an hour after being put to bed, but by the end of a week, the child no longer cried at bedtime. The blue line shows the boy's behavior after an aunt again reinforced his crying and the extinction program was reintroduced.

From Williams, 1959, p. 269.

Extinction of a previously learned behavior can be hastened when some stimulus or cue informs the individual that behaviors that were once reinforced will no longer be reinforced. In the case of the locked door, a sign saying "Door permanently locked—use other entrance" would have greatly reduced the number of times we tried the door before giving up on it. Similarly, when a teacher says, "I will no longer accept papers handed in after the due date," the previously reinforced behavior (handing in late papers) is likely to diminish rapidly if the teacher sticks to the new rule.

Like behaviors, emotions can be extinguished. For example, a child might be fearful on the first day of school. If nothing happens to reinforce the child's fearfulness, the fear will ultimately extinguish. By the same token, students' interest in a subject or enthusiasm for learning may extinguish if they are never given reinforcement in the form of interesting lessons or engaging activities.

Schedules of Reinforcement

The effects of reinforcement on behavior depend on many factors, one of the most important of which is the **schedule of reinforcement.** This term refers to the frequency with which reinforcers are given, the amount of time that elapses between opportunities for reinforcement, and the predictability of reinforcement.

Fixed Ratio (FR).   One common schedule of reinforcement is the **fixed ratio (FR),** where a reinforcer is given after a fixed number of behaviors. For example, a teacher might say, "As soon as you finish ten problems, you may go outside." Regardless of the amount of time it takes, students are reinforced as soon as they finish ten problems. This is an example of an FR10 schedule (ten behaviors for one reinforcer). One common form of a fixed-ratio schedule is where each behavior is reinforced. This is called *continuous reinforcement,* or CRF, though it could just as well be called FR1 because one behavior is required for reinforcement. Putting money in a soda machine is (usually) an example of continuous reinforcement, because one behavior (inserting coins) results in one reinforcer (a soda). Giving correct answers in class is also usually continuously reinforced. The student gives a good answer and the teacher says "Right! Good answer!"

One important process in instruction is gradually increasing reinforcement ratios. Early in a sequence of lessons it may be necessary to reinforce students for every correct answer, such as a single math problem. However, this is inefficient in the long run. As soon as students are answering math problems correctly, it may be possible to reinforce every five problems (FR5), every ten (FR10), and so on. "Thinning out" the reinforcement schedule in this way makes the student more able to work independently without reinforcement, and makes the behavior more resistant to extinction. Ultimately, students may be asked to do entire projects on their own, receiving no reinforcement until the project is completed. As adults, we often assume tasks that take years to complete and years to pay off. (Writing an educational psychology text is one such task!)

Fixed-ratio schedules are effective in motivating individuals to do a great deal of work, especially if the fixed ratio starts with continuous reinforcement (FR1) to get the individual going and moves to high requirements for reinforcement. One reason that high requirements for reinforcement produce higher levels of behavior than low requirements is that reinforcing too frequently can make the value of the reinforcer wear off. Older students who were praised for every math problem would soon grow tired of being praised, and the reinforcer might lose its value.

Variable Ratio (VR).   A **variable ratio** or VR schedule of reinforcement is one in which the number of behaviors required for reinforcement is unpredictable, although it is certain that the behaviors will eventually be reinforced. For example, a slot machine is a variable-ratio reinforcer. It might pay off after one pull one time, after 200 the next, and there is no way to predict which pull will win. In the classroom a variable-ratio schedule exists when students raise their hands to answer questions. They never know when they will be reinforced by being able to give the correct answer, but they may expect to be called upon about one time in thirty (in a class of thirty). This is called a VR30 schedule because, on average, thirty behaviors are required for one reinforcer. Variable-ratio schedules tend to produce high and stable rates of behavior. In fact, almost all gambling games involve VR schedules, and as such they can be quite literally addicting. Similarly, use of frequent random checks of student work can help "addict" students to high achievement.

Variable-ratio schedules are highly resistant to extinction. That is, even after behaviors are no longer being reinforced, people may not give up working for a long time. Because they have learned that it may take a lot of work to be rewarded, they keep on working in the mistaken belief that the *next* effort might just pay off.

This basketball player can't be sure that her shot will go in, but only by trying does she have a chance of success. This exemplifies a variable-ratio schedule of reinforcement, because the number of behaviors required for reinforcement is unpredictable.

Fixed Interval (FI). In **fixed-interval schedules** reinforcement is available only at certain periodic times. The final examination is a classic example of a fixed-interval schedule. Fixed-interval schedules create an interesting pattern of behavior. The individual may do very little until just before reinforcement is available, then put forth a burst of effort as the time for reinforcement approaches. This pattern can be demonstrated with rats and pigeons on fixed-interval schedules, but it is even more apparent in students who cram at the last minute before a test or who write their monthly book reports the night before they are due. These characteristics of fixed-interval schedules suggest that frequent short quizzes may be better than infrequent major exams for encouraging students to give their best effort all the time rather than putting in "all-nighters" before the exam.

Variable Interval (VI). In a **variable-interval schedule** reinforcement is available at some times but not at others, and we have no idea when behavior will be reinforced. An example of this is a teacher making spot checks of students who are doing assignments in class. If the students are working well at the particular moment the teacher comes by, they are reinforced. Since they cannot predict when the teacher will check them, students must be doing good work all the time. People may obey traffic laws out of respect for the law and civic responsibility, but it also helps that the police randomly check drivers' compliance with the law. Troopers hide on overpasses or behind hills so they can get a random sampling of drivers' behavior. If they were always in plain sight, they would be a signal to drive carefully, so the necessity for driving carefully at other times would be reduced.

TEACHERS ON TEACHING

Reinforcement Schedules

What types of reinforcement schedules have you used in your class?

FIXED-RATIO REINFORCEMENT

Paula Ann Berneking, a special education teacher in Louisville, Ky.:

For the entire class I have part of a bulletin board devoted to TREAT. Each day [a student behaves well] that child gets one letter stapled next to his/her name. When the child spells out T-R-E-A-T, he/she gets to choose from the TREAT bag.

VARIABLE-RATIO REINFORCEMENT

Camille Caldemeyer, who teaches fourth grade in Princeton, Ind.:

I have a magic hat that contains a number between 20 and 40. As the week progresses, marks are placed [on the board] when the classroom is too noisy, when directions are not followed, etc. Also, marks may be erased whenever something good happens. On Friday, we count the marks on the board and check them against the number in the hat. If the

number is the same or smaller, a special event (such as a party, extra recess, etc.) is given.

FIXED-INTERVAL REINFORCEMENT

Mary VanDyke, who teaches gifted children in Atchison, Kan.:

I believe that weekly quizzes greatly aid in subjects requiring a good deal of factual knowledge—math, sciences, English. This allows students a chance to see what the teacher considers important and helps with major tests.

VARIABLE-INTERVAL REINFORCEMENT

Walter Roberts Jr., a high school teacher in Gentry, Ark.:

I have a great deal of success with the intermittent reinforcement schedule. Prior to a quiz, I announce, "Either tomorrow or the next day, we will be having five questions over . . ." or "We just might be having a few questions over . . . tomorrow," to encourage preparation for an anticipated test. It works wonders because they know they will eventually have a quiz, but exactly when is left up to me.

Like variable-ratio schedules, variable-interval schedules are very effective for maintaining a high rate of behavior, and are highly resistant to extinction. For example, let's say a teacher has a policy of having students hand in their seatwork every day. Rather than checking every paper, the teacher pulls three at random, and gives these students extra credit if their seatwork was done well. This variable-interval schedule would probably motivate students to do their seatwork carefully. If the teacher secretly stopped spot-checking halfway through the year, the students might never know it, figuring that their own papers just hadn't been pulled to be checked rather than realizing that reinforcement was no longer available for anyone.

Tables 4.1 and 4.2 define and give additional examples of the schedules of reinforcement.

Maintenance

The principle of extinction holds that when reinforcement for a previously learned behavior is withdrawn, the behavior fades away. Does this mean that teachers must reinforce students' behaviors indefinitely or they will disappear?

Not necessarily. For rats in a Skinner box, the withdrawal of reinforcement for bar pressing will inevitably lead to extinction of bar pressing. However, humans live in a much more complex world. Our world is full of *natural* reinforcers for most of the skills and behaviors learned in school. For example, students may require constant reinforcement for behaviors that lead to reading. However, once they can read, they have a skill that unlocks the entire world of books, a world that is highly reinforcing to most students. After a certain point, reinforcement for reading may no longer be necessary because the content of the books themselves maintains the behavior. Similarly, poorly behaved students may need careful, systematic reinforcement for doing schoolwork. After a while, however, they will find out that doing schoolwork

---

TABLE 4.1

SCHEDULES OF REINFORCEMENT

Specific response patterns during reinforcement and extinction characterize each of the four types of schedules.

Schedule	Definition	Response Patterns During Reinforcement	During Extinction
Fixed ratio	Constant number of behaviors required for reinforcement	Steady response rate; pause after reinforcement	Rapid drop in response rate after required number of responses passes without reinforcement
Variable ratio	Variable number of behaviors required for reinforcement	Steady, high response rate	Response rate stays high, then drops off
Fixed interval	Constant amount of time passes before reinforcement is available	Uneven rate, with rapid acceleration at the end of each interval	Rapid drop in response rate after interval passes with no reinforcement
Variable interval	Variable amount of time passes before reinforcement is available	Steady, high response rate	Slow decrease in response rate

Pop Quizzes

TABLE 4.2

EXAMPLES OF REINFORCEMENT IN EVERYDAY LIFE

Continuous reinforcement (reinforcement every time the response is made)	■ Using a token to ride the subway. ■ Kissing your boyfriend or girlfriend. ■ Putting coins in a vending machine to get candy or soda.
Fixed-ratio schedule (reinforcement after a fixed number of responses)	■ Being paid on a piecework basis—in the garment industry workers may be paid so much per 100 dresses sewn. ■ Taking a multi-item test. This is an example of negative reinforcement—as soon as you finish those items on the test, you can leave!
Variable-ratio schedule (reinforcement after a varying number of responses)	■ Playing a slot machine—the machine is programmed to pay off after a certain number of responses have been made, but that number keeps changing. This type of schedule creates a steady rate of responding, because players know if they play long enough, they will win. ■ Hunting—you probably won't hit something every time you fire, but it's not the amount of time that passes, but rather the number of times you shoot that will determine how much game you harvest. And the number of times you shoot will no doubt vary—you won't hit something every time. ■ Sales commissions—you have to talk to many customers before you make a sale, and you never know whether the next one will buy. Again, the number of sales calls you make, not how much time passes, will determine when you are reinforced by a sale. And the number of sales calls will vary.
Fixed-interval schedule (reinforcement of first response after a fixed amount of time has passed)	■ You have an exam coming up and don't study as the days go by, so you have to make up for it all by a certain time, which means cramming. ■ Picking up a salary check, which occurs every week or every two weeks.
Variable-interval schedule (reinforcement of first response after varying amounts of time)	■ Surprise quizzes in a course cause a steady rate of studying because you never know when they'll occur, so you have to be prepared all the time. ■ Dialing a friend on the phone and getting a busy signal. This means that you have to keep dialing every few minutes because you don't know when your friend will hang up. Reinforcement doesn't depend on how many times you dial; it depends on dialing *after* the other person has hung up. ■ Watching a football game, waiting for a touchdown. It could happen anytime—if you leave the room to fix a sandwich, you may miss it, so you have to keep watching continuously.

SOURCE: Adapted from Landy, 1984, p. 219.

pays off in grades, in parental approval, in ability to understand what is going on in class, and in knowledge. These natural reinforcers for doing schoolwork were always available, but the students could not experience them until their schoolwork was improved by more systematic means.

Many behaviors do not need to be reinforced to be maintained because they are *intrinsically reinforcing,* which is to say that engaging in these behaviors is pleasurable in itself. For example, many children love to draw, to figure out problems, or to learn about things even if they are never reinforced for doing so. Many of us even pay good money for books of crossword puzzles or other problem-solving activities, even though after we have completed them no one will ever check our work!

The concept of resistance to extinction, discussed earlier in Schedules of Reinforcement, is very important for understanding maintenance of learned behavior. As noted earlier, when new behaviors are being introduced, reinforcement for correct responses should be frequent and predictable. However, once the behaviors are established, reinforcement for correct responses should become less frequent and less predictable. The reason for this is that variable schedules of reinforcement, and schedules of reinforcement that require many behaviors before reinforcement is given, are much more resistant to extinction than are fixed schedules or "easy" ones. For example, if a teacher praises a student every time the student does a math problem, but then stops praising, the student may stop doing math problems. In contrast, if the teacher gradually increases the number of math problems a student must do to get praised, and praises the student at random intervals (a variable-ratio schedule), then the student will continue to do math problems for a long time with little or no reinforcement from the teacher.

Antecedent Stimulus
Event that comes before a behavior

Cue
Signal as to what behavior(s) will be reinforced or punished

Discrimination and Generalization

Antecedent Stimuli. We have seen that the consequences of behavior strongly influence behavior. Yet it is not only what follows a behavior that has influence. The stimuli that precede a behavior—the antecedents to behavior—also play an important role.

Antecedent stimuli are also known as **cues** because they cue us as to what behavior will be reinforced and/or what behavior will be punished. Cues come in many forms and give us hints as to when we should change our behavior and when

---

FOCUS ON
Reinforcers and Punishers

The rewards that teachers typically use to recognize their students' good work and behavior include praise, gold stars, and good grades. Punishments range from a quick reprimand to a time-out period in the hall or the principal's office.

These methods of reinforcement and punishment usually work, because most students want approval from their teachers and parents. They can fail, however, if students don't value adult approval or have already failed too often in school. Several states now have laws allowing stronger measures to keep students in school.

One of the stronger approaches employs the most coveted of all teen-age perks—the driver's license. States including Florida, West Virginia, Arkansas, Louisiana, and Texas have laws that curtail driving privileges for teenagers under eighteen who don't attend school. Under the Florida law, an applicant for a driver's license must have a satisfactory school attendance record or be enrolled in a training program or an eligible course for a high school equivalency test. Following enactment of a similar law in West Virginia, some students did return to school, but many then left a second time.

Generally, these programs are too new to have proven their effectiveness. However, they do address one problem involved in rewarding or punishing high school students: choosing a consequence of behavior that students value. Such a consequence as losing a driver's license is also more immediate than such long-range deterrents to dropping out as the inability to earn a high salary or to find interesting work.

A different approach to preventing truancy has been taken by Wisconsin lawmakers. Under the Wisconsin law, the state can dock money from a family's welfare check if children in the family skip school too often. Ten absences in a semester triggers scrutiny by school officials, then three more unexcused absences in a month allows state officials to cut $200 from the family's welfare check. Supporters say the measure encourages children to get an education and break the cycle of poverty. Critics say it encourages students and parents to lie about reasons for absenteeism, and, more ominously, gives young people too much control over family finances. Some teenagers have reportedly threatened to skip school unless their parents buy them expensive shoes or stereo equipment.

What do you think of these attempts by lawmakers to keep kids in school? Are the ideas theoretically sound in light of behavioral learning theory? Do you think they will work in practice? Now imagine yourself as a state legislator faced with voting on these issues. Will you vote yea or nay? Why?

Isabel Wilkerson, "Wisconsin Makes Truancy Costly By Tying Welfare to Attendance," *New York Times*, December 11, 1989, p. A1.

"Florida Bars Licenses to Reduce Dropout Toll," *New York Times*, October 4, 1989, p. B9.

Discrimination
Perception of and response to
differences in stimuli

we should not. For example, during a math session most teachers will reinforce students who are working on problems and punish those who are doing nothing. However, after the teacher has announced that math is over and it is time for lunch, the consequences change. The ability to behave one way in the presence of one stimulus—"It's math time"—and a different way in the presence of another stimulus—"It's time for lunch"—is known as *stimulus discrimination*.

■ **Stop and Think**

1. Thinking back on your own learning, cite examples of various strategies used by teachers, such as shaping, extinction, and reinforcement schedules.
2. What effect might the tools of behavioral learning theories have on student motivation?

Discrimination. When is the best time to ask your boss for a raise? When the company is doing well, the boss looks happy, and you've just done something especially good? Or when the company has just gotten a poor earnings report, the boss is glowering, and you've just made a costly error? Obviously, the first situation is more likely to lead to success. You know this because you have learned to *discriminate* between good and bad times to ask your boss to do something for you.

Discrimination is the use of cues, signals, or information to know when behavior is likely to be reinforced. The company's financial condition, the boss's mood, and your recent performance are discriminative stimuli with regard to the chances that your request for a raise will be successful. A pigeon can be trained to peck a disk if it sees a triangle, but refrain from pecking if it sees a square, or even to correctly discriminate between the printed words, "peck" and "don't peck."

For students to learn discriminations they must have feedback on the correctness or incorrectness of their responses. Laboratory studies of discrimination learning have generally found that students most need to know when their responses are incorrect. Praising students for correct answers but not giving them feedback on incorrect answers is not an effective feedback strategy (Barringer and Gholson, 1979; Getsie et al., 1985).

Learning is largely a matter of mastering more and more complex discriminations. For example, all letters, numbers, words, and mathematical symbols are discriminative stimuli. A young child learns to discriminate between the letters "b" and "d." An older student learns the distinction between the words "effective" and "efficient." An educational psychology student learns to discriminate "negative reinforcement" from "punishment." A teacher learns to discriminate facial and verbal cues indicating that students are bored or interested by a lecture.

Applying the concept of discriminative stimuli to classroom instruction and management is easy: Teachers should tell students what behaviors will be reinforced. In theory, a teacher could wait until students did something worthwhile and then reinforce it, but this would be incredibly inefficient. Rather, teachers should give students messages that say, in effect, "To be reinforced (with praise, grades, or stars, for example), these are the things you must do." In this way teachers can avoid having students spend time and effort on the wrong activities. If students know that what they are doing will pay off, they will usually work hard.

Generalization. If students learn to stay in their seats and do careful work in math class, will their behavior also improve in science class? If students can subtract three apples from seven apples, can they also subtract three oranges from seven oranges? If students can interpret symbolism used by Shakespeare, can they also interpret symbolism used by Molière?

These are all questions of **generalization** of behaviors learned under one set of conditions to other situations. Generalization cannot be taken for granted. Usually, when a behavior management program is successfully introduced in one setting, students' behaviors do not automatically improve in other settings. Instead, students learn to discriminate among settings. Even young children readily learn what is encouraged and what is forbidden in kindergarten, what goes at home, and what goes at various friends' houses. Their behavior may be quite different in each setting, according to the different rules and expectations.

For generalization to occur, it usually must be planned for. A successful behavior management program used in social studies class may be transferred to English class to ensure generalization to that setting. Students may need to study the use of symbolism by many playwrights before they acquire the skill to interpret symbolism in playwrights in general.

Obviously, generalization is most likely to occur across similar settings or across similar concepts. A new behavior is more likely to generalize from reading class to social studies class than to recess or home settings. However, even in the most similar-appearing settings, generalizations may not occur. For example, many students will demonstrate complete mastery of spelling or language mechanics and then fail to apply this knowledge to their own compositions. Teachers should not assume that because students can do something under one set of circumstances, they can also do it under a different set of circumstances. Maybe the students don't pick up cues that signal the similarity between the two situations. Or maybe they do pick up the signal but are not motivated to respond.

Such situations demonstrate that the behavioral theories focusing on observable behavior fall short of completely explaining human actions. A behavioral theory that gives us some more answers is called social learning theory.

Generalization
Perception of and response to similarities in stimuli

Modeling
Learning by observing others' behavior

SOCIAL LEARNING THEORY

Social learning theory is a major outgrowth of the behavioral learning theory tradition. Developed by Albert Bandura (1969), it accepts most of the principles of behavioral theories, but focuses to a much greater degree on the effects of cues on behavior and on internal mental processes, emphasizing the effects of thought on action and action on thought (Bandura, 1986). A discussion of the principal concepts of social learning theory follows.

Modeling

Yogi Berra once said, "You can observe a lot by watching." From their first days, children watch the behavior of those around them and try to imitate what they see. One-year-olds have amazing abilities in imitating speech, for example. Children constantly play games based on the behavior they see around them, among family members, friends, and even characters on television.

Bandura noted that the Skinnerian emphasis on the effects of the consequences of behavior largely ignored the phenomena of **modeling**—the imitation of others' behavior—and vicarious experience—learning from others' successes or failures. He

Social learning theory suggests that one important way people learn is by observing and imitating the behavior of others.

felt that much of human learning is not shaped by its consequences, but is more efficiently learned directly from a model (Bandura, 1986). The physical education teacher demonstrates a jumping jack and students imitate. Bandura calls this "no-trial learning" because students do not have to go through a shaping process but can reproduce the correct response immediately.

Bandura's (1977) analysis of observational learning involves four phases: attentional, retention, reproduction, and motivational.

Attentional Phase. The first phase in observational learning is paying attention to a model. In general, students pay attention to models who are attractive, successful, interesting, and popular. This is why so many students copy the dress, hairstyle, and mannerisms of pop culture stars. In the classroom the teacher gains the attention of the students by presenting clear and interesting cues, by using novelty or surprise, and by motivating students to pay attention (for example, by saying, "Listen closely, this will be on your quiz tomorrow").

Retention Phase. Once teachers have students' attention, it is time to model the behavior they want students to imitate and then to give students a chance to practice or rehearse. For example, a teacher might show how to write a script "A." Then students would imitate the teacher's model by trying to write "A's" themselves.

Reproduction During the reproduction phase students try to match their behavior to the model's. In the classroom this takes the form of an assessment of student learning. For example, after seeing the script "A" modeled and practicing it several times, can the student reproduce the letter so that it looks like the teacher's model?

Motivational Phase. The final stage in the observational learning process is motivation. Students will imitate a model because they feel that doing so will increase their own chances to be reinforced. For example, they may imitate a rock star because they see that he is successful and popular, and they hope to capture some of the same popularity for themselves. In fact, it is peer support for imitating popular stars that maintains the imitation. No matter how popular the rock star is, few students would imitate him if their friends did not value imitating him.

In the classroom, the motivational phase of observational learning more often consists of praise or grades given for matching the teacher's model. Students pay attention to the model, practice it, and reproduce it because they have learned that this is what the teacher likes, and that pleasing the teacher pays off.

Effective use of Bandura's principles of modeling can increase achievement. In one study teachers who were taught these principles (ensuring attentiveness, describing each action while doing it, teaching memory aids, and helping students evaluate their own performance) were much more successful in teaching a concept to five-year-olds than were teachers who were not taught the principles (Zimmerman and Kleefeld, 1977).

Vicarious Learning. While most observational learning is motivated by an expectation that correctly imitating the model will lead to reinforcement, it is also important to note that people learn by seeing others reinforced or punished for engaging in certain behaviors. This is why magazine distributors always include happy winners in their advertisements to induce people to enter promotional contests. We may consciously know that our chances of winning are one in several million, but seeing others so handsomely reinforced makes us want to imitate their contest-entering behavior.

Classroom teachers use the principle of **vicarious learning** all the time. When one student is fooling around, teachers often single out others who are working well and reinforce them for doing a good job. The misbehaving student sees that working is reinforced, and (it is hoped) gets back to work.

This technique was systematically studied by Broden et al. (1970). Two disruptive second-graders, "Edwin" and "Greg," sat next to each other. After a baseline period, the teacher began to notice and praise Edwin whenever he was paying attention and doing his classwork. Edwin's behavior improved markedly under this condition. Of greater interest, however, is that Greg's behavior also improved, even though no specific reinforcement for appropriate behavior was directed toward him. Apparently, Greg learned from Edwin's experience.

One of the classic experiments in social learning theory is a study done by Bandura (1965). Children were shown one of three films. In all three an adult modeled aggressive behavior. In one film the model was severely punished. In another the model was praised and given treats. In a third the model was given no consequences. After viewing one of the films, the children were observed playing with toys. The children who had seen the model punished engaged in significantly fewer aggressive acts in their own play than did the children who had seen the model rewarded or had viewed the no-consequences film.

Self-Regulation

Another important concept in social learning theory is **self-regulation.** Bandura (1977) hypothesized that people observe their own behavior, judge it against their own standards, and reinforce or punish themselves. We have all had the experience of knowing we've done a job well and mentally patted ourselves on the back, regardless of what others have said. Similarly, we all know when we've done less than our best. To make these judgments, we have to have expectations for our own performance.

Vicarious Learning
Learning from observing the consequences of others' behavior

Self-regulation
Rewarding or punishing one's own behavior

One student might be delighted to get 90 percent correct on a test, while another might be quite disappointed.

Students can be trained to monitor and regulate their own behaviors. Meichenbaum and Goodman (1971) developed a self-reinforcement strategy in which emotionally disturbed students are trained to say to themselves, "What is my problem? What is my plan? Am I using my plan? How did I do?" (see Meichenbaum, 1977). This strategy has also been used to reduce disruptive behavior of students at many grade levels (Wilson, 1984). For example, Manning (1988) taught disruptive third-graders self-statements to help them remember appropriate behavior and to reinforce it for themselves. As one example, for appropriate hand-raising, students were taught to say to themselves while raising their hands, "If I scream out the answer, others will be disturbed. I will raise my hand and wait my turn. Good for me. See, I can wait!" (Manning, 1988, p. 197). Similar strategies have been successfully applied to helping students monitor their own achievement. For example, poor readers have been taught to ask themselves questions as they read and to summarize paragraphs to help them comprehend text (Kendall, 1981; Bornstein, 1985).

Drabman et al. (1973) designed and evaluated a procedure to teach students to regulate their own behavior. They asked teachers to rate student behaviors each day and reinforce students when they earned high ratings. Then they changed the program and asked students to guess what rating the teacher had given them. The students were reinforced for guessing correctly. Finally, the reinforcers were gradually removed. The students' behavior improved under the reinforcement and guessing conditions, and it remained at its improved level long after the program was ended. The authors explained that students taught to match the teacher's ratings developed their own standards for appropriate behavior and reinforced themselves for meeting those standards.

Information about one's own behavior has often been found to change behavior (Rosenbaum and Drabman, 1982), even when that information is self-provided. For example, Broden, Hall, and Mitts (1971) improved the on-task behavior of an eighth-grader by having her mark down every few minutes whether or not she had been studying in the last few minutes. When coupled with self-reinforcement, self-observation often has important effects on student behavior (O'Leary and Dubey, 1979). Many of us use this principle in studying, saying to ourselves that we will not take a break for lunch until we have finished reading a certain amount of material. During the Watergate hearings one graduate student, a confirmed Nixon hater, put a check in an envelope and addressed it to the "Fairness to President Nixon" committee. He then gave the envelope to a trusted friend to mail if by a given date he had not completed a major paper on which he had been procrastinating for some time. This self-reinforcement program worked: the student completed the paper on time and the friend destroyed the check.

Some reviewers have questioned whether self-reinforcement is really necessary, or whether monitoring one's own progress is equally effective (Hays et al., 1985). The answer is that it probably depends on the task and on other factors. For most school tasks, it may well be enough for students to record or otherwise monitor their own behavior and to mentally congratulate themselves when they make progress toward some important goal.

A lesson from research on self-regulation is that, when assigned a long or complex task, students should be provided with a form for monitoring their progress. For example, a teacher might assign students to write a report on the life of Martin Luther King. Students might be given the following self-monitoring form:

Task Completion Form

———— Located material on Martin Luther King in the library.

———— Read and took notes on material.

———— Wrote first draft of report.

———— Checked draft for sense.

———— Checked draft for mechanics:

    ———— Spelling

    ———— Grammar

    ———— Punctuation

———— Composed final draft typed or neatly handwritten.

The idea behind this form is that breaking down a complex task into smaller pieces encourages students to feel that they are making progress toward their larger goal. Checking off each step allows them to give themselves a mental "pat on the back" that reinforces their efforts.

■ **Stop and Think**

1. If students learn from what they see, what attitudes and values might you expect to be held by the students you plan to teach?
2. Tools of behavioral learning are used to "educate" people outside the school system as well as those in it. Cite examples of the use of behavioral theories in business, the legal system, and family situations.

APPLICATIONS OF BEHAVIORAL LEARNING THEORIES

Behavioral learning theories are so central to educational psychology that they are discussed in many parts of this book. The most direct application of these theories is to classroom management and discipline (Chapter 11). Using principles of behavioral learning theories to motivate students in the classroom is discussed in Chapter 10. Behavioral objectives and task analysis, which show how principles of discrimination and shaping are applied in the classroom, are detailed in Chapter 7 (Organizing for Instruction). Bandura's four phases of observational learning are translated into practical methods in Chapter 8 (The Lesson). Discussed there are means of gaining student attention and motivation, modeling information and skills, having students practice and then demonstrate new skills, and providing feedback and reinforcement to students. Finally, specific instructional methods based on behavioral learning theories, including programmed instruction, mastery learning, and the Keller Plan, are included in Chapter 9 (Accommodating Student Differences).

STRENGTHS AND LIMITATIONS OF BEHAVIORAL LEARNING THEORIES

The basic principles of behavioral learning theories are as firmly established as any in psychology, and have been demonstrated under many different conditions. These principles are useful for explaining much of human behavior, and they are even more useful in changing behavior.

Mary Schulties teaches third grade in a suburban school district. One of her major instructional objectives is to get all her students to memorize the multiplication tables, the "ones" through the "nines." To do this she has written the problems on a large piece of construction paper that she can place on an easel in front of the classroom. If a child comes up in front of the class and says the multiplication tables perfectly one time, he or she gets extra in-class free time and does not have to say them again. If the child misses one, he or she has to spend the extra time studying multiplication.

Only seven of Mary's 28 students have not yet recited their "times tables" perfectly. Billy, who has failed four times previously has been asked to come up front and try again. Mary hands him a wooden pointer as he reaches the front of the room. He is displaying the demeanor of a person about to be executed. Several of the students titter and make faces as he starts.

MARY: Now, Billy, just relax and take your time. We all know you can do it, and we *want* you to do it. We're all pulling for you, aren't we class?

CLASS: [in unison] Yes! (Several students individually shout words of encouragement.)

BILLY: (pointing to each problem in turn) One times one is one. One times two is two. (He continues giving correct answers until he reaches 8 × 7.) Eight times seven is sixty-five.

MARY: Now stop there, Billy. Let's think about that one. What did you say seven times seven is?

BILLY: Uh, forty-nine.

MARY: And what is seven times eight?

BILLY: Fifty-six.

MARY: Well, if seven times eight is fifty-six, then what must eight times seven equal?

BILLY: I don't know! I can't do this!

MARY: OK, now don't be upset. We'll work on it together. You made a really good try! All the way up to the eights! Go on back to your seat and practice.

Billy walks back to his seat with his head hung low. Some of the students look away as he walks by.

It is Friday after school and Mary is sitting in the office of Dr. Jerry Weiser, a school psychologist and the Director of Psychological Services for the school system.

MARY: Thanks for seeing me, Jerry. I've got a problem with my class that I don't know how to handle. I tried to use some of the ideas from the workshop you conducted on behavior modification and, well, they seem to have backfired. I must not be using them correctly.

JERRY: What's the problem?

It is important to recognize, however, that behavioral learning theories are limited in scope. With the exception of social learning theorists, behavioral learning theorists focus almost exclusively on observable behavior. This is one reason that so many of the examples presented in this chapter (and in Chapter 11) involve the management of behavior. Less visible learning processes, such as concept formation, learning from text, problem solving, and thinking, are difficult to observe directly, and have therefore been less often studied by behavioral learning theorists. These processes fall more into the domain of cognitive learning, discussed in Chapters 5 and 6, although social learning theory, which is a direct outgrowth of behavioral learning theories, helps bridge the gap between these two perspectives.

Behavioral and cognitive theories of learning are often posed as competing, opposite models. There are indeed specific areas in which these theories take contradictory positions. However, it is more accurate to see them as complementary rather than competitive—that is, as tackling different problems.

MARY: Well, I've gotten myself into a spot in trying to get the children to memorize the multiplication tables and I don't know how to get out of it.

JERRY: What did you do?

MARY: Well, I made up a chart of the ones through nines and I have the students come up front, point to each one and say them aloud. I remembered what you said about using rewards, so I decided that I would let them have free time when they said them correctly. If there is anything they love, it's free time. But I also praise the children each time they try, no matter what. I've also talked to them about supporting one another.

JERRY: Well, the first thing that comes to mind, Mary, is that it's tough for a third grader to come up front like that. It puts a lot of pressure on them.

MARY: I know, Jerry, but I feel they have to learn to speak in public sooner or later. Some of them will grow up to be teachers, politicians, and school board members. Learning to speak in front of people is important.

JERRY: Well, what's happened?

MARY: All but seven of the children have learned their multiplication tables, but the few who haven't just can't seem to do it, no matter how much help I give them.

JERRY: Can they say them in private?

MARY: Sometimes. But not always even then. Each time they fail I can see how hurt they are, and I think they are beginning to hate multiplication. Jerry, I guess the truth is I wish I had never started this in the first place. But now that I have, I don't know how to get out of it. Should I let the seven children out of doing what I've required the others to do? That just doesn't seem fair. Can you tell me what I did wrong and what I can do to fix it?

QUESTIONS

1. Analyze this case in terms of an appropriate learning theory. For example, how would you explain what has happened in the language of Skinner's operant conditioning theory?
2. What advice should Jerry give Mary? Considering that Mary has attended a behavior modification workshop, how can Jerry take advantage of that to explain to Mary what has happened? Pretend that you are Jerry advising Mary as to how to solve the problem. What actions would you advise her to take that are consistent with the way you have analyzed the case?
3. It is often said that a little learning is a dangerous thing. How might Mary have set up the experience of learning the multiplication tables differently in the first place? On what psychological principles does your recommendation rest?

SUMMARY AND REVIEW OF OBJECTIVES

Definition of Learning. Learning involves the acquisition of abilities that are not innate. It depends on experience, part of which is feedback from the environment.

Theories of Classical and Operant Conditioning. Early research into learning studied the effects of stimuli on reflexive behaviors. Ivan Pavlov contributed the notion of classical conditioning in which neutral stimuli acquire the capacity to evoke responses through their association with unconditioned stimuli. E. L. Thorndike developed the law of effect which emphasized the role of the consequences of present behavior in determining the future behavior. B. F. Skinner continued the study of the relationship between behavior and consequences. As a result, he described a type of learning that he called operant conditioning.

Types of Consequences. Consequences are either reinforcers, which increase the likelihood of a behavior, or punishers, which decrease its likelihood. Reinforcement can be either positive or negative, and either primary or secondary. Punishment involves weakening behavior by either introducing aversive consequences or removing reinforcers.

Schedules of reinforcement refer to the predictability and frequency of reinforcement. A ratio schedule requires a certain amount of behavior before reinforcement is given. An interval schedule is one in which a certain amount of time must pass before reinforcement, regardless of the amount of behavior that occurs. These schedules can be either fixed or variable.

Antecedent stimuli serve as cues indicating which behaviors will be reinforced and/or punished. Discrimination involves using cues to detect differences between stimulus situations. Generalization involves responding to similarities between stimuli. Extinction is the weakening and eventual disappearance of behavior caused by the withdrawal of reinforcement.

Shaping. Shaping is the process of breaking down a task into small steps and giving feedback as each step is taken.

Modeling. Learning from modeling occurs through observation of others' behavior and its consequences. According to Albert Bandura, four phases are involved: attentional, retention, reproduction, and motivational.

STUDY QUESTIONS

1. Which of the following most clearly represents an example of *learning?*
   a. Moving one's hand away from a hot object
   b. Being startled by a loud noise
   c. Feeling thirsty after exercising
   d. Feeling anxious when a teacher announces a pop quiz
   e. All of the above are valid examples
2. Match the following theories or laws of learning with a related experiment (a situation may be used more than once or not at all):
   ____ Classical conditioning
   ____ The Law of Effect
   ____ Operant conditioning
   ____ Social learning theory
   a. Animals learned to press a lever to get food.
   b. The behavior of children was observed after they had seen films in which adults acted aggressively.
   c. Before reading a passage about Buddhism, students reviewed the concepts of Christianity.
   d. Animals used trial-and-error to learn to escape from a box.
   e. Animals exhibited conditioned responses when they heard a bell.
3. A student begins to fear public speaking after being ridiculed by her classmates during a recitation exercise. In classical conditioning terms, her newly acquired fear would be a(n)
   a. conditioned stimulus.
   b. unconditioned stimulus.

   c. unconditional response.
   d. conditioned response.
4. An example of a primary reinforcer is
   a. safety or security.
   b. good grades in school.
   c. money.
   d. praise.
   e. access to toys.
5. Which of the following most clearly illustrates the Premack Principle?
   a. "Take a break and then complete your assignment."
   b. "For talking, spend five minutes in time-out."
   c. "Since directions were not followed by two people, the entire class will lose ten minutes of playground."
   d. "Those who complete their worksheets will be allowed 15 minutes to play the computer game of their choice."
6. Match these types of consequences with the most probable example of each.
   ____ Positive reinforcement
   ____ Negative reinforcement
   ____ Punishment
   a. "Write 'I will not talk' 500 times."
   b. "Students who finish this work will not be assigned homework tonight."
   c. "Good job, class! I'm proud of you!"
7. Extinction occurs as a result of
   a. punishing a response after it occurs.

b.   not rewarding a response after it occurs.

c.   rewarding a response through a continuous schedule.

d.   rewarding a response through an intermittent schedule.

8.   Match the following types of reinforcement schedules with the appropriate description.

_____ Fixed ratio

_____ Variable ratio

_____ Fixed interval

_____ Variable interval

a.   Taking a pop quiz

b.   Being paid for every ten magazine subscriptions sold

c.   Dialing a phone number and having the person you want to talk to answer

d.   Taking a weekly quiz

9.   As the difference between two stimulus settings increases

a.   generalization and discrimination both become easier.

b.   generalization becomes easier but discrimination becomes harder.

c.   generalization becomes harder but discrimination becomes easier.

d.   both generalization and discrimination become harder.

10.   Order the following four phases from Bandura's model in the correct sequence.

a.   Reproduction

b.   Retention

c.   Attentional

d.   Motivational

Answers: 1. *d* 2. *c, d, a* 3. *d* 4. *a* 5. *d* 6. *c, b* 7. *b* 8. *b, c, d, a* 9. *c* 10. *c, b, a, d*

SUGGESTED READINGS

AXELROD, S. (1977). *Behavior modification for the classroom teacher.* New York: McGraw-Hill.

BALDWIN, J. D. and BALDWIN, J. I. (1986). *Behavior principles in everyday life.* Englewood Cliffs, N.J.: Prentice-Hall.

BANDURA, A. (1969). *Principles of behavior modification.* New York: Holt, Rinehart, & Winston.

BANDURA, A. (1977). *Social learning theory.* Englewood Cliffs, N.J.: Prentice-Hall.

HILL, W. F. (1985). *Principles of learning: A handbook of application* (4th ed.). Sherman Oaks, Cal.: Alfred.

MEICHENBAUM, D. H. (1977). *Cognitive behavior modification.* New York: Plenum.

O'LEARY, K. D., and O'LEARY, S. G. (Eds.) (1977). *Classroom management: The successful use of behavior modification* (2nd ed.). New York: Pergamon.

PRESSLEY, M. (1979). Increasing children's self-control through cognitive interventions. *Review of Educational Research, 49,* 319–370.

ROSENBAUM, M. S. and DRABMAN, R. S. (1982). Self-control training in the classroom: A review and critique. *Journal of Applied Behavior Analysis, 15.*

SKINNER, B. F. (1968). *The technology of teaching.* New York: Appleton-Century-Crofts.

SULZER-AZAROFF, B., and MAYER, G. R. (1986). *Achieving educational excellence using behavior strategies.* New York: Holt, Rinehart, & Winston.

WALKER, J. E., and SHEA, T. M. (1980). *Behavior modification: A practical approach for educators* (2nd ed.). St. Louis, Mo.: C. V. Mosby.

Chapter 5

Information Processing and Memory

Chapter Outline

Humans as Information Processors

Information Processing
Sensory Register
Short-Term Memory
Long-Term Memory
Levels of Processing
Allocating Mental Resources
Forgetting
Primacy and Recency Effects
Theory into Practice: Reducing Retroactive Inhibition

Memory Strategies
Verbal Learning
Paired-Associate Learning
Theory into Practice: Paired-Associate Learning
  Strategies
Serial and Free-Recall Learning
Theory into Practice: Serial and Free-Recall Learning
  Strategies
Practice

Chapter Objectives

Understanding how the mind receives, stores, and retrieves information will help you understand how we learn. After reading this chapter you should be able to:

- List the three major components of memory and describe the role that each plays in the processing of information.

- Describe the three ways that our long-term memory codes information.

- Describe theories about memory—and explanations for forgetting.

- Use memory strategies to remember lists of information and pairs of facts.

- Explain the advantages of distributed practice over massed practice.

Information-Processing Theory
Cognitive theory of learning that describes the processing, storage, and retrieval of knowledge from the mind

Sensory Register
Component of the memory system where information is received and held for very short periods of time

Before reading any further, try an experiment. Take a quick look (no more than three seconds) at Figure 5.1 on the following page. Then return to this page.

Now, consider what you just learned. You probably noticed that Figure 5.1 has green boxes and blue arrows, that it has a light brown background, and that it is at the top of the page. You may also have inadvertently noticed information about the room you are in, where the book is placed, what sounds or smells are around you, and so on. You probably saw words like "memory" and "forgotten," and began to bring to consciousness whatever you already know or believe about these topics.

In three seconds, you received an enormous amount of information. If you retained all of it, your mind would soon be overloaded with useless junk. Instead, you began a process of sorting out what was useful and interesting and what was not. You probably did not consciously notice a lot of the extraneous information, such as minor room noises. If you were to study the figure again, you might recall your previous knowledge about memory and about diagrams in order to try to make sense of the figure. A day or a week from now you will forget that the arrows in Figure 5.1 were blue. But you will (it is hoped) remember something about how human memory operates.

The principal business of education is to help students acquire information, skills, learning strategies, and attitudes that they can call on when they need them. Yet we, as educators, cannot simply open up students' heads and pour in knowledge. Information enters our minds in specific ways and is retained there under particular conditions, which educational and cognitive psychologists are understanding better each year. We are constantly surrounded by information—sights, sounds, smells, tastes, and words. The information provided by teachers and schools is only a tiny fraction of the information with which students are bombarded throughout the day. How do we make our way in this sensory jungle? How do we receive, process, and remember information? How can we help students perceive, understand, incorporate, and recall the information presented in school? How can we help them learn to use their own mental capabilities more effectively in order to study, to learn, and to solve complex problems? These questions are addressed in the following two chapters.

INFORMATION PROCESSING

Information constantly enters our minds through our senses. Most of this information is almost immediately discarded, and much of it we may never even be aware of. Some is held in our memories for a short time, and then forgotten. For example, we may remember the seat number on a baseball ticket until we find our seats, at which point we will forget it. However, some information is retained much longer, perhaps for the rest of our lives. What is the process by which information is absorbed, and how can teachers take advantage of this process to help students retain critical information and skills? These are questions that have been addressed by cognitive learning theorists, and that have led to **information-processing theory.**

Research on human memory (see, for example, Atkinson and Shiffrin, 1968; Bransford, 1979; Case, 1985; Siegler, 1986) has helped learning theorists describe the process by which information is remembered (or forgotten). This process is illustrated in Figure 5.1.

Sensory Register

The first component of the memory system that incoming information meets is the **sensory register.** Sensory registers receive large amounts of information from the senses (sight, hearing, touch, smell, taste) and hold it for a very short time, no more

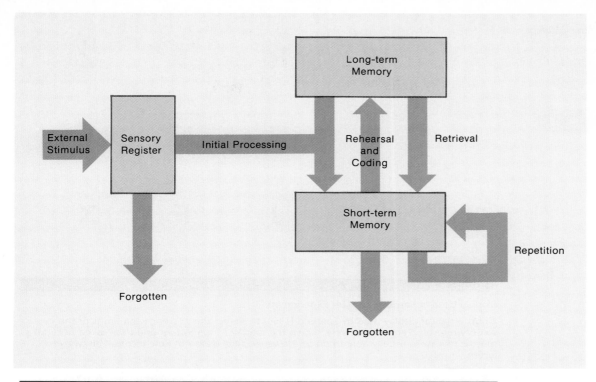

FIGURE 5.1

The Sequence of Information Processing
Information that is to be remembered must first reach a person's senses, then be attended to and transferred from the sensory register to the short-term memory, then be processed again for transfer to long-term memory.

than a couple of seconds. If nothing happens to information held in the sensory registers, it is rapidly lost.

Ingenious experiments have been used to detect the sensory registers. A person might be shown a display like that in Figure 5.2 for a very short period of time, say 50 milliseconds. The person is usually able to report seeing three, four, or five of the letters, but not all twelve of them. Sperling (1960) presented a display like Figure 5.2 to people. After the display disappeared, he signaled viewers to try to recall the top, middle, or bottom row. He found that people could recall any one row almost perfectly. Therefore they must have seen all the letters in the 50 milliseconds and retained them for a short period of time. However, when people tried to recall all twelve letters, the time it took them to do so apparently exceeded the amount of time the letters lasted in their sensory registers, so they lost some of the letters.

The existence of sensory registers has two important educational implications. First, people must pay attention to information if they are to retain it. And second, it takes time to bring all the information seen in a moment into consciousness. For example, if students are bombarded with too much information at once and are not told which aspects of the information they should pay attention to, they may have difficulty learning any of the information at all.

Perception. As soon as stimuli are received by the senses, the mind immediately begins working on some of them. Therefore the sensory images that we are conscious

Perception
A person's interpretation of stimuli

Gestalt Psychology
A psychological movement, started in Germany, that advanced the understanding of perception

Closure
The mental tendency to organize perceptions so they make sense

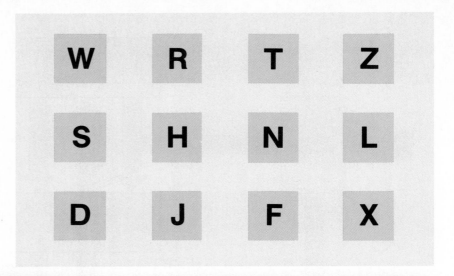

FIGURE 5.2

Display Used in Sensory Register Experiments

This is a typical display used by Sperling (1960) to detect the existence and limits of the sensory register. People who were shown the display for an instant and then asked to recall a specific row were usually able to do so. However, they were not able to recall all twelve letters.

of are not exactly the same as what we saw, heard, or felt; they are what our senses perceived. **Perception** of stimuli is not as straightforward as reception of stimuli; rather, it is influenced by our mental state, past experience, knowledge, motivations, and many other factors.

First, we attend to different stimuli according to rules that have nothing to do with the inherent characteristics of the stimuli. If we are sitting in a building, for example, we may not pay much attention to or even hear a fire engine's siren. If we are driving a car, we pay a great deal more attention. If we are standing outside a burning building waiting for the fire company to arrive, we pay even more attention. Second, we do not record the stimuli we perceive as we see or sense them, but as we know (or assume) they really are. From across a room, a book on a bookshelf looks like a thin strip of paper, but we infer that it is a rectangular form with many pages. We may see the edge of a table and mentally infer the entire table.

Gestalt Psychology. Questions of sensation, perception, and memory occupied the early Greeks and Romans, but in modern times the scientific study of how we receive and process information from the environment largely began with the **Gestalt psychology** movement in Germany (and later the United States and elsewhere) around World War I. *Gestalt* is a German word meaning "form" or "configuration." Gestalt psychologists, such as Max Wertheimer, Kurt Koffka, and Wolfgang Köhler, suggested that we perceive whole units rather than pieces of sensation, that the whole of a sensation is more that its parts. For example, in Figure 5.3 we readily see a circle, a pyramid, a square, and a cube, even though parts of the figures are left out. This illustrates the principle of **closure,** which states that people organize their perceptions so that they are as simple and logical as possible, filling in gaps in perceptions if necessary. This principle also applies when we try to remember an event from the past. We may add details to our memory of the event to make it more comprehensible. For

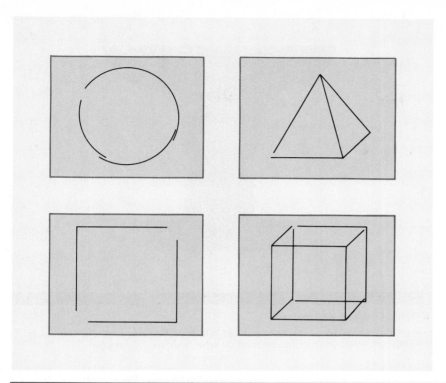

FIGURE 5.3

Closure

Even though these figures are incomplete, they are perceived as a circle, a pyramid, a square, and a cube, which illustrates the mind's tendency to seek closure.

example, in recalling an automobile accident in which one driver was clearly at fault, we might mentally add details that were not actually present to buttress our impression, such as that the innocent driver was wearing a seat belt or had signaled a turn.

Another important principle of Gestalt psychology is that we try to separate figure (that which we focus on) and ground (background). For example, when meeting a friend in a crowded airport, we focus only on the friend's face and generally ignore all other faces. In this circumstance we might miss seeing another friend in the crowd because all faces other than the one we are searching for are relegated to "ground" rather than "figure." A classic case of a **figure-ground relationship** is illustrated in Figure 5.4. Do you see a vase or two faces? If you were told to look for a vase, you might never see the faces (which would be perceived as background), and if you were told to look for faces, you might not see the vase. In Figure 5.5 look at the picture on the left and then at the picture in the center. The picture at the left mentally prepares you to see a young woman, and that is what you perceive. However, if you had first looked at the picture on the right, you would have perceived an older woman in the middle picture.

Attention. When teachers ask students to "pay attention" or "lend me your ears," they are using the words "pay" and "lend" appropriately. Like money, **attention** is a limited resource. When teachers ask students to spend their limited attention capacity

Figure-Ground Relationship
Perceiving selected parts of a stimulus to stand out (figure) from other parts (background)

Attention
The process of focusing on certain stimuli while screening out others

FIGURE 5.4

Example of a Figure-Ground Relationship

Is this a picture of a vase? Or of two faces in profile? Which part of the picture is the figure and which the ground? What you see can depend on what you are looking for.

on whatever they are saying, students must give up actively attending to other stimuli, they must shift their priorities so that other stimuli are screened out. For example, when people listen intently to an interesting speaker, they are unaware of minor body sensations(such as itches or hunger) and other sounds or sights. An experienced speaker knows that when the audience looks restless, its attention is no longer focused on the lecture, but may be turning toward considerations of lunch or other activities, and it is time to recapture the attention of the listeners.

FIGURE 5.5

Effect of Expectations on Perception

Perceptions can be affected by a person's expectations. If you look at the center picture after looking at the picture of the young woman to the left, you probably perceive the center picture as a young woman, too. Now look at the picture to the right. Does the center picture now look like an older woman?

From Leeper, 1935.

Calfee (1976) suggests that there are three aspects of attention. These are alertness, noticing details of the world around us and being sensitive or receptive to stimuli; selectivity, the ability to block out some stimuli and be sensitive to others; and concentration, the ability to focus thoughts on one task.

Gaining Attention. How can teachers focus students' attention on the lesson at hand, in particular on the most important aspects of what is being taught?

There are several ways to gain students' attention, all of which go under the general heading of "arousing student interest." One is to use cues that indicate "this is important." Some teachers raise or lower their voices to signal they are about to impart critical information. Others use gestures, repetition, or position to communicate the same message. Textbook publishers use different colors or typefaces to indicate important points.

Another way to gain attention is to increase the emotional content of material. Some publications accomplish this by choosing very emotional words. This can be why newspaper headlines say "Senate *Kills* Mass Transit Proposal" rather than "Senate *Votes Against* Mass Transit Proposal." Olson and Pau (1966) found that use of such emotionally charged words helped students retain information better than more neutral synonyms.

Attention is also attracted by unusual, inconsistent, or surprising stimuli. For example, science teachers often introduce lessons with a demonstration or magic trick to engage student curiosity (see Berlyne, 1965).

Finally, attention can be gained by informing students that what follows is important to them. For example, teachers can assure attention by telling students, "This will be on tomorrow's test!"

See Chapter 8 for more on how to gain students' attention and focus it on relevant information.

Teachers must hold the attention of their students in order to teach them. Preschool and elementary teachers can use active lesson presentations to arouse their students' interest.

Short-Term Memory

Short-Term Memory
Component of memory where limited amounts of information can be stored for a few seconds

Long-Term Memory
Component of memory where large amounts of information can be stored for long periods of time

Rehearsal
Mental repetition of information, which can improve its retention

Short-Term Memory

Information that a person perceives and pays attention to is transferred to the second component of the memory system, the **short-term memory** (Glanzer, 1982). Short-term memory is a storage system that can hold a limited amount of information for a few seconds. It is the part of memory where information currently being thought about is stored. The thoughts we are conscious of having at any given moment are being held in our short-term memory. When we stop thinking about something, it disappears from our short-term memory.

Information may enter short-term memory from sensory registers or from the third basic component of the memory system, **long-term memory.** Often both things happen at the same time. When we see a robin, our sensory register transfers the image of the robin to our short-term memory. Meanwhile, we may (unconsciously) search our long-term memory for information about birds so we can identify this particular one as a robin. Along with that recognition may come a lot of other information about robins, memories of past experiences with robins, or feelings about robins—all of which were stored in long-term memory but are brought into consciousness (short-term memory) by our mental processing of the sight of the robin.

One way to hold information in short-term memory is to think about it or say it over and over. You have probably remembered a phone number for a short time this way. This process of maintaining an item in short-term memory by repetition is called **rehearsal.** Rehearsal is important in learning because the longer an item remains in short-term memory, the greater the chance that it will be transferred to long-term memory. Without rehearsal, items probably will not stay in short-term memory for more than about thirty seconds. Because short-term memory has a limited capacity, information can also be lost from it by being forced out by other information. You have probably had the experience of looking up a telephone number, being interrupted briefly, and finding that you had forgotten the number.

Teachers must allocate time for rehearsal during classroom lessons. Teaching too much information too rapidly is likely to be ineffective because unless students are given time to mentally rehearse each new piece of information, later information is likely to drive it out of their short-term memories. When teachers stop a lesson to ask students if they have any questions, they are also giving students a few moments to think over and mentally rehearse what they have just learned. This helps students process information in short-term memory, and thereby to establish it in long-term memory. This mental work is critical when students are learning new, difficult material.

Short-term memory is believed to have a capacity of five to seven "bits" of information (Miller, 1956). That is, we can think about only five to seven distinct things at a time. However, any particular "bit" may itself contain a great deal of information. For example, think how difficult it would be to memorize the following shopping list:

Flour	Orange juice	Pepper	Mustard
Soda pop	Parsley	Cake	Butter
Relish	Mayonnaise	Oregano	Canned tomatoes
Potatoes	Milk	Lettuce	Syrup
Hamburger	Hot dogs	Eggs	Onions
Tomato paste	Wine	Spaghetti	Buns
Apples			

This list has too many "bits" of information to remember easily. All twenty-five food items would not fit into short-term memory in random order. However, we could easily memorize the list by organizing it according to familiar patterns. As shown in Table 5.1, we might mentally create three separate "memory files," breakfast, lunch, and dinner. Under each, we expect to find food and beverages, and under lunch and dinner we expect dessert as well. We can then think through the recipes for each item on the menus. In this way, we can recall what we have to buy and need maintain only a few bits of information in our short-term memory. When we enter the store, we are thinking, "I need food for breakfast, lunch, and dinner." First, we bring "breakfast" out of our long-term memory. It contains food (pancakes) and beverage (orange juice). We might think through how we make pancakes step-by-step, and buy each ingredient, plus orange juice as a beverage. When we have done this, we can discard "breakfast" from our short-term memory and replace it with "lunch," and then "dinner," going through the same processes. Note that all we did was to replace twenty-five little bits of information with three big bits that we could then separate into their components.

Short-term memory can be thought of as a bottleneck through which information from the environment reaches long-term memory. The limited capacity of short-term memory is one aspect of information processing that has important implications for the design and practice of instruction. For example, its limited capacity means that we cannot present students with too many ideas at once unless the ideas are so well organized and well connected to information already in the students' long-term memories that their short-term memories (with assistance from their long-term memories) can accommodate them, as in the case of the shopping list just discussed. Other instructional implications of the nature of short-term memory appear throughout this and the following chapters.

Long-Term Memory

Long-term memory is that part of our memory system where we keep information for long periods of time. Long-term memory is thought to be a very large capacity, very long-term memory store. In fact, many theorists believe that we may never forget

TABLE 5.1

EXAMPLE OF ORGANIZATION OF INFORMATION TO FACILITATE MEMORY

A twenty-five-item shopping list that would be very hard to remember in a random order can be organized into a smaller number of familiar categories, making the list easier to recall.

Breakfast		Lunch			Dinner		
Food	Beverage	Food	Beverage	Dessert	Food	Beverage	Dessert
Pancakes: —Flour —Milk —Eggs —Butter —Syrup	Orange Juice	Hot Dogs: —Hot dogs —Buns —Relish —Mustard Potato Salad: —Potatoes —Mayonnaise —Parsley	Soda Pop	Apple	Spaghetti: —Spaghetti —Onions —Hamburger —Canned tomatoes —Tomato paste —Oregano —Pepper Salad: —Lettuce	Wine	Cake

Episodic Memory
A part of long-term memory that stores images of our personal experiences

Semantic Memory
A part of long-term memory that stores facts and general knowledge

Procedural Memory
A part of long-term memory that stores information about how to do things

information in long-term memory; rather, we may just lose the ability to find the information within our memory.

Just as information can be stored in long-term memory a long time, so, too, the capacity of long-term memory seems to be very large. We do not live long enough to fill up our long-term memory.

The differences among sensory registers, short-term memory, and long-term memory are summarized in Table 5.2.

Episodic, Semantic, and Procedural Memory. Theorists divide long-term memory into at least three parts: **episodic memory, semantic memory,** and **procedural memory** (Tulving, 1972, 1985). Episodic memory is our memory of personal experiences, a mental movie of things we saw or heard. When we remember what we had for dinner last night or what happened at our high school prom, we are recalling information stored in our long-term episodic memory. Long-term semantic memory contains the facts and generalized information that we know; concepts, principles, or rules and how to use them; and our problem-solving skills and learning strategies. Most things learned in class lessons are retained in semantic memory. Procedural memory refers to "knowing how" as opposed to "knowing that" (Cotten and Squire, 1980). The abilities to drive, type, or ride a bicycle are examples of skills retained in procedural memory.

Episodic, semantic, and procedural memory differ in that they store and organize information in different ways. Information in episodic memory is stored in the form of images that are organized on the basis of when and where events happened. Information in semantic memory is organized in the form of networks of ideas. Information in procedural memory is stored as a complex of stimulus-response pairings (Oakley, 1981). Let's examine in detail what we mean by these three kinds of memory.

Episodic Memory. What is episodic memory like? We have said that it contains images of experiences organized by when and where they happened. To see this, consider the following demonstrations.

TABLE 5.2

DIFFERENCES AMONG THE THREE STAGES OF MEMORY

The three basic components of memory differ in function, capacity, and organization.

Feature	Sensory Registers	Short-Term Store	Long-Term Store
Entry of information	Preattentive	Requires attention	Rehearsal
Maintenance of information	Not possible	Continued attention Rehearsal	Repetition Organization
Format of information	Literal copy of input	Phonemic Probably visual Possibly semantic	Largely semantic Some auditory and visual
Capacity	Large	Small	No known limit
Information loss	Decay	Displacement Possibly decay	Possibly no loss Loss of accessibility by interference
Trace duration	1/4–2 seconds	Up to 30 seconds	Minutes to years
Retrieval	Readout	Probably automatic Items in consciousness Temporal/phonemic cues	Retrieval cues Possibly search process

Source: Adapted from Craik and Lockhart, 1972, pp. 671–684.

Chapter 5: Information Processing and Memory

Answer this question: In the house in which you lived as a child, when you entered your bedroom, was the head of your bed to the right, left, away from, or pointed toward you? If you are like most people, you answered this question by imagining the bedroom and seeing where the head of the bed was. Now consider this question: What did you do on the night of your senior prom or dance? Most people answer this question by imagining themselves back on that night and describing the events. Finally, suppose you were asked to recall the names of your high school classmates. Suppose further that someone asked you to come to a specific place for one hour a day and try to remember the names. Once psychologist asked graduate students to do just that and to try to verbalize their thinking. Over the course of a month the students continued to recall new names. Even more interestingly, they used space and time cues, which are associated with episodic memory, to imagine incidents that allowed them to recall the names. For example, they might recall the day their social studies teacher came to school dressed as an arctic explorer, and then mentally scan the faces of the students who were there.

These demonstrations indicate that images are important in episodic memory and that cues related to space and time help us retrieve information from this part of memory. You probably have taken an exam and said to yourself, "I should know this answer, I remember reading this section, it was right on the bottom left corner of the page with the diagram in the upper right." Research has confirmed that people can often remember where information was on a page even if they can't remember the information itself (Rothkopf, 1970).

Episodic memories are often difficult to retrieve because most episodes in our lives are repeated so often that later episodes get mixed up in memory with earlier ones, unless something happens during the episode to make it especially memorable. For example, few people remember what they had for lunch a week ago, much less years ago. However, people who happened to be eating lunch at the moment they heard that Pearl Harbor was attacked or that John F. Kennedy was shot, or at the moment they heard they were accepted into college or received a proposal of marriage, may well remember that particular meal (and many other mundane aspects of the setting) forever. The reason for this is that the unforgettable event of that moment gives us access to the episodic (space and time) memories relating to what would usually be forgotten details.

Semantic Memory. Semantic (or "declarative") memory is organized in a very different way (Sylvester, 1985). It is mentally organized in networks of connected ideas or relationships, called **schemata** *(singular: schema)* (Johnson-Laird et al., 1984; Anderson, 1985; Chang, 1986). Recall that the word "scheme" was introduced by Piaget to describe a cognitive framework individuals use to organize their perceptions and experiences. Cognitive-processing theorists similarly use the related terms "schema" and "schemata" to describe networks of concepts individuals have in their memories that enable them to understand and incorporate new information. A schema is like an outline, with different concepts or ideas grouped under larger categories. Various aspects of schemata may be related by series of propositions, or relationships. For example, Figure 5.6 illustrates a simplified schema for the word "bison" showing how this concept is related to other concepts in memory.

In the figure the concept "bison" is linked to several other concepts. These may be linked to still more concepts, which relate both to bison (such as, "How did the Indians hunt bison?") and to broader categories or concepts (such as, "How have conservationists saved many species from extinction?"). Schema theory (Brewer and Nakamura, 1984) holds that we gain access to information held in our semantic long-term memory by mentally following paths like those illustrated in Figure 5.6.

Schemata
Mental networks of related concepts that influence understanding of new information

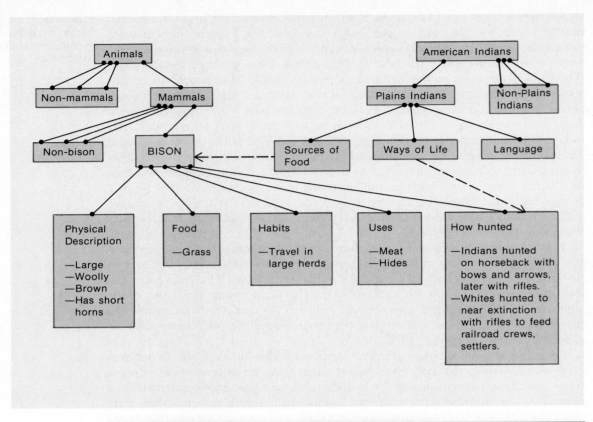

FIGURE 5.6

Schema for the Word "Bison"

Information in long-term semantic memory is organized in networks of related ideas. The concept "bison," for example, falls under the more general concepts "mammals" and "animals," and is related to many other ideas that help differentiate it from other concepts in memory.

For example, we might have deep in our memories the idea that the Spanish introduction of the horse to American Indians revolutionized how the Indians hunted bison. To get to that bit of information, we might start thinking about characteristics of bison, then think about how Indians hunted bison on horseback, then recall (or imagine) how Indians hunted bison before they had horses. Actually, many pathways can be used to get at the same bit of information. In fact, the more different pathways we have leading to a piece of information, and the better established those pathways are, the better access we will have to information in long-term semantic memory (Collins and Loftus, 1975; Anderson, 1985). Remember, the problem of long-term memory is not that information is lost, but that our *access* to information is lost.

One clear implication of schema theory is that new information that fits into a well-developed schema is retained far more readily than information that does not fit into a schema. For example, if we learn that "Bison calves can run soon after they are born," this fits neatly into what we already know about bison and about similar animals (such as horses) that rely on speed to escape from predators. However, if we learned that "Loris babies are born with a strong grasping instinct," this information is less likely to be retained unless we also learn that lorises are furry animals that live in trees.

The uses of schema theory in instruction are discussed in Chapter 6.

Procedural Memory. Procedural memory is the ability to recall how to do something, especially a physical task. This type of memory is apparently stored in a series of stimulus-response pairings. For example, even if we have not ridden a bicycle for a long time, as soon as we get on one, the stimuli begin to evoke responses. When the bike leans to the left (a stimulus), we "instinctively" shift our weight to the right to maintain balance (a response).

■ **Stop and Think**

You've just been introduced to the information-processing perspective on learning. Compare and contrast this perspective to the behavioral viewpoint detailed in the last chapter.

Also, child development experts emphasize the inherent differences among people of different ages. Evaluate the extent to which these differences would affect the application of the information-processing theory to children in lower elementary school, middle school, or high school.

Levels of Processing

The Atkinson-Shiffrin (1968) model of information processing just outlined is not the only one accepted by cognitive psychologists. Another widely accepted model is called **levels-of-processing theory** (Craik and Lockhart, 1972; Crain, 1979), which holds that people subject stimuli to different levels of mental processing, and retain only the information that has been subjected to the most thorough processing. For example, we might perceive a tree, but pay little attention to it. This is the lowest level of processing, and we are unlikely to remember the tree. Second, we might give the tree a name, such as "tree" or "oak." Once named, the tree is somewhat more likely to be remembered. The highest level of processing, however, is giving meaning to the tree. For example, we might remember having climbed the tree, or commented on the tree's unusual shape, or wondered whether the tree would fall on our house if it were struck by lightning. According to levels-of-processing theory, the more we attend to the details of a stimulus, the more mental processing we must do with a stimulus, and the more likely we are to remember it. This was illustrated in a study by Bower and Karlin (1974), who had Stanford undergraduates look at yearbook pictures from Yale. Some of the students were told to classify the pictures as "male" or "female," and some to classify them as "very honest" or "less honest." The students who had to categorize the faces as very honest or less honest remembered them far better than did those who merely categorized them as male or female. Presumably, the "honesty" raters had to do a much higher level of mental processing with the pictures than did the "gender" raters, and for this reason they remembered the faces better. Similarly, students who were asked to rate a series of words as "pleasant" or "unpleasant" recalled over 60 percent more of the words than did students who were only asked to count the letters or identify words with "e" in them (Hyde and Jenkins, 1969).

A concept related to levels-of-processing theory is Paivio's (1971) **dual code theory of memory,** which hypothesizes that information is retained in long-term memory in two forms: visual and verbal (corresponding to episodic and semantic memory, respectively). This theory predicts that information represented both

Levels-of-Processing Theory
Explanation of memory that links recall of a stimulus with the amount of mental processing it receives

Dual Code Theory of Memory
Theory suggesting that information coded both visually and verbally is remembered better than information coded in only one of those two ways

Transfer-Appropriate Processing
A theory which proposes that memory is stronger and lasts longer when the conditions of performance are similar to those under which learning occurred

visually and verbally is recalled better than information represented only one way. For example, we remember a face better if we also know a name, and a name better if we can connect it to a face.

Level-of-processing theory has been modified and extended by the work of Bransford (1979; Bransford et al., 1982) and his associates. They noted that memory did not depend on depth of processing alone, but also on the way in which information was learned and then tested. In a study by Morris, Bransford, and Franks (1977) students were given two types of sentences, involving either the meaning of words (for example, "Does a *dog* have ears?") or rhymes (for example, "Does *dog* rhyme with log?"). As predicted by level-of-processing theory, students could recognize more of the words whose meaning they had to consider than words for which they only had to focus on rhymes—a lower level of processing. Yet when the memory test used rhymes, students recalled more of the words they had learned through rhymes, something not predicted by level-of-processing theory. This led Bransford (1979) to propose a theory of **transfer-appropriate processing,** which holds that the strength and durability of memory depends not only on the depth of processing, but also on the similarity between the conditions under which the material was learned and those under which it is called for. This distinction has great importance for instruction; for example, it helps explain why so many students can recall and apply rules of grammar and punctuation on a multiple-choice or fill-in-the blank test (a format similar to that in which they learned these skills) but be unable to recall or apply the same skills in their own writing. For more on transfer, see Chapter 6.

Allocating Mental Resources

Up to this point we have learned how information is put into memory and how it is stored there. But how do we screen all the information around us to decide what is to be saved in what form, and for how long? How do we sort through information held in long-term memory to find what will help us with our thoughts and actions? How do we use old information to learn new information or skills?

One way to think about how we use our minds is to see information processing as the allocation of limited mental resources to various tasks. We have only so much capacity in short-term memory to use at a given time, so we learn ways to use that capacity efficiently. Consider the following example.

Margaret is baby-sitting for a six-month-old. She is doing her homework, watching a soap opera, and eating lunch. Essentially, she has allocated her mental resources to several activities at the same time. She is putting most of her conscious attention into her homework. But she is vaguely aware of what is going on in the soap opera, aware enough so that when something important happens (young Dr. Smith announces she's in love with her male nurse), she will stop working on her homework to see how it comes out. Margaret is even less consciously aware of the baby, who is sleeping, but in fact she will respond to the slightest noise from him. Finally, she is hardly aware at all of chewing and swallowing her lunch.

Margaret can really devote her full attention to only one thing at a time, but she can give lower levels of attention to other stimuli on "automatic drive." However, there is a limit to how many of these stimuli she can attend to. She makes a conscious or unconscious decision as to which to attend to and which to ignore.

In classrooms students are also attending at some level to many stimuli at once. A critical part of the teacher's task is to focus students' attention on things that matter, reducing distractions and interruptions that diffuse attention.

Automatization.   Not everything requires conscious attention. For instance, our brain monitors breathing and heart rate without our attention. Tasks that require higher-level thinking can also be done without much attention if they have been learned very thoroughly. Think back to elementary school when you learned cursive handwriting. At first you had to make conscious decisions about forming every letter. Your teacher may have told you to watch the slant of the letters and their neatness. Before long, however, you gained experience and could devote much less attention to the act of writing. This process in which tasks require less attention as they become well learned has been called **automatization** by Shiffrin and Schneider (1977). Automatization is important because we want the skills we teach children to become second nature to them to free their short-term memories for more complex tasks.

For example, students' knowledge of the sounds each letter makes and how to decode (read) simple words must become automatic. Students who must put mental effort into sounding out each word in a sentence cannot adequately attend to what the sentence is saying because all their attention (short-term memory) is taken up with the decoding task (La Berge and Samuels, 1974; Perfetti and Lesgold, 1977; Samuels, 1981). Similarly, students must know their multiplication facts automatically so that their mental capacities can be devoted to learning more complex computations and applications of mathematical principles (Greeno, 1978).

Automatization
Process by which thoroughly learned tasks can be performed with little mental effort

FOCUS ON

"Flashbulb Memories"

Where were you on January 28, 1986, when you heard about the explosion of the space shuttle Challenger?

It is likely that you can answer this question with some confidence, and that you can detail the exact time and place when you recall hearing the news. Surprisingly, there is a good chance your recollections will be wrong, according to cognitive psychologist Ulric Neisser.

Neisser has proof. Written reports made by interviewees a day after the event contradict the same people's recollections of three years later.

The Emory University psychology professor saw in the shuttle disaster an opportunity to test a phenomenon called "flashbulb memory"—the vivid recollections that people have of important and emotionally charged events. The morning after the shuttle explosion that killed seven astronauts, Neisser asked 100 students to record where they were when they heard the news. Three years later, he tracked down 44 of the surveyed students and asked them the question again. He scored the accuracy of their responses on a scale of 0 to 7.

Few of the 44 received the top score of 7 on their recollections. Over half were totally wrong. Moreover, many of the students who were extremely confident about their answers were still wrong. Some did not want to accept their mistakes even when confronted with their original 1986 answers.

Most students recalled in the follow-up questioning that they had heard the news when they passed a TV set and stopped to watch. That response, often inaccurate, was probably the result of their ability to recall a few fragments of the experience and then reconstruct a plausible story around these fragments. "After all," Neisser said, "after hearing about [the Challenger explosion], almost all of us sat around that night watching it on television. They remember the television-watching experience."

The concept of flashbulb memory dates back at least to an article written at the turn of the century about people's recollections of how they heard about Abraham Lincoln's assassination. More recently the phenomenon has been used to explain why so many people say they can remember exactly where they were when they heard the news that John F. Kennedy was shot in Dallas on November 22, 1963.

Psychologists theorize that these vivid memories suggest a strong link between emotions and memory and that flashbulb memories are encoded in the brain differently from other events and information. The intriguing question raised by Professor Neisser's survey relates to how accurate these memories really are.

Lauren Neergaard, "Psychologist Finds 'Flashbulb Memories' of Challenger Explosion Off Base," The Associated Press, January 24, 1990.

Richard Restak, M. D., *The Brain,* New York: Bantam Books, 1984.

Interference
A process that occurs when recall of certain information is inhibited by the presence of other information in memory

Retroactive Inhibition
Decreased ability to recall previously learned information caused by learning of new information

Proactive Inhibition
Decreased ability to learn new information because of interference of present knowledge

Students must thoroughly learn basic skills, such as reading simple words, so that their attention can be shifted to higher-level skills, such as understanding the meaning of written material.

Automatization is primarily gained through drill and practice. Just as coaches drill athletes in essential physical skills until they become second nature, so must teachers drill students in certain facts and skills until they are second nature, to free their mental capacities for more complex and important tasks. Gaining automaticity on lower-level processes has enormous consequences for higher-level learning; Bloom (1986), who has studied the role of automaticity in the performances of gifted pianists, mathematicians, athletes, and others, calls automaticity the "hands and feet of genius."

For more on this, see "Overlearning" in the "Practice" section at the end of this chapter.

Forgetting

A discussion of memory is hardly complete without mentioning its opposite and constant companion: forgetting. Why do we remember some things and forget others? Why can we sometimes remember trivial things that happened years ago but not important things that happened yesterday? Most forgetting occurs because information in short-term memory was never transferred to long-term memory. However, it can also occur because we lose our ability to recall information that is in long-term memory.

Interference. One important reason people forget is **interference** (Postman and Underwood, 1973). Interference happens when information gets mixed up with or pushed aside by other information. One form of interference is when people are prevented from mentally rehearsing newly learned information. For example, Peterson and Peterson (1959) gave subjects a simple task, the memorization of sets of three nonsense letters (such as FQB). The subjects were then immediately asked to count backward by threes from a three-digit number (for example, 287, 284, 281, etc.) for up to eighteen seconds. At the end of that time the subjects were asked to recall the letters. They had forgotten far more of them than had subjects who had learned the letters and then simply waited for eighteen seconds to repeat them. The reason for this is that the subjects told to count backward were deprived of the opportunity to mentally rehearse the letters to establish them in their short-term memories. As noted earlier in this chapter, teachers must take into account the limited capacity of short-term memory by allowing students time to absorb or practice (that is, to mentally rehearse) new information before giving them additional instruction.

Another form of interference is called **retroactive inhibition.** This occurs when previously learned information is lost because it is mixed up with new and somewhat similar information. For example, young students might have no trouble recognizing the letter "b" until they are taught the letter "d." Because these letters are similar, students often confuse them. Learning the letter "d" thus interferes with the previously learned recognition of "b." By the same token, a traveler may know how to get around in a particular airport, but then lose that skill to some extent after visiting many similar airports.

Proactive inhibition occurs when learning one set of information interferes with learning of later information. A classic case is an American learning to drive on the left in England. It may be easier for an American nondriver to learn to drive in England than for an experienced American driver because the latter has so thoroughly learned to stay to the right, a potentially fatal error in England.

Figures 5.7 and 5.8 illustrate experiments used to measure retroactive and proactive inhibition.

It should also be noted that learning one thing can often help a person learn similar information. For example, learning Spanish first may help a student learn Italian, a similar language. This would be a case of **proactive facilitation.** On the other hand, learning a second language can help with an already established language. It is often the case, for example, that students find the study of Latin helps them better understand their native English language. This would be **retroactive facilitation.**

For another example, consider teaching. We often have the experience that learning to teach a subject helps us understand the subject better. Since later learning (for example, learning to teach addition of fractions) increases the understanding of

Proactive Facilitation
Increased ability to learn new information due to previously acquired information

Retroactive Facilitation
Increased comprehension of previously learned information due to the acquisition of new information

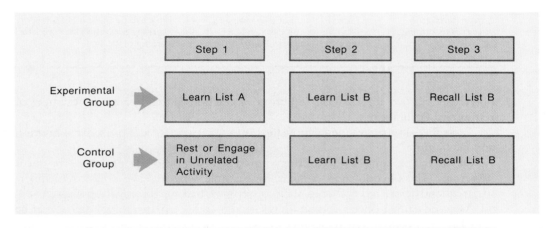

FIGURE 5.7 (ABOVE)

Procedure for Measuring Proactive Inhibition

Researchers found that previously learned material interfered with recall of information learned later. The experimental group probably had trouble recalling List B because of proactive inhibition.

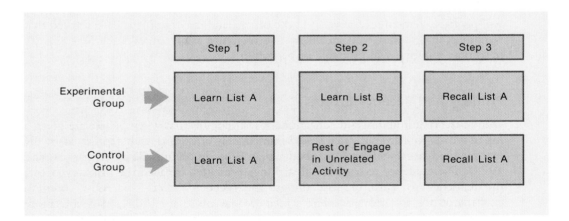

FIGURE 5.8

Procedure for Measuring Retroactive Inhibition

Researchers found that learning new material (List B) interfered with the experimental group's ability to recall information learned earlier (List A), a case of retroactive inhibition. The control group, which did not learn the second list, was better able to recall List A.

Primacy Effect
The tendency for items that appear at the beginning of a list to be more easily recalled than other items

Recency Effect
The tendency for items that appear at the end of a list to be more easily recalled than other items

TABLE 5.3

RETROACTIVE AND PROACTIVE INHIBITION AND FACILITATION

Summary of the effects on memory of retroactive and proactive inhibition and facilitation.

	Effect on Memory	
	Negative	**Positive**
Later learning affects earlier learning	Retroactive inhibition (Example: Learning "d" interferes with learning "b")	Retroactive facilitation (Example: Learning to teach math helps with previously learned math skills)
Earlier learning affects later learning	Proactive inhibition (Example: Learning to drive in the U.S. interferes with learning to drive in the U.K.)	Proactive facilitation (Example: Learning Spanish helps with later learning of Italian)

previously learned information (addition of fractions), this is a prime example of retroactive facilitation.

Table 5.3 summarizes the relationships among retroactive and proactive inhibition and facilitation.

Of all the reasons for forgetting, retroactive inhibition is probably the most important. This phenomenon explains, for example, why we have trouble remembering frequently repeated episodes, such as what we had for dinner a week ago.

As noted earlier, once information is stored in long-term memory, it may never be lost. Elderly people often remember events fifty or sixty years ago better than they recall what happened this morning. Penfield (1969) conducted experiments in which he electrically stimulated various parts of patients' brains. This caused the patients to recall all sorts of things they had thought they had forgotten. What we do lose is access to information in long-term memory, and we lose this most often because later learning interferes with the earlier information. Whatever you remember now about any unique and important event that happened several years ago, such as the death of a close relative or friend, or your marriage or that of someone very close to you, you will probably remember forever. On the other hand, anything you have learned that resembles information you are likely to experience many times, such as a friend's telephone number, will probably be forgotten.

Primacy and Recency Effects

One of the oldest findings in educational psychology is that when people are given a list of words to learn and then tested immediately afterward, they tend to learn the first few and last few items much better than those in the middle of the list (Stigler, 1978). The tendency to learn the first things presented is called the **primacy effect;** the tendency to learn the last things, the **recency effect.** The most common explanation for the primacy effect is that we pay more attention and devote more mental effort to items presented first. As noted earlier in this chapter, mental rehearsal is important in establishing new information in long-term memory. Usually, much more mental rehearsal is devoted to the first items presented than to later items (Rundus and Atkinson, 1970). Recency effects, on the other hand, are due in large part to the fact that little or no other information intervenes between the final items and the test (Greene, 1986).

One implication of retroactive inhibition is that confusing, similar concepts should not be taught too closely in time. Each concept should be taught thoroughly before the next is introduced. For example, students should be completely able to recognize the letter "b" before the letter "d" is introduced. If these letters were introduced at close to the same time, learning of one would inhibit learning of the other. When introduced, the differences between "b" and "d" must be carefully pointed out and discrimination between the two drilled until students can unerringly say which is which. Similarly, teaching someone Spanish and Italian at the same time would be foolish. Students should have a firm grounding in one language before another is introduced. If we were teaching the words "etymology" (the study of words) and "entomology" (the study of insects), we would want to make sure that students readily understood and were able to use one of these terms before we introduced the other.

Another way to reduce retroactive inhibition is to use different methods to teach similar concepts or to vary other aspects of instruction for each concept. For example, Andre (1973) had students study two descriptions of African tribes. For some students, the two passages were organized and printed in the same way. For others, the second passage was organized differently from the first and printed on different-colored paper. Students given the second procedure showed less confusion between the two passages on a later test. Researchers also found that when students were asked to memorize two lists, those

who used the same memorization strategy for both forgot more than those who used a different strategy for each (Andre et al., 1976). This and other research implies that teachers can help students retain information and avoid confusion if they vary their presentation strategies for different material. For example, a teacher might teach about Spain using lectures and discussion, about France using group projects, and about Italy using films. This would help students avoid confusing information about one country with information about the others.

When very similar concepts must logically be taught together, then mnemonic devices may be used to help students avoid confusing them. For example, in teaching about caves, the words "stalactite" and "stalagmite" are sure to be presented together, and sure to be confused. A teacher might reduce the confusion by teaching students to think of the "g" in "stalagmite" as standing for "ground," to help them remember that stalagmites are on the floor of the cave and stalactites on the ceiling. For more on mnemonics, see below.

Finally, it is important to remember that most things that are forgotten were never firmly learned in the first place. The best way to ensure long-term retention of material taught in school is to make certain that students have mastered the essential features of the material. This requires frequent assessment of students' understanding, and reteaching if it turns out that students have not achieved adequate levels of mastery. For more on this, see Chapters 8 and 9.

Who's who? Can't remember? Maybe your history teacher tried to teach you too many new facts before you mastered old ones. (Answer, from left to right: Theodore Roosevelt, Taft, and FDR.)

Verbal Learning
Learning of words or facts under
various controlled conditions

Primacy and recency effects should be considered by teachers. They imply that information taught at the beginning or the end of the period is more likely to be retained than other information. To take advantage of this, teachers might organize their lessons to put the most essential new concepts early in the lesson, and then to summarize at the end. Many teachers take roll, collect lunch money, check homework, and do other noninstructional activities at the beginning of the period. However, it is probably a better idea to postpone these activities, to start the period right away with important concepts and only toward the end of the period deal with necessary administrative tasks. See Chapter 8 for more on this.

■ **Stop and Think**

Without turning any pages, recall several main ideas from the material you just read. If you succeeded, congratulations! If not, analyze why. To what extent is your degree of recollection explained by the information-processing theory just discussed? For example, do you recall more of the information presented most recently, or more of the information at the beginning of the chapter? Do you recall ideas associated with pictures or diagrams? Did you have trouble learning the difference between proactive and retroactive inhibition? If so, which principles of learning and forgetting were demonstrated in your own learning?

MEMORY STRATEGIES

Many of the things that students learn in school are facts that must be remembered. These form the framework on which more complex concepts depend. Factual material must be learned as efficiently and effectively as possible to leave time and mental energy for meaningful learning, such as problem-solving, conceptual, and creative activities (see Chapter 6). If students can memorize the routine things more efficiently, they can "free their minds to spend more time on tasks that involve understanding and reasoning. . . . Even tasks that involve reasoning and understanding require that you remember the facts in order to reason with them and understand them" (Higbee, 1978, p. 150).

Some learning involves memorization of facts or of arbitrary associations between terms. For example, *pomme,* the French word for "apple," is an arbitrary term associated with an object. The capital of Iowa could just as well have been called "Iowapolis" as "Des Moines." Similarly, the figure "2" is an arbitrary representation of the concept "two." Students often learn things as facts before they understand them as concepts or skills. For instance, students may learn the formula for the volume of a cylinder as an arbitrary fact long before they understand *why* the formula is what it is.

Helping people remember factual material has been a concern since ancient times. The Greeks and Romans developed and used techniques for memorizing long messages and speeches. Preliterate societies used memory strategies to pass on oral histories from generation to generation. In recent years cognitive psychologists have rediscovered many of these memory strategies, and developed and researched additional means of helping students learn and retain information.

Research on learning of factual material has been done in two general ways. In many studies psychologists have examined **verbal learning,** or how students learn verbal materials in laboratory settings. For example, students might be asked to learn lists of words or nonsense syllables. Other studies have investigated learning facts from books, lectures, class presentations, movies, and other more typical forms of classroom instruction. These studies have been done both in laboratories and in classrooms.

Verbal Learning

Three types of verbal learning tasks typically seen in the classroom have been identified and studied extensively: the paired-associate task, the serial learning task, and the free-recall learning task.

1. **Paired-associate learning:** This type of task involves learning to respond with one member of a pair when given the other member of the pair. Usually there is a list of pairs to be memorized. In typical experiments the pairs are arbitrary. Educational examples of paired-associate tasks include learning the states' capitals, the names and dates of Civil War battles, the addition and multiplication tables, the atomic weights of the elements, and the spelling of words.

2. **Serial learning:** This involves learning a list of terms in a particular order. Memorization of the notes on the musical staff, the Pledge of Allegiance, the elements in atomic weight order, and poetry and songs are serial learning tasks. Serial learning tasks occur less often in classroom instruction than paired-associate tasks.

3. **Free-recall learning:** These types of tasks also involve memorizing a list, but not in a special order. Recalling the names of the fifty states, types of reinforcement, kinds of poetic feet, and the organ systems in the body are examples of free-recall tasks.

Paired-Associate Learning
A task involving the linkage of two items in a pair so that when one is presented the other can be recalled

Serial Learning
A task requiring recall of a list of items

Free-Recall Learning
A task requiring recall of list of items in any order

Paired-Associate Learning

In paired-associate learning the student must associate a response with each stimulus. For example, the student is given a picture of a bone (the stimulus) and must respond "tibia," or is given the symbol "Au" and must respond "gold." One important aspect of the learning of paired associates is the degree of familiarity the student already has with the stimuli and the responses. For example, it would be far easier to learn to associate foreign words with English words, such as dog—*chien* (French) or dog—*perro* (Spanish) than to learn to associate two foreign words, such as *chien*—*perro*. By the same token, a student who knew Latin could learn medical or legal terms that are Latin or derived from Latin more easily than could someone who was not familiar with Latin.

The first step in learning paired associates is stimulus discrimination. That is, the learner must be able to discriminate among the various stimuli. For example, consider the following lists of Spanish and English words.

A	B
llevar—to carry	*perro*—dog
llorar—to cry	*gato*—cat
llamar—to call	*caballo*—horse

List B is much easier to learn. The similarities among the Spanish words in List A (they are all verbs, all start with "ll," end with "ar," and have the same number of letters and syllables) make them very difficult to tell apart. The English words in List A are also somewhat difficult to discriminate because all are verbs that start with a "c." In contrast, the stimulus-and-response words in List B are easy to discriminate from one another. Because of the problem of retroactive inhibition discussed earlier,

Methods for enhancing paired-associate learning are the most extensively studied of all memory strategies. Several methods of learning such material have been developed and researched. These are called **mnemonics,** a Greek word meaning "aiding the memory" (Higbee, 1979).

IMAGERY

Many powerful memory techniques are based on forming mental images to help remember associations. For example, the French word for fencing is *l'escrime,* pronounced "le scream." It is easy to remember this association (fencing—*l'escrime*) by forming a mental picture of a fencer screaming while being skewered by an opponent, as illustrated in Figure 5.9.

Mental **imagery** can be a very effective aid to memory. For example, Anderson and Hidde (1971) asked students to study a list of sentences that were all of the form "The (occupation—noun) (did—an action)," such as "The doctor opened the closet." Half the students were told to rate the sentences according to how easily they could form a mental image of them. The other half of the group rated the sentences according to how easy it was to pronounce them. The students who had to form mental images recalled three times as many sentences as the other group.

The Keyword Method

One of the most extensively studied methods of using imagery to help paired-associate learning is the **keyword method,** originally developed for teaching foreign language vocabulary but later applied to many other areas (Atkinson, 1975; Atkinson and Raugh, 1975). The example used earlier of employing vivid imagery to recall the French word *l'escrime* is an illustration of the keyword method. In that case, the keyword was "scream." It is called a keyword because it

FIGURE 5.9

Example of the Use of Images to Aid Recall

A student learning French can easily remember that the French word for fencing is *l'escrime* by linking it to the English word "scream"and picturing a fencer screaming.

evokes the connection between the word *l'escrime* and the mental picture. Another illustration given by Atkinson (1975) is learning the Spanish word for duck, *pato*. Since this is pronounced something like "pot-o," the learner is instructed to imagine a duck swimming on a lake with a little pot on its head, or (more contemporarily) a famous cartoon duck smoking marijuana. In this case, "pot" is the keyword linking the image to the new word. The Russian word for building, *zdanie*, pronounced "zdawn'-yeh," might be recalled using the keyword "dawn" by imagining the sun coming up behind a building with an onion dome on top. Atkinson and Raugh (1975) used this method to teach students a list of 120 Russian words over a three-day period. Other students were given English translations of the Russian words and allowed to study as they wished. At the end of the experiment the students who used the keyword method recalled 72 percent of the words, while the other students recalled only 46 percent. This result has been repeated dozens of times, using a wide variety of languages (Pressley et al., 1982), with students from preschoolers to adults. However, young children seem to require pictures of the mental images they are meant to form, while older children (starting in upper elementary school) learn equally well making their own mental images (Pressley and Levin, 1978).

The images used in the keyword method work best if they are vivid and active (Delin, 1969), preferably involving interaction. For example, the German word for room, *zimmer* (pronounced "tsimmer"), might be associated with the keyword "simmer." The German word would probably be better recalled using an image of a distressed person in a bed immersed in a huge, steaming cauldron of water in a large bedroom than using an image of a small pot of water simmering in the corner of a bedroom. The drama, action, and bizarreness of the first image make it memorable, while the second is too commonplace to be easily recalled.

While most research on mnemonic learning strategies has focused on learning foreign language vocabulary, several studies have demonstrated that the same methods can be used for other information, including names of state capitals and English vocabulary words (Levin et al., 1980; Miller et al., 1980). More recent studies applied mnemonics to reading comprehension (Peters et al., 1985), biographical information (McCormick and Levin, 1984), and science facts (Levin et al., 1986). However, it should be noted that most of the research done on use of mnemonic strategies has taken place under rather artificial, laboratorylike conditions, using materials thought to be especially appropriate for these strategies. Evaluations of actual classroom applications of these strategies show more mixed results (Pressley and Levin, 1983). Although the strategies have been relatively successful for teaching foreign language vocabulary (especially nouns) to elementary school students, they have yet to show success in helping students actually speak foreign languages better. However, research is under way on the practical applications of paired-associate learning strategies to a broader range of skills, and it is likely the strategies will prove useful in helping students learn certain kinds of information (see Pressley et al., 1989).

YODAI MNEMONICS

One interesting application of mnemonic strategies primarily using imagery is a method developed in Japan called **Yodai mnemonics,** which means "essence of structure" (Nakane, 1981; Higbee and Kunihira, 1985). This system uses vivid imagery, poems, and songs as aids to memory and understanding. For example, kindergartners were taught operations with fractions. A fraction is called a "bug" whose head is the numerator and whose wing is the denominator. Adding fractions with like denominators is expressed as "count the heads when the wings are the same." Parentheses are called "baskets" and positive and negative numbers are called "male" and "female," so the algebraic expression (a - b) would be referred to as a "male and female bug in a basket" (Higbee and Kunihira, 1985). Be relating these abstract concepts to well-known images and stories, students can apparently comprehend complex operations. A study in Japan showed that students taught mathematics with the Yodai method learned significantly more than traditionally taught students (Machida and Carlson, 1984), and similar results were found in a study applying a form of Yodai mnemonics to the teaching of fractions to U.S. students (Kunihira et al., 1981).

Mnemonics
Strategies to improve memory

Imagery
Use of mental images to improve memory

Keyword Method
Strategy for improving memory by using images to link pairs of items

Yodai Mnemonics
A strategy, developed in Japan, to increase memory by use of vivid imagery, poems, and songs

Stimulus Selection
Choosing aspects of stimuli on which to focus attention

Stimulus Coding
Using aspects of stimuli and mental images to promote recall

Massed Practice
Technique in which facts or skills to be learned are repeated many times over a concentrated period of time

Distributed Practice
Technique in which items to be learned are repeated at intervals over a period of time

presenting the word pairs in List A in the same lesson would be a terrible instructional strategy. Students would be likely to confuse the three Spanish words because of their similar spellings. Rather, students should be completely familiar with one word pair before the next is introduced.

Stimulus selection is a process by which students learning paired associates choose a particular aspect of the stimulus to pay attention to. For example, students may principally pay attention to the first letters of words or to their order on the list. These shortcuts may help them learn a list of paired associates, but will be of little use when the words are presented out of order or in different contexts. Stimulus selection has been demonstrated in pigeons, who were taught to peck when they were shown blue triangles and not peck when they saw red circles. Some pigeons focused on the color, and would peck in response to any blue shape. Others focused on the shape, and pecked in response to any triangle. None, however, focused on both attributes of the blue triangle.

Stimulus coding is a related process in which students may connect a particular image or other association with a stimulus. For example, a student might remember *caballo* means "horse" by thinking of a horse pulling a cab. Stimulus coding is used in many strategies for remembering paired associates.

Finally, students learn the associations between the various stimuli. Methods for making these associations effectively are discussed in the following section.

Serial and Free-Recall Learning

Serial learning is learning facts in a particular order. Learning events on a timeline, the order of operations in long division, or the relative hardnesses of minerals are examples of serial learning. Free-recall learning is learning a list of items that need not be remembered in order, such as the names of the nine Supreme Court justices or the six major exports of New Zealand.

One important thing about learning lists, as in serial and free-recall learning, is that items near the beginning and end of the list are more easily remembered than those in the middle. If, for example, we wished to teach the names of various parts of the body, it would be important to go over the list several times, varying the order of presentation, so that each body part appeared in a different place on the list each time.

Practice

The most common method for committing information to memory is also the most mundane—practice. Does practice make perfect?

Practice is important at several stages of learning. As noted earlier in this chapter, information received in short-term memory must be mentally rehearsed if it is to be retained for more than a few seconds. The information in short-term memory must usually be practiced until it is established in long-term memory.

Massed versus Distributed Practice. Is it better to practice newly learned information intensively until it is thoroughly learned **(massed practice)** or to practice a little each day over a period of time **(distributed practice)**? Massed practice allows for faster initial learning, but for most kinds of learning, distributed practice is better for retention, even over short time periods. This is especially true of factual learning (see, for example, Ash, 1950); "cramming" factual information the night before a test may get you through that test, but the information probably won't be well integrated into

ORGANIZATION

For much serial and free-recall learning, the best memory strategy is to organize the list to be learned into meaningful, easily remembered categories. This was demonstrated earlier in the example of the grocery list that could be organized into breakfast, lunch, and dinner, and then further broken down into recipes for particular foods. This strategy is discussed further in Chapter 6.

LOCI METHOD

Another mnemonic device, used by the ancient Greeks, employs imagery associated with a list of locations (see Anderson, 1980). In the **loci method** the student thinks of a very familiar set of locations, such as rooms in his or her own house, and then imagines each item on the list to be remembered in one specific location. Vivid or bizarre imagery is used to place the object in the location. Once the connections between room or other location and object are established, the learner can recall each place and its contents in order.

The same locations can be mentally "cleared" and used to memorize a different list. However, they would always be used in the same order to ensure that all items on the list were remembered.

PEGWORD METHOD

Yet another imagery method useful for ordered lists is called the **pegword method** (see Paivio, 1971). To use this mnemonic, the student might memorize a list of "pegwords" that rhyme with the numbers one to ten.

To use this method, the student creates mental images relating to items on the list to be learned with particular pegwords. For example, in learning the order of the first ten U.S. presidents, we might picture George Washington eating a bun (one) with his wooden teeth, John Adams tying his shoe (two), Thomas Jefferson hanging by his knees from a branch of a tree (three), and so on.

RHYMING

A very old and quite effective technique for enhancing memory is rhyming. Most of us depend on rhymes such as:

- Thirty days hath September . . .
- "i" before "e" except after "c" . . .
- When two vowels go walking, the first one does the talking.
- In fourteen hundred ninety-two Columbus sailed the ocean blue.
- A B C D E F G
  H I J K L M N O P . . .

Rhymes, songs, and catchy phrases are so effective that we often remember them long after we have forgotten what they refer to. For example, most Americans would recognize most of the following sayings:

- Tippecanoe and Tyler too!
- It's a long way to Tipperary . . .
- Fifty-four forty or fight!
- We are marching to Pretoria . . .
- Damn the torpedoes, full speed ahead!
- Remember the *Maine!*

However, how many of us know who or what Tippecanoe was? (William Henry Harrison, hero of the Battle of Tippecanoe and ninth president of the United States.) Where is Tipperary? (Ireland.) A rapid, nonscientific poll of a half-dozen Ph.D.'s revealed that all of them knew these sayings but few had any idea what they referred to. This illustrates the power of rhymes and sayings to stay with us beyond any reasonable use.

INITIAL-LETTER STRATEGIES

One memory strategy related to organization is taking initial letters of a list to be memorized and making a more easily remembered word or phrase. For example, many trigonometry classes have learned about the imaginary SOH CAH TOA tribe, whose letters help recall: sine = opposite/hypotenuse; cosine = adjacent/hypotenuse; tangent = opposite/adjacent. A strategy for learning from text developed by Dansereau (1985) goes by the catchy title MURDER, for *m*ood, *u*nderstand, *r*ecall, *d*etect, elaborate, and *r*eview (this strategy is discussed in Chapter 6). Gage and Berliner (1984) give the following mnemonic for remembering the order of planets going away from the sun: *M*en *v*ery *e*asily *m*ake *j*ugs *s*erve *u*seful *n*octurnal *p*urposes, for Mercury, Venus, Earth, and so on. To help students remember the steps in long division (estimate, divide, multiply, subtract, compare, bring down) you might try the following mnemonic: *E*very *d*ay *M*artha *s*ees *c*ute *b*oys.

Loci Method
Strategy for remembering lists by picturing items in familiar locations

Pegword Method
Strategy for memorization in which images are used to link lists of facts to a familiar set of words or numbers

Part Learning
Mastering a new material by learning it one part or subskill at a time

Overlearning
Method of improving retention by practicing new knowledge or behaviors after mastery is achieved

This high school orchestra member would probably learn her part best by practicing each day rather than by practicing for long periods of time infrequently.

your long-term memory. Long-term retention of all kinds of information and skills is greatly enhanced by distributed practice. This is the primary purpose of homework (see Chapter 8)—to provide practice on newly learned skills over an extended period of time in order to increase the chances that the skills will be retained.

Part Learning.   It is very difficult for most people to learn a long list all at once. Rather, it is easier to break the list down into smaller lists. This is called **part learning.** Its effectiveness explains why teachers teaching multiplication facts, for example, first have students master the twos table, then the threes, and so on. Note that this strategy helps reduce retroactive inhibition, as the earlier partial lists are thoroughly learned before the next partial list is introduced.

Overlearning.   As noted earlier, one of the most important indicators of long-term retention of information or skills is how well they were learned in the first place. If students practice just long enough to learn something and then do no more, they are likely to forget much of what they have learned. However, if they continue to practice beyond the point where they can recall the answers, retention will increase. This strategy is called **overlearning.** For example, Krueger (1929) had students learn a list of words until they could recite the list with no errors. Then some students were asked to engage in overlearning, to keep practicing the list for an amount of time equal to what it took them to learn the list originally. Four days after the experiment these

What tricks or strategies have you taught students to help them memorize specific facts?

Paul Hashem, who teaches sixth grade in Lackawanna, N.Y., suggests an initial-letter strategy for remembering the order of the planets from the sun. The planets, in order, are Mercury, Venus, Earth, Mars, Jupiter, Saturn, Uranus, Neptune, and Pluto. Students are taught the following sentence, in which the first letters of the words are the first letters of the planets in order: *My very educated mother just served us nine pizzas.*

Camille Caldemeyer, Princeton, Ind., uses a similar strategy to help her fourth-grade students remember the five Great Lakes. The word "homes" contains the first letter of each lake: *Huron, Ontario, Michigan, Erie,* and *Superior.*

Ralph Westenberger, who teaches grades 9–12 in Louisville, Ala., helps students remember how to convert percentages to decimals by relying on their familiarity with the alphabet. He tells them that in changing from *percent* to *decimal*, the decimal is moved to the left (two places) because in going from *p* to *d* in the alphabet, you move to the left. In changing from *decimal* to *percent*, the decimal point is moved to the right because in going from *d* to *p* in the alphabet, you move right.

Mary Dow, Columbus, Ohio, uses words within words to help her fifth-grade students remember that in the pair of words "concave" and "convex"—one of which refers to things that are dished and the other to things that bulge—it is con*cave* that means in, because *caves* go in.

Grayce Dady, who teaches special education in Herkimer, N.Y., uses rhymes—"the more absurd the better"—to help students remember multiplication facts. One of her favorites goes like this:

I ate and ate and got sick on the floor
Eight times eight equals sixty-four.

The rhymes, she says, should be presented with gusto and expression, and they will never be forgotten.

Gretchen L. Powers, who teaches fourth grade in Lynnville, Ind., helps students remember the directions west and east by noting that the first letters of each word spells WE—*West* on the left and *East* on the right, just as on a standard map.

students retained six times as many words as were retained by the students who did not engage in overlearning. By the twenty-eighth day, the non-overlearning group had forgotten all the words, while the overlearning group still had a few.

Overlearning has only a few important applications in instructional practice. It is useful for drilling information that must be accurately recalled for a long time but has little meaning. The prime example of a learning task suitable for overlearning is memorization of multiplication facts, which students should be able to recall automatically and without error. Overlearning of multiplication facts is often accomplished by the regular use of speed drills, mental arithmetic (for example, "Class: What is four times seven minus three divided by five times nine?"), or games. Spelling lists may also be overlearned, particularly for frequently missed words that do not follow regular spelling rules.

■ **Stop and Think**

The first chapter of this book noted that research on learning should be scrutinized for its applicability to real-life situations and to the classroom. With this in mind, consider the relevance of memory strategies to teaching and learning. Would these strategies be useful in a first-grade classroom? In a junior high school Spanish class? In a college-level biology course? How would you adapt these strategies for (1) whole-class instruction or (2) independent study?

Two eleventh grade U.S. history teachers, Tim Baker and George Kowalski, sit talking in George's classroom after school. Tim has taught seven years and George twenty-one years at Garfield High School, the home of the Purple Eagles, the current state high school basketball champions. Tim and George are both members of the Social Studies Department's curriculum committee which is in the process of revising the U.S. history course.

TIM: It really is wonderful to be teaching at a high school with the kind of school spirit we have here at G.H.S.!

GEORGE: Well, having won the state basketball championship twice in the last ten years hasn't hurt any! Not to mention the number of times that Coach Billingsly has gotten us into the finals! Do you realize we were among the top four teams each year in the '80s except 1983 and 1986?

TIM: (smiling) You're very good with facts like that, George, which brings me to the point of our meeting. I think that you and I are the polar extremes on the curriculum committee, and our differences might be the cause of the committee's split. I thought that if we tried to understand and resolve our differences maybe the committee could begin to make progress again.

GEORGE: Well said, Tim, but our disagreement is so fundamental that I'm not sure how we can resolve it. As I see it, you contend that students first need to understand the facts of U.S. History before they can move on to higher order thinking like problem-solving and abstract thought. My contention is just the reverse. We've taught students facts for generations and they forget them right after the test is over. That's because we don't ask them to use the facts in higher order thought. To me, the only way you can learn to think abstractly and solve problems is to try to do so.

TIM: But, George, trying to think abstractly and solve problems in any field must be based on a command of the knowledge in that field. Otherwise, problem solving is a pointless exercise that really amounts to a sharing of ignorance among the uninformed. You've got to learn the fundamentals of the game of basketball before you are capable of executing the complex offensive and defensive plays that Coach Billingsly demands of his players.

GEORGE: No doubt about that, Tim, but that isn't the problem. The problem is never giving the players the opportunity to go beyond the fundamentals. And that's what you do when you stick to lecture and discussion teaching methods and objective multiple-choice and matching tests, with a few short answer items thrown in on the key persons, dates, terms, and events in American history!

TIM: I know that you use a lot of small group and independent study work in your classes and give essay type tests. I remember hearing some students talk about how a couple of your questions really "blew their minds." I believe one was: "What would the United States be like today if the South had won

SUMMARY AND REVIEW OF OBJECTIVES

Components of Memory. The three major components of memory are the sensory register, short-term memory, and long-term memory. The sensory registers are very-short-term memories linked to the senses. Information received by the senses but not attended to will be quickly forgotten. Once information is received, it is processed by the mind in accord with our experiences and mental states. This activity is called perception.

Short-term memory is a storage system that holds five to seven bits of information at any one time. Information enters short-term memory from both the sensory register and the long-term memory. Rehearsal is the process of repeating information in order to hold it in short-term memory.

Long-term memory is the part of the memory system in which a large amount of the Civil War?" The other was: "Why do some Americans refer to the Civil War as the 'War Between the States'?"

GEORGE: (chuckling) Yes, that stirred them up a bit!

TIM: But, George, believe it or not, I've asked my students to write on those two questions from time to time when we're on the Civil War and their answers were terrible! The answers were totally devoid of facts. The kids just wrote their opinions.

GEORGE: But Tim, that's my point! Students have to learn how to use facts—how to organize them and incorporate them into their answers. A basketball player will look terrible the first time he tries a slam-dunk. But, after he learns the technique, it looks easy—and beautiful!

TIM: I can't disagree with you there, George, but I do disagree with you on strategy. Learning the facts is the first step and higher order thinking follows. As I see it, you do the reverse. You begin with higher order thinking by posing problems and questions and hope that the kids will learn the facts to answer the questions. That seems pretty haphazard and risky, like throwing a kid into a lake and asking him to swim.

GEORGE: Tim, the facts and fundamentals are important, but how long are they going to stick with the students if you just drill and test them on the facts? But if you force them to determine and use the facts, they'll remember them long after the test. As I re-call, kids usually forget the facts they cram before an objective test within 48 hours. With my course I'll bet some of the things they've learned are still with them when they're adults and citizens in our society.

TIM: But don't forget, George, our kids have to take objective-type standardized tests that may well determine whether or not they get to college or not. Then, when they're in college, they'll get a chance to do a lot of the higher order thinking that you're talking about.

GEORGE: Well, Tim, I guess we're just at an impasse. I just don't see any way we can reconcile our two positions. Do you?

QUESTIONS

1. How do Tim and George's positions differ on the nature of information processing, memory, and forgetting?
2. What learning strategies are most effective in facilitating the storage, processing, and recall of different types of information? What teaching methods and evaluation procedures seem most compatible with these learning strategies?
3. If you were settling the argument for Tim and George, what advice would you give them from the standpoint of cognitive learning theory? Is there a best way to teach U.S. History so that students not only remember what they have learned but are also able to process the information to answer higher-order questions and later apply it in everyday living?

information is stored for an indefinite time period. Cognitive theories of learning stress the importance of helping students relate information being learned to existing information in long-term memory.

Parts of Long-Term Memory. The three parts of long-term memory are episodic memory, which stores our memories of personal experiences; semantic memory, which stores facts and generalized knowledge in the form of schemata; and procedural memory, which stores knowledge of how to do things. Schemata are networks of related ideas that guide our understanding and action. Information that fits into a well-developed schema is easier to learn than information that cannot be so accommodated.

Remembering and Forgetting. Levels-of-processing theory suggests that learners will remember those things that they process. Students are processing information when they manipulate it, look at it from different perspectives, and analyze it. Dual code theory further suggests the importance of using both visual and verbal coding to learn bits of information.

Interference theory helps explain why we forget. It suggests that students can get confused by—and forget—pieces of similar information. Interference theory states that two situations produce forgetting: proactive inhibition, when learning one task interferes with the retention of tasks learned later; and retroactive inhibition, when learning a second task makes a person forget something learned previously.

Memory Strategies. Teachers can help students remember facts by presenting lessons in an organized way and by teaching students to use memory strategies called mnemonics. Three types of verbal learning are paired-associate learning, serial learning, and free-recall learning.

Paired-associate learning is learning to respond with one member of a pair when given the other member. It involves stimulus discrimination, stimulus selection, and stimulus coding. Students can improve their learning of paired associates by using imagery techniques such as the keyword method.

Serial learning involves recalling a list of items in a specified order, whereas free-recall learning involves recalling the list in any order. Helpful strategies are organization, the loci method, the pegword method, rhyming, and stimulus selection.

Practice. Practice is important to help strengthen associations of newly learned information in memory. Distributed practice, which involves practicing parts of the task over a period of time, is usually preferred over massed practice. Automatization is the process by which tasks require less attention as they become well learned. Skills can become automatic through practice.

STUDY QUESTIONS

1. Which of the following statements about Gestalt psychology is true?
   a. It was developed in the early 1800s in Russia
   b. One of its key principles was schema theory
   c. One of its leading theorists was Tulving
   d. It dealt with how we mentally perceive stimuli
   e. It rejected the principle of closure in favor of a passive model of information processing

2. Sperling's study involving the recall of very briefly displayed letters illustrated the limitations of
   a. long-term memory
   b. short-term memory
   c. rehearsal and coding
   d. retrieval processes
   e. the sensory register

3. Match the following memory components with the characteristics that describe each:
   ____ Episodic memory
   ____ Semantic memory
   ____ Short-term memory
   ____ Sensory register

   a. The memory component from which information is most easily lost
   b. Component in which virtually unlimited amounts of general information can be stored in networks of related schemata
   c. Component that processes new information and also old information that has been brought to consciousness
   d. Storage system in which memories of experiences can be stored for a lifetime

4. A middle-aged college instructor has not played basketball in over 25 years. After agreeing to play for his department in an intramural competition, he finds that many of his old moves and skills quickly return. Which type of memory is most directly involved?
   a. Episodic
   b. Procedural
   c. Semantic
   d. Short-term

5. Which of the following teaching strategies would *not* be recommended for reducing retroactive inhibition?
   a. Be consistent in the methods used when teaching similar concepts

b. Teach one concept thoroughly before introducing the next one

c. Use mnemonic devices to point out differences between the concepts

d. Teach the concepts at different times, such as in separate class periods.

6. A student who has trouble remembering the location of the African countries Ghana and Guinea after learning about the South American country of Guyana has fallen prey to _____ inhibition. Conversely, a student who has trouble learning how to spell "guerrilla" after having earlier learned to spell "gorilla" is being hindered by _____ inhibition.

7. Match the following types of learning tasks with a correct example of each.

_D_ Paired-associate
_A_ Serial
_C_ Free recall

a. Memorizing the names of the world's continents in order by size

b. Paraphrasing each of a series of sentences

c. Memorizing the names, functions, and locations of the major organs in the human body

d. Learning that a group of geese is a gaggle, a group of lions is a pride, a group of birds is a flight, and a group of quails is a bevy

8. Match the following learning tasks with the most appropriate memory strategy:

_B_ Paired-associate
_C_ Serial
_A_ Free recall

a. Loci or pegword method
b. Keyword method
c. Rhyming method

9. Which section(s) of a list of words is/are likely to be most difficult to learn?

a. Middle only
b. Beginning and end
c. Beginning only
d. Middle and end
e. End only

Answers: 1. d 2. c 3. d, b, c 4. b 5. a 6. retroactive, proactive 7. d, a, c 8. b, c, a 9. a.

SUGGESTED READINGS

ANDERSON, J. R. (1985). *Cognitive psychology and its implications* (2nd ed.) San Francisco: Freeman.

ANDERSON, R. C., SPIRO R. J., and MONTAGUE, W. E. (Eds.). (1977). *Schooling and the acquisition of knowledge*. Hillsdale, N.J.: Erlbaum.

BELLEZA, F. S. (1981). Mnemonic devices: Classification, characteristics, and criteria. *Review of Educational Research, 51,* 247–275.

BRANSFORD, J. D. (1979). *Human cognition: Learning, understanding, and remembering*. Belmont, Cal.: Wadsworth.

LEVIN, J. R. (1981). The mnemonic 80's: Keywords in the classroom. *Educational Psychologist, 16,* 65–82.

LOFTUS, E. (1980). *Memory*. Reading, Mass.: Addison-Wesley.

McKEAN, K. (1983, November). Memory. *Discover Magazine,* 19–28.

PRESSLEY, M., and LEVIN, J. (Eds.). (1984). *Cognitive strategy research: I. Educational Applications*. New York: Springer-Verlag.

PRESSLEY, M., ET AL. (1989). The challenges of classroom strategy instruction. *Elementary School Journal, 89,* 301–342.

SIEGLER, R. S. (1986). *Children's thinking*. Englewood Cliffs, N. J.: Prentice-Hall.

SYLWESTER, R. (1985). Research on memory: Major discoveries, major educational challenges. *Educational Leadership, 42,* 69–75.

Chapter 6

Meaningful Learning: The Cognitive Perspective

Chapter Objectives

After reading this chapter you should be able to:

- Use advance organizers.
- Use and teach three strategies for understanding and remembering material in textbooks.
- Teach concepts and problem solving.
- Use both discovery and reception learning.

Consider the following sentences:

1. Enso flrs hmen matn snoi teha erso iakt siae otin tnes esna nrae.
2. Easier that nonsense information to makes than sense is learn.
3. Information that makes sense is easier to learn than nonsense.

Which sentence is easiest to learn and remember? Obviously, Sentence 3. All three sentences have the same letters, and Sentences 2 and 3 have the same words. Yet to learn Sentence 1, we would have to memorize fifty-two separate letters, and to learn Sentence 2, we would have to learn ten separate words. Sentence 3 is easiest because to learn it, we need only learn one concept, a concept that readily fits our common sense and prior knowledge about how learning takes place. We know the individual words, we know the grammar that connects them, and we already have in our minds a vast store of information, experiences, and thoughts about the same topic. For these reasons, Sentence 3 slides smoothly into our understanding.

MAKING INFORMATION MEANINGFUL

The message in Sentence 3 is what this chapter is all about. Most human learning, particularly school learning, involves making sense out of information, sorting it in our minds until it fits in a neat and orderly way, and using old information to help assimilate new learning. We have limited ability to recall rote information—how many telephone numbers can you remember for a month? However, we can retain meaningful information far more easily. Recall that most of the mnemonic strategies discussed in the previous chapter involve adding artificial "meaning" to arbitrary associations in order to take advantage of the much greater ease of learning meaningful information.

The message in Sentence 3 has profound implications for instruction. One of the teacher's most important tasks is to make information meaningful to students, by presenting it in a clear, organized way, by relating it to information already in students' minds, and by making sure that students have truly understood the concepts being taught and can apply them to new situations.

Rote and Meaningful Learning

Ausubel (1961) discussed the distinction between rote learning and meaningful learning. **Rote learning** refers to the memorization of facts or associations, such as the multiplication tables, the chemical symbols for the elements, words in foreign languages, or the names of bones and muscles in the human body. Much of rote learning involves associations that are essentially arbitrary. For example, the chemical symbol for gold (Au) could just as well have been Go or Gd. In contrast, **meaningful learning** is not arbitrary, and it relates to information or concepts learners already have. For example, if we learn that silver is an excellent conductor of electricity, this information relates to our existing information about silver and about electrical conductivity. Further, the association between "silver" and "electrical conductivity" is not arbitrary. Silver really is an excellent conductor, and while we could state the same principle in many ways or in any language, the *meaning* of the statement "Silver is an excellent conductor of electricity" could not be arbitrarily changed.

Inert Knowledge
Learned information that can be applied only to a restricted, often artificial, set of circumstances

When students memorize words and information, they sometimes do so by rote, without learning the information's meaning and context. An important task for teachers is to make information meaningful to students.

We sometimes get the impression that rote learning is "bad," meaningful learning "good." This is not necessarily true. For example, when the doctor tells us we have a fractured tibia, we hope the doctor has mastered the rote association between the word "tibia" and the leg bone it names. Foreign language vocabulary is an important case of rote learning. However, rote learning has gotten a bad name in education because it is overused; we can all remember being taught to parrot facts that were supposed to be meaningful, but that we were forced to learn as rote, meaningless information. William James, in a book called *Talks to Teachers on Psychology* (1912), gave an excellent example of this kind of false learning:

> A friend of mine, visiting a school, was asked to examine a young class in geography. Glancing at the book, she said: "Suppose you should dig a hole in the ground, hundreds of feet deep, how should you find it at the bottom—warmer or colder than on top?" None of the class replying, the teacher said: "I'm sure they know, but I think you don't ask the question quite rightly. Let me try." So, taking the book, she asked: "In what condition is the interior of the globe?" and received the immediate answer from half the class at once. "The interior of the globe is in a condition of igneous fusion." (James, 1912, p. 150)

Clearly, the students had memorized the information without learning its meaning. The information was useless to them because it did not tie in with other information they had.

The Case of the Inert Knowledge.   The "igneous fusion" information that students had memorized in the class James's friend visited is an example of what Bransford et al. (1968a) call **inert knowledge.** This is knowledge that could and should be applicable to a wide range of situations but is only applied to a restricted set of circumstances. Usually, inert knowledge is information or skills learned in school that we cannot apply in life. For example, we all know people who could pass an advanced French test but would be unable to communicate in Paris, or who can solve volume problems in math class but have no idea how much sand to order to fill a sandbox. Many problems in life arise not from a lack of knowledge, but from an inability to use the knowledge we already have.

An interesting experiment by Perfetto et al. (1983) illustrates the concept of inert knowledge. In it, college students were given problems such as the following:

> Uriah Fuller, the famous Israeli superpsychic, can tell you the score of any baseball game *before* the game starts. What is his secret?

> A man living in a small town in the United States married twenty different women in the same town. All are still living and he has never divorced any of them. Yet he has broken no law. Can you explain?

Before seeing the problems, some of the students were given a list of sentences to memorize that were clearly useful in solving the problems; among the sentences were "Before it starts, the score of any game is 0 to 0," and "A minister marries several people each week." Students who were told to use the sentences in their memories as clues performed much better on the problem-solving task than did other students, but students who memorized the clues *but were not told to use them* did no better than students who never saw the clues! What this experiment tells us is that having information in our memory does not at all guarantee that we can bring it out and use it when appropriate. Rather, we need to know how and when to use the information we have.

Teachers can help students learn information in a way that will make it useful as well as meaningful to them. Effective teaching requires an understanding of how to make information *accessible* to students so that they can connect it to other information and apply it outside of the classroom.

Schema Theory and Meaningful Learning

As noted in Chapter 5, meaningful information is stored in long-term memory in networks of connected facts or concepts called schemata. Recall the representation of the concept "bison" presented in Figure 5.6, showing how this one concept was linked to a wide range of other concepts.

The most important principle of schema theory is that information that fits into an existing schema is more easily understood, learned, and retained than information that does not fit into an existing schema (Ausubel, 1968; Anderson and Bower, 1973; Rumelhart and Ortony, 1977). Chapter 5 used the sentence "Bison calves can run soon after they are born" as an example of information that would be easily incorporated into our "bison" schema because we know that (1) bison rely on speed to escape from predators, and (2) more familiar animals (such as horses) that also rely on speed have babies that can run very early. Without all this prior knowledge, "Bison calves can run soon after they are born" would be more difficult to mentally assimilate and easily forgotten. In fact, think back to another example in Chapter 5. Do you remember what special ability loris babies are born with? If you are like most people, you will have to use more mental effort to recall that loris babies have strong grasping reflexes than to recall that bison calves can run soon after their birth, because you probably have a much better-developed schema for bison.

It is thought that most well-developed schemata are organized in hierarchies similar to outlines, with specific information grouped under general categories, which are grouped under still more general categories. This is illustrated in Figure 6.1. Note that in moving from the top to the bottom of the figure, we are going from general

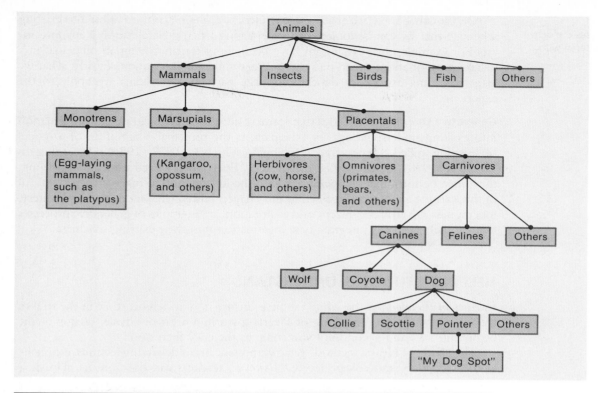

FIGURE 6.1

Example of a Knowledge Structure Arranged as a Hierarchy

A person who understands the place of a particular animal ("Spot") within the animal kingdom might have that information arranged in memory as shown here.

From Royer and Feldman, 1984, p. 225.

(animals) to specific (my dog Spot). The concepts in Figure 6.1 are well "anchored" in the schema (Ausubel, 1963). Any new information relating to this schema will probably be learned and incorporated into the schema much more readily than would information relating to less established schemata or rote learning that does not attach to any schema.

One important insight of schema theory is that meaningful learning requires the active involvement of the learner, who has a host of prior experiences and knowledge to bring to understanding and incorporating new information. For example, consider the following vignette (from Andre, 1984):

> A man goes into a building, he picks up a loaf, he walks to a counter, he picks up his change. He leaves.

What was this story about? You probably thought it was about buying bread in a grocery store. In your mind's eye you probably saw the store, the way the bread was lined up on the shelves, a cash register, and a clerk, none of which were mentioned. However, key words in the story ("loaf," "counter," "change") attach it to all the familiar information about stores and buying bread that already exists in your long-term memory. Just as you could readily perceive the circle, square, and triangle in Figure 5.3 even though they were incomplete, so could you fill in all the details of the bread-buying expedition from your memory.

On the other hand, we are so good at incorporating new information into existing schemata that we can be fooled into generalizing when generalization is inappropriate. For example, the story might have been about a man buying an olive loaf in a delicatessen, or about a man picking up a lazy child at a gas station. Clearly, what we learn from any experience depends in large part on the schema we apply to the experience.

Generative Learning. The idea that learners must actively integrate new information into existing understandings, or schemata, is the principal assumption of a model of learning called **"generative learning"** (Wittrock, 1978, 1986). According to Wittrock (1978), all learning is "discovered." Even when we tell students something, they must perform mental operations with the information to make it their own. All of the learning strategies discussed in this chapter and in Chapter 5, such as imagery, mnemonics, advance organizers, and elaboration, are examples of generative processes that can help students integrate new information into their existing schemata.

HELPING STUDENTS UNDERSTAND

In *Alice in Wonderland* the white rabbit is unsure how to tell his story in the trial of the Knave of Hearts. The King of Hearts gives him a bit of advice: "Begin at the beginning . . . and go on until you come to the end: then stop."

The "King of Hearts method" is a common means of delivering lectures, especially at the secondary and college levels. However, teachers can do more to help their students understand lessons. They can prepare students to learn new material by reminding them of what they already know, they can use questions, and they can help students link and recall new information.

Many aspects of effective lesson presentation are covered in Chapter 8, but the following sections discuss practices derived from cognitive psychology that can help students understand, recall, and apply essential information, concepts, and skills.

Advance Organizers

Read the following passage.

> With the hocked gems financing him our hero bravely defied all scornful laughter that tried to prevent his scheme. Your eyes deceive he had said. An egg, not a table, correctly typifies this unexplored planet. Now three sturdy sisters sought proof. Forging along, sometimes through calm vastness, yet more often through turbulent peaks and valleys, days became weeks as many doubters spread fearful rumors about the edge. At last, from nowhere, welcome winged creatures appeared signifying momentous success. (Dooling and Lachman, 1971, p. 217)

Now read the paragraph again with the following information: the passage is about Christopher Columbus.

Before you knew what the passage was about, it probably made little sense to you. You could understand the words and grammar, and could probably infer that the story involved a voyage of discovery. However, once you learned that the story was about Columbus, you could bring all your prior knowledge about Columbus to bear on comprehending the paragraph, so that seemingly obscure references made sense. The "hocked gems" (Queen Isabella's jewelry), the egg (the shape of the earth), the three sturdy sisters *(Niña, Pinta, Santa Maria),* and the winged creatures (birds) become comprehensible when we know what the story is about.

In terms of schema theory, advance information that the story concerns Columbus activates our schema relating to Columbus. We are ready to receive and incorporate information relating to Columbus, to Isabella and Ferdinand, and to the ships. It is as though we had a filing cabinet with a drawer labeled "Columbus." When we know we are about to hear about Columbus, we mentally open the drawer, which contains files marked "Isabella," "ships," and "scoffers and doubters." We are now ready to file new information in the proper places. If we learned that the *Santa Maria* was wrecked in a storm, we would mentally file that information under "ships." If we learned that most of the educated world agreed with Columbus that the earth was round, we would file that information under "scoffers and doubters." The file drawer analogy is not completely appropriate, however, because the "files" of a schema are all logically connected with one another. Also, we are actively using the information in our "files" to interpret and organize the new information.

David Ausubel (1960, 1963) developed a means called **advance organizers** to orient students to material they were about to learn and to help them recall related information that could be used to assist in incorporating the new information. An advance organizer is an initial statement about a subject to be learned that provides a structure for the new information and relates it to information students already possess. For example, in one study (Ausubel and Youssef, 1963) college students were assigned to read a passage on Buddhism. Before reading the passage, some students were given an advance organizer comparing Buddhism to Christianity, while others read an unrelated passage. The students who were given the advance organizer retained much more of the material than did the other students. Ausubel and Youssef maintained that the reason for this was that the advance organizer activated the students' knowledge of Christianity and the students were able to use that knowledge to incorporate information about a less familiar religion.

Many studies have established that advance organizers increase students' understanding of certain kinds of material (see, for example, Hartley and Davies, 1976; Lawton and Wanska, 1977; Mayer, 1979). Advance organizers seem to be most useful for teaching content that has a well-organized structure that may not be immediately apparent to students. However, they have not generally been found to help students learn factual information that does not lend itself to a clear organization, or subjects that consist of a large number of separate topics (Barnes and Clawson, 1975; Ausubel, 1978).

In addition, methods that activate prior knowledge (such as advance organizers) can be counterproductive if the prior knowledge is weak or lacking (Alvermann, 1985). If students know little about Christianity, relating Buddhism to Christianity might confuse rather than help them.

Advance Organizers
General statements given before instruction that relate new information to existing knowledge

Advance Organizers In Action

Here is an example of a helpful advance organizer:

> A docent (teacher-guide) beginning a tour of an art museum with a group of high school students says, "I want to give you an idea that will help you understand the paintings and sculpture we are about to see. The idea is simply that art, although it is a personal expression, reflects in many ways the culture and times in which it was produced. This may seem obvious to you at first when you look at the differences between Oriental and Western art. However, it is also true that, within each culture, as the culture changes, so the art will change—and that is why we can speak of *periods* of art. The changes are often reflected in the artists' techniques, subject matter, colors, and style. Major changes are often reflected in the forms of art that are produced." The guide then points out examples of one or two changes in these characteristics. She also

asks the students to recall their elementary school days and the differences in their drawings when they were five and six, and when they were older. She likens the different periods of growing up to different cultures.

In the tour that follows, as the students look at paintings and sculpture, the docent points out to them the differences that result from changing times. "Do you see here," she says, "how in this painting the body of the person is almost completely covered by his robes, and there is no hint of a human inside his clothes? In medieval times, the church taught that the body was unimportant and that the soul was everything." Later she remarks, "You see in this painting how the muscularity of the man stands out through his clothing and how he stands firmly on the earth. This represents the Renaissance view that man was at the center of the universe and that his body, mind, and his power were very important indeed." (Joyce and Weil, 1980, p. 75)

Note that the guide first gave her students an organizing framework for understanding the paintings they were about to see: Art reflects aspects of the culture and times in which it was produced. She also related the concept of periods in art history to the students' own experiences by reminding them of how their own artwork changed over time. Thus the guide activated prior knowledge and provided an organizational schema into which information on the paintings themselves would fit. Finally, when the students actually saw some paintings and sculpture, the guide pointed out particulars that related to the schema she had presented earlier.

The use of advance organizers is discussed further in Chapter 8.

Analogies.   Like advance organizers, use of explanatory analogies can contribute to an understanding of the lessons or the text. For example, a teacher could introduce a lesson on the human body's disease-fighting mechanism by telling students to imagine a battle and to consider it as an analogy for the body's fight against infection. Similarly, a teacher could preface a lesson on termite societies by asking students to think of the hierarchy of citizens within a kingdom, using that as an analogy for such insect societies. Such analogies can help students learn new information by relating it to concepts they already have (Vosniadou and Schommer, 1988; Genter, 1989).

Organization of Information

Recall the shopping list presented in Chapter 5. When the list was presented in random order, it was very difficult to memorize, partly because it contained too many items to be held in short-term memory all at once. However, when the list was organized in a logical way, it was meaningful and therefore easy to learn and remember. The specific foods were grouped in familiar recipes (for example, flour, eggs, and milk were grouped under "pancakes"), the recipes and other foods were grouped under "food," "beverage," or "dessert," and these were in turn grouped under "breakfast," "lunch," and "dinner."

Material that is well organized is much easier to learn and remember than material that is poorly organized. Hierarchical organization, in which specific issues are grouped under more general topics, seems particularly helpful for student understanding (Van Patten et al., 1986). For example, in a study by Bower et al. (1969), one group of students was taught 112 words relating to minerals in random order. Another group was taught the same words, but in a definite order. Figure 6.2 shows some of the words organized in a hierarchy. The students were taught the words at levels 1 and 2 in the first of four sessions, those at levels 1, 2, and 3 in the second session, and levels 1–4 in the third and fourth sessions. The students in this second group recalled an average of 100 words, in comparison to only 65 for the group

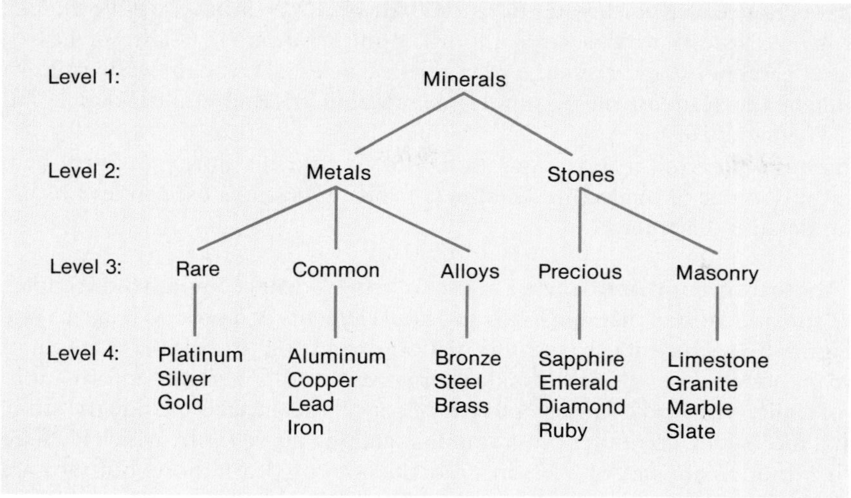

Mathemagenic Behaviors
Strategies, such as previewing
material, that help people learn

FIGURE 6.2

The Hierarchical Structure for Minerals
From Bower et al., 1969.

receiving the random presentation, demonstrating the effectiveness of a coherent, organized presentation.

In teaching complex concepts, it is not only necessary that material be well organized; it is also important that the organizing framework itself be made clear to students (Shimmerlick, 1978). For example, a teacher might introduce *reception learning* (discussed later in this chapter) as follows:

"Now we will discuss reception learning, one application of cognitive theories of learning."

Also, when introducing a new topic, it might be helpful to make the transition from one topic to another clear, as follows:

"So far we have discussed reception learning. Now let's turn to discovery learning, another application of cognitive theories of learning."

Questions

One strategy that helps students learn from written texts, lectures, and other sources of information is the insertion of questions, so that students must stop from time to time to assess their own understanding of what the text or teacher is saying.

Rothkopf (1965) proposed that questions could influence what he called **mathemagenic behavior.** Mathemagenic behavior is any behavior, either internal or external, that helps a person learn. These behaviors include looking at or listening to something to be learned, and relating new information to information in memory. In one study Rothkopf compared the performance of groups that received questions to that of groups that did not. It was clear that students learned material better when they were asked a question about it during instruction than when they were not. Later research on questions inserted in texts (see Rickards, 1979; Crooks, 1988) has tended to support Rothkopf's theory.

However, questions presented *before* the introduction of the instructional material can help students learn material related to the questions but hinder them in learning material that is not related to the questions (Hamilton, 1985; Hamaker, 1986). The solution is to ask questions about *all* important information. In addition, factual questions that paraphrase, rather than repeat, the instructional text help students learn the meaning of the text instead of simply memorizing it (Andre and Sola, 1976; Andre and Womack, 1978).

Like questions inserted in texts, questions put to students during lectures help them learn the content of the lecture (Berliner, 1968). Questions used in lessons are discussed in detail in Chapter 8.

Models.   Another means that teachers can use to help students comprehend complex topics is the introduction of diagrams showing how elements of a process relate to one another. Figure 5.1, which illustrates information processing, is a classic example of a conceptual model. Use of such models organizes and integrates information. Examples of topics that lend themselves to use of conceptual models include the study of electricity, mechanics, computer programming, and the processes by which laws are passed. When models are part of a lesson, students not only learn more, but they are also better able to apply their learning to creatively solve problems (see Mayer, 1989).

Elaboration

Elaboration is a term used by cognitive psychologists to refer to the process of thinking about material to be learned in a way that connects the material to information or ideas already in the learner's mind (Reigeluth, 1983). As an example of the importance of elaboration, Stein et al. (1984) conducted a series of experiments in which students were given lists of phrases to learn, such as "The gray-haired man carried the bottle." Some students were given the same phrases embedded in a more elaborated sentence: "The gray-haired man carried the bottle *of hair dye.*" These students recalled the phrases much better than did those who did not receive the elaboration because the additional words tied the phrase to a well-developed schema already in the students' minds. The connection between "gray-haired man" and "bottle" is arbitrary until we give it meaning by linking these words with the "hair dye" idea.

The principle that elaborated information is easier to understand and remember can be applied to helping students comprehend lessons. Students may be asked to think of connections between ideas, or to relate new concepts to their own lives. For example, it might help students to understand the U.S. annexation of Texas and California if they consider these events from the perspective of Mexicans, or if they compare them to a situation in which a friend borrows a seldom used bicycle, and then decides not to give it back.

In discussing a story or novel, students might be asked from time to time to stop and visualize what is happening or what's about to happen as a means of helping them elaborate their understanding of the material. Elaboration can be taught as a skill to help students comprehend what they read; for more on this, see the section on Metacognitive Strategies later in this chapter.

■ **Stop and Think**
Imagine yourself instructing a group of prospective teachers about techniques for increasing the meaningfulness of lessons. What statements could serve as an advance organizer for this topic? How would you organize the lesson, including in it the topics presented thus far in this chapter? What questions would you pose to students during the lesson?

1. Students sometimes need help to see the various applications of skills and knowledge learned in school. What activities or discussion topics have you used to show students practical uses for their knowledge of math, science, literature, and so forth?

Teachers offered many ideas for showing students the real-world applications of mathematics. These include

- setting up an in-class grocery store and giving students play money so they can practice adding, subtracting, and multiplying.
- giving students a mail-order catalog, a list of people to choose presents for, and a limit on the amount of money they can spend.
- having students prepare food, which involves understanding numbers and measurements in recipes and also telling time if the food has to be cooked
- showing students how to balance checkbooks

Two teachers offered ideas for demonstrating the usefulness of writing skills. Roseanne Swinburne-Sanderfoot, who teaches in Manawa, Wis., writes:

For my middle schoolers, it is easy to come up with real-life situations where we can use our acquired and soon-to-be acquired skills. We have entered contests where each student must submit an essay, and we have also written to companies for

"freebies" that are available to the consumer. In doing these things, we practice careful writing, good spelling, making complete sentences, and addressing envelopes. The possibility of a reward for our efforts makes it more exciting.

Nadine Brock, a third-grade teacher in Galloway, Ohio, says:

A practical way to do a communications unit is to let students put together a class newspaper to be shared with other classes and with parents. Students will write articles for the newspaper, and will learn its various parts.

2. Have you ever taught study strategies to your students? If so, please describe what you taught.

Audrey Sequin, who teaches elementary school in Alpena, Mich., writes:

I help students activate their prior knowledge before reading any material. This helps them better understand their reading. I then give them a purpose for reading the material.

I have also taught students a strategy known as K-W-L. They fill in worksheets on what they *Know* about a particular subject, what they *Want* to know about it, and, after reading about the subject, what they have *Learned* about it. This can also be used as an evaluation tool.

STUDY STRATEGIES

How are you reading this book? Are you underlining or highlighting key sentences? Are you taking notes or summarizing? Are you discussing the main ideas with a classmate? Are you putting the book under your pillow at night and hoping the information will somehow seep into your mind?

These and many other strategies have been used by students since the invention of reading, and have been studied almost as long; even Aristotle wrote on the topic. Yet educational psychologists are still debating which study strategies are most effective.

Underlining

Perhaps the most common study strategy is underlining or highlighting. Yet despite the widespread use of this method, research on it generally finds few benefits (Anderson and Armbruster, 1984; Snowman, 1984). The problem is that most students fail to make decisions about what material is most critical and simply underline too much. When students are asked to underline the *one* sentence in each paragraph that is most important, they do retain more, probably because deciding which is the most important sentence requires a higher level of processing (Snowman, 1984).

Note Taking

Another common study strategy used both in reading and in learning from lectures is note taking. This can be effective for certain types of material because it can require mental processing of main ideas; as in the case of underlining only one sentence per paragraph, note taking requires decisions about what to write. However, the effects of note taking have been found to be inconsistent. Positive effects are most likely when note taking is used with complex, conceptual material in which the critical task is to identify the main ideas (Anderson and Armbruster, 1984). Also, note taking that requires some mental processing is more effective than simply writing down what was read (Kiewra, 1985a, 1988). For example, Bretzing and Kulhavy (1979, 1981) found that writing paraphrase notes (stating the main ideas in different words) and taking notes in preparation to teach others the material were effective note-taking strategies because they required a high degree of mental processing of the information.

One apparently effective means of increasing the value of students' note taking is for the teacher to provide "skeletal" notes before a lecture or reading, giving students categories to direct their own note taking. Several studies have found that this practice, combined with student note taking and review, increases student learning (Kiewra, 1985b).

Summarizing.   Summarization involves writing brief statements that represent the main idea of the information being read. The effectiveness of this strategy depends on how it is used (Hidi and Anderson, 1986). One effective way is to have students write

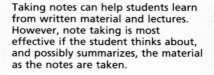

Taking notes can help students learn from written material and lectures. However, note taking is most effective if the student thinks about, and possibly summarizes, the material as the notes are taken.

one-sentence summaries after reading each paragraph (Doctorow et al., 1978). Another is to have students prepare summaries intended to help others learn the material, partly because this activity forces the summarizer to be brief and to seriously consider what is important and what is not (Brown et al., 1983). However, it is important to note that several studies have found no effects of summarization, and the conditions under which this strategy increases comprehension or retention of written material are not well understood (Anderson and Armbruster, 1984; Snowman, 1984).

Outlining, Networking, and Mapping. A related family of study strategies requires the student to represent the material studied in skeletal form. These strategies include outlining, networking, and mapping. Outlining presents the main points of the material in a hierarchical format, with each detail organized under a higher-level category. In networking and mapping, main ideas are identified, and then connections between them are diagrammed. For example, the schematic representation of the concept "bison" shown in Figure 5.6 might have been produced as a network to summarize factual material about bison and their importance to Plains Indians.

Research on outlining, networking, and mapping is limited and inconsistent, but generally finds that these methods are helpful as study aids (Anderson and Armbruster, 1984; Van Patten et al., 1986).

Cooperative Scripts

Many students find it helpful to get together with classmates to discuss material they have read or heard in class. A formalization of this age-old practice has been researched by Dansereau and his colleagues (1985). In it, students work in pairs and take turns summarizing sections of the material for one another. While one student summarizes, the other listens and corrects any errors or omissions. Then the two students switch roles, continuing in this way until they have covered all the material to be learned. A series of studies of this **cooperative scripts** method has consistently found that students who study this way learn and retain far more than students who summarize on their own or who simply read the material (for example, McDonald et al., 1985). It is interesting that while both participants in the cooperative pairs gain from the activity, the larger gains are for the sections students taught to their partners rather than those for which they served as listeners (Spurlin et al., 1984). The Theory into Practice section later in this chapter presents a detailed description of the cooperative scripts procedure. Also, see Chapter 10 for more on cooperative learning.

Student-Generated Questions. The "teacher" in the cooperative scripts team may have learned more than the "learner" because generating questions about material is itself an effective study aid (Anderson and Armbruster, 1984; Wong, 1985). For example, Duell (1978) asked students to make up multiple-choice tests based on the material they were studying. Students who did so retained more of the information than did those who used other methods of study.

Metacognitive Learning Strategies

The term **metacognition** means knowledge about one's own learning (Brown, 1978; Flavell, 1985; Garner and Alexander, 1989), or knowing how to learn. Over the course of their development, students learn such skills as assessing themselves to see

Cooperative Scripts
A study method in which students work in pairs and take turns orally summarizing sections of material to be learned

Metacognition
Monitoring one's own learning behaviors to determine degree of progress and strategies needed for accomplishing instructional goals

Educational psychologists have been concerned for decades with training students to use specific strategies to learn from written material. A result of this work has been the development of **metacognitive strategies** to make students aware of their own learning and able to use more effective study strategies. Traditional learning strategies and recent metacognitive strategies are described in the following sections.

SQ3R/SQ4R

One of the best known study techniques is a procedure called SQ3R, which was developed by Robinson (1961) and modified into a system called **SQ4R** by Thomas and Robinson (1972). The procedure involves teaching pupils a systematic approach to studying instructional texts and other materials. The steps in SQ4R, which is an acronym for survey, question, read, reflect, recite, review, are taught as follows (those steps preceded by an asterisk are also in the original SQ3R method):

1. *Survey* or *scan* the material: Look through the material quickly to get an idea of the general organization and major topics and subtopics. Pay attention to headings and subheadings, and identify what you will be reading about and studying.

2. *Question:* Ask yourself questions about the material as you read it. Use headings to invent questions using the *wh* words: who, what, why, where.

3. *Read:* Read the material. Do not take extensive written notes. Try to answer the questions you pose mentally while reading.

4. *Reflect on the material:* Try to understand and make meaningful the presented information by (1) relating it to things you already know; (2) relating the subtopics in the text to primary concepts or principles; (3) trying to resolve contradictions within the presented information; and (4) trying to use the material to solve simulated problems suggested by the material.

5. *Recite:* Practice remembering the information by asking and answering questions. You may use headings, highlighted words, and notes on major ideas to generate those questions.

6. *Review:* In the final step actively review the material, focusing on asking yourself questions and rereading the material only when you are not sure of the answers.

MURDER

Programs to teach study strategies have been developed for college students who have difficulty with metacognitive strategies (Dansereau et al., 1979). The program's developers used the acronym MURDER to help students remember the strategy. The components of the MURDER strategy are:

- *M*ood—get in the mood for learning.
- *U*nderstand the goals and conditions of the task. To do this, you must identify what you do not understand.
- *R*ecall information relevant to the task. Use such strategies as paraphrasing, imagery, and analyzing key concepts to develop the ability to recall the material.
- *D*etect omissions, errors, and ways of organizing the information. Use resources to clear up any misunderstandings and omissions identified in the *U* step.
- *E*laborate the information into a proper response. Expand upon information and relate it to material in memory by asking yourself questions such as: What questions would I ask the author if I could? How can the material be applied?
- *R*eview the material and focus on information you have not learned well.

These descriptions are based on Dansereau et al., 1979; and Dansereau, 1984. Dansereau also discusses several other support strategies, including goal setting and scheduling, concentrating, and monitoring difficulties. Several studies have shown that training programs based on these procedures can enhance the "individual's capacity for acquiring and using information" (Dansereau, 1984, p. 1).

COOPERATIVE SCRIPTS

In the study strategy called cooperative scripts, discussed earlier in this chapter, students work in pairs and take turns playing roles as "recaller" and "listener." The specific instructions given to students using the cooperative scripts method are as follows (adapted from Spurlin et al., 1984):

1. Decide by coin flip who will serve first as *recaller* and who will serve as *listener*.
2. At the end of each major section (500–600 words), stop reading.
3. The *recaller* summarizes aloud what has been read as completely as possible *without looking at the passage.* The recaller should try to include all of the important ideas and facts in the summary.
4. After the recaller has completed the summary, the *listener* should do the following while looking at the passage:
   a. To improve your own and your partner's understanding of the passage, correct your partner's summary by discussing the important information he or she did not include, and point out any ideas or facts that were summarized incorrectly.
   b. Help yourself and your partner to remember the material better by coming up with *clever* ways of memorizing the important ideas or facts. One way to do this is to relate the information to earlier material and to other things you know. You can also use drawings and mental pictures to aid memory.
5. The recaller can help the listener in correcting and memorizing the summary.
6. After completing and discussing the summary, switch roles as recaller and listener, read the next major section, and then follow the same procedures. Keep switching roles, summarizing, and discussing summaries until you have completed the material.

In assigning students to use cooperative scripts, teachers should establish in advance how much material is to be read before students stop to summarize. With younger students or with difficult material, the passage lengths should be kept relatively short. It is important to note that research establishing the effectiveness of cooperative scripts has taken place entirely at the college level, and therefore applies most directly to college, and perhaps secondary school, students. However, related cooperative learning methods that involve partner reading and discussion have been successfully used at the elementary level (Stevens et al., 1987). For more on this, see Chapter 10.

RECIPROCAL TEACHING

Reciprocal teaching (Palincsar and Brown, 1984) is a method for teaching metacognitive reading comprehension skills to students who are having comprehension difficulties. The following description of reciprocal teaching procedures is adapted from Palincsar (1986).

Introducing Reciprocal Teaching to Students

In introducing reciprocal teaching to students, you might begin as follows:

"For the coming weeks we will be working together to improve your ability to understand what you read. Sometimes we are so busy figuring out what the words are that we fail to pay much attention to what the words and sentences mean. We will be learning a way to pay more attention to what we are reading. I will teach you to do the following activities as you read:

1. To think of important questions that might be asked about what is being read and to be sure that you can answer those questions.
2. To summarize the most important information that you have read.
3. To predict what the author might discuss next in the passage.
4. To point out when something is unclear in the passage or doesn't make sense and then to see if we can make sense of it.

"These activities will help you keep your attention on what you are reading and make sure that you are understanding it.

"The way in which you will learn these four activities is by taking turns in the role of teacher during our reading group sessions. When I am the teacher, I will show you how I read carefully by telling you the questions I made up while reading, by summarizing the most important information I read, and by predicting what I think the author might discuss next. I will also tell you if I found anything I read to be unclear or confusing and how I made sense out of it.

"When you are the teacher, you will first ask the rest of us the questions you made up while reading. You will tell us if our answers are correct. You will summarize the most important information you learned while reading. You will also tell us if you found anything in the passage to be confusing. Several times throughout the story you will also be asked to predict what you think might be discussed next in the passage. When you are the teacher, the rest of us will answer your questions and comment on your summary.

"These are activities that we hope you will learn and use, not only when you are here in reading class, but whenever you want to understand and remember what you are reading—for example, in social studies, science, or history."

DAILY PROCEDURES

1. Pass out the passage for the day.
2. Explain that you will be the teacher for the first segment.
3. Instruct the students to read silently whatever portion of the passage you determine is appropriate. At the beginning, it will probably be easiest to work paragraph by paragraph.
4. When everyone has completed the first segment, model the following:

   "The question that I thought a teacher might ask is _____." Have the students answer your question. They may refer to the text if necessary.

   "I would summarize the important information in this paragraph in the following way _____."

   "From the title of the passage, I would predict that the author will discuss _____."

   If appropriate, "When I read this part, I found the following to be unclear _____."
5. Invite the students to make comments regarding your teaching and the passage. For example:

   "Was there more important information?"

   "Does anyone have more to add to my prediction?"

   "Did anyone find something else confusing?"
6. Assign the next segment to be read silently. Choose a student to act as teacher for this segment. Begin with students who are more verbal and who you suspect will have less difficulty with the activities.
7. Coach the student "teacher" through the activities as necessary. Encourage the other students to participate in the dialogue, but always give the student "teacher" for that segment the opportunity to go first and lead the dialogue. Be sure to give the student "teacher" plenty of feedback and praise for his or her participation.
8. As the training days go by, try to remove yourself more and more from the dialogue so that the student "teacher" initiates the activities himself or herself and other students provide feedback. Your role will continue to be monitoring, keeping students on track, helping them over obstacles. Throughout the training, however, continue to take your turn as teacher, modeling at least once a session.

EXAMPLE OF A RECIPROCAL TEACHING LESSON.

TEACHER: The title of this story is "Genius with Feathers." Let's have some predictions. I will begin by guessing that this story will be about birds that are very smart. Why do I say that?

FIRST STUDENT: Because a genius is someone very smart.

SECOND STUDENT: Because they have feathers.

TEACHER: That's right. Birds are the only animals that have feathers. Let's predict now the kind of information you might read about very smart birds.

THIRD STUDENT: What kinds of birds?

TEACHER: Good question. What kinds would you guess are very smart?

THIRD STUDENT: Parrots or blue jays.

FIRST STUDENT: A cockatoo like the bird on *Baretta*.

TEACHER: What other information would you want to know? *(No response from students.)*

TEACHER: I would like to know what these birds do that is so smart. Any ideas?

SECOND STUDENT: Some birds talk.

FOURTH STUDENT: They can fly.

TEACHER: That's an interesting one. As smart as people are, they can't fly. Well, let's read this first section now and see how many of our predictions were right. I will be the teacher for this section. *(All read the section silently.)*

TEACHER: Who is the genius with feathers?

FIRST STUDENT: Crows.

TEACHER: That's right. We were correct in our prediction that this story would be about birds, but we didn't correctly guess which kind of bird, did we? My summary of the first section would be that it describes the clever things that crows do, which make them seem quite intelligent.

Let's read on. Who will be the teacher for this section? *(Dialogue follows in which the student Jim is chosen to lead the discussion, with the teacher providing corrective feedback.)* (From Palincsar, 1984.)

if they are understanding, figuring out how much time they will need to study something, and choosing an effective plan of attack to study or solve problems. For example, in reading this book, you are bound to come across a paragraph that on first reading you don't understand. What do you do? Perhaps you reread the paragraph more slowly. Perhaps you look for other clues, such as pictures, graphs, or glossary terms to help you understand. Perhaps you read further back in the chapter to see if your difficulty arose because you did not fully understand something that came earlier. These are all examples of metacognitive strategies; you have learned how to know when you are not understanding and how to correct yourself (Zimmerman and Schunk, 1989). Another metacognitive strategy is the ability to predict what is likely to happen or to tell what is sensible and what is not. For example, when you first read the word "reinforcer" in Chapter 4, you knew right away that this did not refer to the little gummed circles of the same name because you knew that that meaning would not fit in the context of this book.

While most students do gradually develop adequate metacognitive skills, others do not. Teaching metacognitive strategies to students can lead to a marked improvement in their achievement. One series of studies on classroom applications of training in metacognitive strategies was conducted by Palincsar and her associates. This method, called "reciprocal teaching" (Palincsar and Brown, 1984), is explained in more detail in the Theory into Practice section on page 175.

Studies of reciprocal teaching methods have found that they significantly increased the reading comprehension of low-achieving junior high school students (Palincsar and Brown, 1984; Palincsar, 1987).

Another successful program for teaching students metacognitive skills to help them comprehend reading materials is called Informed Strategies for Learning, or ISL (Paris, Cross, and Lipson, 1984). In this program, elementary and junior high school students are taught such reading comprehension skills as underlining main ideas, skimming, rereading, paraphrasing, and asking *who, what, why,* and *where* questions.

Simply telling students about effective learning strategies is not enough. Students need training, practice, and feedback on the use of learning strategies; they need to

Metacognitive Strategies
Skills that increase retention by making learners more aware of how they process information

SQ4R
Study strategy that directs the learner to *survey, question, read, reflect, recite,* and *review* material

Reciprocal Teaching
Method that teaches metacognitive skills, through instruction and teacher modeling, to improve the reading performance of students who have poor comprehension

The ability to monitor one's own learning develops gradually. Teachers can help students develop such skills as choosing the best study strategy and assessing their own progress in learning.

Concepts
Categories into which objects, ideas,
and experiences may be grouped

know not only *how* to use them, but also *when* to do so and how to tell if the strategies are working (Baker and Brown, 1984; Ghatala, 1986; Levin, 1986; Paris et al., 1986; Pressley, 1986).

■ **Stop and Think**
Think of study strategies you use such as note taking and underlining. Are these effective for you? How did you learn them? Should they be taught in school? If so, when? (Take into account aspects of cognitive development and school curricula to answer this question.)

Effective Study Strategies: Conclusions

Research on effective study strategies is confusing at best. Few forms of studying are *always* found to be effective, and fewer still are *never* effective. Clearly, the value of study strategies depends on their specifics and on the uses to which they are put. Thomas and Rohwer (1986) have proposed a set of principles of effective studying that apply across particular study methods. These are as follows:

1. *Specificity:* Study strategies must be appropriate to the learning objectives and the types of students with whom they are used. For example, research has found that the same strategies work differently with older and younger students, or with high and low achievers. Writing summaries for others to read may, theoretically, be an effective study method, but it is probably too difficult for young children (Hidi and Anderson, 1986).

2. *Generativity:* One of the most important principles of effective study strategies is that they should involve reworking the material studied, generating something new. This activity forces students to engage in a high level of mental processing, which probably must occur for any study strategy to be effective. Examples of strategies that use a high degree of generativity are writing summaries and generating questions for others, organizing notes into outlines, diagramming relationships among main ideas, and teaching partners about text contents. Strategies low in generativity, such as indiscriminate underlining, taking notes without having to identify main ideas, or writing extensive summaries without having to focus on what is important, have been less successful in helping students learn.

3. *Executive monitoring:* The principle of effective monitoring simply means that students should know how and when to apply their study strategies and how to tell if they are working for them.

4. *Personal efficacy:* Students must have a clear sense that studying will pay off for them if they are to work hard at it. Teachers can create a sense that studying will pay off by giving frequent quizzes and tests based directly on the material students have studied and by making performance on these assessments a major portion of students' grades.

CONCEPT LEARNING

Much meaningful learning involves the learning of **concepts.** A concept is a category under which specific elements may be grouped. For example, a red ball, a red pencil, and a red chair are all instances of the simple concept "red." A green book is a noninstance of the concept "red." If we were shown the red ball, pencil, and chair and asked to say what they have in common, we would produce the concept "red objects." If the green book were also included, we would have to fall back on the much broader concept "objects."

Of course, many concepts are far more complex and less well defined than the concept "red." For example, the concept "justice" is one that people may spend a lifetime trying to understand. This book is engaged primarily in teaching concepts; in fact, at this very moment you are reading about the concept "concept"!

Concepts are generally learned in one of two ways. Most concepts that we learn outside of school we learn by observation. For example, a child learns the concept "car" by hearing certain vehicles referred to as a "car." Initially, the child might include pickup trucks or motorcycles under the concept "car," but as time goes on, the concept is refined until the child can clearly differentiate "car" from "noncar." Similarly, the child learns the more difficult concepts "naughty," "clean," or "fun" by observation and experience.

Other concepts are typically learned by definition. For example, it is very difficult to learn the concepts "aunt" or "uncle" by observation alone. One could observe hundreds of "aunts" and "nonaunts" without deriving a clear concept of "aunt." In this case, the concept is best learned by definition: To be an aunt, one must be a female whose brother or sister (or brother- or sister-in-law) has children. With this definition, instances and noninstances of "aunt" can be readily differentiated.

Teaching of Concepts

Just as concepts can be learned in two ways, so can they be taught in two ways. Students may be given instances and noninstances of a concept and later asked to derive or infer a definition. Or students may be given a definition and then asked to identify instances and noninstances. Some concepts lend themselves to the example-definition approach. For most concepts taught in school, it makes most sense to state a definition, present several instances (and noninstances, if appropriate), and then restate the definition, showing how the instances typify the definition. Use of this pattern, called **rule-example-rule,** has been found to be characteristic of instruction-ally effective teachers (see Chapter 8). For example, the concept "learning" might be defined, as it was at the beginning of Chapter 4, as "a change in an individual caused by experience." Instances might include learning of skills, of information, of behaviors, and of emotions. Noninstances might include maturational changes, such as changes in behaviors or emotions caused by the onset of puberty. Finally, the definition might be restated and discussed in light of the instances and noninstances.

Examples. Teaching concepts involves extensive and skillful use of examples. Tennyson and Park (1980, p. 59) suggest that teachers follow three rules when presenting examples of concepts:

1. Order the examples from easy to difficult.
2. Select examples that differ from one another.
3. Compare and contrast examples and nonexamples.

Consider the concept "mammal." Easy examples are dogs, cats, and humans, and nonexamples are insects, reptiles, and fish. No problem so far. But what about dolphins? Bats? Snakes that bear live young? Kangaroos? Each of these is a more difficult example or nonexample of the concept "mammal" because it challenges the simplistic belief, based on experience, that terrestrial animals that bear live young are

Chapter 6: Meaningful Learning: The Cognitive Perspective

mammals, while fish, birds, and other egg layers are not. The easy examples (dogs versus fish) establish the concept in general, but the more difficult examples (snakes versus whales) test the true boundaries of the concept.

Sometimes students can be given information and asked to infer concepts for themselves. A central principle of discovery learning, discussed later in this chapter, is that whenever possible students should be allowed to discover concepts or principles on their own, with the teacher's guidance but without a definition or principle given in advance. Joyce and Weil (1980) present an example of this kind of concept teaching:

> Mrs. Stern's eighth grade class in Houston, Texas, has been studying the characteristics of the fourteen largest cities in the United States. They have collected data on size, ethnicity of population, types of industry, location, and proximity to natural resources.
>
> Working in committees, the students have collected information and summarized it on a series of charts now pasted up around the room. One Wednesday in November, Mrs. Stern says, "Today let's try a series of exercises designed to help us understand these cities better. I have identified a number of concepts that help us compare and contrast them. I am going to label our charts either *yes* or *no*. If you look at the information we have and think about the populations and the other characteristics, you will identify the ideas that I have in mind. I'm going to start with the city that's a yes and then one that's a no, and so forth. Think about what the yeses have in common. Then write down after the second yes the idea that you think connects these two places, and keep testing those ideas as we go along. Let's begin with our own city," she says. "Houston is a yes."
>
> The students look at the information about Houston, its size, industries, location, ethnic composition. Then she points to Baltimore, Maryland.
>
> "Baltimore is a no," she says. Then she points to San Jose, California. "Here is another yes," she comments.
>
> The students look for a moment at the information about San Jose. Two or three raise their hands.
>
> "I think I know what it is," one offers.
>
> "Hold on to your idea," she replies. "See if you're right." She then selects another yes—Seattle, Washington. Detroit, Michigan, is a no. Miami, Florida, is a yes. She continues until all students think they know what the concept is, and then they begin to share concepts.
>
> "What do you think it is, Jill?"
>
> "The yeses all have mild climates," says Jill; "that is, it doesn't get very cold in any of them."
>
> "It gets pretty cold in Salt Lake City," objects another.
>
> "Yes, but not as cold as in Chicago, Detroit, or Baltimore," another student counters.
>
> "I think the yeses are all rapidly growing cities. Each one of them increased more than 10 percent during the last ten years." There is some discussion about this.
>
> "All the yeses have lots of different industries," volunteers another.
>
> "That's true, but almost all these cities do," replies another student.
>
> Finally the students decide the yeses are all cities that are growing very fast and have relatively mild climates.
>
> "That's right," agrees Mrs. Stern. "That's exactly what I had in mind. Now let's do this again. This time I want to begin with Baltimore, Maryland, and now it is a yes."
>
> The exercise is repeated several times. Students learn that Mrs. Stern has grouped the cities on the basis of their relationship to waterways, natural resources, ethnic composition, and several other dimensions.
>
> The students are beginning to see patterns in their data. Finally she says, "Now, each of

you try to group the cities in a way that you think is important. Then take turns and lead us through this exercise, helping us to see which ones you place in which category. Then we'll discuss the ways we can look at cities and how we can use different categories for different purposes." (Joyce and Weil, 1980, pp. 25–26)

Transfer of Learning
The application of knowledge acquired in one situation to new situations

Note how the teacher forced students to discover the concepts for themselves. An important purpose of this kind of concept teaching is to give students experience informing concepts on their own, a useful skill for high level learning both in and out of school.

TRANSFER OF LEARNING

Students often get so wrapped up in preparing for tests, and teachers in preparing students to take tests, that both forget what the primary purpose of school is: to give students the skills and knowledge necessary for them to function effectively as adults. If a student can fill in blanks on a language arts test but cannot write a clear letter to a friend or a prospective employer, or can multiply with decimals and percents on a math test but cannot figure sales tax, then that student's education has been sadly misdirected. Yet all too frequently students who do very well in school or on tests are unable to transfer their knowledge or skills to real-life situations.

Some principles of **transfer of learning** were discussed in Chapter 4 under Generalization. Essentially, transfer of learning from one situation to another depends on the degree to which the information or skills were learned in the original situation, and on the degree of similarity between the situation in which the skill or concept was learned and the situation to which it is to be applied. These rather obvious principles, known since the beginning of this century (Thorndike and Woodworth, 1901), have important implications for teaching. We cannot simply assume that students will be able to transfer their school learning to practical situations, so we must teach them to use skills in situations like those they are likely to encounter in real life, or in other situations to which we expect learning to transfer. Students must be given specific instruction in how to use their skills and information to solve problems, and be exposed to a variety of problem-solving experiences, if they are to be able to apply much of what they learned in school.

The most important thing to know about transfer of learning is that it cannot be assumed. Just because a student has mastered a skill or concept in one setting or circumstance, there is no guarantee whatsoever that the student will be able to apply this skill or concept to a new setting, even if the setting seems (at least to the teacher) to be very similar (Butterfield, 1988). For example, Lave (1988) describes a man in a Weight Watchers program who was faced with the problem of measuring out a serving of cottage cheese that was three quarters of the usual two-thirds cup allowance. The man, who had passed college calculus, measured out two-thirds of a cup of cottage cheese, dumped it out in a circle on a cutting board, marked a cross on it, and scooped away one quadrant. It never occurred to him to multiply $2/3 \times 3/4 = 1/2$, an operation any sixth grader could do on paper (but few could apply in a practical situation).

Transfer of Concepts

If transfer of learning depends in large part on similarity between the situation in which information is learned and that in which it is applied, then how can we teach in the school setting so that students will be able to apply their knowledge in the very different setting of real life?

Corporate America's ties to the nation's schools are growing increasingly strong. Some businesses are committing millions of dollars to education, others are contributing money and expertise to specialized training programs, and others are setting up schools at the job site.

What do businesses want for their investments of time and money? Primarily, they want schools to turn out a pool of workers who can handle increasingly complex jobs, jobs that often involve computers and technology.

That schools should serve businesses by training future employees is hardly revolutionary. In his 1963 book, *Anti-intellectualism in American Culture,* Richard Hofstadter noted that mass education was founded not on any highfalutin notions about the value of learning for its own sake, but on "the supposed political and economic benefits of education."

Nevertheless, what frictions are created when schools serve the needs of business? Is the concept of helping students transfer school learning to practical situations being abused if high schools become training schools? What freedoms are lost by students who may want to pursue unusual intellectual goals? These are the questions that must be kept in mind as the partnerships between business and schools are evaluated.

Corporations that have committed large amounts of money to education include Coca-Cola, RJR Nabisco, General Electric, and I.B.M. The degree to which the programs are at least partially self-serving varies. I.B.M., for example, which makes computers, is supporting programs that further the use of computers in the classroom. And, RJR Nabisco, whose tobacco division is based in North Carolina, recently announced grants ranging from $300,000 to $750,000 to fifteen innovative schools—four of which are in North Carolina. General Electric, on the other hand, is directing its money to troubled schools, hoping that success there will show the potential for all schools.

A more targeted use of corporate money has been taken by American Express, whose businesses include credit cards and other travel-related services. That company has helped pay for specialized high schools where students learn skills needed in the tourism industry. Three of the "tourism academies" are in New York City and a fourth is in Miami.

There appears to be every reason to applaud Corporate America's new-found support for schools. Business people, do, of course, have children and grandchildren also, for whom they desire the best education possible. But, business is also about making money—and quick returns on the dollar rather than long-term investing ruled the corporate psyche through the 1980s and early 1990s. It is hoped that the businesses that make a commitment to education will stay for the long haul, and will consider the best interests of children ahead of the business's need for profits and for specialized workers.

Lee A. Daniels, "Coca-Cola to Donate $50 million to Education," *New York Times,* November 7, 1989, p. B8.

Lee A. Daniels, "New Corporate Effort to Aid Innovative Schools," *New York Times,* November 1, 1989, p. B9.

Steven A. Holmes, "School Reform: Business Moves In," *New York Times,* February 1, 1990, p. D1.

"Grants to Schools Aim at Innovation," *New York Times,* April 4, 1990, p. B6.

One important principle of transfer is that the ability to apply knowledge in new circumstances depends in part on the variety of circumstances in which we have learned or practiced the information or skill (Bransford, 1979). For example, a few weeks' experience as a parking attendant, driving all sorts of cars, would probably be better than years of experience driving one kind of car for enabling a person to drive a completely new and different car (at least in a parking lot!).

In teaching concepts, one way to increase the chance that the concepts will be appropriately applied to new situations is to give examples from a range of situations. A set of experiments by Nitsch (1977) illustrated this principle. Students were given definitions of words and were then presented with examples to illustrate the concepts. Some were given several examples in the same context, while others received examples from mixed contexts. For example, "minge" is a cowboy word meaning "to gang up on." The examples are shown in Table 6.1.

TABLE 6.1

TEACHING OF CONCEPTS

Research demonstrates that to teach new concepts, teachers should first present examples of the concept used in similar contexts and then offer examples in widely differing contexts. This approach promotes the students' abilities to transfer the concept to new situations.

Concept to be taught: *Minge*
Definition: To gang up on a person or thing.

Same Context Examples	Varied Context Examples
■ The three riders decided to converge on the cow.	■ The band of sailors angrily denounced the captain and threatened a mutiny.
■ Four people took part in branding the horse.	■ A group in the audience booed the inept magician's act.
■ They circled the wolf so it could not escape.	■ The junk dealer was helpless to defend himself from the three thieves.
■ All six cowboys fought against the rustler.	■ All six cowboys fought against the rustler.

Source: Adapted from Nitsch, 1977.

Students given only the same-context examples were able to identify additional examples in the same context, but were less successful in applying the concepts to new contexts. On the other hand, the students who learned with the varied-context examples had some difficulties in learning the concept at first, but once they did, they were able to apply it to new situations. The best strategy was a "hybrid," in which students were given the same-context examples first and then the varied-context examples.

The tricky aspect of teaching for transfer is that the procedures for enhancing transfer are exactly the opposite of those for initial learning. As the Nitsch (1977) study illustrated, teaching a concept in many different contexts was confusing to students if it was done at the beginning of a sequence of instruction, but it enhanced transfer if done after students understood the concept in one setting. The implications of this principle for teaching are extremely important. When introducing a new concept, it is important to use *similar* examples until the concept is well understood, and only then to use diverse examples that still demonstrate the essential aspects of the concept.

As one example of this, consider a series of lessons on evolution. In introducing the concept it would first be important to use clear examples of how animals evolved to increase their chances of survival in their environments, using such examples as the evolution of flippers in seals or the evolution of humps in camels. Then evolution in plants (for example, evolution of a waxy skin on desert plants) might be presented, somewhat broadening the concept. The evolution of social behaviors (such as cooperation in lions, baboons, and humans) might then be discussed, and, finally, phenomena that resemble the evolutionary process (such as the modification of businesses in response to selective pressures of free-market economies) might be explored. The idea here is to first establish the idea of evolution in one clear context (animals) and to gradually broaden the concept until students can see how processes in quite different contexts demonstrate the principle of gradual adaptation under selective pressure. If the lessons had begun with discussions of animals, plants, societies, and businesses, it would have been too confusing. If it had never moved beyond the evolution of animals, however, the concept would not have had much

Problem Solving
The application of knowledge and
skills to achieve certain goals

chance of transferring to different contexts. After learning about the concept of evolution in many different contexts, students are much more likely to be able to apply the concept to a completely new context, such as the evolution of art in response to changes in society.

It is important in teaching for transfer not only to provide many examples, but also to point out in each example how the essential features of the concept are reflected. In the evolution example, the central process might be explained as it applied to each particular case. The development of cooperation among lions, for example, shows how a social trait evolved because groups of lions who cooperated were better able to catch game, to survive, and to ensure that their offspring would survive. Pointing out the essential elements in each example helps students "bridge" a concept to new instances they have never encountered (Perkins and Salomon, 1988).

PROBLEM SOLVING

One indication of transfer of learning is the ability to use information and skills to solve problems. For example, a student might be quite good at adding, subtracting, and multiplying, but have little idea of how to solve this problem:

Sylvia bought four hamburgers at $1.25 each, two orders of french fries at 65 cents and three large sodas at 75 cents. How much change did she get from a ten-dollar bill?

Sylvia's situation is not an unusual one in real life, and the computations involved are not difficult. However, many students (and even some otherwise competent adults) would have difficulty solving this problem. The difficulty of most applications problems in mathematics lies not in the computations, but rather in knowing how to set the problem up so it can be solved. **Problem solving** is a skill that can be taught and learned (Polya, 1957; Silver, 1985). The components of problem-solving skills are discussed in the following sections.

Teachers can help students develop a complete definition of a concept—such as "bird"—by defining it and then offering examples that are both simple and complex.

Chapter 6: Meaningful Learning: The Cognitive Perspective

Means-Ends Analysis

The first step in solving a problem is to identify the goal of the problem and figure out how to proceed. Newell and Simon (1972) suggest that the problem solver repeatedly ask, "What is the difference between where I am now and where I want to be? What can I do to reduce that difference?" For example, in solving Sylvia's problem, the goal is to find out how much change she will receive from a ten-dollar bill after buying food and drinks. We might then break the problem into substeps, each with its own subgoal:

1. Figure how much Sylvia spent on hamburgers.
2. Figure how much Sylvia spent on french fries.
3. Figure how much Sylvia spent on sodas.
4. Figure how much Sylvia spent in total.
5. Figure how much change Sylvia gets from $10.00.

The **means-ends analysis** involves deciding what is going on and what needs to be done. Learning to solve problems requires a great deal of practice with different kinds of problems that demand thought. All too often textbooks in mathematics and other subjects that include many problems fail to present problems that will make students think. For example, they might give students a set of word problems whose solutions require the multiplication of two numbers. Students soon learn that they can solve such problems by looking for any two numbers and multiplying them.

In real life, however, problems do not neatly line themselves up in categories. We may hear, "Joe Smith got a 5 percent raise last week, which amounted to $1200." If we want to figure out how much Joe was making before his raise, the hard part is not doing the calculation, but knowing what calculation is called for. In real life this problem would not be on a page titled "Dividing by Percents"!

The more different kinds of problems students learn to solve, and the more they have to think to solve them, the greater the chance that when faced with real-life problems, they will be able to transfer their skills or knowledge to the new situation.

Extracting Relevant Information. Realistic problems are rarely neat and tidy. Imagine that Sylvia's problem had been as follows:

Sylvia walked into the fast-food restaurant at 6:18 with three friends. Between them, they bought four hamburgers at $1.25 each, two orders of french fries at 65 cents, and three large sodas at 75 cents. Onion rings were on sale for 55 cents. Sylvia's mother told her to be in by 9:00, but she was already twenty-five minutes late by the time she and her friends left the restaurant. Sylvia drove the three miles home at an average of 30 miles per hour. How long was Sylvia in the restaurant?

The first part of this task is to clear away all the extra information to get to the important facts. The means-ends analysis suggests that only time information is relevant, so all the money transactions and the speed of Sylvia's car can be ignored. Careful reading of the problem reveals that Sylvia left the restaurant at 9:25. This (plus her arrival time of 6:18) is all that matters for solving the problem. Once we know what is relevant and what is not, the solution is easy.

Representing the Problem.   For many kinds of problems, graphic representation may be an effective means of finding a solution. Adams (1974) provides a story that illustrates this. A Buddhist monk has to make a pilgrimage and stay overnight in a

Functional Fixedness
Block to solving problems caused by
an inability to see new uses for
familiar objects or ideas

temple that is at the top of a high mountain. The road spirals around and around the mountain. The monk begins walking up the mountain at sunrise. He walks all day long and finally reaches the top at about sunset. He stays all night in the temple and performs his devotions. At sunrise the next day the monk begins walking down the mountain. It takes him much less time than walking up and he is at the bottom shortly after noon. The question is: Is there a point on the road when he was coming down that he passed at the same time of day when he was coming up the mountain?

This can seem a difficult problem because people begin to reason in a variety of ways as they think about the man going up and down. Adams points out one representation that makes the problem easy. Suppose there were two monks, one leaving the top at sunrise and one starting up at sunrise. Would they meet? Of course they would.

Obstacles to Problem Solving.   Sometimes we fail to see the answer to a problem because we cannot free ourselves from familiar knowledge and assumptions. For example, Maier (1930) gave students the following problem:

Two strings are hanging from the ceiling. The strings are of such a length and distance apart that you cannot reach one string while holding onto the other. You have a scissors, a paper clip, a pencil, and a piece of chewing gum in your pocket. Your task is, using just those materials, to tie the strings together.

Many of Maier's students were stumped because they did not consider that the scissors could be used for something besides cutting. To solve the problem, they had to use the scissors as a weight with which to make a pendulum to swing one of the strings toward the other. The problem would have been easier to solve if the word "scissors" had been replaced by "fishing weight," as that object's function is more like that of a pendulum weight. This blocking of a new use of an object by its common use is called **functional fixedness.** For example, Duncker (1945) gave students three boxes, candles, tacks, and matches. In some cases, the candles, tacks, and matches were in the box; in others, they weren't. The task was to attach a candle to the wall in such a way that it could be lighted. The solution is to tack to the wall a box on which the candle can stand. Duncker found that when the other objects were in the box—which emphasized the box's container function—students were less likely to use the box as a candle stand. Other researchers found that when the instructions mentioned the box among the materials to be used, the subjects were more likely to solve the problem. This finding suggests that people erect a mental boundary against using objects not mentioned in the instructions to a problem.

Emotional factors can also contribute to blocks in problem solving. Teachers and parents teach us that it is good to be "right" and bad to be "wrong." Therefore, when faced with problems, we may impose boundaries that don't really exist. People who do well on tests of creative problem solving seem to be less afraid of making mistakes and appearing foolish than those who do poorly. They also seem to treat problem-solving situations more playfully (Getzels and Jackson, 1962). This implies a relaxed, fun atmosphere may be important when teaching problem solving. Students should certainly be encouraged to try different solutions and not be criticized for taking a wrong turn.

Creative Problem Solving

Most of the problems students encounter in school may require careful reading and some thought, but no creativity.

However, many of the problems we face in life are not so cut-and-dried. The scissors-and-string problem discussed earlier is of this type. Life is full of situations

Problem Solving and Creativity

1. What classroom activities have you used to help children learn about problem solving?

Ralph Westenberger, Louisville, Ala., teaches his ninth- to twelfth-grade students to use means-ends analysis with word problems in math books and lessons:

> We in math have an abundance of word problems to aid the student in solving problems in their everyday life. The student can't possibly memorize all the problems, so they have to learn to think before they start working the problems. We teach them to see where they are or what they have to start with, and then see where they want to go and how they might get there by using logical steps. They soon find out that they can't have any success by just guessing and blundering through a problem.

Mr. Westenberger says he also shows students that there are many ways to attack a problem:

> I always try to show them as many different ways to work problems as possible and let students decide which ones they want to use and understand best. I also ask them to speak up if they see an easier way to do it. I never specify one certain way to do something. The students can use any method to work problems as long as it does not violate any laws or principles.

2. What are some of the important things you teach students about solving problems?

Pamela Weiss, who teaches kindergarten in Shawnee Mission, Kans., writes:

> First I have students give some suggestions for possible solutions and tell them that we can try them out. I praise them for their ideas. When we go through the process of trying these ideas, I encourage them to try others if the first ones are unsuccessful. I tell them that they shouldn't expect all the ideas to work.

> Problem solving must be modeled for the class by the teacher. If the kids see you making mistakes and trying something different, they learn to do the same.

3. How do you encourage your students to be creative? What classroom activities have you used that are aimed primarily at encouraging creativity and creative problem solving?

Cheryl Vigue, who teaches elementary school in Pittsfield, Me., writes:

> Maintaining a certain level of excitement or energy in the classroom provides my students with the motivation to be creative. If I can say or do something when they are least expecting it, there is no end to the responses I can elicit from them! While studying aerial views of land areas, I suddenly and without warning jumped onto a chair in the front of the room and let drop a book I was holding. I said, "What part of the book can I see?" Fifteen hands went up.
>
> Besides providing energy, I also let them create their own classroom (bulletin board, seating arrangements, class rules, etc.), so that the room they come to every day is a product of them, not me. I also provide a "hands-on" classroom so that the children have a chance to create with their hands as well as their minds.

Audrey Sequin, an elementary teacher in Alpena, Mich., adds:

> I try to accept almost any student answer—if it's anywhere near what is being discussed. I also often ask other questions instead of just giving an answer. This gives students confidence to take a risk. I remind them that it's OK to be wrong—that we all learn from our mistakes. Above all, I try to be positive with children so they will gain confidence in their creative work.

that call for creative problem solving, as when we have to figure out how to tell someone that we don't want to go out with him without hurting his feelings, or when we have to figure out how to repair a washing machine with a bent paper clip.

Frederiksen (1984) has proposed six elements of a strategy for teaching creative problem solving that are based on a review of research in this area:

1. *Allow time for incubation:* Creative problem solving is quite different from the

analytical, step-by-step process used to solve Sylvia's problems. In creative problem solving, one important principle is to avoid rushing to a solution, but rather to pause and reflect on the problem and think through several alternative solutions before choosing a course of action. Consider the following simple problem:

Roger baked an apple pie in his oven in three-quarters of an hour. How long would it take him to bake three apple pies?

Many students would rush to multiply forty-five minutes by three. However, if they took some time to reflect, most would realize that baking three pies in the same oven would actually take about the same amount of time as one pie!

In teaching this process, teachers must avoid putting time pressures on students. Instead of speed, they should value ingenuity and careful thought.

2. *Suspend judgment:* In creative problem solving, students should be encouraged to suspend judgment, to consider all possibilities before trying out a solution. One specific method based on this principle is called "brainstorming" (Osborn, 1963), where two or more individuals suggest as many solutions to a problem as they can think of, no matter how seemingly ridiculous. Only after all ideas are out is any evaluated as a possible solution. The idea of brainstorming is to avoid focusing on one solution too early and perhaps ignoring better ways to proceed.

3. *Establish appropriate climates:* Creative problem solving is enhanced by a relaxed, even playful environment (Wallach and Kogan, 1965). Perhaps even more importantly, students engaging in creative problem solving must feel that their ideas will be accepted.

4. *Analyze and juxtapose elements:* One method of creative problem solving often suggested is to list major characteristics or specific elements of a problem (Crawford, 1954; Allen, 1962). For example, the scissors-and-string problem mentioned earlier might have been solved by listing characteristics of the strings (one of which might have been that they are too light to be swung together) and of the scissors (one of which is that they have weight).

Careful analysis of the situation might help solve the following problem:

A tennis tournament was set up with a series of rounds. The winner of each match advanced to the next round. If there were an odd number of players in a round, one player (chosen at random) would advance automatically to the next round. In a tournament with 147 players, how many matches would take place before a single winner would be declared?

We might solve this problem the hard way, making diagrams of the various matches. However, careful analysis of the situation would reveal that each match would produce exactly one loser. Therefore it would take 146 matches to produce 146 losers (and one winner).

5. *Teach the underlying cognitive abilities:* Students can be taught specific strategies for approaching creative problem solving. For example, Covington et al. (1974) describe a "Productive Thinking Program" in which students are taught such strategies for solving problems as

- thinking of unusual ideas

- generating many ideas

- planning

- mapping the possibilities

- assembling the facts

- getting the problem clearly in mind

Instrumental Enrichment
A thinking-skills program in which students work through a series of paper-and-pencil exercises designed to develop various intellectual abilities

Students need practice solving many types of problems because situations they will face outside of school often require creative solutions.

6. *Provide practice with feedback.* Perhaps the most effective way to teach problem solving is to provide students with a great deal of practice on a wide variety of problem types, giving feedback not only on the correctness of their solutions but also on the process by which they arrived at the solutions (Michael, 1977).

Teaching Thinking Skills

One of the oldest dreams in education is that there might be some way to make students *smarter*—not just more knowledgeable or skillful, but actually more able to learn new information of all kinds. Perhaps someday someone will come up with a "smart pill" that will have this effect, but in the meantime, several groups of researchers have been developing and evaluating instructional programs designed to increase students' general thinking skills.

The most widely known and extensively researched of several thinking-skills programs currently in use was developed by an Israeli educator, Reuven Feuerstein (1980). In this program, called **Instrumental Enrichment,** students work through a series of paper-and-pencil exercises intended to build such intellectual skills as categorization, comparison, orientation in space, and numerical progressions. Figure 6.3 (from Feuerstein and Jensen, 1980) shows one example of an activity designed to increase "analytic perception." The Instrumental Enrichment treatment is meant to be administered for three to five hours per week over a period of at least two years, usually to underachieving or learning-disabled adolescents. Studies of this duration have found that the program has positive effects on tests of aptitude, such as IQ tests, but generally not on achievement (Savell, Twohig, and Rachford, 1986; Sternberg and Bhana, 1986). Less intensive interventions, particularly those involving fewer than eighty hours of instruction, have rarely been successful. In one study done in

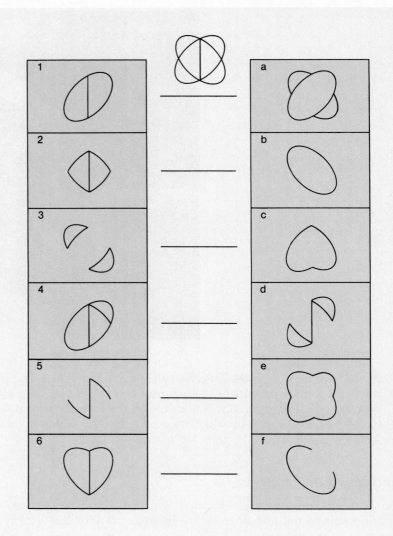

FIGURE 6.3

Examples from Analytic Perception

Look at the figure at the right. For each drawing in the left column, there is a drawing in the right column that completes it. Write the number and the letter of the two forms you combined to make the completion. The child must select the appropriate drawing from the left to complete the one on the right so as to obtain a figure identical to the model at the top of the page. The task requires representation, internalization and labeling of the model, definition of the missing parts, systematic work, and comparison to the model for self-criticism.

From Feuerstein and Jensen, 1980.

Israel (Feuerstein et al., 1981) and one in Venezuela (Ruiz, 1985), positive effects of Instrumental Enrichment on aptitude test scores were still found two years after the program ended.

Many reviewers of the research on Instrumental Enrichment have suggested that this method is simply teaching students how to take IQ tests rather than teaching them anything of real value (Sternberg and Bhana, 1986). Many of the exercises, such as the one reproduced in Figure 6.3, are, in fact, quite similar to items used in nonverbal IQ tests (see, for example, Figure 9.1 in Chapter 9). A similar pattern of results has been found for many other thinking skills programs (Adams, 1989). In fact, researchers have now begun to question whether there are broadly applicable "thinking skills"; the evidence points more toward the existence of teachable thinking skills in specific domains, such as math problem solving or reading comprehension (Perkins and Salomon, 1989).

Until thinking-skills programs can demonstrate effects not only on IQ tests but also on school achievement, their use in schools will probably remain limited (Bransford et al., 1986). However, in recent years researchers have begun to combine teaching of thinking skills with instruction in specific content areas, and preliminary results of these combined models appear to be encouraging (Adams, 1989; Glaser, 1984; Brainin, 1985; Derry and Murphy, 1986).

Critical Thinking

One key objective of schooling is enhancing students' abilities to think critically, to make rational decisions about what to do or what to believe (Hitchcock, 1983). Examples of critical thinking include identifying misleading advertisements, weighing competing evidence, and identifying assumptions or fallacies in arguments. As with any other objective, learning to think critically requires practice—students can be given many dilemmas, logical and illogical arguments, valid and misleading advertisements, and so on (Norris, 1985). Effective teaching of critical thinking depends on setting a classroom tone that encourages the acceptance of divergent perspectives and free discussion. There should be an emphasis on giving reasons for opinions rather than only giving correct answers. Skills in critical thinking are best acquired in relationship to topics with which students are familiar. For example, students will learn more from a unit evaluating Nazi propaganda if they know a great deal about the history of Nazi Germany and the culture of the 1930s and 1940s. Perhaps most important, the goal of teaching critical thinking is to create a critical spirit, which encourages students to question what they hear and to examine their own thinking for logical inconsistencies or fallacies (Norris, 1984).

■ **Stop and Think**

Consider the topics just discussed from the perspective of several types of teachers. First, how might a physical education teacher respond to the following questions?

—List three concepts that you teach to your students.

—List several skills that your students should learn and be able to transfer to other situations, and list strategies for facilitating transfer.

—Describe a problem that your students should learn to solve. Provide strategies for helping them do so.

Now, answer the same questions from the perspective of (1) a grade-school music teacher, (2) a junior high school language arts teacher, and (3) a teacher of the subject and grade level you expect to teach.

COGNITIVE MODELS OF INSTRUCTION

Many of the cognitive psychologists who have studied how learning takes place have also taken the next step and suggested how teaching should be done. Jerome Bruner (1966), David Ausubel (1968), and Robert Gagné (1970) have described three of the

Discovery Learning
Instructional approach in which
students learn from their own active
explorations of concepts and
principles

most prominent cognitive instructional models. These are presented in the remainder of this chapter. It is important to bear in mind that these are theoretical models that have not been researched in schools as practical programs. However, Bruner, Ausubel, and Gagné have had a substantial impact on others, who have developed and evaluated the instructional methods discussed in Chapters 8, 9, and 10.

Jerome Bruner: Discovery Learning

One of the most influential cognitive instructional models is Jerome Bruner's (1966) **discovery learning.** Bruner argued that the teacher's role must be to create situations in which students can learn on their own, rather than to provide prepackaged information to students. Bruner states:

> We teach a subject not to produce little living libraries on that subject, but rather to get a student to think . . . for himself, to consider matters as an historian does, to take part in the process of knowledge-getting. Knowing is a process, not a product. (1966, p. 72)

Bruner suggests that students should learn through their own active involvement with concepts and principles, that they should be encouraged to have experiences and conduct experiments that permit them to discover principles for themselves.

Discovery learning has many applications in science and related subjects. For example, some science museums have a series of cylinders of different sizes and weights, some of which are solid and some hollow. Students are encouraged to "race" the cylinders down a ramp. By careful experimentation, the students can discover principles that determine the speed of the cylinders.

There are several important advantages to discovery learning (see Gilstrap and Martin, 1975). First, it arouses students' curiosity, motivating them to continue to work until they find answers (Berlyne, 1965). Second, this approach can teach independent problem-solving skills, and may force students to analyze and manipulate information rather than to simply absorb it.

Bruner's work was influential in the open schools movement and other humanistic approaches, discussed in Chapter 8.

Constructivist Approaches to Teaching. In recent years, there has been increasing attention paid to methods of teaching built on the idea that students construct meaning for themselves, and that the teacher's role is, therefore, to give students opportunities to experiment with ideas and to help guide their discovery of critical concepts (see, for example, Brown, Collins, and Duguid, 1989; Williams, 1989). Approaches of this kind engage students in "authentic" activities, such as solving complex math problems, reading books, or writing compositions, and then letting students work out or discover (with the teacher's guidance) the basic skills required—computations, decoding, and language mechanics, respectively. Bruner's concept of discovery learning has played an important role in these "constructivist" theories.

As one example of a constructivist approach, consider an example from Lampert (1986). The traditional approach to teaching the multiplication of two-digit by one-digit numbers (e.g., $4 \times 12 = 48$) is to teach students a step-by-step procedure to get the right answer. Later, students are usually given simple word problems using their new skill, such as: "Billy saw some pencils that cost 12 cents each. How much money would he need to buy four of them?"

The discovery learning approach stresses the importance of students learning to learn independently of the teacher. This approach is seen as an important supplement to more structured teaching methods.

The constructivist approach works in exactly the opposite order, beginning with problems (often generated by students themselves) and then letting students figure out how to do the operations. Lampert's example of this appears in Figure 6.4.

The constructivist approach is often called a "top-down" approach to contrast it with the "bottom-up" approach (skills first, then problem solving later) typical of traditional methods. Approaches of this kind are being increasingly used in mathematics (e.g., Schoenfeld, 1985; Burns, 1986), in reading (e.g., Duffy and

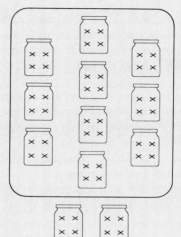

T: Can anyone give me a story that could go with this multiplication . . . 12 x 4?

S1: There were 12 jars, and each had 4 butterflies in it.

T: And if I did this multiplication and found the answer, what would I know about those jars and butterflies?

S1: You'd know you had that many butterflies altogether.

T: Okay, here are the jars. [*Draws a picture to represent the jars of butterflies – see diagram.*] The stars in them will stand for butterflies. Now, it will be easier for us to count how many butterflies there are altogether if we think of the jars in groups. And as usual, the mathematician's favorite number for thinking about groups is?

S2: 10

T: Each of these 10 jars has 4 butterflies in it. [*Draws a loop around 10 jars.*]

T: Suppose I erase my circle and go back to looking at the 12 jars again altogether. Is there any other way I could group them to make it easier for us to count all the butterflies?

S6: You could do 6 and 6.

T: Now, how many do I have in this group?

S7: 24

T: How did you figure that out?

S7: 8 and 8 and 8. [*He puts the 6 jars together into 3 pairs, intuitively finding a grouping that made the figuring easier for him.*]

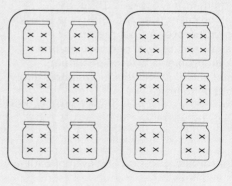

T: That's 3 x 8. It's also 6 x 4. Now, how many are in this group?

S6: 24. It's the same. They both have 6 jars.

T: And now how many are there altogether?

S8: 24 and 24 is 48.

T: Do we get the same number of butterflies as before? Why?

S8: Yeah, because we have the same number of jars and they still have 4 butterflies in each.

FIGURE 6.4

Story Problems for Teaching Multiplication

From Lampert, M. 1986.

Reception Learning
Learning that occurs when students are presented information in organized, teacher-structured lessons

Expository Teaching
Instructional technique in which information is presented to students in an organized, finished form

Roehler, 1986; Palincsar and Brown, 1984), in writing (e.g., Bereiter and Scardamalia, 1987; Graves, 1983), and in other subjects. Constructivist approaches typically make extensive use of cooperative learning, on the theory that students will more easily discover and comprehend difficult concepts if they can talk with each other about the problems. See Chapter 8 for more on applications of constructivist theories.

David Ausubel: Reception Learning

David Ausubel (1968), whose work on advance organizers was discussed earlier in this chapter, has been one of the most vocal critics of discovery learning. He argues that students do not always know what is important or relevant, and that many students need external motivation to do the cognitive work necessary to learn what is taught in school.

Ausubel described an alternative model of instruction, called **reception learning.** Reception theorists suggest that the job of the teacher is to structure the learning situation, to select materials that are appropriate for students, and then present them in well-organized lessons that progress from general ideas to specific details. At the core of Ausubel's approach is what he calls **expository teaching,** which is teacher-planned, systematic instruction on meaningful information.

Although the role of the teacher differs markedly in discovery learning and reception learning, the two approaches do have some common themes. First, both

---

THEORY INTO PRACTICE
Discovery Learning

Teachers who subscribe to Bruner's fundamental goal of making students self-sufficient should encourage independence from the very beginning of the child's school career. But how can you help students gain independence? Perhaps the most appropriate answer from the discovery perspective is to let the students follow their natural interests in achieving competence and satisfying their curiosity. You should encourage students to solve problems on their own or in groups instead of teaching them the answers. Students benefit more from being able to "see" and "do" things than from hearing lectures. You can help students understand difficult concepts by using demonstrations and pictures.

Learning should be flexible and exploratory. If students appear to be struggling with a concept, allow them time to try to solve the problem on their own before providing the solution.

Teachers must also consider the students' attitudes toward learning. According to Bruner, school should arouse children's curiosity, minimize the risk of failure, and be as relevant for the student as possible.

Finally, plan your curriculum so that you periodically

return to important concepts. By doing so, you accomplish a number of goals. First, covering familiar information strengthens it in the students' knowledge structure, especially if the material is presented in different ways. Second, returning to difficult concepts lets you discuss them in more detail. Third, by rethinking a hard problem, students often see solutions that did not appear before. A final reason for presenting material from several perspectives and tackling unresolved problems is to help students improve their intellectual skills, which ultimately allow them to learn independently.

Here are some additional suggestions based on the discovery approach to teaching:

1. Encourage "informed guessing" by asking leading questions.
2. Use a variety of materials and games.
3. Let students satisfy their curiosity even if they pursue ideas not directly related to the lesson.
4. Use a number of examples that contrast the subject matter to related topics.

---

require that students be actively involved in the learning process. Second, both approaches emphasize ways of bringing students' prior knowledge to bear on new learning. Third, both assume that knowledge continually changes once it is "inside" the learner's mind.

Progressive Differentiation
Lesson progression that starts with general concepts, then moves to specifics

Expository teaching consists of three principal stages of lesson presentation.

Phase One: Presentation of Advance Organizer. The advance organizer relates the ideas to be presented in a lesson to information already in students' minds, and provides a broad organizational scheme for the more specific information to be presented.

Phase Two: Presentation of Learning Task or Material. In the second part of the lesson the new material is presented by means of lectures, discussions, films, or student tasks. Ausubel emphasizes the need to maintain student attention, as well as the need for a clear organization of the material to correspond to the structure laid out in the advance organizer. He suggests a process called **progressive differentiation,** which is a step-by-step progression from general concepts to specific information, illustrative examples, and contrasts between new and old concepts.

Phase Three: Strengthening Cognitive Organization. In the third phase of the lesson Ausubel suggests that the teacher try to tie the new information into the structure laid out at the beginning of the lesson, by reminding students of how each specific detail relates to the big picture. Also, students are questioned to see if they have understood the lesson and if they can relate it to their prior knowledge and to the organization described in the advance organizer. Finally, students are given an opportunity to ask questions that extend their understanding beyond the content of the lesson.

Robert Gagné: Events of Learning and Instruction

Robert Gagné (1974, 1977; Gagné and Briggs, 1979) has proposed conditions that must be satisfied if learning is to take place, and has related these conditions to a description of essential "events of instruction," steps in the transmission of information to classroom groups. Gagné's theories have been influential in the research on components of effective lessons presented in Chapter 8. Some of the terminology and concepts presented in this section were revised in Gagné's later work (Gagné, 1977; Gagné and Briggs, 1979). However, the Gagné (1974) formulation is presented here because it sets out the relationship between the events of learning and the events of instruction, both of which are discussed in this section.

Events of Learning. Gagné proposed that an act of learning involves a series of eight events, which are listed in Figure 6.5. The items in boxes represent *internal* events that go on in the mind of the learner, and the words outside the boxes represent *external* events that might be structured by a teacher, by the learner, or by the characteristics of the task. The events of learning are as follows:

1. *Motivation phase:* The learner must be motivated to learn by an expectation that learning will be rewarding. For example, learners might expect that the information will satisfy their curiosity about a subject, will be useful to them, or will help them get a better grade.

2. *Apprehending phase:* The learner must attend to the essential features of an instructional event if learning is to take place. For instance, this could mean paying attention to the relevant aspects of what a lecturer is saying or to the main ideas in a textbook. The lecturer can focus learners' attention on important information by

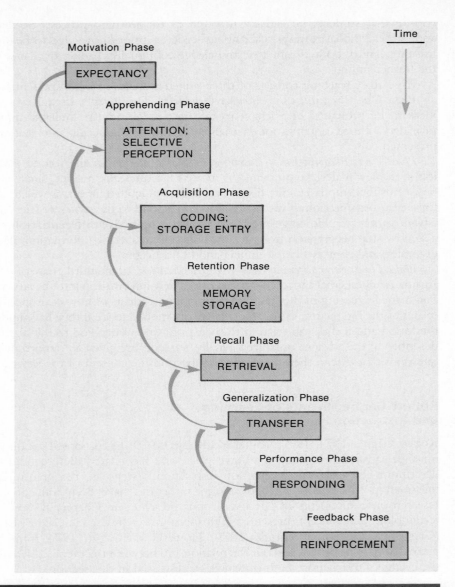

Time

Motivation Phase

EXPECTANCY

Apprehending Phase

ATTENTION;
SELECTIVE
PERCEPTION

Acquisition Phase

CODING;
STORAGE ENTRY

Retention Phase

MEMORY
STORAGE

Recall Phase

RETRIEVAL

Generalization Phase

TRANSFER

Performance Phase

RESPONDING

Feedback Phase

REINFORCEMENT

FIGURE 6.5

Events of Learning

An act of learning is thought to include eight phases. The phases (shown outside the boxes) are external events that can be structured by the learner or teacher. Each is paired with a process within the learner's mind (shown inside the boxes).

From Gagné, 1974, p. 28.

saying (for example): "Listen to the next two words I say, to see if they are different," or "Look at the upper part of this picture" (Gagné, 1974, p. 32). Written materials can do the same by highlighting certain words or sentences, or by using headings, chapter outlines, and notes in the margins.

3. *Acquisition phase.* When the learner is attending to relevant information, the stage is set. The information is presented. As noted earlier in this chapter and in Chapter 5, however, information is not stored directly in memory. Rather, it is

transformed into a meaningful form that relates to information already in the learner's memory. Learners may form mental images of the information or form associations between the new information and old information. Teachers can encourage this process by the use of advance organizers (Ausubel, 1963), by suggesting or demonstrating mental images, by allowing students to see or manipulate objects, or by pointing out relationships between new information and previous knowledge.

4. *Retention phase:* The newly acquired information must be transferred from short-term to long-term memory. This may take place by means of rehearsal, practice, elaboration, or other means.

5. *Recall phase:* It is possible that we can lose access to information in long-term memory. Thus an important part of learning is to learn to gain access to that which we have learned, to recall previously learned information. Access to information is aided by organization: well-organized material grouped by categories or concepts can be more easily recalled than randomly presented material. Recall can also be aided by noting linkages between concepts, particularly between new information and prior knowledge.

6. *Generalization phase:* Usually information is of little value unless it can be applied outside of the context in which it was learned. Thus generalization or transfer of information to new situations is a critical phase in learning. Transfer can be aided by requiring learners to use information in new settings or circumstances, such as asking students to use new arithmetic skills to solve realistic problems, and stating "working rules" ("The angle of incidence equals the angle of reflection") that will apply in many circumstances.

7. *Performance phase:* Learners must demonstrate that they "have it" by some overt performance. For example, students who had just learned subject-verb agreement might show their new knowledge by choosing the correct verb in a sentence such as "A range of subjects (is, are) discussed."

8. *Feedback phase:* Students must receive feedback on their performance indicating whether or not they have understood. This feedback may serve as a reinforcer for successful performance. For example, students in an automobile mechanics course might watch someone assemble a carburetor. After seeing the assembly demonstrated, they might assemble a carburetor themselves and install it in a car (performance phase) and then see if the car starts (feedback phase). If it does, they are reinforced for their learning behaviors. If not, this is valuable information they will use to alter their behavior, reassemble the carburetor, and try again.

Events of Instruction.   Based on his analysis of the critical events of *learning*, Gagné proposed critical events of *instruction*. Note that Gagné does not imply that only teachers can provide instruction; his events of *learning* can be applied as well to discovery learning or independent learning outside of the classroom as to classroom learning. However, his events of instruction do assume that a teacher is presenting one lesson to a group of students.

1. *Activating motivation and informing the learner of the objective:* The first step in the lesson is to get students motivated to learn it. Most often, this is accomplished by arousing students' interest in the content and by pointing out how useful the information will be. For example, the teacher arouses students' interest in learning about fractions of a liter by telling them that this is information they will need in the future, and posing a problem involving buying gasoline for a model airplane. Other means of activating student motivation are discussed in Chapters 8 and 10.

Part of activating student motivation is informing students of what they will be able to do at the end of the lesson. Students need to know *why* they are learning what they are learning as well as *what* they will be learning. Informing the learner of the objective also helps focus student attention on relevant aspects of the lesson. For example, the teacher poses the question, "How can we know how much to ask for if we only want a small amount?" This informs students that by the end of the lesson they should know how to ask for amounts of a liquid that are less than a liter.

2. *Directing attention:* The teacher must direct students' attention to relevant information, to focus their mental energies on critical points. This may be done directly, as when a teacher says, "Notice the markings on the bird's wing," or "Watch for Shakespeare's use of military metaphors in this passage to foretell the events to come." Use of diagrams or writing words or concepts on the chalkboard also focus student attention.

3. *Stimulating recall:* In order to successfully assimilate new information, students need to recall related information already in their memories. The teacher should stimulate recall of relevant prerequisite skills by reminding students of the earlier information and relating it to the new material. For example, the teacher reviews the concept "centimeter" before teaching about "cubic centimeters."

4. *Providing learning guidance:* This stage of the instructional process is where new information is presented and discussed. The form that learning guidance takes depends, however, on the learning objectives. For example, the emphasis in concept learning may be on stating rules and giving examples and nonexamples. In discovery learning, learning guidance may take the form of providing appropriate materials and hints to guide students toward fruitful avenues.

5. *Enhancing retention:* Retention of newly acquired information can be enhanced in several ways. One is to have students practice new skills, as when students practice mathematics problems following a lesson. Another is to provide many examples. Spaced reviews over several days or weeks also aid retention.

6. *Promoting transfer of learning:* Once new information is established in students'

THEORY INTO PRACTICE
Expository Teaching

There are a number of practical issues that are central to expository teaching. For example, all incoming information must be integrated into what students already know if it is to be of lasting importance. This suggests that materials should be organized so that general ideas are presented before specific facts and detail. Advance organizers can help encourage this process of focusing on increasingly smaller details. To do this, each organizer should be more specific than the one before. The first organizers help anchor information at the general level, while later ones anchor more detailed material.

Ausubel suggests that teachers use a **deductive teaching approach.** In other words, they should introduce a topic with general concepts, then gradually include specific examples, always linking the new information to what students already know.

If you teach a unit on the Civil War, for example,

you would want to include advance organizers on important topics such as slavery and the overall military strategies of the North and the South. Remember, the purpose of advance organizers is to activate as much of the students' present relevant background knowledge as possible to help them anchor and interpret new information. Use organizers frequently rather than only when you present major themes.

Here are two additional suggestions for teaching based on the strategies for reception learning:

1. Organize instruction beforehand in a way that leads from the most general concepts to the most inclusive details.
2. Plan brief class discussions before new material is presented so students can share important background information.

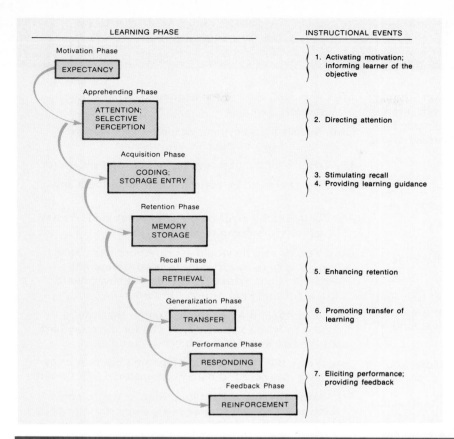

LEARNING PHASE	INSTRUCTIONAL EVENTS

Motivation Phase
EXPECTANCY
1. Activating motivation; informing learner of the objective

Apprehending Phase
ATTENTION; SELECTIVE PERCEPTION
2. Directing attention

Acquisition Phase
CODING; STORAGE ENTRY
3. Stimulating recall
4. Providing learning guidance

Retention Phase
MEMORY STORAGE

Recall Phase
RETRIEVAL
5. Enhancing retention

Generalization Phase
TRANSFER
6. Promoting transfer of learning

Performance Phase
RESPONDING
7. Eliciting performance; providing feedback

Feedback Phase
REINFORCEMENT

FIGURE 6.6

Relation of the Phases of Learning to Instructional Events

Gagné's strategy for lesson presentation suggests that teachers lead students through a series of events that have been identified as necessary for learning.

From Gagné, 1974, p. 119.

memories, the next task is to be sure that students can transfer or generalize principles or concepts to new circumstances, such as problem-solving applications or other fields of study. For example, the teacher promotes transfer of learning by having students consider the relationship of cubic centimeters to liters in a cube of given dimensions rather than a graduated cylinder, to get them to use their new skills in a different context and tie it to a prior skill (finding the volume of a cube).

7. *Eliciting the performance; providing feedback:* At the end of the instructional cycle students must show what they know so that the teacher can tell them whether or not they are on the right track. For example, if students have learned about latitude and longitude, they might be asked to locate Baltimore, London, Sydney, and Calcutta on a globe, and the teacher would indicate whether the latitudes and longitudes given for these cities are correct. The performance may take the form of informal questions, of a brief quiz or test, or of actual performance of a skill.

Relationship Between Events of Learning and Events of Instruction. Gagné's events of instruction are clearly based on his events of learning. The relationship between the two sets of events is illustrated in Figure 6.6.

Greg Ryerson, a sophomore at Van Buren High School, is worried about his upcoming unit exam in advanced placement world history. During sixth period study hall, he goes up to the study hall monitor, Ray Carter, who is a social studies teacher.

MR. CARTER: Can I help you, Greg?

GREG: You sure can, Mr. Carter, if you have time. You teach world history, don't you?

MR. CARTER: Not this year, but, yes, I have taught it many times. It's one of my favorite subjects. What's the problem?

GREG: I'm in Mr. Stadler's advanced placement class and we have this big unit exam coming up on Greece and Rome. I'm really worried about it. I was kind of hoping you might help me.

MR. CARTER: Well, I'm not busy now, but shouldn't you really talk to Mr. Stadler?

GREG: I tried but he said he didn't have time to organize study groups this time. He said that he's the Key Club sponsor and they have to build a float for the homecoming parade and—

MR. CARTER: I get the picture, Greg. OK, why are you worried about the test?

GREG: Well, it covers so much material. I just don't see how I'm going to memorize all this stuff!

MR. CARTER: OK, start at the beginning. What kind of a test is it?

GREG: Mr. Stadler said there would be 100 objective items and two or three essay questions.

MR. CARTER: Will the objective test all be multiple choice?

GREG: No, there will be matching and fill in the blank, too.

MR. CARTER: Did he give you any idea what kind of essay questions he's going to ask?

GREG: Yes. He said he would ask questions like, "How would our life be different today if Greece and Rome had not existed?" I just don't know how to study for that kind of test, Mr. Carter!

MR. CARTER: Well, the first thing, Greg, is that you're going to have to study differently for the essay part of the test than for the objective part. Right?

GREG: Yeah, but this is the first time he's given us essay questions. There's so darn much material, Mr. Carter!

MR. CARTER: The important thing, Greg, is not to panic. Let's see if we can't figure out a study strategy. Let's begin with the objective part. How do you go about reading the material in the text?

GREG: I underline everything important, all the names, dates, battles, and terms. I also take real good notes in class.

MR. CARTER: Then you go over everything you've marked before the exam.

In essence, Gagné's events of instruction are designed to lead learners through the steps they must accomplish to learn. This is not to say that students cannot go through these steps on their own; in many cases, they can and should. However, in circumstances when the teacher is directing instruction, as in traditional classroom lessons, Gagné's events of instruction are keyed to ensuring that the necessary cognitive steps for coding, storing, retrieving, and transferring information are provided for.

For more on Gagné's theories, see Chapters 7 and 8.

■ **Stop and Think**

Evaluate the advantages and disadvantages of an elementary school education based solely on the discovery approach to learning and teaching. Do the same for an education based solely on expository teaching. Now list ways in which your evaluation would change if you were considering a junior high school or high school education.

GREG: That's right.

MR. CARTER: How has that been working?

GREG: Well, OK. But we've only had two big tests before this one, and none of them covered this much material. Take the battles, Mr. Carter. I don't see how I'm going to remember all the Greek battles—not to mention the Roman ones! How do I remember [looking at his notes] the names of the battles of Plataea, Salamis, Marathon, and Thermopylae alone, much less when they were fought, why they were fought, and who won? Usually I can take the first letters and make a word to remember, but what do you do with P, S, M, and T?

MR. CARTER: Well, Greg, maybe you're going about this in the wrong way. You probably need to do more than just memorize the facts.

GREG: But how else can I remember everything, Mr. Carter?

MR. CARTER: It has to be meaningful, Greg! It has to all come alive for you. Take the Battle of Thermopylae in 480 B.C. Now there was a good one! Three hundred Spartans held off 100,000 Persians for three days at a narrow mountain pass to give the Greek city-states time to get their armies organized to meet the Persians.

GREG: That *is* interesting, Mr. Carter, and I wish I had more time to learn about it. But the test is the day after tomorrow!

MR. CARTER: But, Greg, if this material isn't meaningful to you, you'll have real problems with the essay questions. Mr. Stadler will be looking at how well you organize and synthesize your thoughts. You can't write good essay answers if you only memorize names and dates.

GREG: I hear what you're saying, Mr. Carter, but please tell me something.

MR. CARTER: What's that, Greg?

GREG: Please tell how to do that. How do I go about organizing this material so it's meaningful?

QUESTIONS

1. What is the difference between rote and meaningful learning? How can meaningful learning be promoted?
2. What study strategies are most effective in promoting meaningful learning? How is the study strategy used affected by the different types of information being recalled and processed?
3. What advice should Mr. Carter give Greg about the best way to study the material so that it's most meaningful? Since both objective and essay test items are involved, should Greg use more than one strategy?

SUMMARY AND REVIEW OF OBJECTIVES

Advance Organizers. Information that fits easily with what a person already knows can be learned faster than disorganized or totally unfamiliar ideas. When students accommodate newly acquired information with what they already know, they are engaging in meaningful learning as opposed to rote memorization. Advance organizers affect the meaning attached to new information and can help students make sense of it.

Study Skills. Mathemagenic behavior involves any behavior that helps a person learn. One such behavior is answering questions while learning new material. Most effective are (1) paraphrased questions that require the student to think about the meaning of both the material and the question, and (2) questions that occur shortly after the new material is presented. Other recommended strategies include underlining, note taking, summarizing, student-generated questions, outlining, and cooperative scripts.

Metacognition refers to the ability to think about and control one's own thinking process. It is an important aspect of study strategies such as SQ3R, SQ4R, MURDER, and reciprocal teaching. In reciprocal teaching, students learn a prescribed sequence of metacognitive skills, observe the teacher model those skills, and then teach those skills to others.

Concepts. Concepts can be learned by observation or by definition. An effective way to teach concepts is to have students learn them in both these ways. The rule-example-rule approach to teaching concepts suggests that teachers first state a definition, then give examples, and finally restate the definition. Easy examples should be given before hard ones, and teachers should compare and contrast the examples presented.

Problem Solving. Teachers can help students transfer information learned in one setting to other situations. This skill will contribute to the student's problem-solving abilities. Specific aspects of problem solving include focusing on relevant information, analyzing the problem and specifying a goal, and representing the problem in a way that leads to a solution.

Models of Instruction. According to proponents of discovery learning, schools should provide an environment that helps students learn on their own. Advantages of the discovery approach include its ability to arouse the interest of students, to motivate them, and to advance their problem-solving skills. Proponents of expository teaching, on the other hand, believe that the school and the teacher should select, organize, and clearly present information that is appropriate for students.

STUDY QUESTIONS

1. According to cognitive learning theory, which of the following statements is true?
   a. Meaningful learning involves associations that are essentially arbitrary and unalterable.
   b. "Inert knowledge" is another term for the mental schemata learners use in interpreting new information.
   c. Rote learning has little place in the teaching of most school subjects.
   d. Schemata are thought to be organized with specific ideas categorized under more general categories.
   e. All of the above.

2. Which of the following types of questions are considered most likely to facilitate meaningful learning?
   a. Paraphrased questions that occur before the relevant material
   b. Paraphrased questions that occur after the relevant material
   c. Factual questions that occur before the relevant material
   d. Factual questions that occur after the relevant material

3. Which of the following study strategies have been found to consistently enhance learning?
   a. Underlining
   b. Note-taking
   c. Summarizing
   d. Outlining
   e. None of the above

4. Students (and teachers) can improve their comprehension of written material if they use a strategy called SQ4R. The name of this strategy stands for its steps, which are _____, _____, _____, _____, _____, and _____.

5. In the study strategy called "cooperative scripts," the
   a. higher-achieving student is usually designated as the recaller.
   b. desired group size is from 3–5 individuals.
   c. amount of material to be read prior to the summaries should be specified in advance.
   d. listener should generally take a completely passive role.
   e. all of the above.

6. Which of the following best illustrates transfer of learning?
   a. Students who carefully study the week's spelling words do well on the Friday spelling quiz.
   b. A student who excells in mathematics and art goes on to become a skilled architect.
   c. Students recite lines from Shakespeare after being required to memorize the lines.
   d. A student who studied auto mechanics in high school catches on quickly to concepts in physics and chemistry.

7. Which term represents a key component or process of "metacognition"?
   a. Self-monitoring
   b. Part learning
   c. Memorization
   d. Advance organizer
   e. Concept learning
8. A possible weakness associated with Feuerstein's Instrumental Enrichment program is its failure thus far to raise scores on
   a. IQ tests.
   b. school achievement tests.
   c. personality inventories.
   d. creativity measures.

9. Educators who support the use of expository teaching would agree that
   a. teachers should present lessons to students in an organized, finished form.
   b. new knowledge should be kept distinct from prior learning.
   c. students are the best judges of what they should learn.
   d. progressive differentiation should be minimized to the extent possible.

Answers: 1. d 2. b 3. e 4. Survey (Scan), Question, Read, Reflect, Recite, Review 5. c 6. b 7. a 8. b 9. a

SUGGESTED READINGS

ANDERSON, J. R. (1985). *Cognitive psychology and its implications* (2nd ed.). San Francisco: Freeman.

ANDRE, T. (1984). Problem-solving. In G. Phye and T. Andre (Eds.), *Cognitive instructional psychology*. New York: Academic Press.

AUSUBEL, D. B. (1963). *The psychology of meaningful verbal learning*. New York: Grune and Stratton.

BRANSFORD, J. D. (1987). *Enhancing thinking and learning*. New York: W. H. Freeman.

BRUNER, J. D. (1966). *Toward a theory of instruction*. New York: Norton.

DANSEREAU, D. F. (1985). Learning strategy research. In J. Segal, S. Chipman, and K. Glaser (Eds.), *Thinking and learning skills: Relating instruction to basic research*, Vol. 1. Hillsdale, N.J.: Erlbaum.

GAGNÉ, R. (1970). *The conditions of learning* (2nd ed.). New York: Holt, Rinehart & Winston.

JOYCE, B., and WEIL, M. (1980). *Models of teaching*. Englewood Cliffs, N.J.: Prentice-Hall.

NICKERSON, R. S., PERKINS, D. N., and SMITH, E. E. (1985). *The teaching of thinking*. Hillsdale, N.J.: Erlbaum.

PERKINS, D. N., and SALOMON, G. (1988). Teaching for transfer. *Educational Leadership, 46*(1), 22–32.

STERNBERG, R. J., and BHANA, K. (1986). Synthesis of research on the effectiveness of intellectual skills programs: Snake-oil remedies or miracle cures? *Educational Leadership*, (2), 60–67.

TENNYSON, R. D., and PARK, O. (1980). The teaching of concepts: A review of instructional design literature. *Review of Educational Research, 50*, 55–70.

WITTROCK, M. C. (1986). Students' thought processes. In M. C. Wittrock (Ed.), *Handbook of research on teaching* (3rd ed.). New York: Macmillan.

ZIMMERMAN, B. J., and SCHUNK, D. H. (Eds.). (1989). *Self-regulated learning and academic achievement: theory, research, and practice*. New York: Springer.

Chapter 7

Organizing
for Instruction

Chapter Outline

Instructional Objectives
Types of Objectives: Specific versus General
Linking Objectives and Assessment

Taxonomies of Instructional Objectives
Bloom's Taxonomy of Educational Objectives
Taxonomies of Affective and Psychomotor Objectives
Research on Instructional Objectives
Theory into Practice: Planning Courses, Units, and
   Lessons
Task Analysis
Choosing Your Techniques for Teaching

Arranging the Classroom for Effective Instruction

Chapter Objectives

After reading this chapter you should better understand how to set teaching goals and plan strategies to meet those goals. You should also be able to:

■ Write instructional objectives that will guide your lessons and assessments.

■ Set goals that relate to teaching information and cognitive skills, attitudes, and values, and physical skills.

■ Break down a complex skill into its subskills.

■ Arrange desks and other classroom furniture in ways that minimize disruptions.

Effective teaching begins long before the bell rings. Before the teacher begins the lesson, he or she must answer many questions. What content will I teach? How will I arrange the classroom? What teaching methods and materials will I use? How will I motivate students to do their best?

The remaining chapters in this book present principles and strategies that research in educational psychology and the practical experience of successful teachers have established as central to effective teaching. Where the earlier chapters focused on students and learning, we now turn our attention to teachers and teaching: How can teachers present lessons, manage classroom behavior, deal with individual differences, assess student learning, and accomplish the many essential tasks of teaching.

This brief chapter discusses issues teachers must consider before the bell rings: what to teach and how to arrange the classroom.

INSTRUCTIONAL OBJECTIVES

What do you want your students to know or be able to do at the end of today's lesson? What should they know at the end of a series of lessons on a particular subject? What should they know at the end of the course? Knowing the answers to these questions is one of the most important prerequisites for quality instruction. A teacher is like a wilderness guide with a troop of tenderfeet. If the teacher does not have a map or a plan for getting the group where it needs to go, the whole group will surely be lost.

Setting out objectives at the beginning of a course is an essential step in providing a framework into which individual lessons will fit. Without such a framework it is easy to wander off the track, to spend too much time on topics that are not central to the course. One biology teacher spent most of the year teaching biochemistry; her students knew all about the chemical makeup of DNA, red blood cells, chlorophyll, and starch, but little about zoology, botany, anatomy, or other topics usually central to high school biology. Then in late May the teacher panicked because she realized that the class had to do a series of laboratory exercises before the end of the year. On successive days they dissected a frog, an eye, a brain, and a pig fetus! Needless to say, the students learned little from those hurried labs, and little about biology in general. This teacher did not have a master plan, but was deciding week to week (or perhaps day to day) what to teach, thereby losing sight of the big picture—the scope of knowledge that is generally agreed to be important for a high school student to learn in biology class. Few teachers rigidly follow a plan once they make it, but the process of making it is still very helpful (Clark and Peterson, 1986).

An **instructional objective,** sometimes called a behavioral objective, is a statement of skills or concepts students are expected to know at the end of some period of instruction. Typically, an instructional objective is stated in such a way as to make clear how the objective will be measured (see Mager, 1975). Some examples of instructional objectives are:

- Given 100 division facts (such as 27 divided by 3), students will give correct answers to all 100 in three minutes.

- Students will name at least five functions that characterize all living organisms (respiration, reproduction, etc.)

- In an essay students will be able to compare and contrast the artistic styles of van Gogh and Gauguin.

TABLE 7.1

PARTS OF A BEHAVIORAL OBJECTIVES STATEMENT

	Parts		
	Performance	**Conditions**	**Criterion**
	An objective always says what a learner is expected to do.	An objective always describes the conditions under which the performance is to occur.	Wherever possible, an objective describes the criterion of acceptable performance.
QUESTION ANSWERED:	What should the learner be able to do?	Under what conditions do you want the learner to be able to do it?	How well must it be done?
EXAMPLE:	Correctly use adjectives and adverbs.	Given ten sentences with missing modifiers . . .	. . . the student will correctly choose an adjective or adverb in at least nine of the ten sentences.

- Given the statement, "Resolved: The United States should not have entered World War I," students will be able to argue persuasively either for or against the proposition.

Note that even though these objectives vary enormously in the type of learning involved and the level of students to whom they are addressed, they have several things in common. Mager (1975, p. 21), whose work began the behavioral objectives movement, described objectives as having three parts: performance, conditions, and criteria. Explanations and examples are given in Table 7.1.

In practice, the skeleton of a behavioral objective is condition-performance-criterion. First, state the conditions under which learning will be assessed, as in the following:

- Given a ten-item test . . .
- In an essay the student will be able to . . .
- Using a compass and protractor, the student will be able to . . .

The second part of an objective is usually an action verb that indicates what students will be able to do, for example (from Gronlund, 1978):

- Writes
- Distinguishes between
- Identifies
- Matches

Finally, a behavioral objective generally states a criterion for success, as:

- . . . all 100 multiplication facts in three minutes.
- . . . at least five of the nations that sent explorers to the New World.

Sometimes a criterion for success cannot be specified as a "number correct." Even so, success should be specified as clearly as possible, as in the following:

- The student will write a two-page essay describing the social situation of women as portrayed in *A Doll's House*.
- The student will think of at least six possible but creative uses for an eggbeater other than beating eggs.

Though these objectives require judgment on the part of the teacher, they are better than no objective at all because they make it clear to the students what is required of them and on what basis they will be evaluated. When students know a teacher's instructional objectives, they will be able to discriminate between activities that will be rewarded (with good grades, stars, praise) and those that will go unrewarded. Teachers will be more effective if they help students make such discriminations, because when students know what is expected of them and what will be rewarded, they are more likely to work hard.

Types of Objectives: Specific versus General

Instructional objectives must be adapted to the subject matter being taught (Hamilton, 1985). When students must learn well-defined skills or information with a single right answer, specific instructional objectives should be written as follows:

- Given ten problems involving addition of two fractions with like denominators, students will solve at least nine correctly.

Instructional objectives help students know what teachers want. In cooking class, for example, one teacher might require recipes to be followed exactly while another might encourage creativity.

- Given ten sentences missing verbs, students will correctly choose verbs that agree in number in at least eight sentences. Examples are:

My cat and I _____ birthdays in May.
       (has, have)

Each of us _____ to go to college.
       (want, wants)

Some material, of course, does not lend itself to such specific instructional objectives, and it would be a mistake in such cases to adhere to objectives that have numerical criteria (TenBrink, 1986). For example, it would be possible to have an objective as follows:

- The student will list at least five similarities and five differences between the situation of European immigrants in the early 1900s and that of black Americans today.

However, this objective asks for lists, which may not demonstrate any real understanding of the topic. A less specific but more meaningful objective might be:

- In an essay the student will compare and contrast the situation of European immigrants in the early 1900s and that of black Americans today.

This general instructional objective would allow students more flexibility in expressing their understanding of the topic and would promote comprehension rather than memorization of lists of similarities and differences.

Writing Clear Objectives. While instructional objectives should not be more specific than is justified by the topic, they should be specific enough to be meaningful. For example, the objective concerning European immigrants and black Americans might have been written as follows:

- Students will develop a full appreciation for the diversity of peoples who have contributed to the development of American society.

This sounds nice, but what does it mean? Such an objective neither helps the teacher prepare lessons nor helps students understand what is to be taught and how they will be assessed. This type of fuzzy objective was called **word magic** by Dyer (1967).

Mager (1975, p. 20) lists more and less "slippery" words used to describe instructional objectives:

Words Open to Many Interpretations	Words Open to Fewer Interpretations
to know	to write
to understand	to recite
to appreciate	to identify
to *fully* appreciate	to sort
to grasp the significance	to solve
to enjoy	to construct

Word Magic
Objectives that are too general and vague to be useful in measuring student performance

Assessment
A measure of the degree to which instructional objectives have been attained

Linking Objectives and Assessment

Because instructional objectives are stated in terms of how they will be measured, it is clear that objectives are closely linked to **assessment.** An assessment is any measure of the degree to which students have learned the objectives set out for them. Most assessments in schools are tests or quizzes, or informal verbal assessments such as questions in class. However, students can also show their learning by writing an essay, painting a picture, doing a car tune-up, or baking a pineapple upside-down cake.

The principles of test and quiz construction are discussed in Chapter 14, but several aspects of assessment are mentioned here because they are important in understanding instructional objectives.

One critical principle of assessment is that assessments and objectives must be clearly linked. Students learn some proportion of what they are taught; the greater the overlap between what was taught and what is tested, the better students will score on

FOCUS ON
Organizing for Instruction

Organizing for instruction is a never-ending job for both teachers and school administrators. While the focus for teachers is on tasks that directly affect classroom lessons, administrators deal more with the school calendar, and school-based services. These issues, although outside the domain of the teacher, can significantly affect classroom instruction.

Take, for example, summer vacation. Many districts have decided that closing for the summer—an idea that made sense when children were needed on the farm—now is a waste of money and of building space. It also allows children to backslide in their school learning. Research by Barbara Heyns (discussed in Chapter 13) has found that disadvantaged students are particularly likely to lose over the summer months much of what they have learned during the school year. Although less than one percent of U.S. students attend year-round schools, the amount is twice that of five years ago. Year-round schooling is particularly increasing in California, often in response to overcrowding in areas experiencing rapid gains in population. Students often like the practice because they typically get four 3-week vacations during the year, making each 9-week school term less of an ordeal than the standard 9-*month* session. New York City schools are inching toward year-round operation by increasing summer offerings. "Are we backing into an 11-month or 12-month school year? I guess we are," said a New York City school administrator, Bernard Mecklowitz. "And what makes it terrific is that it's all being done on a voluntary basis." Other school districts are taking increased

responsibility for filling gaps in social services, and in the process are taking on the role of community centers. At the Ramón Emeterio Betances School in Hartford, Conn., the doors open at 7 A.M. and don't close until 13 hours later. The longer days allow the school to offer before- and after-school care for children as well as counseling and outreach programs. To the extent that such services benefit the health and well-being of children, they should also improve the teaching environment in the classroom. In fact, a program initiated by Yale psychiatrist James Comer in New Haven, Conn., focusing primarily on the mental health and social adjustment of disadvantaged children has shown gains in the children's academic performance.

Each of these issues reflects the efforts by school officials to meet educational goals, to be fiscally responsible, and to meet the needs of the children and the community in which the school operates. Each also offers teachers a chance to become involved in policy decisions that affect how and what children are taught in school.

Edward B. Fiske, "Lessons," *New York Times,* January 17, 1990, p. B8.

Samuel Weiss, "As Summer Programs Grow, Year-Round School Comes Closer," *New York Times,* August 14, 1989, p. B1.

"Classes the Year Round Pass the Test for Many," *New York Times,* November 8, 1989, p. B12.

the test and the more accurately any need for additional instruction can be determined (Cooley and Leinhardt, 1980). Teaching should be closely linked to instructional objectives, and both should clearly relate to assessment. If any objective is worth teaching, it is worth testing, and vice versa. This idea was illustrated by Mager as follows:

> During class periods of a seventh grade algebra course, a teacher provided a good deal of skillful guidance in the solution of simple equations. . . . When it came time for an examination, however, the test items consisted mainly of word problems, and the students did rather poorly. The teacher's justification for this "sleight of test" was that the students didn't "really understand" algebra if they could not solve word problems.
>
> Perhaps the teacher was right. But the skill of solving equations is considerably different from the skill of solving word problems; if he wanted his students to learn how to solve word problems, he should have taught them how to do so. (1975, p. 82)

Mager's algebra teacher really had one objective in mind (solving word problems), but taught according to another (solving equations). If he had coordinated his objectives, his teaching, and his assessment, he and his students would have been a lot happier, and the students would have had a much better opportunity to learn to solve algebra word problems.

A second critical principle of assessment is that in most cases assessments are *samples* of student knowledge. For example, if students were asked to memorize all fifty state capitals, it would not be necessary to test them on all fifty; five would probably do. The idea here is that if students do not know *which* five they will be tested on, and if the five are representative of the fifty (that is, they include small and large states as well as states from many regions), then students' performance on the five-item test will be a good indicator of their overall knowledge. A student who gets all five correct probably knows all or almost all the state capitals; one who gets two wrong probably knows only about 60 percent (thirty) of the state capitals. Only when every bit of information is essential (as with multiplication facts or conjugations of the verb "to be" in a foreign language) must every bit of information be assessed.

The importance of this principle of assessment for the writing of instructional objectives is that objectives and assessments need not always be expressed in identical terms. For example, the "state capital" objective and its assessment might be as follows:

Objective

The student will be able to name at least 80 percent of the state capitals.

Assessment

Name the capitals of the following states:
1. Massachusetts
2. Alabama
3. Missouri
4. Idaho
5. California

Students might be considered to have mastered the objective if they can correctly name four of the five capitals.

Using Test Questions to Clarify Objectives. One way to specify objectives for a course is to actually prepare test questions before the course begins. This allows the teacher to write general *teaching* objectives and then to clarify them with very specific learning objectives, as in the following examples:

Teaching Objective	Specific Learning Objective (Test Questions)
A. Subtraction of three-digit numbers renaming once or twice	A1. 237 A2. 412 A3. 596 -184 -298 -448
B. Use of language to set mood in Edgar Allen Poe's "The Raven"	B1. How does Poe reinforce the mood of "The Raven" after setting it in the first stanza?
C. Chemical formulas for common substances	Write the chemical formulas for the following: C1. Water _____ C2. Carbon dioxide _____ C3. Coal _____ C4. Table salt _____

Gronlund (1978) suggests a strategy of specifying general objectives and then making them specific by preparing assessments in advance, as in these examples. Gronlund's approach to assessment is described in Chapter 14.

■ **Stop and Think**

Instructional objectives evidently help teachers, but what about students? List some reasons why a teacher should talk with students early in the school year about course objectives. Compare and contrast instructional objectives with the advance organizers described in Chapter 6.

TAXONOMIES OF INSTRUCTIONAL OBJECTIVES

In writing objectives and assessments it is important to consider different skills and different levels of understanding. For example, in a science lesson for second graders on insects, you might want to impart both information (the names of various insects) and an attitude (the importance of insects to the ecosystem). In other subjects, you may try to convey facts and concepts that differ by type. For example, in teaching a lesson on topic sentences in reading, you might have students first repeat a definition of "topic sentence," then identify topic sentences in paragraphs, and finally write their own topic sentences for original paragraphs. Each of these activities demonstrates a different kind of understanding of the concept "topic sentence," and we could not consider this concept adequately taught if students could do only one of these activities. These various lesson goals can be classified by type and degree of complexity. A taxonomy, or system of classification, helps a teacher categorize instructional activities.

Bloom's Taxonomy of Educational Objectives

In 1956 Benjamin Bloom and some fellow researchers published a **taxonomy of educational objectives** that has been extremely influential in the research and practice of education ever since. Bloom and his colleagues categorized objectives from simple to complex, or from factual to conceptual. The key elements of what is commonly called Bloom's taxonomy (Bloom et al., 1956) are:

1. *Knowledge* (recalling information): The lowest level of objectives in Bloom's hierarchy, knowledge refers to such objectives as memorizing math facts or formulas, scientific principles (for example, a body in motion tends to remain in motion), or verb conjugations.

2. *Comprehension* (translating, interpreting, or extrapolating information): Comprehension objectives require that students show an understanding of information as well as the ability to use it. Examples are interpreting the meaning of a diagram, graph, or parable, inferring the principle underlying a science experiment, and predicting what might happen next in a story.

3. *Application* (using principles or abstractions to solve novel or real-life problems): Application objectives require students to use knowledge or principles to solve practical problems. Examples include using geometric principles and knowledge to figure out how many gallons of water to put into a swimming pool of given dimensions, and using knowledge of the relationship between temperature and pressure to explain why a balloon is larger on a hot day than on a cold day.

4. *Analysis* (breaking down complex information or ideas into simpler parts to understand how the parts relate or are organized): Analysis objectives involve

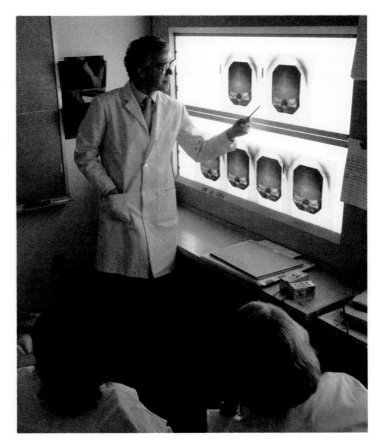

Instructional objectives at all levels of Bloom's taxonomy contribute to a good education. Medical students, for instance, must know not only many facts but also how to apply their knowledge in diverse situations.

having students see the underlying structure of complex information or ideas. Analysis objectives might be contrasting schooling in Western societies with informal education in primitive societies, understanding how the functions of the carburetor and distributor are related in an automobile engine, or identifying the main idea of a short story.

5. *Synthesis* (creation of something that did not exist before): Synthesis objectives involve using skills to create completely new products. Examples would include writing a composition, deriving a mathematical rule, designing a science experiment to solve a problem, and making up a new sentence in a foreign language.

6. *Evaluation* (judging something against a given standard): Evaluation objectives require making value judgments against some criterion or standard. For example, students might be asked to compare the strengths and weaknesses of two home computers in terms of flexibility, power, and available software.

Is Too Much "Knowledge" a Dangerous Thing? Because Bloom's taxonomy is organized from simple to complex, some people interpret it as a ranking of objectives from trivial (knowledge) to important (synthesis, evaluation). However, this is not the intent of the taxonomy. Different levels of objectives are appropriate for different purposes and for students at different stages of development (see Hastings, 1977). For example, students of computer programming often start by learning a single computer language, a task at the simple end of Bloom's taxonomy. Such "low level" knowledge is critical to the accomplishment of "high level" tasks such as programming computers to solve problems. However, when programmers become highly skilled in the use of one language, they often return to square one in Bloom's taxonomy and learn additional languages. The additional knowledge is then applied to ever more complex tasks. Clearly, all levels of understanding are important. Teachers should realize that different subjects lend themselves to different levels of objectives: most objectives in subjects such as mathematics in the early grades fall more appropriately into knowledge, comprehension, and application categories than into "higher-order" skills, while instruction in composition (for example) falls more appropriately into analysis, synthesis, and evaluation categories.

Critics of Bloom's taxonomy (for example, Seddon, 1978; Ormell, 1979) have questioned whether it is a true hierarchy, in the sense that learning higher-order objectives requires mastery of lower-level objectives. In particular, the order of the higher objectives, such as evaluation and synthesis, has been challenged (Madaus et al., 1973). Studies of the meaningfulness of Bloom's taxonomy have found that even trained judges often cannot agree on how to categorize instructional objectives according to the taxonomy (for example, Stoker and Kropp, 1964; Fairbrother, 1975). Again, the disagreements are mostly over the higher categories. Because of these disagreements, Nedelsky (1965) suggested a simplified taxonomy with only three levels: knowledge, understanding, and ability to learn. Despite all the criticism, however, the general form of Bloom's taxonomy has been validated in decades of research, and has guided both research and practice in education since its publication (see De Landsheere, 1977; Seddon, 1978; Furst, 1981).

The primary importance of Bloom's taxonomy is in its reminder that we want students to have many levels of skills. All too often teachers focus quickly on measurable knowledge and comprehension objectives and forget that students cannot be considered proficient in many skills until they can apply or synthesize the skill

(Metfessel et al. 1969). On the other side of the coin, some teachers fail to make certain that students are well rooted in the basics before heading off into "higher-order" objectives.

Behavior Content Matrix
A chart that classifies lesson objectives according to cognitive level

Behavior Content Matrices.   One way to be sure that your objectives cover many levels of Bloom's taxonomy is to write a **behavior content matrix** (Gage and Berliner, 1984). This is simply a chart that shows how a particular concept or skill will be taught and assessed at different cognitive levels. Examples of objectives in a behavior content matrix appear in Table 7.2. Note that for each topic, objectives are listed for some but not all of Bloom's taxonomy. Some topics do not lend themselves to some levels of the taxonomy, and there is no reason that every level should be covered for every topic. However, using a behavior context matrix in setting objectives forces you to consider objectives above the knowledge and comprehension levels.

Outcomes of Learning.   Robert Gagné (1974, 1984), whose "events" of learning and instruction were discussed in Chapter 6, also described a model of the *outcomes* of learning—the types of objectives pursued in instruction. The first three of these outcomes resemble the categories in Bloom's taxonomy.

Gagné's outcomes of learning are important to consider in formulating instructional objectives. For example, verbal information objectives may be expressed and assessed in terms of increases in knowledge, but objectives relating to intellectual skills

TABLE 7.2

EXAMPLES OF OBJECTIVES IN A BEHAVIOR CONTENT MATRIX

A behavior content matrix can remind teachers to develop instructional objectives that address skills at various cognitive levels.

Type of Objective	Example 1: The Area of a Circle	Example 2: Main Idea of a Story	Example 3: The Colonization of Africa
Knowledge	Give the formula for area of a circle.	Define "main idea."	Make a timeline showing how Africa was divided into colonies.
Comprehension		Give examples of ways to find the main idea of a story.	Interpret a map of Africa showing its colonization by European nations.
Application	Apply the formula for area of a circle to real-life problems.		
Analysis		Identify the main idea of a story.	Contrast the goals and methods used in colonizing Africa by the different European nations.
Synthesis	Use knowledge about the areas of circle and volumes of cubes to derive a formula for the volume of a cylinder.	Write a new story based on the main idea of the story read.	Write an essay on the European colonization of Africa from the perspective of a Bantu chief.
Evaluation		Evaluate the story.	

require the student to do something, to discriminate one thing from another, to identify examples and nonexamples of concepts, or to use simple rules to assemble higher-order rules.

Gagné categorized outcomes of learning into five groups, which are summarized in Table 7.3.

1. *Verbal information* corresponds to the "knowledge" level of Bloom's taxonomy; it includes all the facts students must learn, both rote and meaningful (see Chapter 6). Verbal information objectives are the most common in school instruction, particularly in the elementary grades.

2. *Intellectual skill* refers to the "knowing how," as contrasted with the "knowing that" of (verbal) information. The student learns *how* to transform symbols on a page into recognizable words; *how* to convert fractions to decimals; *how* to make verbs agree with subjects of sentences; *how* to turn a French statement into a question; *how* to relate the force acting upon a body to its mass and acceleration (Gagné, 1974, p. 55).

   Gagné further divides intellectual skills into five categories, each building on the previous one. For example, consider the economics concepts "demand" and "price." At the simplest level, the learner must recognize these words, or *discriminate* them from other words. This is a prerequisite for learning the *concepts* of demand and price. These concepts are then *defined* in terms of examples and nonexamples. Once the concepts are clear, a *rule* may be learned. In this case, the rule is "All other things being equal, as demand for a product or service increases, its price also tends to increase." Combining simple rules into *higher-order rules* may then follow. For example, the three simple rules "As demand increases, prices tend to increase," "As supply increases, prices tend to decrease," and "As demand increases, supply tends to increase," might be formed into one higher-order rule: "If demand increases, either supply or price

TABLE 7.3

OUTCOMES OF LEARNING

The outcomes of learning fall into five categories, according to Gagné. Teachers should consider these categories when planning instructional objectives and assessment.

Learning Outcome	Example of Human Performance Made Possible by the Capability
Verbal information	Stating the provisions of the First Amendment to the U.S. Constitution
Intellectual skill	Showing how to do the following:
Discrimination	Distinguishing printed "b's" from "d's"
Concrete concept	Identifying the spatial relation "below"
Defined concept	Classifying a "city" by using a definition
Rule	Demonstrating that water changes state at 100°C.
Higher-order rule	Generating a rule for predicting rainfall, given conditions of location and terrain
Cognitive strategy	Originating a novel plan for disposing of fallen leaves
Attitude	Choosing swimming as a preferred exercise
Motor skill	Planing the edge of a board

SOURCE: Adapted from Gagné, 1974, p. 68.

(or both) will tend to increase. If increased demand leads to increased supply, prices will tend to remain stable; if increased demand does not lead to increased supply; prices will tend to rise."

3. *Cognitive strategy* includes the skills students use to learn and the procedures they employ to assimilate new information and solve problems. As examples of cognitive strategies, recall the step-by-step procedures for solving problems discussed in Chapter 6. Learning cognitive strategies is important for becoming an independent learner—for learning how to learn.

4. and 5. *Attitude* and *motor skill* are also important outcomes of human learning. These are discussed in the following section.

Taxonomies of Affective and Psychomotor Objectives

Learning facts and skills is not the only important goal of instruction. Sometimes the feelings that students have about a subject or about their own skills are at least as important as how much information they learn. Instructional goals related to attitudes and values are called **affective objectives.** Many would argue that a principal purpose of a U.S. history or civics course is to promote values of patriotism and civic responsibility. Considering the high levels of "math phobia" among many adults, it is certainly one purpose of any mathematics course to give students confidence in their ability to use mathematics.

Krathwohl et al. (1964) designed a taxonomy of affective objectives, which can be summarized as follows:

1. *Receiving:* Students show awareness of and willingness to receive information or other stimuli (for example, "I'm willing to receive math instruction").

2. *Responding:* Students indicate a willingness to participate in a given activity, accept certain ideas, and show satisfaction in participating in activities (for example, "I'm eager to participate in group discussions").

3. *Valuing:* Students indicate that they value certain propositions, and express commitment to ideas or activities (for example, "I believe in the importance of civic responsibility in our society").

4. *Organization:* Students integrate and reconcile different values and develop value systems. For example, students might reconcile love for living things and dislike of hunting with the need to avoid overpopulation of deer herds and their own preference for eating meat.

5. *Characterization by value:* A set of values becomes a way of life. Students develop a generalized predisposition to act in a certain way, such as to approach problems confidently and rationally, or to put others' needs above their own.

This taxonomy of affective objectives has played a lesser role in schools than has Bloom's taxonomy of educational objectives. It is probably most important as a reminder that affective objectives should be considered in planning and carrying out instruction (see Eisner, 1969). Love of learning, confidence in learning, and development of prosocial, cooperative attitudes are among the most important objectives teachers should have for their students.

Psychomotor Objectives
Objectives concerned with physical skills that students must master

Educational activities, such as field trips, often are designed to influence students' attitudes and values. Such goals are called affective objectives.

Some objectives that students must attain involve physical skills, such as handwriting, dancing, painting, typing, and many physical education skills. Simpson (1966) has described a taxonomy of **psychomotor objectives,** which progresses from preparedness to imitation to proficiency to automaticity to adaptation.

Research on Instructional Objectives

Three principal reasons are given for writing instructional objectives (Duchastel and Merrill, 1973). One is that this exercise helps organize the teacher's planning. As Mager (1975) puts it, if you're not sure where you're going, you're liable to end up someplace else and not even know it. Another is that establishing instructional objectives helps guide evaluation. Finally, it is hypothesized that development of instructional objectives improves student achievement.

Little is known about the effects of instructional objectives on teachers' planning or on the evaluation process, but in a sense, instructional objectives are helpful in these areas by definition. How could fuzzy planning or no planning at all be better than the specification of clear, concrete objectives? How could fuzzy evaluation be better than evaluation based on well thought out objectives?

In education, however, the ultimate test of any innovation is its effects on students. Here the evidence is less clear. Many researchers have studied the effects on student achievement of telling students in advance the behavioral objectives of a lesson or course. Some (for example, Doty, 1968; Engel, 1968) found that students who were provided with objectives learned more than students who were not. Dalis (1970) compared the achievement effects of presenting tenth-grade students in a three-week health unit with (1) precisely stated objectives, (2) vaguely stated objectives, or (3) no

1. It's August and you're looking ahead to the coming school year—specifically you decide to set some long-term goals for instruction. How do you proceed? What types of questions do you ask yourself?

Joseph Sugamele, who teaches grades 10 and 11 in East Syracuse, N.Y., asks the following questions when planning lessons:

1. Is there a textbook? If so, how does it handle the material I want to cover?
2. How many different methods of teaching can I use, including reading, role playing, audio visual materials, and written responses?
3. How am I going to evaluate whether students have accomplished my goals?
4. If I am going to do group activities, how should I organize the groups? What will groups do? How do I bring the groups back together and synthesize their individual findings?
5. If I am going to use audio-visual material, what is available? Do I have time to preview it and create viewing response guides? Is the vocabulary, fact, and production level appropriate?
6. If I am going to give a reading/writing assignment, is the textbook sufficient or do I need supplemental sources? Will assignments be individual, team, or group work? Do I let students choose or do I assign topics? How do I grade this assignment in relation to other, shorter-term assignments? How much in-class and outside-of-class time should the assignment be given? How can all students share their assignments with other students?
7. If a lesson is going to have a "hands on" component, are there enough different project ideas so every student can do his or her own thing, minimizing competition? How do I evaluate the project?

2. How do you tell students what your long-range instructional goals are for a course?

Teachers write that they use:

- verbal outlines
- questions
- demonstrations of what students will be able to do after the course
- written outlines

Comments from our teachers follow.

Valerie Bang-Jensen, who now teaches kindergarten in Ithaca, N.Y., says:

When I taught sixth grade, I would give the students a verbal overview of a semester and would write an agenda on the board. This helped them develop a sense of how time and subjects can be organized.

Barbara Levin, who taught grades 4 and 5 in Cross Plains, Wis., writes:

Sometimes I asked my fifth-graders to help me plan the science curriculum for the school year. This helped me to capitalize on their interests, and gave them some sense of control over their learning. I did this by listing all units that I was prepared to teach, summarizing them, and then asking the children to rank their preferences.

Gilbert Green, Wilmington, Del., prepares his fifth-graders as follows:

I show examples of the end product, and then students are told the steps or skills required to get there. By telling students course objectives, I help them to see the steps they must take to complete the course

Sandra Dougherty, Shenandoah Junction, W. Va., gives her high school students a course outline:

I distribute a list of objectives to my students, together with a "general" course outline. I emphasize "general" because it allows flexibility in planning as well as spending extra time on skills that may be weak.

3. How do you let students know your objectives for an individual lesson?

Barbara Levin, Cross Plains, Wis.:

I always previewed the lesson orally by telling the children what we would be doing and why we would be doing these things—or what we should be learning. I also reviewed what we did and learned the day before to get them thinking about the topic and how it relates to the upcoming lesson.

objectives. The students given precise objectives learned more than students in the other two groups. On the other hand, several studies found no effects of receiving behavioral objectives (Duchastel and Merrill, 1973). For example, one study found no achievement differences between eleventh-graders receiving specific objectives, general objectives, or no objectives before a social studies lesson (Oswald and Fletcher, 1970).

The situation becomes more complicated when we consider the effects of behavioral objectives on the learning of material not targeted by the objectives. For example, if we tell students before they read *Romeo and Juliet* that they will be tested on questions relating to Juliet, will they learn more or less about Romeo than if they had not been given this specific objective? Once again, the evidence is mixed (see Melton, 1978). In two studies Duchastel (1977) found that students given objectives learned less of the material not included in the objectives than did students not given any objectives. Other studies found either no effect of behavioral objectives on the learning of other material (Morse and Tillman, 1972), or that giving students behavioral objectives relating to some material *increased* their achievement of other skills, which is just the opposite of the Duchastel (1977) findings (Rothkopf and Kaplan, 1972, 1974).

In spite of these mixed research findings, the sum of the research on instructional objectives generally suggests that they should be used. The establishment of instructional objectives and the communication of these objectives to students have never been found to reduce student achievement, and have often been found to increase it. In light of the Duchastel (1977) findings (and in light of common sense), it is important to make sure that instructional objectives communicated to students be broad enough to encompass everything the lesson or course is supposed to teach; there is some danger that giving students too narrow a set of objectives may focus them on some information to the exclusion of other facts and concepts.

Regardless of their effects on student achievement, specification of instructional objectives certainly helps the teacher plan lessons and courses. Perhaps the most convincing support for the establishment of clear instructional objectives is indirect. Cooley and Leinhardt (1980) found that the strongest single factor predicting student reading and math scores was the degree to which students were actually taught the skills tested. This implies that instruction is effective to the degree that objectives, teaching, and assessment are coordinated with one another. Specification of clear instructional objectives is the first step in ensuring that classroom instruction is directed toward giving students critical skills, those we feel are important enough to test.

Task Analysis

In planning lessons, it is important to consider the skills required in the tasks to be taught or assigned. For example, a teacher might ask students to use the school library to write a brief report on a topic of interest. The task seems straightforward enough, but consider the separate skills involved:

- Knowing alphabetical order
- Using the card catalog to find books on a subject
- Using a book index to find information on a topic
- Getting the main idea from expository material

- Planning or outlining a brief report
- Writing expository paragraphs
- Knowing language mechanic skills (such as capitalization, punctuation, and usage)

Task Analysis
Breaking down tasks into fundamental subskills

Of course, these skills could themselves be broken down into subskills, all the way back to letter recognition and handwriting. The teacher must be aware of the subskills involved in any learning task to be certain that students know what they need to know to succeed. Before assigning the library report task, the teacher would need to be sure that students knew, among other things, how to use the card catalog and book indexes, and could comprehend and write expository material. The teacher might teach or review these skills before turning students loose in the library.

Similarly, in teaching a new skill, it is important to consider all the subskills that go into it. Think of all the separate steps involved in long division, in writing chemical formulas, or in identifying topic sentences and supporting details. For that matter, consider the skills that go into making a pizza, as illustrated in Figure 7.1.

The process of breaking tasks or objectives down into their simpler components is called **task analysis** (see Gagné, 1977; Gardner, 1985). In planning a lesson, a three-step process for task analysis may be used:

1. *Identify prerequisite skills:* What should students already know before you teach the lesson? For example, for a lesson on long division, students must know

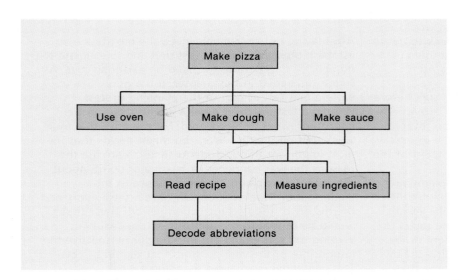

FIGURE 7.1

Example of a Task Analysis

Read the diagram this way: Before students can practice the main skill (making pizza), they must be able to use an oven, make dough, and make sauce. These skills must all be learned before the main skill can be mastered. They are independent of one another and can be learned in any order. Before making dough or making sauce, students must be able to read a recipe and measure ingredients. Finally, to read a recipe, the learner first has to learn how to decode abbreviations.

Adapted from Mager, 1975, p. 100.

Backward Planning Process
Planning instruction by first setting long-range goals, then setting unit objectives, and finally planning daily lessons

their subtraction, multiplication, and division facts, and must be able to subtract and multiply with renaming.

2. *Identify component skills:* In teaching the actual lesson, what subskills must students be taught before they can learn to achieve the larger objective? To return to the long division example, students will need to learn estimating, dividing, multiplying, subtracting, checking, bringing down the next digit, and then repeating the process. Each of these steps must be planned for, taught, and assessed during the lesson.

3. *Plan how component skills will be assembled into the final skill:* The final step in task analysis is to assemble the subskills back into the complete process being

THEORY INTO PRACTICE
Planning Courses, Units, and Lessons

Up to now, this chapter has focused on planning of instruction according to specific instructional objectives. But how does this fit into the larger task of planning an entire course?

In planning a course, it is important to set long-term, middle-term, and short-term objectives before starting to teach. If you were going to drive from Oregon to visit your Aunt Sally in a small town in Ohio, you would first look at a map of the United States to plan how to get to Ohio. Then you would need a more detailed map of Ohio to see how to get to Aunt Sally's town. Finally, you might need a town map or a hand-drawn neighborhood map to find Aunt Sally's house.

Planning course is a little like planning a trip. Before the students arrive for the first day of class, a teacher needs to have a general plan of what will be covered all year, a more specific plan for what will be in the first unit, and a very specific plan for the content of the first lessons. This is illustrated in Table 7.4.

Note that Table 7.4 implies a **backward planning process.** First the course objectives are established. Then unit objectives are designated. Finally, specific lessons are planned. The course objectives list all the topics to be covered during the year. The teacher might divide the number of weeks in the school year (thirty-six) by the number of major topics (eleven) and figure that each will require about three weeks of instruction. More or less than three weeks of instruction could, of course, be reserved for any particular topic, as long as adequate time is allowed for the others. It would be possible to spend a whole semester on any one of the topics in Table 7.4, but in a survey course on life science this would be inappropriate. The teacher must make hard choices about how much time to spend on each topic before the first day of class to avoid spending too much time on early topics and not having enough time

left to do a good job with later ones. Some history teachers always seem to find themselves still on World War I in mid-May, so they have to compress most of the twentieth century into a couple of weeks!

Table 7.4 shows approximate allocations of weeks to each of the topics to be covered. These are just rough estimates to be modified as time goes on.

UNIT OBJECTIVES AND UNIT TESTS

After laying out course objectives, the next task is to establish objectives for the first unit and to estimate the number of class periods to spend on each objective. As suggested earlier in this chapter, it is a good idea to write a unit test as part of the planning process. Writing a test in advance helps you to focus on the important issues to be covered. For example, in a four-week unit on the Civil War, you might decide that the most important things students should learn are the reasons the war happened, a few major points about the military campaigns, the importance of the Emancipation Proclamation, Lincoln's assassination, and the history of the Reconstruction period. These topics would be central to the unit test on the Civil War. Writing this test would put into proper perspective the importance of the various issues that should be covered. This would help you avoid spending a week on the military details of the Battle of Gettysburg, which might be interesting but are of minimal importance relative to the overall objectives.

The test you prepare as part of your course planning may not be exactly what you give at the end of the unit. You may decide to change, add, or delete items to reflect the content you actually covered. But this does not diminish the importance of having decided in advance exactly what objectives you wanted to achieve and how you were going to assess them.

taught. For example, students may be able to estimate, to divide, and to multiply, but this does not necessarily mean they can do long division. The subskills must be integrated into a complete process that students can understand and practice.

Choosing Your Techniques for Teaching

Once you've decided *what* to teach on a given day, you'll have to decide *how* to teach it. Should you lecture? Set up experiments? Show a film? The answer will depend on the topic to be taught, your lesson objectives, and the characteristics of your students.

TABLE 7.4

EXAMPLE OF OBJECTIVES FOR A COURSE IN LIFE SCIENCE

Teachers can allocate instructional time for a course by (1) deciding what topics to cover during the year or semester, (2) deciding how many weeks to spend on each topic, (3) choosing units within each topic, (4) deciding how many days to spend on each, and (5) deciding what each day's lesson should be.

Course Objectives *(Weeks Allocated)*		Unit Objectives *(Days Allocated)*		Lessons
Scientific Method	3	Observation and measurement	4	Lesson 1: • Questions • Observations
Characteristics of living things	3	Prediction and control	2	
Cells	3	Data	3	
Photosynthesis	3	Experiments	3	Lesson 2: • Checking observation with measurement
Respiration	3	Problem solving	3	
Human systems	4			Lesson 3: • Measurement of length
Reproduction	4			
Environment	3			
Adaptation	4			Lesson 4: • Measurement of mass • Measurement of volume
Relationships	3			
Balance	3			

Source: Objectives adapted from Wong et al., 1978.

Many textbooks provide unit tests and objectives, making your task easier. However, even if you have ready-made objectives and tests, it is still important to review their content and change them as necessary to match what you expect to teach.

If you do have to prepare unit tests from scratch, use the guide to test construction described in Chapter 14. Be sure to have the test items cover the various objectives in proportion to their importance to the course as a whole (that is, the more important objectives are covered by more items), and include items that assess different levels of understanding, from knowledge to application to synthesis.

LESSON PLANS AND LESSON ASSESSMENTS

The final step in backward planning is to plan daily lessons. Table 7.4 shows how unit objectives might be broken down into daily lessons. The next step is to plan the content of each lesson. A lesson plan consists of an objective, a plan for presenting information, a plan for giving students practice (if appropriate), a plan for assessing student understanding and, if necessary, a plan for reteaching students (or whole classes) if their understanding is inadequate. The structure of lessons is discussed in detail in Chapter 8.

Variety is important. Students will gain a richer appreciation for, say, biology from a range of experiences—including lectures, microscopic examinations of living organisms, independent research, and discussion.

In addition to planning for variety in the lessons presented on a particular subject, teachers must consider the variety of lesson presentation strategies used on any given day. Hours of lecture can numb the mind of even the most motivated student. Better to plan days that include a mix of activities, some passive, some active, some requiring independent work, some that use groups. This is especially important when teaching elementary school children.

Another way to look at the mix of lessons presented to students is to classify the lessons as either teacher-centered or student-centered. Teacher-centered approaches include traditional lectures and teacher-led lessons. These fall under the label "direct instruction." Student-centered approaches include methods such as discovery learning. Both of these teaching strategies are discussed in Chapter 8, "Effective Instruction." The point here is that teachers should be masters of both approaches, and should be able to use whichever best suits the instructional objectives for a particular lesson.

■ **Stop and Think**

How does the process of organizing for instruction relate to the discussion in Chapters 4, 5, and 6 about how people learn? For instance, describe some memory aids or study strategies that might help students with what Bloom would categorize as knowledge objectives. Also, evaluate how Bloom might categorize the topics of teaching facts, teaching concepts, and teaching for transfer as described in Chapter 6.

ARRANGING THE CLASSROOM FOR EFFECTIVE INSTRUCTION

One important aspect of planning for effective instruction is the physical arrangement of the classroom (see Weinstein, 1979, 1987). Suggestions for room arrangement for elementary and secondary classrooms are presented in Figures 7.2 and 7.3. Researchers have identified four principles of room arrangement for minimizing disturbances and disruptions (Emmer et al., 1984; Evertson et al., 1984). They are as follows:

1. *Keep high-traffic areas free of congestion:* For example, do not put the pencil sharpener where a student using it will block a doorway or disturb another student. Keep students' desks away from doorways, bookshelves, and supply areas to which the class needs frequent access.

2. *Be sure students can be easily seen by the teacher:* Set up student desks so that all students can be seen from the teacher's desk, chalkboard areas, and other instructional areas.

3. *Keep frequently used teaching materials and student supplies readily accessible:* Paper, books, and other supplies should be in easily available, clearly marked areas so that students can find them without teacher help.

4. *Be certain students can see instructional presentations and displays:* Students should be able to see the chalkboard, overhead projector, and instructional areas

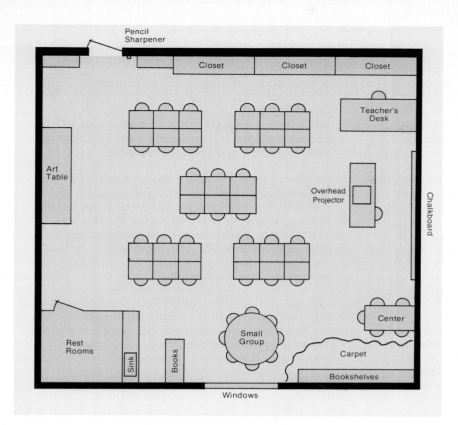

FIGURE 7.2

Elementary Classroom Seating Arrangement

Teachers should arrange classrooms so that disruptions are minimized and all students can see and be seen by the teacher.

From Evertson et al., 1984.

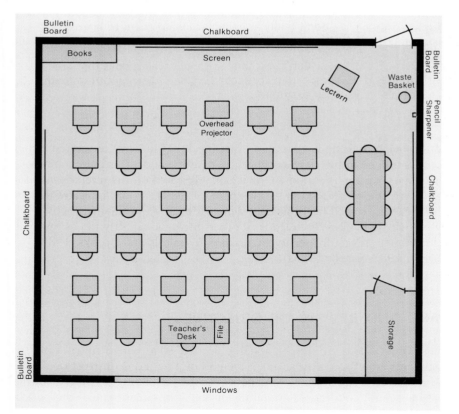

FIGURE 7.3

Secondary School Classroom Seating Arrangement

A traditional row-and-column seating arrangement is appropriate in many junior high school and high school classes.

From Emmer et al., 1984.

Fran Cosco, a beginning second-grade teacher, sits after school is out in the classroom of Sarah Weddings, a third-grade teacher with 17 years experience.

FRAN: I really appreciate your help with these behavioral objectives, Sarah. I know it's all old stuff to you.

SARAH: Well, sort of, but the school system's shift from norm-referenced to criterion-referenced evaluation means that even I will have to change some of my ways. I'm having to rework everything from my behavioral objectives to my report cards. I've written many an objective in my day, but translating them down to the level of the report card is all new to me.

FRAN: That's what I'm finding difficult, too. I learned about behavioral objectives and Bloom's Educational Taxonomy in my coursework, but drawing from them a list of objectives for the report cards is a challenge!

SARAH: And time consuming, too.

FRAN: But, you know, it's not the time that bothers me. It's wondering if this all might be misdirected effort. Writing behavioral objectives for second graders just runs counter to what I think education is all about.

SARAH: What do you mean?

FRAN: What seems important to me in the early grades is that children learn to feel good about themselves and to get along with other children. I have to believe that love and caring are more important to these kids than phonics and math skills.

SARAH: Hmm. I wouldn't totally disagree with you on that, Fran, but don't you think that the skills of learning are important, too? Kids can begin to fall behind really early. It would be a tragedy if we didn't notice that slippage in the lower grades and address it immediately. It seems to me that school achievement might go hand in hand with self esteem and interpersonal skills.

FRAN: I suppose—maybe I got a little carried away. Still, don't you find it hard to specify learning outcomes for kids this young? I know what I want the students to experience but I'm not sure I can specify the learning outcomes.

SARAH: What do you mean?

FRAN: Well, for example, I might want the children to have the fun of going to the zoo. I could probably even list some animals I'd like them to see. But I don't really know what I want them to learn from the experience.

SARAH: Can't you think of *any* learning skills that are important for second graders? How about in math, for example?

without moving their desks or craning their necks. If students are seated far from the action or in places where they can't easily see or hear presentations, they may stop paying attention to the lesson. Research on the interactions of teachers with students seated in various parts of the classroom indicates that students who are seated far from the teacher or away from the main activity rarely participate in class discussions or other instructional activities as much as students who are seated closer to the teacher (Woolfolk and Brooks, 1982; Weinstein, 1987; Good, 1983a).

SUMMARY AND REVIEW OF OBJECTIVES

Instructional Objectives. An instructional objective is a statement of skills or concepts students are expected to know at the end of a period of instruction. Three parts of the instructional objective are performance, or stating what the learner should be able to do; conditions, or stating under what circumstances the perfor-

FRAN: Well, I suppose a child should be able to add two-digit numbers.

SARAH: With or without carrying?

FRAN: Ideally, with both.

SARAH: What about subtraction?

FRAN: Yes, a child should be able to subtract two-digit numbers, at least without borrowing.

SARAH: Anything else?

FRAN: A child should be able to read a clock to the nearest quarter hour. And probably should be able to understand the value of coins and small denomination bills.

SARAH: That's a pretty good list of minimum math skills.

FRAN: But, Sarah, those skills, even if you put them on a report card to check off, aren't what's most important.

SARAH: Human-relations skills again?

FRAN: Yes! And I don't hear anyone talking about putting those kinds of skills on the new report cards.

SARAH: That's true, unless you and I push to get them included.

FRAN: Would you help me with that? Do you think there would be objections?

SARAH: I don't know, but I suspect so. For one thing, a teacher must make some very subjective judgments when assessing a student's human relations skills. Who's to say, for instance, that Tommy is below average in "getting along with others" while Carl is superior in that skill? A teacher might have a tough time supporting that assessment if it were challenged. Also, there's only so much room on a report card, and we're all concerned that we show parents that their kids are learning the basic skills.

FRAN: I know, Sarah, but I just don't get it. What are we supposed to teach: children or subject matter? How can I write behavioral objectives about cognitive skills when more important skills are left out?

QUESTIONS

1. What are behavioral objectives and what are their strengths and weaknesses? What other kinds of instructional objectives are there?
2. On what domains can instructional objectives be focused? What are the cognitive, affective, and psychomotor domains?
3. What advice would you give Fran about writing instructional objectives and identifying the minimum cognitive skills of second graders? What does Fran mean by asking if teachers should teach children or subject matter?

mance will be measured; and criterion, or stating how well the objective must be performed.

The principal reasons for developing instructional objectives are to organize the teacher's planning, to guide evaluation, and to improve student achievement.

The backward planning process starts with the development of long-range goals and moves to a focus on short-range objectives and daily lessons. In using this method, a teacher first lists major topics to be covered during a course. Then each topic is divided into units, with objectives written for each. Finally, daily lessons are planned that will help students meet the unit objectives.

An assessment is any measure of the degree to which students have reached objectives set out for them. Assessments and objectives must be clearly linked. One method that can help clarify instructional objectives is to prepare test items before teaching a course.

Taxonomies of Objectives. Bloom's taxonomy of educational objectives categorizes objectives from simple to complex and from factual to conceptual. The key elements are knowledge, or recalling information; comprehension, or translating or interpreting information; application, or using principles or abstractions to solve novel or real-life problems; analysis, or breaking down complex information into simpler parts; synthesis, or creation of something that did not exist before; and evaluation, or judging something against a given standard. Aside from cognitive skills, other domains in which objectives have been classified are affective objectives which concern students' attitudes and values; and psychomotor objectives which concern mastery of physical skills.

The five categories of learning outcomes described by Gagné are verbal information, which includes all facts that students must learn; intellectual skill, or knowing "how"; cognitive strategy; attitude; and motor skill.

Task Analysis. Task analysis involves breaking down objectives into their components. A three-step process includes identifying prerequisite skills, identifying component skills, and planning how component skills will be integrated into the final skills.

Arranging the Classroom. Four principles of classroom arrangement are: keep high-traffic areas free of congestion, be sure the teacher can see the students, keep frequently used teaching materials and student supplies readily accessible, and be certain students can see instructional presentations and displays.

STUDY QUESTIONS

1. Which of the following objectives satisfies the criteria proposed by Mager?
   a. The student will learn to solve long-division problems involving two-digit numbers.
   b. Without using a calculator, the student will correctly solve 10 out of 12 division problems involving up to two-digit numbers.
   c. The student will understand how to use a calculator in solving long-division problems containing up to two-digit numbers.
   d. Using a calculator, the student will demonstrate mastery of long-division by solving problems involving up to two-digit numbers.

2. The six elements of Bloom's taxonomy of educational objectives are listed below in alphabetical order. Rearrange them so they form a hierarchy from simple to complex tasks.
   a. Analysis
   b. Application
   c. Comprehension
   d. Evaluation
   e. Knowledge
   f. Synthesis

3. A student is shown a model of a space shuttle and asked to explain what its different components are and how they interact. What type of learning is most clearly being emphasized?
   a. Knowledge
   b. Evaluation
   c. Synthesis
   d. Analysis

4. Based on research findings, a desirable outcome of using instructional objectives is
   a. strong and consistent gains in student achievement.
   b. strong and consistent gains in student attitudes toward learning.
   c. better coordination of what is taught and what is tested.
   d. more rapid completion of lessons without declines in achievement.
   e. all of the above.

5. As defined in Gagné's model, an example of verbal information would be
   a. knowing how to write a research report for publication in a professional journal.
   b. knowing which letters are vowels and which are consonants.
   c. appreciating the beauty of the language used and its meanings in a Shakespearian play.
   d. being able to tell someone effective strategies in playing chess.
   e. being able to program a computer.

Answers: 1. b 2. e, c, b, a, f, d 3. d 4. c 5. b

SUGGESTED READINGS

BLOOM, B. S., ENGLEHART, M. B., FURST, E. J., HILL, W. H., and KRATHWOHL, D. R. (1956). *Taxonomy of educational objectives: The classification of educational goals. Handbook 1: The cognitive domain.* New York: Longman.

DUCHASTEL, P. C., and MERRILL, P. F. (1973). The effects of behavioral objectives on learning: A review of empirical studies. *Review of Educational Research, 43,* 53–69.

GRONLUND, N. E. (1978). *Stating objectives for classroom instruction* (2nd ed.). New York: Macmillan.

KRATHWOHL, D. R., BLOOM, B. S., and MASIA, B. B. (1964). *Taxonomy of educational objectives: The classification of educational goals. Handbook II: Affective domain.* New York: David McKay.

MAGER, R. F. (1975). *Preparing instructional objectives.* Belmont, Cal.: Fearon.

MELTON, R. F. (1978). Resolution of conflicting claims concerning the effect of behavioral objectives on student learning. *Review of Educational Research,* 18, 291–302.

SEDDON, G. M. (1978). The properties of Bloom's taxonomy of educational objectives for the cognitive domain. *Review of Educational Research,* 48, 303–323.

TEN BRINK, T. D. (1986). Writing instructional objectives. In J. Cooper (Ed.), *Classroom teaching skills* (3rd ed.) Lexington, Mass.: D.C. Heath.

WEINSTEIN, C. S. (1987). Seating patterns. In M. J. Dunkin (Ed.), *International encyclopedia of teaching and teacher education.* New York: Pergamon.

Chapter 8

Effective Instruction

Chapter Objectives

After reading this chapter about presenting lessons, you should be able to:

- List four factors in quality instruction that are under a teacher's control.
- List steps that are considered fundamental to effective lesson presentation.
- List two widely used forms of direct instruction and describe situations in which each can be used.
- Employ class discussions in appropriate situations.
- Understand the goals of humanistic education.

Effective instruction is not just relating information to students in an appealing way. If it were, we could probably find the best lecturers in the world, make videotapes of their lessons, and show the tapes to students. If you think about why videotaped lessons wouldn't work very well, you will realize how much more is involved in effective instruction than simply giving good lectures. First, the video teacher would have no idea of what students already knew. A particular lesson might be too advanced or too easy for a particular group of students. Second, some students might be learning the lesson quite well, while others were missing key concepts and falling behind. The video teacher would have no way of knowing which students needed additional help and, in any case, would have no way of providing it. There would be no way to question students to find out if they were getting the main points and then to reteach any concept they had missed.

Third, the video teacher would have no way of motivating students to pay attention to the lesson or to really try to learn it. If students failed to pay attention or misbehaved, the video teacher couldn't do anything about it. Finally, the video teacher would never know at the end of a lesson whether students had actually learned the main concepts or skills.

This analysis of video teaching illustrates why teachers must be concerned with many elements of instruction in addition to the presentation of information. Teachers must know how to adapt their instruction to the students' levels of knowledge. They must motivate students to learn, manage student behavior, group students for instruction, and assess the students' learning. These elements of lesson design and classroom orgranization are at least as important as the quality of teachers' lectures.

MODELS OF EFFECTIVE INSTRUCTION

Different teaching situations require different instructional approaches. To teach most effectively, teachers should know how to adapt their lesson presentations to a variety of situations.

To help make sense of all the elements of effective instruction, educational psychologists have proposed "models" of effective instruction. These models explain the critical features of high-quality lessons and how they relate to one another to enhance learning.

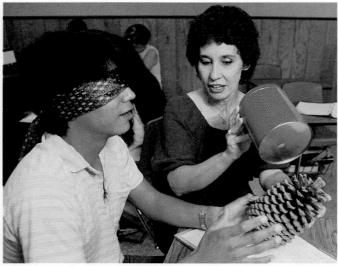

Carroll's Model of School Learning

One of the most influential articles ever published in the field of educational psychology was a paper by John Carroll entitled "A Model of School Learning" (1963). In it he describes teaching in terms of the management of time, resources, and activities to ensure student learning. The model presented by Carroll proposes five elements that contribute to the effectiveness of instruction:

1. *Aptitude:* Students' general abilities to learn.

2. *Ability to understand instruction:* Students' readiness to learn a particular lesson. This is related to abilities, but also to knowledge of prerequisite skills or information needed to understand the next lesson. For example, no matter how able students are, they cannot learn to do long division if they do not know how to multiply and subtract.

3. *Perseverance:* The amount of time students are willing to actively spend learning. Perseverance is mostly a product of students' motivation to learn.

4. *Opportunity:* The amount of time allowed for learning. Opportunity relates to the amount of time teachers spend teaching a particular skill or concept.

5. *Quality of instruction:* The effectiveness with which a lesson is actually delivered. Quality of instruction is high if students learn the material presented in the lesson as rapidly as their abilities and levels of prior knowledge and skills allow.

Carroll discussed these elements in terms of (1) time actually spent on learning and (2) time needed to learn, proposing the following relationship:

$$\text{Degree of Learning} = f(\text{Time Spent/Time Needed})$$

That is, learning is greater the more time students spend on it in relation to the amount of time they need to learn. "Time needed" is a product of aptitude and ability to learn, whereas time actually spent depends on opportunity, quality of instruction, and student perseverence.

What is important about Carroll's model is that it puts the major elements of effective instruction into relationship with one another and discusses them in terms of one variable, time (see Clark, 1987; Carroll, 1989). Many researchers have assumed that degree of learning is primarily a product of student aptitude or intelligence, but what Carroll was implying is that differences in aptitude need not be seen as restricting the *amount* that can be learned, but only as determining the time it takes. In other words, just about anyone can learn just about anything if the quality of instruction is high and if enough time is spent in learning. Carroll's model led directly to Bloom's (1968) theory of mastery learning, discussed in Chapter 9.

Carroll's model mixes two kinds of elements: those that are directly under the control of the teacher, and those that are characteristic of individual students. Aptitude is mostly a characteristic of students over which an individual teacher can have little control. Ability to understand instruction and perseverance are partly controlled by the teacher, but are also partly characteristic of each student. For example, the ability to understand instruction partly depends on the student's ability, but also depends on the teacher's ability to ensure that students have the necessary prerequisites to learn a new lesson. Perseverance results from both the motivation to learn that a student brings to school and from specific strategies a teacher or school

QAIT Model
A model of effective instruction that
focuses on elements that teachers can
directly control

might use to encourage students to do their best. Opportunity (time) and quality of instruction are directly under the control of the teacher or the school.

The QAIT Model of Effective Instruction

Slavin (1987) described a model focusing on the *alterable* elements of Carroll's model, those that the teacher or school can directly change. It is called the QAIT (quality, appropriateness, incentive, time) model of effective instruction.

1. *Quality of instruction:* The degree to which information or skills are presented so that students can easily learn them. Quality of instruction is largely a product of the quality of the curriculum and of the lesson presentation itself.

2. *Appropriate levels of instruction:* The degree to which the teacher makes sure that students are ready to learn a new lesson (that is, have the necessary skills and knowledge to learn it) but have not already learned the lesson. In other words, the level of instruction is appropriate when a lesson is neither too difficult nor too easy for students.

3. *Incentive:* The degree to which the teacher makes sure that students are motivated to work on instructional tasks and to learn the material being presented.

4. *Time:* The degree to which students are given enough time to learn the material being taught.

The shared feature of the four elements in the **QAIT model** is that all must be adequate for instruction to be effective. As noted earlier, effective instruction is not just good teaching. No matter how high the quality of instruction, students will not learn a lesson if they lack the necessary prior skills or information, if they lack the motivation, or if they lack the time they need to learn the lesson. On the other hand, if the quality of instruction is low, then it makes no difference how much students already know, how motivated they are, or how much time they have. Each of the elements of the QAIT model is like a link in a chain, and the chain is only as strong as its weakest link.

The remainder of the section discusses the critical issues involved in each element of the QAIT model.

Quality of Instruction. Quality of instruction refers to the set of activities most people first think of when they think of teaching: lecturing, calling on students, discussing, helping students with seatwork, and so on. When instruction is high in quality, the information presented makes sense to students, is interesting to them, and is easy to remember and apply.

The most important aspect of quality of instruction is the degree to which the lesson makes sense to students. To make lessons make sense, teachers must present material in an orderly, organized way. They need to relate new information to what students already know. They need to use examples, demonstrations, pictures, and diagrams to make ideas vivid for students. They may use such cognitive strategies as advance organizers and memory strategies, which were discussed in Chapters 5 and 6. Sometimes a concept will not make sense to students until they discover it or experience it themselves, or until they discuss it with others.

Another important aspect of quality of instruction is the degree to which the teacher monitors how well students are learning and adapts the pace of instruction so

Effective instruction often requires that teachers use visual aids and demonstrations to help students understand new information.

that it is neither too fast nor too slow. For example, teachers should frequently ask questions to see how much students have grasped. If the answers show that students are keeping up with the lesson, the teacher might move along a little more rapidly. But if students' answers show they are having trouble keeping up, the teacher might review parts of the lesson and slow down the pace.

All these aspects of quality of instruction are discussed further in later sections of this chapter.

Appropriate Levels of Instruction.   Perhaps the most difficult problem of classroom organization is dealing with the fact that students come into class with different levels of knowledge, skills, learning rate, and motivation. This problem requires teachers to provide appropriate levels of instruction. Teaching a class of thirty students (or even a class of ten) is fundamentally different from one-to-one tutoring because of the inevitability of student-to-student differences that affect the success of instruction. Teachers can always be sure that if they teach one lesson to the whole class, some students will learn the material much more quickly than others. In fact, some students may not learn the lesson at all because they lack important prerequisite skills or are not given adequate time (because to give them enough time would waste too much of the time of students who learn rapidly). Recognition of these instructionally important differences leads many teachers to search for ways of individualizing instruction, adapting instruction to meet students' different needs, or grouping students according to their abilities. However, these solutions create new problems that may be more serious than the problems they are meant to solve!

For example, a teacher might give all students materials appropriate to their individual needs and allow them to work at their own rates. This solves the problem of providing appropriate levels of instruction, but creates serious new problems of managing the activities of twenty or thirty students doing twenty or thirty different things. A teacher might group students by ability (for example, Redbirds, Bluebirds, and Yellowbirds) so that each group would have a relatively narrow range of abilities. However, this creates problems, too, because when the teacher is working with the Redbirds, the Bluebirds and Yellowbirds must work without supervision or help.

Methods of accommodating instruction to meet students' different needs are discussed in Chapter 9.

Incentive. Thomas Edison once wrote that "genius is one per cent inspiration and ninety-nine per cent perspiration." The same could probably be said for learning. Learning is work. This is not to say that learning isn't or can't be fun or stimulating, that it has to be a dreary chore—far from it. But it is true that students must exert themselves to pay attention, to conscientiously perform the tasks required of them, and to study, and they must somehow be motivated to do these things. This incentive, or motivation, may come from characteristics of the tasks themselves (for example, the interest value of the material being learned), from characteristics of students (such as their curiosity or positive orientation toward learning), or from rewards provided by the teacher or the school (such as grades and certificates).

If students want to know something, they will be more likely to exert the necessary effort to learn it. This is why there are students who can rattle off the names, batting averages, number of home runs, and all sorts of other information about every player on the Chicago Cubs, but can't name the fifty states or the basic multiplication facts. To such students, baseball facts have great interest value, so they are willing to invest a great deal of effort to master them. Some information is naturally interesting to some or all students, but teachers can do much to *create* interest in a topic by arousing students' curiosity or by showing how knowledge gained in school can be useful outside of school. For example, a baseball fan might be much more interested in learning about computing proportions if told that this information is necessary for computing batting averages!

However, not every subject can be made fascinating to all students at all times. Most students need some kind of recognition or reward if they are to exert maximum effort to learn skills or concepts that may seem unimportant at the moment but will be critical for later learning. For this reason, schools use praise, feedback, grades, certificates, stars, prizes, and other rewards to increase student motivation. These rewards, and general principles of motivation, were discussed in Chapter 4, and are more fully examined in Chapter 10.

Time. The final element of the QAIT model is time. Instruction takes time. More time spent teaching something does not necessarily mean more learning, but if instructional quality, appropriateness of instruction, and incentive are all high, then more time on instruction *will* pay off in greater learning.

The amount of time available for learning depends largely on two factors. The first is the amount of time that the teacher (1) schedules for instruction and (2) actually uses to teach. The other is the amount of time students pay attention to the lesson. Both kinds of time are affected by classroom management and discipline strategies. If students are well behaved, well motivated, and have a sense of purpose and direction, and if teachers are well prepared and well organized, then there is plenty of time for students to learn whatever teachers want to teach. However, many factors, such as interruptions, behavior problems, and poor transitions between activities eat away at the time available for learning (see Karweit, 1989).

Principles of classroom management and discipline are discussed in Chapter 11.

America's high school principals faced a dilemma recently: Should they, in exchange for free TV sets for their classrooms, allow their students to be a captive audience for a daily televised 12-minute newscast that includes commercials?

The newscast, offered by Whittle Communications and called *Channel One*, raised a storm of controversy when it was proposed. Many people criticized the idea as an intrusion of advertising into classroom lessons. On the other side were people who calculated that the benefits of educating students about current events outweighed the two minutes of teaching time lost each day to commercials. Proponents also suggested that while wealthy school districts might have the luxury of snubbing the offer of free TVs, their stand on the moral high ground should not deny a needed educational tool to children in poorer districts.

Weighing the pros and cons of the *Channel One* proposal requires judgments about the dangers of commercialism, the value of lost lesson time, the value to a school of the offered TVs and technology, and about who should control a school's curriculum. Underlying these issues is another question: How effective is television at teaching? Studies of "Sesame Street," educational television's long-running show for preschoolers, prove it is effective for very young children. But what about high school students whose senses have already been dulled by thousands of hours in front of the tube? This question gains added weight when televised instruction is assessed in light of the elements of effective instruction. As the vignette at the beginning of this chapter noted, teachers not only deliver instruction, they must also motivate students, manage them, assess their progress, and perform many other duties in order to teach well.

Therefore, it is likely that shows like *Channel One* can be effective only if they are followed by class discussions. Students are more likely to pay attention and actively process information if they know they will soon discuss topics in the newscast. Discussions should also help students put world events in context by adding needed historical and geographical details.

Another newscast competing for the in-school adolescent audience is CNN "Newsroom," offered by Turner Broadcasting. It is a 15-minute daily broadcast, offered without either the free TV sets or the commercials.

The success of these shows will probably be decided by the size of the audiences they attract. Like any new offering, they are enormously expensive to produce and cannot be kept on the air unless people tune in.

What would you do if you were a school principal faced with deciding whether or not to recommend that your students view one of these shows? Maybe TV can teach some things better than a teacher in front of the classroom. But, should in-school TV come with commercials, as in the case of *Channel One?* Whittle Communications—and its advertisers—think so. What about you?

Walter Goodman, "TV News in the Schools: Which Channel, If Any?" *New York Times,* March 14, 1990, p. C20.

Bill Carter, "Whittle Seen Expanding School News," *New York Times,* June 5, 1989, p. D1.

THE LESSON

Despite the many differences among schools and among subjects and grade levels within the same schools, there is one instructional situation that is common at every level of schooling and for almost every school subject: one teacher trying to transmit information or skills to a class of twenty to thirty students during a period of thirty to sixty minutes. Most teachers spend most of their time teaching class lessons. A typical elementary or secondary teacher might teach 800 to 1,000 class lessons every year!

The lesson is where education takes place. All other aspects of schooling, from buildings to buses to administration, are designed to support the efficient delivery of lessons; they do not educate in themselves. Yet despite the importance of the lesson to the process of education, only in the past fifteen years has research on teaching lessons become central to educational psychology. When educational psychologists finally focused their investigations on the lesson, the result was an explosion of information about what constitutes effective lessons in many subjects and grade levels (see Good and Brophy, 1989; Porter and Brophy, 1988). This chapter presents the principal findings of this research on classroom instruction. It focuses primarily on lessons taught to the class as a whole, on whole-class and small-group discussions, and on humanistic approaches to education.

Parts of the Lesson

A lesson is a process by which information, skills, or concepts are communicated from the teacher to students. There are times when it is best for students to find information on their own, to discover principles working independently of the teacher, or to learn from books, computers, films, or other students. Yet any approach to teaching includes times when the teacher must present material to students in a direct fashion. Although different authors describe it in different ways (see, for example, Block and Anderson, 1975; Gagné and Briggs, 1979; Hunter, 1982; Good et al., 1983; Evertson et al., 1984; Rosenshine and Stevens, 1986), there is general agreement among researchers and teachers as to the sequence of events that characterize effective direct instruction. First, students are brought up-to-date on any skills they might need for today's lesson (for example, the teacher might briefly review yesterday's lesson if today's is a continuation) and are told what they are going to learn. Then most of the lesson time is devoted to the teacher teaching the skills or information, giving students opportunities to practice the skills or express the information, and questioning or quizzing students to see whether or not they are learning the objectives.

A brief description of the parts of a lesson follows:

1. *State learning objectives and orient students to lesson:* Tell students what they will be learning and what performance will be expected of them. "Whet students' appetites" for the lesson by informing them how interesting, important, or personally relevant it will be to them.

2. *Review prerequisites:* Go over any skills or concepts needed to understand today's lesson.

3. *Present new material:* Teach the lesson, presenting information, giving examples, demonstrating concepts, and so on.

4. *Conduct learning probes:* Pose questions to students to assess their level of understanding and correct their misconceptions.

5. *Provide independent practice:* Give students an opportunity to practice new skills or use new information on their own.

6. *Assess performance and provide feedback:* Review independent practice work or give quiz. Give feedback on correct answers, and reteach skills if necessary.

7. *Provide distributed practice and review:* Assign homework to provide distributed practice on the new material. Review material in later lessons and provide a variety of practice opportunities to increase the chances that students will remember what they learned and will be able to apply it in different circumstances.

This general lesson structure would take vastly different forms in different subject areas and at different grade levels. Teachers of older students might take several days for each step of the process, ending with a formal test or quiz; teachers of younger students might go through the entire cycle in a class period, using informal assessments at the end. Two quite different lessons are presented in Figures 8.1 and 8.2 to illustrate how the seven-step lesson structure would be applied to different subjects and grade levels. The first lesson, "Subtraction with Renaming," is an example of the first of a series of lessons directed at a basic math skill. In contrast, the second lesson, "The Origins of World War II," is an example of a lesson directed at higher-order understanding of critical events in history and their causes and interrelationships. Note that the first lesson (see Figure 8.1) proceeds step-by-step and emphasizes frequent learning probes and independent practice to help students thoroughly learn the concepts being taught, while the second (see Figure 8.2) is characterized by an alternation between new information, discussion, and questions to assess comprehension of major concepts.

LESSONS: STEP-BY-STEP

The sequence of activities outlined in these two lessons flows along a logical path, from arousing student interest to presenting new information to allowing students to practice their new knowledge or skills to assessment. This orderly progression is essential to effective lessons at any grade level and in any subject, although the various components and how they are implemented would, of course, look different for different subjects and grades.

A more complete discussion of the lesson parts outlined in the two sample lessons follows.

Orient Students to Lesson

The principle task at the beginning of a lesson is to establish an attitude (or **mental set**) in students that "I'm ready to get down to work; I'm eager to learn the important information or skills the teacher is about to present, and I have a rough idea of what we will be learning."

This "set" can be established in many ways. First, it is important to expect students to be on time to class and to start the lesson immediately when the period begins (Evertson et al., 1984). This establishes a sense of seriousness of purpose that is lost in a "ragged start."

Second, it is important to arouse students' curiosity or interest in the lesson they are about to learn (Gregory, 1975). This was done in the first sample lesson by introducing subtraction with renaming as a skill that would be necessary to decide how many cupcakes the class would need for a party, a situation of some reality and interest to young students. In the second sample lesson the importance of the lesson was "advertised" on the basis that understanding the origins and events of World War II would help students understand events today, and was made personally relevant to students by having them think of a relative who fought in World War II or was deeply affected by it.

A lesson on genetics might be introduced as follows:

"Did you ever wonder why tall parents have taller-than-average children, and red-haired children usually have at least one red-haired parent?

"Think of your own family—if your father and mother are both taller than

FIGURE 8.1

Sample Lesson for Basic Math: Subtraction with Renaming

Lesson Part	Teacher Presentation
1. State learning objective and orient students to lesson.	"There are 32 students in this class. Let's say we were going to have a party, and I was going to get one cupcake for each student in the class. But 5 of you said you didn't like cupcakes. How many cupcakes would I need to get for the students who do like cupcakes? Let's set up the problem on the chalkboard the way we have before, and mark the tens and ones . . ."

tens   ones
  3   2   Students
−   5   Don't like cupcakes

"All right, let's subtract: 2 take away 5 is . . . *hey!* We can't do that! 5 is more than 2, so how can we take 5 away from 2? We can't!

"In this lesson we are going to learn how to subtract when we don't have enough ones. By the end of this lesson, you will be able to show how to rename tens as ones so that you can subtract.

2. Review prerequisites.	"Let's review subtraction when we have enough ones." Put on the chalkboard and have students solve:

$$47 \qquad 56 \qquad 89$$
$$-3 \qquad -23 \qquad -8$$

How many tens are in 23?_____
How many ones are in 30?_____

Give answers, discuss all items missed by many students.

Lesson Part	Teacher Presentation
3A. Present new material (first subskill).	Hand out 5 bundles of 10 popsicle sticks each and 10 individual sticks to each student. Using an overhead projector, explain how to use sticks to show 13, 27, 30. Have students show each number at their own desks. Walk around to check.
4A. Conduct learning probes (first subskill).	Have students show 23 using their sticks. Check desks. Then have students show 40. Check desks. Continue until all students have the idea.
3B. Present new material (second subskill).	Using an overhead projector, explain how to use sticks to show 6 minus 2, and 8 minus 5. Then show 13 and try to take away 5. Ask for suggestions on how this could be done. Show that by removing the rubber band from the ten bundle, we have a total of 13 ones and can remove 5. Have students show this at their desks.
4B. Conduct learning probes (second subskill).	Have students show 12 (check), and then take away 4 by breaking apart the ten bundle. Then have students show 17 and take away 9. Continue until all students have the idea.
3C. Present new material (third subskill).	Give students worksheets showing tens bundles and single units. Explain how to show renaming by crossing out a bundle of ten and rewriting it as 10 units, and then subtracting by crossing out units.
4C. Conduct learning probes (third subskill).	Have students do the first items on the worksheet one at a time, until all students have the idea.
5. Provide independent practice.	Have students continue, completing the worksheet on their own.
6. Assess performance and provide feedback.	Show correct answers to worksheet items on overhead projector. Have students mark their own papers. Ask how many got item no. 1, no. 2, etc., and discuss all items missed by more than a few students. Have students hand in papers.
7. Provide distributed practice and review.	Hand out homework and explain how it is to be done. Review lesson content at start of following lesson and in later lessons.

FIGURE 8.2

Sample Lesson for History: The Origins of World War II

Lesson Part	Teacher Presentation
1. State learning objective and orient students to lesson.	"Today we will begin to discuss the origins and causes of World War II—perhaps the most important event in the twentieth century. The political situation of the world today—the map of Europe, the political predominance of the United States and the Soviet Union, the problems of the Eastern European countries under Soviet domination, even the problems of the Middle East—all can be traced to the rise of Hitler and the bloody struggle that followed. I'm sure many of you have relatives who fought in the war or whose lives were deeply affected by it. Raise your hand if a relative or someone you know well fought in World War II. "Germany today is peaceful and prosperous. How could a man like Hitler have come to power? To understand this, we must first understand what Germany was like in the years following its defeat in World War I and why an unemployed Austrian painter could come to lead one of the largest countries in Europe. "By the end of this lesson you will understand the conditions in Germany that led up the rise of Hitler, the reasons he was successful, and the major events of his rise to power."
2. Review prerequisites.	Have students recall from the previous lesson: ■ The humiliating provisions of the Treaty of Versailles —reparations —demilitarization of the Ruhr —loss of territory and colonies ■ The lack of experience with democracy in Germany
3. Present new material.	Discuss with students: ■ Conditions in Germany before the rise of Hitler —failure of the Weimar Republic —economic problems, inflation, and severe impact of the U.S. Depression —belief that Germany lost World War I because of betrayal by politicians —fear of communism ■ Events in Hitler's rise to power —organization of National Socialist (Nazi) party —Beer-Hall Putsch and Hitler's imprisonment —*Mein Kampf* —organization of Brown Shirts (S.A.) —election and appointment as chancellor
4. Conduct learning probes.	Questions to students throughout lesson should assess student comprehension of the main points.
5. Provide independent practice.	Have students independently write three reasons why the situation in Germany in the 1920s and early 1930s might have been favorable to Hitler's rise, and have students be prepared to defend their answers.
6. Assess performance and provide feedback.	Call on randomly selected students to read and justify their reasons for Hitler's success. Discuss well-justified and poorly justified reasons. Have students hand in papers.
7. Provide distributed practice and review.	Review lesson content at start of next lesson and in later lessons.

average, then you will probably be taller than average. Well, today we are going to have a lesson on the science called *genetics*, in which we will learn how characteristics of parents are passed on to their children."

This introduction might be expected to grab students' interest because it makes the subject personally relevant.

Humor or drama can also establish a positive mental set. One teacher occasionally used a top hat and a wand to capture student interest by "magically" transforming adjectives into adverbs ("sad" into "sadly," for example). The popular and instructionally effective *Sesame Street* and *Electric Company* television programs (Ball and Bogatz, 1970, 1972) use this kind of device constantly to get the attention and hold the interest of young children in basic skills. Of course, such devices can get out of hand to the point where learning is overshadowed by merrymaking. To choose an appropriate device, teachers must know their classes, and they should use the device sparingly to get a lesson rolling rather than as a regular feature of instruction.

Finally, it is important in starting a lesson to give students a "road map" of where the lesson is going and what they will know at the end. As noted in Chapter 7, stating lesson objectives clearly has generally been found to enhance student achievement of those objectives. Also, giving students an outline of the lesson may also help them to incorporate new information (Kiewra, 1985b). Telling students that the material you are about to teach will be tested can be another effective means of increasing attention to the lesson (Hovland et al., 1949).

Review Prerequisites

The second major task in a lesson is to be sure that students have mastered prerequisite skills and to link information already in their minds to the information you are about to present. These are central functions in Ausubel's reception learning theories, discussed in Chapter 6.

If today's lesson is a continuation of yesterday's and you are reasonably sure that students understood yesterday's lesson, then the review may just require reminding them about the earlier lesson and asking a few quick questions before beginning the new one. For instance:

"Yesterday we learned how to add the suffix 'ed' to a word ending in 'y.' Who will tell us how this is done?"

Since today's lesson—adding other suffixes to words ending in "y"—is a direct continuation of yesterday's, this brief reminder is adequate. However, if a new skill or concept is being introduced, and it depends on skills learned much earlier, then more elaborate discussion and assessment of prerequisite skills might be needed. For instance:

"Today we are going to start a new unit on decimals. Decimals are a different way of writing tenths, hundredths, thousandths, and so on. Before we begin, I'd like to review what we know about tenths, hundredths, and thousandths. Can anyone tell me how many hundredths one-tenth would be?"

Sometimes it is necessary to assess students on prerequisite skills before starting a lesson. In the first sample lesson students were briefly quizzed on subtraction without renaming and numeration skills in preparation for a lesson on subtraction with renaming. If students had shown poor understanding of either prerequisite skill, the teacher would have reviewed those skills before going on to the new lesson.

Another reason to review prerequisites is to provide advance organizers. As defined in Chapter 6, advance organizers are introductory statements by the teacher that remind students of what they already know and give them a framework for understanding the new material to be presented. In the second sample lesson the teacher "set the stage" for the new content (Hitler's rise to power) by reviewing the economic, political, and social conditions in Germany that made Hitler's success possible.

Present New Material

Here begins the main body of the lesson—the point at which the teacher presents new information or skills.

Organization. Lessons should be logically organized. Recall from Chapters 5 and 6 that information that has a clear, well-organized structure is retained better than less clearly presented information. Clear structure and systematic progression from subtopic to subtopic are critical features of Ausubel's reception learning and of Gagné's events of instruction (see Chapter 6).

For example, a lesson on the legislative branch of government might be presented as follows:

The Legislative Branch of the Federal Government (First Lesson)

I. Functions and Nature of the Legislative Branch
   A. Passes laws
   B. Approves money for executive branch
   C. Has two houses—House of Representatives and Senate

II. House of Representatives
   A. Designed to be closest to the people
      —representatives elected to two-year terms
      —proportional representation
   B. Responsible for originating money bills

III. Senate
   A. Designed to give greater continuity to legislative branch
      —senators elected to six-year terms
      —each state has two senators
   B. Approves appointments and treaties made by executive branch

This would be a beginning lesson on the legislative branch of the U.S. government (subsequent lessons would present how laws are introduced and passed, checks and balances on legislative power, and so on). It has a clear organization that should be pointed out to students. For example, you might pause at the beginning of the second topic and say, "Now we are going to learn about the lower house of Congress, the House of Representatives." The purpose of this is to help students form a mental outline that will help them remember the material. Clearly laid out structure and transitional statements about the structure of the lesson have been found to increase student understanding (Thompson, 1960; Kallison, 1986).

The better organized students believe a lesson to be, the more they learn from it (Walberg and Anderson, 1968; Belgard et al., 1971). Further, teachers who make smooth, orderly transitions from topic to topic in a lesson have been found to be more instructionally effective than teachers who change topics abruptly or stray from their main points (Smith and Cotten, 1980).

In addition to making clear the organization of a lesson by noting when the next subtopic is being introduced, several researchers (Petrie, 1963; Maddox and Hoole, 1975) have found that instructionally effective teachers give clear indications about the most important elements of the lesson, by saying, for example, "It is particularly important to note that . . ." Important points should be repeated, and brought back into the lesson whenever appropriate. For example, in teaching about the presidential veto in the lesson on the legislative branch of government, it might be good to say:

"Here again, we see the operation of the system of checks and balances we discussed earlier. The executive can veto legislation passed by the Congress, which in turn can withhold funds for actions of the executive. Remember, understanding how this system of checks and balances works is critical to an understanding of how the U.S. government works."

The idea here is to emphasize one of the central concepts of the U.S. government—the system of checks and balances among the executive, legislative, and judicial branches—by bringing it up whenever possible and by labeling it as important.

One carefully controlled experiment found that teachers who used the lesson presentation strategies outlined in this section were more successful than other teachers in increasing student achievement (Clark et al., 1979). The researchers studied the effectiveness of teachers who reviewed main ideas, stated objectives at the beginning of the lesson, outlined lesson content, signaled transitions between parts of the lesson, indicated important points in the lesson, and summarized the parts of the lesson as the lesson proceeded. These teachers' students scored significantly better on the lesson content and learned more than students whose teachers did not do these things.

Clarity. One consistent feature of effective lessons is clarity, the use of direct, simple, and well-organized language to present concepts (McCaleb and White, 1980; Smith and Land, 1981; Land, 1987). Clear presentations avoid the use of vague terms that do not add to the meaning of the lesson, such as the italicized words in the following sentence (from Smith and Land, 1981):

Maybe before we get to *probably* the main idea of the lesson, you should review a *few* prerequisite concepts.

Even more destructive to clarity are "mazes," or false starts, as in:

This mathematics lesson *will enab* . . . will get you to understand *number, uh,* . . . number patterns. (Smith and Land, 1981)

Wandering off into digressions or irrelevant topics or otherwise interrupting the flow of the lesson also detract from clarity. One physics teacher loved to interrupt his own lessons with stories about his experiences in the navy. This was a lot of fun for the students, but added little to their knowledge of physics!

Explanations. Effective teachers have also been found to use many explanations and explanatory words (such as "because," "in order to," "consequently") and to frequently use a pattern of rule-example-rule (see Chapter 6) when presenting new concepts (Rosenshine, 1971; Van Patten et al., 1986). For example:

"Matter may change forms, but it is never destroyed. If I were to burn a piece of paper, it would appear that the paper is gone, but in fact it has been combined with oxygen atoms from the air and changed to a gas (mostly carbon dioxide) and ash. If I could count the atoms in the paper plus the atoms from the air before and after I burned the paper, we could see that the matter involved did not disappear, but merely changed forms."

Note that the rule was stated ("matter . . . is never destroyed"), an example was given, and the rule was restated in explaining how the example illustrates the rule. Also note that a rule-example-rule sequence was used in this book to illustrate the rule-example-rule pattern!

Demonstrations. Cognitive theorists emphasize the importance of seeing and, when appropriate, having "hands-on" experience with concepts and skills (see Chapter 6). Visual representations are maintained in long-term memory far more readily than information that is only heard (see Gagné and Briggs, 1979).

Students can learn more easily from lesson presentations that include visual aids as well as lecture and discussion. Presentations should also be well organized.

Maintaining Attention. Straight, dry lectures can be boring, and bored students quickly stop paying attention to even the most carefully crafted lesson. For this reason, it is important to introduce variety, activity, or humor to enliven the lecture and maintain student attention. For example, use of humor has been found to increase student achievement (Kaplan and Pascoe, 1977; Ziv, 1988), and illustrating the lecture with easily understood graphics can help hold students' attention. On the other hand, too much variation in mode of presentation can hurt achievement if it distracts students from the lesson content (Wyckoff, 1973).

Several studies have established that students learn more from lessons that are presented with enthusiasm and expressiveness than from dry lectures (Coats and Smidchens, 1966; Abrami et al., 1982; Crocker and Brooker, 1986). It is apparently helpful for student interest and achievement to vary types of questions, lengths of lessons, and presentation modes (Rosenshine, 1971). In one sense, teaching is performing, and it appears that some of the qualities we'd seek in a performer are also those that increase the effectiveness of teachers (see Timpson and Tobin, 1982).

Content Coverage and Pace. One of the most important factors in effective teaching is the amount of content covered. Students of teachers who cover more material learn more than other students (e.g., Golem and Leinhardt, 1980; Barr and Dreeben, 1983; Barr, 1987).

This does not necessarily mean that teachers should teach "faster"; obviously, there is such a thing as going too fast and leaving students behind, yet research on instructional pace does imply that most teachers could increase their pace of instruction (Good, Grouws, and Ebmeier, 1983), as long as degree of mastery is not sacrificed. In addition to increasing content coverage, a relatively rapid pace of instruction can help with classroom management (see Chapter 11).

Learning Probes
Methods, such as questioning, that
help teachers find out if students
understand a lesson

Conduct Learning Probes

Imagine an archer who shoots arrows at a target but never finds out how close to the bull's-eye the arrows fall. The archer wouldn't be very accurate to begin with, and would certainly never improve in accuracy.

Similarly, effective teaching requires that teachers be constantly aware of the effects of their instruction. All too often, teachers mistakenly believe that if they have covered a topic well and students appear to be paying attention, then their instruction has been successful. Even students often believe that if they have listened intently to an interesting lecture, they know the material presented. Yet this may not be true! If teachers do not regularly probe students' understanding of the material being presented, students may be left with serious misunderstandings or gaps in knowledge.

The term **learning probe** refers to a variety of ways of asking for brief student responses to lesson content. Learning probes give the teacher feedback on students' levels of understanding, and permit students to "try out" their understanding of a new idea to see if they have it right. Learning probes can take the form of questions to the class, as in the sample lesson on World War II presented in Figure 8.2, or brief written or physical demonstrations of understanding, as in the sample subtraction lesson.

Regardless of whether the response to the learning probe is written, physical, or oral, the purpose of the probe is what Hunter (1982) and Rosenshine and Stevens (1986) call "checking for understanding." That is, the learning probe is used not so much to teach or provide practice as to find out whether students have understood what they just heard. Teachers use the probes to set their pace of instruction. If students are having trouble, teachers must slow down and repeat explanations. If all students show understanding, the teacher can move on to new topics. The following interchange shows how a teacher might use learning probes to uncover student strengths and misunderstandings, and then adjust instruction accordingly. The teacher, Mr. Swift, has written several sentences containing conversation on an overhead projector transparency, and students are learning the correct use of commas and quotation marks:

MR. SWIFT: Now we are ready to punctuate some conversation. Everyone get out a sheet of paper and copy this sentence, adding punctuation where needed:

Take the criminal downstairs Tom said condescendingly.

Is everyone ready? Carl, how did you punctuate the sentence?

CARL: Quote take the criminal downstairs quote comma Tom said condescendingly period.

MR. SWIFT: Close, but you made the most common error people make with quotation marks. Maria, what did you write?

MARIA: I think I made the same mistake Carl did, but I understand now. It should be: Quote take the criminal downstairs comma quote Tom said condescendingly period.

MR. SWIFT: Good. How many got this right the first time? (Half of class raises hands.) Okay, I see we still have some problems with this one. Remember, commas and periods go inside the quotation mark. I know that sometimes this doesn't make much sense, but if English always made sense, a lot of English teachers would be out of work! Think of quotation marks as wrappers for conversation, and the conversation, punctuation and all, goes inside the wrapper. Let's try another.

Drive carefully Tom said recklessly.

Dave?

DAVE: Quote drive carefully comma quote Tom said recklessly period.

MR. SWIFT: Great! How many got it? (All but one or two raise hands.) Wonderful, I think you're all with me. The quotation marks "wrap up" the conversation, including its punctuation. Now let's try one that's a little harder:

I wonder Tom said quizzically whether quotation marks will be on the test.

There are several features worth noting in this interchange. First, Mr. Swift had all students work out the punctuation, called on individuals for answers, and then asked all students whether they got the right answers. This is preferable to asking only one or two students to work (say, on the chalkboard) while the others watch, thus wasting the time of most of the class. When all students have to figure out the punctuation and no one knows whom Mr. Swift will call on, all students actively participate and test their own knowledge, and Mr. Swift gets a quick reading on the level of understanding of the class as a whole.

Note also that when Mr. Swift found that half the class missed the first item, he took time to reteach the skill students were having trouble with, using a different explanation from the one he had used in his first presentation. By giving students the mental image of "quotation marks as wrappers," he helped them remember the order of punctuation in conversation. (Recall that the use of vivid imagery was one of the memory strategies discussed in Chapter 5.) When almost all students got the second item, he moved to the next step, because the class had apparently mastered the first one.

Finally, note that Mr. Swift had plenty of sentences prepared on the overhead projector, so he did not have to use class time to write out sentences. Learning probes should always be brief, and should not be allowed to destroy the tempo of the lesson. By being prepared with sentences for learning probes, Mr. Swift was able to maintain student involvement and interest. In fact, he might have done even better to give students dittos with sentences on them to reduce the time used in copying the sentences.

Questions. Questions to students in the course of the lesson serve many purposes. Questions may be used as Socrates used them, to prompt students to take the next mental step (for example, "Now that we've learned that heating a gas makes it expand, what do you suppose would happen if we cool a gas?"). They may be used to encourage students to think further about information they learned previously or to get a discussion started (for example, "We've learned that if we boil water, it becomes water vapor. Now, water vapor is a colorless, odorless, invisible gas. In that case, why do you suppose we can see steam coming out of a tea kettle?"). With guidance, a class discussion would eventually arrive at the answer, which is that the water vapor recondenses when it hits the relatively cool air—and that what is visible in steam is water droplets, not vapor. Note that this question moves the class discussion to a higher level of Bloom's taxonomy (see Chapter 7).

Finally, questions can be used as learning probes. In fact, any question is to some degree a learning probe, in that the quality of response will indicate to the teacher how well students are learning the lesson.

Research on the frequency of questions indicates that teachers who ask more academically relevant questions are more instructionally effective than those who ask relatively few questions related to the lesson at hand (Dunkin and Biddle, 1974;

Stallings and Kaskowitz, 1974; Gall et al., 1978). This corresponds with cognitive research on questions (discussed in Chapter 6), which also finds that posing questions in the course of instruction increases learning (Andre, 1979; Hamaker, 1986). With elementary-age students, a large number of relatively easy questions on facts or skills seems to be most effective for increasing student achievement, while thought-provoking questions become increasingly effective in secondary schools (Winne, 1979). However, at all levels of schooling it is probable that factual questions will help with factual skills (Clark et al., 1979) and questions that encourage students to think about concepts will help with conceptual skills (Fagan et al., 1981; Redfield and Rousseau, 1981; Gall, 1984).

How to Ask Questions. Teachers typically ask a lot of questions. One study found that teachers asked about 150 questions per hour in elementary science and social studies (Gall, 1970). It seems logical, then, that the way in which teachers ask questions should be an important part of their instructional effectiveness.

One issue regarding questioning that has received much research attention is **wait time,** the length of time the teacher waits for a student to answer a question before giving up. Research has found that teachers tend to give up too rapidly on students they perceive to be low achievers, which tells those students that the teacher expects little from them (Rowe, 1974; Tobin and Capie, 1982).

Teachers who wait approximately three seconds after asking a student a question obtain better learning results than those who give up more rapidly (Tobin, 1986). Further, following up with students who do not respond has been associated with higher achievement (Brophy and Evertson, 1974; Anderson et al., 1979; Larrivee, 1985). Waiting for students to respond, or staying with them when they do not, communicates positive expectations for them (Brophy and Good, 1974). (See Chapter 10 for more on teacher expectations.)

Anderson et al. (1979) found that in reading groups it was better to call on students in a prescribed order (such as around the circle) than to call on them at random, at least in part because this method ensures that all students will be called on. However, the authors expressed doubt that ordered turns would work as well in lessons to the whole class because when students know they will not be called on for some time, they often fail to pay attention. Calling on volunteers is perhaps the most common method, but this allows some students to avoid participating in the lesson by keeping their hands down (Brophy and Evertson, 1974).

Thus research is unclear concerning how students should be called on. Common sense would suggest that when the question is a problem to be worked (as in math), all students should work the problem before any individual is called on. When questions are not problems to be worked, it is probably best to pose the question to the class as a whole and then ask a randomly chosen student (not necessarily a volunteer) to answer. Some teachers even carry around a class list on a clipboard and check off the students called upon to make sure that all get frequent chances to respond. One teacher put her students' names on cards, shuffled them before class, and used the cards to decide whom to call on. This system worked well until one student found the cards after class and removed his name from the deck!

In conducting learning probes it may be especially important to ask questions of students who usually perform above, at, and below the class average to be sure that all students understand the lesson. Also, many researchers favor the frequent use of **choral responses** when there is only one possible correct answer (Becker and Carnine, 1980; Hunter, 1982; Rosenshine and Stevens, 1986). For example, the teacher might say, "Class: In the words listed on the board *(write, wring, wrong)*, what sound does the 'wr' make?" to which the class responds together, "Rrrr!" Similarly, when appropriate, all students can be asked to use hand signals to indicate true or false, to hold up a certain number of fingers to indicate an answer in math, or to write a short answer on a small chalkboard and hold it up on cue (Hunter, 1982). This type of all-pupil response has been found to have a positive effect on student learning (McKenzie, 1979; McKenzie and Henry, 1979). In the subtraction with renaming example used earlier in this chapter, recall that all students worked with popsicle sticks at their desks, and the teacher walked around to check their work. The purpose of these all-student responses is to give students many opportunities to respond and to give the teacher information on the entire class's level of knowledge and confidence.

Provide Independent Practice

The term **independent practice** refers to work students do in class on their own to practice or express newly learned skills or knowledge. For example, after hearing a lesson on solving equations in algebra, students need an opportunity to work several equations on their own without interruptions, both to crystallize their new knowledge and to help the teacher assess their knowledge. Practice is an essential step in the process of transferring new information in short-term memory to long-term memory (see Chapter 5).

Independent practice is most critical when students are learning skills, such as mathematics, reading, grammar, composition, map interpretation, or a foreign language. Students can no more learn arithmetic, writing, or Spanish without practicing them than they could learn to ride a bicycle from lectures alone!

On the other hand, independent practice is less necessary for certain concept lessons, such as the lesson on the rise of Hitler described earlier or a science lesson on the concept of magnetic attraction. In lessons of this kind independent practice can be used to let students rehearse knowledge or concepts on their own, as was done in the World War II lesson, but rehearsal is not as central to this type of lesson as practice of skills is to a subtraction lesson.

Research on **seatwork,** or in-class independent practice, suggests that it is typically both overused and misused (Good and Grouws, 1977; Brophy, 1979; Anderson, 1985). Several researchers have found that student time spent receiving instruction directly from the teacher is more productive than time spent in seatwork (Brophy and Evertson, 1974; Good and Grouws, 1977; Evertson et al., 1980). For example, Evertson et al. (1980) found that the most effective seventh- and eighth-grade math teachers in their sample spent about sixteen minutes on lecture-demonstration and nineteen minutes on seatwork, while the least effective teachers spent less than seven minutes on lecture-demonstration and about twenty-five minutes on seatwork. Yet studies of elementary mathematics and reading find students spending 50 to 70 percent of their class time doing seatwork (Fisher et al., 1978; Rosenshine, 1980). Anderson et al. (1985) have noted that time spent on seatwork is often wasted for students who lack the motivation, reading skills, or self-organization skills to work well on their own. Many students simply give up when they run into difficulties, while others fill out worksheets with little care for correctness. They apparently interpret the task as "finishing the paper" rather than learning the material.

A set of recommendations for effective use of independent practice time, derived from the work of Anderson (1985), Good et al. (1983), and Evertson et al. (1984), follows.

1. Do Not Assign Independent Practice Until You Are Sure Students Can Do It. This is probably the most important principle. Independent practice is *practice,* not

Independent Practice
Component of instruction in which students work by themselves to demonstrate and rehearse new knowledge

Seatwork
Work that students are assigned to do independently during class

instruction, and the students should be able to do most of the items they are assigned to do on their own (Brophy and Good, 1986). In cognitive terms (see Chapter 5), practice serves as rehearsal for transferring information from short-term memory to long-term memory. For this to work, the information must first of all be established in students' short-term memories.

A high success rate on independent practice work can be accomplished in two ways. First, worksheets should be clear and self-explanatory, and should cover content on which all students can succeed. Second, students should never be given independent practice worksheets until they have indicated in learning probes that they can handle the material. For example, a teacher might use the first items of a worksheet as learning probes, assigning them one at a time and discussing each one after students have attempted it, until it is clear that all or almost all students have the right idea.

2. Keep Independent Practice Assignments Short.   There is rarely a justification for long independent practice assignments. About ten minutes of work is adequate for most objectives, but this is far less than what most teachers assign (Rosenshine, 1980). Massed practice (for example, many items at one sitting) has a limited effect on retention; students are more likely to profit from relatively brief independent practice in class supplemented by distributed practice in the form of homework.

3. Give Clear Instructions.   In the lower grades it may be necessary to ask students to read or paraphrase the instructions to be sure that they have understood them.

4. Get Students Started, and Then Avoid Interruptions.   When students start on their independent practice work, circulate among them to be sure that everyone is under way before attending to the problems of individual students or other tasks. Once students have begun, avoid interrupting them.

5. Monitor Independent Work.   It is important to monitor independent work (see Medley, 1979)—for example, by walking around the class while students are doing their assignment. This helps keep students working and makes the teacher easily available for questions.

6. Collect Independent Work and Include It in Student Grades.   A major problem with seatwork as it is often used is that students see no reason to do their best on it because it has little or no bearing on their grades. Students should always know that their seatwork will be collected and will count toward their grade. To this end, it is a good idea to save a few minutes at the end of each class period to briefly read answers to worksheet questions and allow students to check their own papers or exchange worksheets with partners. Then students may pass in their papers for spot checking and recording. This procedure gives students immediate feedback on their seatwork and relieves the teacher of having to check all papers every day.

Assess Performance and Provide Feedback

Every lesson should contain an assessment of the degree to which students have mastered the objectives set for the lesson. This assessment may be done informally by questioning students, may use independent work as an assessment, or may involve a separate quiz. One way or another, however, the effectiveness of the lesson must be

1. Teaching whole-class lessons typically demands that a teacher lecture, or at least be the leader of a lecture/discussion. If you were supervising a student teacher whose lectures clearly bored the students, what would you do?

Linda Jaques, who teaches third grade in Bellwood, Ill., replied:

I would try to help the student teacher understand the nature and characteristics of the students. In an elementary school, I think active participation of students and hands-on activities produce more learning than lectures. I use individual slates during many of my whole-class instruction sessions to encourage active participation!

Dorothy Paulsen, who teaches reading in Wausau, Wisc., suggested:

I would question the student teacher about how he or she felt about the lecture/discussion. With enough real listening to the student teacher, he or she should be able to identify what the problem or problems seem to be. Once the student teacher has identified the problem, the supervisor is able to give some suggestions for resolving or correcting it.

Real listening on the part of the supervisor (instead of making suggestions at the beginning of the conversation) will help the student teacher to evaluate his or her own problem areas. Also, the supervisor will have the opportunity to understand the thinking of the student teacher, and might even learn something from the student teacher.

2. How can new teachers decide how much homework to assign?

Gilbert Green, an elementary teacher in Wilmington, Del., says:

Homework quantity must be based upon need and grade level. Most districts have a guideline on quantity per grade level. If not, one should be established, with parental input. Homework should be assigned so that each night a student must sit down in a proper place and accomplish a given amount. On my own grade level (5th), fifty minutes to one hour is suggested. New teachers should (1) check district policy, (2) ask experienced teachers, and (3) try to analyze the needs of students.

Barbara Levin, Cross Plains, Wis., adds:

Homework should be used to extend the day's lessons. It should not be *just* drill of old material, nor should it ever cover a new concept that the child will not know. Good homework assignments allow children to be creative. For example, the child could find out from parents, relatives, or neighbors about their work or their heritage or about the community's history.

---

assessed, and the results of the assessment should be given to students as soon as possible (Brophy and Evertson, 1976; Gage, 1978; Rosenshine, 1979). Students need to know when they are right and when they are wrong if they are to use feedback to improve their performance (see Barringer and Gholson, 1979).

In addition to assessing the results of each lesson, teachers need to test students from time to time on their learning of larger units of information. In general, more frequent testing results in greater achievement than less frequent testing, but any testing is much more effective than none at all (Bangert-Drowns et al., 1986).

Feedback to students is important, but feedback to teachers on student performance is probably even more important. If students are learning everything they are taught, it may be possible to pick up the pace of instruction. As noted earlier in this chapter, one of the strongest predictors of student achievement is the amount of content covered. A teacher who does not know that students are learning everything being taught may lose an opportunity to cover even more content. On the other hand, if assessment reveals serious misunderstandings, the lesson can be retaught or other steps taken to get students back on track. If some students mastered the lesson and some did not, it may be appropriate to give more instruction just to the students who need it.

Provide Distributed Practice and Review

As noted in Chapter 6, retention of many kinds of knowledge is increased by practice or review spaced out over time (Dempster, 1989). This has several implications for teaching. First, it implies that reviewing and recapitulating important information from earlier lessons enhances learning (Nuthall, 1987). Reviews of important material at long intervals (e.g., monthly) is particularly important to maintain previous skills. In addition, it is important to assign homework in most subjects and grade levels. Homework gives students a chance to practice skills learned in one setting and at one time (school) in another setting at a different time (home). Research on homework finds that it generally does increase achievement, particularly if it is checked and comments on it are given to students (Marshall, 1982; Keith et al., 1986; Elawar and Corno, 1985). However, the effects of homework are not as clear in elementary schools as they are at the secondary level (Cooper, 1989; Epstein, 1988).

■ **Stop and Think**
Recall several recent sessions of your college courses. Analyze the instructor's presentations to see whether the steps of lesson presentation discussed in this chapter were included.

DIRECT INSTRUCTION

Over the past fifteen years educational researchers and practitioners have developed a set of instructional procedures grouped under the name **direct instruction.** Rosenshine (1979) has summarized the principal prescriptions of direct instruction as follows:

> Direct instruction refers to academically focused, teacher-directed classrooms using sequenced and structured materials. It refers to teaching activities where goals are clear to students, time allocated for instruction is sufficient and continuous, coverage of content is extensive, the performance of students is monitored, . . . and feedback to students is immediate and academically oriented. In direct instruction the teacher controls instructional goals, chooses materials appropriate for the students' ability, and paces the instructional episode. Interaction is . . . structured, but not authoritarian. (Rosenshine, 1979, p. 38)

Rosenshine points out that the prescriptions he lists are drawn primarily from research on elementary reading and mathematics, and are therefore most applicable to those subjects and to other objectives characterized by "rational, specific, analytic goals." Given this limitation in scope, direct instruction can be seen as a simple translation of the results of the research on teaching summarized in this chapter and elsewhere (Brophy, 1979; Rosenshine, 1982; Good, 1983b; Brophy and Good, 1986). The principles of direct instruction also have much in common with Ausubel's reception learning and Gagné's events of instruction, described in Chapter 6. Although many researchers and practitioners feel that direct instruction is overly structured, grim, and joyless, and is unlikely to enhance the creativity or affective development of students (for example, Peterson, 1979), there is nothing in the direct instruction prescriptions that demands a grim or joyless classroom environment. In fact, as Rosenshine (1979) notes, just the opposite is the case.

Direct instruction *does,* however, emphasize teacher control of all classroom events, deemphasizes student independence and choice, and recommends against loose structure or discussions unrelated to the task at hand. For example, its prescriptions are directly opposed to Bruner's discovery learning strategies, described in Chapter 6. Yet it is important to note that the goals of direct instruction and discovery learning are quite different. Direct instructional strategies focus primarily on reading, language arts, and mathematics, and can be easily modified for use in such subjects as foreign languages. Discovery learning is focused more on science, social studies, math problem solving, and related areas. To put it simply, few students can be expected to "discover" how to read or compute, but all students need to learn to use their head to explore science and social studies concepts.

Grade Equivalent
Measure of achievement that relates students' scores to expected performance levels at specific grade levels

Research on Direct Instruction Methods

Direct instruction methods fall into two distinct categories. One might be called "master teacher" models (following Rosenshine, 1982) because they are based on the practices of the most effective teachers. This category includes Madeline Hunter's Mastery Teaching model, the Missouri Mathematics Program, and several others.

The other category of direct instruction methods might be called "systematic instruction" models. These are based on principles similar to those behind the master teacher models, but are far more structured. Typically, they provide specific instructional materials and highly organized, systematic methods of teaching, motivating students, managing the classroom, and assessing student progress (see Rosenshine, 1986).

"Master Teacher" Strategies. The best-evaluated of the "master teacher" direct instructional strategies is the Missouri Mathematics Program (MMP). In the first study of this method (Good and Grouws, 1979), fourth-graders whose teachers used the MMP methods learned considerably more than did students whose teachers were not trained in MMP. In one semester MMP students gained 1.24 **grade equivalents** on a standardized mathematics test (on average, students are expected to gain one grade equivalent each year, or only 0.50 per semester). Control students (who did not receive the experimental treatment) gained 0.74 grade equivalents. More recent evaluations of the Missouri Mathematics Program have found smaller positive effects. In three studies MMP students gained somewhat more in mathematics achievement than did control students (Good et al., 1983; Gall et al., 1984; Slavin and Karweit, 1985).

Despite its widespread popularity, evaluations of Madeline Hunter's Mastery Teaching program have not generally found that the students of teachers trained in the model have learned more than other students (Stallings and Krasavage, 1986; Donovan, Sousa, and Walberg, 1987; Mandeville, 1988; Slavin, 1986). A somewhat similar program was found by Stallings (1979) to improve the reading skills of high school students in remedial reading classes, but a second evaluation was less encouraging (Thieme-Busch and Prom, 1983). More successful have been direct instruction models that place a greater emphasis on building teachers' classroom management skills (e.g., Evertson, Weade, Green, and Crawford, 1985), and models that improve teachers' use of reading groups (Anderson, Evertson, and Brophy, 1979).

While the research on applications of "master teacher" models is mixed, most researchers agree that the main elements of these models are essential *minimum* skills that all teachers should have (for example, Gage and Needels, 1989). When studies find no differences between teachers trained in the models and other teachers, it is

Most of the principles of lesson presentation discussed in this chapter have been derived from **process-product studies,** in which observers recorded the teaching practices of teachers whose students consistently achieved at a high level. These principles have been assembled into specific direct instructional programs and evaluated in field experiments (see Chapter 1). That is, other teachers have been trained in the methods used by successful teachers and their students' achievement has been compared to that of students whose teachers did not receive the training. This section describes two of the most widely used direct instruction methods and reviews the field research done to evaluate them.

MADELINE HUNTER'S MASTERY TEACHING

Madeline Hunter's (1982) Mastery Teaching Program provides a general guide to effective lessons in any subject area or grade level. Mastery Teaching lessons proceed in four principal steps: (1) getting students set to learn, (2) input and modeling, (3) checking understanding and guided practice, and (4) independent practice. Descriptions of each follow.

1. Getting Students Set to Learn.

In the first few minutes of class three activities should be completed:

- *Review:* Students should be asked either to answer a few review questions orally or in writing, or to summarize the previous day's lesson. This may go on while the teacher attends to taking roll or other "class-keeping" activities.

- *Anticipatory set:* An "anticipatory set" is created in students by focusing their attention on the material to be presented, reminding them of what they already know, and stimulating their interest in the lesson. This step parallels the earlier suggestion in this chapter that teachers help students get into the proper "mental set" before starting a lesson.

- *Objective:* State the learning objective (as described in Chapter 7).

2. Input and Modeling.

Information should be presented to students in a logical, well-organized sequence, using clear language

and models and demonstrations (if appropriate). Hunter suggests "teaching to both halves of the brain" by first presenting information verbally and then summarizing it on the chalkboard, using simple diagrams, models, and mnemonics (see Chapter 5). She also emphasizes "modeling what you mean" by giving frequent examples of concepts to make their meanings clear, moving from clear and easily understood examples (for example, " 'Book' is a noun," " 'Read' is a verb") to more thought-provoking examples or exceptions (for example, "In the sentence 'I went on a walk,' what part of speech is the word 'walk'?").

3. Checking Understanding and Guided Practice.

Teachers can use many methods to check whether all students understood the information just presented. For example, students might be given a multiple-choice question, such as:

- How many half-steps are there in an octave?
  a. 8
  b. 12
  c. 14
  d. 16

Students might indicate their choices all at the same time by holding up one finger for a, two for b, and so on; or by writing their choice on a small chalkboard and holding it up. This permits the teacher to immediately see how many students are keeping up with the main ideas of the lesson. Teachers can accomplish the same goal by using choral responses or by calling on individual students.

Guided practice refers to methods of giving students problems or questions one or two at a time and checking their answers immediately. The purpose of guided practice is to let students try out their new information and receive immediate feedback on their levels of understanding. The same types of response formats used in checking understanding are also used to check students' work in guided practice. For example, you might have students work a math problem at their desks and then walk around to look at their papers to see that they have the right idea.

4. Independent Practice.

After students indicate understanding of the main points of the lesson, they may be given independent practice. For example, they might be asked to work several math problems, to fill in country names on an outline map, to write main ideas for a series of paragraphs, or to make adjectives and nouns agree in number and gender in a foreign language. Hunter emphasizes that independent practice should be relatively brief, and that practice exercises should be checked as soon as possible so students can find out how they did.

MISSOURI MATHEMATICS PROGRAM

The **Missouri Mathematics Program** (MMP) is based on principles of instruction discovered in research that compared the teaching strategies of teachers who consistently obtained outstanding achievement from their students with those of teachers who were less instructionally successful (Good and Grouws, 1977, 1979). The program primarily applies the prescriptions for lesson components specified by Gagné and Briggs (1979), Rosenshine and Stevens (1986), and others in the direct instruction tradition to the teaching of mathematics at the elementary and middle school levels. The principal features of MMP lessons are summarized in Table 8.1 (adapted from Good et al., 1983).

Similarities Among Direct Instruction Models

One interesting recent development in educational psychology is the extent of agreement among

---

TABLE 8.1

MISSOURI MATHEMATICS PROGRAM

The Missouri Mathematics Program applies the principles of direct instruction to the teaching of mathematics at the elementary and middle school level. A summary of the key instructional behaviors for MMP is shown here.

Opening (First 8 minutes except Mondays)

A. Briefly review the concepts and skills associated with the homework.

B. Collect and deal with homework assignments.

C. Ask several mental computation exercises (for example: "Compute in your head $3 \times 4 - 5 + 3 =$ ").

Development (About 20 minutes)

A. Briefly focus on prerequisite skills and concepts.

B. Focus on meaning and promoting student understanding by using lively explanations, demonstrations, and illustrations. Keep the pace rapid and lively.

C. Assess student comprehension
- –frequent, rapid short-answer questions (but give students enough time to respond)
- –single practice items

D. Repeat and elaborate on the meaning portion as necessary.

Seatwork (About 15 minutes)

A. Provide uninterrupted successful practice. Most students should be getting at least 80 percent of their items correct.

B. Momentum: Keep the ball rolling—get everyone involved, then sustain involvement.

C. Alerting: Let students know their work will be checked at end of period.

D. Accountability: Check the students' work.

TABLE 8.1 *(Continued)*

Homework Assignment

A. Assign homework on a regular basis at the end of each math class.

B. Require about 15 minutes of work to be done at home.

C. Include one or two review problems in homework assignments.

Special Reviews

A. Weekly review/maintenance:
   - —Conduct during the first 20 minutes each Monday.
   - —Focus on skills and concepts covered during the previous week.

B. Monthly review/maintenance:
   - —Conduct every fourth Monday.
   - —Focus on skills and concepts covered since the last monthly review

Source: Adapted from Good et al., 1983.

researchers from quite different backgrounds on what goes into an effective lesson. Table 8.2 shows how different authors have used different language to describe a similar progression of steps.

Despite the obvious similarities among the five models summarized in Table 8.2, there are some differences in emphasis. Only three models, the one presented earlier in this chapter and the prescriptions of Gagné and Rosenshine, emphasize frequent testing (a characteristic that is also central to mastery learning methods, discussed in Chapter 9). Also, three models—the one presented in this text, Hunter's, and Gagné's—emphasize orienting students to the lesson and grabbing student attention.

However, the similarities among the five direct instruction models are more important than their differences. All five emphasize active presentation of information, clear organization, a step-by-step progression from subtopic to subtopic, and the use of many examples, demonstrations, and visual prompts. All five would recommend more teacher-directed instruction and less seatwork than are used in most classrooms. All five emphasize constant assessment of student understanding and altering the pace of instruction according to this information, and all except Gagné's model (which is more a theoretical guide than a practical prescription) present classroom management strategies designed to make effective use of class time and maintain the students' attention.

often because the trained teachers already had most of the direct instruction skills before the training took place! (See Slavin, 1986.)

"Systematic Instruction" Models. The principal evaluations of "systematic instruction" forms of direct instruction were studies of a program called DISTAR[*] and other methods in federally funded Follow Through programs for disadvantaged students in grades 1–3. In the 1970s the federal government funded a large study to find out

[*]Now published under the names *Reading Mastery, Corrective Reading,* and *Distar Arithmetic* by Science Research Associates, Chicago.

TABLE 8.2

COMPONENTS OF EFFECTIVE LESSONS ACCORDING TO VARIOUS AUTHORS

In spite of using different terms, educators from a variety of backgrounds advocate similar methods of lesson presentation.

Slavin (this text)	Gagné (1974, 1977); Gagné & Briggs (1979)	Rosenshine & Stevens (1986)	Madeline Hunter (1982) (Mastery Teaching)	Good & Grouws (1979) (Missouri Math. Program)
1. State learning objectives and orient studies to lesson	Gain and control attention; inform the learner of expected outcomes	Provide overview	Objectives: anticipatory set	Opening
2. Review prerequisites	Stimulate recall of relevant prerequisite capabilities	Review, checking previous day's work	Review	Review homework; mental computations; review prerequisites
3. Present new material	Present the stimuli inherent to the learning task; offer guidance for learning	Present new content/skills	Input and modeling	Development
4. Conduct learning probes	Provide feedback	Initial student practice, checking for understanding, feedback, and correctives	Check understanding and guided practice	Assess student comprehension
5. Provide independent practice		Independent practice	Independent practice	Seatwork
6. Assess performance and provide feedback	Appraise performance	Frequent tests		
7. Provide distributed practice and review	Make provisions for transferability; ensure retention	Homework; weekly and monthly reviews	Homework	Homework; weekly and monthly reviews

which instructional methods were most effective in increasing student achievement. Nine programs were compared. DISTAR and a similar highly structured direct instructional program called Behavior Analysis were by far the most successful for increasing the reading and mathematics achievement of the students (Stallings and Kaskowitz, 1974; Abt Associates, 1976, 1977; Becker and Carnine, 1980). Of the nine programs, only DISTAR brought low-achieving disadvantaged students near the average achievement level of all students in the United States. DISTAR and Behavior Analysis students were also highest in self-esteem. A recent study (Meyer, 1984) followed the progress of students from an inner-city Brooklyn, N.Y., neighborhood who had been in DISTAR classes in grades 1–3, and found that these students were considerably more likely to graduate from high school than were students in a similar Brooklyn school who had not been taught with DISTAR. About 60 percent of the former DISTAR students graduated from high school, compared with only 38 percent of students in the similar school; 34 percent of DISTAR students were accepted into college, versus 17 percent in the other school. Other studies have also found long-term effects of this approach (Meyer et al., 1983; Gersten and Carnine, 1984; Gersten and Keating, 1987).

Thus there is good evidence that a "systematic instruction" form of direct instruction is effective in increasing basic skills, at least for low achieving disadvantaged students in elementary schools. As will be seen in Chapter 9, systematic direct instruction models that use ability grouping and individualized instruction also have had positive effects on student achievement in such basic skills as reading and mathematics.

Direct Instruction: Conclusions.   As of this writing, it is clear that direct instruction methods can improve the teaching of basic skills, but it is equally clear that there is much yet to be learned about how and for what purposes they should be used. The prescriptions derived from studies of effective teachers cannot be uncritically applied in the classroom and expected to make a substantial difference in student achievement. On the other hand, highly structured, systematic instructional programs based on these prescriptions can markedly improve student achievement in basic skills, Still, it is important to remember that the research on direct instruction done up to now has mostly focused on basic reading and mathematics, mostly in the elementary grades. For other subjects and at other grade levels we have less of a basis for believing that direct instruction methods will improve student learning.

■   **Stop and Think**

Compare direct instruction to David Ausubel's theory of reception learning, presented in Chapter 6.

Analyze the prescriptions of direct instruction and list several reasons why this method of teaching is apparently more effective in the elementary grades than in the high school grades, and with the basic skills as opposed to more complex topics and concepts.

DISCUSSIONS

This chapter has so far focused primarily on teaching methods for transmitting knowledge or skills from teacher to students. However, while every subject has a certain body of information, concepts, and skills that must be mastered by students as firmly and as efficiently as possible, there are three kinds of learning objectives that do not fall into this mold (see Gall, 1987). First, in many subjects there are questions that do not have simple answers. There may be one right answer to an algebra problem or one right way to conjugate a German verb, but is there one right set of factors that led up to the Civil War? How were Shakespeare's writings influenced by the politics of his day? Should genetic engineering be banned as a danger to world health? These and many other questions are open to interpretation, so it is important for students to discuss and understand issues instead of simply receiving and rehearsing information or skills. Such subjects as history, government, economics, literature, art, and music contain many issues that lend themselves to discussion because there are no single right answers. Discussing controversial issues has been found to increase

Teachers play a less dominant role in discussions than in traditional lessons. Ideas should be drawn from students, who must be knowledgeable about a topic before it is discussed.

knowledge about the issues as well as encourage deeper understanding of the various sides of an issue (Johnson and Johnson, 1979).

The second category that lends itself to discussion are objectives that do contain single right answers, but that involve difficult concepts that force students to see something in a different way. For example, a science teacher could simply give a lesson on buoyancy and specific gravity. However, since this lesson would challenge a simplistic view of why things float ("Things float because they are light"), students might understand buoyancy and specific gravity better if given an opportunity to make and defend their own theories about why things float, and if they were confronted with such questions as "If things float because they are light, then why does a battleship float?" and "If you threw some things in a lake, they would sink part way but not to the bottom—why would they stop sinking?" In searching together for theories to explain these phenomena, students might gain an appreciation for the meaning of buoyancy and specific gravity that a lecture could not provide. Science and social studies include many concepts that lend themselves to discussion.

The third situation calling for use of discussions is where affective objectives are of particular importance. For example, in a course on civics or government there is much information to be taught about how our government works, but there are also important values to be transmitted, such as civic duty and patriotism. A teacher could teach "six reasons why it is important to vote," but the real objective here is not to teach reasons for voting, but rather to instill respect for the democratic process and a commitment to register and vote when the time comes. Similarly, a discussion of peer pressure might be directed at giving students the skills and the willingness to say "no" when classmates pressure them to engage in illegal, unhealthy, or undesirable behaviors. A long tradition of research in social psychology has established that group discussion, particularly when group members must publicly commit themselves, is far more effective at changing individuals' attitudes and behaviors than even the most persuasive lecture (see Lewin, 1947).

Inquiry Training
Teaching approach aimed at helping
to develop skills in asking questions
and drawing conclusions

Whole-Class Discussion

Discussions take two principal forms. In one the entire class discusses an issue, with the teacher as moderator. In the other students form small groups (usually with four or five students in each group) to discuss a topic, and the teacher moves from group to group, aiding the discussion.

What differentiates a whole-class discussion from a usual lesson is that in discussions the teacher plays a less dominant role. Teachers may guide the discussion and help the class avoid dead ends, but the ideas should be drawn from the students. The following vignette (from Joyce and Weil, 1980, pp. 61–62) illustrates an inquiry-oriented discussion led (but not dominated) by a teacher:

> One morning, as Mrs. Harrison's fourth-grade students are settling down to their arithmetic workbooks, she calls their attention. As they raise their eyes toward her, a light bulb directly over Mrs. Harrison's desk blows out, and the room darkens.
>
> "What happened?" asks one child.
>
> "Can't you see, dopey?" remarks another. "The light bulb blew out."
>
> "Yeah," inquires another, "but what does that mean?"
>
> "Just that. We have all seen a lot of light bulbs blow out, but what does that really mean? What happens?" their teacher prods.
>
> Mrs. Harrison unscrews the light bulb and holds it up. The children gather around, and she passes it among them. After she receives it back, she says, "Well, why don't you see if you can develop a hypothesis about what happened?"
>
> "What's inside the glass?" asks one of the children.
>
> "I'm afraid I can't answer that," she replies. "Can you put it another way?"
>
> "Is there a gas inside?" asks another.
>
> 'No," says Mrs. Harrison. The children look at one another in puzzlement. Finally, one asks, "Is it a vacuum?"
>
> "Yes," nods Mrs. Harrison.
>
> "Is it a complete vacuum? someone inquires.
>
> "Almost," replies Mrs. Harrison.
>
> "What is that little wire made of?" asks another student.
>
> "I can't answer that," says Mrs. Harrison. "Can you put it another way?"
>
> "Is the little wire made of metal?"
>
> "Yes," she agrees.

In asking questions such as these, the children gradually identify the materials that make up the light bulb and the process that caused it to burn out. Finally, they begin to venture hypotheses about what happened. After they have thought up four or five of these, they search through reference books in an effort to verify them.

In this example the teacher used an unplanned event (the bulb burning out) to start a discussion on light bulbs, but the principles she used apply just as well to the more typical case where the teacher introduces a discussion into a lesson planned in advance. The teacher knows the answers to the question at hand ("How does a light bulb work?"), but wants the students to find out for themselves. The lesson is less on light bulbs as such than on how to use scientific methods and other resources to answer questions. The teacher is using a particular strategy called **inquiry training** (Suchman, 1962), in which students are presented with a puzzling event or experiment and must try out theories to explain what happened. The teacher only answers yes-or-no questions, and provides information only when students ask the right questions. This simulates the situation faced by scientists, for whom asking the right questions is the most important step toward finding answers.

The light bulb example is unique in some ways, but it has many characteristics common to most whole-class discussions. First, the teacher took a nondirective role, leaving the primary responsibility for bringing up and exploring ideas to the students. The teacher served as a source of information and as a moderator, but otherwise did not direct the lesson. The teacher encouraged all students to participate, and did not discourage them from making educated guesses or trying out their own theories.

In contrast to the light bulb example, the following vignette describes a situation in which a teacher does not have a specific principle or concept in mind, but rather wants students to explore and develop their own ideas about a topic, using information they have recently learned:

MS. WILSON: In the past few weeks we've been learning about the events leading up to the American Revolution. Of course, since we are all Americans, we tend to take the side of the revolutionaries. We use the term "Patriots" to describe them; King George probably used a less favorable term. Yet many of the colonists were Loyalists, and at times, the Loyalists outnumbered the Patriots. Let's think about how Loyalists would have argued against the idea of independence from Britain.

BETH: I think they'd say King George was a good king.

VINNIE: But what about all the things he did to the colonists?

MS. WILSON: Give some examples.

VINNIE: Like the Intolerable Acts. The colonists had to put up British soldiers in their own houses, and they closed Boston harbor.

TANYA: But those were to punish the colonists for the Boston Tea Party. The Loyalists would say that the Patriots caused all the trouble in the first place.

MS. WILSON: Good point.

FRANK: I think the Loyalists would say, "You may not like everything he does, but King George is still our king."

RICHARD: The Loyalists probably thought the Sons of Liberty were a bunch of hoods.

MS. WILSON: Well, I wouldn't put it quite that way, but I think you're right. What did they do that makes you think that?

RAMON: They destroyed things, and harassed the Loyalists and the British troops. Like they called them names and threw things at them.

MS. WILSON: How do you think Loyalists would feel about the Boston Massacre?

BETH: They'd say those creeps got what they deserved. They'd think that it was Sam Adams's fault for getting everyone all stirred up.

MS. WILSON: Let's think about this another way. We live in California. Our nation's capital, Washington, is 3,000 miles away. We have to pay all kinds of taxes, and a lot of those taxes go to help people in Boston or Baltimore rather than people here. Many of the things our government does make people in

California mad. We've got plenty of food, and we can make just about anything we want to right here. Why don't we have a California Revolution and have our own country?

SARA: But we're part of America!

TANYA: We can't do that! The army would come and put down the revolution!

MS. WILSON: Don't you think that the Loyalists thought some of the same things?

VINNIE: But we can vote and they couldn't.

RAMON: Right. Taxation without representation!

BETH: I'll bet a lot of Loyalists thought the British would win the war and it would be better to stay on the side of the winners.

In this discussion the teacher was not looking for any particular facts about the American Revolution, but rather was trying to get students to use the information they had learned previously to discuss issues from a different perspective. Ms. Wilson let the students determine the direction of the discussion to a substantial degree. Her main tasks were to keep the discussion rolling, to get students to use specifics to defend their positions, to ensure that many students participated, and to help the students avoid dead ends or unproductive avenues.

Information Before Discussion. Before beginning a discussion it is important to make sure that students have an adequate knowledge base. There is nothing so dreary as a discussion in which the participants don't know much about the topic. The light bulb discussion would have been less fruitful if students had not already had a concept of a vacuum and of air as a gas. The American Revolution discussion depended on students' knowledge of the main events preceding the Revolution. Sometimes a discussion can be used before instruction as a means of generating interest in a topic, but at some point students must be given information. This may come in the form of a lesson from the teacher, readings from texts or other books, films, or other media. Full-fledged discussions should be held only after students have some information.

Small-Group Discussions

In a small-group discussion students work in four- to six-member groups to discuss a particular topic. Because small-group discussions require that students work independently of the teacher most of the time, young or poorly organized students need a great deal of preparation and, in fact, may not be able to benefit from them at all. However, most students at or above the fourth grade can profit from small-group discussions.

As with any discussions, small-group discussions should follow the presentation of information through teacher-directed lessons, books, or films. When students know something about a subject, they may start to work in their groups, pulling desks together if necessary to talk and hear one another more easily.

Each group should have a leader appointed by the teacher. Leaders should be responsible, well-organized students, but should not always be the highest-achieving students. Groups may all discuss the same topic, or they may each discuss a different subtopic of a larger topic that the whole class is studying. For example, in a unit on the Great Depression one group might focus on causes of the Depression, another on the collapse of the banking system, a third on the social consequences of the Depression, and a fourth on the New Deal. Each group should be given a series of

1. What types and formats for discussions have worked well in your class?

Teachers gave the following pointers:

- Arrange desks so that students face one another.
- Ensure that students have some knowledge of the subject to be discussed.
- With young children, use role playing to help them get involved in and understand the situation to be discussed.
- With older children, relate discussion topics to material discussed in class or select general topics such as "choosing a career."
- Set up discussions as debates, with the class members divided into two or more opposing teams.

Peggy Boxterman, who teaches fourth grade in Henderson, Nev., sent the following anecdote:

To acquaint students with the Lewis and Clark expedition of 1804–1805, I mentioned the importance of an Indian squaw, Sacajawea. The students could not believe that an Indian woman could make too much difference on such a long trek. So, before the discussion I found a short story on her background. The students used the encyclopedia to look up information on Sacajawea and the Lewis and Clark expedition. We used maps to plot the journey. After a few days of research, we discussed whether Sacajawea was really important to the success of the expedition. There were many pros and a few cons, which made for a very informative discussion.

Terry Olive, Elyria, Ohio, set up a discussion for developmentally handicapped elementary students:

In a recent lesson involving evaporation of water, students were prepared a few days earlier by the start of an experiment. I filled a can with water to a specific point and asked the students where the water would be at the start of our next lesson. I asked several students to explain their predictions and took a vote as to whether they thought the water would be higher, lower, or at the same height.

At the beginning of our next session I asked the same question and reiterated the voting results before "unveiling" the correct answer. The students were then asked where the water went and how it got out of the can. Each question led to another, and students were allowed and encouraged to suggest possibilities.

Dorothy Paulsen, who teaches reading in Wausau, Wisc., has the following guidelines for discussions:

The first and most important thing for any discussion is to be sure that all children have a stake in the discussion. Also, while a discussion should stick to the topic, it should be handled like dinner-table talk at home. Everyone at the table is part of the family, everyone in the family has something to contribute, family members listen to one another, and are not content to leave a topic without some resolution.

Also, teachers should not respond more positively to one student's ideas. All statements should be worked through to a resolution to help students see that it's all right to have errors in thought if you work through those errors to logical solutions. Even the responses that appear to be great at first can be worked through to become even better.

questions to be answered on the topic to be discussed. For example, if the topic were the collapse of the banking system the questions might be:

1. What was the connection between the stock market crash of 1929 and the failures of so many banks?

2. What caused savers to lose confidence in the banks?

3. Why did the banks not have enough funds to pay savers who wished to withdraw their money?

4. Why is a widespread run on banks unlikely today?

The leader's role in each discussion group is to make sure that the group stays on the topic and questions assigned to it, and to ensure that all group members participate. A group secretary can be appointed to write down the group's ideas. At

Humanistic Education
An educational philosophy that
focuses on developing students'
attitudes, feelings, and independent
learning

the end of the discussion the group members may prepare a report on their activities or conclusions to be presented to the rest of the class.

Research on small-group discussions indicates that these activities can increase student achievement more than traditional lessons if the students are well prepared to work in small groups and the group task is well organized (Sharan et al., 1980; Sharan et al., 1984). Not surprisingly, the effects are greater for objectives higher on Bloom's taxonomy than for knowledge or applications objectives. Also, some research suggests that small-group discussions have greater effects on student achievement if students are encouraged to engage in controversy rather than to seek a consensus (Johnson and Johnson, 1979).

■ **Stop and Think**

List objectives from the taxonomies of instructional objectives presented in Chapter 7 that might be achieved through the use of class discussions.

HUMANISTIC EDUCATION

Educational psychology has always had two principal streams of thought. One focuses primarily on the role of education in increasing students' knowledge and skills. This movement currently goes under the name of "direct instruction." The other is more focused on the affective outcomes of schooling, learning how to learn, and enhancing creativity and human potential. This is called the **humanistic education** movement, and it was the dominant force in American education in the early 1970s. At that time A. S. Neill's *Summerhill* (1960) was required reading in many teacher education programs. *Summerhill* describes a school in England where, for example, students were not taught reading until they asked to be taught, no matter how long that took. The philosophy of Summerhill was summarized by its headmaster as follows: "The child is innately wise and realistic. If left to himself, without adult suggestion of any kind, he will develop as far as he is capable of developing" (Neill, 1969, p. 4).

The humanistic movement is a successor to John Dewey's Progressive movement of the 1920s and 1930s (see Withall, 1987). Both were reactions against the overuse of drill and rote learning, which humanistic educators feel to be characteristic of traditional schools (see, for example, Goodman, 1964; Holt, 1964).

Good teachers recognize the strengths of both the humanistic and direct instruction approaches to education. Some students (in some instances) learn best if left to explore and think for themselves. But for other students and in other subjects, learning occurs far more easily if the material is presented to the class as a whole by the teacher. The teacher's challenge is to choose the right mix of approaches to ensure that students not only learn information, skills, and concepts, but also learn how to learn, coming to have confidence in themselves as learners.

Humanistic education programs often include activities that encourage students to learn how to learn. Such activities might include interviewing people, conducting research, or solving business problems.

One of the most important ideas behind humanistic education is that students should have a substantial hand in directing their own education, in choosing what they will study and, to some degree, when and how they will study it. The idea is to make students self-directed, self-motivated learners rather than passive recipients of information. The motivational benefits of students' abilities to choose their own activities have been demonstrated (Campbell, 1964; Wang and Stiles, 1976); students will do more work with greater motivation if they have some choice in what they will study.

Humanistic educators usually put as much value on affective goals of education as on cognitive learning goals, arguing that it is more important that students become responsible, caring, feeling adults than that we squeeze a few more points on a standardized test out of them (Combs, 1967; Jones, 1968; Glasser, 1969; Rogers, 1969). Glasser (1969) and Lefkowitz (1975) developed specific methods for holding "class meetings" to discuss interpersonal problems, values, and feelings. More typically, humanistic educators recommend that teachers emphasize such values as consideration, cooperativeness, mutual respect, and honesty, both by setting an example and by discussing and reinforcing these values when appropriate. Table 8.3 shows a few examples of values listed by Davis (1983) as worth teaching.

Another characteristic typical of humanistic education is the avoidance of grades, standardized testing, and most other formal methods of evaluation. Humanistic educators often recommend using written evaluations, "authentic" evaluations (such as solving real problems or conducting experiments), or no evaluations at all (Kirschenbaum et al., 1971). Although research on graded versus ungraded ("pass-fail") courses indicates that the use of some sort of grading increases student achievement at the college level (see Gold et al., 1971), there is little evidence either way on the effects of grading in elementary or secondary schools, and equally little research comparing written evaluations to letter grades (see Chapter 14 for more on innovative assessment methods).

Another principle of humanistic education is that education should teach students how to learn and to value learning for its own sake. All educators hope that students will develop positive attitudes toward learning and will be able to use various resources to obtain information, but humanistic educators especially emphasize these goals and strongly recommend designing instruction to give students many

TABLE 8.3

VALUES ENCOURAGED IN HUMANISTIC EDUCATION

Honesty

- Not cheating
- Not vandalizing
- Being trustworthy
- Understanding and respecting police

Rights Of Others

- Respecting right of others
- Accepting and respecting individual differences
- Listening
- Helping others
- Empathizing with others' problems

Energy, Environment

- Conserving electricity, gas, coal, wood, metals, paper, school supplies, etc.
- Caring for property, own and others'

Manners

- Sharing
- Doing favors
- Being courteous
- Being considerate of others
- Behaving properly in public

School, Work Habits

- Being prompt
- Following directions
- Being industrious, persevering
- Accepting leadership or participant roles
- Valuing education
- Observing safety rules

Personal Development

- Accepting responsibility
- Valuing physical health, hygiene
- Developing one's talents to the fullest
- Developing self-respect, pride
- Controlling one's temper
- Being courageous, honorable, patriotic
- Appreciating beauty

SOURCE: Adapted from Davis, 1983, pp. 366–367.

opportunities to locate information on their own or with minimal teacher guidance. Humanistic programs therefore generally include frequent use of open-ended activities in which students must find information, make decisions, solve problems, and create their own products. For example, teachers might have students write a history of their school, with students taking responsibility for searching school archives, old yearbooks, and other records, for interviewing older teachers and former students, and for searching the local newspaper's archives for information about the school. To help learn math, students might set up a simulated (or real) store or bank, or pretend to invest in the stock market. Most humanistic educators would recommend frequent field trips and explorations in the world outside school. One teacher took students to visit an old graveyard next to the school. The students' task was to find ways to use the information on headstones to learn about the history of the area and about how people lived many years ago.

Another teacher, before teaching a unit on ancient Egypt, had students visit a local museum to see Egyptian artifacts, without a guide or any information. The students wrote their impressions in a journal, and made hypotheses about the meaning and significance of the artifacts. They then returned to school and studied Egypt for two weeks, learning about Egyptian numbering systems in math, studying the country's geography, comparing ancient and modern Egypt. Students even made their own sarcophagi out of shoe boxes, painting on them the things they personally would like to take with them into the afterlife.

At the end of this activity the class returned to the museum to compare their hypotheses with what they now knew, and to find out how much more they could see in the artifacts than when they knew nothing about ancient Egypt.

It is important to note that these teachers had two quite different kinds of objectives in mind for their students. One was the content itself—the history of an area or the history of Egypt. But the other was at least as important—to give students an experience of finding out something for themselves, of using their brains and their imaginations to learn, of learning how rich the world is in information if only we know how to get at it, of finding out how much fun it is to learn. These are certainly important objectives, although difficult to measure.

Open Schools

The instructional programs most closely associated with the humanistic education movement of the early 1970s are called **open schools** or "open classrooms." The most visible aspect of the open schools movement is still in evidence in many schools today: the classrooms have no walls. However, open-school programs can be done in schools with walls, and traditional instruction can certainly occur in open-space schools.

Open schools vary considerably in their particulars and philosophies, but they do have several features in common. Giaconia and Hedges (1982) list several, which are shown in Table 8.4. Open schools rarely include *all* of the features listed in the table; in fact, some researchers doubt that all the "fundamental" features of open education were ever widely used, even when the open school movement was at its height (Epstein and McPartland, 1975; Marshall, 1981). However, there is no question that many open schools have used most of these elements, giving students a wide variety of instructional opportunities and a wide range of choices as to what and how they will learn. Open classrooms typically use **learning stations,** areas located around the classroom that contain projects, individualized workbooks or units, or other activities. Students choose the order in which they will pursue individual activities, but they

TABLE 8.4

FEATURES OF OPEN EDUCATION

A variety of features are shared by many classrooms that use the open-education approach.

Role of Children in Learning

- Children are active in guiding their own learning.
- Children actively choose materials, methods, and pace of learning.
- Teachers serve as resource persons rather than as directors of classroom activities.
- There is a democratic learning atmosphere.

Diagnostic Evaluation

- Observation, written histories, and samples of student work (rather than conventional tests or grades) are used to evaluate progress.
- Purpose of evaluation is to guide instruction, not to grade or rank students.

Materials to Manipulate

- Diverse materials are used to stimulate student exploration and learning.
- Emphasis is on use of materials students can touch and explore; real-world natural materials are preferred to worksheets and books alone.

Individualized Instruction

- Instruction is based on individual needs and abilities. Students proceed at their own rates.
- Materials are adapted to provide for differences in students' preferred modes of learning.
- Instruction is given to individuals and small groups, rarely to large groups.
- Students set individual goals for learning.

Multiage Grouping

- Students of different ages may work in the same classroom without age distinction.
- Grade levels may not be used to categorize students.

Open Space

- Physical environment of the classroom involves flexible use of space and furnishings.
- Classrooms lack interior walls; many classrooms may share resources and personnel.
- Seating arrangements are flexible.

Team Teaching

- Two or more teachers plan together, share resources, mix students.
- Two or more teachers may completely combine classes in a large area.
- Parents are often used as volunteer aides.

SOURCE: Adapted from Giaconia and Hedges, 1982, pp. 593–594.

typically must accomplish some set of objectives by some time. The particular objectives vary from student to student, and may be negotiated with the teacher. In open classrooms the teacher rarely delivers a lesson to the entire class, but more often spends time with individuals and small groups working on a common activity.

Research on Open Education. Reviews of studies of open versus traditional education have uniformly concluded that the effects of open-education programs did not support the early enthusiasm for them (for example, Horwitz, 1979; Peterson, 1979; Marshall, 1981; Giaconia and Hedges, 1982). Students in open schools generally learn slightly less than do students in traditional programs. On affective outcomes, such as attitudes toward school, cooperativeness, social adjustment, and self-concept, students in open classrooms have scored only slightly better than traditionally taught students; open schools do apparently promote creativity more than traditional programs do, but studies measuring motivation to achieve tend to favor traditional programs (see Giaconia and Hedges, 1982).

Constructivist Approaches to Humanistic Education

As of this writing, humanistic approaches to instruction are once again becoming dominant in many areas of educational psychology and educational practice. However, the focus of modern approaches is different in many ways from the open classroom movement of the 1970s. Modern approaches emphasize discovery learning, experimentation, learning-to-learn, and creativity, all of which were key elements of humanistic education in the 1970s. However, the open classroom placed a greater emphasis on individualized learning, use of separate "learning stations" or "learning activity packets," which students could do on their own. Today's humanistic methods put a much greater emphasis on the role of the teacher in guiding discovery and on the use of cooperative learning and discussion among students. They are largely based on "constructivist" theories of learning (see Chapter 6), which emphasize the need for students to construct meaning for themselves. They emphasize the use of "authentic" activities, learning exercises that resemble the real-life activities for which students are being prepared. For example, new "whole-language" approaches to reading instruction emphasize the use of real literature rather than basal texts, the integration of reading with writing and language arts, student responsibility and choice, and other elements that promote the teaching of reading as meaning rather than as a skill (see Goodman, 1986; Watson, 1989). "Writing process" models emphasize teaching of composition by having students plan, draft, revise, edit, and ultimately "publish" compositions for a real audience, with help and feedback from classmates as well as the teacher at each stage (Calkins, 1983; Graves, 1983). New approaches in mathematics instruction emphasize not only teaching *of* problem solving, but teaching *through* problem solving as well, where students are guided to discover mathematical processes and operations rather than being directly taught (see Lampert, 1986; Burns, 1986).

As noted in Chapter 6, research on the achievement outcomes of these constructivist approaches has produced mixed results. There is strong support for use of writing process models (Hillocks, 1984). A recent review of research comparing whole language to traditional reading approaches concluded that whole language methods were effective in kindergarten as prereading methods, but tended to produce the same or less learning than traditional methods beyond the kindergarten level, particularly with disadvantaged children (Stahl and Miller, 1989). Effects of constructivist mathematics approaches have been mixed (Johnson and Waxman, 1985; Carpenter et al., 1988).

At present, it is too early to make any firm conclusions about constructivist approaches to instruction. Advocates of these approaches typically reject traditional measures of achievement, and therefore question the validity of studies undertaken to evaluate them (see Brown et al., 1989). However, research on constructivist approaches is rapidly accumulating and better answers to questions about these approaches should be available in coming years. Also, it is important to recall that the goals of all humanistic approaches, including those based on constructivist theories, are much broader than improving academic achievement.

Humanistic Education versus Direct Instruction

Which is better, humanistic education or direct instruction? In a way, this is like asking which is a better way to travel, by walking or by swimming. Obviously, walking is better where it is called for (on land) and swimming is better where it is called for (in water). By the same token, direct instruction with clear learning objectives and structured instructional strategies that achieve these objectives is best for teaching well-specified skills that students must master. More humanistic methods are probably most appropriate when the goal is less to teach a particular set of skills or body of knowledge than to teach ways of approaching problems, appreciation of a subject, and openness to different viewpoints.

However, there should not be sharp boundaries between humanistic and direct approaches (Kierstead, 1985). Every teacher must be skilled in both. When the teacher who taught the unit on Egypt (discussed earlier) was presenting lessons on the history of ancient Egypt, she used lesson presentation methods similar to the direct instruction strategies described earlier in this chapter because in those lessons she had a particular body of knowledge to transmit. A math teacher might use direct instructional strategies to teach students how to compute rates, but might then have students use stopwatches to time runners or to predict when two toy cars moving at different speeds will crash.

A recurrent problem in education is not that good ideas are lacking, but that good ideas are overapplied. The open classroom and other humanistic educational methods were applied in the early 1970s to teach everything. This was a mistake, as research later showed. Only the most able and self-motivated students can teach themselves how to read, to add fractions with unlike denominators, or to speak French. Direct, planned, structured instructional methods are needed to teach most students these skills.

On the other hand, while we may not be able to measure the effects of humanistic methods as well as we can those of direct instructional methods, if there is one thing research in educational psychology (and particularly in direct instruction) tells us, it is that students learn what they are taught. If we expect students to be independent learners, we must give them opportunities to learn on their own. If we expect students to value learning for its own sake, we must give them exciting and challenging experiences. If we want them to learn to take responsibility, we must give them responsibility.

Carl Rogers, a psychologist who was one of the major proponents of humanistic approaches to education, put it this way:

> I have come to realize, as I have considered these studies, and puzzled over the design of better studies which should be more informative and conclusive, that findings from such research will never answer our questions. For all such findings must be evaluated in terms of the goals we have for education. If we value primarily the learning of knowledge, then we may discard the conditions I have described as useless, since there is no evidence that they lead to a greater rate or amount of factual knowledge . . . if we value independence, if we are disturbed by the growing conformity of knowledge, of values, of attitudes, which our present system induces, then we may wish to set up conditions of learning which make for uniqueness, for self-direction, and for self-initiated learning. (Rogers, 1969, pp. 239–240)

John Harrison, a fourth-grade teacher in his second year of teaching, sits in the office of Dr. Barbara Payne, the elementary curriculum supervisor for the county school system.

BARBARA: Fire away, John. What can I do for you?

JOHN: Thanks. My trouble is that I haven't been able to hit my stride with this year's group of kids. The class is more diverse than last year's, and I'm not sure my teaching methods are working too well. I seem to have a handful of academic superstars and also a small group that's having real trouble with math and reading. And then there's the fifteen or eighteen kids right in the middle. It just seems like I have two or three classes in one.

BARBARA: I know what you mean. I don't know if this helps much, but what you've got is a very common problem. Almost every teacher faces it to some extent.

JOHN: I know, I talked with my principal about that. His suggestion was that I group the kids for some subjects, but I'm not sure that feels right to me. Last year my students were so similar in their abilities that I was able to be much more flexible with them. Boy, did we do some great projects! We always had time to cover the curriculum, and then some.

BARBARA: Well, different groups of students demand different approaches. Let's look at your present situation. You're familiar with direct instruction, aren't you? That might be your best strategy for working with the low achievers on their basic skills. It would also be good for your whole-class lessons on social studies and the like.

JOHN: Yeah, I tried a form of direct instruction during one of my stints of student teaching but I never got comfortable with it. It all seemed too artificial, structured, and subject-matter oriented to me.

BARBARA: That's a pretty strong reaction!

JOHN: Well, I just felt that I never had time to talk with the kids and see what *they* were thinking and what *they* wanted to learn. They have some pretty good ideas sometimes, you know.

BARBARA: Yes, they do. What teaching strategy have you most enjoyed using?

JOHN: I guess I like the ideas of humanistic education. I've found I'm interested in the whole child, not just the subject matter the child has learned. One science sequence I used last year encouraged the students to think up and solve problems on their own. Those kids took the projects in directions I never would have dreamed of! I also remember seeing the "magic circle" exercises a number of years back where children learned how to communicate and share with others. I even tried it with last year's class a few times, but I was afraid to use it too often because I know this district puts a lot of emphasis on sticking to the curriculum and preparing children for the standardized tests.

BARBARA: Do you see anything wrong with that?

JOHN: I just don't think the test scores say much about the whole child. And when we pay too much attention to scores, we forget about feelings and motivations and creativity. Where do these fit into the curriculum?

BARBARA: Yes, I'll grant you that we might fall short in those areas. But, let's get back to your situation this year. You've got some students who need help with basic skills. Do you think humanistic approaches will help those kids catch up with the average and high achievers in your class?

JOHN: I really don't know. Maybe direct instruction would be better. I might be persuaded about it if I saw my students make real gains. Do you think you could help me work out a mix of approaches that I could use for my various groups of students and the various subjects I teach during the day?

QUESTIONS

1. What are the goals and practices of humanistic education? What is direct instruction? What are the differences, strengths, and weaknesses of the two?
2. To what extent should a teacher be obligated to follow the goals and instructional procedures set out by the school district? To what extent should a teacher's beliefs determine the choice of instructional goals and procedures?
3. What advice would you give John about choosing instructional strategies? Would humanistic teaching procedures work in his classroom situation?

SUMMARY AND REVIEW OF OBJECTIVES

Models of Instruction.   Carroll's model of school learning proposes five elements that contribute to the effectiveness of instruction: aptitude, ability to understand instruction, perseverance, opportunity, and quality of instruction. This model discusses the elements in terms of time needed to learn and time available for learning. It mixes elements under the control of the teacher and those characteristic of the student.

Alterable elements of instruction include quality of instruction, appropriate levels of instruction, incentive, and time. These are identified in the QAIT model of effective instruction.

When the quality of instruction is high, lesson presentations make sense to students, are interesting to them, and are easy to remember and apply. Providing appropriate levels of instruction involves adapting the type and difficulty of materials to student needs. Adequate incentives help to ensure that students will be motivated to learn. Finally, teachers must allocate a sufficient amount of time for students to learn what is taught.

Steps in Lesson Presentation.   The first part of a lesson is to state learning objectives and orient students to the lesson. The principal task here is to establish a mental set so that students are ready to work and learn. Also important is giving students a "road map" of where the lesson is going.

The second part in a lesson is to review prerequisites to ensure that students have already mastered the prior skills needed. Sometimes an assessment of skills is necessary. Reviewing prerequisites can also provide advance organizers for the new task.

Part three is to present the new material. Important aspects of this process are organization, providing explanations and demonstrations, and maintaining attention.

Part four of the lesson, conducting learning probes, involves asking for brief student responses to lesson content. Purposes are to give the teacher feedback on students' understanding and to permit students to try out the new ideas. Questions can be used to prompt students to think further about the information they learned previously. Important issues regarding how teachers ask questions include wait time, the order in which students are called upon, and calling on students at all levels of achievement.

Part five of the lesson is the independent practice or seatwork students do on their own to demonstrate newly learned skills. Researchers make several suggestions for the most effective use of seatwork: do not assign independent practice until you are sure students can do it; keep independent practice assignments short; give clear instructions; get students started and then avoid interruptions; monitor independent work; collect it and include it in student grades.

The sixth part of the lesson is to assess performance and provide feedback. Every lesson should contain an assessment of the degree to which students have mastered the objectives set for the lesson. This provides feedback for both teacher and student.

Part seven of the lesson is to provide distributed practice and review. Retention of many types of knowledge is increased by practice spaced out over time, a finding that supports the use of both homework and review lessons combined with unit tests.

Essentials of Direct Instruction.   Direct instruction emphasizes teacher control of all classroom events, deemphasizes student autonomy, and recommends against loose structure. Direct instructional strategies focus primarily on reading, language, arts, and mathematics. These programs all emphasize active presentation of information; clear organization; a step-by-step progression from subtopic to subtopic; and use of many examples, demonstrations, and visual prompts. Exemplary programs are Madeline Hunter's Mastery Teaching Program and the Missouri Mathematics Program.

Discussions.   In a whole-class discussion the teacher plays a less dominant role than in a regular lesson. When using an inquiry training strategy, the teacher answers only yes-or-no questions and provides information only when students ask the right questions. Before beginning a discussion, teachers should ensure that students have an adequate knowledge base. In a small-group discussion each group should have a leader and a specific series of questions to answer.

Humanistic Education.   The humanistic movement focuses on learning how to learn, creativity, and enhancing human potential. It is based on the idea that students should help direct their own education. Humanistic educators tend to value affective goals of education as highly as cognitive goals and are usually opposed to letter grades, standardized testing, and other formal evaluation methods. Some of the features of open education are the active role children play in learning, the use of diagnostic evaluations only to assess progress, instruction that is individualized, and team teaching. Research has shown the effects of these programs on learning and affective outcomes to be disappointing. Humanistic orientations appear valuable, however, in stressing the importance of developing independent learning skills by giving students opportunities to learn on their own.

STUDY QUESTIONS

1. Which component of the QAIT model is considered an "alterable" element that is necessary for instruction to be effective?

    a. Quality of instruction
    b. Appropriate levels of instruction
    c. Incentive
    d. Time
    e. All of the above

2. Match the following elements from Carroll's model of instruction with the related description of a hypothetical classroom situation.
    ____ Aptitude
    ____ Ability to understand instruction
    ____ Perseverance
    ____ Opportunity
    ____ Quality of instruction

    a. Students have the prerequisite skills needed for all the tasks that will be taught.
    b. The teacher has set aside extra class time to present this lesson.
    c. Students are eager to study until the skills are mastered.
    d. Students have shown great ability to learn.
    e. The lesson is presented in such a way that students learn it as fast as their knowledge and abilities allow.

3. The seven steps in effective lesson presentation are listed below in alphabetical order. Rearrange the items in the order that they should appear in a lesson.

    a. Assess performance and provide feedback.
    b. Conduct learning probes.
    c. Present new material.
    d. Provide distributed practice and review.
    e. Provide independent practice.
    f. Review prerequisites.
    g. State learning objectives and orient students to lesson.

4. Research on questioning suggests that

    a. teachers tend to give low-achievers less time to respond than high-achievers.
    b. if a student doesn't respond immediately, moving quickly to someone else helps to avoid embarassment and keep the exercise moving.
    c. calling on volunteers has proved more effective than selecting students in a prescribed order.
    d. choral responding generally works best when there are several possible correct answers.
    e. an effective procedure is to call on a randomly selected student first and ask the question aloud.

5. In assigning independent practice or seatwork, it is generally recommended that

    a. students' work be collected and included in their grades.
    b. teachers refrain from monitoring students' work while it is in progress.
    c. task difficulty be slightly beyond students' current level of competence.
    d. the tasks be reasonably long, averaging at least half of a class session to complete.

6. Which of the following terms is *not* consistent with the basic orientation of direct instruction?
   a. Immediate feedback
   b. Clear goals
   c. Frequent monitoring of performance
   d. Learner control
   e. Structured interactions

7. Match the following direct instruction methods with the correct descriptions of each.
   ____ Madeline Hunter's Mastery Teaching
   ____ Missouri Mathematics Program
   ____ DISTAR
   a. Principally used with low-achieving children in early elementary grades
   b. A general model that is applicable to virtually any subject area or grade level
   c. A computer-based program for gifted science students
   d. A "master teacher" strategy that has been frequently evaluated in research

8. Which of the following is a feature or emphasis of humanistic instruction?
   a. Letter grades
   b. Affective goals
   c. Standardized testing
   d. Teacher-directed classes
   e. Rote learning

*Answers: 1. c. 2. d. a. c. b. 3. g. f. c. b. c. a. d. 4. a. 5. a. 6. d.
7. b. d. a. 8. b.*

SUGGESTED READINGS

BARR, R. and DREEBAN, R. (1983). *How schools work.* Chicago: University of Chicago Press.

BROOKOVER, W., EFTHIM, H., HATHAWAY, D., LEZOTTE, L., MILLER, S., PASSALACQUA, J. and TORNATSKY, L. (1982). *Creating effective schools.* Holmes Beach, Fla.: Learning Publications.

BROPHY, J. E. (1988). Research on teacher effects: Uses and abuses. *Elementary school journal,* 89, 3–21.

BROPHY, J. E., and GOOD, T. L. (1986). Teacher behavior and student achievement. In M. C. Wittrock (Ed.), *Handbook of research on teaching.* New York: Macmillan.

CARROLL, J. B. (1989). The Carroll model: A 25-year retrospective and prospective view. *Educational Researcher,* 18, 26–31.

GAGE, N. L. and NEEDELS, M. C. (1989). Process-product research on teaching: A review of criticisms. *Elementary School Journal,* 89, 253–300.

GAGNÉ, R. and BRIGGS, L. (1979). *Principles of instructional design* (2nd ed.). New York: Holt, Rinehart & Winston.

GOOD, T., GROUWS, D., and EBMEIER, H. (1983). *Active mathematics teaching.* New York: Longman.

HUNTER, M. (1982). *Mastery teaching.* El Segundo, Cal.: TIP Publications.

JOYCE, B., and WEIL, M. (1980). *Models of teaching.* Englewood Cliffs, N.J.: Prentice-Hall.

PETERSON, P. L., and WALBERG, H. J. (Eds.). (1979). *Research on teaching: Concepts, findings and implications.* Berkeley, Cal.: McCutchan.

ROSENSHINE, B. V., and STEVENS, R. J. (1986). Teaching functions. In M. C. Wittrock (Ed.), *Third handbook of research on teaching.* Chicago: Rand McNally.

SLAVIN, R. E. (Ed.). (1989). *School and classroom organization.* Hillsdale, N.J.: Erlbaum.

Chapter 9

Accommodating Student Differences

Chapter Objectives

After reading this chapter on adapting instruction to meet the needs of students you should be able to:

- List the types of student differences that are most important to consider when teaching a class.

- Understand the concept of intelligence, and the tests used to measure intellectual aptitude.

- Explain the disadvantages of using tracking—or between-class ability grouping—to accommodate student differences.

- Plan a class period in which within-class ability grouping is used to teach basic skills to elementary school students.

- Describe how a unit could be taught using mastery learning.

- Understand how computers can be used to provide individualized instruction.

Mr. Arbuthnot is in fine form. He is presenting a lesson on long division to his fourth-grade class, and feels that he's never been so clear, so interesting, and so well organized. When he asks questions, several students raise their hands, and when he calls on them, they always know the answers. "Arbuthnot, old boy," he says to himself, "I think you're finally getting to these kids!"

At the end of the period he passes out a short quiz to see how well his students have learned the long-division lesson. When the papers are scored, he finds to his shock and disappointment that while about a third of the class got every problem right, another third missed every problem. The remaining students fell somewhere in between. "What went wrong?" he thinks. "Well, no matter, I'll set the situation aright in tomorrow's lesson."

The next day Mr. Arbuthnot is even better prepared, uses vivid examples and diagrams to show how to do long division, and gives an active, exciting lesson. Even more hands than before go up when he asks questions, and the answers are usually correct. However, some of the students are beginning to look bored, particularly those who got perfect papers on the quiz and those who got none right.

Toward the end of the period he gives another brief quiz. The scores are better this time, but there is still a group of students who got none of the problems correct. He is crestfallen. "I had them in the palm of my hand," he thinks. "How could they fail to learn?"

To try to find out what went wrong, he goes over the quiz papers of the students who missed all the problems. He immediately sees a pattern. By the second lesson, almost all students were proceeding correctly in setting up the long-division problems. However, some were making consistent errors in subtraction. Others had apparently forgotten their multiplication facts. Their problems were not with division at all; they simply lacked the prerequisite skills.

"Well," thinks Mr. Arbuthnot, "at least I was doing great with some of the kids." It occurs to him that one of the students who got a perfect paper after the first lesson might be able to give him an idea about how to teach the others better. He asks Teresa how she grasped long division so quickly. "It was easy," she says. "We learned long division last year!"

THE PROBLEM OF STUDENT DIFFERENCES

Mr. Arbuthnot's problem is one that plagues every teacher in every subject at every grade level: how to teach one lesson to a class that contains students with different skills and learning rates. Mr. Arbuthnot started out with a difficult situation. Some of his students lacked basic multiplication and subtraction skills that are crucial for long division. Others already knew long division before he began his lesson, and many probably learned it during the first lesson and did not need the second. If Mr. Arbuthnot stopped to review multiplication and division, he would be wasting the time of the better-prepared students. If he set his pace of instruction according to the needs of his more able students, those with learning problems would never catch up.

Accommodating instruction to student differences is one of the most fundamental problems of education and often leads to politically and emotionally charged policies. For example, most countries outside of North America attempt to deal with the problem of student differences, or student "heterogeneity," by testing children at around ten to twelve years of age and assigning them to different types of schools, only one of which is meant to prepare students for higher education. These systems have long been under attack and are changing in some countries (such as the United Kingdom), but remain in others (such as West Germany). In the United States a similar function is carried out by assignment of students to "college preparatory," "general," and "vocational" **tracks** in high school, and by grouping students in classes according to ability level in junior/middle schools and often in elementary schools as well. Another common means of accommodating instruction to student differences in elementary schools is within-class ability grouping, as in the use of reading groups (Bluebirds, Redbirds, Yellowbirds) that divide students according to their reading performance. The problem of accommodating student differences is so important that many educators have suggested that instruction be completely individualized so that students can work independently at their own rates. In the past twenty-five years this point of view has led to the creation of individualized instructional programs and computer-assisted instruction.

Each of the many ways of accommodating students' differences has its own benefits, but each introduces its own problems, which sometimes outweigh the benefits. This chapter discusses the research on various means of accommodating classroom instruction to student differences. However, first let's consider what student differences are, and which of them teachers must take into account.

Types of Differences

From their first day in school, students differ. They differ on several obvious dimensions that are of little importance to instruction, but they also differ in cognitive abilities and learning rates, which are of great concern to educators. Many students enter kindergarten or first grade knowing the alphabet and numbers up to ten, and some can already read a little. Others lack these skills. As time goes on, initial differences between students tend to increase, so that by junior and senior high school students may enter class with markedly different skills. For example, two fourth-graders who differ by one grade equivalent in reading or mathematics performance are likely to differ by three grade equivalents by the twelfth grade (Coleman et al., 1966).

Intelligence

Perhaps the most important, and certainly the most controversial, of student differences are those found in intelligence. Specific definitions of intelligence vary (see Sternberg and Detterman, 1986), but most psychologists agree that the key components of intelligence are the ability to deal with abstractions, the ability to solve problems, and the ability to learn (Snyderman and Rothman, 1987). Modern theories of intelligence emphasize the idea that there are several different "intelligences," which are distinct enough that individuals are often high in one type and low in another. For example, Sternberg (1986) describes three types of intellectual ability: intelligence, wisdom, and creativity. Gardner and Hatch (1989) describe seven, shown in Table 9.1.

Measurement of Intelligence.   The traditional measure of intelligence is called the *Intelligence Quotient,* or *IQ*. The measurement of IQ was introduced in the early 1900s by Alfred Binet, a French psychologist, to identify children who were unlikely to profit from regular classroom instruction. The scale he developed to measure intelligence assessed a wide range of mental characteristics and skills, such as memory, knowledge, vocabulary, and problem solving. Binet tested a large number of students

Tracks
Classes or curricula targeted for students of a specified achievement or ability level

TABLE 9.1

THE SEVEN INTELLIGENCES

Intelligence	End-States	Core Components
Logical/mathematical	Scientist Mathematician	Sensitivity to, and capacity to discern, logical or numerical patterns; ability to handle long chains of reasoning.
Linguistic	Poet Journalist	Sensitivity to the sounds, rhythms, and meanings of words; sensitivity to the different functions of language.
Musical	Composer Violinist	Abilities to produce and appreciate rhythm, pitch, and timbre; appreciation of the forms of musical expressiveness.
Spatial	Navigator Sculptor	Capacities to perceive the visual-spatial world accurately and to perform transformations on one's initial perceptions.
Bodily/kinesthetic	Dancer Athlete	Abilities to control one's body movements and to handle objects skillfully.
Interpersonal	Therapist Salesman	Capacities to discern and respond appropriately to the moods, temperaments, motivations, and desires of other people.
Intrapersonal	Person with detailed, accurate self-knowledge	Access to one's own feelings and the ability to discriminate among them and draw upon them to guide behavior; knowledge of one's own strengths, weaknesses, desires, and intelligences.

SOURCE: Gardner and Hatch, 1989, p. 6.

of various ages to establish norms (expectations) for overall performance on his tests. He expressed IQ as a ratio of chronological age to "mental age" (the average test score received by a student of a particular age), multiplied by 100. For example, six-year-olds (chronological age [CA] = 6) who score at the average for all six-year-olds (mental age [MA] = 6) would have an IQ of 100 (6/6 × 100 = 100). Six-year-olds who scored at a level typical of seven-year-olds (MA = 7) would have IQs of about 117 (7/6 × 100 = 117).

Over the years the chronological age/mental age comparison has been dropped, and IQ is now defined as having a mean of 100 and a standard deviation of 15 (see Chapter 15 for definitions of standard deviations). Most scores fall near the mean, with small numbers of scores extending well above and below the mean. In theory, about 68 percent of all individuals will have IQs within one standard deviation of the mean, which is to say from 85 (one standard deviation below) to 115 (one standard deviation above). Put another way, on the average, most of us are average!

Intelligence tests are designed to provide a general indication of an individual's aptitudes in many areas of intellectual functioning. The most widely used tests contain many different scales. Figure 9.1 shows items like those used on the Wechsler Adult Intelligence Scale (Wechsler, 1955). Each scale measures a different component of intelligence. Most often, a person who scores well on one scale will also do well on others, but this is not always so; the same person might do very well on general comprehension and similarities, less well on arithmetic reasoning, and poorly on block design, for example. Intelligence tests are administered either to individuals or to groups. Tests administered to groups, such as the Otis-Lennon Mental Ability Tests, the Lorge-Thorndike Intelligence Tests, and the California Test of Mental Maturity, are often given to large groups of students as general assessments of intellectual aptitude. These tests are not as accurate or detailed as intelligence tests administered individually to people by trained psychologists, such as the Wechsler Intelligence Test for Children–Revised (WISC–R) or the Stanford-Binet test. For example, when students are being assessed for possible placement in special education, an individually administered test (most often the WISC–R) is usually administered, along with other tests.

The reason that IQ scores are important is that they are highly predictive of school performance (DeMyer, 1975). That is, students with higher IQs tend, on average, to get better grades, score higher on achievement tests, and so on. By about age six, IQ estimates tend to become relatively stable, and most people's IQs remain about the

FIGURE 9.1

Illustrations of Items Used in Intelligence Testing

Intelligence tests focus on skills such as dealing with abstractions and solving problems. This sample of items resembles those used on the Wechsler Adult Intelligence Scale.

From Thorndike and Hagen 1969, pp. 302–303.

Verbal Subscale

1. General Comprehension.
   Why do people buy fire insurance?
2. Arithmetic Reasoning.
   If eggs cost 60 cents a dozen, what does one egg cost?
3. Similarities.
   In what way are wool and cotton alike?
4. Digit Span.
   Listen carefully, and when I am though, say the numbers right after me.
   7–3–4–1–8–6

   Now I am going to say some more numbers, but I want you to say them backward.
   3–8–4–1–6

Performance Subscale

5. Digit-Symbol Substitution.

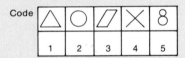

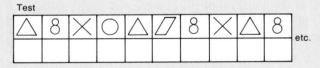

6. Block Design.
   Using the four blocks, make one just like this.

same into adulthood (Hopkins and Bracht, 1975). However, some people will experience substantial changes in their estimated IQ, often because of schooling or other environment influences (Petty and Field, 1980).

The origins of intelligence have been debated for decades, and still cause emotional confrontation. Some psychologists (such as Jensen, 1969) hold that intelligence is overwhelmingly a product of heredity, whereas others (such as Kamin, 1975) just as vehemently hold that intelligence is shaped by factors in a person's social environment, such as the amount a child is read to and talked to. Most investigators believe that both heredity and environment play an important part in intelligence (Schiffetal, 1982; Scarr and McCartney, 1983).

Intense controversy surrounds the use of intelligence tests, most of it revolving around whether the tests are biased in favor of middle-class whites (see, for example, Miele, 1979; Scarr, 1981; Simmons, 1985), causing too many non-white students to be assigned to special education (Mercer, 1973) and causing teachers to expect too little from lower-class students in general (Copper and Good, 1983). Because of evidence that IQ scores used in isolation resulted in the assignment of too many minority students to special education classes, a California judge ruled in *Larry vs. Riles* that IQ tests could no longer be used in that state to classify students as retarded. Many other states are also abandoning the routine use of IQ testing to make placement decisions about students, although individual IQ tests are generally still used, along with other information, for the assessment of students who are experiencing difficulties in school.

Learning Rate

After attending the same class lesson, some students will have learned more than others. Some could have learned the material in less time, and some need more. These are differences in *learning rate,* the amount of time needed to learn a given amount of material. Learning rate is partly a product of intelligence or aptitude for the topic being taught, but other factors are also involved, including motivation and prior knowledge about the subject (recall the discussion of Carroll's model and QAIT in Chapter 8). For example, in a beginning French class, students who have been to France or Quebec or have learned a few words of French may find it easier to learn than those who have no familiarity with the language at all. Even among those who are starting off with equal degrees of ignorance, some students have an "ear" for foreign languages while others do not, and some will have a stronger motivation to learn French than others. All of these factors contribute to the rate at which students will learn the language.

Prior Knowledge

The amount students already know about a subject before it is taught is obviously an important element in determining how rapidly they will learn. Not only does prior knowledge of a subject reduce the additional amount that students must learn, but it also makes further learning easier (Bransford, 1979; Tobias, 1981). Prior knowledge can be knowledge of the actual material to be presented, as was the case with the fourth graders in Mr. Arbuthnot's class who had been taught long division in the third grade. It can also be prerequisite skills, such as knowing how to multiply and subtract before a lesson on long division, or knowing how to interpret maps and globes before a lesson on the discovery of the New World.

Learning Styles

Just as students have different personalities, so do they have different ways of learning (see Messick, 1984). For example, think about how you learn the names of people you meet. Do you learn a name better if you see it written down? If so, you may be a *visual* learner, one who learns best by seeing or reading. If you learn better by hearing, you may be an *auditory* learner. Of course, we all learn in many ways, but some of us learn better in some ways than in others. Students with learning disabilities (see Chapter 12) may have great difficulty learning in one way even if they have no trouble learning in another.

There are several other differences in **learning styles** that educational psychologists have studied. One is **field dependence** versus **field independence** (Witkin et al., 1977). Field-dependent individuals tend to see patterns as a whole, and have difficulty separating out specific aspects of a situation or pattern, while field-independent people are more able to see the parts that make up a large pattern. Field-dependent people tend to be more oriented toward people and social relationships than are field-independent people; for example, they tend to be better at recalling such social information as conversations and relationships, to work best in groups, and to prefer such subjects as history and literature. Field-independent people are more likely to do well with numbers, science, and problem-solving tasks (Shuell, 1981; Witkin and Goodenough, 1981).

Another important cognitive style on which students differ is **impulsivity** versus **reflectivity** (Entwistle, 1981). Impulsive individuals tend to work and make decisions quickly, while reflective types are more likely to take a long time considering all alternatives. Impulsive students are the ones who always finish objective tests early, while reflective students are still chewing on their answers (and possibly their pencils as well) when time is called. Impulsive students tend to concentrate on speed, while reflective ones concentrate on accuracy. Impulsive students can be taught to be reflective by means of self-instruction training (Meichenbaum, 1977), in which they are trained to "talk to themselves" while they work to pace themselves appropriately and reinforce themselves for step-by-step progress. See Chapter 4 for more on this.

Students may also vary in preferences for different learning environments or conditions. For example, Dunn and Dunn (1978, 1987) have found that students differ in preferences regarding such things as the amount of lighting, hard or soft seating, quiet or noisy surroundings, for working alone or with peers, and so on.

Aptitude-Treatment Interactions.   Given the well-documented differences in learning styles and preferences, it would seem logical that different styles of teaching would have different impacts on different learners, yet this common-sense proposition has been difficult to demonstrate conclusively. Studies that have attempted to match teaching styles to learning styles have only inconsistently found any benefits for learning (Corno and Snow, 1985; Pintrich et al., 1986; Whitener, 1989). However, the search for such aptitude-treatment interaction goes on, and a few studies have found positive effects for programs that adapt instruction to an individual's learning style (Dunn et al., 1989; Wilkerson and White, 1988).

Providing Appropriate Instruction

Some student differences can be easily accommodated. For example, the existence of different learning styles is one reason that it makes sense to reinforce verbal presentations with visual cues such as writing on the chalkboard or showing pictures

Learning Styles
Orientations for approaching learning tasks and processing information in certain ways

Field Dependence/Field Independence
A learning style reflecting the degree to which people perceive stimuli as whole patterns (field dependence) as opposed to separating them into parts (field independence)

Impulsivity/Reflectivity
A learning style representing the degree to which tasks are completed slowly with high emphasis on accuracy (reflectivity) as opposed to speed (impulsivity)

Although students differ in levels of skills and knowledge, use of special methods to accommodate differences is not always appropriate because drawbacks of the methods can outweigh benefits.

and diagrams to emphasize important concepts. Other differences in learning style can similarly be accommodated by varying classroom activities, such as alternating active and quiet tasks or individual and group work. Teachers can sometimes work with students on an individual basis and adapt instruction to their learning styles—for example, by reminding impulsive students to take their time, or by teaching overly reflective students strategies for skipping over items they are having problems with so they can complete tests on time.

Differences in prior knowledge and learning rate are more difficult to deal with. All of the common means of accommodating these differences create problems of their own (see Slavin, 1987, 1988), particularly management problems. For this reason, often the best way to deal with these differences is to largely ignore them, to teach the whole class at a single pace, perhaps offering additional help to low-achieving students and giving extra enrichment activities to students who tend to finish assignments rapidly. For example, it is probably less important to accommodate student achievement differences in social studies, science, and English than in mathematics, reading, and foreign languages. This is because in the latter subjects skills build directly on one another, so teaching at one pace to a heterogeneous class may be a disservice to both low and high achievers; low achievers may fail because they lack prerequisite skills, while high achievers may become bored at what is for them a slow pace of instruction. This was the case in Mr. Arbuthnot's mathematics class. In contrast, one pace of instruction in social studies, science, or English is less likely to create problems because topics in these subjects depend less on one another.

The remainder of this chapter discusses strategies for accommodating student achievement differences.

■ **Stop and Think**

Recall a situation from your school career that illustrates the problems created by educationally relevant differences between students. Analyze the nature of the differences. Did they relate to intelligence, prior learning, learning style, learning rate, or a combination of these factors? Recall and evaluate the teacher's response (if any) to the situation.

GROUPING STUDENTS BY ABILITY

Ability Grouping Between Classes

Probably the most common means of dealing with instructionally important differences is to assign students to classes according to their abilities. This **between-class ability grouping** may take many forms. In high schools there may be "college preparatory" and "general" tracks that divide students on the basis of measured ability. In some junior high and middle schools students are assigned to one class by general ability, and they then stay with that class, moving from teacher to teacher. For example, the highest-performing seventh-graders might be assigned to class 7–1, middle-performing students to 7–5, and low-performing students to 7–12. In other junior high/middle schools (and many high schools) students are grouped separately by ability for each subject, so that a student might be in a high-performing math class and an average-performing science class. In high schools this is accomplished by course placements. For example, some ninth-graders take Algebra I, while others who do not qualify for Algebra I take general mathematics. Elementary schools use a wide range of strategies for grouping students, including many of the

patterns used in secondary schools. Often students in elementary schools will be assigned to a mixed-ability class for homeroom, social studies, and science, but regrouped by ability for reading and math. Elementary schools are less likely than secondary schools to use ability grouping *between* classes, but more likely to use ability grouping *within* classes, especially in reading (McPartland et al., 1987).

Research on Between-Class Ability Grouping. Despite the widespread use of between-class ability grouping, and despite evidence that teachers overwhelmingly believe in its necessity and effectiveness (Wilson and Schmits, 1978), research on this strategy does not support its use. Researchers have found that while ability grouping may have slight benefits for students assigned to high-track classes, these benefits are balanced by slight losses for students assigned to low-track classes (for example, Findley and Bryan, 1971; Esposito, 1973; Rosenbaum, 1980; Good and Marshall, 1984; Oakes, 1985; Slavin, 1987b, 1990).

Why is between-class ability grouping so ineffective? Several researchers have explored this question. The primary purpose of ability grouping is to reduce the range of student performance levels teachers must deal with so they can adapt instruction to the needs of a well-defined group. However, grouping is often done on the basis of standardized test scores, intelligence test scores, or other measures of general ability rather than performance in a particular subject. As a result, the reduction in the range of differences that are actually important for a specific class may be too small to make much difference. For example, one study found that dividing students in a particular grade level into two groups on the basis of a measure of general intellectual performance reduced variability in school achievement only 7 percent. Dividing into three groups reduced variability only 17 percent, still not enough to make a substantial difference (Goodlad, 1960). Other researchers have similarly found that ability grouping leaves substantial overlap in performance levels between groups (Barr, in press; Rosenbaum, 1976). Further, concentrating low-achieving students in low-track classes seems to be harmful because it exposes them to too few positive role models (Rosenbaum, 1980). Then, too, many teachers do not like to teach such classes, and may subtly (or not so subtly) communicate low expectations for students in them (Good and Marshall, 1984).

Several studies have found that the quality of instruction is lower in low-track classes than in middle- or high-track classes. For example, teachers of low-track classes are less enthusiastic, less organized, and teach more facts and fewer concepts than do teachers of high-track classes. Instruction in mixed-ability, untracked classes more closely resembles that in high- and middle-track classes than that in low-track classes (Goodlad, 1983; Oakes, 1985).

Perhaps the most damaging effect of tracking is its stigmatizing effect on students assigned to the low tracks, its message to these students that academic success is not within their capabilities. Mallery (1962) reported a comment typical of high school students in the low track: "Around here you're *nothing* if you're not college prep." Schafer and Olexa (1971) interviewed one non–college-prep girl who said that she carried her general-track books upside down to avoid being humiliated walking down the hall. A former delinquent described in an interview how he felt when he went to junior high school and found out he was in the basic track:

> . . . I felt good when I was with my [elementary] class, but when they went and separated us—that changed us. That changed our ideas, our thinking, the way we thought about each other, and turned us to enemies toward each other—because they said I was dumb and they were smart.

Regrouping
A method of ability grouping in which students in mixed-ability classes are assigned to reading or math classes on the basis of their performance levels

Joplin Plan
A regrouping method in which students are assigned to groups for reading instruction across grade lines.

When you first go to junior high school you do feel something inside—it's like a ego. You have been from elementary to junior high, you feel great inside . . . you get this shirt that says Brown Junior High . . . and you are proud of that shirt. But then you go up there and the teacher says—"Well, so and so, you're in the basic section, you can't go with the other kids." The devil with the whole thing—you lose—something in you—like it goes out of you. (Schafer and Olexa, 1971, pp. 62–63)

Students in lower-track classes are far more likely than other students to become delinquent and truant and drop out of school (Schafer and Olexa, 1971; Rosenbaum, 1980; Goodlad, 1983; Oakes, 1985). These problems are certainly due in part to the fact that students in low-track classes are low in academic performance to begin with. However, this is probably not the whole story. For example, students assigned to the low track in junior high school experience a rapid loss of self-esteem (Goodlad, 1983), as the preceding interview illustrates. Slavin and Karweit (1982a) found that fifth- and sixth-graders in urban elementary schools were absent about 8 percent of the time. When these same students entered the tracked junior high school, absenteeism rose almost immediately to 26 percent, with the truancy concentrated among students assigned to the bottom-track classes. The change happened too rapidly to be attributed entirely to characteristics of students; something about the organization of the junior high school apparently convinced a substantial number of students that school was no longer a rewarding place to be.

While individual teachers can rarely set policies on between-class ability grouping, it is useful for all educators to know that research does not support this practice at any grade level, and tracking should be avoided whenever possible. This does not mean that *all* forms of between-class grouping should be abandoned, however. For example, there is probably some justification for acceleration programs, such as offering Algebra I to mathematically talented seventh graders, or offering advanced placement classes in high school. Also, some between-class grouping is bound to occur in secondary schools because some students choose to take advanced courses while others do not. However, the idea that having high, middle, and low sections of the same course can help student achievement has not been supported by research. Mixed-ability classes can be successful at all grade levels, particularly if other more effective means of accommodating student differences are used (see Slavin et al., 1989). These include within-class ability grouping, tutoring for low achievers, and certain individualized instruction programs described in this chapter, as well as cooperative learning strategies presented in Chapter 10.

Regrouping for Reading and Mathematics.   Another form of ability grouping often used in the elementary grades is called **regrouping.** In regrouping plans students are in mixed-ability classes most of the day, but are assigned to reading and/or math classes on the basis of their performance in these subjects. For example, at 9:30 a.m. the fourth-graders in a school may move to a different teacher so that they can receive reading instruction appropriate to their reading levels. One form of regrouping for reading, the **Joplin Plan** (Floyd, 1954), regroups students across grade lines. For example, a reading class at the fourth-grade, first-semester reading level may contain third-, fourth-, and fifth-graders.

One major advantage of regrouping over all-day ability grouping is that in regrouping plans the students spend most of the day in a mixed-ability class. Thus low achievers are not separated out as a class and stigmatized. In the Joplin Plan even the "ability-grouped" reading class has students of all ability levels (but different ages). Perhaps for these reasons, regrouping plans, especially the Joplin Plan, have generally been found to increase student achievement (Slavin, 1987b).

Special Education and Programs for the Gifted. In one sense, provision of separate special education programs for students with serious learning problems is one form of between-class ability grouping, as is provision of separate programs for the academically gifted and talented. These programs for students outside the normal range of individual differences are discussed in Chapter 12.

Ability Grouping Within Classes

Another means of adapting instruction to differences in student performance levels is to group students *within* classes, as is typical in elementary school reading classes. For example, a third-grade teacher might have the "Rockets" group using a 3-1 (third-grade, first-semester) text, the "Stars" using a 3-2 (third-grade, second-semester) text, and the "Planets" using a 4-1 (fourth-grade, first-semester) text.

Within-class ability grouping is far more common in elementary schools than in secondary schools (Goodlad, 1983; McPartland et al., 1987). It is almost universal in elementary reading classes and frequent in math classes, but rarely used in other subjects. In reading, teachers typically have each group working at a different point in a series of reading texts, and allow each group to proceed at its own pace. Teachers who group in math may use different texts with the different groups or, more often, allow groups to proceed at their own rates in the same book, so that the higher-performing group will cover more material than the lower-performing group. In many math classes the teacher teaches one lesson to the whole class, and then meets with two or more ability groups during times when students are doing seatwork to reinforce skills or provide enrichment as needed.

Research on Within-Class Ability Grouping. Research on the achievement effects of within-class ability grouping has taken place almost exclusively in elementary mathematics classes. This is because researchers want to look at teaching situations in

Within-Class Ability Grouping
System of accommodating student differences by dividing a class of students into two or more ability groups for instruction in certain subjects.

Many elementary teachers accommodate student differences in math and reading by assigning students to ability groups. Research shows that such within-class grouping is an effective teaching technique.

which some teachers use within-class ability grouping and others do not, and only in elementary math is this typically true. At other levels and for other subjects, teachers almost unanimously choose either to use or not to use within-class ability grouping. In elementary reading classes, for instance, nearly all teachers do group students, while in elementary subjects other than math and in secondary classes, very few teachers do.

Most studies that have evaluated within-class ability grouping methods in math (where the different groups proceed at different paces on different materials) have found that students in the ability-grouped classes learned more than those in classes that did not use grouping (Slavin, 1987b). Students of high, average, and low achievement levels seem to benefit equally from within-class ability grouping.

The research suggests that small numbers of ability groups are better than large numbers. The two most successful studies (Slavin and Karweit, 1984a) used only two groups, with 60 percent of the students in each class assigned to the high-performing group and 40 percent to the low group. The least successful elementary mathematics study (Wallen and Vowles, 1960) used four groups. All others (for example, Spence, 1958; Dewar, 1964) used three groups. Smaller numbers of groups have the advantage of allowing more direct instruction from the teacher and using less seatwork time and transition time. For example, in a class with two ability groups students must spend at least half of their class time doing seatwork without direct supervision. With three groups this rises to two-thirds of class time.

Teachers who try to teach more than three reading or math groups also may have problems with classroom management. Dividing the class into more than three groups does not decrease the size or range of differences within each group enough to offset these problems (see Hiebert, 1983).

Why is within-class ability grouping apparently so much more effective than between-class grouping? The two strategies do share one goal: reduction in the range of student performance levels for the purpose of adapting instruction to different student needs. However, they differ in most other respects. Within-class ability grouping assignments can be flexible (Weinstein, 1976), while between-class ability grouping tends to be more rigid, as it is hard to change class assignments at midyear. This flexibility allows the teacher using within-class grouping to see how students are actually performing on the material being taught in class, instead of having to depend on less accurate standardized test scores or (even worse) IQ or general-ability test scores to make a one-time placement. Within-class grouping does not concentrate low achievers in a class that teachers dislike teaching and that offers students few good role models for behavior and achievement. Research on within- and between-class ability grouping indicates that teachers using within-class grouping try to accelerate the pace of instruction in their low reading groups to bring the students up to the rest of the class, while teachers of classes containing only low achievers fall behind the pace maintained by higher-achieving classes (Rowan and Miracle, 1983). This may mean that teachers expect and demand more of a low reading group in a heterogeneous class than they do of a low-performing class.

Finally, within-class ability grouping does not seem to have the stigmatizing effect that between-class grouping does. Students identify with their class, not with their reading or math group. While it is clear that students are well aware of reading group status (Cohen and Anthony, 1982), teachers using within-class ability grouping for reading and math do so only for part of the day; the class is completely integrated the rest of the day. In contrast, between-class ability grouping (tracking) usually completely separates students of differing abilities from each other. The ex-delinquent quoted earlier in this chapter, who spoke of his shame at being put in the low track in junior high school, was probably in a low reading group in elementary school, but considered himself part of the class as a whole, which was "separated" when they entered the tracked junior high.

Applicability of Within-Class Ability Grouping. As noted earlier, almost all research on within-class ability grouping has involved elementary mathematics. Do these findings apply to other subjects and grade levels?

One might argue that elementary mathematics is the ideal setting for within-class ability grouping. First, math skills build on one another, so that students who have not mastered one-digit multiplication, for example, will have great difficulty learning two-digit multiplication. This means that there is a danger of moving on in mathematics instruction before everyone has mastered the previous material. Flexible ability grouping may enable teachers to make sure that low-achieving students are learning the skills on which other skills build, while allowing more able students to move through math concepts rapidly. Such subjects as science and social studies do not have this "building block" character to the same degree, so grouping (or other forms of individualization) is probably less necessary. Further, mathematics instruction always requires a fair amount of seatwork to enable students to practice skills they have learned, and students can do this seatwork while the teacher is with another group. Recall that if a teacher is teaching three ability groups, students must spend about two-thirds of their class time doing seatwork without teacher supervision. It would probably be a bad idea for students to spend this much time on worksheets or other unsupervised seatwork activities in science or social studies, where there is less often a need to practice skills.

Seatwork should allow students to practice what they've learned during lessons. Teachers should be sure that students understand seatwork tasks and have enough work to occupy them for the entire period.

Thus it is reasonable to conclude that while within-class ability grouping may be a good idea in elementary mathematics (and might also be effective at the junior or even senior high level), it may not be advisable in such subjects as social studies, science, or secondary English, where differences among students are less instructionally important and where large amounts of unsupervised seatwork would be a poor use of time.

Among some educators, there has been a movement away from the use of reading groups (see Slavin et al., 1989; Barr, in press), but there is little research to indicate whether this is a good idea. On one hand, it seems important to give students reading material on their reading level. On the other, the use of reading groups leads to considerable amounts of seatwork, which, unlike the situation in mathematics, is often of questionable value (Anderson et al., 1985).

General Principles of Ability Grouping. Slavin (1987b) proposed the following general principles of effective ability grouping:

1. Students should remain in heterogeneous (mixed-ability) classes at most times, and be regrouped by ability only in subjects, such as reading and mathematics, in which reducing heterogeneity is particularly important. Students' primary identification should be with a heterogeneous class.

2. Group assignment should be based on performance in a specific skill, not on IQ or general achievement level.

3. Grouping plans should frequently reassess student placements and should be flexible enough to allow for easy reassignment if student performance warrants it.

4. Teachers should vary their level and pace of instruction in regrouped classes to adapt to students' needs.

Ability-Grouped Active Teaching
A method of teaching upper
elementary and middle school math
that uses within-class ability grouping

5. In within-class ability grouping the number of groups should be kept small (two to three groups) so the teacher can provide enough direct instruction to each group.

■ **Stop and Think**

The major arguments against dividing students into separate classes by ability levels are (1) that assessing ability levels for a particular subject is difficult and therefore the assignments are often inappropriate and (2) that the educational progress of the low-ability class is often hampered by motivational problems and a below-average quality of instruction. Evaluate these criticisms based on your experience. Were you ever assigned to a class for high achievers? For low achievers? How does such labeling affect a student's self-image?

Ability-Grouped Active Teaching

Ability-Grouped Active Teaching (AGAT) was developed by Slavin and Karweit (1982b) for use in upper elementary and middle school mathematics classes. AGAT was designed as an ability-grouped version of the Missouri Mathematics Program (MMP), described in Chapter 8. It uses two ability groups rather than the more

TEACHERS ON TEACHING
Ability Grouping

1. If you use within-class ability grouping, please comment on techniques that seem to be key to its success.

Barbara Levin, who has taught middle school in Mount Horeb, Wis., writes:

When I group students I do it on the basis of skills rather than on ability. Using pretests before a unit tells me who needs work on what concepts, and that is my criterion for grouping. These groups stay together for brief periods of time (one, two, or three weeks at most). Groups are rearranged with each new skill, concept, or unit. Kids who master a concept quickly move onto another group to work on a different skill. In subjects that aren't as discreetly skill based as math or reading, I prefer heterogeneous, cooperative groups where children of differing abilities can benefit from working with each other. I mix the cooperative groups up regularly too, so that every child gets to work with different people. I also make sure that everyone in the groups (I like groups of four) has a job, so that no one can be passive and no one can totally dominate.

Valerie Bang-Jensen, who teaches kindergarten in Ithaca, N.Y., says:

I "ability group" for math and reading. The "keys" to its success are: (1) teaching the children how to use centers and activities in the room so that they can work independently while I'm with a group; and (2) regrouping—some of the low readers are in the high-math group and vice versa. I look at each individual's talents in each area.

Audrey Sequin, who teaches elementary school in Alpena, Mich., writes:

The criteria I use for placing students in a reading group include the following:

- the student's score on a reading placement test given at the beginning of the school year,
- my own assessment after hearing the student read aloud and after answering comprehension questions, and
- the student's enthusiasm for reading.

After placing a student in a reading group, I continue to assess and evaluate, and I will reassign students if they are having trouble or show improved comprehension skills. I also believe that many reading strategies can be taught to the whole group.

TABLE 9.2

OUTLINE OF ACTIVITIES FOR ABILITY-GROUPED ACTIVE TEACHING

Teachers who use Ability-Grouped Active Teaching should provide a specific set of instructional activities during each segment of a class period.

Opening (2–4 min.)	1. Students hand in homework.
	2. Students in Teaching Group 1 go immediately to their teaching group area and begin work on starter problems. Students in Teaching Group 2 go to their desks and continue to work on seatwork relating to the previous day's lesson. The teacher helps Teaching Group 2 get started on their seatwork.
Teaching Group Lessons (15–17 min.)	1. Give answers to starter problems. Briefly go over any problems attempted but missed by more than one-quarter of students.
	2. Give answers to seatwork. Briefly go over any problems attempted but missed by more than one-quarter of students. Collect seatwork and starter problems.
	3. Briefly review any prerequisite skills for new lesson (if necessary).
	4. Actively demonstrate new concept or skill, emphasizing the meaning and importance of the skill (8–12 min.).
	5. Assess student comprehension with short answers and supervised practice (1–2 problems at a time).
	6. When success rate is high, move students to seatwork.
Seatwork (15–17 min.)	1. Assign seatwork, start Teaching Group 2 on starter problems, and get Teaching Group 1 started on their seatwork.
	2. Monitor one teaching group's seatwork while you are working with the other group. Recognize students who are working well.
Facts Test (5–7 min.)	1. If students have not all mastered addition, subtraction, multiplication, and division facts, give the class appropriate facts tests twice each week.
Homework Assignment (2 min.)	1. Assign homework every day except Friday.
Quizzes and Tests	1. Give quizzes at logical points in the curriculum, averaging once a week. Before each quiz review the material to be covered in the quiz.
	2. Use quiz score information to adjust pace of instruction.
	3. Give tests at logical points in the curriculum, averaging once a month. Before each test, review the material to be tested.

typical three to increase the amount of time the teacher can spend with each group and to minimize time lost in transitions. Two studies of the effectiveness of AGAT found that students in AGAT classes gained approximately a full grade equivalent more than students in traditionally taught classes in mathematics computations (Slavin and Karweit, 1985). Table 9.2 summarizes the main elements of this approach.

EFFECTIVE USE OF READING GROUPS

Within-class ability grouping is practiced most widely in elementary reading classes, where "Bluebirds," "Yellowbirds," and "Redbirds" have been in use for generations in American schools. However, only recently has educational research

Diagnostic Test
An evaluation that provides
information that can be used to
assign students to ability groups

begun to explore the problem of how best to organize and manage reading groups (see Hiebert, 1983).

In many ways, teaching reading resembles the teaching of other subjects in elementary school, but there are differences. First, more time is usually allotted for teaching reading than for any other single subject, so whereas dividing students into only two groups is recommended for math, a teacher can reasonably manage three groups for reading class. Second, certain activities are unique to reading instruction and to the seatwork that a teacher assigns during reading class. Finally, there is considerable variety in the kinds of activities involved in reading, both in and out of reading groups.

The following section presents a method for using within-class ability groups to teach reading in the elementary grades. The method is based on the work of Anderson et al. (1979, 1982) and Evertson et al. (1984).

Assigning Students to Groups

Most reading programs provide a **diagnostic test** that can be used to place students in reading groups. You may wish to give such tests and use the results (along with any recommendations from last year's teachers as well as grades) to place students in groups. Most teachers use three reading groups; there is seldom justification for having more than three.

Group together students who are performing at similar reading levels, but try to make the lowest group small so that you can provide more individual attention to these students.

Content and Pace of Lessons

In first grade most students are primarily learning to associate symbols (letters) with sounds and words. By the fourth or fifth grade, most students need a great deal of work on comprehension and interpretation. Between the first and fifth grade, reading gradually shifts from an emphasis on sounds, letters, and words to an emphasis on comprehension, although both types of skills are taught (to varying degrees) at all grade levels.

Reading instruction must take into account the needs of the different reading groups. The low reading group probably requires more instructional time than the high group, because the low group is likely to need instruction on basic word skills and comprehension, while the high group may need less basic instruction and more time for independent reading, an activity that demands less teacher involvement.

It is important to assess student understanding frequently to see that the pace of instruction is set appropriately for each reading group and to make sure that all students are catching on to the principal concepts or skills being taught. This assessment can take the form of short quizzes or informal appraisals of skills in the reading group (for example, listening to students read).

Guidelines for Instruction

The following guidelines are adapted from "Principles of Small Group Instruction in Elementary Reading" (Anderson et al., 1982). These principles were derived from a study on first-grade reading instruction (Anderson et al., 1979). In this study the classes whose teachers used the procedures outlined in this section and presented in Table 9.3 gained significantly more in reading achievement than did other classes.

TABLE 9.3

PRINCIPLES OF READING GROUP INSTRUCTION

Specific methods of organizing and teaching elementary school reading groups have been shown to increase student achievement.

General Principles

Length	Instruction should last 25–30 minutes on average.
Academic focus	Teacher must effectively manage reading groups *and* students doing independent work.
Pace	Use small steps to allow high success rates and a brisk pace.
Error rate	Steps are appropriately small if students can correctly answer about 80 percent of the questions.

Organization

Seating	Teacher must be able to see most other students while working with a reading group.
Transitions	Students should move to their reading group from other activities quickly.

Instruction

Lesson start	Start lessons promptly. Prepare needed materials beforehand.
Overviews	Help students establish a mental set by previewing lesson content.
New words	Say new words, show their spelling, and offer phonetic clues.
Independent work	Ensure that students understand seatwork directions by having them demonstrate skills to be practiced.
Group participation	Ensure participation of all by asking students to read aloud, asking questions about words and concepts, calling on students in a systematic way, discouraging call-outs, and checking student progress—especially that of low-achievers.

Questions

Emphasis	Focus on sentence and story comprehension, word recognition, and identifying sounds within words.
Wait time	Wait for an answer as long as student seems to be thinking about the question and may respond.
Help	Simplify or rephrase questions or give feedback if it will help student find an answer.
Answers	Ensure that all students hear correct answers, either from the teacher or another student.
Explanations	Explain reasoning behind an answer if logic or problem-solving skills are involved.
Acknowledgment of correctness	Note correctness of answers, unless the correctness is obvious.

Praise and Criticism

Praise	Give specific, informative praise.
Corrections	Focus on academic content when correcting student responses.

SOURCE: Adapted from Anderson et al., 1982, pp. 2–9.

Cooperative Integrated Reading and Composition
A program that supplements reading-group activities by having students practice related skills in mixed-ability teams

Mastery Learning
System of instruction that emphasizes the achievement of instructional objectives by all students by allowing learning time to vary

These principles have been adapted here to make them relevant to reading instruction in all elementary grades. Specific principles are stated in Table 9.3. The major concepts underlying reading group instruction are:

1. Reading groups should be organized for efficient, sustained focus on the content to be learned.

2. All students should be actively involved in the lesson, not merely attentive.

3. The difficulty level of questions and tasks should be low enough to allow the teacher to move the lesson along at a brisk pace and the students to experience consistent success.

4. Students should receive frequent opportunities to read and respond to questions, and should get clear feedback about the correctness of their performance.

5. Skills should be mastered to the point of overlearning, with new ones gradually phased in while old ones are being mastered.

6. Although instruction takes place in a group setting for efficiency reasons, the teacher should monitor the progress of each individual student and provide each with whatever specific instruction, feedback, or opportunities to practice are necessary.

Cooperative Integrated Reading and Composition

A serious drawback to the use of reading groups is the need for follow-up activities—work students can do at their desks while the teacher is occupied with a reading group. Students do not usually use this time very well, and many teachers believe that follow-up activities are largely intended to keep students busy rather than to teach them.

An innovative approach to the problem of follow-up time in the upper elementary grades is a program called **Cooperative Integrated Reading and Composition,** or CIRC (Madden et al., 1986; Stevens et al., 1987). In this program students work in four-member cooperative learning teams (see Chapter 10). The teams contain two pairs of students from two different reading groups. Rather than working on workbooks during follow-up time, students engage in a series of activities with one another. They take turns reading stories to one another; answer questions about the characters, setting, and plot of each story; practice together on new vocabulary words, reading comprehension skills, and spelling; and write about the stories they have read. Two studies of the CIRC program have found positive effects on students' reading skills, including scores on standardized reading and language tests (Stevens et al., 1987). These findings suggest that many of the problems inherent in the practice of grouping for reading can be solved by combining the use of mixed-ability, cooperative learning groups with the use of homogeneous reading groups.

MASTERY LEARNING

One widely used means of adapting instruction to the needs of diverse students is called **mastery learning** (Block and Anderson, 1975; Block and Burns, 1976; Bloom, 1976). The basic idea behind mastery learning is to make sure that all or almost all students have learned a particular skill to a preestablished level of mastery before moving on to the next skill.

Basic Principles

Mastery learning was first proposed as a solution to the problem of individual differences by Benjamin Bloom (1976), who based his recommendations in part on the earlier work of John Carroll (1963). As discussed in Chapter 8, Carroll had suggested that school learning was related to the amount of time needed to learn what was being taught and the amount of time spent on instruction.

One implication of Carroll's model is that if "time spent" is the same for all students and all students receive the same kind of instruction, then differences in student achievement will primarily reflect differences in student aptitude. However, in 1968 Bloom proposed that rather than providing all students with the same amount of instructional time and allowing *learning* to differ, perhaps we should require that all or almost all students reach a certain level of achievement by allowing *time* to differ. That is, Bloom suggests that we give students as much time and instruction as necessary to bring them all to a reasonable level of learning. If some students appear to be in danger of not learning, then they should be given additional instruction until they do learn.

Bloom (1976) hypothesizes that given additional instructional time, students who do not master their lessons in the time usually allowed should be able to reach achievement levels typically attained by only the most able students. In fact, he proposes that 80 percent of all students should be able to achieve at a level usually attained by only 20 percent of students, and that under these circumstances aptitude or ability should be nearly unrelated to achievement. In a hospital we would not give the same amount of treatment to a patient with a cold as to one with double pneumonia; we treat both patients until they are healthy, giving them as much treatment as they need to reach that goal. Similarly, Bloom argues, we should "treat" students until they reach a preestablished level of mastery. Figure 9.2A shows how, under traditional instructional methods, students start out with a certain distribution of skills. As instruction goes on, "the rich get richer and the poor get poorer"; that is, high-achieving students gain more than low achievers. In contrast, in Figure 9.2B additional instruction is given to low achievers until their performance comes to resemble that of the high achieving students.

Mastery Learning in Practice. The problem inherent in any mastery learning strategy is how to provide the additional instructional time to students who need it. In much of the research on mastery learning, this additional instruction is given outside of regular class time, such as after school or during recess. Students who failed to meet a preestablished mastery criterion (such as 90 percent correct on a quiz) following a lesson were given this extra "corrective instruction" until they could earn a 90 percent score on a similar quiz. Research on mastery learning programs that provide corrective instruction in addition to regular class time has generally found achievement gains, particularly for low achievers (Block and Burns, 1976; Bloom, 1976, 1984; Slavin, 1987c).

Another form of mastery learning, called the Keller Plan (Keller, 1968), has students take tests following a series of lessons. Any students who fail to achieve at a preestablished level of mastery (80–90 percent correct) continue to study or work with fellow students who did achieve mastery until they can pass the tests. In this method students who pass the tests the first time spend much less time on those

In some forms of mastery learning, students are encouraged to increase their learning time by doing homework or studying independently. In other forms, corrective instruction is provided by teachers, tutors, or peers who have achieved mastery.

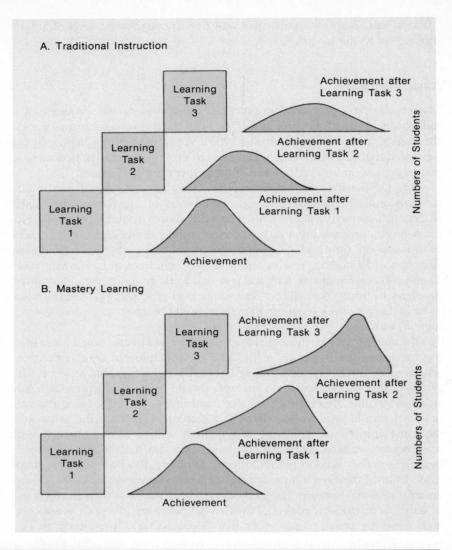

FIGURE 9.2

Theoretical Achievement Distributions During Traditional Instruction and Mastery Learning

When teachers present a series of learning tasks using traditional instruction, they may find that students who do not learn the first task will also fail at the second and that those students, plus others, will fail at the third (as shown in A, on top). However, when teachers make sure that most students thoroughly learn one task before tackling similar but more advanced tasks, they may find that the number of high achievers in their class will increase (as shown in B at bottom).

lessons than students who require several tries. The Keller Plan has been found to be very effective in increasing the academic achievement of students at the college level (Kulik et al., 1979).

Neither the Keller Plan nor forms of mastery learning that require additional instructional time are easily applicable to elementary or secondary education, where amounts of time available are relatively fixed. For example, it is possible to have students stay after school to receive corrective instruction for an experiment lasting a few weeks (see, for example, Tenenbaum, 1982), but this would be difficult to arrange over the long haul. Also, there is some question whether the additional time required for corrective instruction in mastery learning might not be better spent in covering more material. For example, Arlin and Webster (1983) taught an experimental unit on sailing consisting of four chapters. Students in a mastery learning condition received corrective instruction if they missed more than one item on chapter tests, while students in the traditionally taught condition were allowed to go on. Although mastery students scored much better than nonmastery students on a final test, it took them twice as long to complete the unit. Bloom (1976) hypothesizes that as time goes on, students in mastery learning should need less and less corrective instruction, but in a four-year study of a school using mastery learning, Arlin (1984b) found no such trend; in fact, as time went on, the students needed more time for corrective instruction.

Because of the impracticality of providing corrective instruction outside of regular class time, most elementary and secondary schools that use mastery learning use a form developed by Block and Anderson (1975) in which corrective instruction is given during class. The sequence of activities in this approach is described in detail later in this chapter (see Theory into Practice: Mastery Learning).

This form of mastery learning varies the instructional time given to students with different needs by providing corrective instruction to students who need it, while allowing those who do not to do enrichment work. For example, a high school earth

FOCUS ON

Making Low Achievers Repeat a Grade

This problem may face you as a teacher: One student in your class falls far short of the others and becomes below average in academic performance. The student has failed to master many of the critical skills you've taught during the year and tests significantly below grade level on tests of reading and math ability. You wonder whether the student should be held back to repeat a grade.

On an intuitive level, the idea makes sense. Maybe this student just needs more time to master this year's subject matter. Maybe all those critical concepts and skills will suddenly "click" if the student hears them explained by another teacher. Maybe holding this child back will, in a small way, also diminish the problem of individual differences among students.

Research, however, discredits the practice. A review in the *Harvard Education Letter* of 60 studies concluded that whether retained or not, most low-achievers do progress in school, and those who are advanced tend to outperform those who are held back.

Flaws in a New York City program called "Promotional Gates" supports this view. The city scrapped its once-heralded achieve-or-flunk policy after noting that a disproportionate number of those held back eventually dropped out.

Throughout the 1980s, the city required that lagging students be held back at the fourth and seventh grades. In some years, this program caused as many as 10 percent of students in those grades to be held back.

The strategy lost favor, however, when studies in New York and other major cities showed that the older students are when they enter high school, the more likely they are to drop out.

Other states and school districts have been slower to change policy in light of relevant research findings. Many schools in southern states tie student promotion to performance on standardized tests, and Minneapolis, Minn., even allows kindergartners to be held back if they are deemed unready for first grade work.

Furthermore, some educators justify retention by citing its motivating effect on the students who advance each year. They say that the threat of retention is a good motivator and, therefore, should be maintained.

What's best? Research can provide part of the answer, but the debate about retention will continue as long as students differ in ability and as long as the public disagrees over the ultimate mission of the educational system.

From Joseph Berger, "Fernandez to End a Policy on Holding Students Back," *New York Times*, May 3, 1990, p. A1. Edward B. Fiske, "Lessons," *New York Times*, January 1, 1990, p. B5.

The assumption underlying mastery learning is that almost every student can learn the essential skills in a curriculum. This assumption is both communicated to the students and acted upon by the teacher, whose job it is to provide the instruction necessary to make the expectation come true.

The Block and Anderson (1975) form of mastery learning, described in this section, has been used in virtually every subject and at every elementary and secondary grade level.

LESSON PREPARATION

To prepare lessons for mastery learning, follow the lesson presentation guidelines described in Chapter 8. You will need clearly specified objectives for each lesson, teaching materials and practice materials for that objective, and two quizzes.

Formative and Summative Quizzes

At the end of each set of lessons (usually one to two weeks of work), you will need to have prepared two parallel quizzes assessing students' understanding of the lessons just presented. The first of these quizzes is called a **formative quiz,** or a "no-fault" quiz. The second is a **summative quiz,** in other words, a final quiz. "Parallel" means that the quizzes should cover the same content and be equally difficult, but should typically use different items. For example

Formative Quiz

1. $1/3 + 1/4 =$
2. The ____ were all broken.
   a. toy's
   b. toys
   c. toys'
3. The formula for calcium carbonate is ____.
4. The capital of Canada is ____.

Summative Quiz

1. $1/2 + 1/5 =$
2. Whose ____ are these?
   a. books
   b. book's
   c. books'
3. The formula for potassium nitrate is ____.
4. The capital of Canada is ____.

Note that the fourth item ("The capital of Canada is ____") is identical in the formative and summative quizzes. The reason is that this is a specific piece of information the teacher wants the class to know, rather than a general skill to be applied to different problems (as in questions 1–3).

The number and types of questions on the quizzes may vary, but quizzes should not be lengthy; they should require no more than fifteen to twenty minutes for students to complete. The quizzes should focus precisely on assessing students' understanding of the lessons just presented.

Mastery Criteria

You will need to establish what score indicates mastery of a given quiz. **Mastery criteria** are typically set somewhere between 80 and 90 percent correct, although for material that is essential for all students to know (such as multiplication facts), the mastery criterion should be 100 percent. Set the criterion for mastery at the percent correct usually considered A work, which in most schools is 90 percent (Block and Anderson, 1975).

Corrective Instruction

Each time you give a formative quiz, some students are likely to fail to achieve the mastery criterion you set. Since you will be working to bring these students up to an acceptable level of mastery, for every formative quiz you prepare, you will also need to prepare an alternative method of presenting the material for use as **corrective instruction.** For example, if you initially teach a lesson using lecture-discussion, you might prepare corrective instruction using demonstration with pictures or charts. Or you might choose a different textbook, peer tutoring (that is, a student who achieved mastery on the formative quiz might tutor a classmate who did not), adult tutoring, computer-assisted instruction, or programmed instruction to provide the corrective instruction.

Enrichment Activities

Typically, some students will achieve the mastery criterion on the formative quiz. There is no point in giving these students further instruction on the skill or concept covered on the quizzes. Instead, give them **enrichment activities** to keep them usefully occupied while you are providing corrective instruction to other students (unless you decide to have these students tutor classmates who did not achieve mastery).

Enrichment activities should be educationally worthwhile (not busywork), but should not cover upcoming lessons, because all students will receive those lessons anyway. Rather, enrichment activities should broaden students' understanding of the material they have been studying. Applications of skills (such as word problems in math, short essays in language arts, practical science problems in science) are excellent enrichment activities because they allow students to use the information they have just gained. Academic games or brainteasers can be good if, again, they are not just busywork.

MAJOR ACTIVITIES

Mastery learning follows a regular cycle of activities, which is repeated for each major skill or concept taught. Each cycle lasts an average of one to two weeks and its principal activities are:

1. Orient students to mastery.
2. Teach the lesson.
3. Give the formative quiz.
4. Give students either corrective instruction—for those who did not achieve mastery on the formative quiz—or enrichment activities—for those who did achieve mastery.
5. Give the summative quiz to students.

These activities are discussed in greater detail in the following sections.

Orient Students to Mastery

Reserve some classroom time at the outset to orient students to your mastery learning strategy.
Stress the following:

1. The students are going to learn by a method of instruction designed to help all of them learn well.
2. Students will be graded solely on the basis of their performance on the summative quizzes.
3. Students will be graded against a predetermined performance standard and not in relation to the performance of their classmates. Indicate that the standard of A work will be (for example) a score of 90 percent, or eighteen correct answers on a twenty-item quiz. Emphasize that every student can achieve mastery and that mastery, not grades, is the most important goal.
4. Each student who attains the standard will receive an A.

Teach the Lesson

Presentation of the lesson itself in mastery learning may be accomplished using any whole-class instructional method (such as those described in Chapter 8).

Give the Formative "No-Fault" Quiz

Give students the formative quiz when you have completed your planned sequence of lessons.

Give Students Either Corrective Instruction or Enrichment Activities

Give corrective instruction to students who did not achieve the mastery criterion on the formative quiz, and enrichment activities to those who did achieve mastery.

The provision of corrective instruction to students who did not achieve the mastery criterion on the formative quiz is the most important feature of mastery learning, as it is the means by which the strategy addresses the problem of providing appropriate levels of instruction to students with instructionally important differences. Therefore the quality of your corrective instruction is critical to the success of a mastery learning strategy.

As noted earlier in this chapter, the most effective form of mastery learning involves giving corrective instruction outside of regular class time, either during the school day or after school. Aides, special education teachers, peers, parent volunteers, or computers may be used. However, in most cases, practical considerations dictate that corrective instruction be given during regular class time.

If you are giving corrective instruction during regular class time, you will need to divide your class into two groups: students who achieved the mastery criterion on the formative test and those who did not. If the "masters" group is small, you might send these students to a separate area of the room to work on their enrichment materials while you work with the "nonmasters" at their own desks. If the "nonmasters" group is small, you might gather them in a special area for additional instruction.

Make sure that the students doing enrichment activities have plenty to do so that you do not have to interrupt your corrective lessons to answer their questions or otherwise become involved with them.

Give the Summative Quiz and Report the Scores to Students

When you feel that you have given sufficient corrective instruction, have students take the summative quiz. Students who achieved mastery on the formative quiz need not take the summative quiz.

Score the summative quizzes as soon as possible after class (again, you can have students check their own papers or exchange papers for correction in class if you wish). Return graded papers to students. As noted earlier, achieving the mastery criterion should be worth an A; you may set other grades as you like.

By the time of the summative quiz, at least three-quarters of your students should have achieved the mastery criterion (or close to it). If this is not the case, you may repeat the corrective instruction—summative test cycle until at least three-quarters of your students have achieved mastery.

science teacher might teach a lesson on volcanoes and earthquakes. At the end of the lesson students are quizzed. Those who score less than 80 percent receive corrective instruction on concepts they had problems with, while the remaining students do enrichment activities, such as finding out about the San Francisco earthquake or the Mount Vesuvius eruption that buried Pompeii.

Research on this form of mastery learning is much less clear than that on other forms of mastery learning (see Slavin, 1987c). Studies of at least four weeks' duration in which instructional time was the same for mastery and nonmastery classes generally found either no differences in effectiveness (Anderson et al., 1975; Slavin and Karweit, 1984b) or small and short-lived differences favoring the mastery groups (Lueckemeyer and Chiappetta, 1981).

As of this writing, the practical implications of research on mastery learning are only partially clear. First, if the staff time is available to provide corrective instruction in addition to regular classroom instruction, the effects of mastery learning on achievement can be quite positive. Second, any form of mastery learning can help teachers become more clear about their objectives, routinely assess student progress, and modify their instruction according to how well students are learning—all elements of effective instruction (see Chapter 8). Third, when high levels of mastery are needed to form a basis for later learning, mastery learning appears particularly appropriate. For example, many mathematics skills are fundamental for later learning, and these skills might profitably be taught using a mastery approach. Similarly, basic reading skills, map or chart interpretation, essential vocabulary and grammar in foreign languages, and elements of the periodic table lend themselves to mastery learning.

However, the central problem of mastery learning is that it involves a trade-off between the amount of content that can be covered and the degree to which students master each concept (Arlin, 1984a; Slavin, 1987c). The time needed to bring all or almost all students to a preestablished level of mastery must come from somewhere. If corrective instruction is provided during regular class time, it must reduce content coverage. And, as noted in Chapter 8, content coverage is one of the most important predictors of achievement gain (Golem and Leinhardt, 1980). This is not at all to say that mastery learning should be used only when additional time for corrective instruction is available, but merely to emphasize that teachers should be aware of the trade-off involved and make decisions accordingly. Mastery learning should be part of every teacher's skills, for use on material that all students must master, but it is not necessary or effective in every situation.

■ **Stop and Think**

If you have ever taken a class taught with the mastery learning approach, evaluate the effectiveness of this technique relative to more traditional methods of instruction. Consider the amount of material you learned, your retention of that material, and the amount of time spent studying and taking tests. Now think of the grade and subject(s) you plan to teach. For what topics or skills would mastery learning be an appropriate teaching tool?

INDIVIDUALIZED INSTRUCTION

The problem of providing all students with appropriate levels of instruction could be completely solved by simply assigning all students their own teacher. Not surprisingly, studies of one adult—one student tutoring find substantial positive effects of tutoring on student achievement (Glass et al., 1982; Bloom, 1984). One major reason for the effectiveness of tutoring is that the tutor can provide **individualized instruction,** can tailor instruction precisely to a student's needs. If the student learns quickly, the tutor can move to other tasks; if not, the tutor can figure out what the problem is, try another explanation, or just spend more time on the task.

In the real world, providing every student with a tutor is impractical. However, for decades educational innovators have been trying to find ways to get as close as possible to the one-to-one tutoring situation in the typical thirty-to-one classroom. The three strategies for providing individualized instruction discussed in this chapter—programmed instruction, tutoring, and computer-assisted instruction—are the most common means of trying to tailor instruction to the individual needs of diverse students.

Programmed Instruction

The term **programmed instruction** refers to individualized instruction methods in which students work on self-instructional materials at their own levels and rates. For example, one math class might contain some students working on division, others on fractions, others on decimals, and still others on measurement or geometry, all at the same time. The materials students use are meant to be self-instructional, which is to say the students are expected to learn (at least in large part) from the materials, rather than principally from the teacher. For this reason, programmed instruction materials typically break skills down into small subskills, so that students may go step-by-step with little chance of making an error at each step. Figure 9.3 shows an example of a lesson from Individually Prescribed Instruction (IPI), probably the most widely used programmed instruction method when this approach was at its peak of popularity in the mid-1970s.

Formative Quiz
Evaluation designed to determine whether additional instruction is needed

Summative Quiz
Final test of an objective

Mastery Criteria
The standards students must meet to be considered proficient in a skill

Corrective Instruction
Educational activities given to students who initially fail to master an objective; designed to increase the number of students who master educational objectives

Enrichment Activities
Assignments or activities designed to broaden or deepen the knowledge of students who master classroom lessons quickly

Individualized Instruction
Teaching approach in which each student works at his or her own level and rate

Programmed Instruction
Structured lessons that students can work on individually, at their own pace

FIGURE 9.3

Programmed Instruction Skillsheet

Programmed instructional materials are designed to lead a student step-by-step from simple skills to more complex ones.

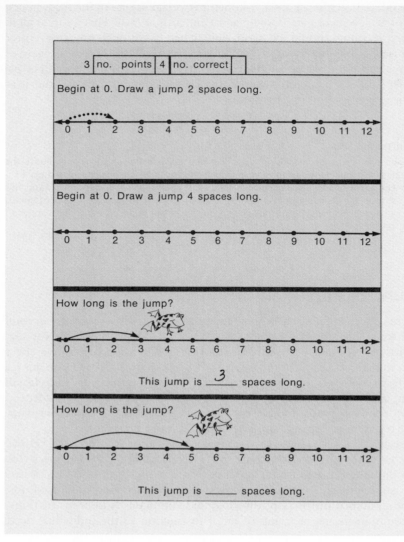

Research on Programmed Instruction. Studies on the first generation of programmed instruction models have been one of the great disappointments of educational research (see Rothrock, 1982). Despite great expectations (for example, Glaser, 1965; Flanagan et al., 1975; Talmage, 1975) and considerable investments, the programmed instruction techniques developed in the 1960s and 1970s have generally failed to show any achievement benefits. The results vary somewhat by subject, but with few exceptions reviewers have concluded that these programmed instruction methods have not lived up to expectations (Miller, 1976; Schoen, 1976; Bangert et al., 1983).

Partly as a result of these disappointing findings and partly because of the expense and difficulty of using programmed instruction, this strategy is seldom employed today as a primary approach to instruction. However, programmed instruction materials are still frequently used in special education (see Chapter 12) and as supplements to more traditional methods. They can help meet the needs of students who perform either above or below the level of the rest of the class, though this function is increasingly being taken over by computer-assisted instruction (discussed later in this chapter).

Team Assisted Individualization

Team Assisted Individualization
Teaching program in which students work on individualized instruction materials in four-member mixed-ability groups

Peer Tutoring
One student teaching another

Programmed instruction may have failed to increase student levels of achievement as expected because the benefits of providing appropriate levels of instruction may have been offset by losses in quality of instruction, student motivation, and instructional time (Slavin, 1987a). For example, quality of instruction may have suffered if teachers had to spend too much time checking materials and managing rather than teaching; student motivation may have suffered because programmed instruction day after day can be boring.

To test this analysis, researchers developed a mathematics instruction program designed to solve the problems of individualized instruction (Slavin, 1985; Slavin et al., 1986). In this program, called **Team Assisted Individualization (TAI),** students work on individualized self-instructional materials at their own levels and rates, just as in earlier programmed instruction methods. However, students do their individualized work in four-member, mixed-ability learning teams. Teammates help each other, check each other's work against answer sheets, and encourage each other to work rapidly and accurately, since the team is rewarded (with certificates and recognition) on the basis of the number and accuracy of assignments completed by all team members. The partners' helping and checking free the teacher to teach groups of students (drawn from the various teams) working at the same point in the individualized program, as in within-class ability grouping. The division of students into three teaching groups solves the problem of quality of instruction by having instruction come from the teacher rather than from written materials alone, and the team reward system solves the problem of incentive by motivating students to work rapidly and accurately and to encourage their teammates to do so. The team reward and student checking systems solve the time problem by motivating students to stay on-task and reducing the time spent waiting for the teacher to check work.

In contrast to research on earlier programmed instruction methods, TAI has been found to be very effective in increasing student mathematics achievement. In six studies involving students in grades 3–6, students in TAI classes gained an average of twice as many grade equivalents in mathematics computations as traditionally taught students. That is, where traditional classes achieved the expected one year's gain, TAI students achieved the equivalent of two years' gain (Slavin, 1985). For example, in one study TAI students gained 1.65 grade equivalents in eighteen weeks, while students using the Missouri Mathematics Program (Good, et al., 1983; described in Chapter 8) gained 0.61 (Slavin and Karweit, 1985).

Tutoring

Peer Tutoring. Students can help one another learn. When one student teaches another, this is called **peer tutoring.** There are two principal types of peer tutoring: cross-age tutoring, where the tutor is several years older than the student being taught, and same-age peer tutoring, where one student tutors a classmate. Cross-age tutoring is more often recommended by researchers than same-age tutoring (Devin-Sheehan et al., 1976), partly because of the obvious fact that older students

Individual tutoring virtually eliminates the problem of student differences. Peers and adults other than classroom teachers can be trained to tutor students.

are more likely to know the material, and partly because students may accept an older student as a tutor but resent having a classmate appointed to tutor them.

Most often, it is recommended that tutors and tutees (the person being taught) be separated by two to three grade levels (Devin-Sheehan et al., 1976). Sometimes cross-age tutoring is used with students in need of special assistance, in which case a few older students may work with a few younger students. Other tutoring schemes have involved, for example, entire fifth-grade classes tutoring entire second-grade classes. In these cases, half of the younger students might be sent to the older students' classroom, while half of the older students are sent to the younger students' classroom. Otherwise peer tutoring may take place in the cafeteria, library, or another school facility. Same-sex pairs are often used in cross-age tutoring, although research does not indicate any advantage of same- or cross-sex pairing for tutoring (Devin-Sheehan et al., 1976).

Research on Peer Tutoring. Research evaluating the effects of peer tutoring on student achievement has generally found that this strategy increases the achievement of both tutees and tutors (Devin-Sheehan et al., 1976; Palincsar et al., 1987; Ehly and Larsen, 1980). In fact, many studies have found greater achievement gains for tutors than for tutees (Cloward, 1967), and peer tutoring is often used as much to improve the achievement of low-achieving older students as to improve that of the students being tutored (Osguthorpe, 1984; Top and Osguthorpe, 1987). As many teachers have noted, the best way to learn something thoroughly is to have to teach it to someone else!

Training of tutors seems to be critical for the effectiveness of peer tutoring (Jenkins and Jenkins, 1987), and some of the most successful tutoring programs have been highly structured "programmed tutoring" models (for example, Ellson et al., 1968). In these models peer tutors are given explicit instructions on how to introduce material. An example of a set of instructions to tutors (Harrison, 1972) appears in Table 9.4.

One caution about the research on peer tutoring: Almost all studies of peer tutoring use tutoring *in addition* to regular instruction, and compare results to those for regular instruction alone. For this reason, at least part of the effectiveness of peer tutoring could be attributed to the extra instruction time than to the value of peer tutoring itself. However, viewed as an addition to regular class instruction, peer tutoring does seem to be an effective way to provide appropriate levels of instruction to students.

Adult Tutoring. As noted earlier in this chapter, one-to-one adult-to-child tutoring is one of the most effective instructional strategies known, and it essentially solves the problem of appropriate levels of instruction. The principal drawback to this method is its cost.

However, it is often possible, on a small scale, to provide adult tutors for students having problems learning in the regular class setting. For example, adult volunteers such as parents or senior citizens may be willing to tutor students. Tutoring is an excellent use of school aides; some school districts hire large numbers of paraprofessional aides precisely for this purpose.

There are some circumstances in which the high costs of one-to-one tutoring can be justified. One of these is for first-graders who are having difficulties learning to read. Failing to learn to read in the lower grades of elementary school is so detrimental to later school achievement that an investment in tutors who can prevent reading failure is worthwhile. A one-to-one tutoring program, Reading Recovery, uses highly trained, certified teachers to work with first-graders who are at risk for failing to learn

---

TABLE 9.4

SAMPLE INSTRUCTIONS FOR TUTORING

Detailed instructions for teaching a student to read.

STEP 1	Tell the student that this exercise will help him or her learn to sound out new words.
STEP 2	Point to the first word and ask the student to *sound* it out. a. If the student reads the word correctly, offer praise; then go on to the next word. b. If the student is unable to read the word or reads it incorrectly, have the student make the individual sounds in the word separately and then blend the sounds. Example: Word: "THIN" *Tutor:* Place your finger over the last two letters in the word and ask, "What sound does the *th* make?" If the student answers correctly, offer praise and go to the next sound. If the student answers incorrectly or fails to answer, say the sound and have the student repeat it. Follow the same procedure for each sound in the word, and then show the student how to blend the separate sounds.
STEP 3	Follow Step 2 for each word on the sheet. Note: *Acceptable performance is reading each word with no pause or break between the various sounds (for example, "fan," not "f . . . an").* Do not go to the next step until the student can read every word in an exercise without hesitation and with no breaks between the various sounds. If a student has a short attention span, do not read every word in the longer exercises in one session.
STEP 4	At the end of the session, praise the student.
STEP 5	Fill out your tutor log.

Source: Adapted from Harrison, 1972, p. 101.

Remediation
Instruction given to students having difficulty learning; supplements whole-class instruction

Students typically learn well from adult tutors. Only the cost of such help prohibits it from being used more frequently.

to read. Research on this strategy has found that students who received tutoring in first grade were still reading significantly better than comparable students at the end of third grade (Pinnell, 1988). Other one-to-one tutoring programs for at-risk first-graders have also found substantial positive effects (Dorval, Wallach, and Wallach, 1978; Slavin et al., in press).

Informal Remediation and Enrichment

Perhaps the most common means of attempting to provide appropriate levels of instruction is to make informal adjustments within whole-class instruction. For example, many teachers teach a lesson, assign seatwork, and while students are doing the seatwork, try to work with students they feel are likely to have problems. Other teachers find time outside of regular class to work with students who need extra help. This extra help is called **remediation.** For students who work very rapidly, teachers will often provide enrichment activities to broaden these students' knowledge or skills in the area being studied. For example, advanced students in an English class might be asked to write a special report on the life of the Brontë sisters. Many schools now have special "gifted and talented" classes for the most able students (see Chapter 12), but even in schools that have such classes there will always be some rapid learners remaining in the regular classes.

There is little or no research on informal means of providing remediation or enrichment; both are usually seen as just standard parts of teaching. However, there is one principle that teachers should be aware of: Do not allow remediation and enrichment activities to interfere with the main course of instruction. One consistent research finding is that time spent with one pupil while the rest of the class has nothing important to do is detrimental to the learning of the class as a whole (see, for example, Stallings and Kaskowitz, 1974).

COMPUTER-ASSISTED INSTRUCTION

One means of individualizing instruction that has been receiving a great deal of attention in recent years is **computer-assisted instruction,** or **CAI.** The decreasing cost and increasing availability of microcomputers in schools have led researchers as well as teachers to become more interested in CAI. Most U.S. schools have at least

TEACHERS ON TEACHING
Styles of Learning and Teaching

1. Educational psychologists theorize that people learn in various ways. Some people seem better able to grasp spoken explanations, while others are more adept at understanding written or visual materials. Also, some can be classified as impulsive decision makers, while others are reflective decision makers. How do you accommodate such differences among students in your teaching?

Margaret Covert Ball, who teaches at Stratford Junior-Senior High in Stratford, Wis., writes:

Recognizing student differences and the ability to work with individual students are the main components of good teaching. Teachers who take into account student's individual learning styles constantly strive to introduce concepts by using a variety of methods. Each student's abilities and strengths should be used to enrich a curriculum. Students who need more concrete information to help process material can be paired with students who use abstract thinking. Together they can process the information relying on both students' strengths.

When introducing a concept it is best to prepare as many different methods as possible. Audio-visual materials should be included when possible. Notes should be introduced orally, using visual clues like the overhead projector, the blackboard, or a prepared summary sheet.

Teachers need to recognize their responsibility to the whole class. They must be constantly searching for clues that a student is confused. Their role is to be traveling around the class answering questions and giving further explanations both for the slower learners and the gifted.

2. Educational psychologists use classroom experiments and observation to study learning and teaching. Teachers do the same thing, though informally, every day. Please describe an observation that has shaped your thinking about some aspect of development, learning, teaching, or motivation.

Roseanne Swinburne-Sanderfoot, who teaches learning disabled students in Manawa, Wis., writes:

Last year the teachers in our district had in-service training on cooperative learning. During the training, we became "students" and took part in various activities, some competitively and some cooperatively. We, as teachers, were allowed to experience the emotions involved in each style of learning. For me, it was much more pleasurable, motivating, and educational to work cooperatively in pairs or in groups.

I decided to experiment with what I learned within my own classroom. I decided to slowly incorporate more cooperative learning into my classroom. I was pleasantly surprised to see the students really working together. They were more enthusiastic, successful, and motivated within the cooperative setting.

By experiencing my own feelings and observing the student's reactions, I am convinced that cooperative learning should be a part of every student's education.

If your class or school has a tutoring program, please describe how it is set up and how successful it is.

Barbara Levin, who has taught middle school in Mount Horeb, Wis., writes:

I have used peer tutoring with the computer in my classroom. For example, each year I teach one group of children how to use a word-processing program, and then they each teach one or two other children. This "each one–teach one" method works very well. Also, If I get a new computer program, I let a few kids figure out how it works, and then have them show the rest of the class. They then become the resident "experts" for that piece of software. Throughout the course of the school year everyone gets a turn to be the leader and the expert about some use of the computer.

one microcomputer (Becker, 1990), and the number of computers per school is rapidly growing.

The idea behind computer-assisted instruction is to use the computer as a tutor to present information, give students practice, assess their level of understanding, and provide additional instruction if needed. In theory, a well-designed CAI program is nearly perfect at providing appropriate levels of instruction, as it can analyze student responses immediately to determine whether to spend more time on a particular topic or skill. The computer can be quite effective in presenting ideas, using pictures or diagrams to reinforce concepts. Finally, for most students, the computer seems to have a motivating quality of its own, so that they work longer and harder when using it than they would on comparable paper-pencil tasks.

Computer-assisted instruction has its roots in programmed instruction and in the behavioral theories of learning discussed in Chapter 4. According to these theories, learning is accelerated by the use of controlled presentation of stimuli, followed by reinforcement based upon the learner's responses. Many CAI programs stress drill and practice exercises; others teach students facts and concepts, while others engage students in complex problem-solving or discovery learning. Whatever their differences, CAI programs generally share the following characteristics: (1) use of a structured curriculum; (2) letting students work at their own pace; (3) giving students controlled, frequent feedback and reinforcement; and (4) measuring performance quickly and giving students information on their performance.

History of CAI

The early work in CAI consisted mostly of drill and practice in mathematics and language arts for elementary school students, especially those who were disadvantaged. Atkinson (1968) developed a reading program that students could use without help from the classroom teacher. First-grade children sat at a computer terminal that had a typewriter keyboard, a television screen, a high-speed filmstrip, and a computer-controlled tape player. They answered questions by touching the screen with a light pen. The computer determined where they were pointing, evaluated their answers, and determined what material should be given next. The reading program taught students letters of the alphabet, basic vocabulary, and other reading skills.

The program was successful, but so expensive that the developers decided to study its use as a supplement to regular classroom teaching. In this role it was still successful. Children who received twelve minutes of computerized reading instruction a day for a school year had reading scores 1.2 grade equivalents ahead of students who received no computer instruction. In a later study first-grade children receiving eight to ten minutes of computer instruction a day for 5.5 months gained 5.05 months in achievement over a control group, and maintained a 4.9-month gain for more than a year (Atkinson and Fletcher, 1972).

By the middle of the 1970s, people involved with CAI felt that the effects of CAI did not justify its costs, and few systems were being used. Then, in 1977, small low-cost microcomputers became available and revolutionized the use of computers in education. A national survey done in 1989 found that over 95 percent of schools have at least one computer, with the average elementary school having seventeen and the average high school having thirty-four. These numbers represent nearly a tenfold increase since the early 1980s (Becker, 1990).

Unfortunately, not all schools have used their new computers wisely. One problem has been a lack of knowledge about **software** (the programs that run the computer), and the fact that not all software on the market is good. To solve this problem, several groups have been organized to develop CAI materials. For example, the Minnesota Educational Computer Consortium (MECC) has distributed materials for elementary and secondary schools. At present many more programs are being written for educational uses of microcomputers. Most of these focus on mathematics and science.

Types of CAI Programs

Drill and Practice Programs.   The most widely used type of computer program is **drill and practice.** This application resembles other teaching techniques such as flashcards and programmed instruction.

The purpose of these programs is to provide practice on skills and knowledge so students can remember and use what they have been taught. The methodology involves repetition of a format in which the computer presents an exercise, the student types in a response, and the computer informs the student if the answer is correct. Drill and practice programs are efficient skill builders, but they usually address lower-level skills and have a narrow range of teaching strategies.

Tutorial Programs.   **Tutorial CAI programs** attempt to put the computer into the role of a teacher instructing an individual student. Their strength is that they actively involve the student in self-paced instruction. Some of the better tutorial programs use the Socratic teaching method, in which the student's learning is guided by a carefully sequenced series of leading questions. Unfortunately, though, most tutorials have a narrow range of teaching strategies, and their "intelligence," or ability to respond in a helpful manner, is often limited. Some progress in the development of tutorials is being made, however. For example, researchers in artificial intelligence have developed tutorials that can analyze a student's natural language and carry on a dialogue. Table 9.5 is an excerpt from a tutorial computer program dealing with the climate around Oregon and Washington.

Simulations.   A **simulation program** is a model of some part of the world. For example, students in one popular simulation reenact the experiences of a family of five who attempt to complete the 2,000-mile journey along the Oregon Trail in 1847. They have $700 and a wagon at the beginning of the trip. The students must decide how much they wish to spend on such items as food, clothing, and ammunition; whether they should hunt or buy food, and so on. Thus they can learn how each of their decisions affects their "journey." The goals of simulations are to teach facts, promote problem solving, develop an understanding of a particular situation, and motivate interest in a subject. Simulations allow students to study events that would otherwise be inaccessible to them because of expense, danger, or time constraints. They are motivating and relatively realistic, and can enhance student learning (Woodward et al., 1988). However, they usually do not check to see if the students are "on the right path." Being simplified models of reality, simulations can degenerate into little more than a "beat the computer" game if their use is not well planned.

Educational Games.   Educational computer games should not be low-level drill and practice exercises transplanted to outer space. In quality games the concepts to be learned are intrinsic to the game's structure and content. For example, one computer

Drill and Practice CAI Programs
Computer programs that let students practice what they have learned and obtain immediate feedback

Tutorial CAI Programs
Programs that teach lessons by varying their content and pace according to student responses

Simulation Programs
Computer programs that model real-life phenomena to promote problem-solving and motivate interest in the areas concerned

TABLE 9.5

DIALOGUE WITH A COMPUTER TUTOR

Some advanced computer tutorial programs can analyze student responses and carry on a dialogue. In this example the student has typed in answers on the computer terminal's keyboard in response to questions shown on the computer screen.

Tutor: Do you know what the climate is like in Washington and Oregon?
    Student: Is it cold?

Tutor: No, it is rather mild. Can you guess about the rainfall there?
    Student: Normal, I guess.

Tutor: Well, the Japan current, which starts in the southeastern Pacific, flows along the coast of Japan and across the North Pacific, ending up off the coast of Washington and Oregon. How do you think that current affects the climate there?
    Student: It's probably rainy.

Tutor: It is indeed very wet, there are rain forests in both Washington and Oregon. What does that tell you about the temperature of the Japan current?
    Student: It's warm.

Tutor: Right. Where do you think the wind blows in that area?
    Student: Towards Washington and Oregon.

Tutor: From where?
    Student: From the sea.

Tutor: Right again. What do you think happens to the moist air blown over Washington and Oregon by those winds?
    Student: It condenses and it rains.

Tutor: Yes, why?
    Student: Because the moist air cools and the clouds can't hold the water, so it rains.
Tutor: OK, what causes the moist air to cool? . . .

SOURCE: From Stevens et al., 1982, p. 18.

game presents coordinate axes on which thirteen "green globs" are scattered randomly. Students type in equations that are graphed by the computer. The object is to destroy all thirteen globs by hitting them with a graph. Players score well when they hit as many globs as possible with each shot. Although students can succeed using only simple, linear functions, higher scores demand more mathematical knowledge. These types of games are designed to develop problem-solving abilities, reinforce skills and knowledge, and motivate interest in learning. However, their goals are not always clear, and, as with simulations, their use can involve no more than "playing" if not integrated into other curricular activities.

Utility Programs. **Utility programs** or general-purpose programs turn the computer into a tool for solving many problems. Perhaps the most widely used are word-processing, or text-editing programs. A word-processing program allows the student to type text into the computer and to delete, insert, or move around portions of the text, save it, and retrieve it later. This may allow children to perceive composition as a flexible, creative process. Writers can gradually shape and form their ideas, try out various ways of expressing themselves, and freely revise. Paper ("hard") copies can be printed out at any stage of the writing process.

Other utility programs can be used along with word processors. Programs are available that automatically check the spelling of every word in a composition. Words not "recognized" are shown to the writer, who decides if the word is misspelled or just not yet part of the program's dictionary (such as the author's name). Other programs check punctuation and capitalization. Some even inform the author about ungrammatical constructions, average sentence length, overuse of certain words or phrases, and phrases that appear sexist. They can also analyze how closely a composition matches standard literary forms, such as an operational manual, a research article, or an eighteenth-century novel.

Research indicates that writers using computers write more, are less worried about making mistakes, take increased pride in their writing, have fewer motor control problems, give more attention to finding errors, and revise more (Daiute, 1982; Watt, 1982). These characteristics are valued by teachers who are guided by modern research, which argues that composition should be viewed as a *process* rather than as a *product*.

Research on CAI

Can computers teach? Several extensive reviews of the research concerning the effectiveness of computer-assisted instruction have been conducted (O'Donnell, 1982; Billings, 1983; Chambers and Sprecher, 1983; Atkinson, 1984; Kulik et al., 1984; Niemiec and Walberg, 1985). These reviews generally agree that CAI can be effective in increasing student achievement, but not always. CAI is often effective when it is used *in addition* to regular classroom instruction, but has smaller and less consistent achievement effects when it entirely replaces classroom instruction. Some reviewers have argued that when the *content* of instruction is carefully controlled, computers are no more effective than other instructional methods (Clark, 1985). For example, one study, which randomly assigned students to use CAI or traditional methods to learn mathematics, found that some CAI methods enhanced learning, whereas some were *less* effective than the traditional teaching methods (Becker, 1990).

There is also some question about whether achievement gains from CAI are maintained over time. For example, Delon (1970) found that a CAI program

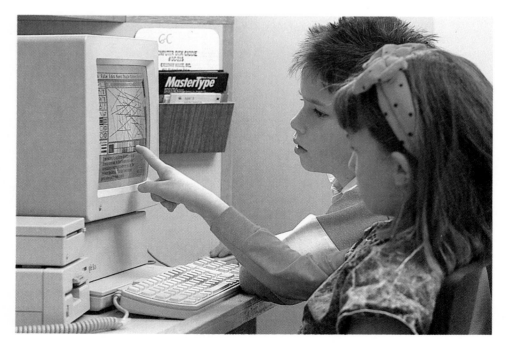

As students are becoming increasingly familiar with computers, schools are groping for effective ways to incorporate computers into classroom instruction.

Two working days before classes begin in the fall, Grace Broward, a fifth-grade teacher, enters the office of the school guidance counselor, Sherry Lawrence. She sees Clare Sims, a sixth-grade teacher with three years experience, jotting down information from student folders.

GRACE: Why hello, Clare! My, you look busy! What are you doing?

CLARE: Hi, Grace. I'm looking up my students' test scores from their cumulative records. I didn't dare ask Sherry to dig them out for me. She's so busy this time of year that I decided to do it myself.

GRACE: What kinds of test scores are you interested in?

CLARE: Mostly IQ scores. I'm using the IQs and the students' other scores to get some idea of their ability.

GRACE: Interesting . . . I've never thought of using IQ scores that way. What will you do with them?

CLARE: For one thing I'll use them to group students for math and reading. I'll also use them when assigning grades.

GRACE: How will you do that?

CLARE: I figure that they can tell me something about a child's motivation. I like to consider everything when giving a child a grade.

GRACE: I'm not sure I completely understand. How do you work it?

CLARE: Well, students who have high ability but do, say, only average work, really shouldn't be given the same grade as a child with low ability who does the same level of work.

GRACE: OK. And how do you use the test scores for grouping?

CLARE: I plan to group high-ability and highly motivated students together and also let them serve as peer tutors for the lower-ability groups. That way everybody wins. Also, I want to arrange for the "high group" to work independently on enrichment activities when they finish classwork first.

GRACE: What will you do with your average and low groups?

CLARE: The average kids will work in a more group-oriented, structured manner. The low-ability students will receive highly structured, individual tutoring from peers and from my teacher's aide. We might also be able to coax some parents to come in and help now and then.

GRACE: That sounds interesting. May I drop in and see it in action some time?

CLARE: Of course. You're welcome any time.

Sherry Lawrence, the guidance counselor, has been working at her desk and overhears part of Grace and Clare's conversation. She moves over to join them.

SHERRY: I couldn't help overhearing your conversation.

significantly increased the mathematics achievement of disadvantaged first-graders. However, by the beginning of the following school year, the differences between the CAI and control classes had completely disappeared.

Use of CAI in schools is still at a relatively primitive stage. One problem is that the cost of maintaining and staffing large numbers of machines, plus the purchase price of the computers and software, make the total expense required to provide meaningful amounts of CAI to all students prohibitive for most school districts. For example, on major study of CAI in mathematics, reading, and language arts found positive effects on the achievement of disadvantaged elementary students who had received ten minutes of computer time per day in each subject (Ragosta, 1983). The researchers calculated that to provide this level of CAI to approximately 380 students would require $100,000 *per year*. Although computers and software get less expensive each year, more than half of the cost of providing computer instruction goes to personnel, maintenance, supplies, insurance, and other items that tend to become more expensive over time (see Levin and Meister, 1986).

Where did you get the idea for using test scores that way?

CLARE: I took a measurement and evaluation course at Teachers' College last semester.

SHERRY: And they suggested this approach?

CLARE: Not really. We studied tests and measurement and I came up with the classroom applications. What do you think, Sherry?

SHERRY: Your idea is interesting. I've just never heard of anyone using IQ scores that way before.

CLARE: Do you see any problem with the idea? Intelligence tests are supposed to be good predictors of student achievement and later success in life.

SHERRY: That's true. But given their standard error of measurement, I'm not sure I would use them to group the kids.

CLARE: I'm really not sure what you're saying, Sherry.

SHERRY: I guess I'm saying that I wonder if they are precise enough as measures of ability differences to use as you suggest. Maybe they help separate the extremes from the middle, but I'm not sure they are accurate enough to separate individual students whose scores may differ by only a few points Drawing the lines would be hard.

CLARE: But I'm dividing the students into only three groups, Sherry—low, average, and high. And, I also use other test scores and my own judgment when I make the assignments.

SHERRY: Have you tried this before?

CLARE: No, but I'm really excited by the possibilities!

SHERRY: Hmmm. You'll have to let us know how it turns out, Clare.

CLARE: Sherry, I get the feeling that you don't think this is a good idea.

SHERRY: Well, I didn't *say* that.

CLARE: I know you didn't, but I'm asking you. Does the plan make sense to you or not? If you really don't think it will work, I'd be interested to know why.

QUESTIONS

1. What do intelligence tests measure? How good a predictor is IQ of school achievement and later success in life?
2. What are the possible drawbacks of Clare's plan? How should Sherry answer Clare?
3. What does Clare assume about IQ tests? How well are her assumptions supported by research?

Use of computers and research on CAI are developing so rapidly that it is difficult to anticipate what the future will bring. However, at this time computers are rarely being used to provide basic instruction. In secondary schools they are primarily used to teach programming and word processing, and in elementary schools they are chiefly used for enrichment (Becker, 1986). Many schools that originally bought computers for CAI have ended up using them to teach computer programming or "computer literacy"—giving students hands-on experience with the computer, but not depending on it to carry a major instructional load (Becker, 1983–1984).

Computer Programming. A popular notion is that learning computer programming (learning to "teach the computer" rather than being taught by it) will increase children's achievement and ability to solve problems. Programming has also been promoted as a virtual synonym for the term "computer literacy."

Much of the research on teaching computer programming to elementary students has focused on the computer language Logo, which was designed to be accessible to young children. Children draw on the computer's display screen by directing the movements of a graphic "turtle," a small triangular point that can move around the screen in response to message sent it by the programmer. Seymour Papert (1980), one of the creators of Logo and a leading supporter of the use of computer programming to expand children's intellectual power, has argued that students who learn Logo will gain in general thinking skills, and others have made similar arguments for the teaching of other computer languages. Research is unclear on the degree to which this is true. Two studies did find a positive effect of extensive experience with Logo on cognitive skills, though not on academic achievement (Clements and Gullo, 1984; Clements, 1986). However, in these studies there was one teacher for every two to three students in the Logo group. Studies with more realistic teacher-student ratios found few effects (duBoulay and Howe, 1982; Pea and Kurland, 1984). When learning of computer programming has effects on thinking skills or other cognitive skills (such as mathematics), the effects are generally restricted to problem-solving skills most similar to those involved in the programming itself (Blume, 1984).

Computer programming is a useful skill in its own right, particularly for high school students interested in technical studies or careers. However, it is doubtful that teaching programming to young students is an efficient way to teach general problem-solving skills, in comparison to direct instruction in problem solving.

▪ Stop and Think

Grouped under the heading "Individualized Instruction" are strategies that share one attribute (providing the appropriate levels of instruction) but differ markedly on other attributes. Recall that the QAIT model (from Chapter 7) focuses on quality of instruction, appropriate levels of instruction, incentives, and time. Assuming that individualized instructional strategies resemble one another in their ability to deliver appropriate levels of instruction, evaluate each on the other three elements in the QAIT model.

APPROPRIATE LEVELS OF INSTRUCTION: REVIEW OF GENERAL PRINCIPLES

This chapter has discussed a number of methods teachers can use to attempt to provide appropriate levels of instruction to students. No one method is ideal for every circumstance. Each solution introduces new problems that must themselves be solved.

Here are a few commonsense principles for providing appropriate levels of instruction in mixed-ability classes:

1. Individualization of instruction always involves costs in terms of efficiency of instruction for the class as a whole. These costs must be minimized. While in certain subjects it is important to provide appropriate levels of instruction to students who learn less rapidly or more rapidly than the rest of the class, this must be done without depriving the rest of the class of high-quality instruction.

2. In some subjects or settings differences among students are not instructionally important, so whole-class instruction may be quite appropriate. In general, subjects in which each skill builds on earlier skills (for example, mathematics, reading) are most in need of some form of individualization.

3. It appears that it is best to meet different needs in the regular, mixed-ability classroom (for example, by using within-class ability grouping, mastery learning, computer-assisted instruction, individualized instruction) rather than using tracking or other between-class ability grouping strategies.

SUMMARY AND REVIEW OF OBJECTIVES

Types of Student Differences. Students differ from one another in a variety of ways, some important to instruction, some not. Differences in intelligence create the most serious problems in instruction. Other important differences are related to prior learning, learning rate, and learning style. Differences in levels of academic achievement among students of the same age tend to increase over time.

Intelligence, and its Measurement. Key components of intelligence are the ability to deal with abstractions, to solve problems, and to learn. The most common measurement of intelligence is the intelligence quotient or IQ. IQ scores have an established mean of 100 and a standard deviation of 15. This means that, theoretically, about two-thirds of all individuals should achieve IQ scores between 85 and 115. Intelligence tests can be administered to individuals or groups. IQ scores are thought to be highly predictive of school achievement, but controversy surrounds the accuracy with which they measure the abilities of children who do not come from white, middle-class families.

Between-Class Ability Grouping. Many schools, particularly at the secondary level, attempt to deal with student differences in level of academic achievement by using between-class ability grouping, or tracking. Often, however, the methods used to categorize students, such as scores on standardized tests, do not measure relevant differences. Research also suggests tracking is detrimental to students assigned to lower-track classes.

Regrouping comprises an alternative to tracking by keeping students in regular (mixed-ability) classes for most of the day, but assigning them to special reading or math classes on the basis of their performance in these subjects.

Within-Class Ability Grouping. Grouping students *within* a class by ability in subjects such as reading or math has proven effective. This method of grouping has the advantages of being flexible, of not segregating low achievers into separate classrooms, and of not stigmatizing students in the lower track. The number of ability groups within a class should be limited to two or three. Ability-Grouped Active Teaching has proved to be an effective within-class grouping program for teaching upper elementary school and middle school mathematics.

Mastery Learning. While standard instructional practices often result in all students receiving equal amounts of instruction, mastery learning suggests that amounts of instructional time should vary so all students have as much time as they need to attain the targeted skills. When this approach is used and corrective instruction given outside of regular class time to students who need it, achievement gains may be seen, especially for low achievers. However, the use of mastery learning often requires decreasing the amount of content covered in favor of increasing achievement levels of the class as a whole. Mastery learning is best used when teaching basic skills.

Computers and Individualized Instruction.   Computers can also help teachers individualize instruction. Types of computer-assisted instruction (CAI) programs include drill and practice, tutorial, simulations, and games. CAI has proven effective when used in addition to regular classroom instruction. Younger students and those who have been identified as low achievers appear to benefit most from CAI. Research findings are unclear regarding the benefits for cognitive development of learning programming languages such as Logo.

Other methods of individualizing instruction include the Keller Plan, programmed instruction, Team Assisted Individualization, tutoring, informal remediation, and enrichment.

STUDY QUESTIONS

1. The type of student differences that creates the most difficult problems for teachers involves variations in
   a. attitude.
   b. fine motor skills.
   c. prior learning.
   d. attention span.
   e. intelligence.
2. Which of the following is true regarding the intelligence quotient (IQ)?
   a. It cannot be used to reliably predict school performance.
   b. It was first introduced by Piaget.
   c. Most scores fall between 85 and 115.
   d. Approximately half the individuals tested score above 110.
3. Which of the following is most likely to occur when students are tracked according to ability?
   a. Students assigned to high tracks and those assigned to low tracks benefit.
   b. Students assigned to low-track classes benefit; high-track students suffer.
   c. Students assigned to high-track classes benefit; low-track students suffer.
   d. Students assigned to high tracks and those assigned to low tracks suffer.
4. A learning style in which students tend to work at a very deliberate pace with emphasis on accuracy is
   a. field dependence.
   b. impulsivity.
   c. receptivity.
   d. reflectivity.
   e. field independence.
5. Match the following types of grouping strategies with the correct description of each.
   ____ Joplin Plan
   ____ Ability-Grouped Active Teaching
   ____ "College Preparatory" and "General" tracks
   ____ Team-Assisted Individualization
   a. A within-class ability grouping method
   b. A regrouping method that extends across grade levels

   c. A cooperative learning method using mixed-ability groups
   d. A between-class ability grouping method
6. Which of the following statements reflects the major philosophy of mastery learning regarding student differences?
   a. Allow level of achievement to vary while holding learning time consistent
   b. Allow both achievement and learning time to vary as much as possible
   c. Keep both level of achievement and learning time consistent
   d. Allow learning time to vary while keeping level of achievement consistent
7. Which of the following is *not* a central feature of mastery learning?
   a. Norm-referenced tests that compare students to each other
   b. Formative quizzes that provide feedback on the student's progress while learning.
   c. Summative quizzes that assess performance at the end of a lesson
   d. Corrective instruction given when mastery is not achieved
   e. Enrichment activities given when mastery is achieved
8. Cross-age tutoring often leads to increased levels of achievement for both the student being taught and the tutor. True or false?
9. A student receives a CAI lesson about the Viet Nam War. She proceeds at her own pace, reading the information provided and answering questions presented intermittently. Based on her responses, either a review or new material is presented in the following segments. This program illustrates the type of CAI called
   a. tutorial.
   b. simulation.
   c. utility.
   d. drill-and-practice.

Answers: 1. *c* 2. *c* 3. *c* 4. *d* 5. *b, a, d, c* 6. *d* 7. *a* 8. *True* 9. *a*

SUGGESTED READINGS

ALESSI, S. M., and TROLLIP, S. R. (1985). *Computer-based instruction*. Englewood Cliffs, N.J.: Prentice-Hall.

ANDERSON, L. M., EVERTSON, C. M., and BROPHY, J. E. (1982). Principles of small group instruction in elementary reading. Occasional Paper No. 58. Institute for Research on Teaching, Michigan State University, East Lansing, Mich.

BECKER, H. J. (1986). *Instructional uses of computers*. Baltimore, Md.: Center for Research on Elementary and Middle Schools, Johns Hopkins University.

BLOCK, J. H., and ANDERSON, L. W. (1975). *Mastery learning in classroom instruction*. New York: Macmillan.

BLOOM, B. S. (1976). *Human characteristics and school learning*. New York: McGraw-Hill.

CALLISON, W. L. (1985). *Using computers in the classroom*. Englewood Cliffs, N.J.: Prentice-Hall.

CORNO, L., and SNOW, R. E. (1986). Adapting teaching to individual differences among learners. In M. C. Wittrock (Ed.), *Handbook of research on teaching* (3rd ed.). New York: Macmillan.

ELLSON, D. G. (1976). Tutoring. In N. L. Gage (Ed.), *The psychology of teaching methods* (pp. 130–165). Chicago: University of Chicago Press.

LEVINE, D. V. (Ed.) (1985). *Improving student achievement through mastery learning programs*. San Francisco: Jossey-Bass.

OAKES, J. (1985). *Keeping track: How schools structure inequality*. New Haven, Conn.: Yale University Press.

PETERSON, P., WILKINSON, L. C., and HALLINAN, M. (Eds.) (1984). *The social context of instruction: Group organization and group processes*. New York: Academic Press.

SLAVIN, R. E., MADDEN, N. A., and STEVENS, R. J. (1989/90). Cooperative learning models for the 3 R's. *Educational Leadership, 47* (4), 22–28.

SLAVIN, R. E. (Ed.) (1989). *School and classroom organization*. Hillsdale, N. J.: Erlbaum.

WANG, M. C., and WALBERG, H. J. (Eds.) (1985). *Adapting instruction to individual differences*. Berkeley, Cal.: McCutchan.

Chapter 10

Motivation

Chapter Outline

Chapter Objectives

After reading this chapter on motivation you should be able to:

- Give examples of basic needs—those that people are motivated to meet for survival—and of growth needs.

- Describe the implication for a person of attributing success or failure to internal or external factors.

- Describe patterns of motivation, such as the motivation to succeed, that can be termed personality characteristics.

- Give examples of how the expectations that teachers have for students can affect student motivation.

- Present lessons that students will be motivated to learn.

Motivation
The influence of needs and desires
on the intensity and direction
of behavior

After delivering a lecture on trigonometry, Ms. O'Connor distributed worksheets to her eleventh-graders. Most of her students got right to work. However, after a few minutes it became apparent that some were working better than others. One student, Frank, put down his pencil and stopped working after the first problem. Marcie and Maria were whispering to each other, hoping Ms. O'Connor wouldn't see them. Carl was trying to catch the eye of one of the prettiest girls in the class, Sara, who was spending her time pretending not to notice him rather than doing her worksheet. Dave was furtively copying answers from Steve.

At the end of the day Ms. O'Connor complained about her class to another math teacher. "My fifth-period class is the pits!" she said. "They're just not motivated!"

MEANING AND IMPORTANCE OF MOTIVATION

Motivation is one of the most important prerequisites for learning. Enormous sums of money are directed toward building, staffing, and equipping schools, and the full authority of the state is exercised to ensure that students will attend them. But all of this is for naught if students do not want to learn.

What makes a student want to learn? The willingness to put effort into learning is a product of many factors, ranging from the student's personality and abilities to characteristics of particular learning tasks, incentives for learning, and settings.

The term "motivation" has little practical meaning by itself; the question is, "motivation to do *what*?" When Ms. O'Connor complains that her class is not motivated, she is mistaken. They are just not motivated to do trigonometry worksheets as much as they are motivated to do other things.

Motivation may vary in both *intensity* and *direction*. Two students may be motivated to play video games, but one of them may be more strongly motivated to do so than the other. Or one student may be strongly motivated to play video games and the other equally strongly motivated to play football. Gage and Berliner (1984) liken motivation to the engine (intensity) and steering wheel (direction) of a car. Actually, though, the intensity and direction of motivations are often difficult to separate. The intensity of a motivation to engage in one activity may depend in large part on the intensity and direction of motivations to engage in alternative activities (see Thibaut and Kelly, 1959). If someone has only enough time and money to go to the movies *or* to play video games, motivation to engage in one of these activities is strongly influenced by the intensity of motivation to engage in the other. In Ms. O'Connor's class Carl might ordinarily have a strong motivation to learn trigonometry, but at the moment he has an even stronger motivation to attract Sara's attention—a goal that has nothing to do with trigonometry.

THEORIES OF MOTIVATION

The first half of this chapter presents contemporary theories of motivation, which seek to explain why people are motivated to do what they do. The second half discusses the classroom use of incentives for learning and presents strategies for increasing students' motivations to do schoolwork.

Motivation and Reinforcers

The concept of motivation is closely tied to the principle that behaviors that have been reinforced in the past are more likely to be repeated than behaviors that have not been reinforced or have been punished (see Chapter 4). In fact, Skinner (1953) and other behavioral theorists would argue that there is no need for separate theories of learning and motivation because motivation is simply a product of reinforcement history. Students who have been reinforced for studying (for example, by receiving good grades or the approval of teachers and parents) will be "motivated" to study, but students who have not been reinforced for studying (because they studied but did not get good grades, or because their teachers or parents did not praise their studying) will be "unmotivated." Finally, students who have been punished for studying (for example, by being made fun of by friends) might be "motivated" to avoid studying. In preference to using the concept of "motivation," a behavioral theorist would describe these situations in terms of the degree to which the students have learned to study or not to study to obtain desired outcomes (see Bandura, 1969).

Why do some students persist in the face of failure while others give up? Why do some students work to please the teacher, others to make good grades, and still others out of interest in the material they are learning? Why do some students achieve far more than would be predicted on the basis of their "ability," and some far less? Examination of reinforcement histories and schedules of reinforcement might provide answers to such questions, but it is usually easier to speak in terms of motivations to satisfy various needs.

Rewards and Reinforcers

With very hungry animals, we can predict that food will be an effective reinforcer. With humans, even hungry ones, we can't be sure what will be a reinforcer and what will not, because the reinforcing value of most potential reinforcers is largely determined by personal or situational factors. As an example of this, think about the value of $50 for an hour's light work. Most of us would view $50 as a powerful reinforcer, more than adequate to get us to do an hour's work. But consider these situations:

1. Mr. Scrooge offers Bill $60 to paint his fence, which Bill thinks is more than enough for the job, so he does his best work. However, when he is done, Mr. Scrooge says, "I don't think you did sixty dollars' worth of work. Here's fifty."

2. Now consider the same situation, except that Mr. Scrooge originally offers Bill $40, and when he is finished praises him for an excellent job and gives him $50.

3. Dave and Barbara meet at a party, like each other immediately, and after the party take a long walk in the moonlight. When they get to Barbara's house, Dave says, "Barbara, I enjoyed spending time with you. Here's fifty dollars I'd like you to have."

4. Janet's aunt offers her $50 to teach little Annette how to play baseball next Saturday. However, if she agrees to do so, Janet will miss her chance to try out for the school baseball team.

In Situations 1, 3, and 4, $50 is not a good reinforcer at all. In Situation 1 Bill's expectations have been raised and then dashed by Mr. Scrooge. Even though the amount of monetary reward is the same in Situation 2, this situation is much more likely to make Bill want to paint Mr. Scrooge's fence again, because in this case his reward exceeds his expectation. In Situation 3 Dave's offer of $50 is insulting, and would certainly not increase Barbara's interest in going out with him in the future. Janet's aunt's offer in Situation 4 would seem generous to Janet under most circumstances, but it is insufficient reinforcement this particular Saturday because it interferes with a more highly valued activity.

These situations illustrate an important point: The reinforcing value of a reward cannot be assumed, because it may depend on many factors. When teachers say, "I want you all to be sure to hand in your book reports on time because they will count toward your grade," the teachers may be assuming that grades are effective reinforcers for most students. However, some students may not care about grades because their parents don't, or because they have a history of failure in school and have decided that grades are unimportant. If a teacher says to a student, "Good work! I knew you could do it if you tried!", this might be reinforcing to a student who had just completed a task he thought was difficult, but punishing to one who thought the task was easy (because the teacher's praise implied that he had to work especially hard to complete the task). As in the case of Bill and Mr. Scrooge, the students' expectations for rewards determine the reinforcing value of any particular reward. It is often difficult to determine students' motivations from their behavior because many different motivations can influence their behavior. Sometimes one type of motivation clearly determines behavior, at other times several motivations are influential. As Figure 10.1 illustrates, the motivation to engage in an activity (in this case, doing a worksheet) depends on the relative strengths of motivations for and against engaging in that activity. Of course, it is not the number of goals on either side of the balance that matters, but their strength; Carl and Sara may be as motivated to do the worksheets as everyone else in Ms. O'Connor's class, but their other motivation—to use the time to socialize—is so strong that it tilts the balance against engaging in the worksheet activity.

Motivation and Needs

While behavioral learning theorists (for example, Skinner, 1953; Bandura, 1969; see Chapter 4) speak in terms of motivation to obtain reinforcers and avoid punishers, other theorists (for example, Murray, 1938; Maslow, 1954; Madsen, 1961) prefer the

FIGURE 10.1

Factors Affecting Student Motivation to Do a Worksheet

Many factors can influence a person's motivation to do something. The factors perceived to be most important usually determine the intensity and direction of behavior.

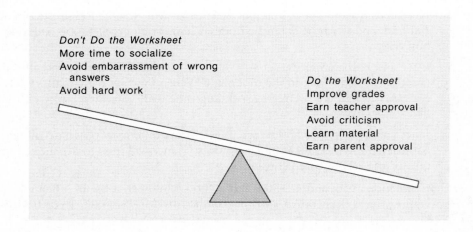

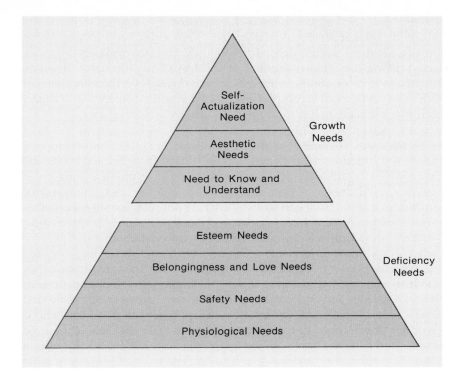

FIGURE 10.2

Maslow's Hierarchy of Needs

Maslow identifies two types of needs, deficiency needs and growth needs. People are motivated to satisfy needs at the bottom of the hierarchy before seeking those at the top.

Adapted from Maslow, 1954.

concept of motivation to satisfy needs. Some basic needs that we all must satisfy are those for food, shelter, love, and maintenance of positive self-esteem. People differ in the degree of importance they attach to each of these needs. Some need constant reaffirmation that they are loved or appreciated, while others have greater needs for physical comfort and security. Also, the same person has different needs at different times; a drink of water would be much more appreciated after a four-mile run than after a four-course meal.

Since people have many needs, which will they try to satisfy at any given moment? To predict this, Maslow (1954) proposed a hierarchy of needs, which is illustrated in Figure 10.2.

In Maslow's theory needs lower in the hierarchy diagrammed in Figure 10.2 must be at least partially satisfied before a person will try to satisfy higher needs. For example, a hungry person or one in physical danger will be less concerned about maintaining a positive self-image than about obtaining food or safety, but once that person is no longer hungry or afraid, self-esteem needs may become paramount. One critical concept introduced by Maslow is the distinction between deficiency needs and growth needs. **Deficiency needs** (physiological, safety, love, and esteem) are those that are critical to physical and psychological well-being; these needs must be satisfied, but once they are, a person's motivation to satisfy them diminishes. In contrast, **growth needs,** such as the need to know and understand things, to appreciate beauty, or to grow and develop in appreciation of others, can never be satisfied completely. In fact, the more people are able to meet their need to know and understand the world around them, the *greater* their motivation may become to learn still more.

Self-Actualization.   Maslow's theory also includes the concept of **self-actualization,** which he defines as "the desire to become everything that one is capable of becoming"

(Maslow, 1954, p. 92). Self-actualization is characterized by acceptance of self and others, spontaneity, openness, relatively deep but "democratic" relationships with others, creativity, humor, and independence—in essence, psychological health. Maslow places striving for self-actualization at the top of his hierarchy of needs, implying that achievement of this most important need depends on the satisfaction of all other needs. The difficulty of accomplishing this is recognized by Maslow (1968), who estimated that fewer than 1 percent of adults achieve self-actualization.

Implications of Maslow's Hierarchy of Needs for Education. The importance of Maslow's theory for education is in the relationship between deficiency needs and growth needs. Obviously, students who are very hungry or in physical danger will have little psychological energy to put into learning. Schools and governmental agencies recognize that if the basic needs of students are not met, learning will suffer, and have responded by providing free breakfast and lunch programs. However, most American students are adequately fed and have few concerns about their physical safety. In schools the most important deficiency needs are those for love and self-esteem. If students do not feel that they are loved and that they are capable, they are unlikely to have a strong motivation to achieve the higher growth objectives, such as the search for knowledge and understanding for their own sake or the creativity and openness to new ideas characteristic of the self-actualizing person. A student who is unsure of his or her "lovableness" or capability will tend to make the "safe" choice: go with the crowd, study for the test without interest in learning the ideas, write a predictable but uncreative essay, and so on. A teacher who is able to put students at ease, to make them feel accepted and respected as individuals, is more likely (in Maslow's view) to help them become eager to learn for the sake of learning and willing to risk being creative and open to new ideas. If they are to become self-directed learners, students must feel that the teacher will respond fairly and consistently to them, and that they will not be ridiculed or punished for honest errors.

Schools often provide snacks or breakfast and lunch because physical needs of the students must be satisfied before they can put energy into learning.

Cognitive Dissonance

The need to maintain a positive self-image is a powerful motivator (Covington, 1984). Much of our behavior is directed toward satisfying our own personal standards; for example, if we believe that we are good and honest people, we are likely to engage in good and honest behavior even when no one is watching, because we want to maintain a positive self-image. If we believe that we are capable and intelligent, we will try to satisfy ourselves in achievement situations that we have behaved capably and intelligently.

However, sometimes the realities of life force us into situations where our behavior or beliefs contradict our positive self-image, or conflict with other behaviors or beliefs. For example, a woman who believes deeply in civil rights might be pleased by the gift of a diamond ring, until she learns that the diamond was mined in South Africa. To maintain her self-image as a dedicated opponent of South Africa's apartheid policies, she must do one of two things: either refuse or exchange the diamond (change her behavior), or rationalize keeping it, perhaps by reasoning that diamond mining employs thousands of black workers who would otherwise be unemployed. With either choice, the woman maintains her self-image.

One situation in which we must often do a great deal of rationalizing to maintain a positive self-image is when we fail at a task at which we feel we should have succeeded. For example, in an episode of *Candid Camera* many years ago a coffee shop distributed sugar packets that could not be opened. The hidden camera recorded many customers trying to open the packets and then deciding that they really preferred unsweetened coffee (exactly like Aesop's fox, who decided that the grapes he couldn't reach were probably sour anyway). One customer, after making an extraordinary effort to open the sugar packet, looked around and then dropped it whole into his coffee! A member of the *Candid Camera* crew approached the man and asked him why he had dropped his sugar packet into his coffee. The man replied that he always did that, that he liked his coffee that way.

The man in the *Candid Camera* episode was responding to an embarrassing situation by rationalizing his strange behavior, hoping to maintain a positive image in others' eyes (and thereby keep his own positive self-image). Similarly, a student who is caught cheating on a test might justify his behavior by stating (and even believing) that "everyone does it," or "the teacher gives unfairly tricky tests, so I felt justified in cheating," or denying (and really believing his denial) that he cheated, despite overwhelming evidence to the contrary.

One psychological theory that deals with behaviors, explanations, and excuses used to maintain a positive self-image is called **cognitive dissonance theory** (Festinger, 1957). This theory holds that people experience tension or discomfort when a deeply held value or belief is challenged by a psychologically inconsistent belief or behavior. To resolve this discomfort, they may change their behaviors or beliefs, or they may develop justifications or excuses that resolve the inconsistency. For example, highly competitive athletes who are otherwise careful about their health might justify taking muscle-enhancing anabolic steroids by rationalizing that the drug will strengthen them and, thereby, help bring victory to their team. This rationalization is potentially very damaging, but underscores the lengths to which people will go to justify their behavior.

In the classic experiment illustrating cognitive dissonance, Festinger (1957) had some college students do a very boring task. Some were paid $20 for doing the task, and some were paid only $1. When asked how much they enjoyed the task and how interesting they thought it was, the subjects who were paid $1 reported that the task

Attribution Theory
An explanation of motivation that
focuses on how people explain
the causes of their own successes
and failures

was interesting and enjoyable, while those paid $20 said that it was boring. Festinger explained this paradoxical finding by noting that the students paid only $1 were faced with a dilemma. They had done a lot of boring work for very little reward. If they perceived the task as boring, then they must be fools for doing it for only a dollar. To avoid this unpleasant conclusion, they could change their perception of the task, viewing it as interesting and the experience as enjoyable and worthwhile. This kind of change in attitude is often unconscious, but real nonetheless. In contrast, the subjects paid $20 did not have to engage in any attitudinal gymnastics to explain why they did the task. They could honestly judge it as boring because they knew why they did it—for the money. People want reassurance that they made the right choice and did the right thing. Other research (Ehrlick et al., 1957) has found that before buying a car people read advertisements for all sorts of cars, but after buying it they mostly read those for the car they bought, seeking reassurance that they had made the right choice and avoiding the dissonance-producing advertisements for the cars that they did not buy.

Importance of Cognitive Dissonance for Education. In educational settings cognitive dissonance theory often applies when students receive unpleasant feedback on their academic performance. For example, Teresa usually gets good grades, but receives a D on a quiz. The mark is inconsistent with her self-image, and causes her discomfort. To resolve this discomfort, Teresa may decide to work harder to make certain that she never gets such a low grade again. On the other hand, she may try to rationalize her low grade: "The questions were tricky, I wasn't feeling well, the teacher didn't tell us the quiz was coming. I wasn't really trying, it was too hot." These excuses would help Teresa account for one D, but suppose she gets several poor grades in a row. Now she might decide that she never did like this subject anyway ("sour grapes"), that the teacher shows favoritism to the boys in the class or is a hard grader. All of these changes in opinions and excuses are directed at avoiding an unpleasant pairing of inconsistent ideas: "I am a good student" and "I am doing poorly in this class, and it is my own fault."

Attribution Theory

Teresa is struggling to find a reason for her poor grades that does not require her to change her perception of herself as a good student. She attributes her poor performance to her teacher, to the subject matter, or to other students—external factors over which she has no control. Or, if she acknowledges that her poor performance is her own fault, she decides it must be a short-term lapse, due to a momentary (but reversible) lack of motivation or attention regarding this unit of instruction.

Attribution theory (see, for example, Weiner, 1979) seeks to understand just such explanations and excuses, particularly when applied to success or failure (wherein lies the theory's greatest importance for education, where success or failure are recurrent themes). Weiner suggests that most explanations for success or failure have three characteristics. The first is whether the cause is seen as internal (within the person) or external. The second is whether it is seen as stable or unstable. The third is whether it is perceived as controllable or not. As in cognitive dissonance theory, a central assumption of attribution theory is that people will attempt to maintain a positive self-image (Covington, 1984). Therefore when anything good happens, they are likely to attribute it to their own efforts or abilities, but when anything bad

TABLE 10.1

ATTRIBUTIONS FOR SUCCESS AND FAILURE

Attribution theory describes and suggests the implications of people's explanations of their successes and failures.

Locus of Control	Stability	
	Stable	Unstable
Internal	**Ability**	**Effort**
Success:	"I'm smart"	"I tried hard"
Failure:	"I'm dumb"	"I didn't really try"
External	**Task Difficulty**	**Luck**
Success:	"It was easy"	"I lucked out"
Failure:	"It was too hard"	"I had bad luck"

SOURCE: Adapted from Weiner, 1979.

Locus of Control
A personality trait that concerns whether people attribute responsibility for their own failure or success to internal factors or to external factors

happens, they will believe that it is due to factors over which they had no control. It has been demonstrated many times that if groups of people are given a task and then told that they either "failed" or "succeeded" (even though all, in fact, were equally successful), those who were told they "failed" will say that their failure was due to bad luck, while those who were told they "succeeded" will attribute their success to skill and intelligence (Forsyth, 1986).

Attribution theory deals primarily with four explanations for success and failure in achievement situations: ability, effort, task difficulty, and luck. Ability and effort attributions are internal to the individual; task difficulty and luck attributions are external. Ability is taken to be a relatively stable, unalterable state; effort can be altered. Similarly, task difficulty is essentially a stable characteristic, while luck is unstable and unpredictable. These four attributions and representative explanations for success and failure are presented in Table 10.1.

Table 10.1 shows how students might seek to explain success and failure differently. When students succeed, they would like to believe that it was because they are smart (an internal, stable attribution), not because they were lucky or because the task was easy, or even because they tried hard (because "trying hard" says little about their likelihood of success in the future). In contrast, students who fail would like to believe that they had bad luck (an external, unstable attribution), which allows for the possibility of succeeding next time (Zuckerman, 1979; Whitley and Frieze, 1985; Marsh, 1986). Of course, over time these attributions may be difficult to maintain. As illustrated in the case of Teresa, a student who gets one bad grade is likely to blame it on bad luck or some other external, unstable cause. After several bad grades, though, an unstable attribution becomes difficult to maintain; no one can be unlucky on tests week after week. Therefore a student like Teresa may switch to a stable but still external attribution. For example, she might decide that the course is too difficult or make some other stable, external attribution that lets her avoid making a stable, internal attribution that would shatter her self-esteem: "I failed because I don't have the ability."

One concept central to attribution theory is **locus of control** (Rotter, 1954). The

Students who believe that success depends on their own efforts and abilities—rather than on luck or other external factors—are likely to work hard and succeed.

word "locus" means "location." A person with an "internal locus of control" is one who believes that success or failure is due to his or her own efforts or abilities. Someone with an "external locus of control" is more likely to believe that other factors, such as luck, task difficulty, or other people's actions, cause success or failure. Locus of control can be very important in explaining a student's school performance. For example, several researchers have found that students high in internal locus of control have better grades and test scores than do students of the same intelligence who are low in internal locus of control (Messer, 1972; Lefcourt, 1976; Nowicki et al., 1978). Brookover et al. (1979) found that locus of control was the most important predictor of a student's academic achievement after ability. The reason is easy to see. Students who believe that success in school is due to luck, the teacher's whims, or other external factors are unlikely to work hard. In contrast, students who believe that success and failure are due primarily to their own efforts can be expected to work hard (provided, of course, they *want* to succeed). In reality, success in a particular class is a product of both students' efforts and abilities (internal factors) and luck, task difficulty, and teacher behaviors (external factors). But the most successful students will tend to *overestimate* the degree to which their own behavior produces success and failure; some experiments have shown that even in situations in which success and failure are completely due to luck, students high in internal locus of control will believe that it was their efforts that made them succeed or fail (see Lefcourt, 1976).

It is important to note that locus of control can change, and depends somewhat on the specific activity or situation. One difficulty in studying the effects of locus of control on achievement is that achievement has a strong effect on it (Weiner, 1980). For example, the same student might have an internal locus of control in academics (because of high academic ability) but an external locus of control in sports (because of low athletic ability). If this student discovered some unsuspected skill in a new sport, he or she might develop an internal locus of control in that sport (but still not in other sports).

Importance of Attributions for Education.   In the classroom students receive constant information concerning their level of performance on academic tasks, either relative to others or relative to some norm of acceptability. This feedback ultimately influences students' self-perceptions (Pintrich and Blumenfeld, 1985). Attribution theory is important in understanding how students might interpret and use feedback on their academic performance, and in suggesting to teachers how they might give feedback that has the greatest motivational value.

Students who believe that their past failures on tasks were due to lack of ability are unlikely to expect to succeed in similar tasks, and are therefore unlikely to exert much effort (Bar-Tal, 1979). Obviously, the belief that you will fail can be self-fulfilling; if students believe they will fail, they may be poorly motivated to do academic work, and this may in turn cause them to fail. Therefore the most damaging idea a teacher can communicate to a student is that the student is hopelessly dumb. Few teachers would say such a thing directly to a student, but the idea can be just as effectively communicated in several other ways. One is to use a competitive grading system (for example, "grading on the curve") and to make grades public and relative student rankings important. This practice may make small differences in achievement level seem large, so that students who receive the poorest grades may decide that they can never learn. Alternatively, a teacher who deemphasizes grades and relative rankings, but expresses the (almost always correct) expectation that all students in the class can learn, is likely to help students see that their chances of success depend, at least

For some students, college is a birthright. Their only decision is which school to attend. For others, many of them minority students, college might as well be the moon. Tuition is staggering, the environment unfamiliar, and the rewards uncertain. Getting there seems impossible.

Fortunately, some high schools and universities are devising ways to nudge more of these students toward higher education. Three modest but successful programs have motivated students with a mix of you-can-do-it pep talk and classes aimed at sharpening academic and language skills.

San Francisco's Mission High School has boosted its percentage of college-bound seniors by bringing college to the high school. In the mid-1980s, only 10 percent of students, who are predominantly Hispanic and Asian, went on to college. By the 1990s, the rate was up to 85 percent, well above the national average of about 50 percent.

Mission High's program, called Step to College, succeeds, according to its founder, Dr. Jacob Perea of the San Francisco State School of Education, because students realize that college attendance can be a real possibility rather than a distant goal. The program allows seniors to attend after-school classes taught by college instructors. Students also have access to facilities and services at nearby San Francisco State College. Furthermore, Mission High students who choose to attend San Francisco State receive support services aimed at discouraging them from dropping out.

A New York City program has boosted the college aspirations of a somewhat different minority student population, foreign-born high schoolers who have all the academic skills for college but who lack proficiency in English.

"School systems aren't really geared to enrich these kinds of students because of the overwhelming demand to concentrate on students who need as much academic help as language help," said Sandra Spector, a program advisor, who teaches English as a Second Language.

New York's Opportunity to Learn program allows

high school students to attend intensive English programs at local colleges and universities during the summer between their junior and senior years. It also provides guidance for the students as they choose a college. Many of the students, who are selected based on the nominations of teachers and guidance counselors, go on from the program to attend top-flight U.S. colleges and universities.

While the Opportunity to Learn Program stresses a vital academic skill, the focus of an inner-city Chicago program is on student self-esteem. "Never Never Never Quit" is the message on the wall of Joyce Oatman's senior class for gifted students at Chicago's Crain High School.

Mrs. Oatman is one of those teachers who, with undying tenacity and enthusiasm, has changed the lives of many students. A 30-year veteran of Crain High School, she has dedicated herself for the last several years to nurturing the talents of those she considers gifted, but who don't necessarily score well on traditional tests. All eight graduating seniors in Mrs. Oatman's class of 1990 were accepted to college—this in a school with a 25 percent drop-out rate, a 33 percent daily rate of absenteeism, and where one of Mrs. Oatman's seniors stands out as the only girl in her homeroom who has not become pregnant.

"There's a whole lot of 'you-can-do-it' encouragement," said Mrs. Oatman. "When they hear it enough, they finally begin to believe it."

What do these programs share? Basically, the notion that more high schoolers might go on to college if they thought themselves capable of college work. Each of these programs deserves praise as a modest effort that might dramatically affect the achievement of students throughout their lives.

From Lee A. Daniels, "College-Bound Immigrants Get Help," *New York Times*, August 9, 1989, p. B8. Louis Freedberg, "High School in West Brings College to Students," *New York Times*, July 5, 1989. Isabel Wilkerson, "Chicago Class for the Gifted Requires More than Brains," *New York Times*, February 21, 1990, p. A1.

somewhat, on their *efforts*—an internal but alterable attribution that lets students anticipate success in the future if they do their best (Ames and Ames, 1984). A stable, internal attribution for success ("I succeed because I am smart") is also a poor attribution for academic success; able students also need to feel that it is their *effort*, not their ability, that leads to academic success. Teachers who emphasize amount of effort as the cause of success as well as failure, and reward effort rather than ability, are more likely to motivate all their students to do their best than teachers who emphasize ability alone (Hunter and Barker, 1987; Raffini, 1986).

Some formal means of rewarding students for effort rather than ability are the use of individualized instruction (see Chapter 9), where the basis of success is progress at the student's own level; the inclusion of "effort" as a component of grading or as a separate grade (see Chapter 14); or the use of rewards for improvement (described later in this chapter).

■ **Stop and Think**

Recall a school situation in which you did worse than you wanted to—maybe one in which you even failed. How did you explain your failure? How would your explanation be classified according to attribution theory?

Now recall a situation in which you succeeded. How would attribution theory classify your explanation for that outcome?

Analyze the effects of these explanations on your subsequent behavior.

Motivation and Personality

The word "motivation" is used to describe a drive, need, or desire to do something. People can be motivated to eat if they haven't eaten in sixteen hours, to go to the movies today, to get better grades in English this year, or to improve the world around them. In other words, the word "motivation" can be applied to behavior in a wide variety of situations.

One use of the concept of motivation is to describe a general tendency to strive toward certain types of goals. In this sense, motivation is often seen as a relatively stable personality characteristic. Some people are motivated to achieve, some to socialize with others—and they express these motivations in many different ways. Motivation as a stable characteristic is a somewhat different concept from motivation to do something specific in a particular situation. For example, anyone may be motivated to eat by being deprived of food long enough (a situational motivation), but some people are more generally interested in food than others (motivation as a personality characteristic). This is not to say that situational and personality motivation are unrelated; motivation as a personality characteristic is largely a product of a person's history of reinforcement.

For example, if children are praised by their parents and teachers for showing interest in the world around them, are successful in school, read well enough to enjoy reading, and are reinforced for reading (both by parents and teachers and by the content of the books themselves), then they will develop a "love of learning" as a general personality trait, and will read and learn even when no one is reinforcing them. However, this personality trait is the result of a long history of *situational* motivations to learn. What this implies is that if, owing to a reinforcement history quite different from that just described, a child fails to develop a love of learning as a personality characteristic, love of learning can still be instilled in the child, and later become part of the child's personality. For example, many children from homes in which learning is not highly valued and in which little reading is done by adults do not develop as much of a "love of learning" as children in more achievement- and reading-oriented families. Yet positive school experiences and reinforcement for learning, curiosity, and reading by teachers can, in time, overcome the lack of encouragement or models at home, and develop love of learning in just about any child. Thus when we speak of motivation as a personality characteristic, it is important to keep in mind that this does not imply that stable, generalized motivations are unalterable, only that they tend to remain constant across a variety of settings and are difficult to change in the short run.

Patterns of Motivation. One dimension along which individuals' personalities differ is the relative strengths of various motives. Some people seem mostly interested in achieving, others in being accepted and liked by other people. Some seek to dominate other people, while others need approval from other people.

McClelland et al. (1953) described four principal motives expressed by different people on the **Thematic Apperception Test, or TAT.** On the TAT, individuals are asked to describe what is happening in an ambiguous picture. People whose descriptions contain many references to goal orientation, success-seeking, and needs for success are scored as high in achievement motivation. For example, if a TAT card depicted a young man speaking with an older man sitting behind a desk, someone high in achievement motivation might describe the young man as an employee asking for a raise. Someone high in affiliation motivation might say instead that the younger man is inviting the older one to play a game of golf, while a person high in power motivation might describe the older man as giving orders to the younger man. Finally, someone high in approval motivation might describe the younger man as asking his boss for a comment on his work.

The reliability and validity of the TAT have been questioned in recent years (Mitchell, 1985), but the concept of motivations as personality characteristics (especially achievement motivation) is still important in personality psychology.

Achievement Motivation

The most important motivation for educational psychology is **achievement motivation** (McClelland and Atkinson, 1948), the generalized tendency to strive for success and to choose goal-oriented, success/failure activities. For example, French (1956) found that given a choice of work partners for a complex task, achievement-motivated students tend to choose a partner who is good at the task, while affiliation-motivated students (who express needs for love and acceptance) are more likely to choose a friendly partner. Achievement-motivated students will persist longer at a task than students less high in achievement motivation, even after they experience failure, and will attribute their failures to lack of effort (an internal but alterable condition) rather than to external factors such as task difficulty or luck. In short, achievement-motivated students want and expect to succeed, and when they fail, they redouble their efforts until they do succeed (see Weiner, 1980).

Not surprisingly, students high in achievement motivation tend to succeed on school tasks (Kestenbaum, 1970). However, it is unclear which causes which: Does high achievement motivation lead to success in school, or does success in school (due to ability or other factors) lead to high achievement motivation? Actually, each contributes to the other; success breeds the desire for more success, which in turn breeds success (Gottfried, 1985). On the other hand, students who do not experience success in achievement settings will tend to lose the motivation to succeed in such settings, and will turn their interest elsewhere (perhaps to social, sports, or even delinquent activities in which they may succeed).

Atkinson (1964), extending McClelland's work on achievement motivation, noted that individuals may be motivated to achieve in either of two ways: to seek success, or to avoid failure. He found that some people were more motivated to avoid failure

Learning Goals
A motivational orientation of students who place primary emphasis on knowledge acquisition and self-improvement

Performance Goals
A motivational orientation of students who place primary emphasis on gaining recognition from others and earning good grades

than to seek success ("failure avoiders"), while others were more motivated to seek success than to avoid failure ("success seekers"). Weiner and Rosenbaum (1965) found that given a choice between doing a puzzle (which had one right answer) or judging pictures (where there was no one answer), success seekers would choose the puzzle and failure avoiders the judgment task. Success seekers' motivation is increased following failure, as they intensify their efforts to succeed. Failure avoiders decrease their efforts following failure (Weiner, 1972).

One very important characteristic of failure avoiders is that they tend to choose either very easy or very difficult tasks. For example, Atkinson and Litwin (1960) found that in a ring toss game, failure avoiders would choose to stand very near the target or very far away, while success seekers would choose an intermediate distance. They hypothesized that failure avoiders preferred either easy tasks (on which failure was unlikely) or such difficult tasks that no one would blame them if they failed. Confirming this idea, Mahone (1960) found that failure avoiders made more unrealistic career choices (given their grades and test scores) than did success seekers, and Isaacson (1964) reported that failure avoiders chose easier and harder college courses than success seekers, who more often signed up for courses of moderate difficulty.

Understanding that it is common for failure avoiders to choose impossibly difficult or ridiculously easy tasks for themselves is very important for the teacher. For example, a poor reader might choose to write a book report on *War and Peace* and, when told that that was too difficult, might choose a simple children's book. Such students are not being devious, but are simply doing their best to maintain a positive self-image in a situation that is difficult for them.

Learning versus Performance Goals.   Dweck (1986; Dweck and Elliott, 1983) and Nicholls (1984) have found that achievement and motivation can be divided according to another dimension of great importance to schools. Some students are motivationally oriented toward **learning goals** (or **mastery goals**), while others are oriented toward **performance goals.** Students with learning goals see the purpose of schooling as gaining competence in the skills being taught, while those with performance goals primarily seek to gain positive judgments of their competence (and avoid negative judgments). Students striving toward learning goals are likely to take difficult courses and to seek challenges, while those with performance goals focus on getting good grades, take easy courses, and avoid challenging situations.

Students with learning as opposed to performance goals do not differ in overall intelligence, but their performance in the classroom can differ markedly. When they run into obstacles, performance-oriented students tend to become discouraged, and their performance is seriously hampered. In contrast, when learning-oriented students encounter obstacles, they tend to keep trying, and their motivation and performance may actually increase (Dweck, 1986). In particular, performance-oriented students who perceive their abilities to be low are likely to fall into a pattern of helplessness, since they feel they have little chance of earning good grades. Learning-oriented students who perceive their ability to be low do not feel this way, since they are concerned with how much they themselves can learn, without regard for the performance of others (Nicholls, 1984).

The most important implication of research on learning versus performance goals is that teachers should try to convince students that learning rather than grades is the purpose of academic work. This can be done by emphasizing the interest value and practical importance of material students are studying, and by deemphasizing grades and other rewards. For example, a teacher might say "Today we're going to learn about events deep in the earth that cause the fiery eruptions of volcanoes!" rather than

"Today we're going to learn about volcanoes so that you can do well on tomorrow's test." In particular, use of highly competitive grading or incentive systems should be avoided (Ames et al., 1977). When students perceive that there is only one standard of success in the classroom and that only a few people can achieve it, those who perceive their ability to be low will be likely to give up in advance (see Rosenholtz and Wilson, 1980; Gamoran, 1984; Cohen, 1986). Table 10.2 (from Ames and Archer, 1988) summarizes the differences in the achievement goals of students with mastery (learning) goals as opposed to those with performance goals.

Learned Helplessness

An extreme form of the motive to avoid failure is called **learned helplessness,** which is a perception that no matter what ones does, one is doomed to failure or ineffectuality: "Nothing I do matters" (Maier et al., 1969). In academic settings learned helplessness can be related to an internal, stable explanation for failure: "I fail because I'm dumb, and that means I will always fail." (Dweck, 1975; Diener and Dweck, 1978).

Learned helplessness can arise from inconsistent, unpredictable use of rewards and punishments by teachers, so that students feel that there is little they can do to be successful. It can be avoided or alleviated by giving students opportunities for success in small steps, immediate feedback, and, most important, consistent expectations and follow-through (see Seligman, 1981). Also, Dweck (1986) has found that focusing on learning goals as opposed to performance goals (see the previous section) can reduce helplessness, since learning goals can be attained to one degree or another by all students.

Achievement Motivation and Attribution Training

As noted earlier, motivation-related personality characteristics can be altered. They are altered in the natural course of things when something happens to change a student's environment, as when students who have vocational but not academic skills move

Learned Helplessness
The expectation, based on experience, that one's actions will ultimately lead to failure

TABLE 10.2

ACHIEVEMENT GOAL ANALYSIS OF CLASSROOM CLIMATE

Climate Dimensions	Mastery Goal	Performance Goal
Success defined as. . .	Improvement, progress	High grades, high normative performance
Value placed on. . .	Effort/learning	Normatively high ability
Reasons for satisfaction. . .	Working hard, challenge	Doing better than others
Teacher oriented toward. . .	How students are learning	How students are performing
View of errors/mistakes. . .	Part of learning	Anxiety eliciting
Focus of attention. . .	Process of learning	Own performance relative to others'
Reasons for effort. . .	Learning something new	High grades, performing better than others
Evaluation criteria. . .	Absolute, progress	Normative

From Ames and Archer, 1988, p. 261.

Expectancy-Valence Model
A theory that relates the probability and incentive value of success to motivation

from a comprehensive high school in which they were doing poorly to a vocational school in which they find success. Such students may break out of a long-standing pattern of external locus of control and low achievement motivation because of their newfound success experience. "Late bloomers," students who have difficulty in their earlier school years but take off in their later years, may also experience lasting changes in motivation-related personality characteristics, as may students who are initially successful in school but who later experience difficulty keeping up.

However, achievement motivation and attributions can also be changed directly by special programs designed for this purpose. For example, DeCharms (1984) worked with black children in inner-city elementary schools to improve their achievement motivation. The DeCharms program emphasized treating students as "origins" rather than "pawns," and teaching them to think of themselves as "origins"—that is to say, masters of their own fates. Students were taught to take personal responsibility for their actions, to choose realistic objectives and plan how to achieve those objectives, and so on. The children trained under the DeCharms program showed substantial increases in achievement as compared to an untrained control group. Trained students also attended school more regularly, and a follow-up study found that they were more likely than untrained students to graduate from high school.

Several studies have found that learned helplessness in the face of repeated failure can be modified by an attribution training program that emphasizes lack of effort, rather than lack of ability, as the cause of poor performance (McCombs, 1984; Fösterling, 1985). For example, Schunk (1982, 1983) found that students who received statements attributing their past successes and failures to effort performed better than did students who received no feedback. Dweck (1975) used a similar procedure and found that it reduced the tendency for failure avoiders to give up after experiencing failure.

■ **Stop and Think**

The motivation theories discussed thus far focus on students' needs, their sense of control over success and failure, and their goals. It was also suggested that experiences shape motivation. With this in mind, evaluate the degree to which these theories are relevant to younger school children versus older ones. Are the theories equally relevant to children of all ages?

Expectancy Theories of Motivation

Edwards (1954) and later Atkinson (1964) developed theories of motivation based on the following formula:

$$\underset{(M)}{\text{Motivation}} = \underset{(P_S)}{\substack{\text{Perceived} \\ \text{probability} \\ \text{of success}}} \times \underset{(I_S)}{\substack{\text{Incentive} \\ \text{value of} \\ \text{success}}}$$

The formula is called an expectancy model, or **expectancy-valence model,** because it largely depends on the person's expectations of reward (see Feather, 1982). What this theory implies is that people's motivation to achieve something depends on the product of their estimation of their chance of success (perceived probability of success, or P_S) and the value they place on success (incentive value of success, or I_S). For example, if Mark says, "I think I can make the honor roll if I try, and it is very important to me to make the honor roll," then he will probably work hard to make the honor roll. However, one very important aspect of the $M = P_S \times I_S$ formula is that it is *multiplicative*, meaning that if people believe that their probability of success is zero *or* if they do not value success, then their motivation will be zero. If Mark would like very much to make the honor roll but feels that he hasn't a prayer of doing so, he will be unmotivated. On the other hand, if his chances are actually good but he doesn't care about making the honor roll, he will also be unmotivated.

Atkinson (1964) added an important aspect to expectancy theory in pointing out that under certain circumstances an overly high probability of success can be detrimental to motivation. If Mark is very able, it may be so easy for him to make the honor roll that he need not do his best. Atkinson (1958) explained this by arguing that there is a relationship between probability of success and incentive value of success such that success in an easy task is not as valued as success in a difficult one. Therefore motivation should be at a maximum at *moderate* levels of probability of success. For example, two evenly matched tennis players will probably play their hardest. Unevenly matched players will not play as hard; the poor player may want very much to win but will have too low a probability of success to try very hard, while the better player will not value winning enough to exert his or her best effort.

Also, people will exert maximum effort to the degree that this increases their probability of success over and above what they could expect with a minimum effort. In the case of the unevenly matched tennis players, the better player is not motivated to do his or her best because winning is extremely likely even with minimal effort; and the poorer player is unmotivated because even with maximum effort, a win is unlikely (see Slavin, 1977a).

Importance of Expectancy Theory for Education.   The most important implication of expectancy theory for education is the commonsense proposition that tasks for students should be neither too easy nor too difficult. Atkinson's (1958) classic experiment illustrates this. In his study college sophomores were given a task and told either that (1) the highest scorer among twenty subjects would be rewarded ($P_S =$

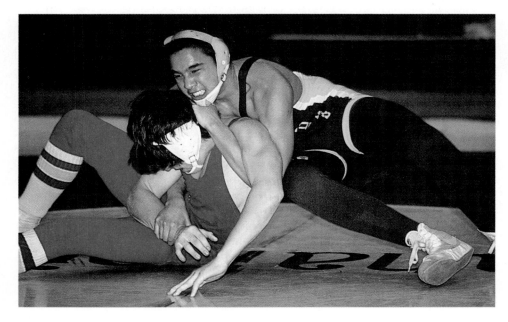

High school wrestling meets that pair competitors according to weight should, according to expectancy theory, lead to even matches and highly motivated competitors.

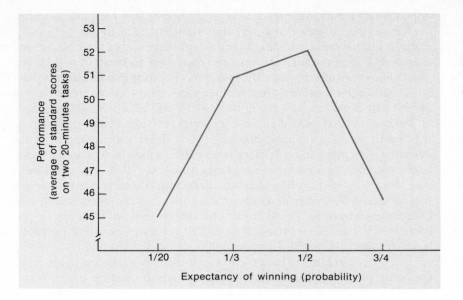

FIGURE 10.3

Expectancy Theory and Motivation

Motivation was found to be highest among college sophomores when the probability of success was neither very high nor very low.

Adapted from Atkinson, 1958, p. 91.

1/20); (2) the highest five scorers in twenty would be rewarded ($P_S = 5/20 = 1/4$); (3) the highest ten scorers would be rewarded ($P_S = 10/20 = 1/2$); or (4) the highest fifteen scorers would be rewarded ($P_S = 15/20 = 3/4$). The results are depicted in Figure 10.3.

As can be seen in Figure 10.3, the students who achieved the most were those who had moderate levels of probability of success (P_S). When the probability of success was too high or too low, achievement fell off. Only students who considered themselves high achievers, and thus thought they had a chance to be the first out of twenty, were likely to be motivated by a one-in-twenty chance to earn the reward if they exerted maximum effort. In contrast, effort made no difference to low achievers in the $P_S = 1/20$ condition, because even with maximum effort they had little hope of success. Similarly, the $P_S = 3/4$ condition was unmotivating for *high* achievers because they knew they would almost certainly be in the top fifteen even if they put out minimal effort. The best probability of success was found to be $P_S = 1/2$, where most students could see that they had a good chance to succeed if they exerted maximum effort, but also a good chance to fail if they did not (see Kukla, 1972b; Slavin, 1977a).

Expectancy theory could not be appropriately interpreted to suggest that questions asked in class or worksheet items should all be moderately difficult or should be answered correctly by only half of all students. An individual question or worksheet item does not usually call for effort, but rather for knowledge gained by previous effort. (Actually, current thought supports the use of relatively easy questions and items; see Chapter 8). Expectancy theory bears more on the criteria for success, as in grading. If some students feel that they are likely to get an A no matter what they do, then their motivation will not be at a maximum. Similarly, if some students feel certain to fail no matter what they do, their motivation will be minimal. Thus grading systems must be set up so that earning an A is difficult (but possible) for as many students as feasible, and earning a low grade is possible for students who exert little effort. Success must be within the reach, but not the easy reach, of all students. Note that establishing moderate, realistic probabilities of success is emphasized by most grouping methods, such as between- and within-class ability grouping, mastery learning, and individualized instruction (see Chapter 9), all of which seek, in different ways, to make success available to all students without making it too easy for some. Also, reward-for-improvement programs (discussed later in this chapter) directly seek to make success equally available (and equally difficult) for all students.

Teacher and Student Expectations

On the first day of class Mr. Erhard called roll. Soon he got to a name that looked familiar.

"Wayne Clements?"
"Here!"
"Do you have a brother named Victor?"
"Yes."
"I remember Victor. He was a terror. I'm going to keep my eye on you!"

As he neared the end of the roll, Mr. Erhard saw that several boys were starting to whisper to one another in the back of the room.

"Wayne! I asked the class to remain silent while I read the roll. Didn't you hear me? I knew I'd have to watch out for you!"

This vignette illustrates how teachers can establish expectations for their students, and how these expectations can be self-fulfilling. Mr. Erhard doesn't know it, but Wayne is generally a well-behaved, conscientious student, quite unlike his older brother, Victor. However, because of his experience with Victor, Mr. Erhard has expressed an expectation that he will have trouble with Wayne. When he saw several boys whispering, it was Wayne he singled out for blame, confirming for himself that Wayne was a troublemaker. After a few periods of this treatment, we might expect Wayne to actually begin playing the role Mr. Erhard has assigned to him.

Research on teachers' expectations for their students has generally found that students do (to some degree) live up to the expectations that their teachers express (directly or indirectly) for them (Brophy and Good, 1974). In one study Rosenthal and Jacobson (1968) tested elementary school students and then picked out a few in each class that they told the teachers were "late bloomers" who should do well this year. In fact, these students were chosen at random, and were of the same ability as their classmates. At the end of the year, when the students were tested again, those who had (falsely) been identified as "late bloomers" were found to have learned more than their classmates in the first and second grades, though this effect was not seen in grades 3–6. The Rosenthal and Jacobson study has been severely criticized (see Elashoff and Snow, 1971), but later evidence has generally supported the idea that teachers' expectations can affect students' behaviors (Cooper and Good, 1983), particularly in the younger grades and when teachers know relatively little about their students' actual achievement levels (Raudenbush, 1984).

What is the process by which teachers' expectations affect student performance? Good and Brophy have described a five-step process (Good and Brophy, 1973, p. 75):

1. The teacher expects specific behavior and achievement from particular students.

2. Because of these expectations, the teacher behaves differently toward different students.

3. This treatment by the teacher tells each student what behavior and achievement the teacher expects from him or her and affects the student's self-concept, achievement, motivation, and level of aspiration.

4. If this teacher treatment is consistent over time, and if the student does not actively resist or change it in some way, it will shape his or her achievement and behavior. High-expectation students will be led to achieve at high levels, but the achievement of low-expectation students will decline.

5. With time, the student's achievement and behavior will conform more and more closely to what was originally expected of him or her.

Communicating Positive Expectations. It is important for teachers to communicate to their students the expectation that they can learn (see Cooper and Tom, 1984). Obviously it is a bad idea to state the contrary, that a particular student cannot learn, and few teachers would explicitly do so. However, there are several implicit ways teachers can communicate positive expectations of their students (or avoid negative ones).

1. *Wait for students to respond:* Rowe (1974) and others have noted that teachers wait longer for answers from students for whom they have high expectations than from other students. Longer wait times may communicate high expectations and increase student achievement (Tobin, 1986, 1987).

2. *Avoid unnecessary achievement distinctions among students:* Grading should be a private matter between students and their teacher, not public information. Reading and math groups may be instructionally necessary in many classrooms (see Chapter 9), but teachers should avoid establishing a rigid hierarchy of groups, should treat the groups equally and respectfully, and should allow for moving a student out of one group and into another when appropriate (see Gamoran, 1984; Rosenholtz and Simpson, 1984). Students usually know who is good in school and who is not, but teachers can still successfully communicate the expectation that all students, not just the most able ones, are capable of learning.

3. *Treat all students equally:* Call on low-achieving students as often as on the high achievers, and spend equal amounts of time with them. In particular, guard against bias. Research finds that teachers often unwittingly hold lower expectations for black students (Baron et al., 1985) and for girls (Good and Findley, 1985).

Anxiety

Anxiety is a constant companion of education. Every student feels some anxiety at some time while in school, but for certain students anxiety seriously inhibits learning or performance, particularly on tests.

The main source of anxiety in school is the fear of failure, and with it, loss of self-esteem (Hill and Wigfield, 1984). Low achievers are particularly likely to feel anxious in school, but they are by no means the only ones; we all know very able, high-achieving students who are also very anxious, terrified to be less than perfect on any school task.

Anxiety can block school performance in several ways (Tobias, 1985). Anxious students may have difficulty learning in the first place; they may have difficulty using or transferring knowledge they do have, and they may have difficulty demonstrating their knowledge on tests. Anxious students are likely to be overly self-conscious in performance settings, which distracts attention from the task at hand (Wine, 1980).

One particularly common form of debilitating anxiety is "math phobia." Many students (and adults) simply freeze up when given math problems, particularly word problems. Girls are especially likely to suffer from serious math anxiety (Richardson and Woolfolk, 1980), at least in part because girls, particularly in adolescence, feel less able in math than boys (Parsons et al., 1982).

There are many strategies teachers can apply to reduce the negative impact of anxiety on learning and performance. Clearly, creating a classroom climate that is accepting, comfortable, and noncompetitive helps. Giving students opportunities to correct errors or improve their work before handing it in also helps anxious children, as does providing clear, unambiguous instructions. In testing situations, teachers can do many things to help anxious students to do their best. One is to avoid time pressure, to give students plenty of time to complete a test and check their work (Hill and Eaton, 1977). Tests that begin with easy problems and only gradually introduce more difficult ones are better for anxious students, and tests with standard, simple answer formats help such students (Phillips et al., 1980).

Test-anxious children can be trained in test-taking skills, and this can have a positive impact on their test performance (Hill and Horton, 1985). Table 10.3 shows some of the key test-taking skills taught in the Hill and Horton study.

■ **Stop and Think**

Did your teachers make success available to all the students in your classes? Recall incidents in which they explicitly did or did not.

INCENTIVES FOR LEARNING

Learning takes work. Euclid, the ancient Greek mathematician who wrote the first geometry textbook, was asked by his king if there were any shortcuts he could use to learn geometry, since he was a very busy man. "I'm sorry," Euclid replied, "but there is no royal road to geometry." The same is true of every other subject: students get out of any course of study only what they put into it.

The remainder of this chapter discusses the means by which students can be motivated to exert the efforts needed to learn. First, the issue of intrinsic motivation—the motivational value of the content itself—is presented. Extrinsic motivation—the use of praise, feedback, and incentives to motivate students to do their best—is then discussed.

Also in this section are specific strategies for enhancing student motivation and suggestions for solving motivational problems common in classrooms, including reward-for-improvement incentive systems and cooperative learning methods.

Many students find classes such as art, intrinsically motivating. In such cases, extrinsic incentives may not be needed to encourage learning.

Intrinsic and Extrinsic Motivation

Sometimes a course of study is so fascinating and useful to students that they are willing to do the work required to learn the material with no incentive other than the interest level of the material itself. For example, many students would gladly take auto mechanics or photography courses and work hard in them, even if they offered no

TABLE 10.3

EXAMPLES OF TEST-TAKING SKILLS AND MOTIVATIONAL DISPOSITIONS

1. General test skills and knowledge:

    a. Be comfortable and sit where you can write easily.

    b. Pay attention when the teacher talks.

    c. The teacher can help you understand how to work on the test, but can't tell you the answer to a problem on the test.

    d. Taking tests is something we learn to do in school.

2. Positive motivation—doing your best:

    a. All I ask is that you do your best. I will be really pleased if you try to do your best.

    b. If you finish a section before time is up, go back and check your answers. Don't disturb others; instead, work quietly at your desk.

    c. Before we begin, remember to carefully listen to me, be quiet, take a deep breath, and feel relaxed.

3. Positive motivation—expectancy reassurance:

    a. Some tests have some very hard problems. Don't worry if you can't do some problems.

    b. It's OK if you aren't sure what the right answer is. Choose the answer you think is best. It's OK to guess.

    c. If you work hard but don't finish a test, don't worry about it! The most important thing to me is that you try hard and do as well as you can. I know you'll do a good job if you try!

4. Test strategy and problem-solving skills:

    a. There is only *one* best answer.

    b. Do what you know first. If you can't answer a problem or it's taking a lot of time move on to the next one. You can come back later if you have time.

    c. Don't rush. If you work *too fast*, you can make careless errors. You have to work carefully.

    d. Don't work too slowly. Do the problems at a moderate rate.

    e. Pay close attention to your work.

    f. Keep track of where you are working on the page by keeping one hand on this spot.

SOURCE: Adapted from Hill and Wigfield, 1984, p. 123.

credit or grades. For these students, the favorite subject itself has enough **intrinsic incentive** value to motivate them to learn. Other students love to learn about insects or dinosaurs or famous people in history, and need little encouragement or reward to do the work necessary to become knowledgeable about their favorite topics.

However, much of what must be learned in school is not inherently interesting or useful to most students in the short run. Students receive about 900 hours of instruction every year, and it is unrealistic to expect that intrinsic interest alone will keep them enthusiastically working day in and day out. For this reason, schools apply a variety of **extrinsic incentives,** reinforcers for learning that are not inherent in the material being learned. Extrinsic reinforcers may range from praise to grades to recognition to prizes or other rewards.

Do Extrinsic Rewards Destroy Intrinsic Motivation? An important question in research on motivation concerns whether or not the providing of extrinsic rewards diminishes intrinsic interest in an activity. In a classic experiment exploring this topic,

Lepper et al. (1973) gave preschoolers an opportunity to draw with felt-tipped markers, which many of them did quite enthusiastically. Then the researchers randomly divided the children into three groups: one was told they would receive a reward for drawing a picture for a visitor (a "Good Player Award"); one was given the same reward as a surprise (not dependent on their drawing); and one received no reward. Over the next four days observers recorded the free-play activities of the children. Those who had received a reward for drawing spent about half as much time drawing with felt-tipped markers as those who had received the "surprise" reward and those who had gotten no reward. The authors suggested that promising extrinsic rewards for an activity that is intrinsically interesting may undermine intrinsic interest by inducing children to expect a reward for doing what they had previously done for nothing. In a later study (Greene and Lepper, 1974) it was found that just telling children they would be watched (through a one-way mirror) had an "undermining" effect similar to that found for a promised reward.

In understanding the results of these studies it is important to recall the conditions of the research. The students chosen for the studies were ones who showed an intrinsic interest in using marking pens; those who did not were excluded from the experiments. Also, drawing with felt-tip pens does not resemble most school tasks. Many children love to draw at home, but few, even those most interested in school subjects, would independently study grammar and punctuation, work math problems, or learn the valences of chemical elements. Further, our most creative and self-motivated scientists, for example, were heavily reinforced as students with grades, science fair prizes, and scholarships for doing science, and virtually all successful artists have been reinforced at some point for engaging in artistic activities. This reinforcement certainly did not undermine their intrinsic interest. Research on older students doing more school-like tasks has generally failed to replicate the results of the Lepper et al. (1973) experiment (Pittman et al, 1983). In fact, the use of rewards sometimes *increases* intrinsic motivation, especially when rewards are contingent on the quality of performance rather than on mere participation in an activity (Bates, 1979; Lepper, 1983), when the task in question is not very interesting (Morgan, 1984), or when the rewards are social (for example, praise) rather than material (Deci, 1975).

The research on the effects of extrinsic rewards on intrinsic motivation does counsel caution in the use of material rewards for intrinsically interesting tasks. Teachers should attempt to make everything they teach as intrinsically interesting as possible, and should avoid handing out material rewards when they are unnecessary, but they should not refrain from using extrinsic rewards when they *are* needed (Lepper, 1983). For example, rewarding young children for doing art projects would be inappropriate, since these activities are usually intrinsically interesting to them, but extrinsic reinforcers are more likely to be needed for teaching grammar skills to junior high school students.

Enhancing Intrinsic Motivation

Classroom instruction must seek to enhance intrinsic motivation as much as possible. This simply means that teachers must try to get their students interested in the material they are presenting, and then present it in an appealing way that both satisfies and increases students' curiosity about the material itself. A discussion of some means of doing this follows (also see Brophy, 1987; Malone and Lepper, 1988; Corno and Rohrkemper, 1985).

Whetting Students' Appetites for Knowledge. As suggested in Chapter 8, it is important to convince students of the importance and interest level of material about to be presented. This is the idea behind the use of an instructional set to begin a lesson. The instructional set relates the lesson about to be presented to students' interests, and if possible shows how the knowledge to be gained will be useful to students. For example, intrinsic motivation to learn a lesson on percents might be increased by introducing the lesson as follows:

"Today we will begin a lesson on percents. Percents are important in our daily lives. For example, when you buy something at the store and a salesperson figures the sales tax, he or she is using percents. When we leave a tip for a waiter or waitress, we use percents. We often hear in the news things like, 'Prices rose seven percent last year.' In a few years many of you will have summer jobs, and if they involve handling money, you'll probably be using percents all the time."

Similarly, a lesson on microorganisms might begin with a statement about the billions of microorganisms that live in and on the human body. A lesson on the settlement of the American Southwest might begin:

"Do you ever wonder why so many cities and towns in California, Arizona, New Mexico, and Texas have Spanish names? San Francisco means 'St. Francis,' Los Angeles means 'The Angels,' and San Antonio means 'St. Anthony.' The literal meaning of Sierra Nevada is 'Snowy Saws,' from the sawtooth shape of the mountains.

"These place names tell us that the American Southwest was settled by people from Spain. This week we will be learning about the Spanish discovery and settlement of this region of our country."

Of course, the purpose of these instructional sets is to arouse student curiosity about the lesson to come, thereby enhancing intrinsic motivation to learn the material.

Another way to enhance students' intrinsic interest is to give them some choice over what they will study or how they will study it (Stipek, 1988).

Maintaining Curiosity. A skillful teacher uses a variety of means to further arouse or maintain curiosity in the course of the lesson. Science teachers, for instance, often use demonstrations that surprise or baffle students and induce them to want to understand why. A floating dime makes students curious about the surface tension of liquids. "Burning" a dollar bill covered with an alcohol-water solution (without harming the dollar bill) certainly increases curiosity about the heat of combustion. Less dramatically, the "subtraction with renaming" lesson described in Chapter 8 got students comfortable with subtracting such numbers as $47 - 3$ and $56 - 23$, but then stumped them with $13 - 5$. Students were shocked out of a comfortable routine and forced to look at the problem in a new way.

Berlyne (1965) discussed the concept of "epistemic curiosity," behavior aimed at acquiring knowledge to master and understand the environment. He hypothesized that epistemic curiosity results from conceptual conflict, as when new information appears to contradict earlier understandings. Berlyne suggests the deliberate use of surprise, doubt, perplexity, bafflement, and contradiction as means of arousing epistemic curiosity. Two examples he gives are teaching about how plants use chlorophyll to carry out photosynthesis, and then introducing the problem of fungi, which do not need sunlight; and teaching about latitude and longitude, and then asking students how they would estimate their location in the middle of the desert.

Interesting and Varied Presentation Modes. The intrinsic motivation to learn something is enhanced by the use of interesting materials (Shirey and Reynolds, 1988), as well as by variety in mode of presentation. For example, student interest in a subject may be maintained by alternating use of films, guest speakers, demonstrations, and so on, although use of each resource must be carefully planned to be sure it focuses on the course objectives and complements the other activities. Use of computers can enhance the intrinsic motivation of most students to learn (Lepper, 1985).

Games and Simulations. One excellent means of increasing interest in a subject is to use games or simulations. A simulation is an exercise in which students take on roles and engage in activities appropriate to those roles. For example, the "American Government Simulation Series" (Stitelman and Coplin, 1969) simulates many aspects of government, such as having students take roles as legislators who must negotiate and trade votes to satisfy their constituents' interests. In "Ghetto" (Toll, 1970) students take on roles as poor people living in the inner city, and must decide how to invest their time in various activities to try to improve their lot. In "Economic System" (Coleman and Harris, 1969) students become economic actors (farmers, producers, consumers) and run a minieconomy. Many simulations are commercially available, including an increasing number designed for use on microcomputers. (For lists and reviews of simulations and games that are commercially available, see Horn and Cleaves, 1980.) However, creative teachers have long used simulations they designed themselves. For example, teachers can have students write their own newspaper; design, manufacture, and market a product; or set up and run a bank.

The advantage of simulations is that they allow students to learn about a subject from the inside. Although research on use of simulations (see Greenblat, 1982; Van

Sickle, 1986) finds that they are generally little or no more effective than traditional instruction for teaching facts and concepts, studies do consistently find that simulations increase students' interest, motivation, and affective learning (Dukes and Seidner, 1978). They certainly impart a different affective knowledge of a subject. For example, it would be easy to teach a lesson about the problems of life in the ghetto, after which students could perhaps pass a test on the main issues. But students who have also had the simulated experience of trying to get an education, stay out of trouble, earn a living, and survive under the very difficult circumstances of the ghetto probably gain a far greater understanding and empathy, though these are difficult to measure.

Nonsimulation games can also increase motivation to learn a given subject. The "spelling bee" is a popular example of a nonsimulation game. Teams-Games-Tournament, or TGT (DeVries and Slavin, 1978), uses games that can be adapted to any subject. There are many math games (see, for example, Crescimbeni, 1965; Allen, 1969). Team games are usually better than individual games; they provide an opportunity for teammates to help one another, and avoid one problem of individual games, which is that more able students consistently win. If all students are put on mixed-ability teams, all have a good chance of success (see Slavin, 1990).

Goal Setting.   One fundamental principle of motivation is that people work harder for goals they themselves set than for goals set for them by others. Klausmeier et al. (1975) developed and evaluated a program that capitalizes on this principle. The program, called Individually Guided Motivation, or IGM, involves having students meet on a regular basis with their teachers to set specific, measurable goals for the week. For example, students might set a minimum number of books they expect to read at home, or a score they expect to attain on an upcoming quiz. At the next goal-setting conference the teacher would discuss student attainment of (or failure to attain) goals, and set new goals for the following week. During these meetings the teacher would help students learn to set ambitious but not unrealistic goals, and would praise them for setting and then achieving their goals.

Research on IGM has found that this method can be effective in increasing student achievement in areas in which goals were set (see Klausmeier et al., 1975).

Incentives for Learning: Basic Principles

While teachers must always try to enhance students' intrinsic motivation to learn academic materials, they must at the same time be concerned about incentives for learning. Not every subject is intrinsically interesting to all students, and students must be motivated to do the hard work necessary to master difficult subjects. The following sections discuss a variety of incentives that can be applied to motivate students to learn academic materials.

Clear Expectations.   Students need to know exactly what they are supposed to do, how they will be evaluated, and what the consequences of success will be. Often student failures on particular tasks stem from confusion about what they are being asked to do (see Brophy, 1982; L. Anderson et al., 1985).

Communicating clear expectations is important when introducing assignments. For example, a teacher might introduce a writing assignment as follows:

"Today, I'd like you all to write a composition about what Thomas Jefferson would think of government in the United States today. I expect your compositions to be about two pages long, and to compare and contrast the plan of government laid out by the founding fathers with the way government actually operates today. Your compositions will be graded on the basis of your ability to describe similarities and differences between the structure and function of the U.S. government in Thomas Jefferson's time and today, as well as on the originality and clarity of your writing. This will be an important part of your six weeks' grade, so I expect you to do your best!"

Note that the teacher is clear about what students are to write, how much material is expected, how the work will be evaluated, and how important the work will be for the students' grades. This clarity assures students that efforts directed at writing a good composition will pay off—in this case, in terms of grades. If the teacher had just said, "I'd like you all to write a composition about what Thomas Jefferson would think about government in the United States today," students might write the wrong thing, write too much or too little, or perhaps emphasize the if-Jefferson-were-alive-today aspect of the assignment rather than the comparative-government aspect. Further, they would be unsure how much importance the teacher intended to place on the mechanics of the composition as compared to its content. Finally, they would have no way of knowing how their efforts would pay off, since the teacher gave no indication of how much emphasis would be given to the compositions in computing grades.

Clarity and Immediacy of Feedback. Another very important requirement for classroom motivation is that feedback on student performance be clear, tied directly to student performance, and occur as soon as possible after student performance. This is important for all students, but especially for young ones. For example, praise for a job well done should specify what the student did well:

"Good work! I like the way you used the guide words in the dictionary to find the words on your worksheet."

"I like that answer. It shows you've been thinking about what I've been saying."

"This is an excellent essay. It started with a statement of the argument you were going to make and then supported the argument with relevant information. I also like the care you took with punctuation and word usage."

Specific feedback is both informative and motivational. It tells students what they did right, so that they will know what to do in the future, and helps give them an effort-based attribution for success ("You succeeded because you worked hard"). In contrast, if students are praised or receive a good grade without any explanation, they are unlikely to learn from the feedback what to do next time to be successful, and may form an ability attribution ("I succeeded because I'm smart") or an external attribution ("I must have succeeded because the teacher likes me, the task was easy, or I lucked out"). As noted earlier in this chapter, effort attributions are most conducive to continuing motivation. Similarly, feedback about mistakes or failures can add to motivation if it focuses only on the performance itself (not on student's general abilities) and if it is alternated with success feedback (see Clifford, 1984).

Immediacy. Immediacy of feedback is also very important (Kulik and Kulik, 1988). If students take a quiz on Monday and don't receive any feedback on it until Friday,

1. How can a teacher encourage a sense of industry in your students?

Richard Thorne, Jr., a sixth-grade teacher in Stoughton, Mass., writes:

By setting a proper example. All pupil work should be corrected and returned the same day or the next day. The teacher should also stress the importance of all lessons.

Curt Fulton, a fifth-grade teacher in Wallkill, N.Y., says:

To answer this question, I would pose another question: How does society encourage these same traits in adults? Most would answer by saying that adequate, appropriate rewards encourage adults to work hard—that is, a paycheck for some, a sense of satisfaction for a job well done for others. As adults, we perform certain tasks with the expectation of some kind of reward. (I don't know of many teachers who would do what they do for free!) We expect our students to perform certain tasks or behaviors, but we forget the reward. We forget the follow-through. It doesn't have to be a "paycheck": it can be some tangible reward that means something to the students, such as free time, parties, or just a friendly smile from the teacher.

2. How would you try to motivate a student who seemed imprisoned by a fear of failure?

Cheryl Groninger, a high school teacher in Annandale, N.J.:

I believe the key to helping a student who has a fear of failure is to provide situations in which the student can experience success. A start can be made by working with the student on an area in which he or she is having difficulty. By guiding the student through the solution of a problem with a series of leading questions, the teacher can give the student the experience of being successful in solving a problem. After a number of such experiences, the student gains self-confidence and will often proceed unaided.

Beth Ohlsson, who teaches in Frederick, Md.:

In these kinds of situations, I do lots of private coaching and hand holding. Mostly, such students need to know I care, and that I'll be there for them even if they fall.

3. How do you guard against carrying unfounded good or bad impressions of students?

Several teachers said they do not look at comments made by students' previous teachers until six weeks, two months, or longer into the school year. For instance, Paul Hashem, a sixth-grade teacher in Lackawanna, N.Y., writes:

I *do not* read the permanent record cards—except for the health card—until the first marking period, at ten weeks. Also, I make it a point *never* to discuss children in a casual, nonprofessional way with my colleagues. Every new school year I have developed a mind-set that goes something like this: "Okay now, every single child in this class is an individual who will react to me differently than to past teachers because of, among other things, personality differences. *Each* child has some unique and positive qualities as well as some undesirable ones, but *all* are in equal need of my talents, love, and understanding, so make an all-out effort to be fair and consistent with all of the children." Also, during the first week of school I have a discussion with the class in which I assure them that this year is a new beginning and we all have an opportunity to start fresh and leave bad habits behind. *No students* are made to feel that their past will automatically come to haunt them.

Anna Grauer, a fifth-grade teacher in Lessport, Pa., made the following comments about teacher expectations:

I have been a teacher long enough to know that children can change from grade to grade. Very often a child suddenly develops an interest in learning, especially a child who was bored and now has more difficult concepts to learn.

Praise that is specific, credible, and contingent on appropriate behavior can be used by teachers to reinforce desired student behavior.

the informational and motivational value of the feedback will be diminished. First, if they made errors on the quiz, they may continue making similar errors all week that might have been averted by feedback on the quiz performance. Second, a long delay between behavior and consequence confuses the relationship between them (see Chapter 4). Young students, especially, may have little idea why they received a particular grade if the performance on which the grade is based took place several days earlier.

Frequency of Assessment, Feedback, and Reward.   Feedback and rewards must be delivered frequently to students to maintain their best efforts. For example, it is unrealistic to expect most students to work hard for six or nine weeks in hope of improving their grade unless they receive frequent feedback. Research in the behavioral learning theories tradition (for example, Bandura, 1969) has established that no matter how powerful a reward is, it may have little impact on behavior if it is given infrequently; small frequent rewards are more effective incentives than large infrequent ones.

Research on frequency of testing has generally found that it is a good idea to give frequent brief quizzes to assess student progress rather than infrequent long tests (Peckham and Roe, 1977; Kjur et al., 1986). It also points up the importance of asking many questions in class, so that student can gain information about their own level of understanding and can receive reinforcement (praise, recognition) for paying attention to lessons.

Value of Rewards.   Expectancy theories of motivation, discussed earlier in this chapter, hold that motivation is a product of the value an individual attaches to success

Individual Learning Expectations

The idea behind ILE is to recognize students for doing better than they have done in the past, for steadily increasing in performance until they are producing excellent work all the time. In this way, all students have an opportunity to earn recognition for academic work simply by doing their best.

LESSONS AND QUIZZES

Instruction is done as described in Chapter 8.

Students should take at least one short quiz per week in any subject(s) in which ILE is being used. Ten items are usually sufficient. Quizzes should be scored in class immediately after being given by having students exchange papers and then having the teacher read the answers. Let students see their own papers, discuss any frequently missed items, and then pass their papers in.

INITIAL BASE SCORES

Base scores represent students' average scores on past quizzes. If you are starting ILE at the beginning of the year, assign initial base scores according to students' grades in the same subjects last year, as shown in the chart on the next page.

Computing Initial Base Scores

Last Year's Grade	Initial Base Score
A	90
A− or B+	85
B	80
B− or C+	75
C	70
C− or D+	65
F	60

If your school uses percentages rather than grades, you may use last year's average as this year's base score. If you are starting to use ILE after you have given some quizzes in your class, use the average percent correct on those quizzes to compute an initial base score.

IMPROVEMENT POINTS

Every time you give a quiz, compare student's quiz scores with their base scores, and give students improvement points as shown in the chart on the next page.

Note that improvement points are given in relationship to past performance. A student who has averaged 75 on previous quizzes and gets an 80 would get the same improvement points (2) as a student who has averaged 90 and gets a 95 this week. However, there is no danger of students "topping out" with too high a base score, since all students get the maximum score (3 improvement points) if they get a perfect paper, regardless of their base score.

FEEDBACK TO STUDENTS

Improvement points should be marked on students' quizzes and returned to them as soon as possible.

In addition, every two weeks, students' improvement scores should be averaged for all quizzes given during that period. Then attractive certificates or other small rewards should be given to students who averaged at least two improvement points. The first time you do this, also send home a note to parents explaining what the certificates are for. Parents are the key to the success of ILE. If they value reports of their children's improvement, and if the teacher emphasizes progress and improvement, then students will value improvement too.

and the individual's estimate of the likelihood of success (see Atkinson and Birch, 1978). One implication of this is that incentives used with students must be valued by them. Some students are not particularly interested in teacher praise or grades, but may value notes home to their parents, a little extra recess time, or a special privilege in the classroom. Practical rewards for use in the classroom are discussed later in this chapter.

Availability of Rewards. Another implication of expectancy theory is that all students must have a chance to be rewarded if they do their best, but no student

Computing Improvement Points

Quiz Score	Improvement Points	Comments
5 or more points below base score	0	"You can do better!"
4 points below to 4 points above base score	1	"About average for you—but you can do better."
5–9 points above base score	2	"Better than your average—good work."
10 or more points above base score or perfect score (regardless of base score)	3	"Super! Much better than average!"

Base Score

<----- — — — — —| |—- — — — — —|— — — — — —| |—- — — —| |— — — — — — —>
           −5 −4   +4 +5   +9 +10 or 100%

| 0 Improvement points | 1 Improvement point | 1 Improvement points | 3 Improvement points |

RECOMPUTING BASE SCORES

At the end of each marking period, average the percent correct scores on each quiz with the past average, and compute a new base score (drop any fraction when you divide). For example, let's say Zelda's past average was 84, and her quiz scores were 90, 95, and 90. You would compute her new base score as follows:

Example of Recomputing Base Scores

   84—Old base score

\+ 90—Quiz 1 score (2 improvement points)

\+ 95—Quiz 2 score (3 improvement points)

\+ 90—Quiz 3 score (2 improvement points)

359/4 = 89¾ (drop fraction) = 89—New base score

Since Zelda's quiz scores were all above her base score (84), her base score increases to 89. Next time it will be somewhat harder for her to earn improvement points.

IMPROVEMENT POINTS AND GRADES

When you give grades, also report average improvement points for the marking period. In general, high improvement points should be reflected in higher grades. For example, a student who averaged two or more might increase from a C to a B or a B to an A. Again, communication to students (and their parents) that effort and improvement are important is critical in making the improvement point system effective.

should have an easy time achieving the maximum reward. This principle is violated by traditional grading practices because some students find it easy to earn A's and B's, while others feel they have little chance of academic success no matter what they do. In this circumstance neither high achievers nor low achievers are likely to exert their best efforts. This is one reason that it is important to reward students for effort, for doing better than they have done in the past, or for making progress, rather than only for getting a high score. Not all students are equally capable of achieving a high score, but all *are* equally capable of exerting effort, exceeding their own past record, or making progress, so these are often better, more equally available criteria for reward.

TABLE 10.4

EXAMPLES OF CLASSROOM REWARDS

Teachers can use many types of rewards to motivate students. Some are used daily, others may be once-in-a-lifetime rewards.

Rewards

Daily	Weekly	Monthly	Yearly	Multiyear
Praise/attention	Quiz grades	Quarter/six-week grades	Final grades	Access to desired activities
Feedback	Positive letter to parents		Honor role/other prizes	Graduation
Stars/smilies	Recognition		Promotion to next grade	College entry
Interest level of lesson	Special privileges			Good job

Extrinsic Motivators

Classroom Rewards. Table 10.4 lists examples of the kinds of rewards teachers have traditionally used in classrooms to maintain student motivation to learn.

Note that some types of rewards are used frequently, while others are used infrequently. For example, praise and recognition are the primary rewards used during daily lessons. They are often used more to influence student attentiveness, effort, and behavior than to reward actual learning performance. On the other hand, grades are more often used to evaluate student learning performance as well as to reward students for learning. Short-term rewards are often "backed up" by longer-term ones. A student may value praise, stars, or "smilies" for daily efforts because they predict success in grades, which themselves may be of value in part because they predict passing from grade to grade, access to desired activities (as when a minimum grade-point average is needed to participate in intramural sports or to gain entry to vocational programs), and ultimately graduation and entry to higher education. Of course, it would be absurd to tell a third-grader to pay attention in class today because it will help him or her get into college and get a good job. Effective short-term rewards take long-term objectives and break them down into attainable milestones.

The following sections discuss incentives used by teachers to enhance student motivation to learn.

Praise. Praise serves many purposes in classroom instruction, but is primarily used to reinforce appropriate behaviors and to give feedback to students on what they are doing right. Overall, it is a good idea to use praise frequently, especially with young children and in classrooms with many low-achieving students (Brophy, 1981). However, what is more important than the *amount* of praise given is the *way* it is given (Nafpaktitis et al., 1985). O'Leary and O'Leary (1977) hold that praise is effective as a classroom motivator to the extent that it is contingent, specific, and credible. By contingent is meant that praise must depend on student performance of well-defined behaviors. For example, if a teacher says, "I'd like you all to open your books to page 279 and work problems 1–10," then praise would be given only to those students who follow directions. Praise should be given only for right answers and appropriate behaviors.

By specificity is meant that the teacher praises students for specific behaviors, not for general "goodness." For example, a teacher might say, "Susan, I'm glad you followed my directions to start work on your composition," rather than "Susan, you're doing great!"

When praise is credible, it is given sincerely for good work. Brophy (1981) notes that when teachers praise low-achieving or disruptive students for good work, they often contradict their words with tone, posture, or other nonverbal cues.

Madsen et al. (1968) present a good summary of the use of contingent, specific, credible praise:

> Give praise and attention to behaviors which facilitate learning. Tell the child what he is being praised for. Try to reinforce behaviors incompatible with those you wish to decrease.

The last part of this statement is important: "Try to reinforce behaviors incompatible with those you wish to decrease." It means, for example, that if you want students to stop getting out of their seats without permission, you should praise them for staying in their seats (which is, of course, incompatible with wandering around). Brophy (1981) lists characteristics of effective and ineffective praise; this list appears in Table 10.5.

In addition to contingency, specificity, and credibility, Brophy's list includes several particularly important principles that reinforce topics discussed earlier in this chapter. For example, Prescriptions 7 and 8 emphasize that praise should be given for good performance relative to a student's usual level of performance. That is, students who usually do well should not be praised for a merely average performance, but students who usually do less well should be praised when they do better. This relates to the principle of accessibility of reward discussed earlier in this chapter; rewards

---

TABLE 10.5

GUIDELINES FOR EFFECTIVE PRAISE

If used properly, praise can be an effective motivator in classroom situations.

Effective Praise	Ineffective Praise
1. Is delivered contingently	1. Is delivered randomly or unsystematically
2. Specifies the particulars of the accomplishment	2. Is restricted to global positive reactions
3. Shows spontaneity, variety, and other signs of credibility; suggests clear attention to the student's accomplishment	3. Shows a bland uniformity, which suggests a conditioned response made with minimal attention
4. Rewards attainment of specified performance criteria (which can include effort criteria, however)	4. Rewards mere participation, without consideration of performance processes or outcomes
5. Provides information to students about their competence or the value of their accomplishments	5. Provides no information at all or gives students information about their status
6. Orients students towards better appreciation of their own task-related behavior and thinking about problem solving	6. Orients students toward comparing themselves with others and thinking about competing
7. Uses students' own prior accomplishments as the context for describing present accomplishments	7. Uses the accomplishments of peers as the context for describing students' present accomplishments
8. Is given in recognition of noteworthy effort or success at difficult tasks (for *this* student)	8. Is given without regard to the effort expended or the meaning of the accomplishment (for *this* student)
9. Attributes success to effort and ability, implying that similar successes can be expected in the future	9. Attributes success to ability alone or to external factors such as luck or easy task
10. Focuses students' attention on their own task-relevant behavior	10. Focuses students' attention on the teacher as an external authority figure who is manipulating them
11. Fosters appreciation of and desirable attributions about task-relevant behavior after the process is completed	11. Intrudes into the ongoing process, distracting attention from task-relevant behavior

Source: Adapted from Brophy, 1981, p. 26.

An effective cooperative learning method is called Student Teams—Achievement Divisions, or STAD (Slavin, 1986, 1990). STAD consists of a regular cycle of teaching, cooperative study in mixed-ability teams, and quiz, with recognition or other rewards provided to teams whose members most exceed their own past records. A guide to the use of STAD follows (see Slavin, 1986, 1990, for more complete descriptions of this and other cooperative learning methods).

PREPARING TO TEACH

Assign students to teams of four or five members each. Four is preferable; make five-member teams only if the class is not divisible by four. To assign the students, rank them from top to bottom on some measure of academic performance (for example, past grades, test scores) and divide the ranked list into quarters, with any extra students in the middle quarters. Then put one student from each quarter on each team, making sure that the teams are well balanced in sex and ethnicity. Extra (middle) students may become fifth members of teams.

Make a worksheet and a short quiz for each unit you plan to teach.

SCHEDULE OF ACTIVITIES

STAD consists of a regular cycle of instructional activities, as follows (see Figure 10.4 on next page):

- *—Teach:* Present the lesson.
- *—Team study:* Students work on worksheets in their teams to master the material.
- *—Test:* Students take individual quizzes.
- *—Team recognition:* Team scores are computed on the basis of team members' improvement scores, and a class newsletter or bulletin board recognizes high-scoring teams.

Descriptions of these activities follow.

TEACHING

Each lesson in STAD begins with a class lesson. Follow the guidelines in Chapter 8 for lesson presentation. The lesson should take one or two class periods.

TEAM STUDY

During team study (one to two class periods) the team members' tasks are to master the material you presented in your lesson and to help their teammates master the material. Students have worksheets and answer sheets they can use to practice the skill being taught and to assess themselves and their teammates. Only two copies of the worksheets and answer sheets are given to each team, to force teammates to work together, but if some students prefer to work alone or want their own copies, you may make additional copies available.

- When you introduce STAD to your class, read off team assignments.

- Have teammates move their desks together or move to team tables, and allow students about ten minutes to decide on a team name.

- Hand out worksheets and answer sheets (two of each per team).

- Tell students on each team to work in pairs or threes. If they are working problems (as in math), each student in a pair or threesome should work the problem, and then check with his or her partner(s). If anyone missed a question, that student's teammates have a responsibility to explain it. If students are working on short-answer questions, they may quiz each other, with partners taking turns holding the answer sheet or attempting to answer the questions.

- Emphasize to students that they are not finished studying until they are sure all their teammates will make 100 percent on the quiz.

- Make sure that students understand that the worksheets are for studying—not for filling out and handing in. That is why it is important for students to have the answer sheets to check themselves and their teammates as they study.

- Have students explain answers to one another instead of just checking each other against the answer sheet.

- When students have questions, have them ask a teammate before asking you.

- While students are working in teams, circulate through the class, praising teams that are working well and sitting in with each team to hear how they are doing.

TEST

Distribute the quiz and give students adequate time to complete it. Do not let students work together on the quiz; at this point they must show what they have learned as individuals. Have students move their desks apart if this is possible.

Either allow students to exchange papers with members of other teams, or collect the quizzes to score after class.

FIGURING INDIVIDUAL AND TEAM SCORES

Team scores in STAD are based on team members' *improvements* over their own past records.

As soon as possible after each quiz you should compute individual improvement scores (using the ILE system described earlier in this chapter) and team scores, and write a class newsletter (or prepare a class bulletin board) to announce the team scores. If at all possible, the announcement of team scores should be made in the first period after the quiz. This makes the connection between doing well and receiving recognition clear to students, which increases their motivation to do their best.

Compute team scores by adding up the improvement points earned by the team members and dividing the sum by the number of team members present on the day of the quiz.

Recognizing Team Accomplishments

As soon as you have calculated points for each student and figured team scores, you should provide some sort of recognition to any teams that averaged two improvement points or more. You might write a newsletter to recognize successful teams, give certificates to team members, or prepare a bulletin board display. It is important to help students value team success. Your own enthusiasm about team scores will help. If you give more than one quiz in a week, combine the quiz results into a single weekly score.

Changing Teams

After five or six weeks of STAD, reassign students to new teams. This gives students who were on low-scoring teams a new chance, allows students to work with other classmates, and keeps the program fresh.

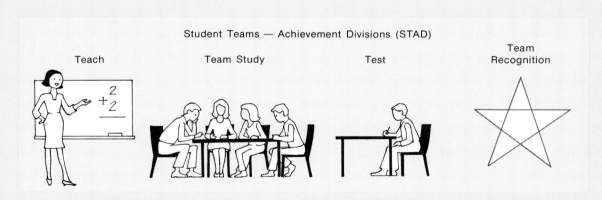

Student Teams — Achievement Divisions (STAD)

Teach   Team Study   Test   Team Recognition

FIGURE 10.4

Basic Schedule of Activities for STAD

Cooperative learning strategies can increase student achievement and improve interpersonal relationships among students. One cooperative learning method, STAD, involves a cycle of activities that includes teaching, team studying, testing, and team recognition.

should be neither too easy nor too difficult for students to obtain. Prescriptions 8 through 11 all relate to the idea that praise should focus on effort and on task mastery, to give students the attribution that success depends on their efforts, not on external factors, as discussed earlier in this chapter.

Feedback.   The word "feedback" means information on the results of one's efforts. The term has been used throughout this book to refer both to information students receive on their performance and to information teachers obtain on the effects of their instruction (see Chapter 8).

Feedback can serve as an incentive. Research on feedback has found that simple provision of information on the results of one's actions can be an adequate reward in some circumstances (Locke et al., 1968; Waller and Gaa, 1974). However, as noted earlier, feedback must be clear and specific and given close in time to performance to be an effective motivator (Bandura, 1969; Kulik and Kulik, 1988).

Grades as Incentives.   The grading systems used in most schools serve three quite different functions at the same time: evaluation, feedback, and incentive (see Slavin, 1978a). This mix of functions makes grades less than ideal for each function. For example, because grades are based largely on ability rather than on effort, they are less than ideal for motivating students to exert maximum effort, as noted earlier in this chapter. Also, grades are given too infrequently to be very useful as either feedback or incentives for young children unable to see the connection between today's work and a grade to be received in six weeks. Grades are effective as incentives for older students, however. Experiments comparing graded and ungraded college classes (for example, Gold et al., 1971) find substantially higher performance in the graded classes. Grades work as incentives in part because they increase the value of other rewards given closer in time to the behaviors they reinforce. For example, when students get stars on their papers, they may value them in part because they are an indication that their grades in that subject may also be good.

The "accessibility" problem of grades—the fact that good grades are too easy for some students but too difficult for others—may be partially diminished by the use of grading systems with many levels. For example, low-performing students may feel rewarded if they simply pass or if they get a C, while their high-performing classmates may not be satisfied unless they get an A. Also, one major reason that students value grades is that their parents value them, and parents are particularly likely to praise their children for *improvements* in their grades. Even though good grades are not equally attainable by all students, improved grades certainly are, except by straight A students.

Principles and procedures for grading are discussed in detail in Chapter 14.

■ **Stop and Think**

What types of incentives encouraged you to work hard in school? Evaluate the pros and cons of those incentives. Would you use them in your future roles as teacher and parent?

REWARDING EFFORT AND IMPROVEMENT

As noted many times in this chapter, incentive systems used in the classroom should focus on student effort, not ability. There are two principal means of rewarding students for putting forth their best efforts. One is to reward effort directly, by praising students for their efforts or, as is done in many schools, giving a separate effort grade or rating along with the usual performance grade or including effort as an important part of students' grades.

Another way is to recognize students' *improvement* over their own past record. The advantage of an improvement score is that it is quantifiable, and does not rely as heavily on teachers' subjective judgments as an "effort" rating does. All but the highest-performing students are equally capable of improvement, and high-performing students can be rewarded for perfect papers, which should be well within their reach.

Slavin (1980; Beady et al., 1981) developed and evaluated a method of rewarding students for improvement called **Individual Learning Expectations,** or **ILE.** It was found that use of ILE significantly increased student achievement in comparison with classes using traditional grading systems. A simplified version of ILE appears earlier in this chapter.

Behavior Modification and Home-Based Reinforcement Strategies

Behavior modification strategies based on behavioral learning theories have been used successfully to increase student motivation to do a wide variety of academic tasks. Also, home-based reinforcement systems, in which information on students' behavior in class is routinely sent home to be reinforced by parents, can be an effective incentive system for student work. These methods are discussed in Chapter 11.

Cooperation and Competition

One aspect of classroom incentive systems that has received considerable research attention in recent years is the **goal structure** of the classroom. This term refers to the degree to which students are in cooperation or competition with one another. If students are in competition, any student's success necessitates another's failure. For example, if the teacher establishes a policy that only one-quarter of the class can get an A, then students are in competition, because if any student gets an A, this means that another cannot get an A. Just the opposite is true of cooperation. If a group of four students is doing a laboratory exercise together, they will all succeed or fail, "sink or swim," together. If one student works hard, this increases the others' chances of success. A third goal structure is individualization, where one individual's success or failure has no consequences for others. For example, if the teacher said, "I will gave an A to all students who average at least 90 percent on all quizzes given this marking period," then the students would be under an individual goal structure, because the success of any one student has no consequences for the success of his or her classmates (see Johnson and Johnson, 1974).

Competitive goal structures have been criticized for discouraging students from helping one another learn (Johnson and Johnson, 1987), for tending to set up a "pecking order" in the classroom (Ames, 1986), and for establishing a situation in which low achievers have little chance of success (Slavin, 1977b). Coleman (1961) noted that an individual student's success in sports is strongly supported by other students because the sports hero brings glory to the team and the school, while students do not encourage one another's academic achievements because in the competitive academic system achievement brings success only to the individual.

Cooperative Learning
A goal structure in which students work in mixed-ability groups and are rewarded on the basis of the success of the group

Cooperative Learning Methods

The past twenty years have seen the development of several practical classroom methods designed to increase the use of cooperative goal structures (see, for example, Johnson and Johnson, 1987; Sharan and Sharan, 1989, 1990; Aronson et al., 1978; Slavin, 1990). In these methods, called **cooperative learning,** students work in mixed-ability groups of four to six members and cooperate with one another to learn academic materials. The groups are usually rewarded according to how much all group members learned (see Sharan, 1980; Slavin, 1990). The idea behind cooperative learning methods is that when groups rather than individuals are rewarded, students will be motivated to help one another master academic materials.

CASE TO CONSIDER
Case 10

Carl Stevenson, a fourth-grade teacher with ten years experience, talks in his classroom after school to Ruth Duncan about Ruth's son, Jeremy.

CARL: I'm glad I was able to reach you, Ruth. I try to talk with every parent by the beginning of the second half of the school year. I know you're busy with your work so I appreciate your taking time to come down today.

RUTH: Oh, I was glad to come. I was just sorry that my husband and I weren't able to make the fall open house. With our own business to run we're always terribly busy, as you might imagine. Anyway, how's Jeremy doing, Carl?

CARL: Well, I'm sure you've noticed from his report cards that he hasn't reached minimum levels in several areas, especially math, and. . . .

RUTH: You know, my husband and I were commenting about how much the report cards have changed. It's not at all like when we were in school and received letter grades.

CARL: Yes, the approach is different. It's called criterion-referenced grading. Rather than comparing the kids to each other so much, we set objectives and assess the degree to which each child meets the goals.

RUTH: I guess that makes sense, but it seems that the old-fashioned grades should also reflect what a child has learned. Anyway, we kept wondering what grades Jeremy would have received under the old grading system.

CARL: Well, let's go over the grading system a little later. I did discuss it with parents at the open house, and I

also sent home explanations with the first report card.

RUTH: Yes, I guess we've just been too busy.

CARL: In any case, Jeremy hasn't reached criterion in several areas. He seems to have trouble applying himself in class, Ruth. He doesn't pay attention well, seems to daydream a lot, and spends a lot of time doodling. He also doesn't turn in his homework all the time. That worries me. What happens to the work I send home with him?

RUTH: I guess we've been remiss there. It seems difficult to force a fourth-grader to do homework. Is this the first year he's had homework to do?

CARL: That's probably true. Teachers primarily use in-class seatwork through the third grade and then begin assigning some homework in the fourth.

RUTH: I've seen him carrying his books home, but when I ask him about the work he's supposed to do, he says it's not much.

CARL: Hmmm. I'd like to see that attitude change. A student's study habits develop early and Jeremy needs to get a good start.

RUTH: I guess you're right, Carl. I'll have to talk with my husband about this. Is there anything else you can tell me about Jeremy's work?

CARL: Well, let's just take a look at the last report card. That way we can discuss some of my key concerns and can also help you understand the grading system. . . .

During class the next day, while Carl's teacher's aide

Research on cooperative learning has established that these methods can be very effective in increasing student achievement in many subjects and grade levels when student groups are rewarded on the basis of the average learning of the group members (Slavin, 1990; Newmann and Thompson, 1987). An example of this form of cooperative learning is Student Teams—Achievement Divisions (STAD; see Slavin, 1986), described in detail subsequently. Team Assisted Individualization (TAI; see Slavin, et al., 1986), described in Chapter 9, is another example of an instructionally effective form of cooperative learning used in mathematics. Cooperative Integrated Reading and Composition (CIRC; see Stevens et al., 1987), also described in Chapter 9, applies principles of cooperative learning to instruction in reading, writing, and language arts in the upper elementary grades. Cooperative

is working with the other children, Carl beckons Jeremy to the front of the room.

CARL: Jeremy, one of the things you have to learn this year is how to add two-digit numbers with carrying. But, before we get to that, I think you need to brush up on your addition problems that don't require carrying. Can we try to do these first five problems on today's worksheet?

JEREMY: I can't do them.

CARL: Now, just a minute. I know that you did problems like this yesterday. Let's try.

JEREMY: But I don't know how! I hate math!

CARL: Well, Jeremy, what do you like to do? I mean, like after school?

JEREMY: Mostly, I play video games and ride my bike.

CARL: Well, don't you want to be able to go to the store and buy video games for yourself?

JEREMY: Sure. . . .

CARL: Well, then you've got to learn to add and subtract. Otherwise you won't know how much money to take to the store and how much the clerk is supposed to give you back. Don't you want to be able to do that for yourself?

JEREMY: I don't care! I'll learn it soon enough. Besides, my mom and dad can help me.

CARL: But what will you do if they're not around?

JEREMY: Then somebody else will be—or I'll learn how. Besides, I could probably do most of those problems if I tried.

CARL: How would you like to help me set up a class store? I could be the clerk and you and the other students could buy toys and games from me. We could use the money from the Monopoly game.

JEREMY: No, I don't think I want do that.

CARL: What do you want to do, Jeremy?

JEREMY: I just want to go back to my desk. I want to draw.

CARL: OK, Jeremy. We'll tackle some of these math problems tomorrow. Would that be all right?

JEREMY: Yeah, OK.

QUESTIONS

1. How can Carl help motivate Jeremy to learn? Is it possible for one person to motivate another or is motivation something inside a person that can occur only when that person chooses to respond? How do the intrinsic and extrinsic views of motivation differ?
2. From a motivational point of view, should a teacher shape the child to the curriculum or shape the curriculum to the individual child's needs? What roles can cooperation and competition play in the fourth grade?
3. What is criterion-referenced grading and how does it relate to motivation? How do other ways of evaluating students relate to motivation?

Most school situations require students to compete against each other for grades or other rewards. Some projects, however, depart from this pattern by requiring students to cooperate.

learning methods have also been found to improve race relations in desegregated classrooms (see Chapter 13), acceptance of mainstreamed, academically handicapped students by their classmates (see Chapter 12), student self-esteem, and other affective outcomes (see Sharan, 1980; Slavin, 1990).

SUMMARY

Motivation and Needs. The reinforcement value of a reward depends on many factors, and the strength of various motivations may be different for different students. In Maslow's theory needs lower on the hierarchy (deficiency needs) must be at least partially satisfied before a person will try to satisfy higher (growth) needs. Maslow's concept of self-actualization, the highest need in the hierarchy, is defined as the desire to become everything that one is capable of becoming.

Individuals Need to Maintain a Positive Self-Image. Cognitive dissonance theory holds that people experience tension or discomfort when one of their deeply held beliefs is challenged by a psychologically inconsistent belief or behavior. Then they develop justifications to resolve the inconsistency. In educational settings cognitive dissonance often occurs when students receive unpleasant feedback about their performance.

Attribution Theory of Motivation. Attribution theory seeks to understand explanations for success or failure. A central assumption is that people will attempt to maintain a positive self-image, so that when good things happen, they tend to attribute them to their own abilities, while they tend to attribute negative events to factors beyond their control. A key concept in this theory is locus of control: a person with an internal locus of control believes that success or failure is due to personal effort or ability; and someone with an external locus of control believes that success or failure is due to external factors, such as luck or task difficulty. Locus of control can help explain school performance in the sense that an internal orientation attributes success largely to personal effort.

Motivation and Personality. The concept of motivation as a personality characteristic can describe a general tendency to strive for certain types of goals. Though motivation tends to remain constant across a variety of settings, it may be an alterable characteristic. In the same way, locus of control can be a relatively stable personality characteristic, though students may have an internal locus of control for some activities and an external locus of control for others. Other motives that may be viewed as personality characteristics include achievement, affiliation, power, and approval motivations. Students with "learning goals" see the purpose of school as gaining knowledge and competence, as opposed to those with "performance goals" who tend to value positive judgments and good grades. Learned helplessness is a perception that a person is doomed to failure, despite his or her actions. Achievement motivation and attributions can be altered by special programs designed for this purpose.

Motivation and Expectations. Expectancy theories of motivation hold that a person's motivation to achieve something depends on the product of that person's estimation of his or her chance of success and the value he or she places on success. Motivation should be at a maximum at moderate levels of probability of success. In educational settings the most important implication of this theory is that students' tasks should be neither too easy nor too difficult. Research on teachers' expectations for their students has generally found that students do tend to live up to the expectations their teachers express for them, so that it is important for teachers to communicate to their students a positive expectation that they can learn.

Applications of Motivation Theory. An incentive is a reinforcer that people can expect to receive if they perform a specific behavior. Some researchers have shown that extrinsic rewards for an intrinsically interesting activity may undermine students' interest, though some form of extrinsic reward is generally needed to motivate students to do their best on school tasks. The use of instructional sets can enhance intrinsic motivation. Other methods include arousing curiosity, using interesting and varied presentation modes, and games and simulations.

The principles of effective use of incentives for learning include clear expectations; clarity and immediacy of feedback; frequency of assessment, feedback, and reward; value of rewards; and availability of rewards. Classroom rewards include praise, which is most effective when it is contingent, specific, and credible. Feedback can serve as an incentive if it is clear and specific and given close in time to performance. Grades serve as evaluations, feedback, and incentives. A fundamental principle of motivation is that people work harder for goals they themselves establish than for goals set by others.

A general method of rewarding effort is to recognize students' improvement over their own past record. One such specific method is Individual Learning Expectations (ILE), based on the idea of recognizing students for doing better than they have done in the past. This method employs quizzes, initial base scores, improvement points, feedback to students, certificates or other small rewards, recomputation of base scores, and improvement points in addition to grades.

Competitive goal structures have been criticized on the basis that they discourage students from helping each other to learn. Cooperative learning methods, on the other hand, have students work in small, mixed-ability groups and cooperate with one another to learn academic material. Student Teams—Achievement Divisions is a method of cooperative learning consisting of mixed-ability groups, a regular cycle of teaching, cooperative study, and quiz, with recognition or other rewards to teams whose members most exceed their own past records.

STUDY QUESTIONS

1. The following needs from Maslow's hierarchy are listed in alphabetical order. Sequence them in the correct order of the hierarchy, starting with the most basic.
   a. Aesthetic
   b. Belongingness and love
   c. Self-esteem
   d. Need to know and understand
   e. Physiological
   f. Safety
   g. Self-actualization
2. Match each theory of motivation with the correct descriptive characteristic.
   ____ Cognitive dissonance
   ____ Attribution
   ____ Expectancy
   a. Motivation hinges on whether success is linked to internal or external factors.
   b. Motivation is triggered by the need to resolve inconsistent perceptions.
   c. Motivational levels depend on value and perceived chance of success.
3. A student with an internal locus of control is likely to attribute a high test grade to
   a. the test being easy.
   b. favored treatment from the teacher.
   c. careful studying.
   d. good luck.
4. Teachers who want their students to try harder regardless of ability level or task difficulty are trying to develop attributions that fall in the _____ category.
   a. internal-stable
   b. internal-unstable
   c. external-stable
   d. external-unstable

5. A student who tends to choose either very easy or very hard tasks would most likely be a(n)
   a. success seeker.
   b. failure avoider.
   c. "origin."
   d. "pawn."
6. Which behavior is characteristics of students who are motivationally oriented toward *learning goals*?
   a. Taking a challenging course
   b. Trying to make the honor roll
   c. Trying to obtain positive recognition from the teacher
   d. Becoming discouraged in the face of obstacles
7. The main idea underlying the Individual Learning Expectations (ILE) model is
   a. a pass-fail grading system.
   b. an ungraded evaluation.
   c. grading on the basis of improvement.
   d. grading on the basis of comparison with other students.
   e. criterion-referenced grading.
8. Match the following goal structures with the correct description of each.
   ____ Competitive
   ____ Cooperative
   ____ Individualized
   a. All succeed or all fail.
   b. One person's success or failure has no influence on another's fate.
   c. Some will succeed and others will fail.

Answers: 1. e, f, b, c, d, a, g. 2. b, a, c. 3. c. 4. b. 5. b. 6. a. 7. c. 8. c, a, b.

SUGGESTED READINGS

AMES, R., and AMES, C. (eds.) (1989) *Research on motivation in education* (Vol. 3). New York: Academic Press.

ARONSON, E. (1980). *The social animal*. San Francisco: Freeman.

ATKINSON, J. W., and BIRCH, D. (1978). *Introduction to motivation* (2nd ed.). New York: Van Nostrand.

BROPHY, J. (1981). Teacher praise: A functional analysis. *Review of Educational Research*, 51:5–32.

BROPHY, J. (1987). Synthesis of research on strategies for motivating students to learn. *Educational Leadership*, 45, 40–48.

COOPER, H. M., and GOOD, T. L. (1983). *Pygmalion grows up: Studies in the expectation communication process*. New York: Longman.

DUKES, R., and SEIDNER, C. (1978). *Learning with simulations and games*. Beverly Hills, Cal.: Sage.

FÖRSTERLING, F. (1985). Attributional retraining: A review. *Psychological Bulletin, 98,* 495–512.

HILL, K. T., and WIGFIELD, A. (1984). Test anxiety: A major educational problem and what can be done about it. *Elementary School Journal, 85,* 105–126.

HUNTER, M., and BARKER, G. (1987). If at first . . .: Attribution theory in the classroom. *Educational Leadership, 45*(2), 50–53.

LEFCOURT, H. (1976). *Locus of control: Current trends in research and theory.* Hillsdale, N.J.: Erlbaum.

LEPPER, M. R. (1983). Extrinsic reward and intrinsic motivation: Implications for the classroom. In J. M. Levine and M. C. Wang (eds.), *Teacher and student perceptions: Implications for learning.* Hillsdale, N.J.: Erlbaum.

MORGAN, M. (1984). Reward-induced decrements and increments in intrinsic motivation. *Review of Educational Research, 54,* 5–30.

SLAVIN, R. E. (1990). *Cooperative learning: Theory, research, and practice.* Englewood Cliffs, N.J.: Prentice-Hall.

STIPEK, D. J. (1988). *Motivation to learn: From theory to practice.* Englewood Cliffs, N.J.: Prentice-Hall.

WEINER, B. (1979). A theory of motivation for some classroom experiences. *Journal of Educational Psychology, 71,* 3–25.

WEINER, B. (1980). *Human motivation.* New York: Holt, Rinehart, & Winston.

Chapter 11

Classroom Management

Chapter Outline

Chapter Objectives

After reading this chapter on classroom
management and discipline you should be able to:

- Plan lessons that make the best use of classroom
  time.

- Prevent most minor incidents of misconduct from
  disrupting lesson presentations.

- List three reinforcers of student misbehavior.

- Use strategies of applied behavior analysis to
  improve student behavior.

It is 11 A.M. in Ms. Green's first-grade classroom. She calls for one reading group to gather at the back of the room. The rest of the class are to remain at their desks.

Three minutes later only one girl has brought her chair to the back. The teacher goes to get the others.

By 11:05, the students are in place, their chairs arrayed in a semicircle. "Oh, I'm sorry, I forgot to tell you to bring your green book," the teacher says.

The students get up, return to their desks, get their green workbooks, and head for the back of the room again. But there is another interruption.

"Get your green books *and* pencils, please." The students return to their desks, and again head for the back of the room. By 11:08, the students are once more gathered around the teacher.

The teacher gets up, walks to her desk, then across to a bookshelf to find her teachers' edition of the green workbook. She returns to the group, and tells the students to open to page 27.

A girl sneezes. The teacher says, "Cover your mouth when you cough. Go to my desk and get a tissue."

"I didn't cough," the student replies.

"Didn't you cough?"

"No."

"I was just looking at you," the teacher responds.

"I didn't cough," the girl maintains. "I sneezed."

"Well, for goodness' sake," the teacher says, "Go to my desk and get a tissue." The girl does not get up.

It is 11:11. The group finally begins the lesson. The teacher tells the students to circle the word "like." One boy is not writing. He does not have a pencil.

"Where's your pencil?" the teacher asks. "You didn't listen." He says he has lost his pencil. She sends him to his desk to look for it, then tells him to use a crayon.

Meanwhile, the students who are not in the group at the back of the room are sitting at their desks with workbooks open. No one is working. Three are pointing pencils at each other, two others watch in apparent fascination. At 11:20 the group completes a few words. The teacher tells the students to get ready for lunch.

She says, "Now, let's see who's ready to go to the cafeteria." She calls the students one at a time, by name, to line up. At 11:25 the lunch bell rings, and the class goes to the cafeteria.

At the end of the twenty-five minute period the class had spent less than nine minutes on actual learning. (Adapted from Salganik, 1980)

Learning takes time. One of the teacher's most critical tasks is to organize the classroom so as to provide enough time on instructionally important tasks for all students to learn. In Ms. Green's class students learned little reading because much of the reading period was taken up with noninstructional activities. The description of Ms. Green's class was taken from observations made by a reporter for the *Baltimore Sun;* it really happened, though "Ms. Green" is not the real name of the teacher observed. Of course, her class was not typical, but the example does illustrate some ways in which time scheduled for instruction is lost. We will return to discuss Ms. Green's class several times.

This chapter focuses on the means available to teachers of managing instructional time effectively, of preventing disruptions that reduce time for instruction, and, when necessary, of taking action to deal with discipline problems. The chapter takes an approach to classroom management and discipline that emphasizes *prevention* of misbehavior, on the theory that effective instruction itself is the best means of avoiding discipline problems. In the past, classroom management has often been seen as an issue of dealing with individual student misbehaviors. Current thinking emphasizes management of the class as a whole in such a way as to make individual misbehaviors rare (Doyle, 1986). Teachers who present interesting, well-organized lessons, who use incentives for learning effectively, who accommodate their instruction to students' levels of preparation, and who plan and manage their own time effectively will have few discipline problems to deal with. Still, every teacher, no matter how effective, will encounter discipline problems sometimes, and this chapter also presents means of handling these problems when they arise.

TIME AND LEARNING

Obviously, if no time is spent teaching a subject, the subject will not be learned. However, within the usual range of time allocated to instruction, how much difference does time make? This has been a focus of considerable research. While it is clear that more time spent in instruction has a positive impact on student achievement, the effects of additional time are often modest or inconsistent (Karweit, 1989). In particular, the typical differences in lengths of school days and school years among different districts have only a minor impact on student achievement (see Karweit, 1981; Walberg, 1988). What seems to be more important is how time is used in class. **Engaged time,** or time on-task, the number of minutes actually spent learning, is the time measure most frequently found to contribute to learning (for example, Marliave et al., 1978; Anderson et al., 1979; Karweit and Slavin, 1981). In other words, the most important aspect of time is the one under the direct control of the teacher—the organization and use of time in the classroom.

Where Does the Time Go?

Time is a limited resource in schools. A typical school is in session for about 6 hours a day for 180 days. While time for educational activities can be expanded by means of homework assignments or (for some students) summer school, the total time available for instruction is essentially set. Out of this six hours (or so) must come time for teaching a variety of subjects, plus time for lunch, recess or physical education, transitions between classes, announcements, and so on. In a forty- to sixty-minute period in a particular subject, many quite different factors reduce the time available for instruction. Figure 11.1 illustrates how time scheduled for mathematics instruction in twelve grade 2–5 classes observed by Karweit and Slavin (1981) was whittled away.

The classes Karweit and Slavin (1981) observed were in schools in and around a rural Maryland town. Overall, the classes were well-organized and businesslike, with dedicated and hardworking teachers. Students were generally well behaved and respectful of authority. However, even in these very good schools the average student spent only 60 percent of the time scheduled for mathematics instruction actually learning mathematics. First of all, about twenty class days were lost to such activities as standardized testing, school events, field trips, and teacher absences. On days when instruction was given, class time was lost because of late starts and noninstructional activities such as discussions of upcoming events, announcements, passing out of materials, and disciplining students. Finally, even when math was being taught, many students were not actually engaged in the instructional activity. Some were daydreaming during lecture or seatwork times, goofing off, or sharpening pencils;

FIGURE 11.1

Where Does the Time Go?

Observations of elementary school mathematics classes showed that the time students actually spend learning in class is only about 60 percent of the time allocated for instruction.

Based on data from Karweit and Slavin, 1981.

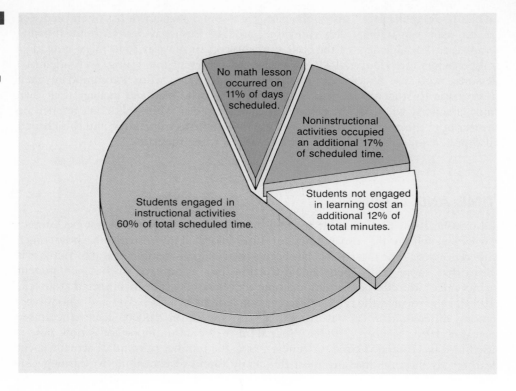

No math lesson occurred on 11% of days scheduled.

Noninstructional activities occupied an additional 17% of scheduled time.

Students not engaged in learning cost an additional 12% of total minutes.

Students engaged in instructional activities 60% of total scheduled time.

others had nothing to do, either because they were finished with their assigned work or had not yet been assigned a task.

Maximizing Periods of Instruction. One way in which much instructional time is lost is through losses of entire days or periods. Many of these losses are inevitable—because of such things as standardized testing days and snow days—and we certainly would not want to abolish important field trips or school assemblies just to get in a few more periods of instruction. However, frequent losses of instructional periods interrupt the flow of instruction and can ultimately deprive students of sufficient time to master the curriculum.

Another source of "lost days," and one that is much more controllable, is teachers' failures to teach a lesson because "today isn't a good day." For example, a teacher might end a unit on a Thursday and not want to begin a new unit until the following Monday. Another teacher might avoid giving a lesson just before or after a holiday.

Making good use of all classroom time is less a matter of squeezing out a few more minutes or hours of instruction each year than of communicating to students that learning is an important business that is worth their time and effort. If a teacher finds excuses not to teach, students may learn that learning is not a serious enterprise. In studying an outstandingly effective inner-city Baltimore elementary school, Salganik (1980) described a third-grade teacher who took her class to the library, which she found locked. She sent a student for the key, and while the class waited, she whispered to her students, "Let's work on our doubles. Nine plus nine? Six plus six?" The class whispered the answers back in unison. Now, did a couple of minutes working on addition facts increase the students' achievement? Of course not. But it probably did help develop a perception that school is for learning, not for marking time.

Allocated Time for Instruction

A principal of an outstanding elementary school in Houston often tells his teachers, "If you don't have a lesson plan for your students, they will have a lesson plan for you." What he means, of course, is that if teachers are not well organized and prepared for class, they may lose control of the class to the students, who are probably more interested in fun and games than in working. This was one major problem experienced by poor Ms. Green. Her students were not bad or lazy, but her lack of organization and preparedness created unnecessary losses of instructional time. She had not established routines so that students would know that at reading group time they had to have a pencil and a green book. Just when she had her students assembled and ready to go, she left them to get her teacher's edition of the workbook, which she should have had ready. She wasted prime instructional time dealing unnecessarily with a student's coughing (or sneezing). She did not give the students in other reading groups a clear assignment and did not monitor them, so they did nothing while she was trying to get her one reading group together. In short, Ms. Green didn't have a clearly laid out lesson plan for her students, so they carried out their own "lesson plan," goofing off instead of reading.

Another term for "instructional time" is **allocated time,** which is the time during which students have an opportunity to learn. When the teacher is lecturing, students can learn by paying attention. When students have seatwork or other tasks, they can learn by doing them. A discussion of some common ways allocated time can be maximized follows.

Avoiding Late Starts, Early Finishes.   A surprising amount of allocated instructional time is lost because the teacher does not start teaching at the beginning of the period. This can be a particular problem is self-contained elementary classes, where there are no bells or fixed schedules to structure the period, but it is also a problem in departmentalized secondary schools, where teachers may spend a long time dealing with late students or other problems before starting the lesson.

A crisp, on-time start to a lesson is important for setting a purposive tone to instruction. If students know that a teacher does not start on time, they may be lackadaisical about getting to class on time, which makes future on-time starts increasingly difficult.

Teachers can also shortchange students if they stop teaching before the end of the period. This is less damaging than a ragged or late start, but is still worth avoiding by planning more instruction than you think you'll need against the possibility that you will finish the lesson early (Evertson, 1982).

Avoiding Interruptions.   One important source of lost allocated time for instruction is interruptions. Interruptions may be externally imposed, as with announcements or the need to sign forms sent from the principal's office, or they may be caused by teachers or students themselves (Behnke, 1979). Interruptions not only directly cut into the time for instruction, they also break the *momentum* of the lesson, which reduces students' attention to the task of hand.

Avoiding interruptions takes planning. For example, some teachers put a "Do not disturb—learning in progress!" sign on the doors to inform would-be interrupters to come back later. One teacher wore a special hat during small-group lessons to remind her other second-graders not to interrupt her during that time. Rather than signing forms or dealing with other "administrivia" at once, some teachers keep a box where students and others can put any forms, and then deal with them after the lesson is over.

Allocated Time
Time during which students have the opportunity to learn

Establishing classroom rules can help prevent disruptions that waste instructional time.

Anything the teacher can delay doing until after a lesson should be delayed. For example, if the teacher has started a lesson and a student walks in late, the teacher should go on with the lesson and deal with the tardiness issue later.

Handling Routine Procedures Smoothly and Quickly.   Some teachers spend too much time on simple classroom routines. For example, Ms. Green spent many minutes getting students ready for lunch because she called them by name, one at a time. This was unnecessary. She could have saved time for instruction by having the students line up for lunch by tables or rows. Early in the school year she could have established a routine that only when the entire table (or row) was quiet and ready to go would they be called to line up. Lining up for lunch would then take seconds, not minutes.

Other procedures must also become routine for students. Early in the school year they must learn classroom rules and procedures. They must know, for example, when they may go to the washroom or sharpen a pencil, and not to ask to do these things at other times. Papers may be collected by having students pass them to the front or to the left, or by having table monitors collect the table's papers. Distribution of materials must also be planned for. It is less important exactly how these tasks are done than that students know clearly what they are to do. Many teachers assign regular classroom helpers to take care of distribution and collection of papers, taking messages to the office, erasing the blackboard, and other routine tasks that are annoying interruptions for teachers but that students love to do. Teachers should use "student power" as much as possible.

The wise teacher also notes in a daily lesson plan what he or she will need and what students will need for a lesson, and then makes sure that these needs are provided for (see Doyle, 1984).

Minimizing Time Spent on Discipline.   Methods of disciplining students are discussed at length later in this chapter. However, one aspect of disciplining should be mentioned at this point. Whenever possible—which is almost always—disciplinary statements or actions should not interrupt the flow of the lesson. A sharp glance, silently moving close to an offending student, or a hand signal, such as putting finger to lips to remind a student to be silent, are usually effective for the kind of minor behavior problems that teachers must constantly deal with, and allow the lesson to proceed without interruption. For example, Ms. Green had no need to get involved with the girl who sneezed. If students need talking to about discipline problems, the time to do it is after the lesson or after school, not in the middle of a lesson. If Diana and Martin are talking during seatwork instead of working, it would be better to say, "Diana and Martin, see me at three o'clock," than to launch into an on-the-spot speech about the importance of being on-task during seatwork times.

Engaged Time

Engaged time (or time on-task) is the time individual students actually spend doing assigned work. Allocated time and engaged time differ in that while allocated time refers to the opportunity for the entire class to engage in learning activities, engaged time may be different for each student, depending on a student's attentiveness and willingness to work. Strategies for maximizing student time on-task are discussed in the following sections. Teacher training programs based on a principles presented in the following sections have been found in several studies to increase student engagement (for example, Emmer et al., 1982; Evertson et al., 1983) and in some cases, learning (Evertson et al., 1985).

Maintaining Momentum and Smoothness of Instruction. Maintaining "momentum" during a lesson is a key to keeping task engagement high. Momentum refers to the avoidance of interruptions or slowdowns (Kounin, 1970). In a class that maintains good momentum, students always have something to do, and once started working are not interrupted. Anyone who has, for example, tried to write a term paper, only to be interrupted by telephone calls, knocks on the door, and other disturbances, knows that these interruptions cause much more damage to concentration and progress than the amount of time they take.

Kounin (1970) gives the following example of teacher-caused slowdowns and interruptions.

> The teacher is just starting a reading group at the reading circle while the rest of the children are engaged in seatwork with workbooks. She sat in front of the reading group and asked, "All right, who can tell me the name of our next chapter?" Before a child was called on to answer, she looked toward the children at seatwork, saying: "Let's wait until the people in Group Two are settled and working." (Actually most are writing in their workbooks.) She then looked at John who was in the seatwork group, naggingly asking, "Did you find your pencil?" John answered something which was inaudible. The teacher got up from her seat, saying "I'd like to know what you did with it." Pause for about two seconds. "Did you eat it?" Another pause. "What happened to it? What color was it? You can't do your work without it." The teacher then went to her desk to get a pencil to give to John, saying, "I'll get you a pencil. Make sure the pencil is here tomorrow morning. And don't tell me you lost that one too. And make it a new one, and see that it's sharpened." The teacher then returned to the reading circle. This pencil transaction lasted 1.4 minutes. (p. 104)

This teacher destroyed the momentum of a reading lesson by spending more than a minute dealing with a child in the seatwork group who did not have a pencil. Of course, during this interchange the entire class—both the reading group and the seatwork group—were off-task, but what is worse, they required much more time to get resettled and back to work after the incident. Just as a lesson was getting under way and students were ready to listen, the teacher broke this chain of activities with a completely unnecessary reprimand for a behavior that could easily have been ignored.

Kounin found momentum to be strongly related to total time on-task, and Brophy and Evertson (1976) and Anderson et al. (1979) found momentum to be related to student achievement. It is significant that some of the features of effective lessons described in Chapters 8 and 9 are largely directed at maintaining momentum. For example, in the Missouri Mathematics Program (MMP; Good et al., 1983), discussed in Chapter 8, the teacher has students try a few problems under his or her watchful eye ("controlled practice") before letting them start their seatwork, to make sure that the flow from lesson to seatwork is not interrupted by student questions and problems.

"Smoothness" is another term used by Kounin (1970) to refer to continued focus on a meaningful sequence of instruction. Smooth instruction avoids jumping without transitions from topic to topic, or from the lesson to other activities, which produces "jarring breaks in the activity flow" (Kounin, 1970, p. 97). For example:

> The teacher was conducting a recitation with a subgroup. She was walking towards a child who was reciting when she passed by the fish bowl. She suddenly stopped walking toward the boy, and stopped at the fish bowl, saying: "Oh my, I forgot to feed the fish!" She then got some fish food from a nearby shelf and started to feed the fish, saying: "My, see how hungry it is." She then turned to a girl, saying: "See, Margaret, you forgot to feed the fish. You can see how hungry it is. See how quickly it comes up to eat." (Kounin, 1970, pp. 98–99)

This example illustrates how smoothness and momentum are related. The teacher jumped from her lesson to housekeeping to (unnecessary) disciplining, interrupting one student's recitation and making it virtually impossible for the other students to focus on the lesson. As with momentum, smoothness was found to be strongly associated with student time on-task (Kounin, 1970) and achievement (Brophy and Evertson, 1976; Anderson et al., 1979).

Managing Transitions. Transitions are changes from one activity to another, as from lecture to seatwork, subject to subject, or lesson to lunch. Elementary classes have been found to have an average of thirty-one major transitions a day, occupying 15 percent of class time (Burns, 1984). Transitions are the "seams" of class management at which classroom order is most likely to come apart; Anderson et al. (1979) and Evertson et al. (1980) found that teachers' efficiency at managing transitions between activities was positively related to their students' achievement.

Following are three rules for the management of transitions:

1. When making a transition, the teacher should give a clear signal to which the students have been taught to respond (Arlin, 1979; Doyle, 1984).

For example, in the elementary grades some teachers use a bell to indicate to students that they should immediately be quiet and listen to instructions.

2. Before the transition is made, students must be absolutely certain about what they are to do when the signal is given (Arlin, 1979).

For example, a teacher might say, "When I say 'Go,' I want you all to put your books away and get out the compositions you started yesterday. Is everyone ready? All right, go!"

When giving instructions to students to begin independent seatwork, the teacher can help get started with the activity before letting them work independently, as in the following example:

"Today we are going to find guide words for different pages in the dictionary. Everyone should have a ditto sheet with the words on it and a dictionary. Class, hold up your ditto sheet. [They do.] Now hold up your dictionary. [They do.] Good. Now turn to page 102. [The teacher walks around to see that everyone does so.] Look at the top of the page and put your finger on the first guide word. [The teacher walks around to check on this.] Class, what is the first guide word?"

CLASS: "Carrot!"

"Good. The first guide word is carrot. Now look to the right on the same page. Class, what word do you see there?"

CLASS: "Carve!"

"Right. The guide words are carrot and carve. Now turn to page 555 and find the guide words. [Students do this.] Class, what is the first guide word on page 555?"

CLASS: "Scheme!"

"Class, what is the second guide word?"

CLASS: "Scissors!"

"Great! Now do the first problem on your ditto sheet by yourselves, and then stop."

The teacher would then check whether all or almost all students have the first item correct before telling them to complete the worksheet. The idea, of course, is to make sure that students know exactly what they are to do before they start doing it.

3. Make transitions all at once.

Students should be trained to make transitions all at once, rather than one student at a time. The teacher should usually give directions to the class as a whole or to well-defined groups, as follows:

"Class, I want you all to put away your laboratory materials and prepare for dismissal as quickly and quietly as you can. . . . I see that Table 3 is quiet and ready. Table 3, please line up quietly. Table 6, line up. Table 1 . . . Table 4. Everyone else may line up quietly. Let's go!"

Maintaining Group Focus During Lessons. "Maintaining group focus" refers to the use of classroom organization strategies and questioning techniques that ensure that all students in the class stay involved in the lesson, even when only one student is called on by the teacher. Two principal components of Kounin's "maintaining group focus" were found to be significantly related to students' on-task behavior: accountability and group alerting.

Kounin (1970) uses the term "accountability" to mean "the degree to which the teacher holds the children accountable and responsible for their task performances during recitation sessions" (p. 119). Examples of strategies for increasing accountability are the use of choral responses, having all students hold up their work so the teacher can see it (see Chapter 8), circulating among the students to see what they are doing, and drawing other children into the performance of one child (for example, "I want you all to watch what Suzanne is doing so you can tell me whether you agree or disagree with her answer").

The idea behind these strategies is to maintain the involvement of all students in all parts of the lesson. A study of third- and fourth-graders found that students raised their hands an average of once every six minutes, and gave an answer only once every fifteen minutes, with some students hardly ever participating (Potter, 1977). This is not enough participation to ensure student attention. Teachers should be concerned not only about drawing all students into class activities, but also about avoiding activities that relegate most students to the role of spectator for long periods. For example, a very common teaching error is to have one or two students work out a lengthy problem on the chalkboard or read an extended passage while the rest of the class has nothing to do. Such strategies waste the time of much of the class, break the momentum of the lesson, and leave the door open for misbehavior (Gump, 1982).

Group alerting refers to questioning strategies (see Chapter 8) designed to keep all students "on their toes" during a lecture or discussion. One example of group alerting is creating suspense before calling on a student by saying, "Given triangle ABC, if we know the measures of sides A and B and of angle AB, what else can we find out about the triangle? . . . (Pause) . . . Maria?" Note that this keeps the whole class thinking until Maria's name is called. The opposite effect would have been created by saying, "Maria, given triangle ABC . . . ," because only Maria would have been alerted. Calling on students in a random order is another example of group alerting, as is letting students know that they may be asked questions about the last

Students are less likely to misbehave if they are actively involved in interesting lessons.

Withitness
The degree to which the teacher is aware of, and responsive to, student behavior

Overlapping
A teacher's ability to respond to behavior problems without interrupting a classroom lesson

reciter's answers. For example, the teacher might follow up Maria's answer with, "What is the name of the postulate that Maria used? . . . Ralph?"

Maintaining Group Focus During Seatwork.   During times when students are doing seatwork and the teacher is available to work with them, it is important to monitor the seatwork activities and to informally check individual students' work. That is, the teacher should circulate among the students' desks to see how they are doing. This allows the teacher to identify any problems students are having before they waste seatwork time practicing errors or giving up in frustration.

While seatwork times provide excellent opportunities for providing individual help to students who are struggling to keep up with the class, teachers should resist the temptation to work too long with an individual student. Interactions with students during seatwork should be as brief as possible (Brophy and Evertson, 1976; Anderson et al., 1979), because if the teacher gets tied down with any one student, the rest of the class may drift off-task or run into problems of their own (Doyle, 1984).

Withitness.   **Withitness** is another term coined by Kounin (1970). It describes teachers' actions that indicate awareness of students' behavior at all times. Kounin calls this awareness "having eyes in the back of one's head." Teachers who are "with it" can respond immediately to student misbehavior and know who started what. Teachers who lack withitness can make the error of scolding the wrong student, as in the following instance:

> Lucy and John, who were sitting at the same table as Jane, started to whisper. Robert watched this and he too got into the act. Then Jane giggled and said something to John. Then Mary leaned over and whispered to Jane. At this point, the teacher said, "Mary and Jane, stop that!" (Adapted from Kounin, 1970, p. 80).

By responding only to Mary and Jane, who were late to get involved in the whispering and giggling incident, the teacher indicated that she did not know what was going on. A single incident of this kind may make little difference, but after many such incidents students recognize the teacher's tendency to respond inappropriately to their behavior.

Another example of a lack of withitness is responding too late to a sequence of misbehavior. Lucy and John's whispering could have been easily nipped in the bud, perhaps with just a glance or a finger to the lips. By the time the whispering had escalated to giggling and spread to several students, it took a full stop in the lesson to rectify the situation.

Kounin (1970) found the withitness of teachers to be strongly related to their effectiveness as class managers, and Brophy and Evertson (1976) and Anderson et al. (1979) found that "withit" teachers also produced better student achievement.

A major component of "withitness" is scanning the class frequently and establishing eye contact with individual students. Several studies have found that more effective managers frequently scan the classroom visually, to monitor the pace of activity as well as individual students' behaviors (Emmer et al., 1980; Evertson and Emmer, 1982; Brooks, 1985).

Overlapping.   **Overlapping** refers to the teacher's ability to attend to interruptions or behavior problems while continuing a lesson or other instructional activity. For example, one teacher was teaching a lesson on reading comprehension when he saw a student looking at a book unrelated to the lesson. Without interrupting his lesson, he walked over to the student, took her book, closed it, and put it on her desk, all

Problems of Classroom Management

1. A teacher's job would be easier if classroom distractions never occurred. For example, how would you suggest a young teacher handle a situation like the following: You're 10 minutes into a well-crafted, 40-minute English lesson when the custodian appears—finally!—to fix a troublesome light. The very presence of someone else in the room breaks your momentum and the students' concentration, and the custodian's tinkering with the fixture could disrupt the remainder of the class. Short of asking the custodian to leave, what do you do?

Gretchen L. Powers, who teaches elementary school in Lynnville, Ind., said:

During summer vacation the custodians clean all the classrooms and leave the adjustable desks at the same height. Because fourth graders vary widely in height, it is necessary to ask the custodian to readjust the desks the first or second day of school in the fall. The custodians are very busy at this time, so I am delighted to have them come whenever possible. I often use the custodian's visit to discuss with students the many people who are involved in education. We mention not only teachers and principals, but also the cooks, bus drivers, secretaries, custodians, plumbers, electricians, etc. It is important for the children to realize that there are many people who are working hard to see that each child receives a quality education.

Myrta Gerren, who teaches elementary school in Hartville, Ohio, actually faced the situation of the troublesome light. Here's what she said:

This situation actually happened this year in my first-grade class. If the light was to be fixed that day, it had to be fixed during my reading class. I called attention to the fact that it was very nice of Mr. Rinker to take time out of his busy day to fix the light. I then called the children to the rug at the front of the room and involved them in a high-interest activity. Since they were more interested in what was going on in our class and since they had looked at the light at the beginning, I had no difficulty keeping their interest. When I noticed that he was finished and about to leave I said, "What do we tell Mr. Rinker for fixing our light?" The class responded with a hearty, "Thank you." I then sent the children to their seats for some oral reading. They were ready for the switch.

As long as a teacher can remain cool and in charge, everything goes fine. Letting the children see what is happening by calling attention to the distraction at first and then removing them from the vicinity by doing something with high-level interest works best.

2. Classroom situations can be stressful. How do you prevent yourself from becoming angry? How do you allow students to let off steam during or after a stressful situation?

Pam Woolsey, who teaches junior high in Knoxville, Ill.:

We all become angry sometimes; it is a natural response. However, it is necessary to direct your anger at the problem and not the person, and explain the reason it causes anger for you. Students cannot be allowed outbursts of angry rage, but a little sulking in a class can be tolerated.

Patricia James, who teaches ninth grade in Elizabeth City, N.C.:

Allowing students to go to the restroom or some other "time-out" place after a stressful situation allows the situation to defuse. I also try to remember myself at that age, and consider how I would want my children treated in a similar situation.

while continuing to speak to the class. This took care of the student's misbehavior without slowing the momentum of the lesson; the rest of the class hardly noticed that the event occurred.

Another example of a teacher doing a good job of overlapping is as follows:

The teacher is at the reading circle and Lucy is reading aloud while standing. Johnny, who was doing seatwork at his desk, walks up toward the teacher, holding his workbook. The teacher glances at Johnny, then looks back at Lucy, nodding at Lucy, as

Lucy continues to read aloud. The teacher remains seated and takes Johnny's workbook. She turns to Lucy, saying, "That was a hard word, Lucy, and you pronounced it right." She checks about three more answers in Johnny's book saying, "That's fine, you can go ahead and do the next page now," and resumes looking at the reading book as Lucy continues reading. (Kounin, 1970, p. 84)

Now, Johnny's interruption of the reading group might have been avoided altogether by a good classroom manager, who would have assigned enough work to keep all students productively busy during reading circle time, and given clear instructions on what they were to do when they finished their seatwork. However, interruptions are sometimes unavoidable, and the ability to keep the main activity going while handling them is strongly related to overall classroom order (Kounin, 1970; Copeland, 1983) and to achievement (Brophy and Evertson, 1976; Anderson et. al., 1979).

Engaged Time versus Engaging Instruction: A Caution

This chapter began with the example of poor Ms. Green, whose class management problems were greatly interfering with her ability to teach. Her example is certainly not one to emulate. However, it is possible to go too far in the other direction, emphasizing time on-task to the exclusion of all other considerations. For example, in a study of time on-task in elementary mathematics, one teacher's class was found to be engaged essentially 100 percent of the time. The teacher accomplished this by walking up and down the rows of desks looking for the slightest flicker of inattention. This class learned very little math over the course of the year.

Several recent studies have found that increasing time on-task in classes in which students were already reasonably well behaved did not increase student achievement (Blackadar and Nachtigal, 1986; Slavin, 1986; Stallings and Krasavage, 1986). An overemphasis on time on-task can be detrimental to learning in several ways. For example, complex tasks involving creativity and uncertainty tend to produce lower levels of time on-task than simple cut-and-dried tasks (Atwood, 1983; Doyle and Carter, 1984). Yet it would clearly be a poor instructional strategy to avoid complex or uncertain tasks in order to keep time on-task high. Maintaining classroom order is an important goal of teaching, but it is only one of many (see Doyle, 1983, 1986; Slavin, 1987).

■ **Stop and Think**

What do you suppose will be the classroom management issue that you will face most frequently in the grade and subject you plan to teach? What will be the most serious (though not necessarily the most frequent) issue? Keep these situations in mind as you review the material you have already read, and as you read further.

Classroom Rules and Behavior

Starting the Year Properly.   Emmer et al. (1980) and Evertson and Emmer (1982) studied teacher's actions at the beginning of the school year and correlated them with students' behaviors later in the year. They found that the first days of school were critical in establishing classroom order. They compared teachers whose classes were mostly on-task over the course of the school year with teachers whose classes were less consistently on-task, and found that the better classroom managers engaged in certain activities during the first days of school significantly more often than did the less effective managers. A list of six characteristics of effective classroom managers follows.

1. More effective managers had a clear, specific plan for introducing students to classroom rules and procedures, and spent as many days as necessary carrying out their plan until students knew how to line up, ask for help, and so on.

2. More effective managers worked with the whole class initially (even if they planned to group students later). They were involved with the whole class at all times, rarely leaving any students without something to do or without supervision. For example, more effective managers seldom worked with an individual student unless the rest of the class was productively occupied (Sanford and Evertson, 1981; Doyle, 1984).

3. More effective managers spent much of the first days of school introducing procedures and discussing class rules (often encouraging students to suggest rules themselves). These teachers usually reminded students of class rules every day for at least the first week of school.

4. More effective managers taught students specific procedures. For example, some had students practice lining up quickly and quietly; others taught students to respond to a signal, such as a bell, a flick of the light switch, or a call for attention.

5. As first activities, more effective managers used simple, enjoyable tasks. Materials for the first lessons were well prepared, clearly presented, and varied. Students were asked to get right to work on the first day of school, and were then given instructions on procedures gradually, to avoid overloading them with too much information at a time.

6. More effective managers responded immediately to stop any misbehavior.

Setting Class Rules. As already noted, one of the first management-related tasks at the start of the year is setting class rules. Three principles govern this process. First, class rules should be few in number. Second, they should make sense and be seen as fair by students. Third, they should be clearly explained and deliberately taught to students (Emmer et al., 1980; Brooks, 1985). A major purpose of clearly explaining general class rules is to give a "moral authority" for specific procedures. For example, all students will understand and support a rule such as "respect others' property." This simple rule can be invoked to cover such obvious misbehaviors as stealing or destroying materials, but also gives a reason for putting materials away, cleaning up litter, and refraining from marking up textbooks. Students may be asked to help set the rules, or they may be given a set of rules and asked to give examples of these rules. Class discussions give students a feeling of participation in setting rational rules that everyone can live by. When the class as a whole has agreed on a set of rules, offenders know that they are transgressing community norms, not the teacher's arbitrary regulations.

One all-purpose set of class rules follows:

1. *Be courteous to others:* This rule forbids interrupting others or speaking out of turn, teasing or laughing at others, fighting, and so on.

2. *Respect others' property.*

3. *Be on-task:* This includes listening when the teacher or other students are

A major task for elementary teachers is to teach students how to behave in school. These teachers usually find young students eager to please and to learn.

The preceding sections discuss classroom management issues from a general instructional perspective. However, it is important to note (following Brophy and Evertson, 1976) how management concerns differ in classrooms at various levels.

ELEMENTARY SCHOOL (K–5)

A major component of the teacher's task as students first begin formal education is to socialize them to norms and behaviors expected in school. Considerable time and attention must be given to teaching students rules and procedures. Luckily, children in the early grades are typically highly motivated and eager to please; the teacher's task is more to channel their enthusiasm into productive activities and to familiarize them with classroom routines than to motivate them or reinforce compliance with rules. When young children misbehave, it is often out of misunderstanding of what is required of them rather than willfulness or orneriness.

One management-related complication in the early grades is the almost universal use of ability grouping (at least in reading). Many of the management issues discussed in the previous sections crop up frequently when a teacher is working with one group and others are expected to work independently. Since independent work skills must be developed in young children, the teacher must maintain a balancing act between giving attention to reading or math groups and seeing that the remainder of the class has enough work to do and knows how to do it. (Anderson et al., 1979; Morine-Dershimer, 1983).

By the second or third grade, most students know classroom routines and procedures. Classroom management issues begin to revolve around maintenance of momentum in lessons and enforcing compliance with rules that are reasonably well understood. The continued widespread use of within-class ability grouping is still an important management concern.

MIDDLE/JUNIOR HIGH SCHOOL GRADES (5–9)

In early adolescence students undergo several changes that have importance for classroom management. On the one hand, they now have the cognitive and social skills to appreciate the need for the class to operate smoothly and for people to be courteous and respectful toward one another. On the other, they become more likely to resist authority, and peer norms (which often oppose school-supported norms) take on great importance. Misbehavior in class may be applauded by peers. Aggressive behavior among students increases, as does interest in the opposite sex. Also, while almost every first-grader enters school feeling that he or she is a capable learner (Stipek, 1981) by upper elementary and middle school some students feel that they have little chance of academic success. Some of these students seek a delinquent or antiestablishment identity because they feel prosocial avenues are closed off to them.

In most schools departmentalization is introduced in the upper elementary or middle school grades. Passing from class to class becomes an important management issue. Tracking is more common in departmentalized schools, creating the phenomenon of the poorly motivated, poorly behaved low-track class (see Chapter 9). At the same time, the use of within-class ability grouping decreases.

While younger students typically respect their teachers, respect must be earned in junior and senior high school classes. Fairness, consistency, and lack of favoritism or bias are important at all grade levels, but vital with adolescents.

HIGH SCHOOL GRADES (9–12)

By the time students enter high school, many of the worst behaved and least motivated of them have dropped out (Combs and Cooley, 1968; Tseng, 1972). Others have mentally dropped out and are merely marking time until they reach the legal school-leaving age (sixteen in most states), or are just barely passing courses, waiting for graduation. On the other hand, many students are highly motivated to do well and pose few management problems.

As in middle and junior high schools, the primary management task for the teacher is to motivate students to follow rules and procedures and to learn the material being presented. Since high school students have many interests that compete with academics, high school teachers must be particularly concerned with the interest level and relevance of their lessons (Allen, 1986).

talking, working on seatwork, continuing to work during any interruptions, staying in one's seat, being at one's seat and ready to work when the bell rings, and following directions.

4. *Raise hands to be recognized:* This is a rule against calling out or getting out of one's seat for assistance.

DISCIPLINE

The preceding sections of this chapter discussed means of organizing classroom activities to maximize time for instruction and minimize time for such minor disturbances as students talking out of turn, getting out of their seats without permission, and not paying attention. Provision of interesting lessons, efficient use of class time, and careful structuring of instructional activities will prevent most such minor behavior problems, and many more serious ones as well. For example, Kounin (1970) found that teacher behaviors associated with high time on-task were also associated with fewer serious behavior problems. Time off-task can lead to more serious problems; many behavior problems arise because students are frustrated or bored in school. Instructional programs that actively involve students and provide all of them with opportunities for success may prevent such problems.

However, effective lessons and "good classkeeping" are not the only means of preventing or dealing with inappropriate behavior. Besides structuring classes so as to reduce the frequency of behavior problems, teachers must have strategies for dealing with behavior problems when they do occur (see Cairns, 1987).

Structure and Freedom

Before considering disciplinary strategies, it is important to reflect on their purpose. Students should learn much more in school than the "3 R's." Hopefully, they learn that they are competent learners, and that learning is enjoyable and satisfying. A classroom environment that is warm, supportive, and accepting is critical in developing these attitudes.

A healthy classroom environment cannot be created if students do not respect teachers or teachers do not respect students. The teacher is the leader of the classroom and is responsible for the welfare of the entire class. Though teachers should involve students in setting class rules and take student needs or input into account when organizing the classroom, ultimately teachers are the leaders who establish and enforce rules that students must live by. These class rules and procedures should become second nature to students. Teachers who have not established their authority in the classroom are likely to spend much too much time dealing with behavior problems or yelling at students to be instructionally effective. Furthermore, the clearer the structure and routine procedures in the classroom, the more freedom the teacher can allow students. The following sections discuss strategies for dealing with typical discipline problems.

Managing Routine Misbehavior

The great majority of behavior problems a teacher must deal are relatively minor disruptions—behaviors that would be appropriate on the playing field but not in the classroom. These include talking out of turn, getting up without permission, failing to follow class rules or procedures, and inattention—nothing really serious, but behaviors that must be minimized for learning to occur.

The Principle of Least Intervention.   In dealing with routine classroom behavior problems, the most important principle is that misbehaviors should be corrected using the simplest intervention that will work. Many studies have found that the amount of time spent disciplining students is negatively related to student achievement (for example, Stallings and Kaskowitz, 1974; Evertson et al., 1980; Crocker and Brooker, 1986). The teacher's main goal in dealing with routine misbehavior is to do so in a way that both is effective and avoids unnecessarily disrupting the lesson. If at all possible, "the show must go on" while any behavior problems are dealt with. A continuum of strategies for dealing with minor misbehaviors, from least disruptive to most, is discussed in the following sections. These strategies are to employ (1) prevention, (2) nonverbal cues, (3) praise of incompatible, correct behavior, (4) praise for other students, (5) verbal reminders, (6) repeated reminders, and (7) consequences.

1. *Prevention:* The easiest behavior problems to deal with are those that never occur in the first place. As illustrated earlier in this chapter, behavior problems can be prevented by presenting interesting and lively lessons, making class rules and procedures clear, keeping students busy on meaningful tasks, and using other effective techniques of basic classroom management (Doyle, 1983, 1986).

Varying the content of lessons, using a variety of materials and approaches, displaying humor and enthusiasm, can all reduce boredom-caused behavior problems (Kounin, 1970). Frustration caused by material that is too difficult or assignments that are unrealistically long can be avoided by breaking down assignments into smaller steps and doing a better job of preparing students to work on their own. Fatigue can be reduced by allowing short breaks, by varying activities, and by scheduling difficult subjects in the morning, when students are fresh.

2. *Nonverbal cues:* Much routine classroom misbehavior can be eliminated without breaking the momentum of the lesson by the use of simple nonverbal cues (Woolfolk and Brooks, 1985). Making eye contact with a misbehaving student may be enough to stop misbehavior. For example, if two students are whispering, the teacher might simply catch the eye of one or both of them. Moving close to a student who is misbehaving also usually alerts the student to shape up. If these fail, a light hand on the student's shoulder is likely to be effective (although touch should be used cautiously with adolescents, who may be touchy about touching). These nonverbal strategies all clearly convey the same message: "I see what you are doing and don't like it. Please get back to work." The advantage of communicating this message nonverbally is that the lesson need not be interrupted. In contrast, verbal reprimands can cause a "ripple effect"; many students stop working while one is being reprimanded (Kounin, 1970). Instead of interrupting the flow of concentration for many to deal with the behavior of one, nonverbal cues usually have an effect only on the student who is misbehaving, as was illustrated earlier in this chapter by the teacher who continued his lesson while silently closing and putting away a book one student was reading. That student was the only one in the class who paid much attention to the whole episode.

3. *Praise of incompatible, correct behavior:* As noted in Chapter 10, praise can be a powerful motivator for many students. One strategy for reducing misbehavior in class is to make sure to praise students for behaviors that are incompatible with the misbehavior you want to reduce. That is, catch students in the act of doing *right*. If

students often get out of their seats without permission, praise them on the occasions when they do get to work right away.

4. *Praise of other students:* It is often possible to get one student to behave by praising others for behaving. For example, if Polly is goofing off, the teacher might say, "I'm glad to see so many students working so well—Jake is doing a good job, Carol is doing well, José and Michelle are working nicely . . ." When Polly finally does get to work, the teacher should praise her too, without dwelling on her past inattention, as follows: "I see James and Walter and Polly doing a good job."

5. *Simple verbal reminder:* If a nonverbal cue is impossible or ineffective, a simple verbal reminder may help bring a student into line. The reminder should be given immediately after students misbehave; delayed reminders are usually ineffective (Aronfreed and Reber, 1965). If possible, the reminder should state what students are supposed to be doing rather than dwelling on what they are doing wrong. For example, it is better to say, "John, please attend to your own work," than "John, stop copying off of Alfredo's paper." Stating the reminder positively communicates more positive expectations for future behavior than does a negative statement (see Good and Brophy, 1984). Also, the remainder should focus on the behavior, not on the student. While a particular student *behavior* may be intolerable, the student himself or herself is always accepted and welcome in the classroom (see Ginott, 1972).

6. *Repeated reminders:* Most often a nonverbal cue, reinforcement of other students, or a simple reminder will be enough to end minor misbehavior. However, sometimes students test the teacher's resolve by failing to do what has been asked of them or by arguing or giving excuses. This "testing" will diminish over time if students learn that teachers mean what they say and will use appropriate measures to enforce an orderly, productive classroom environment.

When a student refuses to comply with a simple reminder, one strategy to attempt first is a repetition of the reminder, ignoring any irrelevant excuse or argument. Canter and Canter (1976), in a program called "Assertive Discipline," call this strategy the "broken record." Teachers should decide what they want the student to do, state this clearly to the student ("statement of want"), and then repeat it until the student complies. An example of the "broken record" from Canter and Canter (1976, p. 80) follows:

Teachers can try to halt misbehavior by reminding students of the behavior that is appropriate. Such reminders can be repeated if at first they are ineffective.

TEACHER: "Craig, I want you to start your project now." (Statement of want)

CRAIG: "I will as soon as I finish my game. Just a few more minutes."

TEACHER (firmly): "Craig, I understand, but I want you to start your project now." (Broken record)

CRAIG: "You never give me enough time with the games."

TEACHER (calmly, firmly): "That's not the point, I want you to start your project now."

CRAIG: "I don't like doing my project."

TEACHER (firmly): "I understand, but I want you to start your project."

CRAIG: "Wow, you really mean it. I'll get to work."

This teacher avoided a lengthy argument with a student by simply repeating the request. When Craig said, "You never give me enough time with the games," and "I don't like doing my project," he was not inviting a serious discussion, but was simply

A punishment is a consequence that a person will try to avoid.

procrastinating and testing the teacher's resolve. Rather than going off on a tangent with him, the teacher calmly restated the request, turning aside his excuses with "That's not the point . . . " and "I understand, but . . . " Of course, if Craig had a legitimate issue to discuss or a valid complaint, the teacher would have dealt with it, but all too often students' arguments or excuses are nothing more than a means of drawing out an interaction with the teacher to avoid getting down to work.

7. *Applying consequences:* In the (hopefully) rare case when all previous steps have been ineffective in getting the student to comply with a clearly stated and reasonable request, the final step is to pose a choice to the student: Either comply or suffer the consequences. Examples of consequences are sending the student out of class, making the student miss a few minutes of recess or some other privilege, having the student stay after school, and calling the student's parents. A consequence for not complying with the teacher's request should be mildly unpleasant, short in duration, and applied as soon as possible after the behavior occurs. Certainty is far more important than severity; students must know that consequences follow misbehavior as night follows day. One disadvantage of using severe or long-lasting punishment (for example, no recess for a week) is that it can create resentment in the student and a defiant attitude. Also, it may be difficult to follow through on severe or long-lasting consequences. Mild but certain consequences communicate, "I cannot tolerate that sort of *behavior,* but I care about *you* and want you to rejoin the class as soon as you are ready."

Before presenting a student with a consequence for noncompliance, teachers must be absolutely certain they can and will follow through if necessary. When teachers say, "You may choose to get to work right away or you may choose to spend five minutes of your recess doing your work here," they must be certain that someone will be available to monitor the student in the classroom during recess. Empty or vague threats ("You stop that or I'll make you wish you had!" or "You get to work or I'll have you suspended for a month!") are worse than useless. If teachers are not prepared to follow through with consequences, students will learn to shrug them off.

After a consequence has been applied, the teacher should avoid referring to the incident. For example, when the student returns from a ten-minute exclusion from class, the teacher should accept him or her back without any sarcasm or recriminations. The student now deserves a fresh start.

Managing More Serious Behavior Problems

The previous section discussed how to deal with behaviors that might be appropriate on the playing field but are out of line in the classroom. There are other behaviors that are not appropriate anywhere. These include fighting, stealing, destruction of property, and gross disrespect for teachers or other school staff. These are far less common than routine classroom misbehavior, but far more serious.

For serious misbehaviors, swift and certain consequences must be applied. Any delay in punishment, or any uncertainty that the punishment will be applied, may make the consequences ineffective (Aronfreed and Reber, 1965; Solomon et al., 1968). For most students, the most effective consequence for serious misbehavior is a call to the student's parent by the teacher, principal, or vice principal. If the behavior is repeated, the parents should be called in for a conference to help work out a plan for solving the problem. Behavior modification programs can also be effectively used to reduce serious behavior problems. These strategies are described in the following sections.

The topic of classroom management revolves around who controls the classroom: the teacher or the students. No wonder the topic makes people anxious! Plan some remedies for this anxiety: list people in a school who can help you with classroom management problems. Review what you already know about being a good manager. Think about steps you'll take to remain calm and in command when the first "crisis" hits.

APPLIED BEHAVIOR ANALYSIS

Behavioral learning theories, described in Chapter 4, have direct application to classroom management. Simply put, behavioral learning theories hold that behaviors that are not reinforced or are punished will diminish in frequency. The strategies for dealing with misbehavior discussed in the previous sections were based directly on behavioral learning theories: appropriate behaviors are strengthened by praise, and inappropriate ones are diminished by ignoring them or by mild but certain punishment. The following section presents an analysis of classroom behavior in terms of behavioral concepts, and gives specific behavior modification strategies for preventing and dealing with misbehavior.

What Maintains Student Misbehavior?

A basic principle of behavioral learning theories is that if any behavior persists over time, it must be maintained by some reinforcer. To reduce misbehavior in the classroom, we must understand which reinforcers maintain misbehavior in the first place.

The most common reinforcer for classroom misbehavior is attention—from the teacher, the peer group, or both. Students receiving one-to-one tutoring rarely misbehave, both because they already have the undivided attention of an adult and because no classmates are present to attend to any negative behavior. However, in the typical classroom students have to go out of their way to get the teacher's personal attention, and they have an audience of peers who may encourage or applaud their misdeeds.

Teacher's Attention.   Sometimes students misbehave because they want the teacher's attention, even if it is negative. This is a more common reason for misbehavior than many teachers think (see Hamblin et al., 1971). A puzzled teacher might say, "I don't know what is wrong with Nathan. I have to stay with him all day to keep him working! Sometimes I get exasperated and yell at him. My words fall off him like water off a duck's back. He even smiles when I'm scolding him!"

When students appear to misbehave to gain the teacher's attention, the solution is relatively easy: pay attention to those students when they are doing well, and ignore them (as much as possible) when they misbehave. When ignoring their actions is impossible, time-out (for example, sending these students to the principal's office) will be more effective than scolding—in fact, scolding acts as a reinforcer for many students.

Peers' Attention.   Another very common reason that students misbehave is to get the attention and approval of their peers. The classic instance of this is the "class clown," who is obviously performing for the amusement of his or her classmates. However,

1. Young children cannot be expected to control themselves as well as older children. When young students disrupt the class, how do you deal with them?

Sharon Reed, a first-grade teacher in Bozeman, Mont., notes the importance of setting and sticking to rules:

> Establishing guidelines in the first days of school is the simplest way I have found for keeping discipline problems to a minimum. Each situation and the consequences are spelled out for the children. As they occur, I call attention to the guidelines, recalling our earlier discussion. Once is enough for a reminder. After that, I act quietly and swiftly and carry out the appropriate discipline as outlined in those first days. This would usually involve removing the child from the group and reprimanding in private. The impact of my reaction is noticed by the class and the teacher's word is established.
>
> Most discipline can be handled by a look, a touch, or a gentle reprimand.

2. Adolescence is a time when many people challenge authority. What measures have you found helpful when a junior high or high school student challenges your authority as a teacher?

Pam Woolsey, junior high math teacher in Knoxville, Ill., mentions the importance of the teacher's relationship to the students:

> I like to earn my students' respect, not demand it. It is necessary to always be the professional and not the occasional adolescent with them. They must see you as an adult—not necessarily popular with them all, but fair and consistent.

Patricia Padgett, a high school teacher in Pleasanton, Cal.:

> I do active listening—stating what I see/hear is the student's position and thereby acknowledging his or her right to have a position (and one that is different from mine). Then I reiterate the format of the teaching situation—I'm there to teach and the student's behavior is interfering, therefore it must stop. I also talk about what students' "developmental" tasks are à la Eric Erikson, and support their learning how to handle time, decisions, etc.

Patricia Rentschler, a ninth-grade teacher in Terre Haute, Ind.:

> I've used the hall for disciplining students. I may send the student to the dean. I may ask the dean to come to my room. My job isn't to embarrass, but to teach. Good teaching and being well prepared solve many problems before they happen, but a teacher should not hesitate to call for help if the situation is taking up too much class time.

Patricia James, who teaches ninth grade in Elizabeth City, N.C.:

> I give the student a choice: Follow the rules or take the consequences. I also try to give them a way out. A cornered adolescent can be dangerous and will do almost anything rather than look foolish or back down in front of peers. Use of humor also helps, as well as asking students for their solution to the situation.

many other forms of misbehavior are motivated primarily by peer attention and approval—in fact, few students completely disregard the potential impact of their behavior on their classmates. For example, students who refuse to do what the teacher has asked are consciously or unconsciously weighing the effect of their defiance on their standing among their classmates.

Even preschoolers and early elementary students misbehave to gain peer attention, but beginning around the third grade (and especially during the middle/junior high school years), it is particularly likely that student misbehavior is linked to peer attention and support. As students enter adolescence, the peer group takes on extreme importance, and peer norms begin to favor independence from authority. When older children and teenagers engage in serious delinquent acts (such as vandalism, theft, and assault), they are usually supported by a delinquent peer group (Cloward and Ohlin, 1960).

Strategies for reducing peer-supported misbehavior are quite different from those for dealing with misbehavior meant to capture the teacher's attention. Ignoring misbehavior will be ineffective if the misbehavior is reinforced by peers. For example, if a student is balancing a book on his or her head and the class is laughing, the behavior can hardly be ignored, because it will continue as long as the class is interested (and will encourage others to behave likewise). Further, scolding may only attract more attention from classmates, or worse, enhance the student's standing among peers. Similarly, if two students are whispering or talking to each other, they are reinforcing each other for misbehaving, and ignoring their behavior will only encourage more of it.

There are two primary responses to peer-supported misbehavior. One is to remove the offender from the classroom to deprive him or her of peer attention. Another is to use **group contingencies,** strategies in which the entire class (or groups of students within the class) is rewarded on the basis of everyone's behavior. Under group contingencies, all students benefit from their classmates' good behavior, so peer support for misbehavior is removed. Group contingencies and other behavior management strategies for peer-supported misbehavior are described in more detail in the following sections.

Release from Boredom, Frustration, or Fatigue. A third important reinforcer for misbehavior is release from boredom, frustration, fatigue, or unpleasant activities. As explained in Chapter 4, escaping or avoiding an unpleasant stimulus is a reinforcer. Some students see much of what happens in school as unpleasant, boring, frustrating, or tiring. This is particularly true of students who experience repeated failure in school; for them, the classroom may be an endless psychological torture. But even the most able and motivated students feel bored or frustrated at times.

Students often misbehave just to escape from unpleasant activities. This can be clearly seen with students who frequently ask permission to get a drink of water, go to the washroom, or sharpen their pencils. Such students are more likely to make these requests during seatwork than during lecture, because seatwork can be frustrating or anxiety-provoking for students who have little confidence in their academic abilities.

More serious misbehaviors can also be partially or completely motivated by a desire for release from boredom, frustration, or fatigue. A student may misbehave just to stir things up. Sometimes students misbehave precisely so that they will be sent out of the classroom. Obviously, then, sending such a student to the hall or the principal's office can be counterproductive.

The best solution for misbehaviors arising from boredom, frustration, or fatigue is prevention. Students rarely misbehave during interesting, varied, engaging lessons. Actively involving students in lessons can head off misbehaviors due to boredom or fatigue. Use of cooperative learning methods or other means of involving students in an active way can be helpful. Frustration may be avoided by the use of materials that ensure a high success rate for all, by making sure that all students are challenged but none are overwhelmed. Changing instruction and assessments to help students succeed can be an effective means of resolving frustration-related behavior problems. For example, Becker et al. (1967) used a combination of praise and small rewards to increase the on-task behavior of first- and second-graders with serious behavior problems. Either praise alone or praise plus reward were effective with most students, but not with one low-achieving student. However, when he was given a special reading tutor, his misbehavior virtually disappeared (even when he was not with the

Group Contingencies
Class rewards that depend on the behavior of all students

Students sometimes misbehave out of boredom or out of a desire for attention from fellow students.

tutor). The experience of success at his own level was apparently enough to remove the need to escape from frustration and failure by misbehaving.

APPLIED BEHAVIOR ANALYSIS AND CLASSROOM MANAGEMENT

The behavior management strategies outlined in the previous sections (for example, nonverbal cues, reminders, mild but certain punishment) might be described as informal applications of behavioral learning theories. These practices, plus the prevention of misbehavior by the use of efficient class management and engaging lessons, will be sufficient to create a good learning environment in most classrooms.

However, in some classrooms more systematic behavior modification methods are needed. In classrooms in which most students are well-behaved but a few have persistent behavior problems, individual behavior modification strategies can be effective. In classrooms in which many students have behavior problems, particularly when there is peer support for misbehavior, whole-class behavior modification strategies or group contingencies may be needed. Such strategies are most often required when many low-achieving or poorly motivated students are put in one class, as often happens in lower-class neighborhood schools, in special education classes, and in schools that use tracking or other between-class ability grouping methods.

Setting up and using any behavior modification program requires following a series of steps that proceeds from the observation of the behavior through program implementation to program evaluation (see Medland and Vitale, 1984). The steps listed here are part, to a greater or lesser extent, of the four behavior modification programs that are discussed in the next section:

1. Identify target behavior(s) and reinforcer(s).

2. Establish a baseline for the target behavior.

3. Choose a reinforcer and criteria for reinforcement.

4. If necessary, choose a punisher and criteria for punishment.

5. Observe behavior during program implementation and compare it to baseline.

6. When the behavior modification program is working, reduce the frequency of reinforcement.

Individual Behavior Modification Strategies

Individual behavior modification strategies are useful for coping with individual students who have persistent behavior problems in school. Strategies for dealing with this sort of chronic behavior problem follow (see Sulzer-Azaroff and Mayer, 1986).

1. *Identify target behavior(s) and reinforcer(s).* The first step in implementing a behavior modification program is to observe the misbehaving student to identify one or a small number of behaviors to target first and to see what reinforcers maintain the behavior(s). Another purpose of this observation is to establish a baseline against which to compare improvements. A structured individual behavior modification program should aim to change only one behavior or a small set of closely related behaviors. Tackling too many behaviors at a time risks failing with all of them because the student may not clearly see what he or she must do to be reinforced.

The first behavior targeted should be one that is serious, easy to observe, and, most importantly, occurs frequently. For example, if a child gets into fights in the playground every few days but gets out of his or her seat without permission several times per hour, you would start with the out-of-seat behavior and deal with the fighting later. Ironically, the more frequent and persistent a behavior, the easier it is to extinguish. This is because positive or negative consequences can be applied frequently, making the connection between behavior and consequence clear to the student.

As noted earlier, three reinforcers maintain most classroom misbehavior: teacher's attention, peers' attention, and release from boredom, frustration, or fatigue. In observing a student, try to determine which reinforcer(s) are maintaining the target behavior. If a student misbehaves in league with others (for example, talks without permission, swears, teases, fights) or if a student's misbehavior usually attracts the attention of others (for example, clowning, sassing the teacher), then you might conclude that the behavior is peer-supported. If the behavior does not attract much peer attention but always requires teacher attention (for example, getting out of seat without permission, constantly asking for help when help is not needed, refusing to work without constant prodding), then you might conclude that the behavior is supported by your own attention.

2. *Establish a baseline for the target behavior.* On several successive days (at least three) observe the student to see how often the target behavior occurs. Before you do this, you will need to clearly define exactly what constitutes the behavior. For example, if the target behavior is "bothering classmates," you will have to decide what specific behaviors constitute "bothering" (perhaps teasing, poking, interrupting, taking materials).

Baseline measurements may be taken in terms of frequency (for example, how many times Charles got out of his seat without permission) or time (how many minutes Charles was out of his seat). Frequency records are usually easier to keep; you can simply make a tally on a sheet of paper on your desk.

3. *Decide on a reinforcer and a criterion for reinforcement.* Behavioral learning theories and behavior modification practice strongly favor the use of reinforcers for appropriate behavior rather than punishers for inappropriate behavior. The reasons for this are practical as well as ethical. Punishment often creates resentment, so that even if it solves one problem, it may create others (see Skinner, 1968). Also, punishment must be consistently applied. In contrast, successful reinforcement programs are supposed to be faded out over time. While reinforcers must be consistently given for appropriate behavior at the beginning of a behavior modification program, they should be given less and less consistently as behavior improves. Finally, an ethical note. Even where punishment would work as well as reinforcement, it should be avoided because it is not conducive to the creation of a happy, healthy classroom environment. Punishment of one kind or another is necessary in some circumstances, and it should be used without qualms when reinforcement strategies are impossible or ineffective. However, a program of punishment for misbehavior should always be the last option considered, never the first.

Typical classroom reinforcers include praise, privileges, and tangible rewards. In a carefully structured behavior modification program, praise can be extremely effective in improving student behavior. For example, Kirby and Shields (1972) had a teacher praise an underachieving seventh-grader immediately when he did his math work, and ignore him when he was not on-task. The boy's rate of correct answers per minute tripled during the time when feedback and praise were given. Eventually the teacher praised him after every two problems, then every four, and later after every eight problems, and his problem-solving behavior remained at a high level. These results are illustrated in Figure 11.2. During Baseline 1 and Baseline 2 the teacher did not praise the boy for his math work; the difference made by the "praise and immediate feedback" treatment is apparent in the figure.

Praise is especially effective for students who misbehave to get the teacher's attention. It is often a good idea to start a behavior modification program using praise for appropriate behavior to see if this is sufficient, but to be prepared to use stronger reinforcers if praise is not enough (see Becker et al., 1967).

Ignoring inappropriate behavior is often the counterpart of praising appropriate behavior. However, this strategy is effective only if misbehavior is maintained by the teacher's attention. Zimmerman and Zimmerman (1962) give two examples of this. One emotionally disturbed eleven-year-old, David, when asked to spell words, would mumble letters completely unconnected with the words. The teacher would coax him for some time, giving the first letter and other clues and encouraging him to get

FIGURE 11.2

Reinforcing Good Behavior with Praise

The number of math problems a seventh-grade boy answered correctly per minute tripled when he was immediately praised for doing his work. The boy's work was not praised immediately during the baseline period.

From Kirby and Shields, 1972, p. 82.

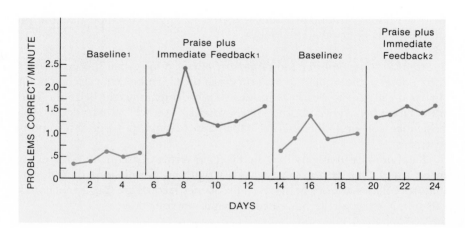

started. This went on for weeks. Then the teacher decided to ignore David until he wrote a word correctly. She gave him an easy word and asked him to write it. He said, "I can't spell it," and hemmed and hawed for several minutes, during which time the teacher paid no attention to him. Finally he wrote the word correctly. The teacher looked up and said, "Good, now we can go on." This procedure was repeated for ten words, each of which took less and less time. At the end the teacher praised David, wrote an A on the paper, and asked him to help her color some Easter baskets, which he did gladly. Over the next week David's bizarre spelling and other inappropriate work behaviors disappeared entirely.

Another eleven-year-old emotionally disturbed boy, Sam, had terrific temper tantrums. Several adults and other children would routinely gather around to watch him lie on the floor, kicking and screaming.

After many such tantrums the teacher tried a different approach. One day Sam had a tantrum in the classroom before the other students arrived. The teacher ignored him completely, continuing to work at her desk. After about three minutes of screaming and crying, Sam looked up at the teacher. She said that she would be glad to work with him when he was ready. Sam cried and screamed with diminishing loudness for another five minutes, then lifted his head and said he was ready. The teacher smiled, said, "Good, now let's get to work," and worked with Sam for the rest of the period. A similar approach was used for a few later incidents of tantrums. If the tantrums occurred when other students were in the classroom, the teacher took Sam into an empty room to have his tantrum, but otherwise ignored him until he was calm. At all other times she made a point of giving Sam a lot of personal attention. Soon the tantrums disappeared. Interestingly, many other inappropriate behaviors disappeared along with the tantrums. Positive "spillover" effects of this kind are common outcomes of successful behavior modification programs.

In the cases of David and Sam, the teacher's well-meaning efforts to help were in fact reinforcing the misbehavior. For example, David's bizarre spellings gained him a lot of attention, which he thrived on. When the attention was withdrawn, and he received attention only for spelling correctly, he was glad to comply, because his needs were as well satisfied by praise as by the coaxing he had received for his misspellings.

In addition to praise, many teachers find it useful to give students stars, "smilies," or other small rewards when they behave appropriately. Some teachers use a rubber stamp to mark students' papers with a symbol indicating good work. These small rewards make the teacher's praise more concrete and visible, and also let students take their work home and receive praise from their parents.

4. If necessary, decide on punishers and criteria for punishment. When a serious behavior problem does not respond to a well-designed reinforcement program, punishment may be necessary.

A punisher is any unpleasant stimulus that an individual will try to avoid. Common punishers used in schools are reprimands, being sent out of class or the principal's office, and detention or missed recess. Corporal punishment (for example, spanking) is illegal in some states and districts (see Sulzer-Azaroff and Mayer, 1986) and highly restricted in others, though the practice is still often seen (Rose, 1984). However, corporal punishment is neither a necessary nor an effective response to misbehavior in school.

O'Leary and O'Leary (1972, p. 152) list seven principles for the effective and humane use of punishment:

1. Use punishment sparingly.

Time-Out
Removing a student from a situation in which misbehavior was being reinforced

2. Make it clear to the child why he or she is being punished.

3. Provide the child with an alternative means of obtaining some positive reinforcement.

4. Reinforce the child for behaviors incompatible with those you wish to weaken (for example, if you punish for being off-task, also reinforce for being on-task).

5. Avoid physical punishment.

6. Avoid punishing while you are in a very angry or emotional state.

7. Punish when a behavior starts rather than when it ends (see Walters et al., 1965).

Many studies have demonstrated the effectiveness of certain, mild punishment for reducing inappropriate behavior. For example, Hall et al. (1971) evaluated a program in which each of ten emotionally disturbed boys received check marks next to their names every time they got out of their seats without permission. Each check mark equaled five minutes after school. This procedure reduced out-of-seat behaviors for the boys from an average of 23 per session to 2.2 per session. O'Leary et al. (1970) found that softly delivered, firm reprimands for misbehaviors were much more effective than yelling.

One effective punisher is called **time-out.** The teacher tells a misbehaving student to go to a separate part of the classroom, the hall, the principal's or vice principal's office, or another teacher's class. The place where the student is sent should be uninteresting and out of view of classmates. An empty room may be best, although Canter and Canter (1976) suggest that pairs of teachers agree in advance that if one teacher's students need time-out, they can be sent to the other's classroom.

One advantage of time-out procedures is that they remove the student from the attention of his or her classmates. Therefore time-out may be especially effective for students whose misbehavior is primarily motivated by peer attention.

Teachers should assign time-outs infrequently, but when they do assign them, they should do so calmly and surely: the student is to go straight to the time-out area and stay there until the prescribed time is up. Time-out assignments should be brief; about five minutes is usually adequate. However, timing should begin only after the student settles down; if the student yells or argues, that time should not count. During time-out no one should speak to the student. Teachers should not scold the student during time-out. Students should be told why they are being given time-out, but not otherwise lectured. If the principal's office is used, the principal should be asked not to speak to the student.

Time-out procedures have been successfully used to reduce disruptive talking by junior high school girls (Madsen and Madsen, 1968), aggression, temper tantrums, and destruction of materials by retarded children (Birnbrauer et al., 1965), and for many other misbehaviors in various settings.

5. *Observe behavior and compare to baseline.* It is important to assess the effectiveness of your program. A behavior modification program usually works within a few days. If behavior is not improving after a week, try a different system or different reinforcers.

6. *When the behavior management program is working, reduce the frequency of reinforcement.* Once a behavior modification program has been in operation for a while and the student's behavior has improved and stabilized at a new level, the

frequency of reinforcement can be reduced. Initially, reinforcers might be applied to every instance of appropriate behavior; as time goes on, every other instance, then every several instances, might be reinforced. Reducing the frequency of reinforcement helps maintain the new behaviors over the long run, and aids in extending the behaviors to other settings.

Home-Based Reinforcement Strategies
Behavior modification strategies in which a student's school behavior is reported to parents, who supply rewards

Home-Based Reinforcement

Home-based reinforcement strategies are perhaps the most practical and effective behavior modification–based classroom management methods (see Barth, 1979). Teachers give students a daily or weekly "report card" to take home, and parents are instructed to provide special privileges or rewards to students on the basis of these teacher reports. Home-based reinforcement is not exactly a new idea; a museum in Vermont displays weekly "report cards" from the 1860s.

Home-based reinforcement methods have been used to improve the behavior of individual disruptive children in classrooms (Sluyter and Hawkins, 1972) as well as that of entire disruptive classrooms (Ayllon et al., 1975). Dougherty and Dougherty (1977) used home-based reinforcement to motivate students to hand in homework, complete their schoolwork, and refrain from talking without permission.

Home-based reinforcement has several advantages over other, equally effective behavior management strategies. First, parents can give much more potent rewards and privileges than schools can. For example, parents control access to such activities as television, trips to the store, and going out with friends. Parents also know what their own children like and therefore can provide more individual privileges than the school.

Second, home-based reinforcement gives parents frequent good news about their children. Parents of disruptive children usually hear from the school only when their child has done something wrong. This is bad for parent-school relations, and leads to much blame and finger-pointing.

Third, home-based reinforcement is easy to administer. Any adults who deal with the child (other teachers, bus drivers, playground or lunch monitors) can be involved in the program by having a student carry a "daily report card" all day (Runge et al. 1975).

Finally, over time "daily report cards" can be replaced by "weekly report cards" and then "biweekly report cards" without loss in effectiveness (Dougherty and Dougherty, 1977), until the school's usual six- or nine-week report cards can be used.

When home-based reinforcement programs are used, the responsibility for rewarding a child's good behavior rests with the parents. One reward might be to do a special activity with the child.

Example of a Daily Report Card Program.   Figure 11.3 presents a daily report card for Homer Heath, an elementary school student. His teacher, Ms. Casa, rated his behavior and schoolwork at the end of each academic period, and she arranged to have the lunch monitor and the recess monitor rate his behavior when Homer was with them. Homer was responsible for carrying his report card with him at all times and for making sure that it was marked and initialed at the end of each period. Whenever he made at least 30 points, his parents agreed to give him a special privilege—his father was to read him a story before bedtime and let him stay up fifteen minutes longer than usual. Whenever he forgot to bring home his report card, his parents were to assume that he did not meet the criterion.

If Homer had been a junior or senior high school student, or if he had been in departmentalized elementary school (where he changed classes for each subject), he would have carried his report card to every class and each teacher would have marked

STUDENT HOMER H.	DAILY REPORT CARD	DATE MARCH 21	

PERIOD	BEHAVIOR	SCHOOLWORK	TEACHER
READING	1 2 ③ 4	1 ② 3 4	Ms. Casa
MATH	1 2 3 ④	1 2 3 ④	Ms. Casa
LUNCH	1 2 ③ 4		Mr. Mason
RECESS	1 2 ③ 4		Ms. Hauser
LANGUAGE	1 2 3 ④	1 2 3 ④	Ms. Casa
SCIENCE/SOC. STUD.	1 2 ③ 4	1 2 ③ 4	Ms. Casa
	1 = Poor	1 = Assignments not completed.	
	2 = Fair	2 = Assignments completed poorly.	
	3 = Good	3 = Assignments completed adequately.	
	4 = Excellent	4 = Assignments completed — excellent!	

TOTAL RATING: 33   ☺   SCORE NEEDED: 30

FIGURE 11.3

Example of a Daily Report Card

Teachers who use a home-based reinforcement program must set up a daily report card so that a student's work and behavior can be assessed and reported to the student's parents.
From Dougherty and Dougherty, 1977.

it. Obviously, this would take some coordination among the teachers, but the effort would certainly be worthwhile if the daily report card dramatically reduced his misbehaviors and increased his academic output, as it has in dozens of studies evaluating this method (Barth, 1979).

Whole-Class Behavior Modification

Behavior modification–based classroom management strategies are often applied to the class as a whole, so that all students are reinforced (or punished) for their behavior under the same rules (see Litow and Pumroy, 1975). For example, if the teacher says, "Any student who finishes the worksheet may go to recess," this is a simple whole-class behavior modification system; all students have the same opportunity to be rewarded according to the same standard.

As is the case with all the behavior modification–based classroom management programs discussed in this chapter, whole-class behavior modification strategies have been consistently found to have strong, often dramatic effects on student behavior. For example, O'Leary and Becker (1967) evaluated a program in which emotionally disturbed third-graders were given points according to a rating of their academic behaviors (in seat, facing front, raising hand, working, paying attention, desk clear).

Daily Report Cards

Steps for setting up and implementing a daily report card system are as follows:

1. *Decide on behaviors to include in the daily report card:* Choose a behavior or set of behaviors on which the daily report card is to be based. Devise a rating scheme for each behavior, and construct a standard report card form. Your daily report card might be more or less elaborate than the one in Figure 11.3. For example, you might break "behavior" down into more precise categories, such as "getting along with others," "staying on-task," and "following class rules." If a student's sole problem is fighting, then the card might only have a rating for "getting along with others."

Students need not be rated every period; one rating at the end of the day may be enough. In fact, the easiest form of a home-based reinforcement program would be to give students whose behavior meets a high criterion a "good behavior certificate" to take home each day. However, for young children or those with serious behavior problems, one rating at the end of the whole day may be too long a wait and too vague a criterion to be effective.

2. *Explain the program to parents:* Since home-based reinforcement programs depend on parent participation, it is critical to inform parents about the program and to obtain their cooperation. Ayllon et al. (1975), who worked in an inner-city school where most households were headed by single working women, asked parents to attend a two-hour meeting and called or visited those who could not attend. However, other researchers (Edlund, 1969; Dougherty and Dougherty, 1977; Lahey et al., 1977) found that writing letters to parents worked quite well, and Karraker (1972) reported the home-based reinforcement programs involving one-hour parent conferences, fifteen-minute conferences, or one-page letters to parents were equally effective.

However they are notified and involved, parents should be told what the daily report card means, and asked to reward their children whenever they bring home a good report card. In presenting the program to parents, teachers should explain what parents might do to reward their children. Communications with parents should be brief, positive, and informal; they should generate a feeling that "we're going to solve this together." The program should focus on rewarding good behavior rather than punishing bad behavior (see Runge et al., 1975).

Examples of rewards parents might use at home (adapted from Walker and Shea, 1980) are:

- Special activities with a parent (for example, reading, flying a kite, building a model, shopping, playing a game, going to the zoo).
- Special foods.
- Baking cookies or cooking.
- Operating equipment usually reserved for adults (for example, the dishwasher or vacuum cleaner).
- Access to special games, toys, equipment.
- Small rewards (such as coloring books, paper, comic books, erasers, stickers).
- Additional play time, television time, and the like.
- Having a friend spend the night.
- Later bedtime or curfew.

Parents should be encouraged to choose rewards they can give every day (that is, nothing too expensive or difficult).

The best rewards are ones that build closeness between parent and child, such as doing special activities together. Many children who have behavior problems in school also have them at home, and may have less than ideal relationships with their parents. Home-based reinforcement programs provide an opportunity for parents to show their love for their child at a time when the child has something to be proud of. A special time with Dad can be especially valuable as a reward for good behavior in school and for building the father-son or father-daughter relationship.

3. *When behavior improves, reduce the frequency of the report:* When home-based reinforcement works, it often works dramatically (Dickerson et al., 1973). Once the behavior of students has improved and has stabilized, it is time to decrease the frequency of the reports to parents. Report cards might then be issued only weekly. As noted in Chapter 4, the best way to ensure maintenance is to "thin out" the reinforcement schedule—that is, to increase the interval between reinforcers.

FIGURE 11.4

Token Reinforcement Program

The percent of class time during which students misbehaved fell dramatically when "good behavior" points were given that could be traded for desired items.

From O'Leary and Becker, 1967, p. 639.

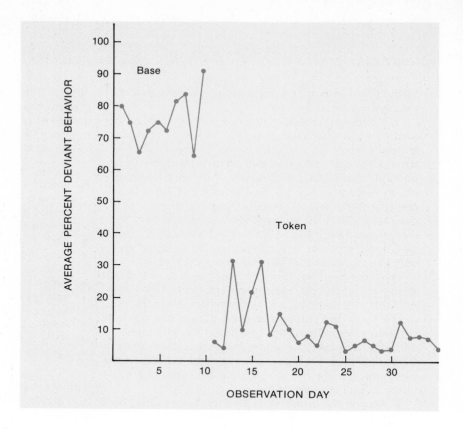

The points (or "tokens") could be exchanged at the end of each day for items such as candy, pennants, comic books, perfume, or kites. Disruptive behavior among the students dropped from 76 percent of class time to 10 percent almost as soon as the program was introduced. These results are illustrated in Figure 11.4.

Similar results have been obtained in many studies in a wide variety of settings using a wide variety of point systems and reinforcers. Broden et al. (1970a) gave junior high school special education students points for being in seat and doing assignments quietly, and charged them points for misbehavior. Students could exchange their points for privileges, such as a pass to go to lunch five minutes early, the opportunity to move their desks to a new location, or a five-minute quiet break during class time. This system increased students' on-task time from 39 percent of class time to 83 percent. Working with low-achieving eleventh- and twelfth-graders, McAllister et al. (1969) found that consistently praising students for being quiet and working reduced "talking without permission" behavior from 25 percent of class time to 5 percent. Ayllon and Roberts (1974) gave students in a regular fifth-grade class who were experiencing serious discipline problems points each day for completing reading assignments at 80 percent correct, with extra points for perfect papers. Students could exchange these points for a variety of rewards, such as ten minutes of extra recess time, access to a movie, the privilege of changing their seat in the cafeteria, or the opportunity to have their lowest test grade removed. "Auctions" were held for such privileges as being ball captain or "assistant teacher" for a week. This program increased the accuracy of students' work from 48 to 70 percent, and substantially reduced inappropriate behavior (even though the points were only for completing assignments accurately, not for behavior per se).

Because of their difficulty and expense, token reinforcement systems are rarely used today except in special education. In general, they have given way to more practical group contingencies and home-based reinforcement systems.

Group Contingencies

A group contingency is a reinforcement system in which an entire group is rewarded on the basis of the behavior of the group members. Teachers have always used group contingencies, as "We'll go to lunch as soon as *all students* have put their work away and are quiet." When the teacher says this, any one student can cause the entire class to be late to lunch. Or the teacher might say, "If the class averages at least ninety on tomorrow's quiz, then you'll all be excused from homework for the rest of the week." This group contingency would depend of the average performance of all group members rather than on any single student.

One important advantage of group contingencies is that they are easier to administer than other behavior modification–based classroom management strategies. For one thing, record keeping for a group contingency is usually much easier. Also, most often the whole class is either rewarded or not rewarded, which avoids having to do one thing with some students and something else with others. For example, suppose a teacher says, "If the whole class follows the class rules this morning, we will have five extra minutes of recess." If the class does earn the extra recess, they all get it together; the teacher need not arrange to have some students stay out longer while others are called inside.

The theory behind group contingencies is that when a group is rewarded on the basis of the behavior of its members, the group members will encourage one another to do whatever helps the group gain the reward (Hayes, 1976; Slavin, 1990). Group contingencies can turn the same peer pressure that often *supports* misbehaviors to *opposing* misbehavior. When the class can earn extra recess only if all students are well behaved all morning, no one is liable to find it funny when Joan balances a book on her head or Quinn sasses the teacher.

Group contingencies have been successfully used in many forms and for many purposes. Barrish et al. (1969) divided a fourth-grade class into two teams during math period. When the teacher saw any member of a team disobeying class rules, the whole team received a check mark on the chalkboard. If a team had five or fewer check marks at the end of the period, all team members would take part in a free-time activity at the end of the day. If both teams got more than five check marks, the one that got fewer would receive the free time. Figure 11.5 shows the results of the program.

Note that in math period talking without permission and out-of-seat behavior dropped dramatically during the "good behavior game," resumed when the "game" was removed, and dropped again when the "game" was reinstated. When the program was then extended to reading period, similar results were obtained.

Winett and Vachon (1974) evaluated a simple group contingency in an inner-city fifth-grade class. The teacher simply rated the class's behavior during an afternoon instructional period. The class was rated on such things as attention, noise level, work quality, and amount of work done. At the end of class the teacher totaled the ratings and explained them to students. This group feedback strategy alone (with no rewards) produced an increase in appropriate behavior from 62 percent of class time to 76

FIGURE 11.5

Group Contingency Program

Rewarding teams of fourth-graders for good behavior caused a dramatic decrease in the percent of one-minute intervals during which students talked out of turn or got out of their seats. During the baseline and reversal periods, the teacher used routine classroom management strategies.

From Barrish et al., 1969, p. 122.

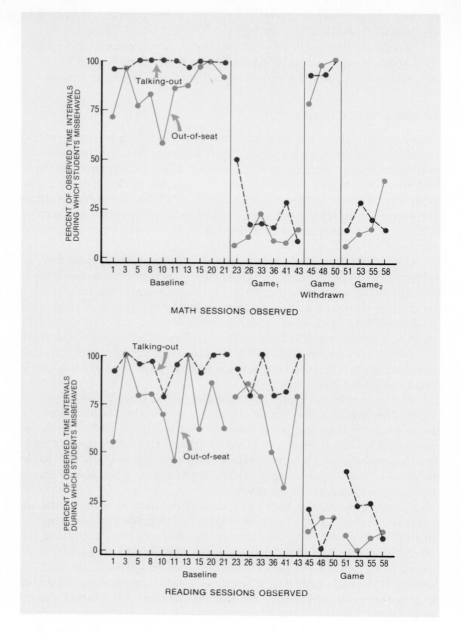

percent. When the class was given an opportunity to earn free time, games, or a chance to go outside if they got an "excellent" total rating, appropriate behavior rose to 84 percent of class time.

Ethics of Behavioral Methods

The behavior analysis strategies described in this chapter are powerful. Properly applied, they will usually bring the behavior of even the most disruptive students to manageable levels. However, there is a danger that teachers may use behavior

Group Contingency Programs

As noted earlier, a group contingency behavior management program can be as simple as the statement, "Class, if you are all in your seat, on-task, and quiet this morning, you may have five extra minutes of recess," However, a little more structure than this can increase the effectiveness of the group contingency.

1. *Decide which behaviors will be reinforced.* As in any whole-class behavior modification program, the first step in setting up a group contingency is to establish a set of class rules.

2. *Set up a point system:* There are essentially three ways to implement a group contingency behavior management program. One is to simply rate class behavior each period or during each activity. That is, an elementary school class might receive 0–5 points during each individual instructional period such as reading, language arts, and math. A secondary class might receive one overall rating each period, or separate ratings for behavior and completed assignments. Students would then be rewarded each day or week if they exceeded a preestablished number of points.

Another way to set up a group contingency is to rate the class at various times during the day. For example, you might set a timer to ring on the average of once every ten minutes (but varying randomly from one to twenty minutes). If the whole class is conforming to class rules when the timer rings, then the class earns a point. The same program can be used without the timer if the teacher gives the class a point every ten minutes or so if all students are conforming to class rules. Canter and Canter (1976) suggest that teachers use a bag of marbles and a jar, putting a marble into the jar from time to time whenever the class is following rules. Each marble would be worth thirty seconds of extra recess. In secondary schools, where extra recess in not possible, each marble might represent thirty seconds of "break time" held at the end of the period on Friday.

3. *Consider deducting points for serious misbehavior:* The group contingency reward system by itself should help improve student behavior. However, it may still be necessary to react to occasional serious misbehavior. For example, you might deduct 10 points for any instance of fighting or of serious disrespect for the teacher. When points must be deducted, do not negotiate with students about it. Just deduct them, explaining why they must be deducted and reminding students that they may earn them back if they follow class rules.

4. *When behavior improves, reduce the frequency of the points and reinforcers:* Initially, the group contingency should be applied every day. When the class's behavior improves and stabilizes at a new level for about a week, you may change to giving rewards once a week. Ultimately, the class may "graduate" from the point-and-reward system entirely, though feedback and praise based on class behavior should continue.

5. *Combine group and individual contingencies if necessary:* The use of group contingencies need not rule out individual contingencies for students who need them. For example, students who continue to have problems in a class using a group contingency might still receive daily or weekly report cards to take home to their parents.

modification techniques to overcontrol students. They may be so concerned about getting students to sit down, stay quiet, and look productive that they lose sight of the fact that school is for learning, not for social control. Winett and Winkler (1972) wrote an excellent article entitled "Current Behavior Modification in the Classroom: Be Still, Be Quiet, Be Docile," in which they warned that behavior modification–based classroom management systems are being misused if teachers mistakenly believe that a quiet class is a learning class. This point parallels the basic premise of the QAIT model of effective instruction presented in Chapter 8. Behavior management systems can increase time for learning, but unless quality of instruction, appropriate levels of instruction, and incentives for learning are also adequate, the additional time may be wasted.

Some people object to behavior modification on the basis that it is "bribing" students to do what they ought to do anyway, or that it is "mind control." However, it is important to remember that all classrooms use rewards and punishers (such as grades, praise, scolding, suspension). Behavior modification strategies simply use these rewards in a more systematic way, and avoid punishers as much as possible.

■ **Stop and Think**

The focus of this chapter has been on the prevention of behavior that disrupts the classroom. Consider now the opposite case, the nonparticipating student. How might applied behavior analysis be used for a case such as this, say for a young student who is shy and withdrawn?

SERIOUS BEHAVIOR PROBLEMS AND DELINQUENCY

Everyone misbehaves. There is hardly a person on earth who has not at some time done something he or she knew to be wrong, or even illegal. However, some people's misbehavior is far more frequent and/or serious than others', and students who fall into this category cause their teachers and school administrators (not to mention their parents and themselves) a disproportionate amount of trouble and concern.

Serious misbehavior in schools is not evenly distributed among students or schools. Clarizio and McCoy (1976) have estimated that 15 percent of all boys, but only 5 percent of girls, have moderate to severe behavior problems; and about 30 percent of all students (again, disproportionately boys) have problems that are mild to severe. Serious delinquency is far more common among students from impoverished backgrounds, particularly in urban locations. Students with poor family relationships are also much more likely than other students to become involved in serious misbehavior and delinquency, as are students who are low in achievement and those who experience attendance problems (see Wolfgang et al., 1972).

Even though some types of students are more prone to misbehavior than others, these characteristics do not *cause* misbehavior. Some students misbehave because they perceive that the rewards for misbehavior outweigh the rewards for good behavior. For example, students who do not experience success in school may perceive that the potential rewards for hard work and good behavior are small, so they turn to other sources of rewards. Some put their energies into sports, others into social activities. Some, particularly those who are failing in many different domains, find their niche in groups that hold norms against achievement and other prosocial behavior. This can all happen very early, as soon as some students realize that they are unlikely to do well in school or to receive much support at home, from peers, or from the school itself for their academic efforts. Over time, students who fail in school and get into minor behavior difficulties may fall in with a delinquent subgroup and begin to engage in serious delinquent or even criminal behavior. The role of the delinquent peer group in maintaining delinquent behavior cannot be overstated. Delinquent acts among adolescents and preadolescents are usually done in groups and are supported by antisocial peer norms (Cloward and Ohlin, 1960).

Preventing Serious Misbehavior and Delinquency

The school has an important role to play in preventing or managing serious misbehavior and delinquency, but the student and the school are only one part of the story; delinquent behavior often involves the police, courts, social service agencies, as

Rookie teachers bring bundles of enthusiasm to their new jobs—and also some anxieties about their knowledge and competence. Frequently among their nightmares is the specter of an uncooperative, uncontrollable student who disrupts lessons, irritates other students, and generally bedevils the classroom environment.

Luckily, researchers are finding ways of helping such students. Their advances offer hope that students who have problems with behavior can learn to succeed in school and can lead productive lives thereafter.

One example is the work by psychologists and educators with aggressive boys. The techniques being tried include helping the boys learn how to make friends and teaching their parents effective techniques for discipline. Adding urgency to the work is research that links youthful aggression to adult criminal behavior.

Dr. Robert Selwan, of the Harvard Medical School, has observed that an early problem for many aggressive boys is difficulty in making friends. "In almost every case the boys have never had a close friend," Dr. Selwan said. "They want to be friends, but don't know how."

His approach has been to pair an aggressive boy with one who is overly withdrawn. He then nurtures a friendship by having the boys spend time on activities they both enjoy. Over time, the boys learn to negotiate solutions to their disagreements instead of resorting to anger, withdrawal, or fighting.

"We show them that you don't have to control everything to have fun and that they both can get what they want," he said.

In similar research with boys four to nine years of age, Dr. Ronald Prinz, a psychologist at the University of South Carolina, has taught parents better management and discipline skills, encouraging them to use more praise than punishment with their boys. The parents are taught to identify problem behaviors very specifically, to make very clear requests for changes in behavior,

and, if that doesn't work, to use a time-out period as punishment. The intent of the approach is to break patterns of escalating tensions, confrontation, and defiance that often characterize difficult relationships.

Another program, in Los Angeles, works with young children who are at risk of developing behavior problems because they were exposed to drugs in their mother's womb. The thirty or so preschoolers and kindergartners in the program are of normal intelligence, but show signs of learning disabilities and behavior disorders.

Although the Los Angeles program is small, the problem it addresses will soon be huge. Some experts predict that the number of drug-exposed children in some inner-city schools may grow to 40 percent to 60 percent of the schools' population. Moreover, the prenatal drug exposure is typically only one of many tragic complications in the lives of these youngsters. Many in the Los Angeles program have been shuttled between numerous relatives and foster homes, and some children tell stories during circle time of fights at home and of parents being put in jail.

The good news is that the program's early intervention seems to help. Some children have improved their ability to concentrate; others have learned to work through their frustrations instead of exploding into anger; others have graduated from the program into regular kindergarten or first-grade classes. The keys to success seem to be abundant caring and love from teachers and staff, the maintenance of daily routines, and the avoidance of abrupt transitions, which cause great difficulty for many of these children.

Daniel Goleman, "Taming Unruly Boys: Old Techniques and New Approaches," *New York Times,* February 1, 1990, p. B10.

Cathy Trost, "As Drug Babies Grow Older, Schools Strive to Meet their Needs," *Wall Street Journal,* December 27, 1989, p. 1.

well as student's parents and peers. However, there are a few general principles that should guide the school's prevention of delinquency and serious misbehaviors (see Wolfgang and Glickman, 1980; Weis and Sederstrom, 1981):

1. *School and classroom rules must be clearly expressed and consistently enforced.* Expectations that students will conform to school rules must be consistently expressed (Gottfredson, 1984). For example, graffiti or other vandalism must be repaired at once, so that other students do not get the idea that misbehavior is common or sanctioned.

2. *Truancy must be reduced by any means possible.* Truancy and delinquency are strongly related (Gold, 1970); when students are out of school, they are often in the community making trouble. While there are few proven methods available to schools that are known to reduce delinquency in the community, there are effective means of reducing truancy. Brooks (1975) had high school teachers sign cards carried by students with serious attendance problems at the end of each period they attended. Students received a "ticket" for each period attended, plus bonus tickets for good behavior in class and for going five days without missing a class. The tickets were used in a drawing for a variety of prizes. Before the program began, the target students were absent 60 percent of all school days. During the program absences dropped to 19 percent of school days. Over the same period, truancy among students not in the program increased from 59 to 79 percent.

Barber and Kagey (1977) markedly increased attendance in an entire elementary school by making full participation in once-a-month parties depend on student attendance. Several activities were provided during the parties, and students could earn access to some or all of them according to the numbers of day they attended.

Fiordaliso et al. (1977) increased attendance among chronically truant junior high school students by having the school call their parents whenever the students were present several days in a row. The number of days before calling depended on how severe the student's truancy had been; parents of the most truant students, who had been absent six or more days per month, were called after the student attended for only three consecutive days.

In these and other studies truancy was successfully reduced using behavior modification principles. Since truancy is one aspect of delinquency over which the school does have some control, reducing it should be an important part of any delinquency prevention program.

3. *Tracking (between-class ability grouping) should be avoided if possible.* Low-track classes are ideal breeding grounds for antisocial delinquent peer groups (Howard, 1978). Similarly, behavioral and academic problems should be dealt with in the context of the regular class as much as possible, rather than in separate special education classes (Safer, 1982; Madden and Slavin, 1983b). Individualization in the regular, heterogeneous classroom is the best means of dealing with most behavioral as well as academic deficits (Calhoun and Elliott, 1977).

4. *In secondary schools the curriculum should be differentiated to allow for instruction relevant to non–college-bound students.* This means making available vocational courses, as well as other curricular offerings related to the life experiences and needs of students.

5. *Classroom management strategies should be used to reduce inappropriate behavior before it escalates into delinquency.* Improving students' behavior and success in school can prevent delinquency. For example, Hawkins et al. (1988) used preventative classroom management methods such as those emphasized in this chapter along with interactive teaching and cooperative learning to help low-achieving seventh-graders. In comparison with control-group students, the students who were involved in the program were suspended and expelled less often, had better attitudes toward school, and were more likely to expect to complete high school. Use of behavior modification–based programs for misbehavior in class can also contribute to the

prevention of delinquency. Group contingencies can be especially effective with predelinquent students because they can deprive students of peer support for misbehavior.

As noted earlier, peer support is central to the great majority of delinquent acts by older students. For example, Graubard (1969) used a group contingency with emotionally disturbed, delinquent preadolescents. Students earned points for following class rules, which they helped formulate. Every few minutes a "bonus bell" was rung. If all students were following class rules when the bell rang, they all received ten "bonus points." All students in the class were rewarded if *every* student earned a certain minimum number of points. Under this system, students continually reminded their classmates that inappropriate behavior affected them all. As a result, inappropriate behavior dropped markedly, and declined even further when individual contingencies were added to the group contingencies.

Graubard (1969) contrasted the group contingency approach to the traditional "artichoke" method, in which "the teacher attempts to peel the child away from the [delinquent] group just as one peels artichoke leaves off the stem" (p. 268). Because of the power of peer pressure among delinquent students, Graubard argued, individual students cannot easily be "peeled." A more promising strategy is to deal with the "artichoke" as a whole, to use group contingencies to change peer group norms.

6. *Involve the student's home in any response to serious misbehavior.* When misbehavior occurs, parents should be notified. If it persists, they should be involved in establishing a program, such as a home-based reinforcement program, to coordinate home and school responses to misbehavior.

7. *Avoid the use of suspension (and expulsion) as punishment for all but the most serious misbehavior* (see Chobot and Garibaldi, 1982; Moles, 1984). Suspension often exacerbates truancy problems, both because it makes students fall behind in their work and because it gives them experience in the use of time out of school. In-school suspension, detention, and other penalties are more effective.

8. *When students misbehave, they should be punished, but when punishment is applied, it should be brief.* Being sent to a time-out area or detention room is a common punishment and effective for most students. Loss of privileges may be used. However, whatever punishment is used should not last too long. It is better to make a student miss two days of football practice than to throw him off the team, because once the student is off the team, the school may have little else to offer or withhold.

9. *When misbehavior occurs, punish it, but then reintegrate the student.* Serious misbehavior must be consistently and firmly punished, but once the punishment is over, the student should be allowed to participate in educational programs without reminders or continuing penalties. Every child has within him or herself the capacity for good behavior as well as for misbehavior. The school must be the ally of the good in each child at the same time it is the enemy of misbehavior. Overly harsh penalties, or penalties that do not allow the student to reenter the classroom on an equal footing with others, risk pushing students into the antisocial, delinquent subculture. When a student has paid his or her debt by losing privileges, experiencing detention, or whatever, he or she must be fully reaccepted as a member of the class.

Sue Simpson, a sixth-grade teacher in her second year of teaching, meets with Dr. John Cravens, a school psychologist and director of psychological services for the countywide school system, in his office.

JOHN: Sue, it's good to see you again! How can I help you?

SUE: Thanks for seeing me, John. Ever since the behavior modification workshops that you held for the teachers in our school, I've tried to put the ideas I learned there to work in my class. But I'm afraid they're not working, or I'm doing something wrong.

JOHN: Why don't you tell me what you are doing. Maybe we can figure out how to change it.

SUE: Well, I remembered how important you said it was to praise desirable behavior and try to ignore undesirable behavior and I've made that a regular practice. I praise all the children regularly, and, at first, it seemed to make a difference.

JOHN: Do you praise contingently?

SUE: What do you mean?

JOHN: Praise them only when they do something worth praising and as soon as possible after they do it.

SUE: Well, yes, I guess. At least as often as I can. I certainly try to be positive and let the children know that I care for them.

JOHN: Well—.

SUE: [interrupting] But the most important thing that I've done is to set up a group-reinforcement system with the whole class.

JOHN: How did you do that?

SUE: First, I took your reinforcement menu idea and asked the children what activities they'd like to do during reward time, which we have on Fridays. As a group we decided how good citizens should behave in the classroom. So, I made up a big poster with each child's name down the side and the list of good behaviors across the top. I give them a gold star each time I see them be a good citizen or make at least a B on an assignment.

JOHN: Well, then, what did they get to exchange the gold stars for?

SUE: They get to exchange them for the reward time activities that they choose for Fridays.

JOHN: And how did that system work?

SUE: It seemed to work fine at first but then the children seemed to lose interest.

JOHN: What happened?

SUE: Well, misbehavior began to increase and fewer students made B's. At that point I tried using group social-reinforcement procedures.

JOHN: What did you do?

SUE: I cleared a space on the bulletin board and asked the students to bring in snapshots of themselves. I told them that each week I was going to put up the pictures and work of the five students who did the best work that week and who displayed the best citizenship.

JOHN: Uh huh, then what happened?

SUE: That seemed to work fine for a while, too. I spent time each Friday praising the five children and their

SUMMARY

Using Class Time Well. Methods of maximizing allocated time include avoiding late starts and early finishes, avoiding interruptions, handling routine procedures smoothly and quickly, anticipating needs, and minimizing time spent on discipline. Engaged time, or time on-task, is the time individual students spend actually doing assigned work, which can be maximized by proper arrangement of the classroom, starting the year properly, setting class rules, maintaining momentum, maintaining smoothness of instruction, managing transitions, maintaining group focus, withitness, and overlapping.

A major component of the teacher's task with early elementary student (K–2) is socialization to expected behavior. Ability grouping presents a special complication work and then had the entire class applaud their efforts. Unfortunately, it was usually the same five students at first, but after a while some of the other students began to make it. In fact, none of the original five that seemed to be there every Friday at first have made it for over a month. I've begun to worry about them.

JOHN: Tell me this, Sue. What did the kids do on Fridays during reward time if they didn't each get enough gold stars to participate?

SUE: They sat at their seats and did their regular work.

JOHN: So things have gotten worse in your room recently?

SUE: Yes, I'd say they have in the last three or four weeks.

JOHN: What's happened?

SUE: Well, the quality of the work has gone down, even among my best students, and more and more students are not eligible for reward time. Also, it has become harder to find student work worth putting on the bulletin board. Last Friday there were only three students whose work and good citizenship were worth putting up. Some of the better students have become lazy in their work and have developed discipline problems.

JOHN: What kinds of discipline problems?

SUE: Oh, they sometimes sass back, or clown around to get attention, or sit and waste time when they should be working. I just really don't know what to do, John. I've thought about using the response cost that you talked about by taking away gold stars, but they don't seem to care about the gold stars anymore. I'm just at my wits end, John! Why isn't behavior modification working? What can I do?

JOHN: I'd suggest, Sue, that it's time to go back to basics. These applications of behavioral theory can be powerful, but, as you've found, they're also tricky to apply. And, they *can* take time that might be better spent on instruction. How about trying this for a month: Put away the gold stars and the bulletin board displays and focus instead on presenting really interesting, informative lessons to your students. Don't forget to praise them for their good efforts, but also don't let the praising get in the way of your lesson. What do you think? Is it worth a try?

SUE: Sure. And, as a matter of fact, I think it will be a relief to concentrate more on my teaching again.

JOHN: OK, then. Let's talk again in about a month. And, please feel free to call if you need some help in the meantime.

QUESTIONS

1. How well has Sue applied the principles of behavior modification to her classroom? What errors has she made?
2. What does John mean by "going back to basics"? What does he seem to suggest as the best way to minimize classroom discipline problems?
3. What classroom management model would you feel most comfortable using in an elementary school classroom?

because while the teacher works with one group, others must work independently. In the middle elementary grades (2–5) classroom management revolves around maintenance of momentum in lessons and enforcing compliance with rules that are reasonably well understood by students. In the middle/junior high school grades (5–9) students become more likely to resist authority and embrace peer norms. During the high school grades (9–12) teachers must be concerned with the interest level and relevance of their lessons and the use of incentives to motivate students to do academic work.

Handling Routine Misbehavior. One principle of classroom discipline is good management of routine misbehavior. The principle of least intervention means using the simplest methods that will work. There is a continuum of strategies from least disruptive to most: prevention of misbehavior; nonverbal cues, such as eye contact, which can stop a minor misbehavior; praise of incompatible, correct behavior; praise of other students who are behaving; simple verbal reminders given immediately after students misbehave; repetition of verbal reminders; and application of consequences when students refuse to comply. For serious behavior problems, swift and certain consequences must be applied. A call to the student's parents can be effective.

The Reinforcers of Misbehavior. The most common reinforcer for classroom misbehavior is attention from teachers or peers. When the student misbehaves to get the teacher's attention, one effective strategy is to pay attention to correct behavior while ignoring misbehavior as much as possible; scolding often acts as a reinforcer. Strategies for reducing peer-supported misbehavior include time-out (removing the child from the classroom) and group contingencies (rewarding the class only when everyone's behavior is good). Teachers can prevent the kind of misbehavior that results from boredom and fatigue by actively involving students in lessons. Misbehavior arising from frustration may be prevented through the use of materials that ensure a high success rate.

The Application of Behavior Analysis. Individual behavior modification strategies are useful for students with persistent behavior problems in school. The first step is observation to identify problematic behaviors and reinforcers. Step two is establishment of a baseline for target behavior. Step three is deciding on a reinforcer and a criterion for reinforcement. Step four is deciding on punishers and criteria for punishment (if necessary). Step five is observing behavior and comparing it to the baseline. Step six is reducing the frequency of reinforcement once the behavior management program is working.

Home-based reinforcement strategies involve giving students daily or weekly "report cards" to take home, and instructing parents to provide rewards on the basis of these reports. The steps to setting up such a program include deciding on behaviors to use for the daily report card and explaining the program to parents.

The steps in setting up a whole-class behavior modification program include establishing a point system and reinforcers, and considering the deduction of points for misconduct.

A group contingency is a reinforcement system in which an entire group is rewarded on the basis of the behavior of the group members. An advantage of this type of program is that it is easier to administer than an individual one. The use of group contingencies need not rule out individual contingencies.

The danger of behavior modification techniques is that they can be used to overcontrol students. Behavior modification strategies always emphasize praise and reinforcement, reserving punishment as a last resort.

There are few sure methods of preventing delinquency, but some general principles are: clearly expressing and consistently enforcing classroom rules; reducing truancy however possible; avoiding the use of between-class ability grouping; using behavior modification classroom management strategies; involving parents in any response to serious misbehavior; avoiding the use of suspension; applying only brief punishment; and reintegrating students after punishment.

STUDY QUESTIONS

1. According to research, which of the following would be most likely to increase student achievement?

   a. Increasing allocated time for instruction by 10 percent above what it is normally.

b. Increasing engaged time to 100% of the allocated classroom time.

c. Increasing engaged time by 10% above what it is normally.

d. Decreasing allocated time by late starts and early finishes.

2. A teacher begins the social studies lesson by asking, "Cassandra, what are some of the reasons the textbook lists for requiring people to pay taxes?" Which principle recommended by Kounin has the teacher clearly *not* followed?

a. Accountability
b. Withitness
c. Overlapping
d. Group alerting

3. Match the following terms with the correct definition for each.

_____ Accountability
_____ Group alerting
_____ Withitness
_____ Overlapping

a. Monitoring, and responding when necessary, to the behavior of all students.

b. Using questioning strategies that hold the attention of all students.

c. Maintaining the flow of instruction in spite of small interruptions.

d. Involving all students in all parts of a lecture or discussion.

4. According to the principle of least intervention, in which order should the following management methods be used when dealing with discipline problems?

a. Repeated reminders.
b. Consequences, such as suspension.

c. Nonverbal cues, such as a head shake at two note passers.

d. Verbal reminders about what a student *should* be doing.

5. Match the reinforcement sought by a misbehaving student with the appropriate teacher response. Student is misbehaving to seek

_____ teacher attention
_____ peer attention
_____ release from frustrations

a. send student to time-out area.
b. use teaching methods that provide appropriate levels of instruction.
c. ignore misbehavior, praise good behavior.

6. Sequence the following steps of a behavior modification program in the order in which they should be used.

a. Select and use reinforcers and, if necessary, punishers.
b. Establish a baseline for target behavior.
c. Fade out reinforcement.
d. Identify target behavior and its reinforcer(s).
e. Observe behavior during program, compare to baseline.

7. Which of the following procedures should be avoided in trying to prevent delinquency?

a. Making vocational courses available in the school curriculum.
b. Using group contingencies for managing classroom behavior.
c. Involving the students' parents when serious misbehavior occurs.
d. Using suspension as a punishment for misbehavior.

Answers: 1. c, 2. d, 3. d, b, a, c, 4. c, d, a, b, 5. c, a, b, 6. d, b, a, e, 7. d.

SUGGESTED READINGS

AMERICAN ASSOCIATION OF SCHOOL ADMINISTRATORS (1982). *Time on task: Using instructional time more effectively*. Arlington, Va.: AASA.

BARTH, R. (1979). Home-based reinforcement of school behavior: A review and analysis. *Review of Educational Research, 49*, 436–458.

CANTER, L., and CANTER, M. (1976). *Assertive discipline*. Los Angeles: Lee Canter and Associates.

DOYLE, W. (1986). Classroom organization and management. In M. C. WITTROCK (Ed.), *Handbook of research on teaching* (3rd ed.). New York: Macmillan.

DUKE, D. L. (Ed.) (1982). *Helping teachers manage classrooms*. Alexandria, Va.: Association for Supervision and Curriculum Development.

DUKE, D. L. and MECKEL, A. M. (1984). *Teacher's guide to classroom management*. New York: Random House.

EMMER, E. T., EVERTSON, C. M., SANFORD, J. P., CLEMENTS, B. S., and WORSHAM, M. E. (1989). *Classroom management for secondary teachers* (2nd ed.). Englewood Cliffs, N.J.: Prentice-Hall.

EPSTEIN, C. (1979). *Classroom management and teaching: Persistent problems and rational solutions*. Reston, Va.: Reston.

EVERTSON, C. M., EMMER, E. T., CLEMENTS, B. S., SANFORD, J. P., and WORSHAM, M. E. (1989). *Classroom management for elementary teachers* (2nd ed.). Englewood Cliffs, N.J.: Prentice-Hall.

HOWARD, E. R. (1978). *School discipline desk book*. West Nyack, N.Y.: Parker.

KOUNIN, E. R. (1970). *Discipline and group management in classrooms*. New York: Holt, Rinehart & Winston.

MEDLAND, M., and VITALE, M. (1984). *Management of classrooms*. New York: Holt, Rinehart & Winston.

SAFER, D. J. (1982). *School programs for disruptive adolescents*. Baltimore, Md.: University Park Press.

SULZER-AZAROFF, B. and MAYER, G. R. (1986). *Achieving educational excellence using behavioral strategies*. New York: Holt, Rinehart & Winston.

WALKER, J. E., and SHEA, T. M. (1980). *Behavior modification: A practical approach for educators* (2nd ed.). St. Louis: C. V. Mosby.

WOLFGANG, C. H., and GLICKMAN, C. D. (1980). *Solving discipline problems: Strategies for classroom teachers*. Boston: Allyn and Bacon.

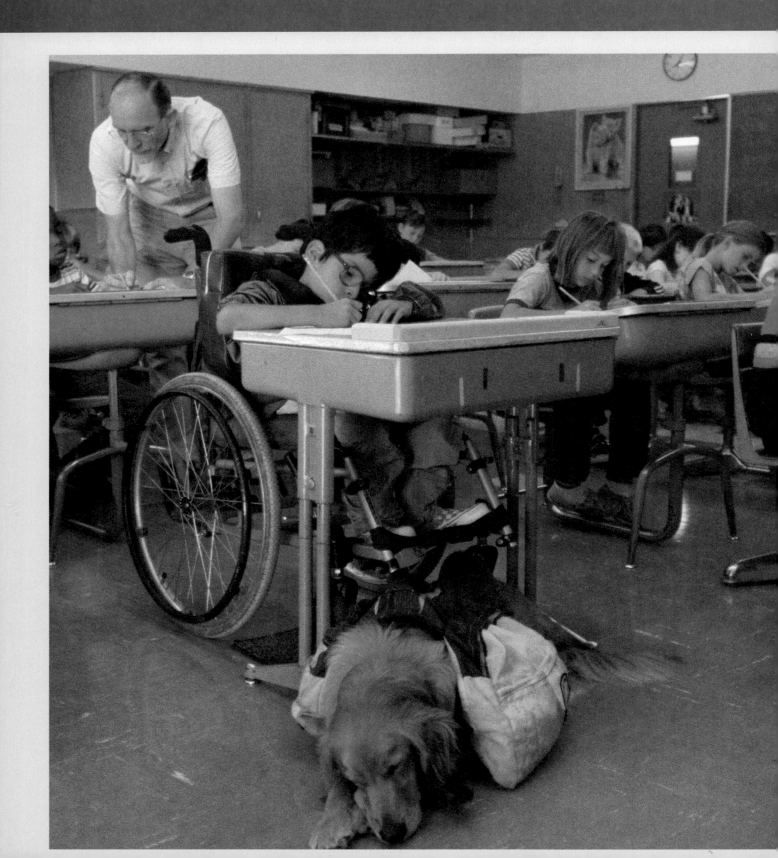

Chapter 12

Exceptional Students

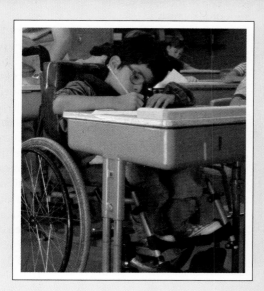

Chapter Outline

Chapter Objectives

After reading this chapter on exceptional children and special education, you should be able to:

- Define and list characteristics of the major types of exceptionalities.

- Describe the continuum of educational services available for students with varying degrees of special need.

- Describe the procedure for developing Individualized Education Programs.

- Define "mainstreaming" and describe its benefits.

- Describe how to meet both the academic and social needs of handicapped children who are mainstreamed.

Exceptionality
Mental, emotional, or physical
condition that creates special
educational needs

WHO IS AN "EXCEPTIONAL STUDENT"?

In one sense, all children are exceptional. No two are exactly alike in their ways of learning and behaving, in their activities and preferences, skills and motivations. All students would benefit from a program uniquely tailored to their individual needs.

However, schools cannot practically meet the precise needs of every student. For the sake of efficiency, students are grouped into classes and given common instructional experiences designed to provide the greatest benefit to the largest number at a moderate cost. This system works reasonably well for the great majority of students. However, some students do not fit easily into this mold. Some have physical or sensory disabilities, such as hearing or vision impairment or orthopedic handicaps, that restrict their ability to participate in the regular classroom program without special assistance. Other students suffer from general mental retardation or emotional problems, or have learning disabilities that make it difficult for them to learn in the regular classroom without special assistance. Finally, some students have such outstanding talents that the regular classroom teacher is unable to provide for their unique needs without help.

Exceptionality is defined more by the problems a student creates for the instructional program than by the characteristics of the student. For example, Mercer (1973) notes that most children are labeled "mentally retarded" only after they enter school, and that many children whose behavior at home is well within normal limits may still be labeled "exceptional" by the school system (Edgerton, 1984). She introduced the concept of "six-hour retardation" to describe students who are only "retarded" in school.

The definition of exceptionality is somewhat circular. Exceptional children are those in need of special educational services. Who needs special educational services? Exceptional children, of course. In general, exceptionalities fall into four categories: mental, emotional, speech or language, and physical. Mental exceptionalities are the most common and include mental retardation, specific learning disabilities, and other learning problems.

How Many Students Are "Exceptional"?

Some exceptionalities, such as deafness and blindness, are relatively easy to define and measure. Others, such as mental retardation, learning disabilities, and emotional disturbance, are much harder to define, and their definitions have evolved over time. In fact, there has been a dramatic change over the past fifteen years in these categories, with substantially increasing numbers of students with learning problems being categorized as learning disabled. Table 12.1 shows the percentages of all students in each category of exceptionality in 1976–1977, 1982–1983, and 1986–1987. Note that while most of the easily defined physical impairments have remained fairly stable, the relative number of students categorized as learning disabled has steadily increased and the use of the category "mentally retarded" has diminished.

Other than the changes over time among the categories, there are several pieces of information worthy of note in Table 12.1. First, notice that the overall percentage of students receiving special education in 1986–1987 was almost 11 percent; about one out of every nine students aged three to twenty-one was categorized as exceptional. Second, serious physical disabilities, such as deafness, blindness, and orthopedic handicaps, are relatively rare. Learning problems, speech disorders, and emotional disturbance are considerably more common, accounting for about 94 percent of all students receiving special education services. Because learning-disabled and speech-

TABLE 12.1

PERCENT OF CHILDREN SERVED IN EDUCATIONAL PROGRAMS FOR THE HANDICAPPED

The largest segments of the school-age handicapped population are people with speech impairments, learning disabilities, and mental retardation. The size of the different segments changes somewhat as definitions of the handicaps change.

	Percent of Children Aged 3–21 Served		
Type of Handicap	1976–1977	1982–1983	1986–1987
All conditions	8.33	10.73	10.97
Learning disabled	1.80	4.39	4.80
Mentally retarded	2.16	1.91	1.61
Emotionally disturbed	0.64	0.89	0.96
Speech impaired	2.94	2.85	2.85
Hard of hearing and deaf	0.20	0.18	0.16
Visually handicapped	0.09	0.07	0.07
Orthopedically handicapped	0.20	0.14	0.14
Other health impaired	0.32	0.13	0.13
Multihandicapped	—	0.16	0.24
Deaf-blind	—	0.01	0.01

SOURCE: Adapted from National Center for Educational Statistics, 1988.

impaired students are most often taught in regular classes (usually with special services for a few hours or less each day), regular classroom teachers are most likely to be teaching students with these exceptionalities. Based on the prevalence of various exceptionalities and the percentage of students with various problems who are taught in a regular classroom at least part of the day, it can be estimated that in a class of thirty a regular classroom teacher will, on average, have one learning-disabled student and one with a speech impairment. In contrast, only about one class in forty is likely to have a student who is hard of hearing, visually impaired, or otherwise physically handicapped.

TYPES OF EXCEPTIONAL STUDENTS

What's in a Label?

To receive special education services, a student must fall into one of a small number of categories of handicaps. These general "labels," such as "learning disabled," "mentally retarded," or "orthopedically handicapped," in fact cover a wide diversity of problems. As experience and research produce a clearer understanding of handicaps, categories evolve. For example, many students who would previously have been called mildly retarded are now identified as learning disabled. In fact, the practical distinctions among slow learners, learning-disabled students, and mildly retarded students are difficult to make consistently, and vary from district to district and from tester to tester (see Ysseldyke and Algozzine, 1982; Gerber and Semmel, 1984).

Even though labels are neither exact nor unchanging, they are a useful "shorthand" to indicate the type and severity of a student's handicaps, as long as we

Intelligence Quotient
An intelligence test score that for people of average intelligence should be near 100

Normal Curve
Bell-shaped symmetrical distribution of scores in which most scores fall near the mean, with progressively fewer occurring as distance from the mean increases

Mental Retardation
Condition, usually present at birth, that results in below-average intellectual skills and poor adaptive behavior

The test most widely used to measure the IQ of children is the Wechsler Intelligence Scale for Children–Revised.

remember the limitations of the labels. The following sections discuss characteristics of students with the types of handicaps most commonly seen in schools.

Mental Exceptionalities

As noted earlier, the majority of handicapped students have learning problems of one kind or another. Therefore classroom teachers are far more likely to have handicapped students with learning disabilities and mild retardation than with other exceptionalities.

IQ. To understand how children come to be categorized as mentally retarded, learning disabled, or gifted, it is first important to recall (from Chapter 9) the concept of IQ, or **intelligence quotient.**

Figure 12.1 illustrates the distribution of IQs on a form of the Stanford-Binet Intelligence Scale, one commonly used IQ test. Note that the IQ scores form a bell-shaped curve, called a **normal curve.** Most scores fall near the mean, with small numbers of scores extending well above and below the mean.

Students with IQs between 80 and 120 are rarely considered exceptional, unless they have serious deficits in specific areas of performance (see "Learning Disabilities" later in this section). Seventy-nine percent of all students fall in this range, and another 13 percent fall above IQ 120. This leaves only about 8 percent of the population below IQ 80. Note that of this group, the great majority of scores fall between IQ 70 and 80, and very few scores fall below 60.

Mental Retardation. **Mental retardation** is defined by the American Association on Mental Deficiency (AAMD) as follows: "Mental retardation refers to significantly subaverage general intellectual functioning resulting in or associated with impairments in adaptive behavior and manifested during the developmental period" (Grossman, 1983). People who are mentally retarded typically have general learning

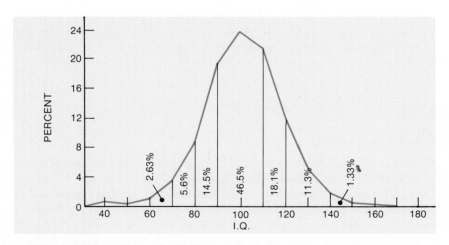

FIGURE 12.1

Distribution of Intelligence Test Scores

The distribution of intelligence test scores resembles a bell-shaped curve, called a normal curve. Scores from 80 to 120 are in the low-average to high-average range.

Adapted from Terman and Merrill, 1960, p. 18. Reprinted from Kirk, 1972, p. 9.

TABLE 12.2

CLASSIFICATION SYSTEMS FOR MENTAL RETARDATION

Two systems are commonly used to classify the severity of mental retardation. Both are based on IQ.

System	IQ 100 95 90 85 80 75 70 65 60 50–55 45 35–40 30 20–25 15 10 5
American Association on Mental Deficiency	Mild | Moderate | Severe | Profound
American Educators	Educable | Trainable | Severely and Profoundly Handicapped

SOURCE: Adapted from Hallahan and Kauffman, 1982, p. 43.

Educable Mentally Retarded
Category of mental retardation applied to those with mild handicaps, whose learning problems are often identified only after they enter school

Trainable Mentally Retarded
Category of mental retardation applied to those with moderate handicaps, whose education usually focuses on self-help skills

problems manifested in all of their intellectual functioning, in and out of school. Also, mental retardation is generally considered to be present at birth or soon after even if it is not detected until later in life. Mild retardation is not usually diagnosed until children enter school (Robinson and Robinson, 1976).

Mental retardation is usually classified according to the severity of mental impairment. Many classification schemes have been used, but the most common categorize children in terms of their measured IQs. The AAMD defines one set of categories, but most school districts use a simpler system. Both are illustrated in Table 12.2.

The AAMD definitions set an IQ of 69 or below as a defining characteristic of mental retardation. Definitions of retardation vary from district to district, but generally use a similar criterion. However, IQ should never be the sole criterion of whether a child is considered retarded. For example, most districts take into account a student's school and home performance, scores on other tests, and cultural background.

The distinction between educable and trainable mentally retarded students is an important one. Typically, programs for those who are **educable mentally retarded** (EMR) focus on basic academic skills, while those for people who are **trainable mentally retarded** (TMR) emphasize self-help, vocational skills, and such "independent living skills" as learning to ride buses, to identify the words "walk" and "don't walk," and the like.

Mental retardation has many causes. For most mentally retarded students, there is no specific syndrome that explains their retardation. Some may be children of retarded or nearly retarded parents, or grow up in such a deprived environment that they lack the early mental stimulation necessary for success in school. These are called cultural-familial causes. Other causes of retardation can be more clearly identified. These include genetic chromosomal abnormalities, such as Down syndrome; certain diseases passed from mother to child, such as rubella (German measles), syphilis, and herpes simplex; prenatal problems, such as alcohol abuse by the mother; and delivery problems that cut off oxygen to the brain of the newborn.

While most mentally retarded children were retarded from birth, some became retarded because of diseases, such as encephalitis or meningitis, or because of accidents. One cause of mild retardation among youngsters in poverty stricken neighborhoods is lead poisoning, which usually results from children eating flakes of old paint that contains lead.

Characteristics of Mentally Retarded Students.   The term "mental retardation" refers to a wide range of learning deficits and behavioral characteristics. Mildly retarded students may appear physically normal, may behave acceptably outside of school, and may eventually lead normal lives, hold jobs, and raise families. These individuals have little in common with severely and profoundly retarded children, who are likely to have much more pervasive learning problems and a less optimistic long-term outlook. Table 12.3 lists the principal characteristics, educational outlook, and ultimate social and vocational outlook for people with mild, moderate, severe, and profound mental retardation.

One of the best responses to mental retardation is early intervention. Studies have shown that programs to provide cognitively stimulating environments to retarded or at-risk children before formal school entry and programs to increase the skills of parents of handicapped children can have an important impact on the later school success of these children (Casto and Mastropieri, 1986; Garber, 1988).

Classroom teachers (that is, those who are not special education teachers) are most likely to be involved with students in the mild or educable mentally retarded category.

TABLE 12.3

DEVELOPMENTAL CHARACTERISTICS OF THE MENTALLY RETARDED

The severity of a person's mental retardation affects development, the type of education or training that is appropriate, and prospects for self-sufficiency in adulthood.

Degree of Mental Retardation	Preschool Age (0–5) Maturation and Development	School Age (6–20) Training and Education	Adult (21 and over) Social and Vocational Adequacy
Mild	Can develop social and communication skills; minimal retardation in sensorimotor areas; often not distinguished from normal until later age.	Can learn academic skills up to approximately sixth-grade level by late teens. Can be guided toward social conformity. Termed "educable."	Can usually achieve social and vocational skills adequate to minimum self-support, but may need guidance and assistance when under unusual social or economic stress.
Moderate	Can talk or learn to communicate; poor social awareness; fair motor development; profits from training in self-help; can be managed with moderate supervision.	Can profit from training in social and occupational skills; unlikely to progress beyond second-grade level in academic subjects; may learn to travel alone in familiar places.	May achieve self-maintenance in unskilled or semiskilled work under sheltered conditions; needs supervision and guidance when under mild social or economic stress.
Severe	Poor motor development; speech is minimal; generally unable to profit from training in self-help; little or no communication skills.	Can talk or learn to communicate; can be trained in elemental health habits; profits from systematic habit training.	May contribute partially to self-maintenance under complete supervision; can develop self-protection skills to a minimal useful level in controlled environment.
Profound	Gross retardation; minimal capacity for functioning in sensorimotor areas; needs nursing care.	Some motor development present; may respond to minimal or limited training in self-help.	Some motor and speech development; may achieve very limited self-care; needs nursing care.

SOURCE: U.S. Department of Health, Education and Welfare, 1969.

These children often spend part of their school day in regular classes. Mildly retarded students are rarely identified until they enter school because their behavior is often within or near the normal range at home. Educational programs for mildly retarded students focus on building academic skills that will permit them to function independently in society, because with appropriate education they can be expected to lead normal lives.

In contrast, moderately retarded, or trainable, children are usually seriously delayed both socially and academically. The goal of education is to enable these students to live semi-independently (for example, in a group home) and to work in a sheltered environment. Contact with nonhandicapped students is important for moderately and mildly retarded students. Programs for mentally retarded students held in regular school buildings usually allow these students to participate with their nonhandicapped peers in activities for which academic performance is least important, such as lunch, recess, physical education, art, and music.

Adapting instruction to meet the needs of mildly retarded students placed in regular academic classes is discussed later in this chapter.

Learning Disabilities. The term **learning disabilities** is relatively new and, as noted earlier, the use of this category has increased rapidly over the past decade. Exact definitions of learning disabilities vary, but one definition accepted by the federal government and used in most states is as follows: "Specific learning disability means a disorder in one or more of the basic psychological processes involved in understanding or in using language, spoken or written, which may manifest itself in an imperfect ability to listen, think, speak, read, write, spell, or to do mathematical calculations . . ." (*Federal Register,* 1977, p. 65083). This definition goes on to imply that children should be labeled learning disabled if they are having difficulties in school that are *not* attributable to some other type of problem such as mental retardation or cultural or economic deprivation.

All definitions of learning disabilities share the following characteristics (adapted from Hallahan and Kauffman, 1976):

1. There is academic retardation in relation to the student's intelligence.
2. An uneven pattern of development exists.
3. The person may or may not have demonstrable central nervous system dysfunction (such as brain damage).
4. Learning problems are *not* due to environmental disadvantage.
5. Learning problems are *not* due to mental retardation or emotional disturbance.

As a rule, learning-disabled children are identified after entering school, often when they encounter difficulty with school-related tasks. Many districts use tests measuring visual and auditory reception, memory, and association to assess learning disabilities.

Characteristics of Learning-Disabled Students. As the term has been more and more broadly applied in recent years, learning disabilities have come to encompass a wide range of learning problems. Some of the most frequently mentioned characteristics of learning-disabled students are:

1. Uneven patterns of strengths and weaknesses in learning performance.
2. Lack of coordination and balance.

Learning Disability
Disorder that impedes academic progress of people who are not mentally retarded or emotionally disturbed

Attention Deficit
The inability to concentrate for long periods of time

3. Attention deficits, impulsivity, and hyperactivity (inability to sit still, pay attention, and concentrate).

4. Specific disorders of memory, thinking, or language.

Not all learning-disabled students have all of these characteristics; some who are diagnosed as learning disabled have only one or two. "Classic" learning disabilities have been found in people who are normal or even gifted in many areas, but have specific problems in one area. For instance, Nelson Rockefeller was said to suffer from dyslexia, an impairment of the ability to read, but it did not stop him from serving as governor of New York and vice president of the United States. A minority of learning-disabled students show evidence of neurological dysfunction. These students may have somewhat atypical patterns of brain waves as measured by EEGs (electroencephalograms).

However, the percentage of students now categorized as learning disabled who have truly specific learning disabilities is small. In some school districts a student who falls more than two grade levels behind expectations and has an IQ in the normal range (for example, above 80) is likely to be called learning disabled.

One frequent characteristic of learning-disabled students is an **attention deficit,** or inability to pay attention in class or to concentrate for long periods (Swanson, 1980). This is normal in preschoolers, and among first- or second-graders may simply indicate a developmental lag of little importance in the long run. However, beyond that point, attention deficits can become serious problems (McKinney and Speece, 1986).

Emotional and behavioral problems often compound learning disabilities. Learning-disabled students are frequently emotionally unstable, behaviorally impulsive, and likely to misbehave. The great majority of children with attention deficits are also hyperactive, meaning they are unable to sit still (Whalen, 1983). Emotional problems and hyperactivity are discussed under "Serious Emotional Disturbance" later in this chapter. On average, learning disabled students have lower self-esteem than do nondisabled students (Chapman, 1988).

Boys are much more likely than girls to be labeled learning disabled. In 1980, 4.4 percent of all boys in elementary and secondary schools were diagnosed as learning disabled, compared to only 1.8 percent of girls (National Center for Educational Statistics, 1985).

Good classroom instruction for most learning-disabled students is similar in most ways to good instruction for nonhandicapped students (Larrivee, 1985; Leinhardt and Bickel, 1987). However, some adaptations in instruction strategies may be necessary to meet their needs. These are discussed at the end of this chapter.

Giftedness

Who are the gifted? Almost everyone, according to their parents, and in fact many students do have outstanding talents or skills in some area. Giftedness was once defined almost entirely in terms of superior IQ or demonstrated ability, such as outstanding performance in mathematics or chess, but the definition now encompasses students with superior abilities in any of a wide range of activities, including the arts. For this reason, the term "gifted and talented" is coming to be used more often than simply "gifted." However, high IQ is still considered part of the definition of "gifted and talented," and most students so categorized have IQs well within the superior range, above 130.

The 1978 Gifted and Talented Act indicated that "the gifted and talented are children . . . who are identified . . . as possessing demonstrated or potential abilities that give evidence of high performance capabilities in areas such as intellectual, creative, specific academic or leadership ability or in the performing or visual arts and to by reason thereof require services or activities not ordinarily provided by the school" (Public Law 95–561, Section 902). This definition is meant to include students who possess extraordinary capabilities in any number of activities, not just those areas that are part of the school curriculum. According to these rather vague criteria (see Gallagher, 1979), somewhere between 3 and 5 percent of all students are "gifted and talented" (Mitchell and Erickson, 1980). However, the percentage of students identified as gifted and talented varies from less than 1 percent in North Dakota to almost 10 percent in New Jersey (National Center for Educational Statistics, 1988). This does not mean that New Jersey's students are especially talented, rather it indicates the vast differences found in defining and identifying the gifted and talented in different states.

Characteristics of Gifted and Talented Children.   Gifted children typically have strong motivation (Renzulli, 1978). They are also academically superior, usually learn to read early, and, in general, do excellent work in most school areas.

One of the most important studies of the gifted, begun by Louis Terman in 1926, is following 1,528 individuals who had IQs over 140 as children. Terman's research exploded the myth that high-IQ individuals were brainy but physically and socially inept. In fact, Terman found that children with outstanding IQs were larger, stronger, and better coordinated than other children, and became better adjusted and more emotionally stable adults (Terman, 1959).

Education of the Gifted.   How to educate gifted students is a matter of debate (see Torrance, 1986). Some programs for gifted and talented children involve special secondary schools for students gifted in science or in the arts. Some programs are special classes for high achievers in regular schools. One debate in this area concerns *acceleration* versus *enrichment*. Advocates of acceleration (e.g., Stanley, 1979; Van Tassel-Baska, 1989) argue that gifted students should be encouraged to move through the school curriculum rapidly, perhaps skipping grades and going to college at an early age. Others (for example, Gallagher, 1976) maintain that rather than moving students through school more rapidly, programs for the gifted should engage them in more problem-solving and creative activities.

Research on the gifted provides more support (in terms of student achievement gains) for acceleration than for enrichment (Daurio, 1979; Kulik and Kulik, 1984). However, as Fox (1979) points out, this may be because the outcomes of enrichment, such as creativity or problem-solving skills, are difficult to measure.

Acceleration programs for the gifted often involve the teaching of advanced mathematics to students at early ages, as in Stanley's (1979) Study of Mathematically Precocious Youth (SMPY) program. This program had a stated goal of getting mathematically talented seventh- and eighth-graders from Algebra I through second-year college mathematics (Calculus III, linear algebra, and differential equations) in as short a time as possible.

Enrichment programs take many forms. Many successful enrichment programs have involved self-directed or independent study (Parke, 1983; Reiss and Cellerino, 1983). Others have provided gifted students with adult mentors (Nash et al., 1980). Renzulli (1977) suggests an emphasis on three types of activities: general exploratory

1. Enrichment activities are useful for students who quickly master required material or who finish classroom assignments ahead of others. Please describe enrichment activities you have used.

Ann Taylor, specialist teacher in grades 4–6 in Dallas, Tex., writes:

I hung colored ribbons with clothespins sewn on at six-inch intervals, to which I attached index cards with various assignments. This was work to be done for extra credit. Each color was number-weighted. For example, activities on the yellow ribbon were worth three points, those on the red ribbon five points, etc. The more points, the more involved the activity. A variety of activities was always provided: drawing cartoons, research, short stories, poems, solving a code, working a crossword. Both fast and slower students loved this approach.

2. Skipping a grade is sometimes proposed when children are far ahead of their peers. What are some of the benefits and potential problems of skipping?

Walter Roberts, Jr., a high school teacher in Gentry, Ark., notes that academic benefits must be weighed against the potential social problems:

Promoting students ahead of their peers for academic excellence is better in the long run as it provides the chance to learn material at a faster rate. However, it does place "underaged" students in a stressful situation. While academically the students may be able to compete with their new classmates, emotionally they may find that the new world places

strains on their abilities to cope with older pupils. In school we often neglect the emotional stresses placed on children to produce up to our expectations, and while I think that some of our expectations are too low, we should never forget that too much pressure for even the simplest of tasks can cause anyone to fail. (If we ever forget what it feels like to be that ninth- or eleventh-grader we are teaching, and how awkward adolescence is, then we need to get out of the classroom in a hurry!)

3. Some gifted and talented students fail to reach their full potential because of lack of educational and career planning. When told they can do anything they want, they wait too long to commit themselves to any one endeavor. How would you help a multitalented student find direction and make educational and career choices?

Ann Taylor, Dallas, Tex.:

In our schools this is handled as follows: Elementary students are assigned to talented and gifted classes in which they choose the field in which they are most interested. They do research that involves an interview with someone in the field. Then they write a paper or present a slide film at a night program for parents. In high school, if they apply and are chosen, they are given time off to follow an executive in the field of their choice. Many discover they are not interested in the field after this experience, which saves them from majoring in the wrong thing in college.

activities, such as allowing students to find out about topics on their own; group training activities, such as games and simulations to promote creativity and problem-solving skills; and individual and small-group investigations of real problems, such as writing books or newspapers, interviewing elderly people to write oral histories of an area, and conducting geological or archaeological investigations.

The main problem with enrichment programs for the gifted is simply stated: there are few activities suggested for gifted students that would not be beneficial for *all* students. What student would fail to profit from more opportunities for problem solving, cultural enrichment, and exploration? However, the gifted may be better able to take advantage of enrichment programs, not so much because of their talents, but because they are able to master the regular curriculum rapidly enough to allow them the time to engage in more exploratory activities.

Serious Emotional Disturbance

Emotionally Disturbed
Category of exceptionality
characterized by problems with
learning, interpersonal relationships,
and controlling feelings and behavior

All students are likely to have emotional problems at some point in their school career, but about 1 percent have such serious, long-lasting, and pervasive emotional disorders that they require special education. As in the case of learning disabilities, seriously emotionally disturbed students are far more likely to be boys than girls, by a ratio of more than three to one (National Center for Educational Statistics, 1985).

A seriously **emotionally disturbed** child has been defined as one whose educational performance is adversely affected over a long period of time to a marked degree by any of the following conditions:

1. An inability to learn that cannot be explained by intellectual, sensory, or health factors.

2. An inability to build or maintain satisfactory interpersonal relationships with peers and teachers.

3. Inappropriate types of behavior or feelings under normal circumstances.

4. A general, pervasive mood of unhappiness or depression.

5. A tendency to develop physical symptoms, pains, or fears associated with personal or school problems.

One problem in identifying emotional disturbance is that the term covers a wide range of behaviors, from aggression or hyperactivity to withdrawal or inability to make friends (Kauffman, 1981). Also, emotionally disturbed children quite frequently have other handicaps, such as learning disabilities or mental retardation, and it is often hard to tell whether an emotional problem is causing the diminished academic performance or school failure is causing the emotional problem.

Procedures used to identify children with serious emotional disturbances include observation, behavior rating scales and inventories, and personality testing. Observation is the most direct method and requires the least amount of inference on the teacher's part (Taylor, 1984). However, although observation can help document the behavior under question, a trained professional's judgment is required in deciding the amount, frequency, or degree of behavior that must be present for a student to be characterized as "disturbed" or "disordered."

Behavior rating scales are used primarily by teachers and provide a more standard measure of various categories of behavior characteristics. For example, a behavior rating scale might include a number of items (descriptions of behaviors such as "Is hostile and aggressive toward peers") that are grouped according to various "behavior factors" (such as withdrawal, immaturity, aggression). This information provides a comparison between the behavior of one student and that of others, as well as a profile that shows the student's behavioral difficulties.

Characteristics of Students with Emotional Disturbances. Scores of characteristics are associated with emotional disturbance (Kneedler, 1984). The important issue is the *degree* of the behavior problem. Virtually any behavior that is exhibited excessively over a long period of time might be considered an indication of emotional disturbance.

There are, however, some general characteristics displayed by most students identified as emotionally disturbed. These include poor academic achievement, poor interpersonal relationships, and poor self-esteem (Kneedler, 1984). Quay (1979) surveyed the literature on the reported characteristics and noted four general categories or factors: conduct disorder, anxiety-withdrawal, immaturity, and socialized-aggressive disorder. Children who fall into the "conduct disorder" category are characterized frequently as disobedient, distractible, selfish, jealous, destructive, impertinent, resistive, and disruptive. Hyperactivity (see below) is also associated with this factor, although this term is sometimes used by itself to describe certain students. Quay noted that three of these factors represent behaviors that are either maladaptive or a source of personal distress. The fourth factor, "socialized-aggressive," seems to be tied more to poor home conditions that model or reward aggressive behavior.

Aggressive Behavior.   Most children engage in aggressive "acting-out" behavior from time to time. However, emotionally disturbed students with conduct disorders are likely to frequently engage in fighting, stealing, destruction of property, refusal to obey teachers, and other behaviors unacceptable in school. These students tend to be disliked by their peers, their teachers, and even (sometimes especially) their parents. They typically do not respond to punishment or threats, though they may be skilled at avoiding punishment.

Not only do aggressive children pose a threat to the school and to their peers, they can also put themselves in grave danger. Aggressive children, particularly boys, are likely to develop serious emotional problems later in life, to have difficulty holding jobs, and to become involved in criminal behavior (Robins, 1974).

The most effective treatments for aggressive emotionally disturbed students are well-structured, consistently applied behavior modification programs, such as those described in Chapter 11 (see Patterson et al., 1975). Many times these programs can be used in the regular classroom, and thus avoid segregating the student with a group of equally aggressive peers (Madden and Slavin, 1983a). Successful treatments for seriously emotionally disturbed students have also used special education resource rooms one or two hours a day for highly structured behavior modification programs, tutoring, and other assistance (Glavin et al., 1971).

Withdrawn and Immature Behavior.   While the aggressive child causes distressing problems to teachers and peers, children who are withdrawn, immature, low in self-image, or depressed can be just as disturbed. Typically, such students have few friends, or may play with children much younger than themselves. They may have elaborate fantasies or daydreams, and may have either very low self-images or grandiose visions of themselves. Some may be overly anxious about their health, and may feel genuinely ill when under stress. Some emotionally disturbed students exhibit school phobia, refusing to attend school or running away from school.

Unlike aggressive emotionally disturbed children, who may appear quite normal when they are not being aggressive, withdrawn and immature children often appear odd or awkward at all times. Their drawings and compositions frequently exhibit unusual or bizarre thinking.

Withdrawn and immature students almost always suffer from a lack of social skills. Some of the more successful therapies for these children involve teaching them the social skills that other students absorb without special instruction. Such programs have improved the social behavior of withdrawn, friendless students, and have increased their acceptance by their classmates (see Gottlieb and Leyser, 1981; Gresham, 1981; Strain and Kerr, 1981).

Hyperactivity.   One very common emotional/behavioral problem is **hyperactivity,** an inability to sit still or to concentrate for any length of time. Hyperactive children exhibit excessive restlessness and short attention span. It is estimated that 5 percent of all elementary school students are hyperactive (O'Leary, 1980). Hyperactivity is particularly common among learning-disabled students and is much more frequently seen in boys than in girls.

Hyperactive children are usually impulsive, acting before they think or without regard for the situation they are in, and they find it hard to sit still (Shaywitz and Shaywitz, 1988). These students are often described as "always on the go," as though "driven by a motor" (American Psychiatric Association, 1982).

Students who are diagnosed as hyperactive are often given a stimulant medication, such as Ritalin. More than a million children take Ritalin, and this number has been rising in recent years (Weiss, 1989). These drugs usually do make hyperactive children more manageable and sometimes improve their academic performance (Gadow, 1981; Ottenbacher and Cooper, 1983), but they can also have serious side effects, such as insomnia, weight loss, and blood pressure changes (Hersen, 1986). Further, students who receive drugs for hyperactivity during the elementary years often become seriously behaviorally disordered in adolescence, perhaps because they have not really learned to control their behavior.

Nondrug therapies, such as the classroom management methods described in Chapter 11, can be as effective or more effective than medication (see, for example, Rappaport et al., 1982) and should be seriously and systematically applied before drug therapy is tried (O'Leary, 1980; Walden and Thompson, 1981). Kneedler (1984, p. 91) suggested that classroom teachers "(1) take a cautious view of the use of medication, (2) view drugs as a treatment to turn to only when other approaches have failed, and (3) recognize that medication alone is never enough; it always needs to be used in combination with other educational approaches."

Other Severe Emotional Disturbances. A very small number of children, about one in a thousand, suffer from severe emotional disturbances such as childhood schizophrenia or other psychotic disorders or autism (Kauffman, 1985). Psychotic children, including schizophrenics, are likely to live in a fantasy world and to have few or no normal relationships with others. Autistic children are typically extremely withdrawn, and have such severe difficulties with language that they may be entirely mute. They (and often psychotic children as well) may engage in self-stimulation, such as rocking, twirling objects, or flapping their hands. However, they may have normal or even outstanding abilities in certain areas.

Behavioral Disorders

The term "emotional disturbance" is usually limited to behavioral disorders that are long-lasting and pervasive and that interfere with academic performance. However, there are several other behavioral disorders that are not defined as emotional disturbance but are serious enough to merit attention from teachers and other school staff.

Drug and Alcohol Abuse. Unfortunately, drug and alcohol abuse in many schools is an everyday occurrence. While drug abuse is no longer increasing in prevalence, as it did through the 1970s, it is still at a high level (see U.S. Department of Health and Human Services, 1987). Figure 12.2 shows that more than half of all seniors reported using marijuana at some time, and about a quarter of them had used marijuana within the past month. Five percent of the seniors reported *daily* use of marijuana, and a

FIGURE 12.2

Prevalence and Recency of Use

Eleven Types of Drugs, Class of 1986

Source: U.S. Department of Health and Human Services, 1987.

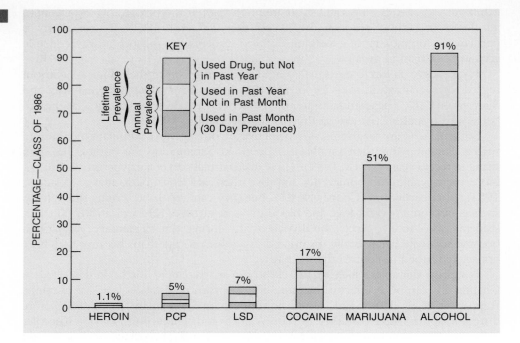

similar proportion reported daily alcohol use. These daily use figures are at about half their 1979 levels. Alarmingly, there has been a trend toward students using drugs at earlier grades; almost 20 percent of eighth graders have used some illicit drugs, usually marijuana.

One of the main factors in drug and alcohol use is peer pressure (Zucker, 1979). Another risk factor for alcohol abuse is parents drinking at home (Lawson et al., 1983). Occasional drug and alcohol use are only slightly more common among boys than girls, but heavy drinking or daily marijuana use is twice as common among boys, and boys are more likely to use cocaine and heroin. Students planning to go to college are equally likely to use marijuana as those who do not have college plans, but are less likely to use other drugs (National Institute on Drug Abuse, 1985).

Not surprisingly, heavy use of drugs and alcohol can seriously impair students' academic performance. The drug-use statistics cited for high school seniors probably understate the problem, because many drug and alcohol users never make it to the senior class.

If a teacher suspects that a student is using drugs or alcohol, or has problems in the home that might lead to such behavior, it is a good idea to consult the school counselor or other appropriate school staff members. Also, there are now several drug- and alcohol-abuse prevention programs available (for example, Gern and Gern, 1986; Botvin, 1984; National Clearinghouse for Drug Abuse Information, 1986).

Juvenile Delinquency. Approximately 3 percent of all adolescents engage in behaviors serious enough to cause them to be referred to juvenile court (Arnold and Brungardt, 1983). Juvenile delinquency and its prevention are discussed in Chapter 11.

Family Issues: Divorce and Death. Many factors can affect families and disrupt a child's sense of security and self-worth. Changes in the family structure can leave a child depressed, angry, unsure, and lonely. Two such phenomena are divorce and death of a family member. It is estimated that 30 percent of all children will be affected by divorce and another 15 to 20 percent will live in a one-parent household because of separation, death of a parent, or other factors.

Researchers have investigated the effects of divorce on children. Longfellow (1979) summarized one such survey. At ages seven and eight children showed feelings of sadness and loss, fear and insecurity. They felt abandoned and rejected. Children aged nine and ten reported that they were ashamed and outraged, yet also lonely and rejected. The children who were thirteen to eighteen years old reported anger, shame, sadness, and embarassment. In a five-year follow-up study Wallerstein and Ketty (1980) reported that 34 percent of those surveyed were happy and 29 percent were doing reasonably well; 37 percent, however, still reported feelings of depression.

Death or serious illness in a child's family is also likely to cause anxiety, depression, or behavior problems. Young children may not fully understand what death means. If a student experiences a death in his or her family, the teacher should at least acknowledge it, and perhaps take the opportunity to discuss the topic of death, but then return the student to a regular routine as soon as possible.

Child Abuse and Neglect. The Child Abuse Prevention and Treatment Act (1974) defines child abuse and neglect as "physical or mental injury, sexual abuse, negligent treatment, or maltreatment of a child under the age of eighteen by a person who is responsible for the child's welfare under circumstances which indicate that the child's health or welfare is harmed or threatened thereby." Certain social and cultural factors seem to increase the chances of child abuse. These include parents' history of being abused, poverty and undereducation, and a physically violent environment (Kauffman, 1981). Other factors linked to child abuse and neglect are large families, young parents, and lower socioeconomic status (Baldwin and Oliver, 1975). There are also attributes of the child that are associated with the problem. These include unattractiveness, irritability, and defiance (Kauffman, 1981).

When students seem depressed or angry, teachers should be aware that the cause could be a problem at home, such as a death in the family or divorce.

Speech Disorders
Articulation problems occurring most
frequently among children in the
early elementary school grades

TABLE 12.4

SYMPTOMS OF CHILD ABUSE AND NEGLECT

Teachers have an ethical and legal responsibility to report suspected cases of child abuse and neglect. To meet this responsibility, they must know the symptoms of maltreatment.

Abuse	Neglect
1. Evidence of repeated injury	1. Clothing inappropriate for the weather
2. New injuries before previous ones have healed	2. Torn, tattered, unwashed clothing
3. Frequent complaints about abdominal pain	3. Poor skin hygiene
4. Evidence of bruises	4. Rejection by other children because of body odor
5. Bruises of different ages	5. Need for glasses, dental work, hearing aid, or other health services
6. Welts	6. Lack of proper nourishment
7. Wounds, cuts, or bruises	7. Consistent tiredness or sleepiness in class
8. Scalding liquid burns with well-defined parameters	8. Consistent very early school arrival
9. Caustic burns	9. Frequent absenteeism or chronic tardiness
10. Frostbite	10. Tendency to hang around school after dismissal
11. Cigarette burns	

SOURCE: Berdine and Blackhurst, 1981, pp. 44. Reprinted by permission of Scott Foresman and Company.

Teachers have both an ethical responsibility and (in most states) a legal one to report incidents of suspected child abuse or neglect (Rose, 1980). Although it is sometimes difficult to differentiate the characteristics of abuse and neglect from other sources of injury (such as accidents), it is better to be on the safe side so that the situation can be investigated. Most reporting laws protect teachers who report suspected child abuse in good faith (Beezer, 1985). All teachers should learn the procedures to follow if they suspect that a student has been abused or neglected. Table 12.4 presents several symptoms of abuse and neglect that are described in publication of the Council for Exceptional Children entitled *Child Abuse and Neglect: A Primer for School Personnel* (Kline, 1977).

Communication Disorders

One of the most common exceptionalities is communication disorders—problems with speech and language. About one in every forty students has a communication disorder serious enough to warrant speech therapy or other special education services.

While the terms "speech" and "language" are often used interchangeably, they are not the same. Language is the communication of ideas using symbols, and includes written language, sign language, gesture, and other modes of communication in addition to oral speech. Speech refers to the formation and sequencing of sounds. It is quite possible to have a speech disorder without a language disorder, or a language disorder without a speech disorder.

Speech Disorders. There are many kinds of **speech disorders.** The most common are articulation (or phonological) disorders, such as omissions, distortions, or substitutions of sounds. For example, some students have difficulty pronouncing "r's," saying "sowee" for "sorry." Others have lisps, substituting "th" for "s," saying "thnake" for "snake."

Misarticulated words are common and developmentally normal for many children in kindergarten and first grade but drop off rapidly through the school years. Figure 12.3 shows that moderate and extreme deviations in articulation diminish over the school years, with or without speech therapy (Shriberg, 1980). For this reason, speech therapists will often decide not to work with a child with a mild articulation problem. However, speech therapy is called for if a student cannot be understood, or if the problem is causing the student psychological or social difficulties (such as teasing).

A less common but often more troublesome speech disorder is stuttering, the "abnormal timing of speech sound initiation" (Perkins, 1980). Everyone stutters sometimes, but children with a serious problem stutter to a degree that impairs their ability to communicate. Stutterers may prolong sounds ("wwwwwe wwwwwent to the store") or they may have difficulty making any sound at times. It is often particular sounds or words or situations that give stutterers difficulties. Unfortunately, anxiety increases stuttering, creating a vicious cycle: when stutterers are afraid of stuttering, their fear makes them stutter.

FIGURE 12.3

Prevalence of Speech Impairment by Grade Level

Articulation problems are most common among children in the early elementary grades. These problems, as well as stuttering, generally fall off with age.

From Hull and Hull, 1973, p. 200.

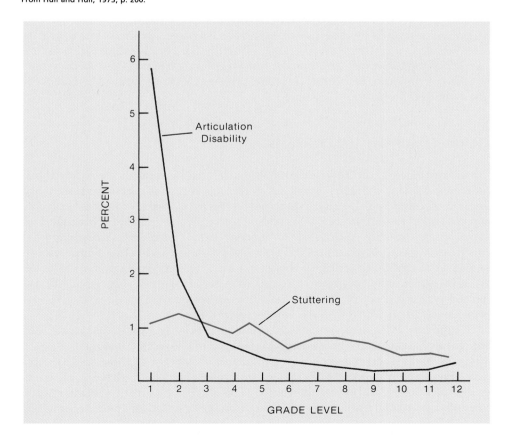

With or without therapy, stuttering usually disappears by early adolescence. However, as in the case of articulation problems, speech therapy is often prescribed for stuttering because of the psychological and social problems it causes youngsters.

Speech Disorders and the Classroom Teacher. Speech disorders of all kinds are diagnosed by and treated by speech pathologists or speech therapists. The classroom teacher's role is less important here than with the mental exceptionalities. However, the classroom teacher does have one crucial role to play: displaying acceptance of students with speech disorders. Recall (from Figure 12.3) that most speech disorders will eventually resolve themselves. The lasting damage is more often psychological than phonological; students with speech disorders often undergo a great deal of teasing and social rejection. Teachers can model acceptance of the child with speech disorders in several ways. First, they should be patient with students who are stuttering or have trouble producing words, never finishing a student's sentence or allowing others to do so. Second, they should avoid putting students with speech problems into high-pressure situations requiring quick verbal responses. Third, teachers should refrain from correcting students' articulation in class.

Language Disorders. Language disorders are impairments of the ability to understand language or to express ideas in one's native language. Problems due to limited English-speaking ability for students whose first language is not English are not considered language disorders (these are discussed in Chapter 13).

Difficulties in understanding language *(receptive language disorders)* or in communicating *(expressive language disorders)* may result from such physical problems as hearing or speech impairment. If not, they are likely to indicate mental retardation or learning disabilities. Many students from disadvantaged backgrounds come to school with what appear to be receptive or expressive language disorders, but that in fact result from a lack of experience in standard English. Preschool programs rich in verbal experience and direct instruction in the fundamentals of language have been found to be effective in overcoming the language problems characteristic of children from disadvantaged homes (see Chapter 3).

Children with Physical Problems

Visual Impairments. Most visual problems exhibited by students are correctable. In other words, many children require glasses or another type of corrective lens. A visual disorder is considered a visual handicap only if it is not correctable. It is estimated that approximately 1 out of every 1,000 children is visually handicapped. Those with such handicaps are usually referred to as blind or partially sighted. According to the American Medical Association (1934), a legally blind child is one whose vision is judged to be 20/200 or less in the better eye even with correction, or whose field of vision is significantly narrower than that of a person with normal vision. Partially sighted persons, according to this classification system, are those whose vision is between 20/70 and 20/200 in the better eye with correction.

Kauffman (1981) noted that it is a misconception to assume that legally blind individuals have no sight. In one large study Willis (1976) found that only 18 percent of legally blind students were totally blind, and 52 percent of these students could read large- or regular-print books rather than Braille (an alphabet that uses raised dots to represent letters and is read by touch). This implies that many visually impaired students can be taught using only a modification of usual teaching materials. Hallahan and Kauffman (1982) offered an educational definition of visual handicap that depends on the amount of adaptation required in the school setting. They suggested that "the blind are those who are so severely impaired that they must be taught to read by Braille, while the partially sighted can read print even though they need to use magnifying devices or books with large print" (p. 337).

Classroom teachers should be aware of the signs that indicate a child is having a visual problem. Undoubtedly, children who have difficulty seeing also have difficulty in many areas of learning because classroom lessons typically use a tremendous amount of visual material. The National Society for the Prevention of Blindness (1969) suggested several symptoms of visual problems that teachers and parents should be aware of. These include (1) holding one's head in an awkward position or holding material very close to the eyes; (2) tuning out when information is presented on the blackboard; (3) constant questioning as to what is going on in the classroom; (4) being inordinately affected by glare; (5) a pronounced squint, excessive rubbing of the eyes, or pushing the eyeballs; and (6) physical eye problems such as redness, swelling, or crusting. If you notice any of these problems, you should refer the student for appropriate vision screening.

Students who hold reading materials very close to their eyes or who exhibit other symptoms of vision problems should be referred for an eye examination.

Hearing Impairments. Hearing impairments range from complete deafness to problems that can be alleviated with a hearing aid. The appropriate classification of an individual depends on the measures required to compensate for the problem. Davis (1970) indicated the educational implications that correspond to the various degrees of hearing loss (see Table 12.5).

The amount of adaptation required for a teacher to communicate with a hearing-impaired student obviously depends on the degree of hearing loss. Many children can communicate adequately by listening to your voice and watching your lips. Others might need a hearing aid, while those with more severe problems will

TABLE 12.5

EDUCATIONAL SIGNIFICANCE OF HEARING IMPAIRMENTS

Students with mild hearing losses may need only to be seated in an advantageous location to understand a teacher's presentations. Greater accommodation must be made for students with more severe hearing impairments.

Levels of Loss	Sound Intensity for Perception (Decibels [dB])	Educational Implications
Mild	27–40 dB	May have difficulty with distant sounds. May need preferential seating and speech therapy.
Moderate	41–55 dB	Understands conversational speech. May miss class discussion. May require hearing aids and speech therapy.
Moderately severe	56–70 dB	Will require hearing aids, auditory training, speech and language training of an intensive nature.
Severe	71–90 dB	Can only hear loud sounds close up. Sometimes considered deaf. Needs intensive special education, hearing aids, speech and language training.
Profound	91 dB +	May be aware of loud sounds and vibrations. Relies on vision rather than hearing for information processing. Considered deaf.

SOURCE: Davis and Silverman, 1970. Reprinted by permission of Holt, Rinehart, and Winston.

Cerebral Palsy
Disorder in ability to control
movements caused by damage to the
motor area of the brain

need to use a nonverbal form of communication such as sign language. Following are several suggestions that you should keep in mind (Blackhurst and Berdine, 1981):

1. Seat hard-of-hearing children in the front of the room, slightly off center toward the windows. This will allow them to see your face in the best light.

2. If the hearing problem is predominantly in one ear, students should sit in a front corner seat so that their better ear is toward you.

3. Speak at the student's eye level whenever possible.

4. Give important information and instructions while facing the class. Avoid talking to the chalkboard.

5. Do not use exaggerated lip movements when speaking.

6. Learn how to assist a child with a hearing aid.

Cerebral Palsy.   **Cerebral palsy** is a motor impairment caused by brain damage. The damage can be produced by any number of factors that result in oxygen deprivation—poisoning, cerebral bleeding, or direct injury. The damage usually occurs before, during, or shortly after birth, and causes some degree of paralysis, weakness, or incoordination (Eiben and Crocker, 1983). Cerebral palsy is not a "disease" that is contagious, nor does it get progressively worse. Not all cerebral-palsied individuals are retarded. The damage to the brain is in the motor area, and may not be associated with damage to other areas of the brain. Children with cerebral palsy may have normal intelligence.

The severity of cerebral palsy varies tremendously. Some people have virtually no voluntary control over any of their movements, while others have a motor problem that is barely discernible. In the more severe cases there is great difficulty in speaking. Obviously, the degree of severity affects the amount of adaptation that is necessary in the classroom. Increasingly sophisticated adaptive equipment, particularly in the area of communication, is now available to allow students with cerebral palsy to participate in regular as well as special education classes.

Seizure Disorders.   Seizure disorders, or epilepsy, are caused by an abnormal amount of electrical discharge to the brain. Witnessing a seizure can be a frightening experience for an unknowledgeable observer.

There are several types of seizures that a child might experience. The first type, "grand mal," is a major seizure characterized by loss of consciousness, rigidity, shaking, and jerking. Before a grand mal seizure some type of "aura" might be experienced, a peculiar sensation in which certain sounds are heard, odors smelled, or images seen. If a child has an identifiable aura, this will often give him or her enough time to lie down. Immediately after the seizure, these children go into a deep sleep. The most violent part of a grand mal seizure lasts only about three to four minutes, but during it care must be taken that the children do not hurt themselves by biting their lips or tongues or involuntarily striking furniture or other objects.

Heward and Orlansky (1980, p. 249) offered the following suggestions for when a student has a seizure:

1. Ease the child to the floor and loosen his collar. You cannot stop the seizure. Let it run its course and do not try to revive the child.

2. Remove hard, sharp, or hot objects that may injure the child, but do not interfere with his movements.

3. Do not force anything between the child's teeth. If the child's mouth is already open, you might place a soft object, like a handkerchief, between the side teeth. Be careful not to get your fingers caught between the teeth.

4. Turn the head to one side for release of saliva. Place something soft under his head.

5. When the child regains consciousness, let him rest if he wishes.

6. If the seizure lasts beyond a few minutes, or if the child seems to pass from one seizure to another without gaining consciousness, call the school nurse or doctor for instructions and notify the parents. This rarely happens, but should be treated immediately.

A few other suggestions are also helpful. If you know that a child in your class is prone to having seizures, discuss this with the class so that they won't be surprised. The important thing is for everyone to remain calm.

A "petit mal seizure" is much less severe than a grand mal but occurs much more frequently. In this type of seizure the student will experience brief lapses of consciousness. During these short intervals (usually about five to fifteen seconds) the student might look blank, stare, and have a fluttering of the eyelids. Petit mal seizures often go unnoticed or are misinterpreted as a short attention span or a behavior problem.

Between seizures, epileptic children are usually quite normal, and new medications developed over the past decade have allowed most seizure disorders to be partially or completely controlled.

■ **Stop and Think**
A benefit of thinking about "exceptional children" is that it demands a reevaluation of what is "normal"—and what we as a society value. Consider, for example, the following:
- A young child's behavior seems "normal" at home but is unacceptable at school. What should change, the child or the school situation?
- A shy preadolescent is teased by peers because she stutters. Who needs counseling, the young girl or the classmates who tease her?
- A dyslexic junior high schooler falls behind in social studies because the teacher relies solely on long reading assignments to convey important information. Should only the student's reading problem be addressed, or should the teacher's instructional strategy also change?

SPECIAL EDUCATION

Special education refers to any program provided for handicapped children instead of, or in addition to, the regular classroom program. The practice of special education has changed dramatically in recent years and is still evolving. One of the most important changes is that federal legislation is now critical in setting standards for special education services administered by states and local districts.

Public Law 94–142

Twenty years ago education of exceptional children was quite different from what it is today. Many handicapped students received no special services at all. Those who did get special services usually attended separate schools or institutions for the retarded, emotionally disturbed, deaf, or blind.

Special Education
Programs that address the needs of students with mental, emotional, or physical handicaps

Public Law 94–142
Federal law requiring provision of special education services to eligible students

Mainstreaming
The placement, for all or part of the school day, of handicapped children in regular classes

Individualized Education Program
School program tailored to the needs of a handicapped child

In the late 1960s the special education system came under attack (see, for example, Dunn, 1968; Christoplos and Renz, 1969). Critics argued that the seriously handicapped were too often shut away in state institutions with inadequate educational services or left at home with no services at all, and that the mildly handicapped (particularly those with mild mental retardation) were being isolated in special programs that failed to teach them the skills they needed to function in society.

As a result of these and other factors, in 1975 Congress passed **Public Law 94–142,** the Education For All Handicapped Act. PL94–142, as it is commonly called, has profoundly affected both special and regular education throughout the United States. It prescribes the services that all handicapped children must receive and gives them and their parents legal rights that they did not previously possess.

A basic component of PL94–142 is that every handicapped child is entitled to special education appropriate to the child's needs at public expense. This means, for example, that school districts or states must provide special education to the severely retarded and handicapped.

Least Restrictive Environment. The provision of PL94–142 of greatest importance to regular classroom teachers is that handicapped students must be assigned to the "least restrictive placement" appropriate to their needs. This provision gives a legal basis for the practice of **mainstreaming,** or placing handicapped students with nonhandicapped peers for as much of their instructional program as possible. This means that regular classroom teachers are likely to have in their classes students with mild handicaps (such as learning disabilities, mild mental retardation, physical handicaps, or speech problems) who may leave class for special instruction part of the day. It also means that classes for students with more serious handicaps are likely to be located in regular school facilities, and that these students will probably attend some activities with their nonhandicapped peers. The continuum of services for exceptional students and the issue of mainstreaming are discussed later in this chapter.

Individualized Education Program (IEP). Another important requirement of PL94–142 is that every handicapped student must have an **Individualized Education Program,** or IEP, which guides the services the student receives. The IEP describes a student's problems and delineates a specific course of action to address these problems. Generally, it is prepared by special education teachers and a special education supervisor or school psychologist in consultation with the principal, counselor, and the classroom teacher, and it must be consented to by the student's parent. The idea behind the use of IEPs is to give everyone concerned with the education of a handicapped child an opportunity to help formulate the child's instructional program. The requirement that a parent sign the IEP is designed to ensure parental awareness of and approval of what the school proposes to do with the child; a parent may hold the school accountable if the child does not receive the promised services.

The law requires that evaluations of students for possible placement in special education programs be done by qualified professionals. Although classroom and special education teachers will typically be involved in the evaluation process, teachers are not generally allowed to give the psychological tests (such as IQ tests) that are used for placement decisions.

PL94–142 gives handicapped children and their parents legal safeguards with regard to special education placement and programs. For example, if parents feel that a child has been diagnosed incorrectly or assigned to the wrong program, or if they are unsatisfied with the services a child is receiving, they may bring a grievance against

Mainstreaming allows handicapped and nonhandicapped students to learn together. Research shows that students with mild academic disorders learn better in regular as opposed to special education classes.

the school district. Also, the law specifies that parents be notified about all placement decisions, conferences, and changes in program. This aspect of PL94–142 requires that decisions concerning special education placements be made cooperatively between the school and the parents.

A Continuum of Special Education Services

An important aspect of an IEP is a special education program appropriate to the student's needs. Every school district provides a range of special education services, from placement in the regular class with special adaptations or assistance to placement in special schools or hospitals. A typical continuum of services is illustrated in Table 12.6.

In general, students with more severe handicaps receive more "restrictive" services than those with less severe handicaps. For example, a severely retarded student is unlikely to be placed in a regular classroom during academic periods, while a student with a speech problem or a mild learning disability is likely to be in a regular classroom for most or all of the school day. However, severity of handicap is not the sole criterion for placement; also considered is the appropriateness of the various settings for an individual student's needs. For example, a student in a wheelchair with a severe orthopedic handicap can easily attend and profit from regular classes, while a student with a hearing deficit might not.

Table 12.7 shows the percentages of handicapped students who receive special education services in various settings. Note that with the exception of the physically handicapped, few students received special education outside of a regular school building. The great majority of learning-disabled and speech-impaired students attend regular classes part or most of the day, usually supplemented by one or more hours per day in a special education resource room. This is also true for the majority of physically handicapped students and almost half of all emotionally disturbed students.

TABLE 12.6

A CONTINUUM OF SPECIAL EDUCATION SERVICES

Special education services range from consultation to residential school placement or home and hospital care.

Level	Type of Service	Typical Recipients
1.	Direct or indirect consultation, support for regular teacher	Those with mild handicaps
2.	Special education up to 1 hour per day	Most children with speech impairments, some learning-disabled (LD) children
3.	Special education 1–3 hours per day; resource program	Most LD children, some emotionally disturbed (ED) children
4.	Special education more than 3 hours per day; self-contained special education	Most educable mentally retarded (EMR) children, some ED and LD children
5.	Special day school	Most ED and trainable mentally retarded (TMR) children
6.	Special residential school	Some ED children
7.	Home/hospital	Some health-impaired children

SOURCE: Based on the 1978 Maryland State Board of Education Guidelines and 1982 data.

TABLE 12.7

PERCENT OF HANDICAPPED CHILDREN SERVED IN VARIOUS ENVIRONMENTS

The likelihood that a student will spend most of the school day in a regular classroom or will receive more specialized services depends on the type of handicap as well as its severity.

Types of Handicap	Regular Class	Resource Room	Special Class	Special School	Other Environment
Learning disabled	16	61	21	2	—
Mentally retarded	5	28	53	14	1
Emotionally disturbed	12	34	33	18	3
Speech impaired	65	26	5	4	1
Hard of hearing and deaf	21	24	31	24	1
Visually handicapped	33	30	19	18	1
Orthopedically handicapped	18	21	34	20	7
Other health impaired	24	26	33	7	11
Multihandicapped	3	14	44	37	2
Deaf-blind	5	16	24	54	2

SOURCE: Adapted from National Center for Education Statistics, 1988.

Most other handicapped students attend special classes located in regular school buildings. The continuum of services available to handicapped students, from least to most restrictive, is described in the following sections.

Regular Classroom Placement. The needs of many handicapped students can be met in the regular classroom with little or no outside assistance. For example, students who have mild vision or hearing problems may simply be seated near the front of the room. Students with mild to moderate learning disabilities may have their needs met in the regular classroom if the teacher uses strategies (such as those described in Chapter 9) for accommodating student differences. For example, the use of instructional aides, tutors, or parent volunteers can allow exceptional students to remain in the regular classroom. Classroom teachers can often adapt their instruction to make it easier for students to succeed. For example, one teacher noticed that a student with perceptual problems was having difficulties with arithmetic because he could not line up his numbers. She solved the problem by giving him graph paper to work on. Another teacher had an emotionally disturbed student who wandered the classroom and otherwise behaved unacceptably. Rather than recommending special education, the teacher arranged with the student's parents that he would send home a report on the student's behavior each day, and the parents would reward the student with special privileges for a good report. This program (later reduced to one report per week) greatly improved the students' behavior (See Chapter 11 for more on behavior management).

Research generally shows that the most effective strategies for dealing with learning and behavior problems are those used in the regular classroom. Special education options should usually be explored only after serious efforts have been made to solve students' problems in the regular classroom (see Madden and Slavin, 1983a).

Consultation and Itinerant Services.   Many school districts provide classroom teachers with consultants to help them adapt their instruction to the needs of handicapped students. Consulting teachers typically are trained in special as well as regular education. They may come into the classroom to observe the behavior of a student having trouble, but most often suggest solutions to the regular teacher rather than working directly with students. Research on consultation generally finds that well-designed consulting models can be effective in assisting teachers to maintain mildly handicapped students, particularly those with learning disabilities, in the regular class (Cantrell and Cantrell, 1976; Graden, Casey, and Bonstrom, 1985; Fuchs and Fuchs, 1989).

For some types of handicaps, itinerant (traveling) teachers may provide special services to students a few times a week. This pattern of service is typical of programs for students with speech and language disorders.

Resource Room Placement.   Many handicapped students are assigned to regular classes for most of their school day, but participate in resource programs at other times. Most often resource programs focus on teaching reading, plus (somewhat less often) language arts, mathematics, and (occasionally) other subjects. Resource room programs usually involve small numbers of students working with a special education teacher. Ideally, the resource teacher meets regularly with the classroom teacher to coordinate programs for students and to suggest ways the regular classroom teacher can adapt instruction to the needs of the students when they are in the regular class.

Sometimes resource teachers work right in the regular classroom. For example, a resource teacher might work with one reading group while the regular classroom teacher works with another. A major advantage of this arrangement is that it avoids pulling students out of class, which is both inefficient, because of the transition time it requires, and potentially demeaning, because the students in need of special help are excluded from class for some period of time. Team teaching involving regular and special teachers also makes communication between the teachers much easier.

Special Class Placement with Part-Time Mainstreaming.   Many students are assigned to special classes taught by a special education teacher, but are mainstreamed with nonhandicapped students part of the school day. Most often these handicapped students join regular students for music, art, and physical education, and somewhat less often for social studies, science, mathematics, or (least often) reading. One important difference between this category of special services and the resource room model is that in the case of the resource room, the student's primary placement is in the regular class; the regular classroom teacher is the homeroom teacher and generally takes responsibility for the student's complete program, with the resource teacher providing extra support. In the case of a student assigned to special education and mainstreamed part of the day, the situation is reversed. The special education teacher serves as the homeroom teacher and takes primary responsibility for the student.

Self-Contained Special Education.   A self-contained special education program is a class located in a regular school but largely separate from the regular instructional program. Until the mainstreaming movement began in the early 1970s, this (along with separate schools for the retarded and handicapped) was the typical placement for handicapped students. Self-contained programs are taught by special education teachers with relatively few contacts with the regular instructional program.

Some students attend separate, special day schools. These are typically students

Classroom teachers have important roles related to the education of handicapped children. They are important in referring students to receive special services, in participating in the assessment of students, and in preparing and implementing IEPs. This section describes the process by which classroom teachers seek special education services for students (see Odle and Galtelli, 1980; Turnbull and Brantley, 1982). An example of an IEP appears in Figure 12.4 on pages 430 and 431.

INITIAL REFERRAL

Referrals for special education assessment can be made by parents, physicians, principals, or teachers. Classroom teachers most often initiate referrals for children with suspected learning disabilities, mental retardation, speech impairment, or emotional disturbance; most other handicaps are diagnosed before students enter school.

In most schools initial referrals are made to the building principal, who contacts relevant school district staff.

SCREENING AND ASSESSMENT

As soon as the student is referred for assessment, an initial determination is made to accept or reject the referral. In practice, almost all referrals are accepted. The evaluation/placement team may look at the student's school records and interview classroom teachers and others who know the student. If the team members decide to accept the referral, they must obtain parental permission to do a comprehensive assessment.

Members of the evaluation/placement team include professionals designated by the school district plus the parents of the referred student and, if appropriate, the referred student. If the referral has to do with learning or emotional problems, a school psychologist or guidance counselor will usually be involved; if it has to do with speech or language problems, a speech pathologist or speech teacher will typically serve on the team. The building principal usually chairs the team, but may designate a special education teacher or other professional to do so.

The referred student is then given a battery of tests to assess strengths and weaknesses. For learning and emotional problems, these tests are usually given by a school psychologist; specific achievement tests (such as reading or mathematics assessments) are often given by special education or reading teachers.

WRITING THE IEP

When the comprehensive assessment is complete, the evaluation/placement team members meet to consider the best placement for the student. If they determine that special education is necessary, they will prepare an IEP. Usually the special education teacher and/or the classroom teacher prepares the IEP. The student's parent(s) must sign a consent form regarding the placement decision, and in many school districts a parent must also sign the IEP. This means that parents can (and in some cases do) refuse to have their children placed in special education programs.

At a minimum, the IEP must contain the following information (see Odle and Galtelli, 1980, p. 248):

with severe handicaps, such as severe retardation or physical disabilities, or those whose presence might be disruptive to the regular school, such as students with serious emotional disturbances. In addition, small numbers of handicapped students attend special residential schools. These schools may be for profoundly handicapped students with relatively rare disabilities that require special treatment.

Other Special Services. In addition to the placements just described, other special services are often needed by exceptional students. For example, school psychologists are often involved in the process of diagnosing handicapped students, and sometimes participate in the preparation of Individualized Education Plans. In addition, they

1. *Statements indicating the child's present level of performance:* This typically includes the results of specific tests as well as descriptions of classroom functioning. Behavior rating checklists, work samples, or other observation forms may be used to clarify a student's strengths and weaknesses.

2. *Goals indicating anticipated progress during the year:* For example, a student might have goals of reading at a fourth-grade level as measured by a standardized test, of improving classroom behavior so that disciplinary referrals are reduced to zero, or of completing a bricklaying course in a vocational education program.

3. *Intermediate (shorter-term) instructional objectives:* A student having difficulties in reading might be given an intermediate objective to complete a certain number of individualized reading comprehension units per month, or an emotionally disturbed student might be expected to get along with peers better and avoid fights.

4. *A statement of the specific special education and related services to be provided as well as the extent to which the student will participate in regular education programs:* The IEP might specify that a student will receive two thirty-minute sessions with a speech therapist each week. An IEP for a learning-disabled student might specify forty-five minutes per day of instruction from a resource teacher in reading, plus consultation between the resource teacher and the classroom teacher on ways to adapt instruction in the regular classroom. A mentally retarded student might be assigned to a self-contained special education class, but the IEP might specify that the student participate in the regular physical education program. Any adaptations necessary to accommodate students in the regular class, such as wheelchair ramps, large-type books, cassette tapes, or simply being placed near the front of the classroom, would be specified in the IEP.

5. *The projected date for the initiation of services and the anticipated duration of services:* Once the IEP is written, students must receive services within a reasonable time period. They may not be put on a waiting list—the school district must provide or contract for the indicated services.

6. *Evaluation criteria and procedures for measuring progress toward goals on at least an annual basis.*

The IEP should specify a strategy for remediating students' deficits. In particular, the IEP should state what objectives the student is to achieve and how those objectives are to be attained and measured. It is critical to direct special education services toward a well-specified set of learning or behavior objectives, rather than simply deciding that a student falls into some category and therefore should receive some service. Ideally, special education for mildly handicapped students should be a short-term, intensive treatment to give student the skills needed in a regular class. All too often a student assigned to special education remains there indefinitely, even after the problem for which the student was initially referred has been remediated.

Note that IEPs must be updated at least once a year. The updating provides an opportunity to change programs that are not working, or to reduce or terminate special education services when the student no longer needs them.

may counsel the student or consult with the teacher about behavioral and learning problems.

Speech and language therapists generally work with students on a one-to-one basis, though some small-group instruction may be provided for students with similar problems. They also consult with teachers about ways to address student difficulties.

Physical and occupational therapists treat motor difficulties under the direction of a physician. Students who have physical disabilities may see a physical or occupational therapist whose treatment focuses on the development of motor skills as well as on the correction and prevention of motor problems. Physical therapists usually concentrate on gross motor problems, such as difficulties with walking, while occupational

FIGURE 12.4

Individualized Education Program

From Hallahan and Kauffman, 1986, pp. 33–35.

INDIVIDUALIZED EDUCATION PROGRAM

Confidential Information

School Year ___84-85___

Name ___Patrick Milton___ DOB ___11/7/72___ School ___Field___ Grade ___6___

Handicapping condition ___Learning Disability___ Date of IEP meeting ___10/15/84___ (M-D-Y) Notification to parent ___11/12/84___ (M-D-Y)

Initiation and anticipated duration of services ___11/84___ (M-Y) to ___11/85___ (M-Y) Eligibility/Triennial ___10/12/84___ (M-D-Y) Plan to be reviewed no later than ___3/85___ (M-Y)

Educational/Vocational Program

Special Education Services

Work with LD resource teacher on reading and language arts; may be taught in group of up to five students; summer school (1985) recommended.

Total Amount ___ Times/Wk. ___5___ Hrs./Day ___

Regular Education Services

Regular sixth grade

Total Amount ___ Times/Wk. ___5___ Hrs./Day ___5___

Related Services

Type	Amount
Speech-language sessions with speech-language therapist for 30 minutes 2 times/week to work on lateral lisp and improve oral fluency.	

Physical Education

Adapted Class Amount ___None___

Regular Class Amount ___As scheduled___

Transportation

Special ___NA -- walk to sch.___ Regular ___

Current Level of Performance

Reading: Second grade, first semester; special difficulty with word-attack skills; knows 70 basic sight words. Language Arts: Cursive writing mostly illegible; not able to construct sentences in composition; mostly phonetic spelling; poor ability to give verbal descriptions. Math and other areas: Completes work with 80% or better accuracy at grade level. Work Habits: Consistently completes about 20% of language arts assignments with about 80% accuracy.

Participants in Plan Development

Name	Title
Marie Milton	Mother
Melissa Borden	LD resource teacher
Tim Triumph	Sixth grade teacher
Evan Gorley	Principal
Kate Nona	Speech-language therapist
Ron Horsely	School psychologist

For High School Students ONLY (to be initially completed at 9th grade IEP meeting and reviewed annually).

This student is a candidate for: High School Diploma ___; Special Ed. Certificate ___; GED Equivalency Diploma ___.
Is the Minimum Competency Test to be administered this school year? Yes ___ No ___ If yes, attach addendum.

White: Confidential Folder Yellow: Parent Copy

INDIVIDUALIZED EDUCATION PROGRAM

School Year 84 - 85

ANNUAL GOAL: The student _Patrick Milton_ will _complete all assigned work in language arts and reading with 90% or better accuracy at Fifth grade level by September 1985_

PROGRESS REPORTS

SHORT TERM OBJECTIVES	Grading Periods		COMMENTS
Objective: Given 200 sight words from his reader, Pat will read them with 90% accuracy.	1	✕	
Beginning Skill Level: 2² (Ginn); knows 70 Dolch words	2	12/84	
	3	3/85	P- Learning average of 2 new sight words/school day
Date Initiated: 11/21/84	4		M- Now knows all Dolch words and all words in reader
Objective: Given a topic with which he is familiar, Pat will write at least 5 complete sentences on the topic within 30 minutes.	1	✕	
Beginning Skill Level:	2	12/84	P- Will write 2 or 3 sentences before refusing to continue; tells sentence from nonsentence with 75% accuracy.
Does not know sentence from nonsentence.	3	3/85	P-
Date Initiated: 11/21/84	4		
Objective: Given instructions to copy 5 lines of printed material from a book, Pat will write the material on lined paper using cursive letters so that another teacher can immediately decipher	1	✕	
Beginning Skill Level: at least 90% of the material.	2	12/84	P- Most written work now 60% legible; 75% legible when copying.
Only letters legible 80% of the time are e, p, w.	3	3/85	M- Nearly all written work is legible.
Date Initiated: 11/21/84	4		
Objective: Given 50 sight words from his reading book and 50 CVCE words, Pat will read them with 100% accuracy; given the same words from dictation,	1	✕	
Beginning Skill Level: he will spell them with 95% accuracy.	2	12/84	P- Reads CVCE words with 95% accuracy and writes them with 80% accuracy.
Tested spelling grade level = 2.	3	3/85	
Date Initiated: 11/21/84	4		

Evaluation Procedures: Annual goals will be evaluated during the annual review. Short term objectives will be monitored at each nine week marking period. Beginning skill level indicates the student's performance prior to instruction.

Progress Key: No mark–Objective not initiated   **P**–Progressing on the Objective   **D**–Having difficulty with the objective (comment to describe difficulty)

M–Objective mastered   **M/R**–Objective mastered, but needs review to maintain mastery

White: Confidential Folder   Yellow: Parent Progress Report   Pink: Teacher Working Copy   Goldenrod: Parent Original therapists are concerned with fine motor problems, such as handwriting, as well as with self-help and job skills.

School social workers and pupil personnel workers serve as a major link between the school and the family, and are likely to become involved when problems at home are affecting students' school performance or behavior.

For handicapped students who are unable to attend school because of a lengthy illness or complications related to a disability, instruction is often provided while they are at home or in the hospital. Such instruction is designed to maintain and continue a student's academic progress. Homebound instruction is intended for short periods of time.

MAINSTREAMING

The "least restrictive placement" clause of PL94–142 has revolutionized the practice of special as well as regular education. As already noted, it requires that exceptional students be assigned to the least restrictive placement appropriate to their needs. The effect of this provision has been to greatly increase contacts between nonhandicapped and handicapped students. In general, all types of handicapped students have moved one or two notches "up" the continuum of special education services. Students who were once placed in special schools are now generally put in separate classrooms in regular schools. Students who were once placed in separate classrooms in regular schools, particularly mildly retarded and learning-disabled students, are now most often assigned to regular classes for most of their instruction.

Many (perhaps most) classroom teachers have students identified as handicapped, who are usually receiving some type of special educational services part of the day. Most of these mainstreamed students are categorized as learning disabled, speech

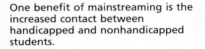
One benefit of mainstreaming is the increased contact between handicapped and nonhandicapped students.

1. How can you encourage exceptional—and regular—students to focus not on *disabilities* they or others may have but on abilities?

Phaedra Damianakos, a third-grade teacher in New York City:

In this world everyone has problems. Who is perfect? A teacher must reinforce the idea that shortcomings, whether errors in schoolwork or disabilities, are not all-important. The important thing is what you *can* do and what you *do* do in society to enrich the whole. This is not an easy task: "Ad astra per aspera" ("To the stars through difficulties"). Does one contribute one's talents to the betterment of the group, or does one hoard and "fade into the woodwork"? A teacher must stress ability, not disability, whether real or imagined.

2. For students with physical or mental disabilities, social integration in the class may be as important as academic success. How would you help an exceptional student feel like an accepted member of your class?

Donna Lloyd, who teaches elementary school in Maybrook, N.Y., wrote:

Learning-disabled children have certain strengths, as do all children. It is upon these strengths that we try to build their self-esteem. I feel that if the teacher shows love, warmth, and understanding toward *all* students, then students will usually accept each other. In the case of physical disabilities, a certain curiosity must be satisfied with elementary children. A growing number of books on various disabilities are available for children to read and these could be displayed in the classroom. Simulation activities in which children pretend they are handicapped in one way or another can also be helpful in fostering an understanding of a person with that disability.

Kaye Cutchen, who teaches middle school in Eufaula, Ala., wrote:

Without calling attention unnecessarily to the exceptional student, I would try to make sure that he or she understands all instructions and assignments.

I would seat the exceptional student near several outgoing students who would give the exceptional student an immediate sense of belonging in the class.

During group work I would make every effort to place the exceptional student in a group that includes students of various ability levels, and I would certainly include some students not so high in ability that they would make the exceptional student feel inadequate.

I would offer genuine praise for any work that the exceptional student does that deserves praise. False praise is quickly identified by most any student.

3. The instruction of exceptional students is often the shared responsibility of several teachers, with the student "mainstreamed" into an ordinary classroom for some activities and pulled out to work with specialized teachers for others. What types of cooperation between the various teachers are necessary for this educational arrangement to work?

Donna Lloyd, who teaches elementary school in Maybrook, N.Y., wrote:

To make such an arrangement work, *a lot* of cooperation is needed among the teachers involved, as well as flexibility. Time for the teachers to communicate with each other regarding the mainstreamed child is vital. This often presents a problem when the time cannot be worked into an 8:30 to 3:30 schedule. Time for this communication must often be arranged either before or after school. If this communication does not exist, school can become even more confusing or disruptive, especially for a learning disabled child who needs the structure and stability of a secure environment.

Karen Schilling, who teaches elementary school in Platteville, Wis., wrote:

Thinking of the special educators as team teachers of the regular educator will help foster cooperative thinking. Sharing of lesson plans and class plans on a regular basis will keep the team informed.

The classroom teacher needs to actively seek the assistance of the special educator in the preparation or modification of lessons to accommodate learning weakness.

The special educator should spend part of each day in the regular classroom focusing on the special education students, but assisting all other students, too.

impaired, mildly retarded, or emotionally disturbed. High-quality mainstreaming can dramatically improve the achievement and self-confidence of these students. Unfortunately, some classroom teachers are uncomfortable about having handicapped students in their classes, and many feel poorly prepared to accommodate their needs (Gickling and Theobald, 1975; Alexander and Strain, 1978). It occasionally happens that a teacher will present a lesson to twenty-nine students while one handicapped, supposedly mainstreamed child, sits in the back of the room coloring a picture or doing nothing at all.

Mainstreaming solves several important problems. It allows mildly handicapped students to interact with nonhandicapped peers and to learn normal behavior. The problems of self-contained special education classes are similar to those of the low track in schools that use tracking (see Chapter 9): lumping together students with problems labels them as "special," deprives them of appropriate role models, and creates classes that are difficult to manage.

However, mainstreaming also *creates* problems. When mainstreamed students are performing below the level of the rest of the class, the teacher must adapt instruction to the mainstreamed students' levels. The attitudes of the nonhandicapped students toward their handicapped classmates are often negative (Gottleib and Leyser, 1981), which frequently defeats the social integration goals of mainstreaming.

Research on Mainstreaming

Research on mainstreaming has focused on students with learning disabilities and mild retardation, whose deficits can be termed "mild academic handicaps" (Madden and Slavin, 1983b; MacMillan, et al., 1986) Several studies have compared students with mild academic handicaps in special education classes to those in regular classes. In general, these students learn somewhat better in regular classes. When the regular teacher uses an instructional method designed to accommodate a wide range of student abilities, students with mild handicaps generally learn much better in the regular classroom than in special education. One outstanding study on this topic was done by Calhoun and Elliott (1977), who compared educable mentally retarded (EMR) students and emotionally disturbed (ED) students in regular and special classes. Regular as well as special education classes used the same individualized materials, and teachers (trained in special education) were rotated across classes to ensure that the only difference between the regular and special programs was the presence of nonhandicapped classmates.

The results of the Calhoun and Elliott (1977) study are depicted in Figure 12.5. Note that the study continued for three years. Each year the EMR and ED students in regular classes (blue lines) gained in achievement in comparison to similar students in the special classes (red lines). Since the students were initially randomly assigned (for example, by coin flip) to special or regular classes and all other factors were held constant, the differences shown in Figure 12.5 can only be attributed to the superiority of regular class placement.

Research on programs for regular classrooms containing students with mild academic handicaps indicates that the most successful strategy for these students is to use individualized instructional programs, as was done in the Calhoun and Elliott (1977) study. For example, the Team Assisted Individualization (TAI) and Cooperative Integrated Reading and Composition (CIRC) programs described in Chapter 9 have both been found to improve the achievement of mainstreamed

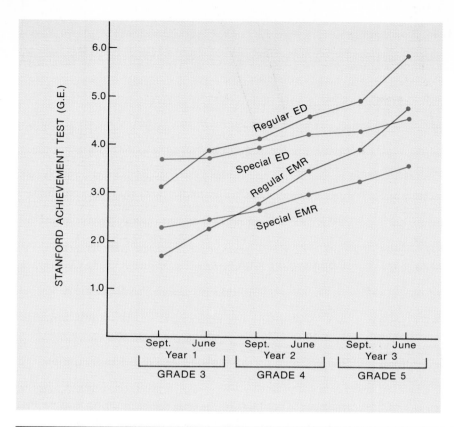

FIGURE 12.5

Achievement of Students in Regular and Special Education Classes

Placement in regular rather than special education classes resulted in higher achievement levels over three years for emotionally disturbed and educable mentally retarded students.

From Madden and Slavin, 1983a, p. 525. Based on data from Calhoun and Elliott, 1977.

learning-disabled students, in comparison to mainstreamed students in traditionally organized classes (Slavin et al., 1984c; Madden et al., 1986). Highly structured resource room programs that use programmed instruction and behavior modification techniques (see Chapter 4) to supplement the regular teacher's reading and mathematics instruction have also been found to be effective (Glavin et al., 1971).

One of the reasons for the growth in the 1950s of segregated classes for students with academic handicaps was the observation that these students were poorly accepted by their classmates (Johnson, 1950). Now that these students are being reintegrated into regular classes, problems of social acceptance are reappearing (see Gottlieb and Leyser, 1981). Improving the social acceptance of academically handicapped students is a critical task of mainstreaming.

One consistently effective means of doing this is to involve the academically handicapped students in cooperative learning teams with their nonhandicapped classmates. For example, a study of Student Teams—Achievement Divisions (described in Chapter 10) in classes containing learning-disabled students found that STAD reduced the social rejection of the learning-disabled students while significantly increasing their achievement (Madden and Slavin, 1983a). Other cooperative learning

Whether classroom teachers use individualized instruction, cooperative learning, or other means of accommodating student differences, they need to know how to adapt lessons to address the needs of students with learning or emotional problems. This section discusses ways of adapting classroom instruction so handicapped learners can succeed.

When students have difficulty with instruction or materials in learning situations, the recommendation is frequently to adapt or modify the instruction or the materials (see Burnett, 1987). Teachers are often uncertain what is meant by this suggestion, and they sometimes think that the only adaptation possible is to rewrite the entire lesson or to design entirely new materials. The particular adaptation required depends on the student's needs (Lambie, 1980), and could be anything from format adaptation to rewriting textbook materials to lower the reading level or designing materials to incorporate specific features needed by an individual student (Allen et al., 1982). In this section three common types of adaptations for accommodating handicapped students in regular classrooms are described.

FORMAT ADAPTATIONS FOR WRITTEN ASSIGNMENTS

Teachers can sometimes help handicapped students by changing the format in which a task is presented, without changing the actual task. Handicapped students may require changes of this type for a variety of reasons: (1) an assignment is too long; (2) the spacing on the page is too close to allow the student to focus on individual items; (3) the directions for the task are insufficient or confusing; or (4) the models or examples for the task are either absent, misleading, or insufficient. The critical concept here is that while task and response remain the same, adaptations are made in the way the material is presented.

To make adaptations in the length of an assignment, you might present only one portion of it at a time. When that portion is completed, you would present the next portion. For instance, the assignment might be twenty subtraction problems arranged in five rows of four problems each. You might have students complete five small assignments by cutting the paper into five strips and presenting one row at a time. Or you might teach children to divide the assignment into manageable "chunks" themselves, completing one "chunk," then checking with you or taking a short break before continuing with the next "chunk."

For some handicapped students, adaptations will need to be made because the items on the page are too close together to allow them to concentrate attention on one item at a time or to write in a complete response. You may need to cut the items apart and mount them on other paper. Again, the task has not changed, only the format.

Occasionally, the directions for a task or assignment must be simplified. For example, you might substitute in a set of directions the word "circle" for "draw a ring around." You could also teach students the words commonly found in directions (Cohen and deBettencourt, 1983). By teaching students how to understand such words, you will make them more independent learners. Models or examples presented with a task may also need to be changed, so that they more closely resemble the task to be completed.

ADAPTATIONS IN CONTENT

In some instances, handicapped students may require an adaptation in the content being presented. One such

programs have found similar effects on the social acceptance of students with mild academic handicaps (Ballard et al., 1977; Slavin et al., 1984b).

In traditionally organized classes, many behaviors have been found to be characteristic of teachers who are especially effective in improving the achievement of mainstreamed students. Among them were the following behaviors identified in a series of studies by Larrivee (1985):

1. Efficient use of time, avoiding spending inordinate amounts of time in transitions, discipline, and unstructured activities.

2. Providing positive, sustaining feedback to students (for example, staying with

situation is when so much new information is presented that the student is unable to process it quickly. Another is when handicapped students lack a prerequisite skill or concept necessary to complete a task.

Adaptations in the amount of content being presented may be made by isolating each single concept (Gallagher, 1979), and then teaching and requiring mastery of each concept as a separate unit before proceeding to the next concept. Although this type of adaptation requires teaching and practicing smaller units of material, the same content will be covered in the end.

Adaptations required because students lack essential prerequisites may be as simple as explaining vocabulary or concepts prior to teaching a lesson. Teachers often do this as a part of their lesson (for example, when they introduce new words at the beginning of a reading lesson). More complex adaptations are required when students lack prerequisite skills or concepts that cannot be explained easily or when they do not have a skill necessary to learn the lesson. For example, if the math lesson involves solving word problems that require the division of three-digit numerals and the student has not yet learned how to divide three-digit numerals, this skill would have to be taught before the word problems could be addressed.

ADAPTATIONS IN MODES OF COMMUNICATION

Some handicapped students require adaptations either in the way they receive information or the way they demonstrate their knowledge of specific information. Many students who are unable to learn information when their only means of getting it is through reading can learn if the information is made available in other forms. You should be creative in considering the possibilities. You might have students watch a demonstration, filmstrip, film, videotape, television program, or play. Or you might have them listen to an audiotape, lecture/discussion, or debate.

A different type of adaptation may be required if a student cannot respond as the task directs. Since the most common method of having students respond is in writing, students who cannot write or having writing problems may appear to lack knowledge of the particular task when their actual problem is in communicating what they know. If a student has a writing problem, you might ask the student to tell you about the concept in a private conversation, record the student's response on a tape recorder, or ask the student to present an oral report to the class. Or you might let the student represent the knowledge by drawing a picture or diagram or by constructing a model or diorama.

TEACHING OF LEARNING STRATEGIES

Many learning disabled students do poorly in school because they have failed to "learn how to learn." Programs directed at helping students learn such strategies as note taking, summarization, and memorization methods have been very successful with learning disabled adolescents (Deshler and Schumaker, 1986). Reciprocal teaching, a method for helping normal students learn metacognitive strategies for reading, is described in Chapter 6. It has also been successful with learning disabled adolescents (Palincsar, 1987).

a student who gives a wrong answer and helping him or her reach the correct answer rather than moving on to the next student).

3. Responding supportively (rather than critically) to students.

4. Asking questions to which students are likely to be able to respond correctly.

5. Using classroom management strategies that maintain the continuity of the lesson and minimize discipline problems (see Chapter 11).

In other words, teacher behaviors associated with effective teaching for mainstreaming students are essentially the same as those that improve achievement for all students (Leinhardt and Bickel, 1987).

A current theme in special education is to consider the needs of exceptional children not only during their school years but also before they enter school and after they graduate. Already the benefits of mainstreaming are evident as young people with disabilities such as Down syndrome find themselves employable in real jobs. What might be other long-term benefits (or problems) of integrating special needs students into "regular" classrooms?

Computers and the Handicapped Student

Computers can provide individualized instructions to academically handicapped students in regular as well as special education classes. There are four major advantages in using computers to help exceptional children learn. First, computers can help individualize instruction in terms of method of delivery, type and frequency of reinforcement, rate of presentation, and level of instruction. Second, computers can give immediate corrective feedback and emphasize the active role of children in learning. Third, they can hold the attention of children who are easily distractible. Finally, computer instruction is motivating and patient.

Handicapped children seem to like learning from computers. Poorly motivated students have become more enthusiastic about their studies (Cartwright and Derevensky, 1976). They feel more "in control" because they are being taught in a context that is positive, reinforcing and nonthreatening.

One valuable approach using computers is to provide academically handicapped children with activities in which they can explore, construct, and communicate. Word processors serve this purpose, and other programs have been specifically designed for handicapped children. For example, in CARIS (Computer Animated Reading Instruction System) children can select words for sentences by touching a computer screen with a light pen. The computer then generates a brief animated cartoon acting out the meaning of the sentence. Many combinations of words can be explored. Advantages of this program include the control that children have when using it and the immediate visual feedback it supplies.

Educators are finding that computers can help teach exceptional students.

During their school years, children with disabilities are protected from academic and social isolation by the provisions of Public Law 94–142. No such protection exists after graduation, but a convergence of factors has opened doors for the disabled to find work and be more productive members of society.

Although no reliable nationwide statistics exist, anecdotal reports point to an increased number of job opportunities for people with mental retardation and physical disabilities. A generation ago, the only readily available work for these people was at sheltered workshops, where the tasks were menial and the wages far below the national minimum.

Contributing to this change have been a pair of factors, the institution of Public Law 94–142 and projected shortages in the pool of workers.

Public Law 94–142, which encourages students with disabilities to be educated alongside nonhandicapped children, was passed by Congress in 1975. As a result, the first wave of children to fully benefit from the law is now entering the work force. Not only do these young people expect to be integral members of society, but their presence in the classroom has made fellow students and teachers more accepting of them.

The second factor to increased opportunities for the handicapped is the shrinking of the traditional labor pool. A decline in the birthrate during the 1960s and 1970s, coupled with a projected surge in retirements near the year 2000, has sent employers looking for new sources of labor.

Companies that have hired significant numbers of people with disabilities include McDonald's, Pizza Hut, and the Marriott Corporation. A study by Pizza Hut showed that disabled workers stay at their jobs four to five times longer than other workers. For the company, that means less money spent to hire and train new employees.

At the Marriott Corporation, Matthew Starr is a good example of how a company can match a handicapped worker to a job. Mr. Starr, who is in his early twenties, has Down syndrome and is classified as mildly retarded. He washes pots and pans at a Maryland Marriott hotel for 40 hours a week at $3.60 an hour.

Mr. Starr does his job by rote—giving each pot or pan equal treatment whether it needs it or not. A supervisor spent ten weeks closely guiding Mr. Starr as he learned the job and even after a year, Mr. Starr still has a coach that he can contact by beeper if the pots back up and his frustration builds. His coach, Laurie Patterson, also supervises five other retarded workers at Marriott.

As one might expect, a person can get tired of washing pots. Luckily, Marriott does promote its workers when possible, and Mr. Starr hopes to move on soon to a better paying job in the company's mailroom.

"What we're learning is not to make distinctions among handicapped and nonhandicapped workers," said Kathleen Alexander, vice-president for personnel services at Marriott. "It sounds Pollyanna-ish, but we're focusing on what's the job to be done and who can we get to do it."

The original proponents of Public Law 94–142 probably couldn't be more pleased.

From Peter T. Kilborn, "For the Retarded, Independence in Real Jobs," *New York Times*, January 2, 1990, p. A1. Kathleen Teltsch, "As the Labor Pool Dwindles, Doors Open for the Disabled," *New York Times*, June 22, 1989, p. A1.

Buddy Systems and Peer Tutoring

One way to help meet the needs of handicapped students in the regular classroom is to provide these students with assistance from nonhandicapped classmates, using either a "buddy system" to help with noninstructional needs or peer tutoring to help with learning problems.

A nonhandicapped student who volunteers to be a handicapped student's "buddy" can help the handicapped student cope with the routine tasks of classroom life. For example, a nonhandicapped buddy can guide a visually impaired student, help an academically handicapped student when directions are not understood, or deliver cues or prompts as needed in some classes. In middle and high school settings a nonhandicapped buddy can take notes for a hearing-impaired or learning-disabled student by making carbons or photocopies of his or her own notes. The nonhandicapped buddy can also ensure that the exceptional student has located the correct textbook page during a lesson, and has the materials necessary for a class. The primary responsibility of the buddy is to help the handicapped student adjust to the regular classroom, to answer questions, and to provide direction for activities. Use of this resource allows the regular classroom teacher to address more important questions related to instructional activities.

Another way of helping handicapped students within the regular classroom is to use peer tutoring (Scruggs and Richter, 1986). Teachers who use peers to tutor in their classroom should ensure that these tutors are carefully trained. This means the peer tutor must be taught how to provide assistance by modeling and explaining, how to give specific positive and corrective feedback, and when to allow the handicapped student to work alone. When peer tutoring involves a handicapped student and a nonhandicapped student, both may benefit: the handicapped student by acquring academic concepts and the tutor by gaining a better acceptance and understanding of handicapped students. Sometimes handicapped students themselves tutor younger nonhandicapped students, and this generally benefits both students (Osguthorpe and Scruggs, 1986). See Chapter 9 for more on peer tutoring.

Coordination with Special Education Personnel

When a handicapped student is integrated into the regular classroom, the classroom teacher often works with one or more special educators to ensure the student's successful integration (Turnbull and Schulz, 1979). The classroom teacher may participate in conferences with groups of special education personnel who are involved in a particular student's case, the special education personnel may at times be present in the regular classroom, or the classroom teacher may consult with a special educator at regular intervals. Whatever the arrangement, the classroom teacher and the special educator(s) must recognize that each has expertise crucial to the

Educationally handicapped students often spend part of each day in a "regular" classroom and part of the day with a special education teacher.

At the end of a lesson on fractions, Ralph Martin assigned his class of twenty-six fourth-graders a page of fractions problems. Twenty-five students got right to work, but one student, Ann Willis, sat still, doing nothing. Ann is a learning disabled student who is mainstreamed for math.

Ralph sighed inwardly, and walked over to Ann.

RALPH: Are you having trouble with this?

ANN: I don't get it.

RALPH: Weren't you listening to the lesson?

ANN: Yeah, but I didn't understand it.

At this point, Mr. Martin sees several other students with their hands up.

RALPH: Well, do your best, and I'll check in with you later.

Later that day, Mr. Martin meets with Sally Jackson, a special education teacher who has Ann for an hour each day in a resource room.

RALPH: I'm really concerned about Ann. She's not doing anything in my math class. What good can it possibly do her to just sit there?

SALLY: What problem is she having?

RALPH: She just doesn't do anything! I taught a lesson on fractions to the class, and gave out a worksheet. She handed it in blank!

SALLY: Did you talk with her about it?

RALPH: Sure! But I've got twenty-six kids, and a lot of them have problems too. I can't drop everything to teach one student all the time.

SALLY: I've often found with Ann that she understands more than she seems to, but doesn't show it because she lacks confidence and because she gets confused about directions. Could you go over the directions with her, and then praise her when she completes the first few items?

RALPH: I guess, but as I say, I can't take too much time from the rest of the class. Why can't you keep her with you? You've only got eight kids at a time so you can give them a lot more individual attention.

SALLY: I could do that, but I'm concerned that kids who spend most of the day in the resource room get cut off from their regular classmates, and get classified as "those special ed kids."

RALPH: That sounds fine in theory, but everyone in my class knows that Ann is a little strange. She doesn't have any friends that I know of; she just sits by herself at lunch.

SALLY: Ralph, I know it's hard for you in some ways, but I'd really like to make this situation work for Ann. She has some problems, but I think she can make it in your class if you and I work together on it. Here's an idea: Give me a copy of the math work you're planning to do each day, and I'll go over it with Ann before she goes to your class, so she'll already have a good idea of what she's supposed to do. Maybe I could modify the task sometimes so she can have more success at it.

RALPH: Well, maybe that will help. Since you're so set on it, I'll give it a try, But I'm not expecting any miracles.

QUESTIONS

1. Discuss the pros and cons of mainstreaming a student like Ann.
2. Will Sally's plan work? What other things might Sally or Ralph try to help Ann be successful in Ralph's math class?
3. What might Sally or Ralph do to help Ann make friends and be accepted by her classmates?

handicapped student's success. The regular classroom teacher is the expert on how the classroom is organized and operates on a day-to-day basis, the curriculum of the classroom, and what expectations are placed on students for performance. The special educator, on the other hand, is the expert on the characteristics of a particular group of handicapped students, the special learning and behavioral strengths and deficits of the student who is being mainstreamed, and instructional techniques for a particular group of handicapped students. All this information is important to the successful integration of handicapped students, which is why communication between the regular and special education teacher is so necessary (Laurie, et al., 1978; Leinhardt and Bickel, 1987).

Communication should begin before handicapped students are placed in the regular classroom and should continue throughout the placement. Both teachers must have up-to-date information about the student's performance in each setting to plan and coordinate an effective program. Only then can instruction targeted to improving the student's performance in the regular classroom be designed and presented. In addition, generalization of skills and behaviors from one setting to the other will be enhanced.

Social Integration of Handicapped Students

Placement of handicapped students in the regular classroom is only one part of their integration into that environment. These students must be integrated socially as well as instructionally. The classroom teacher plays a critical role in the social integration of handicapped students. Much has been written about the effects of teacher expectations on student achievement and behavior (see Chapter 10). When integrating handicapped students, the teacher's attitude toward these students is important not only for teacher-student interactions but also as a model for the nonhandicapped students in the classroom. Simpson (1980) identified the attitudes of people such as teachers as a factor in influencing the attitudes of regular class students.

The research on attitudes toward handicapped individuals provides several strategies that might be useful to the regular classroom teacher who wants to influence the attitudes of nonhandicapped students. One strategy is to use cooperative learning methods. Another is to provide information to the regular students about various handicaps, perhaps using specially designed materials (for examples see Barnes et al., 1978; Bookbinder, 1978). There are several sources of literature written about individuals with various handicaps (for example, Baskin and Harris, 1977; Dreyer, 1977).

SUMMARY AND REVIEW OF OBJECTIVES

Types of Exceptionalities. Exceptionalities can be categorized as mental, emotional, speech or language, and physical. Almost 11 percent of students receive special education; 94 percent of these are given special education for learning disorders, speech problems, or emotional disturbances.

Mental retardation refers to significantly subaverage general intellectual functioning resulting in impairments in adaptive behavior. IQ measurements, plus other information, are most commonly used to diagnose mental retardation. Programs for *educable* mentally retarded children focus on basic academic skills, while those for *trainable* mentally retarded children emphasize self-help, vocational skills, and independent living skills.

Specific learning disability is most often characterized by disorders of memory, thinking, and language. Such a disability may affect a student's ability to listen, think, speak, read, write, spell, or do mathematical calculations. The most widely used criterion for identifying learning-disabled students is some difficulty in school-related tasks without an indication of mental retardation or emotional disturbance.

Most students characterized as gifted have IQs over 130 and typically have superior cognitive and creative skills and strong motivation. One debate concerning programs for gifted students centers on acceleration—moving students rapidly through a curriculum—versus enrichment—engaging them in supplemental problem-solving and creative activities.

A wide range of behaviors is covered by the term "emotional disturbance." These include aggression, hyperactivity, withdrawal, and immature behavior. Procedures to identify severe emotional disturbances include observation, behavior rating scales and inventories, and personality testing.

There are other behavior disorders, not due to emotional disturbance, that interfere with academic performance. These include drug and alcohol use, juvenile delinquency, depression or anger due to family problems, and psychological problems due to child abuse and neglect.

Many children in the early elementary grades have articulation problems, which is a common type of speech disorder. Mild articulation problems often disappear as children advance through elementary school. Other problems with communication include stuttering and language disorders.

Children with physical handicaps include those with visual, hearing, or neurological impairments, congenital problems—such as cerebral palsy or seizures—and those with orthopedic handicaps.

Continuum of Special Education Services.   Special education refers to any program provided for handicapped children instead of, or in addition to, the regular classroom program. Public Law 94–142 requires that school districts provide free and appropriate public education for handicapped children. Components of special education programs include use of the least restrictive environment, Individualized Education Programs, legal safeguards with regard to special education and placement programs, and student evaluation and placement.

In an Individualized Education Program (IEP) the appropriateness of a setting and school resource are considered with regard to students' needs. Regular classroom placement is often most appropriate for students with mild or moderate vision or hearing problems or learning disabilities. Consultants, resource room placement, special class placement with part-time mainstreaming, self-contained special education, special day or residential schools, and homebound and hospital instruction are additional alternatives.

Development of Individualized Education Programs.   Parents, physicians, principals, or teachers often make the initial referral for special education assessment. An evaluation/placement team, composed of professionals designated by the school district along with parents, makes decisions about the diagnosis and placement. A preliminary screening involves a look at the student's school records and perhaps an interview with the student's teacher. A comprehensive assessment is a battery of tests to assess the student's strengths and weaknesses. An IEP that is appropriate to the student's needs is then developed. The IEP must contain statements indicating the child's present level of performance, annual goals, intermediate objectives, a statement of special education and related services to be provided, projected date for the initiation of services and their anticipated duration, and evaluation criteria and procedures for measuring progress.

Mainstreaming.   Mainstreaming gives mildly handicapped students an opportunity to interact with their nonhandicapped peers and diminishes the effects of labeling of handicapped students. Research shows that when the regular class uses an instructional method designed to accommodate a wide range of student abilities, students with mild handicaps tend to learn better in regular classes than in special education. A consistently effective means of improving the social acceptance of mainstreamed academically handicapped students is to involve them in cooperative groups with their nonhandicapped classmates.

Meeting Needs of Mainstreamed Students.   Problems with mainstreaming include adapting instruction and encouraging other students to have a positive attitude toward the handicapped student. Three common types of adaptations useful for accommodating exceptional students are format adaptations, or changes in certain aspects of the task's presentation such as length, spacing, directions, or models; adaptations in content; and adaptations in receiving and demonstrating knowledge. Computers can aid in individualizing instruction by giving immediate corrective feedback, by holding student attention, and by motivating the student. The buddy system involves pairing handicapped students with nonhandicapped students. In peer tutoring, nonhandicapped students are trained to help handicapped students. Communication between regular and special education teachers is necessary for the successful integration of handicapped students into the classroom.

STUDY QUESTIONS

1. Which of the following exceptionalities would be most common in a junior high class?
   a. Deafness
   b. Articulation problem
   c. Learning disability
   d. Physical handicap
2. Almost four out of five students have IQs in which of the following ranges?
   a. 50–75
   b. 60–90
   c. 70–110
   d. 80–120
   e. 90–110
3. An individual with a learning disability is likely to
   a. be mentally retarded.
   b. have memory or language difficulties.
   c. be environmentally disadvantaged.
   d. have motor impairments.
4. Educable mental retardation implies
   a. a mild handicap with ability to learn academic skills.
   b. an IQ in the range of 90–100.
   c. a moderate degree of retardation with ability to learn self-help skills.
   d. a. and b. are correct.

5. Two major options for adapting educational programs to the needs of gifted and talented students are _____ and _____ programs.
6. Number the following special education options in order from least restrictive (1) to most restrictive (4).
   —— Resource room placement
   —— Regular classroom placement
   —— Special day school
   —— Self-contained special education classroom
7. Research regarding mainstreaming has shown students with mild handicaps to
   a. learn poorly under individualized instruction as opposed to group instruction.
   b. become fearful and confused when introduced to computer-based activities, such as LOGO.
   c. perform better in regular classrooms than in special education classrooms.
   d. show better social development in special education classrooms than in regular classrooms.

Answers: 1. c   2. d   3. b   4. a   5. acceleration, enrichment   6. 2, 1, 4, 3   7. c

SUGGESTED READINGS

GALLAGHER, P. A. (1979). *Teaching students with behavior disorders: Techniques for classroom instruction.* Denver, Colo.: Love.

GOTTLIEB, J., and LEYSER, Y. (1981). Friendship between mentally retarded and nonretarded children. In S. Asher and J. Gottman (Eds.), *The development of children's friendship.* Cambridge: Cambridge University Press.

HALLAHAN, D. P., and KAUFFMAN, J. M. (1988). *Exceptional children* (4th ed.). Englewood Cliffs, N.J.: Prentice-Hall.

HIXON, T. J., SCHRIBERG, L. D., and SAXMAN, J. H. (Eds.). (1980). *Introduction to communication disorders.* Englewood Cliffs, N.J.: Prentice-Hall.

LARRIVEE, B. (1985). *Effective teaching behaviors for successful mainstreaming.* New York: Longman.

LEINHARDT, G., and PALLAY, A. (1982). Restrictive educational settings: Exile or haven? *Review of Educational Research, 52,* 557–578.

MADDEN, N. A., and SLAVIN, R. E. (1983). Mainstreaming students with mild academic handicaps: Academic and social outcomes. *Review of Educational Research,* 53, 519–569.

MACMILLAN, D. L., KEOGH, B. K., and JONES, R. L. (1986). Special educational research on mildly handicapped learners. In M. C. WITTROCK (Ed.), *Handbook of research on teaching* (3rd ed.). New York: Macmillan.

MATSON, J. L., and MULICH, J. A. (Eds.). (1983). *Handbook of mental retardation.* New York: Pergamon.

O'LEARY, K. D. (1980). Pills or skills for hyperactive children. *Journal of Applied Behavior Analysis,* 13, 191–204.

RENZULLI, J. S. (1977). *The enrichment triad model: A guide for developing defensible programs for the gifted and talented.* Wethersfield, Conn.: Creative Learning Press.

TAYLOR, R. (1984). *Assessment of exceptional students: Educational and psychological procedures.* Englewood Cliffs, N.J.: Prentice-Hall.

TORRANCE, E. P. (1986). Teaching creative and gifted learners. In M. C. WITTROCK (Ed.), *Handbook of research on teaching* (3rd ed.). New York: Macmillan.

TURNBULL, A. P., and BRANTLEY, J. C. (1982). *Mainstreaming: Developing and implementing individualized education programs* (2nd ed.). Columbus, Ohio: Merrill.

YSSELDYKE, J., and ALGOZZINE, B. (1982). *Critical issues in special and remedial education.* Boston: Houghton Mifflin.

Chapter 13

Social Class, Ethnicity, and Gender

Chapter Objectives

After reading this chapter on social class, ethnicity, and gender, you should better understand how and why these variables affect school performance, and you should be able to:

- List ways in which social class affects upbringing and achievement.

- Describe the role of the federal government in helping students from disadvantaged backgrounds.

- Define "ethnic group," and contrast it with "social class."

- Understand the issues that are of special importance to teachers in desegregated schools and in schools where some students speak little or no English.

- Describe some gender differences that are biologically based and some that are learned, and understand how to avoid reinforcing sex stereotypes.

Culture
The language, attitudes, ways of
behaving, and other aspects of life
that characterize a group of people

Throughout the twentieth century the schools have served as the principal engine of social mobility. Most middle-class Americans today are descended from immigrants who arrived with little, worked hard, and sent their children to school so that they could attain the success and security denied to their poorly educated parents. The school is almost always the ladder by which the children of the poor climb out of poverty.

The very foundation of our political philosophy is that every American must have an equal opportunity to reach his or her full potential. Since success in school is so central to success in life, children from all social-class backgrounds, all ethnic groups, and both sexes must have equal opportunities to succeed in school.

This chapter describes the characteristics of students from different social-class, ethnic, and linguistic backgrounds, and discusses educational issues related to these factors, including desegregation, bilingual education, compensatory education, and intergroup relations. It also discusses gender differences and equal treatment of boys and girls.

Teachers are more than instructors of students. They are builders of tomorrow's society. A critical part of every teacher's role is to make certain that the equal opportunity we hold to be central to our nationhood is translated into equal opportunity in day-to-day life in the classroom. This chapter was written with this goal in mind.

THE IMPACT OF CULTURAL DIVERSITY

If you have ever traveled to a foreign country, you noticed differences in behaviors, attitudes, dress, language, and food. In fact, part of the fun of traveling is in discovering these differences in **culture.**

Even though we usually think of cultural differences as being mostly national differences, there is probably as much cultural diversity within the United States as between the United States and other industrialized nations. The life of a middle-class family in the United States or Canada is probably more like that of a middle-class family in Italy, Ireland, or Israel than it is like that of a poor family living a mile away. Yet while we value cultural differences between nations, we are often less tolerant toward differences within our own society. Our tendency is to value characteristics of mainstream, high-status groups and devalue those of other groups.

By the time children enter school, they have absorbed many aspects of the culture in which they were raised: the language, attitudes, ways of behaving, food preferences, and so on. Many of the behaviors associated with being brought up in a particular culture have important consequences for classroom instruction. For example, the school expects children to speak standard English. This is easy for students from homes where standard English is spoken but difficult for those whose families speak other languages or significantly divergent dialects of English. The school also expects students to be highly verbal, to spend most of their time working independently, and to compete with other students for grades and recognition. However, many cultures within our society value cooperation and peer orientation rather than independence and competitiveness. Since the culture of the school reflects mainstream middle-class values, and since most teachers are middle-class themselves, the child from a different culture is often at a disadvantage. Understanding the backgrounds from which students come is critical for effectively teaching them both academic material and the behaviors and expectations of the school.

SOCIAL CLASS

One important way in which students differ from one another is in social class. Even in small rural towns in which almost everyone is the same in ethnicity, religion, and basic world outlook, we can safely assume that the children of the town's banker, doctor, and teachers have a different upbringing from that experienced by the children of farmhands or domestic workers.

Social class, or **socioeconomic status (SES),** is defined by sociologists in terms of an individual's income, occupation, education, and prestige in society. These factors tend to go together, so SES is most often based on a combination of the individual's income and years of education, because these are most easily measured (see, for example, Duncan et al., 1972).

However, social class indicates more than level of income and education. Along with social class goes a pervasive set of behaviors, expectations, and attitudes. Students' social-class origins are likely to profoundly affect attitudes and behaviors in school. Students from lower-class backgrounds are less likely than middle-class students to enter school knowing how to count, to name letters, to cut with scissors, or to name colors. They are less likely to perform well in school than are children from middle-class homes (Duncan et al., 1972; Boocock, 1980). Of course, these differences are only true on average; many lower-class parents do an outstanding job of supporting their children's success in school, and there are many lower-class children whose achievement is very high.

Much research has focused on the differences in child-rearing practices between the average middle-class and the average lower-class family. One important class difference involves the quality of language parents use with their children. Hess and Shipman (1970) studied mothers of different social classes and their four-year-old children. The researchers asked the mothers to teach some simple tasks to their children. The middle-class mothers used much more expressive language, gave clearer directions, and took their children's perspective better than the lower-class mothers. For example, a middle-class mother explained one task as follows:

> "All right Susan, this board is the place where we put the little toys; first of all you're supposed to learn how to place them according to color. Can you do that? The things that are all the same color you put in one section; in the second section you put another group of colors, and in the third section you put the last group of colors. Can you do that? Or would you like to see me do it first?" (Hess and Shipman, 1970, p. 182)

In contrast, the lower-class mothers used less elaborate language, gave less clear directions, and were more likely to communicate "Do it because I told you to" than to explain why and how the task was to be done. One lower-class mother's instructions were as follows:

> "I've got some chairs and cars, do you want to play the game?" Child does not respond. Mother continues: "O.K., what's this?" Child: "A wagon?" Mother: "Hm?" Child: "A wagon?" Mother: "This is not a wagon. What's this?" (Hess and Shipman, 1970, p. 182)

Hess and Shipman's (1970) findings suggest that lower-class children receive an upbringing less consistent with what they will be expected to do in school than middle-class children do. By the time they enter school, middle-class children are likely to be masters at following directions, explaining and understanding reasons, and comprehending and using complex language, while lower-class children will probably have less experience in all these areas.

Socioeconomic Status
A measure of prestige within a social group, usually based on income and education (often abbreviated SES)

Children whose parents encourage them to learn have an advantage over children from homes where parents provide few educational opportunities.

Chapter 13: Social Class, Ethnicity, and Gender

Another important difference between middle-class and lower-class families is in the kinds of activities parents tend to do with their children. Middle-class children are likely to express high expectations for their children, and to reward them for intellectual development. They are likely to provide good models for language use, to talk and read to their children frequently, and to encourage reading and other learning activities. They are particularly apt to provide all sorts of learning opportunities for children at home, such as books, encyclopedias, records, puzzles, and, increasingly, home computers. These parents are also likely to expose their children to learning experiences outside the home, such as museums, concerts, and zoos (see Bloom, 1964).

One very interesting study underscored the link between social class and school achievement. This study found that students from families of different social-class backgrounds achieved quite similarly during the school year. However, over the summer students from poorer families lost much of the achievement they had gained, while those in wealthier families gained in achievement level (Heyns, 1978). These results (for white students only) are illustrated in Figure 13.1

Note that the poorest students (whose parents made less than $9,000) lost ground in knowledge over the summer, while the wealthiest students (whose parents made at least $15,000) gained. Similar patterns were seen for black students; in fact, the poorest group of black students, whose families made less than $4,000, lost more than half of the word knowledge they had gained in the fifth grade in only three summer months, while the wealthiest black students gained a third more during the summer over their school-year gains (Heyns, 1978).

What the Heyns data suggest is that home environment influences not only academic readiness for school but also the level of achievement throughout students' careers in school. Middle-class children are learning all summer and, presumably, at

FIGURE 13.1

Social-Class and Achievement Levels

As a group, white students from middle- and upper-income families gained in levels of achievement during the summer recess between fifth and sixth grade, while the achievement levels of white students from lower-income families slipped.

Adapted from Heyns, 1978, p. 48.

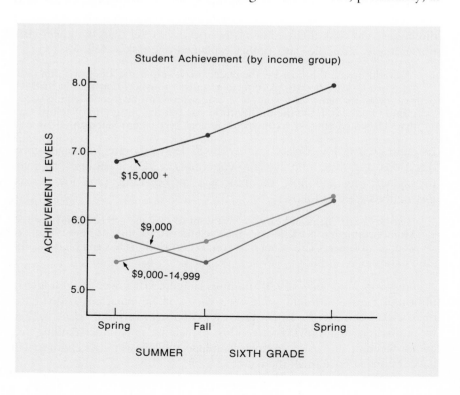

other times when they are at home. Lower-class children are receiving less academically relevant stimulation at home, and are more likely to be forgetting what they learned in school.

Schools as Middle-Class Institutions

Students from backgrounds other than the mainstream middle class have difficulties in school in part because their upbringing emphasizes behaviors different from those valued in the school. The problem is that the school overwhelmingly represents the values and expectations of the middle class. Two of these values are individuality and future time orientation (see Boykin, 1986).

Individuality. Most American classrooms operate on the assumption that children should do their own work. Helping others is often defined as cheating. Students are expected to compete for grades, for the teacher's attention and praise, and for other rewards. Competition and individual work are values instilled early on in middle-class homes.

However, students from lower-class white families (Pepitone, 1985) and from some minority groups (Kneller, 1965; Richmond and Weiner, 1973; Kagan, 1983) are less willing to compete and more interested in cooperating with their peers than are middle-class Anglo-Americans. These students have learned from an early age to rely on their friends and family, and have always also helped and been helped by others. Not surprisingly, students who are most oriented toward cooperation with others learn best in cooperation with others, while those who prefer to compete learn best in competition with others (Wheeler, 1977; Kagan et al., 1985). Because of the mismatch between the cooperative orientation of many lower-class and minority children and the competitive orientation of the school, Kagan et al. (1985) have argued that there is a "structural bias" in traditional classrooms that works against these children. He recommends the use of cooperative learning strategies (see Chapter 10) at least part of the time with these students so that they receive instruction consistent with their cultural orientations.

Future Time Orientation. Schools are geared to reward behavior "sometime in the future." That future may be the end of the day, but more likely is the end of the week, the grading period, or even the school year. Therefore, success in school requires the ability to forgo the gratification of doing something now for the sake of a future reward. Middle-class children are likely to have learned not only to work for a delayed reward, but also to plan their own actions so that they accomplish tasks on schedule. Schools demand this type of behavior all the time. An example would be a social studies project assigned on Monday and due on Friday. Lower-class pupils may have difficulty pacing their work so that they can complete the project when required. However, all students can learn to manage their time and to develop and carry out plans if they are given many opportunities to do so.

Implications for Teachers. Children enter school with varying degrees of skills needed for success. Their behaviors, attitudes, and values also vary. However, just because some children initially don't know what is expected of them and have fewer entry-level skills than others does not mean that they are destined for academic failure. While there is a positive correlation between social class and achievement, it should not by any means be assumed that this relationship holds for all children from

Compensatory Education
Programs designed to supplement the education of non-achieving disadvantaged students

Chapter 1
A federal program that gives school districts money to improve educational services for disadvantaged students

lower-social-class families. There are many exceptions. Lower-class families can provide home environments quite supportive of their children's success in school. Autobiographies of people who have overcome poverty often refer to the influence of strong parents with high standards, who expected nothing less than the best from their children and did what they could to help them achieve. While educators need to be aware of the problems encountered by many lower-class pupils, they also need to avoid converting this knowledge into stereotypes. In fact, there is evidence that middle-class teachers often have low expectations for lower-class students (Rist, 1978) and that these low expectations can be a cause of low achievement (Alexander et al., 1987).

In addition to differences in the home life and behaviors of children by social class, we also see differences in what their parents expect from the school. Middle-class parents, when asked what they expect schools to teach, give such replies as "responsibility," "self-direction," "creativity." It is not that middle-class parents don't want their children to learn basic academic skills. Rather, they take that as a given and expect more from the schools. Lower-class parents, on the other hand, more often want the school to teach their children the basics—reading, writing, and arithmetic. These parents want a no-frills, no-nonsense education in which children are taught to be obedient and responsive to authority (see Kohn, 1969). They are typically opposed to activities aimed at teaching children to "think for themselves" if they feel that these activities will take time away from the basics. Lower-class parents' own experiences with school contribute to their expectations. These parents may not have succeeded in school themselves, so they don't assume that their children will be academically successful.

Compensatory Education

Programs designed to overcome the problems associated with being brought up in an impoverished environment are called **compensatory education.** Compensatory education programs supplement the education of students from disadvantaged backgrounds who are experiencing trouble in school or who are felt to be in danger of having school problems. Two such programs, Head Start and Follow Through, were discussed in Chapter 3. These programs are designed to give disadvantaged preschool and primary children the skills necessary for a good start in school. However, the largest compensatory education program, and the one most likely to affect regular classroom teachers, is called **Chapter 1** (formerly Title I), a federally funded program that gives schools money to provide extra services for students who are from disadvantaged homes and are having trouble in school. Title I was begun in 1965 as part of President Johnson's War on Poverty. The purpose of Title I was stated as follows:

> In recognition of the special educational needs of children of low-income families and the impact that concentrations of low-income families have on the ability of local educational agencies to support adequate educational programs, the Congress hereby declares it to be the policy of the United States to provide financial assistance . . . to local educational agencies serving areas with concentrations of children from low-income families.

During the Reagan administration, the legislation relating to Title I programs was changed in the Education Consolidation and Improvement Act of 1981. Compensatory education programs were included under Chapter 1 of this act, which is why Title I programs are now called Chapter 1. More than 90 percent of all school

1. Schools tend to reward middle-class behaviors such as working independently or developing and sticking to a plan that promises a reward far in the future. However, the experience of lower-class children may not have helped them develop these behaviors. Their experience may suggest that seeking immediate gratification is less risky than working toward a distant goal. If you have students (lower-class or otherwise) whose outlook on life seems to hinder their progress, what should you do?

Judy Weeks, who teaches elementary school in Dyersburg, Tenn., wrote:

I deal mainly with lower socioeconomic status students. It takes tremendous patience and adherence to detail to develop enough trust with these children so they *can* defer immediate gratification and stick to a plan for future reward. At first, you must find some means of immediate, concrete gratification and gradually move toward postponed, intangible rewards. (It takes years, sometimes, and it must be started from "square one," to some extent, with each new adult supervisor.)

I try to be consistent—do what I say I'll do. I have the same rules and rewards for everyone to help combat these children's feelings of inferiority and their constant vigilance against being treated unfairly.

J. Burrow, who teaches elementary school in Frisco, Texas, wrote:

I believe all children can learn. But first, self-esteem and self-worth need to be there. Give children concrete and immediate reasons why they need to try. I truly believe a child can and will achieve according to what you, the teacher, expect of him or her. Children need a person who is going to see to it that they work toward a goal.

2. How do you encourage healthy social interaction among your students?

Curt Fulton, who teaches in Wallkill, N.Y., wrote:

In addition to breaking up my class numerically, I color-code the names. By combining different color-coded groups for group interaction activities, I can make sure that the students get opportunities to work with different people in the class. The color coding also helps when a teacher needs to put children into groups quickly without a lot of confusion.

Richard Thorne, Jr., who teaches elementary school in Stoughton, Mass., wrote:

Social interaction is encouraged through group projects and activities. Building a geodesic dome display in the classroom encourages the students to work together. Good behavior is periodically rewarded by group games and activities.

3. Every classroom has cliques, some of which are segregated by race or ethnicity. What should a teacher do to encourage students to know and respect one another both in the classroom and outside of it?

Nancy Letts, who teaches gifted and talented students in White Plains, N.Y., wrote:

Cooperative learning has been one of the most effective ways that I know to combat cliques of any kind in the classroom. Groups of three or four students are selected to work together, and each is given a very directed task. The goal is stated again and again: it is your responsibility to make certain that each member of your group knows as much as any other. Students are taught the skills needed to work cooperatively and the reasons for doing so are constantly reinforced.

Cooperative learning is another technique which teachers must learn. It takes time to learn and time to teach, but the results have been wonderfully gratifying at eliminating cliques based on culture, gender, or intelligence.

Deanna Seed, who teaches elementary school in Placerville, Calif., wrote:

Too much emphasis has been placed on boy-girl differences and that has become a major concern for classroom cliques.

Separate lines for boys and girls give subtle messages to students. "People" lines are used with my students. Some days I may have students line up according to eye color, hair color, height, school subject preference, public official preference, family heritage, hobbies, or personal strengths in areas such as soccer or math.

This exemplifies the fact that we all have likenesses and differences and one is not valued more than another.

districts, 75 percent of elementary schools, and 34 percent of middle schools and high schools provide Chapter 1 services (Birman et al., 1987). In addition, many states supplement Chapter 1 with their own compensatory education programs.

Chapter 1 is not merely a transfer of money from the federal government to local school districts. According to the federal guidelines, Chapter 1 funds must be used to "supplement, not supplant" local educational efforts. This means that most school districts cannot use the money to reduce class size for all students or increase teachers' salaries; it must go directly toward increasing the academic achievement of disadvantaged students. The exception is that schools serving very disadvantaged neighborhoods—in which at least 75 percent of the students receive a free lunch—can use Chapter 1 money to improve the school as a whole.

Chapter 1 programs can take many forms. Most often a special Chapter 1 teacher provides remedial help to disadvantaged students experiencing difficulties in reading and, in many cases, in other subjects as well (Birman et al., 1987). Programs of this type are called "pull-out" programs because the students are "pulled out" of their regular classes.

Pull-out programs have come under increasing criticism in recent years. A large-scale study of Chapter 1 pull-out programs found that students left without Chapter 1 services in the regular classroom achieved just as well as, and sometimes better than, students pulled out for special assistance (Glass and Smith, 1977). One major problem with pull-out programs is that there is often little coordination between the regular teacher and the Chapter 1 teacher, so that students who need the most consistent and structured instruction often have to deal with two completely different approaches (Cohen et al., 1978; Johnston et al., 1985). One study found that half of a group of Chapter 1 teachers could not even name the reading text *series* their students were using in regular class; two-thirds could not name the specific book (Johnston et al., 1985). These researchers argue that Chapter 1 programs must be directed at ensuring the success of students in the regular classroom, and should therefore be closely coordinated with the regular teacher's instructional activities. For example, if a student is having trouble in the regular class with finding the main ideas of paragraphs, the Chapter 1 teacher should be working on main ideas, perhaps using the same instructional materials the classroom teacher is using.

Increasingly, school districts are avoiding the problems of pull-out programs by having the Chapter 1 teacher or aide work as a team teacher in the regular reading classroom (see Harpring, 1985). This way, two teachers can give reading lessons to two groups of students at the same time, which avoids some of the problems of within-class ability grouping (see Chapter 9). Team teaching can also increase the levels of communication and collaboration between the regular classroom teacher and the Chapter 1 teacher. However, such "in-class" models of Chapter 1 services have not been found to be any more effective than pull-out programs (Archambault, 1989). Many other innovative programs have been found to accelerate the achievement gains of disadvantaged students. Among these are tutoring programs, "continuous progress" programs in which students are frequently assessed and regrouped as they proceed through a sequence of skills, and other structured step-by-step instructional programs with clear objectives and frequent assessments of students' attainment of these objectives (see Slavin and Madden, 1987; Slavin, Karweit, and Madden, 1989).

Research on Compensatory Education. Early research on Title 1 programs found few positive effects on students (Glass and Smith, 1977; NIE, 1978). However, later studies focusing on Title I/Chapter 1 programs that were well implemented found that these programs do help disadvantaged students gain one grade equivalent each year; that is, although (on average) they do not significantly accelerate disadvantaged students, they keep them from falling further behind. Without compensatory programs, students eligible for Title I/Chapter 1 gain only about two-thirds of a grade equivalent each year, which means they fall further behind each year (Cooley and Leinhardt, 1980).

The largest and most carefully controlled study of compensatory education found consistent benefits of the program, particularly for students in the early grades (Carter, 1984). These results are illustrated in Figure 13.2. Note that in Grades 1, 2, and 3 needy students receiving Title I services started at the same achievement level as other needy students not in Title I. By the end of the year, the Title I students significantly exceeded the non–Title I needy students. However, as in the early studies, Title I programs did not narrow the achievement gap between needy and regular students, although it did keep the gap from widening (see also Kennedy et al., 1986).

Research on effective practices in Title I/Chapter 1 classes finds that, in general, practices that work well in regular classes also work well in Chapter 1 classes. For example, more instructional time, time on-task, and other indicators of effective

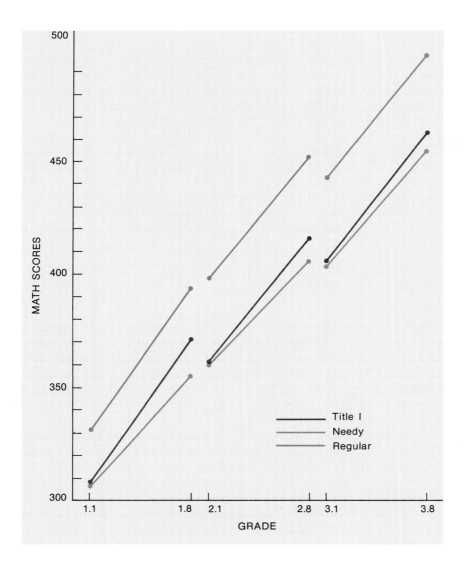

FIGURE 13.2

Effect of Title I Programs on Achievement

Needy students who participated in Title I programs gained more in math than needy students not in special programs. However, the extra help did not close the gap in achievement between needy and regular students.

From Carter, 1984, p. 7.

Ethnic Group
Group of people who share
characteristics such as race, religion,
and/or place of origin

classroom management are important predictors of achievement gain in Title I/Chapter 1 classes (Stein et al., 1989; Cooley, 1981; Crawford, 1989).

■ **Stop and Think**

Schools are a meeting place for a wide variety of groups, including children of different ages and backgrounds, teachers with various agendas, and administrators. Out of this mix evolves an educational institution that imposes unfamiliar rules and expectations on every person who enters. List from your early days in kindergarten or first grade some ways of behaving or speaking that seemed foreign to you at that time. Evaluate how well your home environment prepared you for school. Now imagine a first day at school for a child from a culture that differs significantly from a school's predominant culture. Describe some situations that child might find strange.

ETHNICITY AND RACE

A major determinant of the culture in which students will grow up is their ethnic origin. An **ethnic group** is one in which individuals have a shared sense of identity, usually because of a common place of origin (such as Swedish, Polish, or Greek Americans), religion (such as Jewish Americans), or race (such as black or Asian Americans).

Most "Anglo-Americans" identify with some ethnic group, such as Polish, Italian, Irish, Greek, or German. Identification with these groups may affect a family's traditions, holidays, food preferences, and, to some extent, outlook on the world. However, white ethnic groups have been largely absorbed into mainstream American society, so the differences among them have few educational implications.

The situation is quite different for other ethnic groups. In particular, blacks, Hispanics, and American Indians have yet to be fully accepted into mainstream American society, and have not yet attained the economic success or security achieved by the white ethnic groups. Students from these ethnic groups face special problems in school, and have been the focus of two of the most emotional issues in American education over the past thirty years: desegregation and bilingual education. The following sections discuss the situation of students of different ethnic backgrounds in schools today.

Racial and Ethnic Composition of the United States

The U.S. Census Bureau estimates of the racial and national origins of the population of the United States for 1970 and 1980 appear in Table 13.1. Note the relative increases in most categories (especially "other") of racial and ethnic origins besides non-Hispanic whites. The story told by the numbers in Table 13.1 is that the United States is rapidly becoming more culturally diverse. By the year 2000, one-third of all Americans will be non-white (Hodgkinson, 1985).

Academic Achievement of Minority Students. If minority students achieved at the same level as Anglo-Americans, there would probably be little concern about ethnic group differences in American schools. Unfortunately, they don't. On virtually every test of academic achievement, black, Hispanic, and American Indian students score significantly lower than their Anglo-American classmates.

Table 13.2 (from Levine and Havinghurst, 1989) shows the standardized test scores and socioeconomic status of high school sophomores according to their racial

TABLE 13.1

RACIAL AND ETHNIC COMPOSITION OF THE UNITED STATES

Non-Hispanic whites form the largest racial and ethnic group within the United States, followed by non-Hispanic blacks and Hispanics. However, the size of the minority population increased relative to the U.S. population as a whole between 1970 and 1980.

	Percent of Total Population	
	1970	1980
White (non-Hispanic)	83.3	77.1
Black (non-Hispanic)	10.9	11.4
Hispanic	4.5	6.4
American Indian	0.4	0.6
Chinese	0.2	0.4
Filipino	0.2	0.3
Japanese	0.3	0.3
Asian Indian	—	0.2
Korean	—	0.2
Vietnamese	—	0.1
Other	0.2	3.0
	100.0	100.0

SOURCE: Adapted from U.S. Census Bureau, 1981.

TABLE 13.2

TEST SCORE DIFFERENCES AMONG RACIAL/ETHNIC GROUPS

As groups, white and Asian American high school sophomores were above average in performance on standardized tests and in socioeconomic status in 1980. Other racial and ethnic groups, taken as whole, were below average.

Level and Subject	Standardized Scores								
	Total	White	Black	All Hispanic	Mexican	Puerto Rican	Cuban	Asian American	American Indian
Sophomores									
Vocabulary	50.0	52.0	42.4	44.9	44.2	44.0	48.1	51.6	45.0
Reading	50.0	51.7	44.2	45.1	44.6	44.5	48.6	51.6	46.2
Math part 1	50.0	51.8	43.1	44.9	44.5	43.9	48.0	55.7	44.6
Math part 2	50.0	51.3	44.9	46.2	45.7	45.5	49.3	55.5	46.2
Science	50.0	52.1	41.6	44.5	44.0	42.9	46.3	51.5	46.1
Writing	50.0	51.8	43.3	44.9	44.8	43.3	46.8	53.7	46.0
Civics	50.0	51.3	45.7	45.9	45.7	46.0	45.6	51.0	45.5
Socioeconomic status	50.0	51.3	46.1	46.0	45.0	44.2	47.3	51.7	47.2

SOURCE: Levine and Havinghurst, 1989, p. 381.

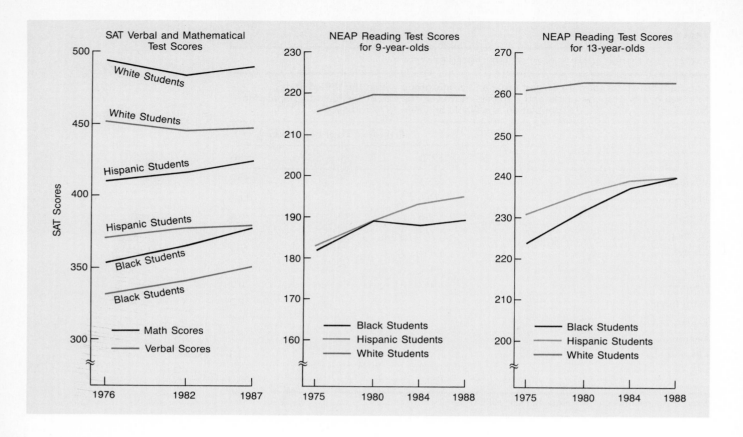

SAT Verbal and Mathematical Test Scores

500
White Students
450
White Students
Hispanic Students
400
SAT Scores
Hispanic Students
350
Black Students
Black Students
300
— Math Scores
— Verbal Scores

1976   1982   1987

NEAP Reading Test Scores for 9-year-olds

230
220
210
200
190
180
170
160

— Black Students
— Hispanic Students
— White Students

1975   1980   1984   1988

NEAP Reading Test Scores for 13-year-olds

270
260
250
240
230
220
210
200

— Black Students
— Hispanic Students
— White Students

1975   1980   1984   1988

FIGURE 13.3

Trends in Standardized Test Scores by Group

As a group, white students score higher on standardized tests than black and Hispanic students. However, the gap in achievement differences has narrowed because of relative improvements in the scores earned by blacks and Hispanics.

From College Entrance Examination Board, 1985, and Digest of Education Statistics, 1988.

and ethnic groups. All scores were set at a mean of 50.0, so numbers below 50 indicate scores below the mean. There are two points to be made about Table 13.2. First, blacks, Hispanics, and American Indians score below the mean for whites (and for Asian Americans) on all tests. Second, note how closely the socioeconomic status scores correspond to the achievement test scores. This suggests that the ethnic group differences shown in Table 13.2 are highly associated with differences in social-class background and upbringing.

One recent development in the academic performance of minority students is heartening: the achievement gap between them and Anglo-Americans is narrowing. For example, black and Hispanic students are gaining more rapidly than whites on Scholastic Achievement Tests (SATs) each year, as is shown in Figure 13.3. Figure 13.3 also shows the trends in performance on the National Assessment of Educational Progress (NAEP) reading tests for nine- and thirteen-year-olds in 1975, 1980, 1984, and 1988. Gains have been particularly dramatic for the lowest-achieving minority children (Carroll, 1987). Although black and Hispanic students are gaining in achievement more rapidly than whites, they still have a long way to go. Similar patterns appear in every subject assessed by the National Assessment of Educational Progress: the gap between whites and minorities remains wide, but is diminishing over time (see Burton and Jones, 1982; Jones, 1984).

Why do minority students score so far below Anglo-Americans on achievement tests? The most important reason is that in our society blacks, Hispanics (particularly

Mexican Americans and Puerto Ricans), and Indians tend to occupy the lowest rungs of the socioeconomic ladder. Consequently, families in these groups are often unable to provide their children with the stimulation and academic preparation typical of a middle-class upbringing. Chronic unemployment, epidemic in minority communities, has a negative effect on family life.

Another important disadvantage faced by minority students is that they often attend academically inferior, overcrowded urban schools. Middle-class and working-class families throughout the United States buy their way out of center-city schools by moving to the suburbs or sending their children to private or parochial schools, leaving the public schools to serve those without the resources to afford alternatives.

The low achievement of minority students may well be a "temporary" problem; in a decade or two, as minorities increasingly achieve economic security and enter the middle class, their children's achievement will come to resemble that of other groups. In the 1920s it was widely believed that immigrants from southern and eastern Europe (such as Italians, Greeks, Poles, and Jews) were hopelessly backward and perhaps retarded (see, for example, Kirkpatrick, 1926), yet the children and grandchildren of these immigrants now achieve as well as the descendants of the Founding Fathers. However, we cannot afford to wait a decade or two. The school is one institution that can break the cycle of poverty, by giving children from impoverished backgrounds the opportunity to succeed.

Desegregation

Before 1954, black, white, and Hispanic students were legally required to attend separate schools in twenty states plus the District of Columbia, and segregated schools were common in the remaining states. Minority students were often bused miles past their nearest public school to separate schools. The doctrine of "separate but equal"

Teachers in integrated schools can promote friendships among students from different racial and ethnic groups by providing opportunities for the students to work together.

Teaching in Desegregated Schools

In most ways the problems of desegregated schools are no different from those of schools in general. However, there are some issues that are of special significance to teachers in desegregated schools.

FAIRNESS AND BALANCE

Fairness is always important in education, but it becomes crucial in desegregated schools. Teachers and other school staff must give every evidence of being evenhanded. Students must never have any justification for believing that "students like me [whites, blacks, Hispanics] don't get a fair chance in this school."

All students in a desegregated school must feel that students like themselves have an equal opportunity to succeed and achieve recognition. To this end, it is important that all groups be represented on the school cheerleading squad, student council, and other high-status groups (Crain et al., 1982). Also, many teachers unintentionally show bias by calling on minority students less often in class, a pattern that should be avoided (Cunkin and Doenau, 1987).

To help ensure fairness and balance, many secondary schools appoint integrated human relations committees to receive and discuss complaints from students concerning unfair treatment, and to recommend changes in school policies or practices to the school administration. These committees may be appointed by the principal or by the student government. The use of human relations committees has been found to be associated with positive intergroup relations (Forehand and Ragosta, 1976; Crain et al., 1982).

Fairness and balance must also be shown in instructional materials. Most student texts now feature minority individuals in high-status, nonstereotyped roles, but the teacher should review texts and other materials for bias or stereotyping and avoid those that have these tendencies.

It should go without saying that teachers in desegregated schools (or in any schools for that matter) must refrain from communicating bias or stereotypes. In general, it is better for teachers to discuss racial or ethnic relations openly than to pretend to be color-blind. In particular, the teacher must unequivocally communicate that racial or ethnic bias is intolerable in the classroom or the school. During a time of tension between British and American officers during World War II, General Eisenhower had a staff colonel demoted and transferred for calling a British officer a "British SOB." Eisenhower remarked that if he had just called the officer an SOB, that would have been fine; it was the addition of the word "British" that made his behavior unacceptable. By the same token, the classroom teacher cannot let racial taunts or even jokes go by, but must tell students that they will not be tolerated, and if they occur, forceful action will be taken.

---

education for minority students was upheld in several Supreme Court decisions. However, in 1954 the Supreme Court struck down this practice in the landmark *Brown vs. Board of Education of Topeka* case, on the grounds that separate education was inherently unequal. *Brown vs. Board of Education* did away with legal segregation, but it was many years before large numbers of black and white students were attending school together. In the 1970s a series of Supreme Court decisions found that the continued segregation of many schools throughout the United States was due to past discriminatory practices, such as the drawing of school boundary lines deliberately to separate Hispanic or black from white neighborhoods. These decisions forced local school districts to desegregate their schools by any means necessary. Many districts were given specific standards for the proportions of minority students that could be assigned to any particular school. For example, a district in which 45 percent of the students were black might be required to have a black population of 35–55 percent in its schools. To achieve desegregation, some school districts simply changed school attendance areas, while others created special "magnet schools" (such as schools for the performing arts, for talented and gifted students, or for special vocational preparation) to induce students to attend schools outside of their own neighbor-

AVOIDING RESEGREGATION

When, as it often happens, racial or ethnic desegregation also means combining students from different social classes, it is likely there will be achievement differences between majority and minority students. In this situation tracking or between-class ability grouping may create racially or ethnically identifiable classes, with high-track classes for whites and low-track classes for blacks, Hispanics, or Indians. There are good reasons to avoid between-class ability grouping in all schools (see Chapter 9); it is critical to avoid them in desegregated schools (Rosenbaum, 1980; Slavin, 1989).

INTERGROUP RELATIONS

One strength of the desegregated school is that it allows for the development of friendships and respect across racial or ethnic boundaries. However, research on desegregation tends to find that these positive relationships do not arise merely because students from different backgrounds attend the same schools (Gerard and Miller, 1975; Epstein, 1985). Rather, interactions among students of different races or ethnicities must be structured to increase the chances that they will lead to positive relationships. Gordon Allport (1954) described the conditions under which intergroup contact leads to positive intergroup relations.

Prejudice . . . my be reduced by equal status contact between majority and minority groups in the pursuit of common goals. The effect is greatly enhanced if this contact is sanctioned by institutional supports . . . and if it is of a sort that leads to the perception of common interests and common humanity between members of the two groups. (Allport, 1954, p. 281)

Essentially, Allport argued that intergroup contact does not lead to positive intergroup relations unless individuals from different groups are given opportunities to know one another as individuals and to work together toward common goals. Later research has largely supported Allport's theory (see Slavin, 1985). For example, in desegregated high schools, students who have participated in integrated sports are much more likely to have friends of an ethnic group different from their own than are other students (Slavin and Madden, 1979).

Research on cooperative learning (see Chapter 10) in desegregated classrooms consistently finds that these methods improve relationships across racial and ethnic lines (Slavin, 1985c). In some cases, the positive effects on intergroup friendships of working in cooperative, integrated learning teams have been found to long outlast the teams themselves (Slavin, 1979; Ziegler, 1981) and to extend to relationships formed outside of school (Oishi et al., 1983).

hoods. However, in many large, urban districts, segregation of neighborhoods is so extensive that students must be bused to achieve racially balanced schools.

School desegregation is supposed to increase the academic achievement of minority students by giving them the higher quality of schooling assumed to be received by whites and by giving them opportunities to interact with more middle-class, achievement-oriented peers. All too often, however, the schools to which minority students are bused are no better than the segregated schools they left behind, and the outflow of middle-class families from urban areas (which was well under way before busing began) often means that lower-class black or Hispanic students are integrated with similarly lower-class whites (Rossell, 1983).

Perhaps for these reasons the overall effect of desegregation on the academic achievement of minority students has been small, though positive (St. John, 1975). However, when desegregation begins in elementary school, and particularly when it involves busing minority children to high-quality schools with substantially middle-class student bodies, desegregation can have a significant effect on the achievement of minority students (Crain and Mahard, 1978, 1983). This effect is not thought to result from sitting next to whites, but rather from attending a better school. One

Bilingual Education
Instructional program for students who speak little or no English in which some instruction is provided in their native language

important outcome of desegregation is that blacks who attend desegregated schools are more likely than other blacks to attend desegregated colleges, to work in integrated settings, and to attain higher incomes (Braddock, 1985).

LANGUAGE MINORITIES

In the early 1980s, 13.3 percent of all U.S. children age five to fourteen were from families in which the primary language spoken was not English. This segment of the school-age population is increasing. Most of these students' families speak Spanish, and they are primarily located in the Southwest and in the New York City, Miami, and Chicago areas (Arias, 1986). However, many other language-minority students speak any of dozens of Asian or European languages.

Language-minority students present a dilemma to the educational system. Clearly those who have limited proficiency in English need to learn English. However, until they are proficient in English, should they be taught math or social studies in their first language or in English? Should they be taught to read their first language? These questions are not just pedagogical; they have political and cultural significance that has provoked emotional debate. One issue is that many Hispanic parents wish to have their children instructed in the Spanish language and culture in order to maintain their Hispanic identity and pride. Many educators and others concerned with the problem feel that the students should be fully integrated into American society, and fear that bilingualism and biculturalism will be detrimental to our country's "melting pot" tradition. For example, in Miami non-Hispanic leaders have expressed concern that because of the substantial Cuban American population in the area, Spanish has become as accepted as English, and the ability to speak Spanish is being required for all but the lowest-level jobs. Responding to similar fears, California has designated English as the state's only official language (see Suhor, 1989).

Several years ago all students were simply put in classes taught in English and expected to do the best they could. In the Southwest teachers once patrolled playgrounds to make sure that students did not speak Spanish to one another. One entirely Mexican American school in Texas was described as follows: "They have what they call 'Spanish detention' and if the child is caught speaking Spanish, he is usually held after school for an hour or an hour and a half. If he persists, he may be spanked by the principal" (Carter and Segura, 1979, p. 187). As a result, many students from Spanish-speaking homes fared poorly in school, and came to believe that their language and culture were inferior to the English language and the Anglo culture.

Today "Spanish detention" and other institutionalized attempts to discriminate against the use of Spanish have disappeared, but students from non–English-speaking backgrounds continue to experience serious problems in school. For example, students whose usual language is not English are more than twice as likely to be performing below grade level than are students from similar cultural backgrounds whose usual language is English (Durán, 1983).

Bilingual Education

The term **bilingual education** refers to programs for students with limited proficiency in English that teach the students in their own language part of the time while English

Proponents of a fully integrated society must feel they have fought the same battles year after year and generation after generation.

It has been almost 40 years since a landmark court decision struck down institutionalized segregation of the races. Nevertheless, cities across the United States still have their black ghettos, white enclaves, and Hispanic barrios.

Moreover, two generations of children have entered and graduated from largely desegregated public schools, yet racial incidents have recently marred student life on a handful of college campuses. Some black high school graduates now base their college choices on their perceptions of a college's tolerance for minority students.

The causes of continued racial and ethnic divisions include the depth of racism's roots in history and—surprisingly—the way humans learn and think. The schema theory that explains human learning and memory may also shed light on the seeds of racism.

The crux of schema theory (see Chapter 5) is a description of the way the human mind organizes information. As people receive new perceptions, they try to categorize these perceptions under already established categories in memory.

The possible link between schema theory and racism is seen in the way humans classify other people and in the meaning they give to those classifications as they gain new perceptions and information.

A young child, for example, builds an understanding about the human race from encounters with an ever-widening circle of people. At first, the child may categorize people into only two groups: primary caregivers (usually mom and dad) and strangers. Then the child may recognize other family members and friends. Slowly further categories are identified, and the child may decide at some point that some types of people—such as big kids at the playground or people who are dirty—are best avoided.

In a multiracial community, the child will notice and possibly form mental categories for people who look different from the child. The meaning that the child attaches to any of these categories and the child's ability to be flexible in categorizing people shapes the child's racial sensitivity.

"Once you categorize people into groups in any way, you tend to like people in your own group more than those in other groups," states Dr. Samuel Gaert-

ner, a psychologist at the University of Delaware. He further states that "It happens in many situations apart from race relations. You see it often, for instance, in a corporate merger, when people in the acquiring company continue to stereotype people from the acquired company with disdain, and those from the acquired company resent what they see as a favored status for those with the acquiring firm."

Contributing to the tenacity of racial attitudes is the mind's tendency to avoid cognitive dissonance. That is, once an idea is planted or a category formed, people look for confirmation of that idea. Experiences or perceptions that contradict the established ideas may be dismissed or discounted as aberrations.

Hence, if an older person plants in a child's mind a shorthand description for some group of people, the child may readily accept any further perceptions that confirm the stereotype. For example, a child who hears Polish jokes told at the dinner table may accept the implied assumptions about Polish people. That child may feel free to laugh at and share similar jokes with friends at school.

Schools have had some success in breaking down racial, ethnic, and sexual stereotypes. The use of cooperative learning groups that intentionally mix children of various racial and ethnic groups have increased cross-cultural friendships among classmates.

In addition, a school in Pittsburgh has been started as a laboratory for developing better race relations. The school, which carries the imposing name of the Prospect Middle School Center for Multiracial, Multicultural, and Multiethnic Education, opened in 1989 in hopes of developing programs for use throughout Pittsburgh's school system. The school system serves almost 40,000 students, of which about half are white and half are black. Also, schools in some 25 cities have added anti-bias lessons to their curriculums.

These are small but promising steps in the fight to open people's minds and promote harmony between society's various groups.

From Daniel Goleman, "Psychologists Find Ways to Break Racism's Hold," *New York Times*, September 5, 1989, p. C1. "Anti-Bias Classes in Georgia," *New York Times*, January 1, 1990, p. B7. "School as a Model for Race Relations," *New York Times*, July 11, 1989.

is being learned. The rationale for bilingual education was given by the U.S. Commission on Civil Rights (1975):

> Lack of English proficiency is the major reason for language minority students' academic failure. Bilingual education is intended to ensure that students do not fall behind in subject matter content while they are learning English, as they would likely do in an all-English program, since limited English proficiency will no longer impede their academic progress.

Bilingual programs vary enormously in content and quality. At a minimum, they include instruction in English as a second language for students with limited English proficiency. Typically, bilingual programs offer some instruction in Spanish. (The largest number of bilingual programs in the United States by far are in Spanish, so the examples in this section all refer to Spanish. However, the same general principles apply to bilingual programs in other languages.) The programs differ in the degree to which Hispanic culture is taught to all students. Also, a few bilingual programs teach Spanish to all students, whether or not their primary language is Spanish (Genesee, 1985). To the degree that a program emphasizes Hispanic *culture* as well as language, it is called "bilingual-bicultural." The U.S. Office of Education (1970) defined an ideal bilingual-bicultural program as follows:

> The use of two languages, one which is English, as mediums of instruction for the same pupil population in a well-organized program that encompasses part or all of the curriculum and includes the study of the history and culture associated with the mother

Bilingual education programs strive both to help language-minority students learn English and to teach them math, reading, and other school subjects.

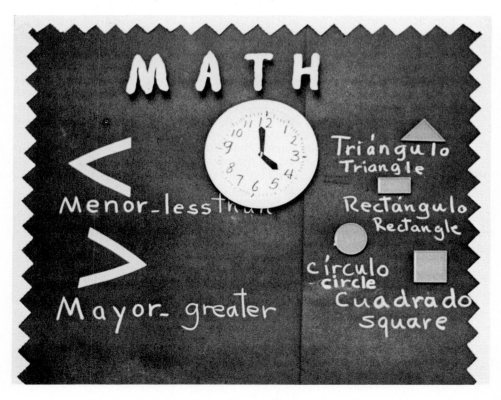

tongue; a complete program develops and maintains the children's self-esteem and legitimate pride in both cultures. (p. 1)

However, Carter and Segura (1979) state that few bilingual programs approach this ideal. Most are simply transitional programs designed to support students in Spanish until they are able to make it in the regular classroom in English. For example, most bilingual programs begin teaching students with limited English proficiency in their primary language in kindergarten but move them to English-only classes by the end of the first or second grade. More rarely, students may continue receiving instruction in their primary language until the sixth grade. Students may receive anywhere from thirty minutes to several hours of instruction per week in their primary language, but at least half of their instruction will be in English from the very beginning (Ramirez, 1986). Some programs that are called "bilingual education" in fact provide nothing more than instruction in English as a second language.

Research on Bilingual Education.   Reviews of research focusing on the best-designed studies of good quality bilingual programs have found positive results (Dulay and Burt, 1977; Zeppert and Cruz, 1977; Hakuta and Gould, 1987; Willig, 1985; Wong-Fillmore and Valadez, 1986). Researchers have never found bilingual programs to be harmful to students, and the programs are often beneficial for the achievement of Hispanic students in English as well as in subjects they learned in Spanish. In fact, one important rationale for maintaining bilingual programs is the finding that the learning of a second language is facilitated by skills in one's native language (Haruta and Garcia, 1989; Cummins, 1986). But more research on this important topic is needed to identify the types of programs most likely to improve the achievement of language-minority students (Gunderson, 1982).

Bilingualism itself has not been found to interfere with performance in either language, and in fact has been found in Canadian studies to increase achievement in areas other than the language studied (Perl and Lambert, 1962). This evidence has been cited as a reason to promote bilingual education for *all* students; the United States is one of the few countries in the world in which most students graduate from high school knowing only their own language (National Commission on Excellence in Education, 1983).

Bilingual education has many problems, however. One is the lack of teachers who are themselves completely bilingual. This is a particular problem for bilingual education in the languages of the most recent immigrants, such as those from Southeast Asia. A second problem is in making the transition from the bilingual program to the all-English mainstream program. Third, the goals of bilingual education sometimes conflict with those of desegregation by removing language-minority students from classes containing Anglo-American students. Despite all these problems, the alternative to bilingual education—leaving students in the regular class with no support or with part-time instruction in English as a second language (sometimes known as the "sink or swim" approach)—has not been found to be beneficial for students' English language development, and risks having the language-minority child fail in school. For example, language-minority children are often assigned to special education because of academic difficulties that are in fact due to lack of proficiency in English (Cummins, 1984).

■ **Stop and Think**
At the heart of the debate over bilingual education are questions about the goals of the U.S. system of education. Should schools ease children into mainstream culture by focusing

As the cultural diversity of our society increases, so does the cultural diversity of our classrooms. This presents teachers with some problems, but also many opportunities.

The most important task in teaching a class of students from different cultures is to be sure that all students have an equal opportunity for success. As in the desegregated classroom, fairness and balance in dealing with students are essential.

Another important task is to make all students feel that their culture is valued. For example, teachers can encourage students from different cultures to discuss or demonstrate their traditions, such as having Hispanic children bring in *piñatas* or describe Three Kings Day, having Vietnamese children describe their Tet celebration, or having Arabic children discuss Ramadan. Teachers should present lessons about the histories of the nations from which their students come, in particular, ways in which these cultures contributed to ours. Schools can also plan fairs to which children from different cultures bring ethnic foods or handicrafts to share with others. An ideal activity is to have students from different cultures teach one another to cook the foods characteristic of their cultures, as a way of showing that all children have unique expertise derived from their own upbringing. Of course, activities of this kind are as beneficial for Anglos, who are learning about other cultures, as they are for non-Anglos. America is becoming more of a mosaic than a melting pot (Towson, 1985); knowledge about and appreciation for the cultural backgrounds of all who live here is essential for everyone.

Regardless of the kind of bilingual program being used (if any), language-minority students will spend time in classes taught in English. One common strategy for dealing with the comprehension problems of these students is to use a "buddy system," in which students with limited proficiency in English are paired with bilingual students. The "buddy" translates or clarifies the teacher's instructions. In one Maryland classroom a teacher arranged a triad; one student who was bilingual in English and Spanish translated instructions to one who was bilingual in Spanish and Korean, who translated for one who spoke only Korean! Buddy systems are especially important in schools containing too small a number of students speaking a particular language to justify a bilingual program or even daily instruction in English as a second language. Even if one buddy is only a little more proficient in English than the other, the two together are likely to be better able to figure out what the teacher is saying than each would be alone.

As noted earlier, students from non-Anglo backgrounds tend to be less competitive and more peer-oriented than Anglo-Americans. The constant individual competition found in school is not motivating to these students, and may even be repugnant to them. For this reason, cooperative learning activities should be used at least part of the time, particularly in classes containing students from Mexican-American and American-Indian backgrounds, who are likely to strongly prefer cooperative activities (see California State Department of Education, 1983; Kagan et al., 1985). Cooperative learning has been found to be particularly beneficial for the achievement of minority students; it also improves their relationships with Anglo-American students (Kagan, 1985; Slavin, 1985).

on English instruction? Or, might children learn both English and other school subjects better if some instruction were given in the child's native tongue? In regard to the second question, should the United States, whose primary language is English, endorse the continued use of foreign languages? What do you think should be the nation's priorities? List some of the classroom implications of your choice.

GENDER DIFFERENCES

The first sections of this chapter dealt with sociological differences among various social classes and racial and ethnic communities. In this section, we consider differences in the socialization of males and females. Such differences affect student attitudes, behaviors, and school readiness. To more fully understand gender differences in achievement and behavior, we will focus on the rapidly growing body of research on variations in early socialization experiences, the interaction of social class and race with gender, and the ways in which schools can avoid sex-role stereotyping.

Actual versus Learned Gender Differences

Like race, sex is a visible, permanent attribute with which a child is born. Cross-cultural research indicates that the sex role is one of the first learned by individuals and that all societies treat males differently from females. Therefore sex-role behavior is learned behavior. However, the range of roles occupied by males and females across cultures is broad. What is considered "natural" behavior for each of the sexes is in fact based more on cultural belief than biological necessity. Nevertheless, the extent to which biological differences or gender socialization affects behavioral patterns and achievement is still a much debated topic. The consensus of a large body of research is that no matter what the inherent biological differences, much of the observed differences between males and females can be clearly linked to differences in early socialization experiences.

Perhaps the most comprehensive review of the research on gender differences was done by Eleanor Maccoby and Carol Jacklin (1974). After reviewing the published research on how the sexes differ in intellectual abilities, motivation, self-concept, and social behavior, they concluded that there are only four areas in which there is any convincing "real" evidence of differences between males and females that cannot be explained simply by socialization or culture: verbal aptitude, visual-spatial aptitude, mathematical aptitude, and aggression.

1. Females exhibit greater verbal aptitude than males. Their verbal skills show up earlier in childhood and mature more rapidly. Caution should be exercised here, however. Boocock (1980) states that more recent research indicates that "the magnitude of sex differences varies considerably from one task or population to another, and a number of recent studies have shown no significant sex differences in verbal ability" (p. 89).

2. Males apparently exceed females in visual-spatial aptitude. This difference is one of the few that may be genetically based: "Biological research indicates that spatial ability is highly heritable, transmitted via chromosome combinations that are more common to males than females" (Boocock, 1980). However, research purporting to show a male advantage in visual-spatial aptitude has been sharply criticized in recent years (see Fennema and Sherman, 1977; Carlan et al., 1985).

3. Males exceed females in mathematical aptitude, although, as with verbal ability, the magnitude of the difference varies from one study to another. Research indicates that there are no sex differences in acquisition of quantitative concepts or mastery of basic mathematical skills during the grade school years (Peterson and Fennema, 1985), though one recent study found a slight advantage for sixth-grade girls in math computations, while boys did slightly better in story problems (Marshall, 1984). Later variations may be due to males' greater visual-spatial aptitude, or to the fact that girls are less likely than boys to select higher mathematics courses.

4. Males are more aggressive than females both physically and verbally. This difference has also been noted in cross-cultural studies. The likelihood is high that this difference is biological; levels of aggression are related to levels of sex hormones and have been manipulated experimentally through the administration of these hormones.

Perhaps as interesting as the areas in which Maccoby and Jacklin found evidence for gender differences are those areas in which there is no evidence of gender differences: (1) females are not more "social" than males; (2) females are not more "suggestible" than males; (3) females do not have lower self-esteem than males; and (4) females are not better than males at rote learning and simple repetitive tasks.

Gender Differences in Early Socialization

If there are so few genetically based differences between males and females, why do so many differences exist? These behavioral differences originate out of different experiences, including reinforcement by adults for different types of behavior.

Male and female babies are treated differently from the time they are born. The wrapping of the infant in either a pink or blue blanket symbolizes the variations in experience that will greet the child from birth onward. Studies indicate that adults describe boy or girl babies wrapped in blue blankets as more active than the same babies wrapped in pink. Other masculine traits are also ascribed to those wrapped in blue (Smith and Lloyd, 1978). Additionally, newborn babies are given sex-appropriate reinforcement as early as three weeks of age (Moss, 1967). By six months, girl babies are being talked to and handled by their mothers more than boys. By thirteen months, female infants have begun to reciprocate the mother's interest by touching her more than males of the same age do. Around the ages of three or four children have begun to make gender distinctions and preferences. Thus children enter school having been successfully socialized into appropriate sex-role behavior for their age (Jacklin, 1983).

According to Kagan (1964), parents want their daughters to be passive, nurturing, and dependent, and their sons to be aggressive and independent. Therefore they punish independence in daughters and passivity in sons. Children respond to these influences because they want to please their parents and to avoid rejection. In early childhood males are subjected more to physical punishments, and girls to psychological punishments such as the threat of withdrawal of love. Because of these early differences in socialization, females tend to be more conforming and more concerned about displaying socially desirable behavior than males are (Deaux, 1984).

Gender Differences and the School

The early socialization into appropriate sex-role behavior continues throughout life. The schools contribute to this socialization. Though interactions between socialization experiences and achievement are complex and it is difficult to make generalizations, there are a number of ways in which the school differentiates between the sexes. Boys receive more disapproval and blame from their teachers than girls do (Brophy and Evertson, 1981). But they also engage in more interactions with their teachers in such areas as approval, instruction giving, and being listened to (Meyer and Thompson, 1963). Teachers tend to punish females more promptly and explicitly for

Avoiding Gender Bias in Teaching

There are three principal ways in which teachers (usually without being aware of it) exhibit gender bias in classroom teaching: reinforcing gender stereotypes, maintaining sex separation, and treating boys and girls differently as students. (See Klein, 1985; Sadker and Sadker, 1985.)

AVOIDING STEREOTYPES

Teachers should avoid promoting sexual stereotypes. For example, they can assign jobs in the classroom without regard to gender, avoiding automatically appointing boys as "group leader" and girls as "secretary," and can ask both boys and girls to help in physical activities. Teachers should also refrain from stating stereotypes, such as "Boys don't cry" and "Girls don't fight," and should avoid such terms as "tomboy" (Sadker and Sadker, 1982). Teachers should encourage students who show an interest in activities and careers that do not correspond to cultural stereotypes, for example, a girl who likes math and science.

PROMOTING INTEGRATION

One factor that leads to gender stereotyping is the tendency for boys and girls (particularly in elementary school) to have few friends of the other sex and to engage mostly in activities with members of their own sex. Teachers sometimes encourage this by having boys and girls line up separately, assigning them to sex-segregated tables, and organizing separate sports activities for boys and girls. As a result, interaction between boys and girls in schools is rare relative to that between students of the same sex (Lockheed, 1984). However, in classes where cross-sex collaboration is encouraged, children have less stereotyped views of the abilities of boys and girls (Lockheed and Harris, 1982).

Not surprisingly, cooperative learning activities (see Chapter 10) can increase cross-sex interactions and friendships (DeVries and Edwards, 1974; Lockheed et al., 1979; Oishi et al., 1983).

EQUAL TREATMENT OF GIRLS AND BOYS

Too often girls and boys are not treated equally by teachers. Observational studies of classroom interactions have found that teachers interact more with boys than with girls (Sadker and Sadker, 1985) and ask boys more questions (Jackson and Lahaderne, 1976), in particular more abstract questions (Sikes, 1972). In one study researchers showed teachers videotapes of classroom scenes and asked them whether boys or girls participated more. Most teachers responded that the girls talked more, even though in fact the boys participated more than the girls by a ratio of three to one (Sadker and Sadker, 1985). The authors interpreted this finding as indicating that teachers expect girls to participate less, and thus see low rates of participation as normal.

Teachers must be careful to allow all students equal opportunities to participate in class, to take leadership roles, and to engage in all kinds of activities. While there are a few behavioral differences between boys and girls, these differences tend to be small; they do not justify unequal treatment of boys and girls in the classroom.

aggressive behavior than they do males. Torrance (1962) found that the creative behavior of males was rewarded by teachers three times as often as that of females. Other differentiations are subtle, as when girls are directed to the house corner while boys are provided with blocks, or in music class when boys are given the drums to play and girls the triangles.

Sex bias is often found in curriculum materials, although this is rapidly changing. One study (U.S. Department of HEW, 1975) of 134 children's reading texts found that males were shown in 147 different jobs whereas females were shown in only 26. Additionally, all of the occupations for women could be classified as "woman's work." This study of children's textbooks also found that the central figure in a story was usually male. Moreover, the characters in these stories who displayed ingenuity,

Children learn about sex roles from their experiences at home and in school.

creativity, autonomy, or self-respect were boys four times as often as they were girls. By 1978 all major publishers of textbooks had issued guidelines to avoid sex bias in content, so this situation is improving. However, while major efforts have been made to decrease sex-role stereotyping in storybooks for children, this effort has not been as successful in textbooks for such subjects as science, math, or social studies (Klein, 1985).

Gender Differences in Achievement

Just as debate rages over the relative contributions of heredity and environment to IQ, so, too, do experts debate the contributions of physiological, psychological, and sociological factors to the academic achievement patterns of males and females.

Basically, there are no important gender differences found in either general academic ability or in IQ scores. However, variations in the socialization of males and of females do affect achievement.

According to Boocock (1980), "Test scores . . . indicate that on all measures there is considerable overlap between the distribution of scores for the two sexes; and that on tests of total or composite abilities, the sexes do not differ consistently, and superior or highly developed ability is more or less equally distributed among boys and girls" (p. 89).

Nevertheless, males do consistently score higher than females in mathematics, while females score higher on tests of verbal skill. The gap between males and females in math achievement has narrowed, though, as the number of females enrolling in math courses has risen.

Girls have an initial academic advantage over males; in elementary school they consistently outperform males in grades, and maintain this grade advantage into high school, even in math and science (Sadker et al., 1989). At the elementary level males are six times more likely than females to have reading problems and, as noted in Chapter 12, are much more likely to be learning disabled or emotionally disturbed. However, from the beginning of school boys tend to express more interest than females in mathematics and science. This difference increases with age. Studies of students who are extremely gifted in mathematics found that gifted boys outnumbered gifted girls by a substantial ratio (Benbow and Stanley, 1980).

Social-Class and Sex-Role Differences

Socialization of children into male and female roles varies from family to family, but there are characteristic differences between middle- and lower-class families. For example, middle-class parents make fewer distinctions than do lower-class parents between desirable behaviors for boys and for girls (Kohn, 1976) and are less rigid about sex-role distinctions. While middle-class parents do encourage femininity in their daughters, they also urge a degree of independence and assertiveness. This shows up in their encouragement of their daughters to excel in sports and school. As a result of these experiences, middle-class girls show later awareness of sex typing and are less traditional in their sex-role concepts than are lower-class females.

Lower-class parents, on the other hand, tend to be concerned that there be clear differences between the behavior of boys and girls and between men and women. This means that lower-class parents are more likely to punish daughters than sons for refusing to do as they are told or for engaging in aggressive behavior, such as fighting. Males are socialized to be independent and assertive. As a consequence, children from these families tend to have more traditional sex-role standards than do those from the middle class and are able to differentiate between sex roles at an earlier age. Additionally, lower-class parents are likely to see the pursuit of excellence in sports or schoolwork as "masculine" and to discourage their daughters from devoting too much time to either.

Sons also experience social-class differences in sex-role socialization. Middle-class parents permit their sons to be more expressive, nurturing, and tender. Working-class parents see these traits as "sissy" and actively discourage them among their sons:

> In summary, then, middle-class parents are interested in seeing both their sons and daughters develop a greater range of traits along *both* instrumental and expressive lines. In contrast, blue-collar parents encourage traditional sex-role behavior in both boys and girls. (Weitzman, 1979, p. 71)

■ **Stop and Think**

School experiences shape a child's sense of identity. What experiences during your grade school years showed you that society expected different things from boys and girls? What experiences reinforced this discovery during high school?

If you were a school principal, what, if any, actions would you take to ensure equal educational opportunities for girls and boys? What steps would you take to encourage students to be as free as possible from sex-role expectations as they set their goals for education and for work?

John Zalinski, a high school English teacher, was waiting for his fourth period class to arrive when he heard shouting in the hall. He went out to see what was happening and found Victor Rinaldi and Sam Worthington in a scuffle. He and another teacher separated the two students, and John asked them what was going on.

SAM: He called me a nigger!

VICTOR: He's always pushing me around! He and his friends always act superior, like they don't want to have anything to do with white guys!

A number of students in the hall were throwing in their own comments; the black students were siding with Sam, the whites with Victor. Mr. Zalinkski asked all the students to come into his classroom.

MR. ZALINSKI: We were supposed to talk about *Romeo and Juliet* today, but something happened just now that is much more important. I've been seeing something in this class that I don't like, and I was afraid something like this would happen. I've seen a lot of teasing and taunting between white and black students, and I'm not seeing much positive talk between the two groups. In this school, we take fairness and equal treatment very seriously, and we just can't tolerate racial problems.

ALTHEA: If everything's so fair and equal, how come all the cheerleaders are white?

MR. ZALINSKI: We've always had elections for cheerleaders and it just so happens that the white cheerleaders won the election.

SAM: That's 'cause it "just so happens" that there's more whites in this school, and they won't vote for blacks for anything!

MR. ZALINSKI: Well, that may be, but this discussion isn't getting us anywhere. What are we going to do about what happened in the hall just now?

VICTOR: Those black kids are always making trouble.

MR. ZALINSKI: What do you mean "those black kids"? Do all black kids make trouble? Don't white kids make trouble too? You were certainly making trouble out in the hall there.

VICTOR: Well, my dad says black people are no good.

MR. ZALINSKI: You know, I'm willing to bet that when the first Rinaldi came to America, people called him all kinds of names, and said that Italians were no good. I know that when my grandfather came from Poland, people called him a "Polack" and said that Polacks were no good.

ALTHEA: Yeah, but when we came to America we came in chains, and racists like Victor want to keep us there!

SAM: And this whole school treats us like we're freaks. I think everyone would like to go back to the days when Woodrow Wilson High School was the great white school on the hill!

QUESTIONS

1. What should Mr. Zalinski say to his class? What should he do in response to the fight between Sam and Victor?
2. How might Mr. Zalinski have prevented the racial problems in his class? What might the school have done to improve race relations?
3. What are the benefits and problems of desegregation?

SUMMARY AND REVIEW OF OBJECTIVES

Social Class Differences. Social class or socioeconomic status (SES) is defined in terms of an individual's income, occupation, education, and prestige in society. The social class of a student's family can profoundly influence the student's attitudes toward school.

Low SES groups tend to lag in school achievement because of (1) the inability of their families to provide the same stimulation and academic preparation that wealthier families can often provide, and (2) the assignment of children from low SES homes to academically inferior, overcrowded schools. Home environment affects not only a child's readiness for school but also achievement throughout the school years.

Middle-class values, such as independence, competitiveness, and goal-setting, are reflected in the school system. In contrast, many lower-class families stress cooperation and reliance on family and friends.

Low achievement among lower-social-class pupils is not an inevitable result of lower-class origins, but of the characteristics of individual families and of the middle-class orientation within the schools.

Government Aid to the Disadvantaged.   Compensatory education programs are designed to supplement the education of students from disadvantaged backgrounds. As part of federally mandated (Chapter I) compensatory education, pull-out programs provide a special teacher who helps disadvantaged students in reading or other subjects. Team teaching can contribute to communication and collaboration between the regular classroom teacher and the Chapter I teacher. Research shows that well-implemented Chapter I programs can help disadvantaged students to avoid falling farther behind in school.

Ethnic Groups and Social Class.   An ethnic group is one in which individuals have a shared sense of identity, usually because of a common place of origin, religion, or race. Blacks, Hispanics, and American Indians tend to score below the mean for whites on standardized tests; socioeconomic scores correspond closely with achievement test scores.

Desegregation.   School desegregation is supposed to increase the academic achievement of minority students by giving them the higher-quality schooling assumed to be received by whites, and by allowing them to interact more with the middle class, though this ideal is often not realized.

Issues that are particularly important in desegregated schools are fairness, equal opportunity for all students, avoiding resegregation, and structuring interactions so that they will lead to positive intergroup relationships.

Bilingual education refers to programs for students with limited proficiency in English. These programs offer instruction to students in their own language while they learn English. Programs that emphasize Hispanic culture as well as the Spanish language are called bilingual-bicultural. There is no research showing that bilingual programs are harmful to students, and there is evidence that they are often beneficial for the achievement of Hispanic students in English as well as in subjects taught to them in Spanish. Difficulties in bilingual programs include the lack of bilingual teachers and making the transition into all-English mainstream programs. Two important tasks in teaching a class of students from many cultures are ensuring that all students have an equal opportunity for success and making certain that all students feel their culture is valued.

Gender Differences.   Research shows that many observed differences between males and females can be linked to differences in early socialization experiences. Four areas of male-female differences cannot be fully explained by socialization or culture: verbal aptitude, visual-spatial aptitude, mathematical aptitude, and aggression. Males and females are treated differently from birth, and learn to behave in ways considered appropriate for their sex. There are no gender differences in general academic ability, nor are there differences in male/female IQ scores. Males consistently score higher than females in mathematics, while females score higher in verbal ability. Middle-class parents make fewer distinctions than do lower-class parents between desirable behavior for boys and girls. The three main tasks for teachers in avoiding gender bias in the classroom are shunning stereotypes, promoting integration of male and female students, and treating boys and girls equally.

STUDY QUESTIONS

1. Which of the following is *not* defined as an indicator of socioeconomic status (SES)?
   a. Occupation
   b. Race
   c. Income
   d. Education

2. In teaching simple tasks to their children, lower-class mothers are more likely than middle-class mothers to
   a. explain why the task needs to be done.
   b. give clear directions.
   c. take the child's perspective.
   d. demand that the task be done.

3. The purpose of Chapter 1 programs is to
   a. provide money to schools for special services to disadvantaged students.
   b. promote the use of bilingual education with language minority students.
   c. use government money to improve home and neighborhood environments.
   d. monitor and reduce the use of sexist teaching materials in public school teaching materials.

4. The socioeconomic status of various racial/ethnic groups and the groups' scores on standardized tests appear to be
   a. positively correlated.
   b. negatively correlated.
   c. uncorrelated

5. Which of the following is *not* a disadvantage or limitation of bilingual programs?
   a. Such programs generally interfere with performance in either the native language or English.
   b. The transition from a bilingual program to an all-English program may be difficult for many students.
   c. There are insufficient bilingual teachers to support such programs.
   d. The class groupings that result may conflict with the goals of desegregation.

6. Which of the following areas of differences between males and females seems *most* attributable to socialization or cultural influences?
   a. Differences in spatial ability
   b. Differences in mathematical ability
   c. Differences in self-concept
   d. Differences in verbal ability

7. Lower-class parents would tend to be less supportive than middle-class parents of
   a. a girl striving for academic excellence.
   b. a boy trying out for the cheerleading team.
   c. a girl hitting another child in retaliation.
   d. all of the above

Answers: 1. b, 2. d, 3. a, 4. a, 5. a, 6. c, 7. d

SUGGESTED READINGS

BOOCOCK, S. S. (1980). *Sociology of education* (2nd ed.). Boston: Houghton Mifflin.

CALIFORNIA STATE DEPARTMENT OF EDUCATION (1983). *Basic principles for the education of language-minority students: An overview.* Sacramento, Cal.: Author.

CARTER, T. P., and SEGURA, R. D. (1979). *Mexican Americans in school: A decade of change.* Princeton, N.J.: College Entrance Examination Board.

COOLEY, W. W. (1981). Effectiveness in compensatory education. *Educational Leadership,* 38, 298–301.

CRAIN, R. L., MAHARD, R. E., and NAROT, R. E. (1982). *Making desegregation work: How schools create social climate.* Cambridge, Mass.: Ballinger.

FOREHAND, G., and RAGOSTA, M. (1976). *A handbook for integrated schooling.* Washington, D.C.: U.S. Department of Education.

HAWLEY, W. D., CRAIN, R. L., ROSSELL, C. H., SMYLIE, M. A., FERNANDEZ, R. R., SCHOFIELD, J. W., TOMPKINS, R., TRENT, W. T., and ZLOTNIK, M. S. (1983). *Strategies for effective desegration.* Lexington, Mass.: D.C. Health.

KLEIN, S. (1985). *Handbook for achieving sex equity through education.* Baltimore, Md.: Johns Hopkins University Press.

LEVINE, D. V., and HAVINGHURST, R. S. (1989). *Society and education.* (7th ed.). Boston: Allyn and Bacon.

LOCKHEED, M. E., HARRIS, A. M., and FINKELSTEIN, F. J. (1979). *Curriculum and research for equity: A training manual for*

Chapter 13: Social Class, Ethnicity, and Gender

promoting sex equity in the classroom. Princeton. N.J.: Educational Testing Service.

MACCOBY, E. E., and JACKLIN, C. N. (1974). *The psychology of sex differences*. Stanford, Cal.: Stanford University Press.

MARLAND, M. (Ed.) (1983). *Sex differentiation and schooling*. London: Heinemann.

SADKER, M. P., and SADKER, D. M. (1982). *Sex equity handbook for schools*. New York: Longman.

SLAVIN, R. E. (1985). Cooperative learning: Applying contact theory in desegregated schools. *Journal of Social Issues, 41,* 45–62.

SLAVIN, R. E., KARWEIT, N. L., and MADDEN, N. A. (1989). *Effective programs for students at risk*. Boston: Allyn and Bacon.

WONG-FILLMORE, L., and VALADEZ, C. (1986). Teaching bilingual learners. In M. C. Wittrock (Ed.), *Handbook of research on teaching* (3rd ed.). New York: Macmillan.

Chapter 14

Student Evaluation: Tests and Grades

Chapter Objectives

After reading this chapter on tests and grading you should be able to:

- List several reasons for evaluating students.

- Write a table of specifications for a test that links assessment to instructional objectives.

- Develop tests that accurately measure skills and knowledge, using appropriate types of questions.

- Assign letter grades that represent levels of student performance fairly.

Many of us, when asked to recall a course we took in junior or senior high school, may not be able to recall a single thing we learned in the course. We might, however, be able to remember the grade we got in it. Even students who don't particularly like math can (and do) accurately compute their grade point averages to the second or third decimal point.

Students spend substantial amounts of their school time taking quizzes and tests, and teachers spend even more time making and marking these tests and otherwise evaluating students' performance. There is probably no aspect of schooling that teachers and students dislike more, but there is also probably no aspect of schooling that is more durable. Chances are that you will receive a grade in the course for which you are reading this chapter, chances are you won't like working for this grade, and chances are your professor won't like giving it—but like it or not, the grade will be given.

Simon and Bellanca (1976, p. 1) put it this way:

> No level of education is free from it; no teacher or student can hide from it. The cry of "Wad-Ja-Get?" is all around us.
>
> The "Wad-Ja-Get?" refrain that accompanies the grading system in American education is as pervasive as our questions about higher taxes, increased smog, and rising inflation. Students, from kindergarten through graduate school, feel the ache of the "Wad-Ja-Get?" syndrome; most know that it dominates more of their learning than they would ever care to admit. Teachers likewise deal with the grading problem, from the first day they enter a classroom until the moment they file their last record book and retire. School administrators spend countless hours on "Wad-Ja-Get?" as well; they grapple with parents—who have already grappled with their children's teachers—about the "fairness" and "rightness" of grades.
>
> Wherever teaching and learning go on, grades are a grim reality for most people; that much is clear. But beyond the reality is an enormous amount of confusion and arguing about grading, a phenomenon that—by touching the lives of almost every human being—has an impact incredibly wide and deep. To ignore the complexity of the grading issue is to live in a fantasy world where houses are made of gingerbread, the stork delivers babies, and failure has no effect on a person's life.

STUDENT EVALUATION

Given that tests and grades are about as popular as ants at a picnic, why do we use them? We use them because, one way or another, we must periodically check students' learning. Tests and grades tell teachers, students, and parents how students are doing in school. Teachers can use tests to see whether their instruction was effective and to find out which students need additional help. Students can use them to see whether their studying strategies are paying off. Parents need grades to find out how their children are doing in school; grades serve as the one consistent form of communication between school and home. Schools need grades and standardized tests to make student placements. States and school districts need tests to evaluate schools and, in some cases, teachers. Ultimately, colleges use grades and standardized test scores to decide whom to admit.

Ebel (1980b) defended the use of tests and grades as follows:

> There are those on most school and college faculties who are not in favor of evaluating sudents, that is, giving tests and assigning grades. They may consider themselves to be good teachers. . . . But, unless the achievements of their pupils are evaluated, they can provide no solid evidence that they are in fact good teachers. . . . For the essential task of the teacher is to facilitate student learning. . . . The best way to determine how

much learning has occurred is to observe how successfully the student can cope with tasks that require learning; this means testing. It also means grading, for grades can provide concise, meaningful indications of the degree of a student's success in learning. (p. 47)

Ebel argues that the problem is not evaluation per se, but inadequate or inappropriate use of evaluation. We must evaluate student learning; few would argue otherwise. Research on the use of tests finds that students learn more in courses that use tests than in those that do not (Bangert-Drowns et al., 1986). But *how* should we evaluate? That is the topic of this chapter.

Student evaluation refers to all the means used in schools to formally measure student performance. These include quizzes and tests, written evaluations, and grades. Student evaluation usually focuses on academic achievement, but many schools also evaluate behaviors and attitudes. For example, one national survey of report cards found that most elementary schools provided descriptions of students' behavior (such as "Follows directions," "Listens attentively," "Works with others," "Uses time wisely"). In upper elementary, middle, and high school the prevalence of behavior reports successively diminishes, but even many high schools rate students on such criteria as "Works up to ability," "Is prepared," and "Is responsible" (Chansky, 1975).

Student Evaluations
Formal assessments of student performance using tests, written reports, and grades

WHY DO WE EVALUATE?

One problem with student evaluation is that we expect one grade or score to serve many purposes, yet an evaluation that is optimal for one use may be inappropriate for another (see Slavin, 1978). Before discussing *how* we should evaluate students, let's consider *why* we evaluate them.

Student evaluations serve six primary purposes:

1. Incentives to increase student effort
2. Feedback to students
3. Feedback to teachers
4. Information to parents
5. Information for selection and certification
6. Information for accountability

Evaluations as Incentives

One important use of evaluations is to motivate students to give their best efforts. This use of evaluations was discussed in Chapter 10. In essence, high grades, stars, and prizes are given as rewards for good work. These are primarily valued by elementary students because they are valued by their parents, and by high school students because they are important for getting into college.

Natriello and Dornbusch (1984) and Natriello (1989) have suggested criteria that must be satisfied if evaluations are to increase student effort (see also Crooks, 1988). An adaptation of their criteria follows.

1. *Important evaluations:* Evaluations are effective to the degree that they are important to students. For example, grades will be less effective as incentives for students whose parents pay little attention to their grades than for students

Evaluations can help motivate students if the students—and their parents—consider the evaluations important.

whose parents care a great deal about them. They will be more effective for students planning to go to competitive colleges (which require high grades for admission) than for other students. Natriello and Dornbusch (1984) state that evaluations will be important to students to the degree that they are seen as *central* to their attainment of valued objectives and *influential* in attaining those objectives.

2. *Soundly based evaluations:* Evaluations must be closely related to a student's actual performance. Students must feel that the only way to succeed in school is to work hard on school tasks, and that hard work will pay off. They must also feel that evaluations are fair, objective measures of their performance. To the degree that students believe they can outfox the system and get away with shoddy efforts, or that the system is rigged against them, evaluations will have little impact on their efforts. Students should have every opportunity to show what they really know on tests. Reducing test anxiety, a serious problem for many students (Hembree, 1988; Hill and Wigfield, 1984) is one way to increase the soundness of evaluations. This can be done by giving plenty of time for tests, by reducing pressure, and by linking tests closely to course content.

3. *Consistent standards:* Evaluations will be effective to the degree that students perceive them to be equal for all students. For example, if students feel that some of their classmates are evaluated more leniently than others, this will reduce the effectiveness of the evaluation system.

4. *Clear criteria:* The criteria for success must be clear to students; they should know precisely what is required to obtain a good grade or other positive evaluation (see Schunk, 1983).

5. *Reliable interpretations of evaluations:* Students often interpret evaluations (and their own efforts) in light of the social context of the evaluation. For example, students in a low-track class might believe that doing any homework at all shows a high level of effort, because their classmates are doing none; or these

students might view a C as an adequate grade, since many of their classmates are failing.

6. *Frequent evaluations:* There is evidence that the more frequently evaluations take place, the more students generally achieve (Bloom et al., 1971; Peckham and Roe, 1977). Frequent, brief quizzes are better than infrequent, long tests because they require that students pay attention all the time rather than cram for the occasional exam, because they give students more timely feedback, and because they provide reinforcement for hard work closer in time to when the work was done.

7. *Challenging evaluations:* Evaluations should be challenging for all students, but impossible for none. This can be done by evaluating students according to their improvement over their own past performance, a strategy found to increase their achievement (Slavin, 1980). Evaluation systems should be set up to encourage students always to be "reaching" for success, just as runners set goals for finishing a mile a little bit faster than their previous best time.

The practical implications of these principles will be discussed in the sections on "Achievement Tests" and "Grading and Evaluating" later in this chapter.

Informational Value of Evaluations

Evaluations as Feedback to Students. Imagine that a store owner tried several strategies to increase business—first advertising in the newspaper, then sending fliers to homes near the store, and finally holding a sale. However, suppose that after trying each strategy, the store owner failed to record and compare the store's revenue. Without "taking stock" this way, the owner would learn little about the effectiveness of any of the strategies, and might well be wasting time and money.

In the same way, students need to know the results of their efforts. Regular evaluation gives them feedback on their strengths and weaknesses. For example, suppose a teacher had students write compositions, and then gave back written evaluations. Some students might find out that they need to work more on content, others on the use of modifiers, still others on language mechanics. This information would help students improve their writing much more than would a grade with no explanation.

To be useful as feedback, evaluations should be as specific as possible. For example, Page (1958) found that students who were given written comments as well as grades on their papers achieved more than those who were given letter grades only. Later studies failed to find such differences (see Stewart and White, 1976), but when the teacher's comments added information not provided by the letter grade alone, they helped students understand how to improve. For example, Cross and Cross (1980–81) found that students who received written feedback in addition to letter grades were more likely than other students to feel that their efforts, rather than luck or other external factors, determined their success in school.

Evaluations as Feedback to Teachers. One of the most important (and often overlooked) functions of evaluating student learning is to provide feedback to teachers on the effectiveness of their instruction. As noted in Chapter 8, teachers cannot expect to be optimally effective if they do not know whether students have grasped the main points of their lessons. Asking questions in class gives the teacher some idea of how well students have learned, but in many subjects brief, frequent quizzes are necessary to provide more detailed indications of students' progress. Recall that most of the effective instructional strategies discussed in Chapters 8, 9, and 10, including the Missouri Mathematics Program and Student Teams Achievement Divisions, use frequent brief quizzes to provide feedback to teachers (as well as to students themselves) on the degree to which students have mastered the lesson objectives.

Evaluations as Information to Parents.   A report card is called a report card because it "reports" information on student progress to parents. This reporting function of evaluation is important for several reasons. First, routine school evaluations of many kinds (test scores, stars, and certificates as well as report card grades) keep parents informed about their children's schoolwork. For example, if a student's grades are dropping, the parents may know why and may be able to help the student get back on track. Second, grades and other evaluations set up informal "home-based reinforcement" systems. Recall from Chapter 11 that many studies have found that reporting regularly to parents when students do good work, and asking parents to reinforce good reports, improves student behavior and achievement (Barth, 1979). Without much prompting, most parents naturally reinforce their children for bringing home good grades, thereby making grades more important and more effective as incentives (Natriello and Dornbusch, 1984).

Evaluations as Information for Selection.   Some sociologists (such as Sørensen, 1984) see as a primary purpose of schools the sorting of students into societal roles; if schools do not actually determine who will be a butcher, a baker, or a candlestick maker, they do substantially influence who will be a laborer, a skilled worker, a white-collar worker, or a professional. This sorting function takes place gradually over years of schooling. In the early grades students are sorted into reading groups and, in many cases, into tracks that may remain stable over many years (Barker-Lunn, 1970). Tracking becomes more widespread and systematic by junior high or middle school, when students begin to be selected into different courses (McPartland, Coldiron, and Braddock, 1987). For example, some ninth-graders are allowed to take Algebra I, while others take pre-algebra or general mathematics. In high school students are usually steered toward college preparatory, general, or vocational tracks, and of course a major sorting takes place when students are accepted into various colleges and training programs. Throughout the school years some students are selected into special education or gifted programs or into other special programs with limited enrollments.

Closely related to selection is certification, a use of tests to qualify students for promotion or for access to various occupations. For example, many states and local districts have minimum competency tests that students must pass to advance from grade to grade or to graduate from high school. Bar exams for lawyers, board examinations for medical students, and tests for teachers, such as the National Teachers' Examination, are examples of certification tests that control access to professions.

The most important criterion for an effective certification test is the degree to which a high score on the test predicts success in the activity for which students are being certified. For example, if a score on the National Teachers' Examination had no relationship to performance as a teacher, it would be of little value.

Evaluations as Information for Accountability.   Often, evaluations of students are used to evaluate teachers, schools, districts, or even states. Many states have statewide testing programs that allow the states to rank every school in terms of student performance. Most school districts use these tests for similar purposes. These test scores are often used in making decisions about the hiring and firing of principals and sometimes even superintendents. Consequently, these tests are taken very seriously. In addition, student test scores are often used to evaluate teachers.

■ **Stop and Think**

Do you or any close friends suffer from extreme anxiety before tests? What are the roots of this anxiety? How can a teacher help students to approach tests with confidence so that they can do their best?

EVALUATION STRATEGIES

As implied in the previous sections, evaluation strategies effective for any one purpose may be ineffective for other purposes. Table 14.1 summarizes the optimal characteristics of evaluations conducted for various purposes. Note, for example, that evaluation frequency and timeliness (how soon evaluations should be made after the student's performance) are critical when evaluations are used to increase incentive and to provide feedback to students and teachers, but when evaluations are used to provide information to parents, for selection decisions, and for accountability, the emphasis is on reliable comparability among students.

To understand how evaluations can be used most effectively in classroom instruction, two critical concepts must be grasped: formative versus summative evaluation, and norm-referenced versus criterion-referenced evaluation.

TABLE 14.1

OPTIMAL CHARACTERISTICS OF EVALUATION FOR VARIOUS FUNCTIONS

Evaluation strategies used as incentives have different characteristics than strategies used for various types of feedback or for selection.

Evaluation Function	Optimal Frequency	Importance of Timeliness	Importance of Comparability to Other Students	Importance of Tie to Curriculum
Incentive	Very frequent	Important	Moderately important	Important
Feedback to students	Very frequent	Crucial	Unimportant	Crucial
Feedback to teachers	Very frequent	Crucial	Unimportant	Crucial
Information to parents	Moderately frequent	Unimportant	Important	Moderately important
Information for selection and certification	Infrequent	Unimportant	Crucial	Moderately important
Information for accountability	Infrequent	Unimportant	Crucial	Important

Formative versus Summative Evaluation

The distinction between formative and summative evaluation was introduced in the discussion of mastery learning in Chapter 9, but this distinction also applies to a broader range of evaluation issues. Essentially, a **formative evaluation** asks "How are we doing?" while a **summative evaluation** asks "How did we do?" Formative, or diagnostic, tests are given to discover strengths and weaknesses in learning, to make midcourse corrections in pace or content of instruction. Formative evaluation is useful to the degree that is informative, closely tied to the curriculum being taught, timely, and frequent. For example, frequent quizzes given and scored immediately after specific lessons might serve as formative evaluations, providing feedback to teachers and students that they can use to improve students' learning.

In contrast, summative evaluation refers to final tests of student knowledge. Summative evaluation may or may not be frequent, but it must be reliable and (in general) should allow for comparisons among students. Summative evaluations should also be closely tied to formative evaluations and to course objectives.

In mastery learning, both summative and formative tests are given frequently. However, in other contexts the term "formative evaluation" usually refers to routine quizzes that evaluate students' progress during instruction, while "summative evaluation" refers to grading, standardized testing, or other final assessments of student achievement.

Norm-Referenced versus Criterion-Referenced Evaluation

Norm-referenced evaluations focus on comparisons of a student's scores to those of other students. Within a classroom "grading on the curve" gives us an idea of how a student has performed in comparison with classmates. A student may also have a grade-level or school rank, and in standardized testing, student scores may be compared with those of a nationally representative norm group (see Chapter 15).

Criterion-referenced evaluations focus on assessing students' mastery of specific skills, regardless of how other students did on the same skills. Criterion-referenced evaluations are closely tied to the curriculum being taught and to the lesson or course objectives. Table 14.2 (from Gronlund, 1982, p. 15) compares the principal features and purposes of criterion-referenced and norm-referenced testing.

Formative evaluation is almost always criterion-referenced. In formative testing, we want to know, for example, who is having trouble with Newton's Laws of Thermodynamics, not which student is first, fifteenth, or thirtieth in the class in physics knowledge. Summative testing, however, may be either criterion-referenced or norm-referenced. Even if it is criterion-referenced, however, we usually want to know on a summative test how each student did compared to other students (see "Comparative Evaluations" later in this chapter).

Matching Strategies with Goals

Considering all the factors discussed up to this point, what is the best strategy for evaluating students? The first answer is that there is clearly no *one* best strategy; as illustrated in Table 14.1, the best means of accomplishing any one objective of evaluation may be inappropriate for other objectives. Therefore teachers must choose different types of evaluation for different purposes.

TABLE 14.2

COMPARISON OF TWO APPROACHES TO ACHIEVEMENT TESTING

Norm-referenced tests and criterion-referenced tests serve different purposes and have different features.

	Norm-Referenced Testing	Criterion-Referenced Testing
Principal use	Survey testing	Mastery testing
Major emphasis	Measures individual differences in achievement.	Describes tasks students can perform.
Interpretation of results	Compares performance to that of other individuals.	Compares performance to a clearly specified achievement domain
Content coverage	Typically covers a broad area of achievement.	Typically focuses on a limited set of learning tasks.
Nature of test plan	Table of specifications is commonly used.	Detailed domain specifications are favored.
Item selection procedures	Items are selected that provide maximum discrimination among individuals (to obtain high score variability). Easy items are typically eliminated from the test.	All items needed to adequately describe performance are included. No attempt is made to alter item difficulty or to eliminate easy items to increase score variability.
Performance standards	Level of performance is determined by *relative* position in some known group (ranks fifth in a group of twenty).	Level of performance is commonly determined by *absolute* standards (demonstrates mastery by defining 90 percent of the technical terms).

SOURCE: Gronlund, 1982, p. 15.

At a minimum, two types of evaluation should be used, one directed at providing incentive and feedback, and the other at ranking individual students relative to the larger group. The characteristics of these types of feedback are listed in Table 14.3.

Incentive/Feedback Evaluation. Traditional grades are often inadequate as incentives to encourage students to give their best efforts and as feedback to teachers and students (see Slavin, 1978a). The principal problem is that grades are given too infrequently, are too far removed in time from student performance, and are poorly tied to specific student behaviors. Recall from Chapter 4 that the effectiveness of reinforcers and of feedback diminishes rapidly if there is much delay between behavior and consequences. By the same token, research has found that achievement is higher in classrooms where students receive immediate feedback on their quizzes than in those classrooms where feedback is delayed (Kulik and Kulik, 1988).

TABLE 14.3

OPTIMAL CHARACTERISTICS OF INCENTIVE/FEEDBACK AND COMPARATIVE EVALUATIONS

Evaluations used for incentive and feedback should be very frequent, while evaluations for comparative purposes can be infrequent. The two types of evaluations differ on other counts, too.

Incentive/Feedback	Comparative
Very frequently (daily, weekly)	Infrequent (every 6–9 weeks at most)
Very timely (immediate feedback)	Timeliness not important
Criterion-referenced, closely tied to curriculum	Norm-referenced, reliable

Tests take significant amounts of class time but are an important part of the instructional process.

Another reason grades are less than ideal as incentives is that they are usually based on comparative standards. In effect, it is relatively easy for high-ability students to achieve A's and B's, but very difficult for low achievers to do so. As a result, high achievers do less work than they are capable of doing, and, in particular, low achievers give up. As noted in Chapter 10, a reward that is too easy or too difficult to attain, or that is felt to be a result of ability rather than of effort, is a poor motivator (Atkinson and Birch, 1978; Weiner, 1979).

For these reasons, traditional grades must be supplemented by evaluations better designed for incentive and feedback. For example, teachers might give daily quizzes of five or ten items that are scored in class immediately after completion. These would give both students and teachers the information they need to adjust their teaching and learning strategies and to rectify any deficiencies revealed by their evaluations. If the quiz results were made important by having them count toward course grades or by giving students with perfect papers special recognition or certificates, then they would serve as effective incentives, rewarding effective studying behavior soon after it occurs. Use of the Individual Learning Expectations (ILE) strategy (Slavin, 1980) by itself or as part of Student Teams Achievement Divisions (Slavin, 1978b) adds the element of having students measured against their own past achievement. The emphasis is on improvement through increased effort rather than on high scores attained largely through ability or prior knowledge. (See Chapter 10 for more on these methods.)

Comparative Evaluations. There comes a time when we do need to know how well students are doing in comparison to others. This information is important to give parents and students themselves a realistic picture of student performance. For example, students who have outstanding skills in science ought to know that they are exceptional, not only in the context of their class or school, but also in a broader state or national context. In general, students need to form accurate perceptions of their strengths and weaknesses to guide their decisions about their futures.

Comparative evaluations are traditionally provided by grades and by standardized tests (see Chapter 15). Unlike the incentive/feedback evaluations discussed earlier, comparative evaluations need not be conducted frequently. Rather, the emphasis in comparative evaluation must be on fair, unbiased, reliable assessment of student performance. Comparative evaluations should assess what students can do, and nothing else. Student grades should be based on demonstrated knowledge of the course content, not on politeness, good behavior, neatness, or punctuality, because the purpose of a grade is to give an accurate assessment of student performance, not to reward or punish students for their behavior. (Behavior management, discussed in Chapter 11, can be accomplished more effectively using strategies that do not involve grades.)

However, grades are imperfect as comparative evaluators because many teachers consider subjective factors when assigning grades. One solution in secondary schools is for teachers in a given department to get together to write "departmental exams" for each course. For example, a high school science department might decide on common objectives for all chemistry classes, and then make up common unit or final tests. This would ensure that students in all classes are evaluated on the same criteria.

Comparative evaluations and other summative assessments of student performance must be firmly based on the objectives established at the beginning of the course (see Chapter 7), and must be consistent with the formative incentive/feedback evaluations. We would certainly not want a situation in which students who are doing well on week-to-week assessments fail the summative evaluations because there is a lack of correspondence between the two forms of evaluation. For example, if the summative test uses essay questions to assess higher-order skills, then similar essay questions must be used all along as formative tests.

For more on comparative evaluation, see "Grading and Evaluating," later in this chapter.

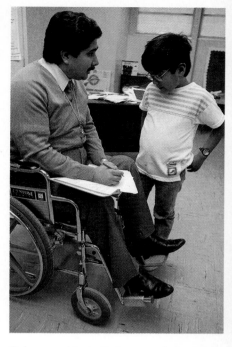

Quizzes and tests that are graded quickly can provide feedback and incentive for students as well as guidance for teachers regarding student progress.

■ **Stop and Think**

After taking hundreds of tests in your school career, what strategy of testing have you found most helpful to mastering and remembering course material? What type of tests encouraged you only to memorize information, and then forget it soon after the test?

ACHIEVEMENT TESTS

Basic Principles of Achievement Testing

Achievement testing is one of the most important classroom activities. Achievement tests are used (1) to predict student performance in a course of study, (2) to diagnose student difficulties, (3) to serve as formative tests of student progress, and (4) to serve as summative tests of learning. From 5 to 15 percent of all class time is used in written testing (Dorr-Bremme and Herman, 1986; Haertel, 1986). Writing good achievement tests is thus a critical skill for effective teaching.

Gronlund (1982) listed six principles to keep in mind in preparing achievement tests:

1. Achievement tests should measure clearly defined learning objectives that are in harmony with instructional objectives.

Perhaps the most important principle of achievement testing is that the tests should correspond with the course objectives and with the instruction actually provided. An achievement test should never be a surprise for students; rather, it should assess the students' grasp of the most important concepts or skills the lesson or course is supposed to teach. Further, assessments should tap the true objectives of the course, not easy-to-measure substitutes. For example, a course on twentieth-century art should probably use a test in which students are asked to discuss or to compare art works, not to match artists with their paintings (see Fredericksen, 1984).

2. Achievement tests should measure a representative sample of the learning tasks included in the instruction.

With rare exceptions (such as multiplication facts), achievement tests do not assess every skill or fact students are supposed to have learned. Rather, they sample from among all the learning objectives. If students do not know in advance which questions will be on a test, then they must study the entire course content to do well. However, the test items must be *representative* of all the objectives and content covered. For example, if an English literature course spent eight weeks on Shakespeare and two weeks on other Elizabethan authors, the test should have about four times as many items relating to Shakespeare as to the others.

Items chosen to represent a particular objective must be central to that objective. There is no place in achievement testing for tricky or obscure questions. For example, a unit test on the American Revolution should ask questions relating to the causes, principal events, and outcomes of that struggle, not who rowed George Washington across the Delaware.*

3. Achievement tests should include the types of test items that are most appropriate for measuring the desired learning outcomes.

Items on achievement tests should correspond as closely as possible to the ultimate instructional objectives. For example, in mathematics problem solving our goal is to enable students to solve problems they will encounter outside of school. Thus multiple-choice items might be inappropriate for this kind of exam because in real life we are rarely presented with four options as possible solutions to a problem.

4. Achievement tests should fit the particular uses that will be made of the results.

Each type of achievement test has its own requirements. For example, a test used for diagnosis would focus on particular skills students might need help with. A diagnostic test of elementary arithmetic might contain items on subtraction involving zeros in the minuend (for example, $307 - 127$), a skill with which many students have trouble. In contrast, a test used to predict future performance might assess a student's general abilities and breadth of knowledge. Formative tests should be very closely tied to material recently presented, while summative tests should survey broader areas of knowledge or skills.

5. Achievement tests should be as reliable as possible and should be interpreted with caution.

*Answer: John Glover and his Marblehead Marines.

1. Students know they've taken a good test when they walk away from it feeling they've learned something. How do you ensure that the various evaluation techniques you use not only rank your students but also motivate them and help them learn?

Margaret Ball, who teaches at Stratford High in Stratford, Wisc., wrote:

I feel it is every educator's responsibility to use varied approaches to testing. To vary testing methods, the following steps should be followed:

1. Identify the concepts that you want to test for mastery.
2. Examine each, thinking through ways that mastery could be measured. Ask yourself such questions as:
   —Should I use matching answers, short answers, or other conventional methods?
   —Could I vary the method by using a diagram (visual) or auditory clues?
   —Do I have any hands-on material to use during testing?
   —Should I give different tests for different situations? Can I experiment with classes?

When using a multisensory approach, students seem to motivate themselves. A multisensory approach helps students recognize that they, too, can learn and measure their learning.

Gail C. Hartman, who teaches elementary school in Hobbs, N.M., wrote:

I have provided each child with his or her own graph on which results from each week's math test can be graphed and a child can easily see his or her own progress. The children do not feel pressured by the results of other children in the class; rather attention has been focused on the child's own progress. I have found that this encouraged them to improve and they actually look forward to the weekly timed tests.

2. Some teachers find it helpful to use pretests. Have you done this? In what situation? How has it helped you with your teaching?

Mary Van Dyke, Atchison, Kan.:

Pretests are extremely important tools, especially for students who have high academic skills. All independent activities, research skills, and subjects are first presented on pretests to eliminate wasting time on areas already mastered. The same test may be given after the study to measure growth. This allows students to become familiar with what is to be learned.

John Kobza, a ninth-grade teacher in Merrillville, Ind.:

I have given open-book pretests. This gives the students a chance to research the material, so when I lecture they will have some knowledge of what I am talking about.

Marta Lustgraaf, Council Bluffs, Iowa:

I often use pretests when working with basic skills that were taught in the elementary grades. This lets me know whether I need to lightly review the skills, go on to more advanced skills, or reteach the basic skills in-depth. It saves valuable class time. Transitions from one skill to another are also much easier if you know where to begin. Pretests also help you group students for better teaching and learning.

3. What post-test activities or explanations have you found most help students learn from their mistakes on tests?

Dyanne Buckelew, who teachers fourth grade in Puryear, Tenn., writes:

In class we review all test questions and correct answers. Material is used again in the following lessons to refocus on concepts. As we move to other material, I try to relate the new material to the things we have already covered, either by comparing the similarities or by contrasting the differences.

Carol Hyneman, who teaches sixth grade in Princeton, Ind., writes:

When I go over the tests with students, I explain to them that I, too, can make errors in grading. I ask that they watch their papers carefully to ensure that I do not mark an item wrong that is correct. I have found that students do pay careful attention during this activity when they are looking for a teacher error. Sometimes they find errors not in their favor, and I always reward this honest behavior by allowing them to keep the unearned credit, and I comment on their honesty.

Reliability
A measure of the consistency of test scores obtained from the same students at different times

Table of Specifications
List of instructional objectives and expected levels of understanding that guides test development

A test is reliable to the degree that students tested a second time would fall in the same rank order (see Chapter 15, "Reliability"). In general, **reliability** of achievement tests is increased by using relatively large numbers of items and by using few items that almost all students get right or that almost all students miss. The use of clearly written items that focus directly on the objectives actually taught also enhances test reliability. Still, no matter how rigorously reliability is built into a test, there will always be some error of measurement. Students have good and bad days, or may be lucky or unlucky guessers. Some students are "test-wise" and usually test well; others are "test anxious" and test far below their actual knowledge or potential. Therefore, no single test score should be viewed with excessive confidence. Any test score is only an approximation of a student's true knowledge or skills, and should be interpreted as such.

6. Achievement tests should improve learning.

    Achievement tests of all kinds, particularly formative tests, provide important information on students' learning progress. Achievement testing should be seen as part of the instructional process, and used to improve instruction and guide student learning (Foos and Fisher, 1988). This means that achievement test results should be clearly communicated to students soon after the test is taken; in the case of formative testing, students should be given the results immediately. Teachers should use the results of formative as well as summative tests to guide instruction, to locate strong and weak points in students' understandings, and to set an appropriate pace of instruction. Including review items on each test (and telling students you will do so) provides distributed practice of course content, an important aid for learning and retaining knowledge (Dempster, 1987).

Tables of Specifications

Gronlund's (1982) first principle—that achievement tests should measure well-specified objectives—is an important guide to the content of any achievement test. The first step in the test development process is to decide which concept domains the test will measure and how many test items will be allocated to each concept. Gronlund (1982) and Bloom et al. (1971) suggest teachers make up a **table of specifications** listing the various objectives taught and different levels of understanding to be assessed. The "levels of understanding" may correspond to Bloom's taxonomy of educational objectives (Bloom et al., 1956). Bloom et al. (1971) suggest classifying test items for each objective according to six categories, shown in Table 14.4, a table of specifications for a chemistry unit. Table 14.5 shows a table of specifications on testing (from Gronlund, 1982).

Note that the tables of specifications vary for each type of course and that they are nearly identical to behavior content matrixes, discussed in Chapter 7. This is as it should be: a behavior content matrix is used to lay out objectives for a course, and the table of specifications tests those objectives. Gronlund's (1982) format (Table 14.5) specifies the number of items to be used to test each concept at each level of understanding, according to the importance of each concept. For example, he has determined that the topics "Principles of Testing" and "Planning the Test" are twice as important as the other two topics and has accordingly allocated twice the number of items to these topics.

TABLE 14.4

TABLE OF SPECIFICATIONS FOR A CHEMISTRY UNIT

This table of specifications classifies test items (circled numbers) and objectives according to six categories ranging from knowledge of terms to ability to apply knowledge.

A. Knowledge of Terms	B. Knowledge of Facts	C. Knowledge of Rules and Principles	D. Skill in Using Processes and Procedures	E. Ability to Make Translations	F. Ability to Make Applications
Atom (1)		Boyle's law (12)			
Molecule (2)		Properties of a gas (13)		Substance into diagram (22)	Writing and solving equations to fit experimental situations
Element (3)		Atomic theory (16)			
Compound (4)	Diatomic gases (11)	Chemical formula (19)		Compound into formula (21)	(28)
Diatomic (5)					
Chemical formula (6)		Avogadro's hypothesis (14)			(23)
Avogadro's number (7)		Gay-Lussac's law (15)			(24)
Mole (8)		Grams to moles (18)			(25)
Atomic weight (9)		Molecular weight (17)	Molecular weight (20)		(26)
Molecular weight (10)					(27)
					(29)

SOURCE: Bloom et al., 1971, p. 121.

TABLE 14.5

TABLE OF SPECIFICATIONS FOR A TEST ON TESTING

Tables of specifications can be used to allocate test items among important topics and levels of understanding.

Content Outcomes	Knows			Comprehends Principles	Applies Principles	Total Number of Items
	Terms	Facts	Procedures			
Role of tests in instruction	4	4		2		10
Principles of testing	4	3	2	6	5	20
Norm-referenced versus criterion-referenced	4	3	3			10
Planning the test	3	5	5	2	5	20
Total number of items	15	15	10	10	10	60

SOURCE: Gronlund, 1982, p. 26.

Once you know the concept domains to be tested, it is time to write items. There is one overall principle to apply in writing achievement test items: Every item should separate students who know the material from those who do not. Test-wiseness (the ability to do well on a test by picking up answer clues from the questions or by using other strategies that disguise the test taker's ignorance of the content being assessed) should never be rewarded. Students who do not know the material should not be able to bluff or guess their way through a test.

The various types of test items and their advantages and disadvantages are discussed in the following sections.

MULTIPLE-CHOICE ITEMS

Considered by some educators to be the most useful and flexible of all test forms (Lindeman and Merenda, 1979; Gronlund, 1982), multiple-choice items can be used in tests for most school subjects. The basic form of the multiple-choice item is a stem followed by choices, or alternatives. The stem may be a question or a partial statement that is completed by one of several choices. There is no truly optimum number of choices, but four or five are most common—one correct response and others referred to as **distractors**.

Here are two types, one with a question stem and the other a completion stem:

1. What color results from the mixture of equal parts of yellow and blue paint?
   a. Red
   b. Green (correct choice)
   c. Gray
   d. Black

2. The actual election of the U.S. president to office is done by
   a. all registered voters
   b. the Supreme Court
   c. the Electoral College (correct choice)
   d. our Congressional representatives

When writing a multiple-choice item keep two goals in mind. First, a knowledgeable student should be able to choose the correct answer and not be "distracted" by the wrong alternatives. Second, you should minimize the chance that a student ignorant of the subject matter can guess the correct answer. To achieve this, the distractors (the wrong choices) must look plausible to the uninformed: their wording and form must not identify them readily as bad answers. Hence, one of the tasks in writing a good multiple-choice item is to identify two or three plausible, but not tricky, distractors.

Here are some guidelines for constructing multiple-choice items.

1. Make the stem sufficiently specific to stand on its own without qualification.

   In other words, the stem should contain enough information to set the context for the concepts in it. At the same time, the stem should not be too wordy; a test is not the place to incorporate instruction that should have been given in the lessons.

   Here is an example of a stem for which insufficient context has been established.

   Behavior modification is
   a. punishment
   b. classical conditioning
   c. self-actualization
   d. reinforcement contingencies

   An improved version of this stem is

   Which of the following alternatives best characterizes the modern clinical use of behavior modification?
   a. punishment
   b. classical conditioning
   c. self-actualization
   d. reinforcement contingencies (correct choice)

2. Do not put too much information into the stem or require too much reading. Avoid complicated sentences unless the purpose of the item is to measure a student's ability to deal with new information or to interpret a paragraph.

3. The stem and every choice in the list of potential answers ought to fit grammatically. In addition, phrases or words that would commonly begin each of the alternatives should be part of the stem. It is also a sound idea to have the same grammatical form (say, a verb) at the beginning of each choice.

For example:

The task of statistics is to
a. *make* the social sciences as respectable as the physical sciences
b. *reduce* large masses of data to an interpretable form (correct choice)
c. *predict* human behavior
d. *make* the investigation of human beings more precise and rigorous

4. Special care must be taken when using no-exception words such as "never," "all," "none," and "always." In multiple-choice items these words often give clues to the test-wise but concept-ignorant student. However, by including these no-exception words in *correct* choices, it is possible to discriminate knowledgeable from ignorant students.

   Hill (1977) notes that such qualifying words as "often," "sometimes," "seldom," "usually," "typically," "generally," and "ordinarily" are most often found in correct responses (or ones that are true), and along with the no-exception words should be avoided whenever possible.

5. Avoid making the correct choice either the longest or shortest of the alternatives (usually the longest, because absolutely correct answers often require qualification and precision).

6. Be cautious in using "None of the above" as an alternative because it too often reduces the possible correct choices to one or two items (Lindeman and Merenda, 1979).

   Here are two examples illustrating how a student may know very little and get the correct answer. In the first one, by knowing only one of the choices is incorrect, a student will reduce the number of plausible choices from four to two:

Research suited to investigate the effects of a new instructional program on mathematics achievement is
a. historical
b. experimental (correct choice)
c. correlational
d. all of the above

The student who knows that "historical" is not a good choice also knows that d must be incorrect and the answer must be b or c.

In the second example notice that the correct response, "all of the above," may be determined by being familiar with only two of the three presidents' careers:

Which of the following were U.S. presidents during wars?
a. F. Roosevelt
b. L. Johnson
c. Lincoln
d. all of the above

7. After a test, discuss the items with students and note their interpretations of the wording of the items.

   Students often interpret certain phrases quite differently from what the teacher intended. Such information is very useful in revising items for the next test, as well as for learning about students' understandings.

8. Do not include a choice that is transparently absurd. All choices should sound plausible to a student who has not studied or otherwise become familiar with the subject.

   Example with an absurd choice:

During the Civil War the main philosophical differences between the North and the South focused on
a. religious values
b. agricultural and industrial interests
c. secular human values
d. the climate (not a philosophical choice)

In effect this item has only three choices.

Besides these guidelines for writing multiple-choice items, here are some suggestions about format:

- List the choices vertically rather than side by side.
- Use letters rather than numerals to label the choices, especially on scientific and mathematical tests.
- Use word structures that make the stem agree with the choices according to acceptable grammatical

practice. For example, a completion-type stem would require that each of the choices begin with a lower-case letter (unless it begins with a proper noun), and a direct question type of stem usually calls for choices to begin with a capital letter.

- Avoid overusing one letter position as the correct choice; instead, correct choices should appear in random letter positions.

TRUE-FALSE ITEMS

True-false items can be seen as one form of multiple choice. They are most useful when a comparison of two alternatives is called for, as in the following: Controversy over the use of behavioral objectives in setting goals is caused more by differences in terminology than by real differences in philosophies. (False)

The main drawback of true-false items is that students have a 50 percent chance of guessing correctly. For this reason, multiple-choice or other formats are generally preferable.

FILL-IN-THE-BLANK ITEMS

When there is only one possible correct answer, the best item format is completion, or "fill in the blank," as in the following examples:

1. The largest city in Germany is_____.

2. What is 15% of $198.00?_____.

3. The measure of electric resistance is the_____

The advantage of completion items is that they can reduce the element of test-wiseness to near zero. For example, compare the following items:

1. The capital of Maine is_____.

2. The capital of Maine is_____.
   a. Sacramento
   b. Augusta
   c. Juneau
   d. Boston

A student who has no idea what the capital of Maine is could pick Augusta from the list in item 2 because it is easy to rule out the other three cities. In item 1, however, the student has to know the answer.

Completion items are especially useful in mathematics, where use of multiple-choice may help give the answer away or reward guessing. For example:

$$
\begin{array}{ll}
4037 & \text{a. } 4196 \\
\underline{-159} & \text{b. } 4122 \\
 & \text{c. } 3878 \text{ (correct answer)} \\
 & \text{d. } 3978
\end{array}
$$

If students subtract and get an answer other than any of those listed, they know they have to keep trying. In some cases, they can narrow the alternatives by estimating rather than knowing how to compute the answer.

It is critical to avoid ambiguity in completion items. In some subject areas this can be difficult because two or more answers will reasonably fit a fragment that does not specify the context. Here are two examples:

1. The Battle of Hastings was in_____. (Date or place?)

2. "H_2O" represents_____. ("Water" or "two parts hydrogen and one part oxygen"?)

MATCHING ITEMS

Matching items are commonly presented in the form of two lists, say A and B. For each item in List A, the student has to select one item in List B. The basis for choosing must be clearly explained in the directions. Matching items can be used to cover a large amount of content; that is, a large number of concepts should appear in the two lists. The primary cognitive skill being tested by matching exercises is recall.

A logistical difficulty with matching items is deciding on the number of concepts to put in each list. If both lists have the same number of items, and no item in B may be used more than once, then a student is able to answer at least one item by default. Or the student may be uncertain about one matching pair and become confused, switch a correct pair, and thus mismatch two items. Since the student cannot mismatch only one pair under these conditions, a "double jeopardy" situation has been created. It is possible to get around this problem by making List B contain more alternatives than the items in List A, and by allowing the alternatives in List B to be selected more than once as correct choices to match with items in List A.

Finally, each list of items to be matched should have no more than six items. Longer lists only confuse students and tend to measure perseverance rather than knowledge. If you find you have too many matched pairs for one question, divide the list into two questions.

SHORT ESSAY ITEMS

Short essay questions allow students to respond in their own words. The most common form for a short essay item includes a question for the student to answer. The answer may range from a sentence or two to a page of, say, 100 to 150 words.

The essay form can elicit a wide variety of responses, from giving definitions of terms to comparing and contrasting important concepts or events. These items are especially suited for assessing the ability of students to analyze, synthesize, and evaluate. Hence teachers may use them to appraise a student's progress in organizing data and applying concepts at the highest levels of instructional objectives. Of course, these items depend heavily on writing skills and the ability to phrase ideas.

One of the crucial faults teachers make in writing essay items is failing to clearly specify the approximate detail required in the response and its expected length. Stating how much weight an item has relative to the entire test is generally not sufficient to tell students how much detail must be incorporated in a response. Here's an illustration of this point:

Bad essay item: Discuss Canadian politics.
Improvement: In a 400-word essay, identify at least three ways in which the Canadian prime minister and the U.S. president differ in their obligations to their respective constituencies.

A short essay item, like all test items, should be linked directly to instructional objectives taught in the lessons. Consequently, the short essay item should contain specific information that students are to address. Some teachers seem reluctant to name the particulars that they wish the student to dicuss, as if they believe that recalling a word or phrase in the instructions is giving away too much information. But if recall of a name is what a teacher is attempting to measure, then there are other, more suitable forms of test items to use.

Short essay items have a number of advantages in addition to letting students state ideas in their own words. Essay items are not susceptible to correct guesses. They can be used to measure creative abilities, such as writing talent or imagination in constructing hypothetical events. Short essay items may require students to combine several concepts in their response in order to measure their global perspective of the topic.

On the negative side is the problem of reliability in scoring essay responses. Some studies demonstrate that independent marking of the same essay response by several teachers results in appraisals ranging from excellent to a failing grade. This gross difference in evaluations indicates a wide range of marking criteria and standards among teachers of similar backgrounds (Lindeman and Merenda, 1979).

A second drawback of essay items is that essay responses take considerable time to evaluate. The time a teacher might have saved by writing one essay item instead of several other kinds of items must be paid back when grading the essays.

Here are some additional suggestions for writing short essay items:

1. Match items with the instructional objectives.
2. Write a response to the item before you give the test to estimate the time students will need to respond. About four times the teacher's time is a fair gauge. (Model responses are discussed in the next section.)
3. Do not use such general directives in an item as "discuss," "give your opinion about . . . ," "tell all you know about. . . ." Rather, carefully choose specific response verbs such as "compare," "contrast," "identify," "list and define," and "explain the difference."

EVALUATING SHORT ESSAY ITEMS

After writing a short essay item—and clearly specifying the content that is to be included in the response—you must have a clear idea of how you will mark various pieces of a student's response. Of course, you want to use the same standards and criteria for all students' responses to that item.

The first step is to write a model response or a

detailed outline of the essential elements students are being directed to include in their responses. You will compare students' responses to this model.

If you intend to use evaluative comments but no letter grades, your outline or model will serve as a guide for pointing out to students omissions and errors in their responses, as well as the good points of their answers. If you are using letter grades to make the essays, you will compare elements of students' responses with the contents of your model and give suitable credit to responses that match the relative weights of elements in the model.

If possible, you should ask a colleague to assess the validity of the elements and their weights in your model response. Going a bit further and having the colleague apply the model criteria to one or more student responses could increase the reliability of your marking.

One issue relating to essay tests is whether and how much to count grammar, spelling, and other technical features. If you do count these, give students separate grades in content and in mechanics so that they will know the basis on which their work was evaluated.

PROBLEM-SOLVING ITEMS

In many subjects, such as mathematics and the physical and social sciences, instructional objectives include the development of skills in problem solving. Many academic disciplines have specific and unique procedures for problem solving. Unlike some school tasks with rigid procedures and right or wrong answers, problem solving involves organizing, selecting, and applying complex procedures that have at least several important steps or components. It is important to appraise the students' work in each of these steps or components.

Here is a seventh-grade-level mathematical problem and a seventh-grader's response to it. In the discussion of evaluating problem solving to follow, the essential components are described in specific terms, but they can be applied to all disciplines.

Problem:

Suppose two gamblers are playing a game in which the loser must pay an amount equal to what the other gambler has at the time. Now, if Player A won the first and third games, and Player B won the second game, and they finished the three games with $12 each, with how much money did each begin the first game?

A Student's Response:

After game	A had	B had
3	$12.00	$12.00
2	6.00	18.00
1	15.00	9.00
In the beginning	$ 7.50	$16.50

When I started with Game 1, I guessed and guessed but I couldn't make it come out to 12 and 12. Then I decided to start at Game 3 and work backwards. It worked!

How may we objectively evaluate such a response?

EVALUATING PROBLEM SOLVING

As should be done when evaluating short essay items, a plan to appraise problem-solving responses should begin by writing either a model response or, perhaps more practically, an outline of the essential components or procedures involved in problem solving. As with essays, problem-solving responses may take several different yet valid approaches. The outline must be flexible enough to accommodate all valid possibilities.

In problem solving there are several important components that fit most disciplines. These include understanding the problem to be solved, attacking the problem systematically, and arriving at a reasonable answer. The student's response to the mathematics problem described previously includes each of these. Following is a detailed list of elements common to most problem solving. Such a list can guide the evaluation of a student's problem-solving abilities. In the blank spaces to the right of the list, a teacher can indicate weightings appropriate to each element.

Problem-Solving Evaluation Elements:

1. Problem organization
   a. Representation by table, graph, chart, etc.
   _____
   b. Representation fits the problem _____
   c. Global understanding of the problem
   _____

2. Procedures (mathematical: trial-and-error, working

backwards, experimental process, empirical induction)

    a. A viable procedure was attempted _____

    b. Procedure was carried to a final solution _____

    c. Computation (if any) was correct _____

3. Solution (mathematical: a table, number, figure, graph, etc.)

    a. Answer was reasonable _____

    b. Answer was checked _____

    c. Answer was correct _____

4. Logic specific to the detail or application of the given information was sound _____

This or a similar method of evaluation permits students to see their strengths and weaknesses at using the steps expected in such subjects as science, mathematics, business, and social studies. The evaluation thus becomes an important teaching tool.

Partial Credit. If you wish to give partial credit for an answer that contains correct elements, or want to inform students about the value of their responses, you must devise ways to do this consistently from student to student. The following points offer some guidance:

1. Write model responses before giving partial credit for such work as essay writing, mathematical problem solving, laboratory assignments, or any work that you evaluate according to the quality of its various stages.

2. Tell students in sufficient detail the meaning of the grades you give in order to communicate the value of the work.

    Weightings or evaluative statements may be made regarding the most important aspects of the student's work. The following examples illustrate outlines of exemplary student work from mathematics and social studies or literature.

From mathematics. Students are given this problem:

In a single-elimination tennis tournament 40 players are to play for the singles championship. Determine how many matches must be played.

Evaluation

    a. Evidence that the student understood the prob-

lem; demonstrated by depicting the problem with a graph, table, chart, equation, etc. (3 points)

    b. The use of a method for solving the problem that had potential for yielding a correct solution—for example, systematic trial-and-error, empirical induction, elimination, working backward. (5 points)

    c. Generalization to other problems of this kind. (1 point)

    d. Arrival at a correct solution. (3 points)

The four components in the evaluation were assigned points according to the weight the teacher judged each to be worth in the context of the course of study and the purpose of the test. Teachers can give full credit for a correct answer even if all the work is not shown in the response, provided they know that students can do the work in their heads.

From social studies or literature. Students are asked to respond with a 100-word essay to this item:

Compare and contrast the development of Eskimo and Navajo tools on the basis of the climates in which these two peoples live.

Evaluation

    a. The response gives evidence of specific and accurate recall of the climates in which Eskimos and Navajos live (1 point) and of Eskimo and Navajo tools. (1 point)

    b. The essay develops with continuity of thought and logic (3 points)

    c. An accurate rationale is provided for the use of the various tools in the respective climates of Eskimos' and Navajos' lands. (3 points)

    d. An analysis comparing and contrasting the similarities and differences between the two groups and their tool development is given. (8 points)

    e. The response concludes with a summary and closure. (1 point)

These two examples should suggest ways to evaluate items in other subject areas as well. Giving partial credit for much of the work students do certainly results in a more complete evaluation of student progress than marking the work merely right or wrong. The examples show how to organize an "objective" style for evaluating work that does not lend itself to the simple forms of multiple-choice, true-false, completion, and matching items. Points do not have to be used to evaluate components of the responses. In many situations some kind of evaluative descriptors might be more meaningful. Evaluative descriptors are statements describing strong and weak features of a response to an item, a question, or a project. In the mathematics example, a teacher's evaluative descriptor for (a) might read "You have *drawn an excellent chart showing that you understand the meaning of the problem,* and that is very good, but it seems *you were careless* when you entered several important numbers in your chart."

CONGRUENCE BETWEEN TEST ITEMS AND INSTRUCTIONAL OBJECTIVES

Once you have written items corresponding to your table of specifications, look over the test in its entirety and evaluate it against the following standards:

1. Do the items emphasize the same things you emphasized in day-to-day instruction?

2. Has an important area of content or any objective been overlooked or underemphasized?

3. Does the test cover all levels of instructional objectives included in the lessons?

4. Does the language of the items correspond to the language and reading level you used in the lessons?

5. Is there a reasonable balance between what the items measure and the amount of time that will be required for students to develop a response?

6. Did you write model answers or essential component outlines for the short essay items? Does the weighting of each item reflect its relative value among all the other items?

Evaluation restricted to information acquired from paper-and-pencil tests provides only certain kinds of information about children's progress in school. Other sources and strategies for appraisal of student work must be used, including checklists, interviews, classroom simulations and role-playing activities, and anecdotal records. To do this systematically, you may keep a journal or log to record concise and cogent evaluative information on each student throughout the school year.

ALTERNATIVES TO TRADITIONAL TESTS

In recent years there has been a movement away from traditional paper-and-pencil testing toward forms of testing that focus more on what students can do. For example, many teachers maintain portfolios of student writings that show the development of a composition from first draft to final product (Wolf, 1989). Students may be asked to indicate their learning in more "authentic" ways. For example, ninth-graders might be asked to conduct an oral history by reading about some recent event or issue and interviewing the people involved. The quality of the oral histories, done over a period of weeks, would indicate the degree of the students' mastery of the social studies concepts involved (Wiggins, 1989). A model for this type of "exhibition of mastery" assessment model (Sizer, 1984) is the doctoral thesis, an extended project required for Ph.D.'s that is intended to show not only what students *know,* but what they can *do* (Archibald and Newmann, 1988).

GRADING AND EVALUATING

One of the most perplexing and often controversial tasks a teacher faces is grading student work (Kirschenbaum et al., 1971; Aiken, 1983). Is grading necessary? Research on pass-fail courses at the college level (Gold et al., 1971; Hales et al., 1971) indicates that students do perform considerably better under graded than under pass-fail systems. Other forms of evaluation may be superior to grades, but it is clear that *some* form of summative student evaluation is necessary, and at the moment grading of one kind or another is the predominant form used in American schools.

Chapter 14: Student Evaluation: Tests and Grades

According to a study conducted by Burton (1983), primary, intermediate, and secondary school teachers view the *purpose* of grading differently. More than half (52 percent) of the primary grade teachers in the study said that their main reason for giving grades was that the school district required it; the evaluative and other functions of grades were not most important in their view. Furthermore, many of the primary teachers tended to blame grading practices on the college systems. In contrast, middle school and high school teachers listed "to inform students" as the most important reason for grading. They cited letter grading as a "service" to students and said that teachers "owed" it to them as part of their education.

As for methods used to assign grades, about as many elementary school teachers used numerical scores to give overall grades in school work as depended on "their own professional judgments." Elementary teachers also listed student participation and enthusiasm as an important "second" criterion for grading. By comparison, about 85 percent of the middle and high school teachers said they assign grades according to paper-and-pencil test results (Burton, 1983).

Grading Criteria

There are many sets of grading criteria, perhaps as many variations as there are teachers who assign grades. But regardless of the level of school they teach in, teachers generally agree on the need to explain the meaning of grades they give students (Burton, 1983). Grades should communicate at least the relative value of a student's work in a class. They should also help students understand better what is expected of them and how they might improve.

For teachers and schools that use letter grades, there are some general meanings attached to the letters. The popular interpretations are:

A = superior; exceptional; outstanding attainment

B = very good, but not superior; above average

C = competent, but not remarkable work or performance

D = minimum passing, but weaknesses are indicated

F = failure to pass; serious weaknesses demonstrated

When students receive grades, they should also be given an explanation of what each grade means. Policies regarding grading can differ from school to school and grade to grade.

Assigning Letter Grades

All school districts have a policy or common practice for assigning report card grades. Most use A–B–C–D–F or A–B–C–D–E letter grades, but many (particularly at the elementary level) use various versions of outstanding–satisfactory–unsatisfactory. Some simply report percentage grades. The criteria upon which grades are based vary enormously from district to district. Secondary schools usually give one grade for each subject taken, but most elementary schools and some secondary schools include ratings on effort or behavior as well as on performance.

The criteria for giving letter grades may be specified by a school administration, but most often grading criteria are set by individual teachers using very broad guidelines. In practice, few teachers could get away with either giving half their students A's or with failing too many students, but between these two extremes teachers may have considerable leeway.

Absolute Grading Standards
Preestablished performance criteria
required for different grades

Relative Grading Standard
A system of allocating grades to
students on the basis of their
positions in a group or class

Absolute Grading Standards.   Grades may be given according to absolute or relative standards. **Absolute grading standards** might consist of preestablished percentage scores required for a given grade, as in the following example:

Grade	% Correct
A	90–100%
B	80–89%
C	70–79%
D	60–69%
F	Less than 60%

In another form of absolute standards, called criterion-referenced grading, the teacher looks at a test and decides in advance what performance constitutes outstanding (A), above-average (B), average (C), below-average (D), and inadequate (F) mastery of the instructional objective.

Absolute percentage standards have one important disadvantage. This is that student scores may depend on the difficulty of the tests they are given. For example, on a true-false test a student can pass (if a passing grade is 60 percent) by knowing only 20 percent of the answers and guessing on the rest (getting 50 percent of the remaining 80 percent of the items by chance). On a difficult test of, for example, mathematics problem solving that uses a completion (fill-in-the-blank) format where guessing is impossible, 60 percent could be a respectable score. For this reason, use of absolute percentage criteria should be tempered with some degree of criterion-referenced standards (if school policies allow it). That is, a teacher might use a 60–70–80–90 percent standard in most circumstances, but establish (and announce to students) tougher standards for a test students are likely to find easy, and easier standards for a test on which a moderate percent-correct score might indicate adequate mastery of a concept.

Relative Grading Standards.   A **relative grading standard** exists whenever a teacher gives students grades according to the students' rank in their class or grade. The classic form of relative grading is specifying what percentage of students will be given A's, B's, and so on. This practice is called "grading on the curve" because it typically allocates grades to students on the basis of their position on a "normal curve" of scores, as follows (Cureton, 1971):

Grade	% Of Students
A	7
B	24
C	38
D	24
F	7

Figure 14.1 gives an example of grading on the curve, using a 7–24–38–24–7 percent grade distribution. In this class of thirty-two students we can allow for two or three A's (7% of 32 is 2.24), seven or eight B's, and so on. The scores are listed from

FIGURE 14.1

Step 1: Figure how many students will get each letter grade.

A. Total number of students equals 32

B. GRADE	% of STUDENTS (Based on normal curve)	No. of STUDENTS
A	7%	2–3
B	24%	7–8
C	38%	12–13
D	24%	7–8
F	7%	2–3

Step 2: Use tallies to note distribution of grades. Count tallies and distribute grades according to normal curve.

SCORE

30	II	(3)	} A
29	I		
28	IIII		
27	II	(8)	} B
26	II		
25	ШH		
24	III	(13)	} C
23	ШH		
22	II		
21	I		
20			
19	II	(6)	} D
18			
17	I		
16			
15			
14	I		
13			} F
12		(2)	
11	I		
10 or less			

Example of Grading on the Curve

When teachers distribute letter grades according to a normal curve, they should start by figuring the number of students to be given each grade. Then they should use tally marks to note the distribution of grades. When a normal curve is used, C will be the grade most frequently given.

top to bottom, and tallies are placed to indicate how many students got each score. Then we count the tallies from the top to indicate which scores will be assigned each grade.

Grading on the curve and other relative grading standards have the advantage of placing students' scores in relation to one another, without regard to the difficulty of a particular test. However, relative grading standards have serious drawbacks. One is that because they hold the number of A's and B's constant, students in high-track classes (in schools using tracking) must get much higher scores to earn an A or B than students in low-track classes—a situation that might be good for the motivation of some students but one that is likely to be widely seen as unfair. This problem is often dealt with by giving relatively more A's and B's in high-track classes than in average or low-track ones. Another disadvantage of grading on the curve is that it creates competition among students; when one student earns an A, this diminishes the chances that others may do so. This can inhibit students from helping one another and can hurt social relations among classmates (see Ames et al., 1977).

Strict grading on the curve, as well as guidelines for numbers of A's and B's, has been disappearing in recent years. For one thing, there has been a general "grade

The tables are being turned as experts search for new ways to test teachers. Students might recognize the proposed methods as similar to the age-old classroom activity show and tell.

Lee Shulman, a Stanford University education professor who is developing the new teacher-testing methods, thinks he might be on to something. "There is a growing sense that there is something fundamentally wrong with the usual standardized tests and that something else will replace them," he said. "We think we've got an alternative."

The "usual standardized tests" to which he is referring are the multiple choice tests that teachers take to receive their licenses. These tests measure general knowledge and familiarity with teaching methods. Beyond that, the traditional method of teacher evaluation is for a principal or senior teacher to observe a teacher at work in the classroom. These methods have drawn fire as too narrow (in the case of the standardized tests) or too time-consuming (in the case of the in-class evaluations).

Professor Shulman likens the new method of teacher evaluation to the portfolio of an artist or a writer. Teachers who took part in a trial of the evaluation technique submitted examples of their skills in such teaching situations as working with entire classes, small groups, and individuals. The portfolio examples included written logs, photographs, videotapes, and samples of student work.

Now the challenge for the Stanford researchers is to find a way to rate the quality of the portfolios. The hurdles are to maintain objectivity and keep costs down. Those factors are the chief advantages of standardized tests. The factors of objectivity and cost present greater hurdles when educators consider using portfolios rather than standardized tests to rate the achievement of students.

Spurring the development of new evaluation techniques is a plan by the National Board of Professional Teaching Standards to certify elementary and high school teachers. The board has released guidelines for such certification and hopes to begin awarding the credentials in 1993. The goal of the certification program is to boost the image of teachers, to increase salaries, and to draw brighter young people into the profession. The board also hopes that board-certified teachers could break out of the traditional "flat" teaching career path by taking on additional tasks and responsibilities.

From Edward B. Fiske, "Lessons," New York Times, August 9, 1989, p. B8. Edward B. Fiske, "Lessons," New York Times," July 19, 1989, p. B6.

inflation," so that more A's and B's are given now than in the past; C is no longer the expected average grade, but often indicates below-average performance. At present, the most common approach to grading involves teachers looking at student scores on a given test, taking into account the difficulty of the test and the overall performance of the class, and assigning grades in such a way that about the "right number" of students earn A's and B's and the "right number" fail. Teachers vary considerably in their estimates of what these "right numbers" should be, but within a school there is often an unspoken norm about how many students should be given A's and how many should fail. New teachers may seek guidance from experienced teachers about the school's common practice with regard to grading. Many teachers set grading criteria by constructing a table of tallies like that shown in Figure 14.1 and assigning grades by looking for "clumps" of students at, above, and below the class average—again, taking into account the approximate number of A's and B's they want to give, how difficult the test was, and perhaps other factors.

Other Approaches to Grading. Several other approaches to grading are used in conjunction with innovative instructional approaches. In contract grading (see

Chapter 10) students negotiate a particular amount of work or level of performance they will achieve to receive a given grade. For example, a student might agree to complete five book reports of a given length in a marking period to receive an A. **Mastery grading,** an important part of mastery learning (see Chapter 9), involves establishing a standard of mastery, such as 80 or 90 percent correct, on a given test. All students who achieve that standard receive an A; students who do not achieve it the first time receive corrective instruction and then can take the test again to try to achieve the mastery criterion. Individualized instructional programs (see Chapter 9) often use **continuous progress grading,** in which students' evaluations depend on how many units they complete in a given time period, regardless of the level of the units. Sometimes continuous progress evaluation involves simply reporting to students and parents the specific skills students have mastered, without any indication of how the student is doing in relation to other students.

Mastery Grading
Grading procedure used in mastery learning, in which all students who achieve the mastery criterion can earn the highest available grade

Continuous Progress Grading
Evaluation based on the number of units completed in a given time period

■ **Stop and Think**
Critics of the United States education system complain about "grade inflation," which occurs when teachers give too many A's and not enough F's. Do you see this as a problem? If so, how should educators respond?

Report Card Grades

Most schools give report cards four or six times per year, that is, every nine or six weeks (Chansky, 1975). Report card grades are most often derived from some combination of the following factors:

- Average scores on quizzes and tests
- Average scores on homework
- Average scores on seatwork
- "Class participation" (academic behaviors in class, answers to class questions, etc.)
- Deportment (classroom behavior, tardiness, attitude)
- Effort

One important principle in report card grading is that grades should never be a surprise to students. Students should always know how their grades will be computed, whether classwork and homework are included, whether class participation and effort are taken into account. Being clear about standards for grading helps avoid many complaints about unexpectedly low grades and, more importantly, lets students know exactly what they must do to improve their grades.

Another important principle is that grades should be private. There is no need for students to know one another's grades, and making grades public only invites invidious comparisons among students (see Simpson, 1981).

Finally, it is important to restate that grades are only one method of student evaluation. Written evaluations that add information to that provided by the grade can provide useful information to parents and students (Burton, 1983).

Ray Mason is a beginning teacher in a large urban high school. During the teachers' preschool planning period two weeks before classes begin in August, he meets with Toni Sue Garrick, the social studies chairwoman, in her classroom.

TONI SUE: So, that's what I generally do in the area of discipline, Ray. I'd say that the most important thing to remember is that an ounce of prevention is worth a pound of cure. Don't let things build up; nip them in the bud.

RAY: Thanks, Toni, I'll remember that. Do you have another minute to tell me about the school's grading policy?

TONI SUE: Sure. Where do you want to begin?

RAY: Well, we do have a policy, I assume?

TONI SUE: I guess you could say so. If you look on the report cards you'll notice that 94 to 100 is an A, 88 to 94 is a B, and so forth. Anything below 70 is failing.

RAY: What if no one gets in the 94 to 100 range on a test?

TONI SUE: Then you either don't give any A's, if you think the test was fair, or you adjust the scale by adding on points to every student's score.

RAY: OK. Are we supposed to give a certain percentage of A's, a certain percentage of B's, and so forth?

TONI SUE: There's no rigid policy, but if you give too many A's and B's that could become a problem.

RAY: How many are too many?

TONI SUE: Well, certainly there should be more B's than A's, and more C's than either A's or B's. I guess you could say that if you try to approximate the normal bell-shaped curve idea in a general, flexible way you would be on solid ground.

RAY: Then the percentage of D's should roughly correspond to the percentage of B's, and the F's should correspond to the A's?

TONI SUE: Well, not necessarily. I usually have fewer D's and F's than I do A's and B's. But then again, it all depends on the ability level of the students. In an advanced placement course like European history, I seldom give D's and F's. However, in the sophomore-level world history course I usually end up giving a few less D's and F's than A's and B's, but they fairly closely approximate one another.

RAY: Have there been any big problems with grading differences among teachers?

TONI SUE: Well, I remember a few years back when a young teacher gave almost all A's and B's. It didn't come to light until the students began comparing their grades at report card time. Some other teachers and parents were quite upset.

RAY: What happened?

TONI SUE: Oh, we—the administration, that is—talked with the young woman and smoothed things over. She was very bright and easy to work with. I think she's at another school now and is doing a fine job.

SUMMARY AND REVIEW OF OBJECTIVES

Reasons for Evaluation. Evaluations serve many purposes, including motivating students to learn, informing students about their work, guiding teachers in lesson planning, and informing parents about their children's progress in school.

Teachers should try to match the type of evaluation to the goal of evaluation. For example, formative quizzes can be used during instruction to guide the pace and content of lessons and to motivate students to study. Summative tests after instruction can measure student skills and knowledge. In addition, teachers must choose in each situation whether it is most appropriate to base the evaluation on the degree of mastery of a specific skill (criterion-referenced evaluation) or on the level of proficiency relative to other students (norm-referenced evaluation).

RAY: I see. Toni, in my history classes I plan to give weekly quizzes, mid-unit and unit exams, and to assign individual and small-group projects. I was wondering whether I should give objective or essay exams?

TONI SUE: I'd recommend objective exams to offset the subjectivity involved in grading individual and group projects. While good objective tests are harder to write, they are certainly worth the effort when it comes to defending the scores and grades. Students and parents have a hard time arguing grading bias, favoritism, or subjectivity when you give objective tests. Also, I figure that objective tests help prepare the kids to take standardized achievement tests. It seems that everyone is concerned with increasing the overall performance of our students on those tests, and I think we should do everything we can as teachers to help.

RAY: I see what you mean. OK, one more thing. I guess I'm a little afraid of some of the parents and the fact that some of their children will be receiving D's and F's in my class.

TONI SUE: I know what you mean. Parents can be difficult and confrontive at times. I guess I've found that if the students and parents think you're fair, you'll have few problems. Spell out very clearly what you expect from the students and what the grading procedures are. And, if you do choose to use objective tests, I don't think you'll have any problem defending yourself. If you run into an unreasonable parent,

well, that's what we're here for. We'll be glad to sit in on parent conferences with you. After all, our society was founded on competition—and competition means failing sometimes as well as succeeding. Our kids have to learn how to deal with failure as well as success. And parents should understand that, too—but we still may have to remind them of it sometimes. Don't worry, Ray. You'll do fine. It will all work out.

RAY: Thanks, Toni Sue! I really appreciate your support and guidance.

QUESTIONS

1. What kind of evaluation strategy has Toni Sue described to Ray? How does it differ from a criterion-referenced approach? What are its strengths and weaknesses?
2. How valid are Toni Sue's arguments concerning objective testing? What are the strengths and weaknesses of objective and subjective tests?
3. How valid are Toni Sue's arguments regarding competition and failure?
4. If you were put on a committee to evaluate and revise this high school's evaluation and grading policies and procedures, what would you recommend and why?

Linking Tests to Instructional Objectives. In developing tests, the content of the test should match that of classroom lessons, the test should sample the content students expect it to sample, and reliable scoring should be possible.

Writing Good Test Questions. Some guidelines for multiple-choice items are: (1) make the stem sufficiently specific to stand on its own; (2) avoid complicated sentences in the stem; (3) try to avoid overuse of "no-exception" items such as "always" and "never"; (4) avoid making the correct choice significantly longer or shorter than others; (5) generally avoid "none of the above" and "all of the above" answers; (6) discuss the items with students after the test; and (7) do not include transparently absurd answers.

True-false items are sometimes useful for the comparison of two alternatives, but have the disadvantage of a 50 percent guessing probability. Accordingly, multiple-choice formats are generally preferable.

Important considerations for writing short essay questions include matching items with instructional objectives, providing clear indications of content and length of the expected response, and writing a response to the item before giving the test to estimate the time students will need to complete it. Problem-solving evaluation elements include problem organization, procedures, solution, and logic.

Assigning Letter Grades. Grading criteria can be based on absolute grading standards (a type of criterion-referenced grading) or on relative standards (a form of norm-referencing). Grading on a curve is an example of a relative grading standard. Other approaches to grading include mastery grading systems and continuous progress grading.

STUDY QUESTIONS

1. Education researchers have suggested that seven criteria must be satisfied if evaluations are to increase effort. Identify at least *four* of those criteria.
2. Match the following types of evaluations with the correct descriptions.
   —— Norm-referenced
   —— Criterion-referenced
   —— Formative
   —— Summative
   a. Follows conclusion of instructional unit as a final test of knowledge.
   b. Measures performance against standard of mastery.
   c. Given during instruction; can guide lesson presentations.
   d. Measures achievement of one student relative to others.
3. The purpose of devising a table of specifications in testing is to
   a. indicate the types of learning to be assessed for different instructional objectives.
   b. indicate the make-up of a test with regard to number of multiple-choice items, essay questions, etc.
   c. define clear scoring criteria for each essay or open-ended question used in a test.
   d. compare the students' scores on a standardized test to those of the national sample.
   e. define the normal curve percentile ranks for different letter grades.
4. Which of the following is recommended in constructing multiple-choice items?

   a. Making the stem short and general, such as "Testing is:"
   b. Frequently using "none of the above" as a distractor
   c. Listing choices horizontally rather than vertically
   d. Making distractors plausible
   e. Using numbers, wherever feasible, instead of letters in listing distractors

5. Match the following grading strategies with the correct descriptions. (One description does not apply to any.)
   —— Contract grading
   —— Mastery grading
   —— Relative grading standards
   a. Students' grades depend on their achievement relative to that of classmates.
   b. Students are assigned a group activity and are graded as a group.
   c. Students can contribute to the establishment of grading criteria.
   d. All students who reach a uniform level of proficiency get the highest grade.

Answers: 1. Evaluations are: important to students; soundly based on performances; applied consistently; judged on clear criteria; interpreted reliably; given frequently; challenging, but not overly difficult. 2. d, b, c, a 3. a 4. d 5. c, d, a

SUGGESTED READINGS

BERK, R. A. (Ed.) (1986) *Performance assessment: Methods and applications.* Baltimore, Md.: Johns Hopkins University Press.

BLOOM, B. S., HASTINGS, J. T. and MADAUS, G. F. (1971). *Handbook of formative and summative evaluation of student learning.* New York: McGraw-Hill.

CROOKS, T. (1988). The impact of classroom evaluation practices on students. *Review of Educational Research, 58,* 438–481.

EBEL, R. L. (1980). Evaluation of students: Implications for effective teaching. *Educational Evaluation and Policy Analysis, 2,* 47–51.

GRONLUND, N. D. (1982). *Constructing achievement tests* (3rd ed.) Englewood Cliffs, N.J.: Prentice-Hall.

LINDEMAN, R. H. and MERENDA, P. F. (1979). *Educational measurement.* Glenview, Ill.: Scott, Foresman.

NATRIELLO, G., and DORNBUSCH, S. M. (1984). *Teacher evaluative standards and student effort.* New York: Longman.

STIGGINS, R. (1987). Design and development of performance assessments. *Educational measurement: Issues and practices, 6* (3), 33–42.

Chapter 15

Using and Interpreting Standardized Tests

Chapter Outline

What Are Standardized Tests?
Uses of Standardized Tests
Selection and Placement
Diagnosis
Evaluation and Accountability

Types of Standardized Tests
Aptitude Tests
Achievement Tests

Interpreting Standardized Tests
Types of Scores
Validity, Reliability, and Bias
Theory into Practice: Interpreting Standardized
    Test Results

Selecting Standardized Tests
Why Are You Testing in the First Place?
The Uses of Standardized Tests in the Schools
Problems and Issues in Standardized Testing

Chapter Objectives

After reading this chapter on standardized testing, you should be able to:

- List three general purposes for which standardized tests are used in schools.

- Describe the differences between aptitude tests and achievement tests, and between norm-referenced tests and criterion-referenced tests.

- Interpret various types of scores used to report achievement on standardized tests, such as percentiles, grade equivalents, stanines, normal curve equivalents, and z-scores.

- Assess the validity of a standardized test in terms of content, predictive ability, and quality relative to other tests.

Standardized Tests
Tests that are usually commercially prepared for nationwide use to provide accurate and meaningful information on students' levels of performance relative to others at their age or grade levels

Norms
Standards derived from giving a test to a sample of people similar to those who will take the test and that can be used to interpret scores of future test takers

Do you remember taking SATs, ACTs, or other college entrance examinations? Did you ever wonder how those tests were constructed, what the scores meant, and to what degree your scores represented what you really knew or could really do?

The SATs and other college entrance examinations are examples of **standardized tests.** Unlike the teacher-made tests discussed in Chapter 14, a standardized test is typically given to thousands of students who are similar to those for whom the test is designed. This allows the test publisher to establish norms, or standards, against which any individual score can be compared. For example, if a representative national sample of fourth-graders had an average score of thirty-seven items correct on a fifty-item standardized test, then we might say that fourth-graders who score above thirty-seven are "above national norms" on this test, while those who score below thirty-seven are "below national norms."

Standardized tests of many kinds are being administered more and more frequently by schools at all levels. This chapter discusses how and why standardized tests are used, and how scores on these tests can be interpreted and applied to make important educational decisions.

WHAT ARE STANDARDIZED TESTS?

Standardized tests are usually used to provide a yardstick against which to compare individuals or groups of students that teacher-made tests cannot provide. For example, suppose a child's parents asked a teacher how their daughter is doing in math. The teacher says, "Fine, she got a score of 81 percent on our latest math test." For some purposes, this information would be adequate. But for others, we might want to know much more. How does 81 percent compare to the scores of other students in this class? How about other students in the school, the district, the state, or the whole country? In some contexts the score of 81 percent might help qualify the girl for a special program for the mathematically gifted; in others it might suggest the need for remedial instruction. Also, suppose the teacher found that the class averaged 85 percent correct on the math test. How is this class doing compared to other math classes or to students nationwide? A teacher-made test cannot yield this information.

Standardized tests are typically carefully constructed to provide accurate, meaningful information on students' levels of performance. Most often curriculum experts establish what students at a particular age should know about a subject or should be able to do. Then questions are written to assess the various skills or information students are expected to possess. The questions are tried out on various groups of students. Items that almost all students get right or almost all miss are usually dropped, as are items that students find unclear or confusing. Patterns of scores are carefully examined. If students who score well on most items do no better than lower-scoring students on a particular item, that item will probably be dropped.

Eventually a final test will be developed and given to a large selected group of students from all over the country. Usually attempts are made to ensure that this group resembles the larger population of students who will ultimately use the test. For example, a test of geometry for eleventh-graders might be given to a sampling of eleventh-graders in urban, rural, and suburban locations, in different regions of the country, in public as well as private schools, and to students with different levels of preparation in mathematics. This step establishes the **norms** for the test, which provide an indication of how an average student will score. Finally, a testing manual is prepared, explaining how the test is to be given, scored, and interpreted. This particular standardized test is now ready for general use.

USES OF STANDARDIZED TESTS

The test development process creates tests whose scores have meaning outside the confines of a particular classroom or school. These scores are used in a variety of ways. Explanations of some of the most important functions of standardized testing follow.

Selection and Placement

Standardized tests are often used to select students for entry or placement in specific programs. For example, the SATs (Scholastic Aptitude Test) or ACTs (American College Testing Program) you probably took in high school were used to help your college admissions board decide whether to accept you as a student. Similarly, admission to special programs for gifted and talented students might depend on standardized test scores. Standardized tests might also be used to decide whether to place students in special education programs or to assign students to "tracks" or ability groups. For example, high schools may use standardized tests to decide which students to place in "college preparatory," "general," or "vocational" programs, while elementary schools may use them to place students in reading groups (see Chapter 9 for between- and within-class ability grouping). Standardized tests are sometimes used to determine eligibility for grade-to-grade promotion, graduation from high school, or entry into an occupation.

Diagnosis

Often standardized tests are used to diagnose learning problems or strengths. For example, a student who is performing poorly in school might be given a battery of tests to determine whether the student has a learning disability or is mentally retarded. At the same time the testing might identify specific deficits in need of remediation. Diagnostic tests of reading skills are frequently used to identify a student's particular reading problem. For example, a diagnostic test might indicate that a student's decoding skills are fine but that his or her reading comprehension is poor.

Evaluation and Accountability

Perhaps the most common use of standardized testing is to evaluate the progress of students and the effectiveness of teachers and schools. For example, parents often want to know how their children are doing in comparison with what is expected of children at their grade level. Of course, standardized test scores are meaningful as evaluation only if used along with other information, such as students' actual performance in school and in other contexts. Many students who score poorly on standardized tests excel in school, college, or occupations; either they have trouble taking tests well or they have important skills that are not measured by such tests.

The use of standardized tests to assess teachers, schools, and districts has increased dramatically in recent years. Most states now have statewide testing programs, in which students at selected grade levels take standardized achievement tests and/or "minimum competency tests." Scores on these tests are used to evaluate the state's educational program as a whole, and to compare the performance of individual school districts, schools, and teachers. These comparisons go under the general heading of "accountability programs," and are described later in this chapter.

TYPES OF STANDARDIZED TESTS

Three kinds of standardized tests are commonly used in school settings: aptitude tests, norm-referenced achievement tests, and criterion-referenced achievement tests.

An **aptitude test** is designed to assess students' abilities. It is meant to predict the ability of students to learn or perform particular types of tasks rather than to measure how much the students have already learned. The most widely used aptitude tests measure general intellectual aptitude, but many other, more specific tests measure particular aptitudes such as mechanical or perceptual abilities or reading readiness. The SAT, for example, is meant to predict a student's aptitude for college studies. An aptitude test is successful to the degree that it predicts performance. For example, a reading readiness test given to kindergartners that did not accurately predict how well the students would read when they reached first or second grade would be of little use.

A norm-referenced achievement test, which was discussed in Chapter 14, is an assessment of a student's knowledge of a particular content area, such as mathematics, reading, or Spanish. It provides scores that can be compared with those of a representative group of students, and it is constructed to show differences among students. Typically, norm-referenced achievement tests assess some but not all of the skills taught in any one school. A norm-referenced achievement test cannot be too specific because it is designed for nationwide use even though the curricula for any given subject vary from district to district. For example, if some seventh graders learn about base-two arithmetic or Venn diagrams and others do not, then these topics would be unlikely to appear on a standardized mathematics tests.

A criterion-referenced achievement test also assesses a student's knowledge of subject matter, but rather than comparing the achievement of an individual student against national norms, it is designed to measure the degree to which the student has mastered certain well-specified skills. The information produced by a criterion-

The tests that Boy Scouts and Girl Scouts must pass to receive merit badges are examples of criterion-referenced achievement tests, which are designed to measure mastery of specific skills.

referenced test is quite specific: "Thirty-seven percent of Arkansas fifth-graders can fill in the names of the major Western European nations on an outline map" or "Ninety-three percent of twelfth-graders at Alexander Hamilton High School know that increasing the temperature of a gas in a closed container increases the gas's pressure." Sometimes criterion-referenced test scores are used to make comparisons from school to school or from district to district, but there is typically no representative "norming group" used. If a group of curriculum experts decides that every fifth-grader in Arkansas should be able to fill in an outline map of Western Europe, then the "norm" for that item is 100 percent; it is of less interest whether Arkansas fifth-graders score better or worse on this item than students in other states. What is more important is that, overall, students improve each year on this item.

While aptitude tests, norm-referenced achievement tests, and criterion-referenced tests are each distinct in theory, there is, in fact, considerable overlap among them. For example, school learning definitely affects students' aptitude test scores, and a student who scores well on one type of test will usually score well on another. In fact, many testing theorists claim that aptitude and achievement tests are so highly correlated that both should be considered achievement tests (see, for example, Sternberg and Detterman, 1986; Ebel, 1980a; Anastasi, 1981).

The following sections discuss the types of aptitude and achievement tests most often given in schools.

Aptitude Tests

General Intelligence Tests. The most common kind of aptitude tests given in school are tests of **intelligence,** or general aptitude for school learning. The intelligence quotient, or IQ, is the score most often associated with intelligence testing, but other types of scores are also used.

Intelligence tests are designed to provide a general indication of individuals' aptitudes in many areas of intellectual functioning. Intelligence itself is seen as the ability to deal with abstractions, to learn, and to solve problems (Estes, 1982; Snyderman and Rothman, 1987; Sternberg, 1982, 1986), and tests of intelligence focus on these skills. Intelligence tests give students a wide variety of questions to answer and problems to solve.

Intelligence tests are administered either to individuals or to groups. Tests administered to groups, such as the Otis-Lennon Mental Ability Tests, the Lorge-Thorndike Intelligence Tests, and the California Test of Mental Maturity, are often given to large groups of students as general assessments of intellectual aptitude. These tests are not as accurate or detailed as intelligence tests administered to people individually by trained psychologists, such as the Wechsler Intelligence Test for Children–Revised (WISC–R) or the Stanford-Binet. For example, when students are being assessed for possible placement in special education, an individually adminis- tered test (most often the WISC–R) is usually administered, along with other tests (for more on intelligence and its assessment, see Chapter 9).

Multifactor Aptitude Tests. One other form of the aptitude test that provides a breakdown of more specific skills is the **multifactor aptitude battery.** A number of such tests are available, with a range of content and emphases. They include scholastic abilities tests such as the SAT; a number of elementary and secondary school tests, such as the Differential Aptitude Test, the Cognitive Abilities Test, and the Test of Cognitive Skills; reading readiness tests, such as the Metropolitan Reading Readiness

Intelligence
General aptitude for learning, often measured by ability to deal with abstractions and to solve problems

Multifactor Aptitude Battery
Test that predicts ability to learn a variety of specific skills and types of knowledge

Achievement Battery
Standardized test that includes
several subtests designed to measure
knowledge of particular subjects

Test, and various developmental scales for preschool children. At a minimum, most of these tests provide not only overall aptitude scores but also subscores for verbal and nonverbal aptitudes. Often subscores are even more finely divided to describe more specific abilities.

Achievement Tests

While aptitude tests focus on knowledge acquired both in school and out, achievement tests focus on skills or abilities that are traditionally taught in the schools. In general, standardized achievement tests fall into one of four categories: achievement batteries, diagnostic tests, single-subject achievement measures, and criterion-referenced achievement measures.

Achievement Batteries.   Standardized **achievement batteries,** such as the California Achievement Test, the Iowa Tests of Basic Skills, the Comprehensive Test of Basic Skills, the Stanford Achievement Test, and the Metropolitan Achievement Tests, are used to measure individual or group achievement in a variety of subject areas. These "survey" batteries include several small tests, each on a different subject area, and are usually administered to a group over a period of several days. Many of the achievement batteries available for use in the schools are similar in construction and content. However, because of slight differences between the tests in the instructional objectives and subject matter sampled within the subtests, it is important before selecting a particular test to examine it carefully for its match with a specific school curriculum and for its appropriateness relative to school goals. Often achievement batteries have several forms for various age or grade levels so that achievement can be monitored over a period of several years. Table 15.1 shows testing time devoted to various subskills for a number of standardized tests available in 1981 for use in the third grade. The table shows clear differences between the content covered in each. For example, note that the California Achievement Test and the Iowa Tests of Basic Skills devoted considerable time to reference and study skills, while the Metropolitan Achievement Tests and Stanford Achievement Test did not assess these skills at all.

Diagnostic Tests.   Diagnostic tests differ from achievement batteries in that they generally focus on a specific content area and emphasize those skills thought to be important for mastery of that subject matter. Diagnostic tests produce much more detailed information than other achievement tests. For example, a standardized mathematics test often produces scores for math computations, concepts, and applications, whereas a diagnostic test would give scores on more specific skills, such as adding decimals or solving two-step word problems. Diagnostic tests are mostly available for reading and mathematics, and are intended to show specific areas of strength and weakness in these skills. The results can be used to guide remedial instruction, or to structure learning experiences for students who are expected to learn the skill.

Specific Subject Achievement Tests.   Most classroom tests for assessing skills in specific subjects are made up by teachers. However, schools can purchase specific subject achievement tests for almost any subject. A problem with many of these tests is that unless they are tied to the particular curriculum and instructional strategies used in the classroom, they may not adequately represent the content that has been taught. If standardized achievement tests are considered for evaluating learning in

TABLE 15.1

SKILLS COVERED IN ELEMENTARY SCHOOL ACHIEVEMENT TESTS

Four achievement batteries used in third grade differ in the percent of time devoted to various subskills. Teachers and school administrators should select achievement tests that closely match instructional objectives in their schools.

Learning Areas	% Testing Time			
	California Achievement Test	Iowa Tests of Basic Skills	Metropolitan Achievement Tests (Survey)	Stanford Achievement Test
Reading comprehension	20.8%	17.2%	21.0%	10.9%
Vocabulary	6.0	6.1	0.0	7.8
Language	18.4	16.4	21.0	17.1
Spelling	4.2	4.9	0.0	6.2
Fundamentals of arithmetic	14.9	18.4	21.0	17.1
Arithmetic reasoning	20.8	10.2	0.0	10.9
Reference/study skills	14.9	26.6	0.0	0.0
Listening comprehension	0.0	0.0	0.0	10.9
Social studies	0.0	0.0*	18.4	9.3
Science	0.0	0.0*	18.4	9.3
Total working time (minutes)	168	244	190	320

*Optional subtests are available.

Note that these data may not reflect current forms of the various tests.

Source: Ahmann and Glock, 1981, p. 297.

specific areas, the content of the test should be closely examined for its match with the curriculum, instruction, and general teaching goals.

Criterion-Referenced Tests. Criterion-referenced tests differ from norm-referenced standardized tests in a number of ways, most notably in regard to scoring. Such tests can take the form of a survey battery, a diagnostic test, or a single-subject test. In contrast to norm-referenced tests that are designed for use by schools with varying curricula, criterion-referenced tests are often constructed around a well-defined set of objectives. For many tests, these objectives can be chosen by the school district, building administrator, or teacher, to be applied in a specific situation. The items on the test are selected to match specific instructional objectives, often with three to five items measuring each objective. For this reason, these tests are sometimes referred to as objective-referenced tests. Criterion-referenced tests also differ from norm-referenced tests in that measurement with the criterion-referenced test often focuses on students' performance with regard to specific objectives rather than on the test as a whole. Therefore the tests can indicate which objectives individual students or the class as a whole have mastered. Test results can be used to guide future instruction or remedial activities.

Finally, criterion-referenced tests differ from other achievement tests in the way they are scored and how the results are interpreted. With criterion-referenced tests, it is generally the score for each objective that is important. Results could show, for example, how many students can multiply two digits by two digits or how many can write a business letter correctly. Moreover, students' scores on the total test or on objectives are interpreted with respect to some criterion of adequate performance independent of group performance. Examples of criterion-referenced tests include tests for drivers and pilots, when we want to know who can drive or fly, not who is in the top 20 percent of drivers or pilots.

Score reports for criterion-referenced tests are frequently in the form of the number of items that the student got correct on each objective. From these data, the teacher can gauge whether the student has mastered the objective.

When criterion-referenced tests are used for making decisions about mastery of a subject or topic, some procedure must be employed to determine the test score cutoff point for mastery. Most procedures for the establishment of a **cutoff score** rely on the professional judgment of teachers and other school personnel. Qualified professionals examine each item in a test and judge the probability that a student with an acceptable level of proficiency would get the item correct. They then base the cutoff score for mastery or proficiency on these probabilities. See Berk (1986) for more on the setting of performance standards for criterion-referenced tests.

■ **Stop and Think**

A relatively small number of publishers and educators control the development, marketing, and scoring of the standardized tests that are so critical to student success. However, only by having uniform testing and scoring can such tests be termed "standardized" and used to compare students across the country and, indeed, around the world. What are the advantages and disadvantages of the current system of standardized testing?

INTERPRETING STANDARDIZED TESTS

After students take a standardized test, one of two things happens. The tests are sent for computer scoring to the central office or the test publisher or, less often, teachers or other school staff score the tests themselves, consulting test manuals to interpret the scores. In either case, the students' raw scores (the number correct on each subtest) are translated into one or more **derived scores,** such as percentiles, grade equivalents, or normal curve equivalents, which relate the students' scores to those of the group on which the test was normed. Each of these statistics has its own meaning, described in the following sections.

Types of Scores

Percentiles. A **percentile score,** or percentile rank (sometimes abbreviated in test reports as %ILE), indicates the percentage of students in the norming group who scored lower than a particular score. For example, students who achieve at the median for the norming group (that is, equal numbers of students scored better or worse than that score) would have a percentile rank of 50, because their scores exceeded those of 50 percent of the students in the norming group. If you ranked a group of thirty students from bottom to top on test scores, the twenty-fifth student from the bottom would score in the 83rd percentile ($25/30 \times 100 = 83.3$).

Grade Equivalents. **Grade-equivalent scores** relate students' scores to the average scores obtained by students at a particular grade level. Let's say a norming group

Standardized Test Scores

Take this two-question test to gauge your understanding of how standardized test scores are reported:

1. True or False. To say a student is reading *at grade level* is to say the student has mastered reading skills appropriate for that grade.

2. True or False. College students whose SAT scores match the average for their college class can assume that half their fellow students have scores above them and half have scores below them.

Common sense suggests these statements are true. In reality, both are false—and each reveals some of the obfuscation surrounding standardized test scores.

The reports by school districts of the percent of students reading at or above grade level is a closely watched measure of school success. A report by the Knoxville, Tenn., schools might say, for example, that 80 percent of fourth graders are reading at or above grade level. A Knoxville parent might then assume that little Johnny and most of his classmates are almost geniuses—or at least a bit ahead of teacher expectations.

Unfortunately, the parents would be misreading the test results. The concept of *at grade level* has little relationship to what the students *should* know. Rather, the score that defines *at grade level* is a score statistically in the middle of scores earned by students in a particular grade. To be *at grade level,* then, is to be average among one's peers, not to have met some specified level of mastery.

The confusion surrounding these statistics are convenient for school officials. Not only do the scores not report what common sense might suggest, but with test norms revised very infrequently—say every ten years or so—the accuracy of the "average" score is even questionable. As schools emphasized basic skills and better test scores during the 1980s, their tests scores crept up in relation to norms set early in the decade. Fewer schools could have boasted of steady improvement if the tests had been renormed.

Lest anyone think that only elementary and secondary schools use statistics to their convenience, here's a game played by colleges: the manipulation of SAT scores for public relations purposes.

Consider, for example, the student with a combined math and verbal SAT score of 1100 who is choosing among three colleges and universities. State U. reports the highest average score for its previous year's incoming class, a nearby private college has the next highest average, and almost matching that average is a branch of the state college system.

To blindly assume that State U. has the brightest students and toughest admissions standards would be wrong. Here are a few of the methods and rationales the schools might use for massaging the statistics.

State U. might have wanted to boost its average by carefully defining the concept of "entering freshmen." Some schools, for example, exclude from the calculations students who do not enter in September (possibly because they are required to start in the summer to take remedial courses) and those given special consideration in admissions, such as athletes or the children of alumni.

Conversely, the private college might have wanted to deflate its average score so as not to scare away potential applicants. It may have feared that high school students would read the published average as a minimum. A reasonable way of understating scores is to calculate both the mean and the median and to then choose the lower of the two.

Finally, the local state college branch might have reported the average of all *accepted* students, a number that can be assumed to be higher than the average of the students who actually chose to *attend* the school.

Sound confusing? It is. Which is the lesson in all this. Seemingly simple scores hide critical assumptions and definitions. Be aware that statistics can be used as public relations tools as well as conveyors of hard facts.

From Edward B. Fiske, "Lessons," *New York Times,* May 31, 1989. Edward B. Fiske, "Lessons, *New York Times,* July 12, 1989.

achieved an average raw score of 20 on a reading test at the beginning of fifth grade. This score would be established as a grade equivalent of 5.0. If a sixth-grade norming group achieved a fall test score of 30, this would be established as a grade equivalent of 6.0. Now let's say a fifth-grader achieved a raw score of 25. This is halfway between the score for 5.0 and that for 6.0, so this student would be assigned a grade equivalent of 5.5. The number after the decimal point is referred to as "months," so a grade equivalent of 5.5 would be read "five years, five months." In theory, a student in the third month of fifth grade should have a score of 5.3 (five years, three months), and so on.

The advantage of grade equivalents is that they are easy to interpret and make some intuitive sense. For example, if an average student gains one grade equivalent each year, we call this achieving at expected levels. If we know a student is performing "two years below grade level" (say, a ninth-grader who scores at a level typical of seventh-graders), this gives us some understanding of how poorly the student is doing.

However, grade-equivalent scores should be interpreted only as rough approximations (see Coleman and Karweit, 1972). For one thing, students do not gain steadily in achievement from month to month. For another, scores far from the expected grade level do not mean what they appear to mean. A fourth-grader who scores at, say, 7.4 grade equivalents is by no means ready for seventh-grade work; this score just means that the fourth-grader has thoroughly mastered fourth-grade work, and has scored as well as a seventh-grader would *on a fourth-grade test*. Obviously, the average seventh-grader knows a great deal more than what would be on a fourth-grade test, so there is no real comparison between a fourth-grader who scores at 7.4 grade equivalents and a seventh-grader who does so.

Shifting definitions of grade-level expectations can also confuse the interpretation of scores. For example, New York City school administrators were pleased during the late 1980s to report that 67 percent of students were reading at or above grade level. However, after national concern about the "Lake Wobegon Effect," wherein much more than 50 percent of students were scoring "above average" (Cannell, 1987), test makers renormed their tests. As a result, administrators in New York City could then claim only 49 percent of their students were reading at or above grade level (Fiske, 1989).

Another common misinterpretation of grade-equivalent scores is that if the gap between low-achieving and average students increases over time, the low achievers are "getting worse." In fact, achievement scores become more variable over the school years. A student who stays at the 16th percentile throughout elementary and secondary school will fall behind in grade equivalents, as illustrated in Figure 15.1, but that student is remaining at the same point relative to age-mates. When all these cautions are kept in mind, grade-equivalent scores are a useful and understandable "shorthand" for describing students' scores.

Standard Scores.   Several kinds of scores describe test results according to their place on the normal curve. A normal curve, which was discussed in Chapter 12, describes a distribution of scores in which most fall near the mean, or average, with a smaller number of scores appearing the farther we go above or below the mean. A frequency graph of a normal distribution produces a bell-shaped curve. For example, Figure 15.2 shows a frequency distribution from a test with a mean score of 50. Each "x" indicates one student who got a particular score; there are 10 x's at 50, so we know that ten students got this score. Nine students got 49's and 51's, and so on, with very few students making scores above 60 or below 40. Normal distributions like the one shown in Figure 15.2 are common in nature; for example, height and weight are normally distributed throughout the general population of biologically normal people. Standardized tests are designed so that extremely few students will get every item or no item correct, so scores on them are typically normally distributed.

One important concept related to normal distributions is the **standard deviation,** a measure of the dispersion of scores. The standard deviation is, roughly speaking, the

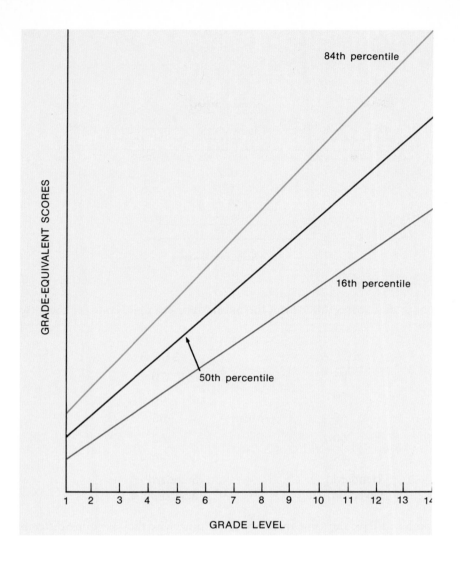

FIGURE 15.1

Increasing Gap in Grade-Equivalent Scores over Years of Schooling

A student who scores at the 16th percentile on a test in elementary school will have a corresponding grade-equivalent score relatively close to that of a student in the 84th percentile. However, two students who rank correspondingly high and low as measured by percentile in secondary school would find their grade-equivalent scores relatively far apart.

Coleman and Karweit, 1972, p. 97.

GRADE-EQUIVALENT SCORES

84th percentile

16th percentile

50th percentile

GRADE LEVEL

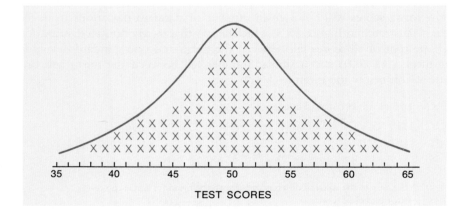

TEST SCORES

FIGURE 15.2

Frequency of Scores Forming a Normal Curve

If 100 people take a test and the score for each is marked by an x on a graph, the result could suggest a normal curve. In a normal distribution most scores are at or near the mean (in this case, 50) and the number of scores further from the mean progressively decreases.

Slavin, 1984b, p. 165.

FIGURE 15.3

Standard Deviation

When test scores are normally distributed, knowledge of how far a given score lies from the mean in terms of standard deviations indicates what percent of scores are higher and lower.

Slavin, 1984b, p. 167.

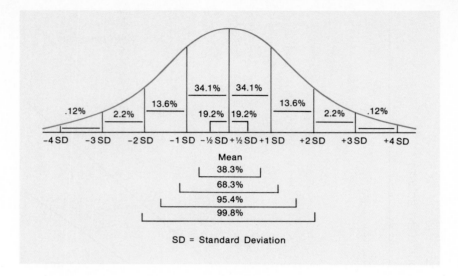

SD = Standard Deviation

average amount that scores differ from the mean.* For example, consider these two sets of scores:

SET A		SET B
85		70
70		68
65	←Mean→	65
60		62
45		60
Standard deviation: 14.6		Standard deviation: 4.1

Note that both sets have the same mean (65), but otherwise they are quite different, with Set A being more "spread out" than Set B. This is reflected in that Set A has a much larger standard deviation (14.6) than Set B (4.1). The standard deviation of a set of normally distributed scores indicates how spread out the distribution will be. Furthermore, when scores or other data are normally distributed, it allows us to predict how many scores will fall a given number of standard deviations from the mean. This is illustrated in Figure 15.3, which shows that in any normal distribution about 34.1 percent of all scores fall between the mean and one standard deviation above the mean (+1 SD), and a similar number fall between the mean and one standard deviation below the mean (−1 SD).

*The formula for finding standard deviation is:

$$\sqrt{\frac{\Sigma(x - \bar{x})^2}{N - 1}}$$

where $\Sigma(x - \bar{x})^2$ = the sum of the squared differences between the mean ($\bar{x}$) and each score
N = the number of scores

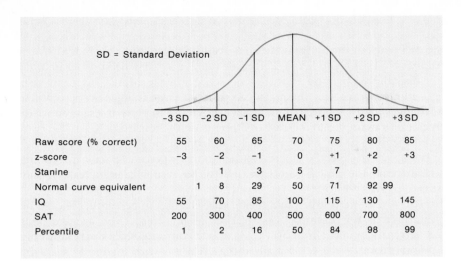

	-3 SD	-2 SD	-1 SD	MEAN	+1 SD	+2 SD	+3 SD
Raw score (% correct)	55	60	65	70	75	80	85
z-score	-3	-2	-1	0	+1	+2	+3
Stanine		1	3	5	7	9	
Normal curve equivalent		1	8	29	50	71	92 99
IQ	55	70	85	100	115	130	145
SAT	200	300	400	500	600	700	800
Percentile		1	2	16	50	84	98 99

SD = Standard Deviation

Stanine
A type of standardized score ranging from 1 to 9, having a mean of 5 and a standard deviation of 2

Normal Curve Equivalent
Set of standardized scores ranging from 1 to 99, having a mean of 50 and a standard deviation of about 21

z-Scores
Set of standardized scores having a mean of zero and a standard deviation of 1

FIGURE 15.4

Relationship Between Various Types of Scores
Raw scores that are normally distributed can be reported in a variety of ways. Each reporting method is characterized by its mean, by the range between high and low scores, and by the standard deviation interval.

Scores on standardized tests are often reported in terms of how far they lie from the mean as measured by standard deviation units. For example, IQ scores are normed so that there is a mean of 100 and a standard deviation of 15. This means that the average person will score 100; someone scoring one standard deviation above the mean will score 115; someone scoring one standard deviation below will score 85; and so on. Thus, about 68.2 percent of all IQ scores (that is, more than two-thirds) fall between 85 (−1 SD) and 115 (+1 SD). SAT scores are also normed according to standard deviations, with the mean set at 500 and a standard deviation of 100. That puts more than two-thirds of all scores between 400 and 600. It is important to note that SAT scores, though highly correlated with IQ scores, cannot be directly transformed into IQ scores because the norming groups are different. IQ scores are normed on a sample of all individuals of a given age, while SAT scores are normed on college-bound seniors only (since non–college-bound seniors do not usually take the test).

One standard score that is sometimes used is the **stanine** (from the words "standard nine"). Stanines have a mean of 5 and a standard deviation of 2, so each stanine represents .5 standard deviations. Stanine scores are reported as whole numbers, so a person who earned a stanine score of 7 (+1 SD) actually fell somewhere between .75 SD and 1.25 SD above the mean.

Another form of a standard score that is being increasingly used is the **normal curve equivalent,** or NCE. A normal curve equivalent can range from 1 to 99, with a mean of 50 and a standard deviation of approximately 21. NCE scores are similar to percentiles, except that, unlike percentile scores, intervals between NCE scores are equal. Another standard score, used more often in statistics than in reporting standardized test results, is the **z-score,** which sets the mean of a distribution at zero and the standard deviation at 1. Figure 15.4 shows how a set of scores with a mean percent correct of 70 percent and a standard deviation of 5 would be represented in

Validity
A measure of the degree to which a test is appropriate for its intended use

Content Validity
A measure of the match between the content of a test and the content of the instruction that preceded it

z-scores, stanines, normal curve equivalents, percentile scores, and equivalent IQ and SAT scores.

Note the difference in the figure between percentile scores and all standard scores (z-score, stanine, NCE, IQ, and SAT). Percentile scores are "bunched up" around the middle of the distribution because most students score near the mean. This means that small changes in raw scores near the mean can produce large changes in percentiles. In contrast, changes in raw scores make a smaller difference in percentiles far above or below the mean. For example, an increase of 5 points on the test from 70 to 75 moves a student from the 50th to the 84th percentile, an increase of 34 "percentile points," but 5 more points (from 75 to 80) increases the student's percentile rank by only 14 points. At the extreme, the same 5 points, from 80 to 85, results in an increase of only 1 percentile point, from 98 to 99.

This characteristic of percentile ranks means that changes in percentiles should be cautiously interpreted. For example, one teacher might brag, "My 'average' kids increased 23 percentile points (from 50 to 73), while your *supposedly* smart kids only gained 15 points (from 84 to 99). I really did a great job with them!" In fact, the bragging teacher's students gained only 3 points in raw score, or .6 standard deviation, while the other teacher's students gained 10 points in raw score, or 2 standard deviations!

Validity, Reliability, and Bias

When teachers and administrators decide that a standardized test should be used in school, they have to choose which test to use. There are hundreds of tests available for various purposes, so more criteria need to be established to help guide this choice.

In making the test selection decision, there are three primary questions to ask:

1. What is the test to be used for? That is, what do I want the results to tell me?

2. How accurate can I expect the results to be?

3. Is the test biased against certain students?

These questions correspond to three aspects of tests that are fundamental to test selection: validity, reliability, and bias.

The **validity** of a test refers to whether the text provides the type of information desired. The criteria used to evaluate the validity of a test vary according to the test's purpose. For example, if a test is being selected to help teachers and administrators determine which students are likely to have some difficulty with one or more aspects of instruction, the primary concern will be how the test predicts future academic performance. On the other hand, if the concern is a description of current achievement levels of a group of students, primary interest will focus on the accuracy of that description. In short, validity deals with the relevance of a test for its intended purpose.

Because of the various roles that tests are expected to play in the schools and their education process, there are several types of validity that may be of concern to test users. These fall into one of three basic classes: content validity, predictive validity, and construct validity.

Content Validity. The most important criterion for the usefulness of a test—especially an achievement test—is whether it assesses what the user wants it to assess (Popham, 1981). This criterion is called **content validity.** Content validity in achievement testing refers to the degree of overlap between what is taught (or what should be taught) and what is tested. Content validity is determined by carefully comparing the content of a test with the objectives of a course or program.

Often an evaluation of content validity begins with a close examination of the table of specifications that has been constructed for the test (tables of specifications for teacher-made tests were discussed in Chapter 14). The table of specifications serves as a road map for item construction and test development. Tables showing the classification by subject matter of questions of a given test series should also be examined. Table 15.2 shows part of a categorization of items by skill area for the Science Research Associates Achievement Series. Notice in this table that general achievement skill areas are listed. Numbers in the table refer to the numbers of the items measuring each skill and therefore reveal the emphasis placed on each skill area. Of course, tables such as these vary widely depending upon the subject matter that the test is intended to cover. These tables can usually be found in the test manual. Such tables provide valuable information for making decisions regarding which test to use for a given purpose and the proper interpretation of the test results.

If the content specifications listed in the test manual are reasonably representative of the classroom instructional goals, then the test can be thought of as content valid. For example, some mathematics achievement tests focus mostly on computations and word problems, while others devote fewer items to these skills and more to such topics as sets, measurement, estimation, inference, or mathematical properties. A school using a mathematics program that does not cover the latter topics in any depth would do best to choose a test that focuses on topics that it did teach.

This discussion illustrates a very important point: A test that is content-valid for one purpose may be completely inappropriate for another. There is no such thing as a general measure of content validity for a test; content validity cannot be determined without considering the skills the test is supposed to assess.

TABLE 15.2

A PORTION OF A TABLE CATEGORIZING ITEMS ON AN ACHIEVEMENT TEST

This partial categorization of items for an SRA achievement series shows skill areas tested and the numbers of the items allocated to each skill. Such tables, which are usually found in test manuals, should guide test selection.

Skill Area	Item Numbers
Language Arts: Spelling	1–40
Mathematics: Concepts	
Numeration	1, 5, 9, 15 16, 24, 30, 35, 37, 39
Operations	4, 31, 32, 40
Problem Solving	3, 6, 13, 21, 23, 25, 27, 33
Geometry	17, 19, 20, 26, 29, 34, 36, 38
Measurement	2, 7, 8, 10, 11, 12, 14, 18, 22, 28
Mathematics: Computation	
Whole Numbers $(+ \ -)$	1, 2, 3, 6, 7, 12, 14, 16, 21, 22, 23, 25, 31, 35, 40
Whole Numbers $(\times \ \div)$	4, 5, 8, 10, 11, 13, 15, 17, 19, 20, 24, 27, 28, 29, 30, 32, 34, 36
Fractions $(+ \ -)$	18, 37, 39
Fractions $(\times \ \div)$	33
Decimals & Percents	9, 26, 38

SOURCE: SRA Assessment Survey Achievement Series, Teacher's Guide, Forms E and F, "Using Test Results," 1972." p. 57.

Predictive Validity
A measure of the ability of a test to predict future behavior

Achievement tests are high in content validity if they cover the material that students have been taught.

Of course, the instructional activities in a classroom are guided largely by curriculum. Consequently, the three factors relevant to the evaluation of content validity are the test content, the instructional content, and the curriculum content. Two terms have been used with respect to the determination of validity: "instructional validity," which refers to the extent of overlap between the content of the test and that of the instruction, and "curricular validity," which refers to the extent of overlap between the test content and the curriculum content. Evaluating the extent to which the content taught in school matches the content contained in a test is a rather subjective procedure that relies heavily on professional judgment (see Deno, 1985).

It can be argued that for the purpose of standardized testing, instructional content and test content need not form a perfect match. This is true for two reasons. First, it may be that a test measures what educators feel students *should* be learning, and what needs to be changed is the instruction, not the test. For instance, in the mathematics achievement test example discussed earlier, it may be that teachers are doing little instruction in sets and estimation, but perhaps they should be doing more, and therefore a test of those skills may be appropriate as a means of encouraging teachers to focus on those topics. Second, some generalization of skills or knowledge can be expected. For example a test might ask for the next number in the following series:

$$1, 4, 9, 16, 25, \underline{\quad ? \quad}$$

The particular skill assessed by that item may not be taught as such, but any student who understands squares of numbers would readily supply the correct answer, 36.

Predictive Validity.   The **predictive validity** of a test refers to its contribution to the prediction of future behavior. For example, if we are using a test to predict future school performance, one way to examine its accuracy is to relate the test scores to some measure of performance in the future. If an appropriate level of correspondence exists between the test and future performance, the test could then be used to provide predictive information for students.

For example, test scores on SATs and ACTs have been shown to relate, to a reasonable degree, to performance in college, and are therefore used (along with high school grades and other information) by many college admissions officers in deciding which applicants to accept.

Construct Validity. **Construct validity** refers to the degree to which test scores relate to other scores, and whether this correspondence makes sense in terms of what the test is supposed to measure (see Haertel, 1985). For example, consider a test of mechanical aptitude. Of course, such a test should be strongly related to a student's ability to build things. However, general intelligence might also predict (to some degree) how well a student can build things, so it is possible that what appears to be a test of mechanical aptitude is in fact a test of general intelligence. To document the construct validity of the mechanical aptitude test, the test designer might show that the test predicts actual mechanical performance much better than does a test of general intelligence.

■ **Stop and Think**

A child's performance on a standardized test is influenced by many factors in addition to intelligence. These include the child's native language, facility with the language in which the test is given, test-taking experience, and ability to concentrate. How would you help a student who scored poorly on a standardized test and, as a result, was not afforded appropriate educational opportunities? How could you help such students prepare for future tests?

Reliability. While the validation process relates to the skills and knowledge measured by a test, the reliability of a test relates to the accuracy with which these skills and knowledge are measured (see Chapter 14). When a test is administered, there are a number of aspects related to both the test itself and the circumstances surrounding its administration that could cause the results to be inaccurate. In theory, if a student were to take the same test twice, we would expect the student to obtain the same score both times. The extent to which this would not occur is the subject of reliability. Ambiguous test items, testing experience, inconsistent motivation, and anxiety all affect test scores and could cause scores for different administrations of the same test to differ. At a very simplistic level, if it could be shown that individuals rank similarly on two administrations of the same test, then some confidence could be placed in the test's reliability. The extent to which the ranking does not hold could be attributed to error, and therefore inconsistency in the test results. If the inconsistency is high, it would be difficult to place much faith in a particular test score.

When Is Reliability Adequate? Reliability is measured on a scale from 0 (total unreliability) to 1.0 (total reliability). If the reliability of a test were 1.0, each student who took it would get precisely the same score each time he or she took the test (or would fall in exactly the same rank order). Adequate reliability is the minimum requirement of a test's value; a test lacking reliability cannot be considered valid. Reliabilities of published achievement and aptitude tests generally range above 0.80, which is considered quite adequate. Small differences in reliability between two standardized tests are of little importance. In practice, in achievement and aptitude testing, it is validity, not reliability, that is the principal criterion of a test's value for a particular purpose, because reliabilities of these measures tend to be uniformly high. Reliability takes on greater importance in testing of attitudes or such difficult-to-

Interpreting Standardized Test Results

In recent years test publishers have been making available increasing amounts of information on students' standardized test scores. This section presents a guide to interpreting test reports for one widely used standardized test of academic performance, the Comprehensive Tests of Basic Skills (CTBS)

CLASS RECORD FORMS

Figure 15.5 on page 528 shows a sample class record sheet for the CTBS, Form U, Level G, given to a fifth-grade class. The letters on the class record sheet refer to the principal parts of the form, as follows:

A *Identification data:* This section identifies the class that took the test, in this case Ms. Jones's class at Washington Elementary School. The grade (5.1) indicates that the students were in the first month of the fifth grade.
B *List of students:* Students may be listed alphabetically or in order from highest to lowest total score.
C *Form and level:* This indicates that students took Form U, Level G, of the CTBS. Level G is the test level that is appropriate for students in grades 4.6 (fourth grade, sixth month) to 6.9, according to the CTBS manuals. Form U refers to the particular version of the CTBS used; the CTBS and most other achievement batteries make available two parallel forms of the same test, which consist of different items but are identical in every other respect.
D, E, *and* H *Scores:* The CTBS gives grade equivalents (GE), scale scores (SS), normal curve equivalents (NCE), national percentiles (NP), national stanines (NS), and local percentiles (LP).

National percentiles and national stanines relate student scores to those of the national norming group. Local percentiles relate scores to local (usually school district) norms. For example, in a high-achieving school district a student might be performing at the 75th percentile according to national norms, but only at the 50th percentile according to the school district's distribution of scores. Scale scores cannot be interpreted directly, but are useful for certain research purposes.
F *Tests and subtests:* Scores are listed for each test (such as reading) and subject (such as vocabulary and comprehension).

G *Individual performance information:* Robert Lee's scores indicate that he is performing below grade-level expectations in total reading (GE = 2.5). The same information is communicated in a different way by his normal curve equivalent score (NCE = 21 on a scale from 0 to 99), his national percentile score (NP = 8; his score exceeded that of only 8 percent of all students), his national stanine (NS = 2), and his local percentile (LP = 5). On the other hand, he performed somewhat above grade-level expectations in total mathematics (GE = 5.7).

It is important to keep in mind that the different ways of reporting a student's scores are not independent measures of performance. If a student's score is lower than it should be (for example, the student was tired on the day of the testing) or higher than it should be (for example, the student cheated), then all of the forms of the same score will reflect the same degree of error. If Robert Lee's reading score is too low because he forgot his glasses on the day the reading tests were given, the fact that his grade equivalent, NCE, percentile, and stanine scores are all low does not provide any additional evidence that his test score is valid.

Quartermonth interpolation: Many standardized tests adjust norms according to the month the test was taken. Ms. Jones's class took the test in the fifth quartermonth (or week) of the school year. If the norming group of fifth-graders had taken the test in the seventh week of school, for example, the scores in Ms. Jones's class would have been slightly adjusted to reflect the fact that they had had slightly less instruction before taking the test than the norming group did.

Not shown in Figure 15.5 are class means, the average of the scores received by all students in the class, or school means. This information would be useful in placing the class and school according to national and local norms, and in giving teachers an idea of where individual students rank in terms of their own schools or classes.

INDIVIDUAL TEST RECORD

An individual test record is usually provided for each student who took a standardized test. An example of a

CTBS individual test record for one student, Robert Lee, appears in Figure 15.6 on page 529. The meanings of the letters in the figure are as follows:

A *Identification data:* Same as for the class record sheet, plus the student's name.

B and C *Scores:* Robert Lee's scores are listed according to the same criteria as in the class record sheet.

D *Confidence band:* For each subtest and test, a "confidence band" is given around the student's national percentile score. A confidence band indicates the possible error associated with a given score. For example, Robert Lee would probably not always score in exactly the 15th percentile in vocabulary, as he did in the example. However, there is a 95 percent chance that he would score between the 10th and the 30th percentiles, as indicated by the x's for vocabulary. Confidence bands are useful in indicating true versus chance differences between scores. If two confidence bands overlap considerably, the two scores may be considered equivalent. If they do not, they may be considered truly different. For example, Robert Lee's vocabulary percentile is 15, but his comprehension percentile is only 6. Is he better in vocabulary than in comprehension? Since his confidence bands for those subtests overlap completely, we cannot conclude that there is any meaningful difference between his scores on those subtests. In contrast, his total reading score (NP = 8) is significantly lower than his total language score (NP = 37); the confidence bands around those scores do not overlap at all. Confidence bands can also be useful in comparing students to one another. They tend to show that small differences between scores are of little consequence, and may well be due to chance.

E *Stanine bands:* The national percentile confidence bands can also be presented in terms of stanines.

F and G *Objectives scores:* Each student's degree of mastery of particular subobjectives may be indicated on an individual test record. The asterisks denote a confidence band around students' scores on each subskill (the scores are indicated by 0 or 00 in the middle of the band). Students' levels of mastery of each objective are indicated by a "−" for non-mastery, a "P" for partial mastery, and a "+" for mastery. For example, Robert Lee demonstrated partial mastery of "multimeaning words" and

Educators must ensure that students and parents understand the results of standardized tests.

mastery of "meaning of affixes" in the vocabulary sub test.

These objectives scores are somewhat useful in pointing to students' strengths and weaknesses, but should not be taken too literally, as they are based on a small number of items that may or may not be closely tied to school district objectives.

H *Number of items not reached:* The CTBS provides an indication of the number of items at the end of a test that students did not attempt. This is useful information. If a student attempted all the items on a particular subskill but missed most of them, the student probably needs help on that subskill. However, if a student did poorly on a subskill because it was located at the end of a section and the student just didn't get that far, this has a different meaning.

Test reports for standardized tests other than the CTBS are organized somewhat differently, but usually contain similar information.

Class Record Sheet

ctbs Comprehensive Tests of Basic Skills

CLASS JONES
SCHOOL WASHINGTON
CITY ANYCITY
DISTRICT WAYNE USD
STATE CA

(A) GRADE 05.1   TEST DATE 10/81   RUN DATE 11/10/81

CTB ID 91190   BATCH 738A   GROUP 001/001

PAGE 2   001501

Students	Form & Level	Scores	Word Attack	Vocab	Compr	Total (Reading)	Spell-ing	Mech	Expr	Total (Lang)	Compu	Conc/Appli	Total (Math)	Total Battery †	Ref Skills	Science	Social Studies
GROVES WILLIA	U G	GE		4.4	3.3	3.7	4.2	4.7	4.7	4.7	3.8	4.6	4.1	4.2	4.9	4.8	2.4
		SS		649	605	627	636	666	669	648	648	653	651	649	648	637	580
		NCE		42	30	35	34	45	45	26	43	33	37	37	46	47	17
		NP		35	18	23	22	41	45	13	37	21	27	30	43	44	6
		NS		4	3	3	3	5	5	3	4	3	4	4	5	5	2
		LP		34	13	23	30	41	39	14	39	23	30	30	39	52	7
HUNG SALLY	U G	GE		2.2	2.1	2.1	4.5	2.9	2.9	2.9	4.2	3.4	3.9	2.7	3.3	2.1	4.2
		SS		537	517	527	652	591	577	584	665	621	643	585	604	521	650
		NCE		14	18	11	40	23	21	32	32	27	29	17	34	19	38
		NP		4	6	3	32	10	10	20	20	13	16	6	23	7	28
		NS		1	2	2	4	2	2	3	3	3	3	2	4	2	4
		LP		4	4	4	38	18	9	13	27	14	16	5	11	16	39
JEFFERSON DINAH	U G	GE		5.8	4.4	4.9	6.6	4.9	5.0	4.8	4.8	5.6	5.1	4.9	5.5	5.2	5.2
		SS		684	665	675	693	671	675	673	686	674	680	676	672	649	679
		NCE		58	41	47	60	48	48	47	44	55	50	47	55	51	52
		NP		64	34	44	69	46	47	39	39	59	50	44	60	52	53
		NS		6	4	5	6	5	5	5	5	5	5	5	6	5	5
		LP		63	39	48	75	45	50	52	55	59	59	48	61	57	59
KARRELSON INGE	U G	GE		7.1	9.3	8.4	9.4	5.6	8.3	6.6	4.8	7.0	5.8	6.9	6.7	6.0	8.6
		SS		706	775	741	730	686	707	697	686	694	690	709	697	667	721
		NCE		69	74	72	77	55	65	59	44	69	58	64	64	57	73
		NP		82	88	85	90	59	76	66	39	82	65	74	74	63	87
		NS		7	7	7	6	6	6	6	4	7	6	6	6	6	7
		LP		80	91	91	88	55	75	71	55	86	82	79	86	71	95
LEE ROBERT S	U G	GE		3.2	2.1	2.5	4.0	5.1	4.3	4.6	4.9	6.5	5.7	4.0	5.5	3.9	4.7
		SS		607	517	562	630	676	651	664	689	689	689	638	672	608	664
		NCE		29	18	21	32	50	43	46	46	65	57	34	55	37	44
		NP		15	6	8	20	50	29	37	43	76	63	22	60	27	39
		NS		3	2	2	4	5	4	5	5	6	6	3	4	4	4
		LP		16	4	5	25	50	32	34	71	79	77	23	61	34	52
MADISON RACHEL	U G	GE		5.1	4.8	4.9	5.6	2.3	5.0	3.6	4.4	4.4	4.3	4.2	4.3	4.6	5.4
		SS		668	684	676	681	560	675	618	671	649	660	651	621	630	682
		NCE		50	46	45	55	17	48	35	35	32	38	38	38	44	53
		NP		50	42	45	59	6	47	16	24	32	28	28	29	39	55
		NS		5	5	5	5	2	5	3	4	4	4	4	4	4	5
		LP		48	52	54	63	11	50	23	32	32	29	38	23	45	64

Score Codes
• : Maximum Score Obtained
A : No Valid Attempt
X : No Score Available

CTBS U G-201 CRS

GE : GRADE EQUIVALENT   SS : SCALE SCORE
NCE : NORMAL CURVE EQUIVALENT   NP : NATIONAL PERCENTILE
NS : NATIONAL STANINE   LP : LOCAL PERCENTILE

CTBS LEVEL(S): G
CTBS FORM(S): U
(|) : CTBS NORMS INTERPOLATED TO QUARTERMONTH 05

Published by CTB/McGraw-Hill, Del Monte Research Park, Monterey, California 93940
Copyright © 1981 by McGraw-Hill, Inc. All rights reserved. Printed in the U.S.A.

† TOTAL BATTERY INCLUDES TOTAL READING, TOTAL LANGUAGE, AND TOTAL MATHEMATICS.

FIGURE 15.5

Sample Class Record Sheet for a Standardized Test

When a class of students takes a standardized test, the results may be reported on a form similar to that shown here.

CTB/McGraw-Hill, 1981, p. 18.

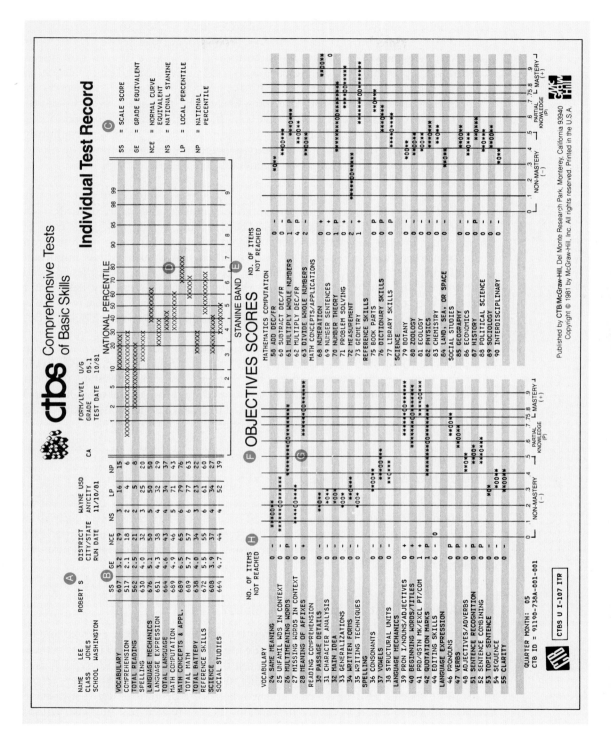

FIGURE 15.6

Sample Individual Test Record for a Standardized Test

Score reports for individuals who take standardized tests may include overall scores and scores on specific objectives.

From CTB/McGraw-Hill, 1981, p. 19.

define constructs as creativity, because in these cases high reliability of measurement is harder to achieve.

One important factor affecting reliability is the length of a test. The longer the test, the greater its reliability, other things being equal. This means that even though a test may be highly reliable overall, specific subscales may be less so. For example, a standardized test may provide a reliable score for a student on general reference skills. A teacher might, however, wish to see how students did on one specific skill such as map reading, represented on the reference skills test by three items. Test publishers are increasingly providing just such detailed "diagnostic" information. However, the reliability of that three-item map skills scale is likely to be low (again, even though the overall reliability of the reference skills test is high). For this reason, interpretation of subscale scores based on small numbers of items should be done very cautiously. Another factor that contributes to reliability is range of item difficulties. The greater the range, the greater the reliability (in general).

Criterion-Referenced Tests. The reliability of a criterion-referenced test must be examined from a somewhat different perspective because of the nature of the test and the score interpretation. In criterion-referenced testing, a person's proficiency on specific skills, or standing with respect to the criterion, is of primary interest. From this perspective, variability of scores between different test takers is less important. Consequently, items for a criterion-referenced test are constructed with less concern for item difficulty and more for whether the item reflects a difficulty level that is consistent with the criterion, and traditional reliability estimates for these tests can be expected to be somewhat lower than those for norm-referenced tests (see Berk, 1986).

Test Bias. One major issue in the interpretation of standardized test scores is whether tests are biased against lower-class or minority students (Scheuneman, 1984). In one sense, this is a question of test validity; a test that gave an unfair advantage to one or another category of student could not be considered valid for general use. Of greatest concern is the possibility that tests may be biased because their items assess knowledge or skills common to one culture but not another.

SELECTING STANDARDIZED TESTS

Where can educators find out about various standardized tests? How can they choose from among the dozens of norm-referenced or criterion-referenced tests likely to be available for assessment of any conceivable type of aptitude or achievement? The following section discusses the steps involved in selecting standardized tests for classroom use.

Why Are You Testing in the First Place?

The first step in choosing a standardized test is to clarify what is to be assessed and the purposes of the testing. For example, if you were testing to select students for a special program for the gifted, you would want a test high in predictive validity (such as an aptitude test), since your purpose is to predict future performance. If you were testing to diagnose specific student deficits, you would want a diagnostic test that provides detailed information on a variety of subskills closely related to your instructional objectives. If you were testing to see how many students had mastered particular skills, you would choose a criterion-referenced test. One of the most common errors in standardized testing is using tests for purposes other than those for which they were designed. For example, as noted earlier, test publishers now often provide detailed breakdowns of norm-referenced standardized achievement scores so that schools can identify particular areas on which their students show weaknesses. However, these subscores are based on small numbers of items, which are hardly representative of the content taught in school. These scores are fine if interpreted very cautiously, but to use them to guide changes in curricula or teaching methods would be inappropriate; broad-range achievement tests do not usually have enough items on any particular subskill or enough overlap with curricula to be useful as diagnostic tools.

Locating Information on Standardized Tests. The principal source of information on all published tests it the *Mental Measurements Yearbook,* or MMY (Mitchell, 1985), which reviews more than a thousand tests of all kinds. The MMY describes the tests and includes reviews of their strengths and weaknesses by experts in psychological and educational assessment. Another useful source is *Test Critiques* (Keyser and Sweet-land, 1984–85). In addition, test evaluations are available from the Center for the Study of Evaluation, University of California at Los Angeles. Other data regarding test characteristics, reliability, validity, and norming procedures can be found in manuals or technical bulletins available from test publishers.

What to Look For in Choosing a Standardized Test. Popham (1981) has described eight criteria on which tests should be evaluated. These criteria are summarized in Table 15.3, a test review format Popham suggests be used by educators evaluating achievement tests.

1. *Description of measured behavior:* First, Popham recommends a careful look at the test's description of the behavior or skills it is supposed to measure to make sure

---

TABLE 15.3

SAMPLE FORMAT FOR EVALUATING TESTS

Eight features of standardized tests should be evaluated when such tests are considered for use in schools.

Test _____

	Rating		
Evaluative Factor	Strong	Acceptable	Weak
1. Description of measured behavior	_____	_____	_____
2. Items per measured behavior	_____	_____	_____
3. Scope of measurement	_____	_____	_____
4. Reliability	_____	_____	_____
5. Validity	_____	_____	_____
6. Comparative data	_____	_____	_____
7. Ease of administration	_____	_____	_____
8. Absence of cultural bias	_____	_____	_____

Source: Popham, 1981, p. 63.

the test covers the content or skills you want it to cover. The description may take the form of a table of specifications from which items were generated.

2. *Items per measured behavior:* A test may cover the skills you wish to assess, but may not provide enough items on particular behaviors you feel are critical. Popham suggests as a rule of thumb that for any important educational decision, at least ten items are needed to provide a reliable indicator of student mastery. For example, if a test is to judge whether students need instruction in solving simultaneous equations involving two variables, it should contain at least ten items on this subskill. This is why broad-scale standardized tests cannot be used to diagnose specific student deficits; they have too few items on any particular subskill.

3. *Scope of measurement:* Scope of measurement refers to the breadth of skills a test is suppose to measure. Given a finite amount of time for testing, there are only so many behaviors we can measure reliably. Thus there is a trade-off between scope of measurement and items per behavior. An SAT test, for instance, produces reliable scores for verbal and quantitative aptitude because it contains a wide variety of items assessing many behaviors. In other words, the SAT has an extremely broad scope of measurement, which it achieves by having small numbers of items per behavior. In contrast, a criterion-referenced test of language mechanics skills might have a narrower scope, focusing on capitalization, punctuation, usage, and grammar skills, with many items assessing each behavior. An extremely narrow scope might be appropriate for a specific test assessing mastery of punctuation of dialogue. In evaluating a particular test for classroom use, it is important to make certain that the test's scope of measurement assesses the full range of behaviors you wish to assess, but no more.

4. *Reliability:* Adequate reliability is the absolute minimum requirement for test adequacy. As noted earlier, published achievement tests of many items are almost always adequate in reliability, although subscale scores based on only a few items may not be.

5. *Validity:* Test publishers often present several kinds of information to demonstrate that their tests measure what they are supposed to measure. This information, and your own determination of the test's validity for the use you are planning, are crucial elements of test selection.

6. *Comparative data:* One of the most important advantages of standardized tests is that they allow you to compare any individual's score with those of some well-specified norming group. Therefore it is critical that the norming group really represent all students of a particular kind, and that the norming data be carefully collected and clearly described. For example, if a test gives separate "private school norms," you would want to know what kinds of private schools are meant. Did the test publishers include parochial schools? Christian academies? Prep schools? Independent schools? If they included all of these, did they include them in the same proportions they are of all private schools? Did the norming group represent all regions of the country, and urban, suburban, and rural locations? One particularly important aspect of comparative data is how recently the norms were established. Out-of-date norms might give inflated scores in certain skills because students now taking the test may have had more instruction in the skills than students in the norming group.

7. *Ease of administration:* A test might be good on most criteria, but so cumbersome, difficult to administer, or time-consuming that you would want to avoid it. A test might also be hard to score and not provide a computer scoring service. The costs of tests and of test-scoring services have risen sharply in recent years, and these must be considered.

Preparing Students for Standardized Tests

As standardized testing has taken on increasing importance in the evaluation of students, teachers, and schools, so too has the preparation of students to take these tests. Of course, the best way to prepare students for tests is to do a good job of teaching them the material. However, there is also a need to help many students become "test-wise," to help them show what they really know on standardized tests and to help them get as good a score as possible.

There are many ethical issues involved in helping students do well on standardized tests (Teddlie and Stringfield, in press). For example, one way to help students score well is to know the test items in advance and teach them the answers. This clearly is cheating. A much more ethically ambiguous case arises when teachers know what is on the test and teach only objectives that they know will be tested. For example, if a standardized test did not assess Roman numerals, a math teacher might skip this topic in order to spend more time on an objective that is tested. This practice is criticized as "teaching to the test." On one hand it could be argued that it is unfair to test students on material that they have not been taught, and that instruction should therefore be closely aligned with tests (Cohen, 1987). On the other hand, a standardized test can only assess a small sample of all objectives taught in school. Gearing instruction toward those objectives that will be on the test, to the exclusion of all others, would produce a very narrow curriculum. An ethical compromise might be to teach the full range of objectives, not just those on the test.

Beyond matching instructional content with test objectives there are many ways to help students learn to do well on tests in general. Research has found that students can be taught to be "test-wise," and that this increases their standardized test scores (Anastasi, 1981; Kulik, Kulik, and Bangert, 1984). Questions have been raised about the effectiveness of programs that prepare students for the Scholastic Aptitude Test. The consensus among researchers is now that coaching is effective, particularly for minority and low-achieving students (Messick, 1982).

Some ways of helping students to prepare for standardized tests follow (see Sarnacki, 1979):

1. Give students practice with similar item formats. For example, if a test will use multiple-choice formats, give students practice with similar formats in routine classroom quizzes and tests. If tests use unusual formats, such as verbal analogies (i.e., BIG:SMALL::HONEST:_____), give students practice with this type of item.
2. Suggest that students skip over difficult or time-consuming items and return to them later.
3. If there is no penalty for guessing on a test, suggest to students that they always fill in some answer. If there is a penalty for guessing, students should still be encouraged to guess if they can narrow down the options to two.
4. Suggest that students read all options on a multiple-choice test before choosing one. Sometimes one answer is correct, but there may be a better answer.
5. Suggest to students that they use all available time. If they finish early, they should go back over their answers.

8. *Absence of cultural bias:* It should go without saying that a test with any kind of overt cultural bias should be rejected. For example, a test whose items always refer to doctors as "he" or give Hispanic names only to menial workers should not be used. Recent forms of widely used tests have almost always been carefully edited to remove cultural or gender bias, but older or less widely used tests should be carefully read to detect sterotyping or other cultural bias.

The Uses of Standardized Tests in the Schools

Standardized tests can contribute to improving the schooling process. The results of some standardized tests provide information regarding appropriate student placement and diagnostic information important in remediation. In addition, achievement tests can guide curriculum development and revision where areas of weakness appear (see Ebel, 1980a). A broader view of the role of standardized tests in the schools suggests uses in guidance and counseling as well. This is true not only in the areas of achievement and aptitude testing, but also for more specialized types of measures such as vocational interest inventories and other psychological scales that are used in the counseling of students in the schools.

Standardized tests also have some administrative roles. Academic achievement tests, for instance, are often used to evaluate the relative success of competing educational programs or strategies. For example, if a teacher or school tries out an innovative teaching strategy, tests can be used to find out whether it was more successful than previous methods. Also, district-wide test results often serve as a yardstick for citizens to judge the success of their local schools. Tests can also contribute to accountability, to evaluate relative teaching strengths and weaknesses of faculty. In all of these uses it is important to remember that educating students is a complex process and that standardized tests provide only a small portion of the information that is necessary for evaluating teachers, programs, or schools.

Accountability. A growing trend over the past decade has been to hold teachers and schools accountable for what students learn. Most states and school districts have implemented regular standardized testing programs and publish the results on a school-by-school basis. Not surprisingly, principals and other administrators watch these scores the way business owners watch their profit sheets. In many districts the scores of each teacher's students are made available to the school administration and may be used in decisions about hiring, firing, promotion, and transfer.

Even more recently many states and districts have established minimum competency tests that students must pass either to graduate from high school or to be promoted from grade to grade (see Lerner, 1981). These are typically criterion-referenced tests focusing on important skills students are expected to have mastered. School districts using minimum competency tests also usually establish special remedial programs—often during the summer—to help students pass the tests and qualify for promotion or graduation.

The accountability movement stems in part from the public's loss of confidence in American education. State legislators (among others), upset by examples of students graduating from high school unable to read or compute, have demanded that schools establish higher standards and that students achieve them.

The accountability movement has its critics, however. Many argue that minimum competency testing focuses school on minimums rather than maximums. Others are concerned that schools will teach only what is tested, emphasizing reading and mathematics at the expense of, for instance, science, and social studies. Teachers and principals point out that accountability assessments fail to take into account differences among students; a school or classroom may test low because the students are from impoverished backgrounds rather than because they were given poor instruction.

Regardless of these criticisms, accountability is probably here to stay. One advantage of accountability is that it does force schools and teachers to pay attention to students who might otherwise "fall between the cracks" and to help those who need the most help. Another is that it encourages schools to search out improved instructional methods and guarantees routine evaluation of any innovations they try. For example, one principal had several teachers using an effective reading program. A new teacher said she didn't like the program and preferred to use her own. "Fine," the principal said, "if your program produces as much gain as ours, more power to you." As it turned out, the teacher's program did not increase reading scores as much as the

1. A good score on a standardized test suggests two things: (1) that the test taker knew the material, and (2) that he or she was skilled at taking tests. While it can be assumed that a teacher will devote time to guaranteeing the first, what about the second? How should you prepare students for taking standardized tests?

Richard Thorne Jr., who teaches elementary school in Stoughton, Mass., wrote:

> The best preparation for taking standardized tests is a sound program of teaching and learning all year long. Test taking skills should be taught one week before the standardized test will be taken. This should be done by practicing items similar in format to those the pupils will encounter on the tests. No professional educator would "teach the test." To do so would render the results meaningless.

Krissy Potusna, who teaches elementary school in Ransom, Ill., wrote:

> I think you should begin by giving the students sample tests in which the level is below what they're actually capable of. Next, you should use some of the testing techniques used in the standardized tests (multiple choice, for example) in tests given in class. If you begin this at the beginning of the year, the students will be accustomed to the methods and find the standardized tests easier. They will feel less confusion and pressure.

Lloyd Stableford, who teaches middle school in Westport, Conn., wrote:

> Given that so much of education is evaluated through testing by teachers, students are generally well prepared for a variety of tests well before standardized tests are ever taken. In addition to this, the Connecticut State Mastery Test encourages the giving of a pretest that highlights the possible tests to be given.
>
> One consequence of the recent state testing requirements is a decided pressure by the administration on the staff to prepare students for the tests, to establish a correct testing atmosphere, and to remind students of the seriousness of the tests. Given all of this, the students are very well prepared for the week of testing.

2. How can you use standardized test scores in planning for an upcoming year?

Mary Bruskotter, Fort Jennings, Ohio:

> Some tests give a readout of the correct and incorrect responses of all students on each test question. This shows areas of weakness for the group. In this small school at which I teach, we can see at a glance what areas need to be worked on.

principal's, so she dropped her own method and used his. The standardized tests of reading skills gave the principal and the teacher a fair standard against which to evaluate their programs, so (presumably) they ended up with the better program.

Problems and Issues in Standardized Testing

As with any educational practice, there are a number of controversial issues related to standardized testing. Many of these issues can be addressed through careful consideration of the need for standardized testing, appropriate test selection, and appropriate interpretation of test results.

Restricted Test Format. Because most standardized tests are designed for administration to a group and for ease in administration and scoring, the response format is objective, usually employing multiple-choice questions. Some professionals in education believe that this format does not allow students to demonstrate complex cognitive skills, and so does not provide a complete picture of their abilities. Examples of such skills include reading in the early grades, creative writing, and complex

Some states require high school students to pass a test before graduating. The test is designed to ensure that seniors have achieved at least a minimum level of competency in important skills.

Chapter 15: Using and Interpreting Standardized Tests

Jerry Natkin, who is beginning his seventh year of teaching and his first year as head of the English Department, and Roscoe Carnes, who is beginning his fourth year as an art teacher, sit talking in the teachers' lounge of the only high school in a medium-sized city. This is the first opportunity the two friends have had to talk since school began one week ago.

ROSCOE: Jerry, congratulations on being elected to head the English Department! Couldn't have happened to a better man!

JERRY: I don't know about that, Roscoe, but thanks.

ROSCOE: Now that you're the chairman, what are your plans for the department?

JERRY: I figure that as 'chair' my first job is to locate a good table to work on!

ROSCOE: Oh, brother! I can see that becoming chairman hasn't helped the quality of your jokes any!

JERRY: No, seriously, I guess my first priority is to do something about the standardized test situation in this school.

ROSCOE: What situation is that?

JERRY: I guess you artists don't worry too much about such things. But those of us in academics worry a lot about declining standardized test scores.

ROSCOE: OK, ease off. What do you want to do about the scores, Jerry?

JERRY: Well, we have to get them up. I've looked back at the last ten years of testing records and the trend isn't pretty. Last year's students scored a couple of percentage points below the kids of five years ago, and even further below the average scores of ten years ago. I wonder if these kids just aren't learning.

ROSCOE: Or maybe they're just not able to show what they know on those tests.

JERRY: It could be. Anyway, I want the members of the English Department to examine what they are teaching to make sure that the content of the state standardized test is being covered in our courses. I also want them to include in their own exams the kinds of objective test items that are on the state test—so the kids will become familiar with them. I think we can easily increase the school's overall average score and also our number of state finalists each year.

ROSCOE: But, Jerry, aren't you then "teaching to the test"?

JERRY: Sure I am. What's wrong with that?

ROSCOE: But the state exam is practically all multiple choice! What about higher-order learning like problem solving and creative thinking?

JERRY: You don't have to encourage English teachers to teach higher-order thinking! That's always part of our courses.

problem solving in math and science. These skills can be measured, of course, using evaluation methods other than multiple-choice tests that can be scored by computer.

Truth-in-Testing. In the history of standardized testing it is an unfortunate fact that some individuals who were tested were not well informed as to why they were being tested, what was to be tested, and how the resulting scores were to be used. Current freedom-of-information practices are slowly changing this situation. In recent years more information regarding tests and testing practices has been provided to test takers. Often the administration of a standardized test is preceded by a thorough discussion of the testing process, and the results of testing are frequently accompanied by booklets that help explain them to students and parents. Schools often set up "practice" sessions designed to familiarize students with a test's form and general content. In addition, recent legislation such as the New York "truth-in-testing" law requires that the results of standardized tests be released to students, and, if requested, a copy of the exam and keyed correct responses be provided as well. While the intent of such laws is to increase access to information regarding testing, test publishers and

ROSCOE: But Jerry, If you get the whole department focusing on the test, they might start neglecting higher-order learning. Minimums do have a way of becoming maximums, you know.

JERRY: If I can get the English Department to do anything as a group, I'll be a miracle worker! But I have no doubt we can both cover the material better and also include higher-order objectives. The main thing we need to do is push the kids more.

ROSCOE: How are you going to do that?

JERRY: Maybe we can get some of the parents involved with working with the kids at home using sample test items and such. Achievement tests may be imperfect, but they're the best measuring devices we have in education and one thing is sure: Kids who score high on them make better grades and do better in life.

ROSCOE: I don't know about that, Jerry. I—

JERRY: And, another thing: the thing I hear teachers complain about most is the lack of feedback they get on the job, and how they never know when they've accomplished something. Well, achievement test scores can tell you that. They're like a scoreboard at a football game lighting up and telling everyone you've scored a touchdown. We need that in education.

ROSCOE: I'm not sure whether standardized tests are a good measure of English proficiency or not, but they sure won't contribute anything in my field.

JERRY: Yes, I've got to admit that art and music education people have a problem. Why don't you give your students tests of creativity, Roscoe?

ROSCOE: Jerry, are you serious? Do you really think art teachers should coach kids so they can do well on some artificial measure of creativity? Is that what art is all about?

JERRY: Now, Roscoe, don't get excited. I said that I—

ROSCOE: Jerry, do you really think that standardized test scores should be guiding your educational goals for the English Department?

QUESTIONS

1. What kinds of learning do standardized achievement tests measure? What are higher-order and lower-order learning?
2. What does it mean to "teach to the test"? What does Roscoe mean when he talks about "minimums becoming maximums"?
3. How would you evaluate Jerry's plan to improve test scores? Will it work? Is it a good idea? What can schools do to involve parents in the education of their children?

other specialists fear that such requirements will eventually decrease the validity of the test results; obviously, if students can obtain tests in advance, they can memorize the answers rather than learning the material. Since the test construction process is an expensive one, the concern for item secrecy has implications for both test availability and the cost of testing.

Trends in Testing. Early in the accountability movement, critics often recommended that widescale testing be discontinued entirely. Today, however, there is a recognition among educators that since tests are almost certainly here to stay, we had better turn our attention toward making better tests and other means of assessment (Shepard, 1989). One critic put it this way:

> We *should* "teach to the test." The catch is to design and then teach to . . . tests so that practicing for and taking the tests actually enhances rather than impedes education. (Wiggins, 1989, p. 41)

One important trend in testing is a movement toward the testing of higher-order skills (such as problem solving). In reading, there is a movement away from assessing isolated skills and toward an emphasis on comprehension of longer sections and on the metacognitive awareness of reading strategies (Valencia et al., 1989; Roeber and Dutcher, 1989). Some school districts are experimenting with "portfolio" assessments, in which student work is accumulated over time to show how students are progressing (Wolf, 1989; Wiggins, 1989). There is also a trend toward more "authentic" testing. For example, the Connecticut statewide assessment in science has students show that they can design experiments, control variables, construct electrical circuits, and use microscopes; in foreign language students must write letters and converse with interviewers (Baron, 1989).

SUMMARY AND REVIEW OF OBJECTIVES

Purposes of Standardized Testing.   One use of standardized tests is to aid in making selection and placement decisions. Tests such as the Scholastic Aptitude Test (SAT) and the American College Testing Program (ACT), for example, give college admissions officers information regarding the likelihood of a student's success in college. Standardized tests may also be used to certify proficiency in a given subject area. Two other uses are diagnosis of learning difficulties and assessment of student progress. Each of these functions involves comparing test scores with a criterion, either group performance or some other standard.

The word "standardized" in reference to testing describes tests that are uniform in content, administration, and scoring, and therefore allow for the comparison of results across classrooms, schools, and school districts. Development of standardized tests involves writing test items that assess knowledge students are expected to possess, inspecting all items for clarity, administering the test to a group that is representative of those for whom the test is intended, and determining average scores.

Types of Standardized Tests.   Aptitude tests are most often used for selection, placement, and diagnosis; they attempt to assess the abilities of individuals and to predict their future performance. General aptitude tests include intelligence tests, which attempt to provide a measure of individual aptitude in a variety of cognitive areas. These tests may be administered either to individuals or to groups. A multifactor aptitude battery provides a breakdown of more specific skills.

Achievement tests are designed to measure student proficiency. Achievement batteries are used to measure individual or group achievement in a variety of subject areas by including several small tests, each on a different subject area. Diagnostic tests generally focus on a specific content area and emphasize skills thought to be important in mastery of that subject matter.

The interpretation of standardized test scores involves comparison with a standard. Criterion referencing is an interpretation of scores with respect to a fixed performance level, while norm referencing is an interpretation of scores with respect to other people who took the test.

Interpreting Test Scores.   Most standardized aptitude tests use norm-referenced scoring. The norming group, a representative sample of the group for whom the test is intended, serves as a comparative basis for interpretation of the scores. Derived scores are interpretations of raw scores and provide information about the standing of a particular score relative to those earned by the norming group. A percentile score, for instance, expresses the percentage of scores in the norming group that fall below a particular score. Grade-equivalent scores express performance as the grade and month at which a particular score is thought to represent typical performance. A grade-equivalent score does not necessarily imply that the student possesses readiness for the grade level indicated, and thus needs to be interpreted cautiously. Other ways of reporting scores include using stanines, normal curve equivalents, and z-scores.

Measuring Validity.   The validity of a test refers to whether the test provides the type of information desired. Three aspects of a test that relate to content validity are the content of the test, of the instruction, and of the curriculum. Predictive validity refers to a test's prediction of future behavior. Construct validity refers to the degree to which the test actually measures the particular construct (trait or aptitude) in question, and thus correlates with tests of the same or similar constructs.

In the test selection process the general goals and content of the test should be similar to those of the setting in which the test is used; reliability and validity should be investigated; and the question of whether there is a need for the test should be considered. One criticism of standardized testing is that the response format does not allow students to demonstrate complex cognitive skills. Another is that the test content may shape the classroom curriculum. Truth-in-testing laws require that results of standardized tests and exam questions and answers be released to students on request.

STUDY QUESTIONS

1. Which of the following types of standardized test is designed to predict future performance?
   a. Norm-referenced achievement test
   b. Criterion-referenced achievement test
   c. Aptitude test
   d. Diagnostic test
2. Which of the following score reports would apply to a sixth-grade student who has scored at the national mean on a standardized test?
   a. %ILE = 40, Stanine = 9, z = 0
   b. NCE = 50, z = 0, %ILE = 50
   c. GE = 7.2, Stanine = 5, NCE = 100
   d. z = 3, NCE = 60, %ILE = 50
3. Both the first-period and fifth-period classes averaged 75 on the math final, but student scores in the first class were much more spread out. The first-period class therefore has a larger
   a. mean.
   b. median.

   c. standard deviation.
   d. normal curve equivalent.
4. A seventh-grader earns a grade equivalent of 9.4 on a standardized exam. Which of the following can be assumed?
   a. She is ready to tackle ninth-grade work.
   b. The standardized exam is too easy and needs to be renormed.
   c. She has scored as well on the test as the average ninth-grader would.
   d. All of the above.
5. When students take a certain aptitude test twice they score about the same both times. This result implies that the test has high
   a. predictive validity.
   b. content validity.
   c. construct validity.
   d. reliability.

Answers: 1. c 2. b 3. c 4. c 5. d

SUGGESTED READINGS

ARCHBALD, D., and NEWMANN, F. (1988). *Beyond standardized testing: Authentic academic achievement in the secondary school.* Reston, Va.: NASSP.

AMERICAN PSYCHOLOGICAL ASSOCIATION (1974). *Standards for educational and psychological tests.* Washington, D.C.: APA.

COLE, N. S. (1981). Bias in testing. *American Psychologist, 36,* 1067–1077.

GREEN, B. F. (1981). A primer of testing. *American Psychologist, 36,* 1001–1011.

GRONLUND, N. E. (1976). *Measurement and evaluation in teaching* (3rd ed.). New York: Macmillan.

HOPKINS, K. D., and STANLEY, J. C. (1981). *Educational and psychological evaluation* (6th ed.). Englewood Cliffs, N.J.: Prentice-Hall.

LERNER, B. (1981). The minimum competency testing movement: Social, scientific, and legal implications. *American Psychologist, 36,* 1057–1066.

OAKLAND, T. (Ed.) (1977). *Psychological and educational assessment of minority children.* New York: Brunner/Mazel.

POPHAM, W. J. (1981). *Modern educational measurement.* Englewood Cliffs, N.J.: Prentice-Hall.

SLAVIN, R. E. (1984). *Research methods in education: A practical guide.* Englewood Cliffs, N.J.: Prentice-Hall.

Glossary

Ability-Grouped Active Teaching. A method of teaching upper elementary and middle school math that uses within-class ability grouping. (p. 288)

Absolute grading standards. Preestablished performance criteria required for different grades. (p. 500)

Accommodation. Modifying existing schemes to fit new situations. (p. 27)

Achievement battery. Standardized test that includes several subtests designed to measure knowledge of particular subjects. (p. 514)

Achievement motivation. The desire to experience success and to participate in activities in which success is dependent on personal effort and abilities. (p. 329)

Advance organizers. General statements given before instruction that relate new information to existing knowledge. (p. 167)

Affective objectives. Objectives concerned with student attitudes and values. (p. 217)

Allocated time. Time during which students have the opportunity to learn. (p. 365)

Antecedent stimulus. Event that comes before a behavior. (p. 117)

Aptitude test. A test designed to measure general abilities and to predict future performance. (p. 512)

Assessment. A measure of the degree to which instructional objectives have been attained. (p. 210)

Assimilation. Interpreting new experiences in relation to existing schemes. (p. 26)

Attention. The process of focusing on certain stimuli while screening out others. (p. 133)

Attention deficit. The inability to concentrate for long periods of time. (p. 410)

Attribution theory. An explanation of motivation that focuses on how people explain the causes of their own successes and failures. (p. 324)

Authoritarian parents. Parents who strictly enforce their authority over their children. (p. 65)

Authoritative parents. Parents who mix firm guidance with respect and warmth toward their children. (p. 65)

Automatization. Process by which thoroughly learned tasks can be performed with little mental effort. (p. 143)

Autonomous morality. Stage at which a person understands that people make rules, and that punishments are not automatic. (p. 45)

Aversive stimulus. A condition that a person tries to avoid or escape. (p. 106)

Backward planning process. Planning instruction by first setting long-range goals, then setting unit objectives, and finally planning daily lessons. (p. 222)

Behavior content matrix. A chart that classifies lesson objectives according to cognitive level. (p. 215)

Behavioral learning theories. Explanations of learning that emphasize observable changes in behavior. (p. 99)

Between-class ability grouping. System in which students are assigned to classes according to achievement and abilities. (p. 282)

Bilingual education. Instructional program for students who speak little or no English in which some instruction is provided in their native language. (p. 462)

Centration. Paying attention to only one aspect of an object or a situation. (p. 31)

Cerebral palsy. Disorder in ability to control movements caused by damage to the motor area of the brain. (p. 422)

Chapter 1. A federal program that gives school districts money to improve educational services for low-achieving disadvantaged students. (p. 452)

Choral response. A response to a question made by an entire class in unison. (p. 248)

Classical conditioning. Associating a previously neutral stimulus with an unconditioned stimulus to evoke a conditioned response. (p. 100)

Closure. The mental tendency to organize perceptions so they make sense. (p. 132)

Cognitive dissonance theory. An explanation of the discomfort people feel when new perceptions or behaviors clash with long-held beliefs. (p. 323)

Cognitive learning theories. Explanations of learning that focus on mental processes. (p. 99)

Compensatory education. Programs designed to supplement the education of non-achieving disadvantaged students. (p. 452)

Compensatory preschool programs. Programs designed to prepare disadvantaged children for entry into kindergarten and first grade. (p. 63)

Computer-assisted instruction. Individualized instruction administered by a computer. (p. 305)

Concepts. Categories into which objects, ideas, and experiences may be grouped. (p. 178)

Concrete operational stage. Stage at which children develop skills of logical reasoning and conservation but can use these skills only when dealing with familiar situations. (p. 34)

Consequence. A condition that follows a behavior and affects the frequency of future behavior. (p. 104)

Conservation. The concept that certain properties of an object (such as weight) remain the same regardless of changes in other properties (such as length). (p. 29)

Construct validity. The degree to which test scores relate to scores from measures of the same or similar variables (constructs). (p. 525)

Content validity. A measure of the match between the content of a test and the content of the instruction that preceded it. (p. 522)

Continuous progress grading. Evaluation based on the number of units completed in a given time period. (p. 503)

Control group. Group that receives no special treatment during an experiment. (p. 11)

Cooperative Integrated Reading and Composition. A program that supplements reading-group activities by having students practice related skills in mixed-ability teams. (p. 292)

Cooperative learning. A goal structure in which students work in mixed-ability groups and are rewarded on the basis of the success of the group. (p. 354)

Cooperative scripts. A study method in which students work in pairs and take turns orally summarizing sections of material to be learned. (p. 173)

Corrective instruction. Educational activities given to students who initially fail to master an objective, designed to increase the number of students who master educational objectives. (p. 299)

Correlational coefficients. Numbers ranging from $+1.0$ to -1.0 that describe the direction and strength of the relationship between two or more variables. (p. 15)

Correlational study. Research into the relationships between variables as they naturally occur. (p. 13)

Criterion-referenced evaluations. Assessments that rate how thoroughly students have mastered specific skills or areas of knowledge. (p. 484)

Cue. Signal as to what behavior(s) will be reinforced or punished. (p. 117)

Culture. The language, attitudes, ways of behaving, and other aspects of life that characterize a group of people. (p. 448)

Cut-off score. Score designated as the minimum necessary to demonstrate mastery of a subject. (p. 516)

Deductive teaching approach. Method of lesson presentation in which general ideas precede specifics. (p. 198)

Deficiency needs. Basic requirements for physical and psychological well-being as identified by Maslow. (p. 321)

Derived score. A value computed from raw scores that relates students' performances to those of a norming group; examples are percentiles and grade equivalents. (p. 516)

Descriptive research. Study aimed at identifying and gathering detailed information about something of interest. (p. 16)

Diagnostic test. An evaluation that provides information that can be used to identify specific areas of strength and weakness. (p. 290)

Direct instruction. Approach to teaching in which lessons are goal-oriented and structured by the teacher. (p. 252)

Discovery learning. Instructional approach in which students learn through their own active explorations of concepts and principles. (p. 192)

Discrimination. Perception of and response to differences in stimuli. (p. 118)

Distractors. Incorrect responses offered as alternative answers to a multiple-choice question. (p. 499)

Distributed practice. Technique in which items to be learned are repeated at intervals over a period of time. (p. 152)

Drill and practice CAI programs. Computer programs that let students practice what they've learned and obtain immediate feedback. (p. 307)

Dual code theory of memory. Theory suggesting that information coded both visually and verbally is remembered better than information coded only one of those two ways. (p. 141)

Educable mentally retarded. Category of mental retardation applied to those with mild handicaps, whose learning problems are often identified only after school entry. (p. 407)

Educational Psychology. The study of learning and teaching. (p. 3)

Egocentric. The belief that everyone views the world as you do. (p. 32)

Elaboration. The process of thinking about new material in a way that helps to connect it with existing knowledge. (p. 170)

Emotionally disturbed. Category of exceptionality characterized by problems with learning, interpersonal relationships, and control of feelings and behavior. (p. 413)

Engaged time. Time students spend actually learning; same as time on-task. (p. 363)

Enrichment activities. Assignments or activities designed to broaden or deepen the knowledge of students who master classroom lessons quickly. (p. 299)

Episodic memory. A part of long-term memory that stores images of our personal experiences. (p. 138)

Equilibration. The process of restoring balance between present understanding and new experiences. (p. 27)

Ethnic group. Group of people who share characteristics such as race, religion, and/or place of origin. (p. 456)

Exceptionality. Mental, emotional, and physical condition that creates special educational needs. (p. 404)

Expectancy valence model. A theory that relates the probability and incentive of success to motivation. (p. 332)

Experiment. Procedure used to test the effects of a treatment. (p. 10)

Experimental group. Group that receives treatment during an experiment. (p. 11)

Expository teaching. Instructional technique in which information is presented to students in an organized, finished form. (p. 194)

External validity. Degree to which results of an experiment can be applied to real-life situations. (p. 12)

Extinction. Eliminating or decreasing a behavior by removing reinforcement for it. (p. 111)

Extrinsic incentive. A reward that is external to the activity, such as recognition or a good grade. (p. 338)

Field dependence/field independence. A learning style reflecting the degree to which people perceive stimuli as whole patterns (field dependence) as opposed to separating them into parts (field independence). (p. 281)

Figure-ground relationship. Perceiving selected parts of a stimulus to stand out (figure) from other parts (background). (p. 133)

Fine motor activity. A physical action of the fine muscles of the hand involving precision and dexterity. (p. 58)

Fixed-interval schedule (FI). Dispensing reinforcement for behavior emitted following a constant amount of time. (p. 114)

Fixed-ratio schedule (FR). Dispensing reinforcement following a constant number of correct behaviors. (p. 113)

Formal operations. Stage at which the ability to deal with hypothetical situations and to reason abstractly is acquired. (p. 35)

Formative evaluations. Tests or assessments administered during units of instruction that measure progress and guide the content and pace of lessons. (p. 484)

Formative quiz. Evaluation designed to determine whether additional instruction is needed. (p. 299)

Free recall learning. A task requiring recall of a list of items in any order. (p. 149)

Functional fixedness. Block to solving problems caused by an inability to see new uses for familiar objects or ideas. (p. 186)

Generalization. Perception of and response to similarities in stimuli. (p. 119)

Generative learning. A theory that emphasizes the active integration of new information with existing schemata. (p. 166)

Gestalt psychology. A psychological movement, started in Germany, that advanced the understanding of perception. (p. 132)

Goal structure. The degree to which students are placed in competitive or cooperative relationships in earning classroom rewards. (p. 353)

Grade equivalent. Measure of achievement that relates students' scores to expected performance levels at specific grade levels. (p. 253)

Grade equivalent score. Standard score that relates students' raw scores to the average scores obtained by norming groups at different grade levels. (p. 516)

Gross motor activity. A physical action, such as running or throwing, that involves the limbs and large muscles. (p. 58)

Group alerting. Methods of questioning that encourage students to pay attention during lectures and discussions. (p. 369)

Group contingencies. Class rewards that depend on the behavior of all students. (p. 381)

Growth needs. Needs for knowing, appreciating, and understanding, which people try to satisfy after their basic needs are met. (p. 321)

Heteronomous morality. Stage at which children think that rules are unchangeable and that breaking them leads automatically to punishment. (p. 45)

Home-based reinforcement strategies. Behavior modification strategy in which a student's school behavior is reported to parents, who supply rewards. (p. 387)

Humanistic education. An educational philosophy that focuses on developing students' attitudes, feelings, and independent learning. (p. 264)

Hyperactivity. Condition characterized by extreme restlessness and short attention spans relative to peers. (p. 414)

Identity diffusion. The adolescent's inability to develop a clear sense of self. (p. 84)

Identity foreclosure. The premature choice of a role, often done to reinforce self-concept. (p. 84)

Imagery. Use of mental images to improve memory. (p. 152)

Impulsivity/reflectivity. A learning style representing the degree to which tasks are completed slowly with high emphasis on accuracy (reflectivity) is opposed to speed (impulsivity). (p. 281)

Independent practice. Component of instruction in which students work by themselves to demonstrate and rehearse new knowledge. (p. 249)

Individualized Education Program. School program tailored to the needs of an exceptional child. (p. 424)

Individualized instruction. Teaching approach in which each student learns at his or her own level and pace. (p. 299)

Individual Learning Expectations. A teaching method that includes evaluation of students' improvement relative to past achievement. (p. 353)

Inert knowledge. Learned information that can be applied to only a restricted, often artificial set of circumstances. (p. 163)

Inferred reality. The meaning of stimuli in the context of relevant information. (p. 34)

Information-processing theory. Cognitive theory of learning that describes the processing, storage, and retrieval of knowledge from the mind. (p. 130)

Inquiry training. Teaching approach aimed at helping students to develop skills in asking questions and drawing conclusions. (p. 260)

Instructional objectives. A statement of information or tasks that students should master after one or more lessons. (p. 206)

Instrumental enrichment. A thinking-skills program in which students work through a series of paper-and-pencil exercises designed to develop various intellectual abilities. (p. 189)

Intelligence. General aptitude for learning, often measured by ability to deal with abstractions and to solve problems. (p. 513)

Intelligence quotient. An intelligence test score that for people of average intelligence should be near 100. (p. 406)

Interference. A process that occurs when recall of certain information is inhibited by the presence of other information in memory. (p. 144)

Internal validity. The degree to which an experiment's results can be attributed to the treatment in question, not to other factors. (p. 11)

Interpersonal Theory of Psychiatry. A theory that focuses on a person's relationships and need for security. (p. 86)

Intrinsic incentive. An aspect of an activity that people enjoy and, therefore, find motivating. (p. 338)

Joplin Plan. A regrouping method in which students are assigned to groups for reading instruction across grade lines. (p. 284)

Keyword method. Strategy for improving memory by using images to link pairs of items. (p. 152)

Laboratory experiment. Experiment in which conditions are highly controlled. (p. 11)

Law of Effect. An act followed by a favorable effect is more likely to be repeated in similar situations; an act followed by an unfavorable effect is less likely to be repeated. (p. 102)

Learned helplessness. The expectation, based on experience, that one's actions will ultimately lead to failure. (p. 331)

Learning. A change in an individual that results from experience. (p. 98)

Learning disability. Disorder that impedes academic progress of people who are not mentally retarded or emotionally disturbed. (p. 409)

Learning goals. A motivational orientation of students who place primary emphasis on knowledge acquisition and self-improvement. (p. 330)

Learning probes. Methods, such as questioning, that help teachers find out if students understand a lesson. (p. 246)

Learning stations. Areas where students work on individualized units or other independent activities. (p. 266)

Learning styles. Orientations for approaching learning tasks and processing information in certain ways. (p. 281)

Levels of processing theory. Explanation of memory that links recall of a stimulus with the amount of mental processing it receives. (p. 141)

Loci method. Strategy of remembering lists by picturing items in familiar locations. (p. 154)

Locus of control. A personality trait that concerns whether people attribute responsibility for their own failure or success to internal factors or to external factors. (p. 325)

Long-term memory. Component of memory where large amounts of information can be stored for long periods of time. (p. 136)

Madeline Hunter's Mastery Teaching Program. A general guide to using direct instructional methods. (p. 258)

Mainstreaming. The placement, for all or part of the school day, of handicapped children in regular classes. (p. 424)

Massed practice. Technique in which facts or skills to be learned are repeated many times over a concentrated period of time. (p. 152)

Mastery criteria. The standards students must meet to be considered proficient in a skill. (p. 299)

Mastery grading. Grading procedure used in mastery learning in which all students who achieve a mastery criterion can earn the highest available grade. (p. 503)

Mastery learning. System of instruction that emphasizes the achievement of instructional objectives by all students by allowing learning time to vary. (p. 292)

Mathemagenic behaviors. Strategies, such as previewing material, that help people learn. (p. 169)

Meaningful learning. Mental processing of new information leading to its linkage with previously learned knowledge. (p. 162)

Means-ends analysis. Problem-solving technique that encourages identifying the goal (ends) of a problem, the current situation, and what needs to be done (means) to reduce the difference between the two conditions. (p. 185)

Mental retardation. Condition, usually present at birth, that results in below average intellectual skills and poor adaptive behavior. (p. 406)

Mental set. Students' readiness to begin a lesson. (p. 239)

Metacognition. Monitoring one's own learning behaviors to determine degree of progress and strategies needed for accomplishing instructional goals. (p. 173)

Metacognitive strategies. Skills that increase retention by making learners more aware of how they process information. (p. 177)

Missouri Mathematics Program. A method of teaching math using direct instruction. (p. 258)

Mnemonics. Strategies to improve memory. (p. 152)

Modeling. Learning by observing others' behavior. (p. 119)

Moral dilemmas. Hypothetical situations that require a person to consider values of right and wrong. (p. 48)

Motivation. The influence of needs and desires on the intensity and direction of behavior. (p. 318)

Multidimensional classroom. Classroom in which children are shown many paths to success. (p. 48)

Multifactor aptitude battery. Test that predicts ability to learn a variety of specific skills and types of knowledge. (p. 513)

Negative correlation. Relationship in which high scores on one variable correspond to low scores on another. (p. 14)

Negative reinforcer. Release from an unpleasant situation to strengthen behavior. (p. 106)

Neutral stimulus. A stimulus that does not naturally prompt a particular response. (p. 99)

Normal curve. Bell-shaped symmetrical distribution of scores in which most scores fall near the mean, with progressively fewer occurring as distance from the mean increases. (p. 406)

Normal curve equivalent. Set of standardized scores ranging from 1 to 99, having a mean of 50 and a standard deviation of about 21. (p. 521)

Norm-referenced evaluations. Assessments that compare the performance of one student against the performance of others. (p. 484)

Norms. Standards derived from giving a test to a sample of people similar to those who will take the test and that can be used to interpret scores of future test takers. (p. 510)

Object permanence. Knowing an object exists when it is out of sight. (p. 28)

Open schools. Schools in which students are actively involved in deciding what and how they will study. (p. 266)

Operant conditioning. Using consequences to control the occurrence of behavior. (p. 102)

Operations. Actions carried out through logical mental processes. (p. 31)

Overlapping. A teacher's ability to respond to behavior problems without interrupting a classroom lesson. (p. 370)

Overlearning. Method of improving retention by practicing new knowledge or behaviors after mastery is achieved. (p. 154)

Paired-associate learning. A task involving the linkage of two items in a pair so that when one is presented the other can be recalled. (p. 149)

Parenting styles. General patterns of behavior used by parents when dealing with their children. (p. 65)

Part learning. Mastering new material by learning it one part or subskill at a time. (p. 154)

Pedagogy. Methods of instruction. (p. 2)

Peers. People who are equal in age or status. (p. 65)

Peer tutoring. One student teaching another. (p. 301)

Pegword method. Strategy for memorization in which images are used to link lists of facts to a familiar set of words or numbers. (p. 154)

Perceived appearances. How something appears to the eye. (p. 34)

Percentile score. Derived score that designates what percent of the norming group earned raw scores lower than a particular score. (p. 516)

Perception. A person's interpretation of stimuli. (p. 132)

Performance goals. A motivational orientation of students who place primary emphasis on gaining recognition from others and earning good grades. (p. 330)

Permissive parents. Parents who give their children great freedom. (p. 65)

Positive correlation. Relationship in which high scores on one variable correspond to high scores on another. (p. 13)

Positive reinforcer. Consequence given to strengthen behavior. (p. 104)

Predictive validity. A measure of the ability of a test to predict future behavior. (p. 524)

Premack principle. Using favored activities to reinforce participation in less desired activities. (p. 106)

Preoperational stage. Stage at which children learn to mentally represent things. (p. 29)

Pretend play. Creative activity in which children put themselves into imaginary roles or situations. (p. 67)

Primacy effect. The tendency for items that appear at the beginning of a list to be more easily recalled than other items. (p. 146)

Primary reinforcer. Food, water, or other consequence that satisfies basic needs. (p. 104)

Principle. Explanation of the relationship between factors. (p. 6)

Proactive facilitation. Increased ability to learn new information due to previously acquired information. (p. 145)

Proactive inhibition. Decreased ability to learn new information because of interference of present knowledge. (p. 144)

Problem solving. The application of knowledge and skills to achieve certain goals. (p. 184)

Procedural memory. A part of long-term memory that stores information about how to do things. (p. 138)

Process-product studies. Research approach in which the methods used by effective teachers are recorded through classroom observation. (p. 258)

Programmed instruction. Structured lessons that students can work on individually, at their own pace. (p. 299)

Progressive differentiation. Lesson progression that starts with general concepts, then moves to specifics. (p. 195)

Prosocial behaviors. Actions that show respect and caring for others. (p. 66)

Proximal zone of development. Level of development immediately above a person's present level. (p. 38)

Psychomotor objectives. Objectives concerned with physical skills that students must master. (p. 218)

Psychosocial theory. A set of principles that relates social environment to psychological development. (p. 38)

Puberty. Developmental stage at which a person becomes capable of reproduction. (p. 79)

Public Law 94-142. Federal law requiring provision of special education services to eligible students. (p. 424)

Punishment. Using unpleasant consequences to weaken a behavior. (p. 106)

QAIT model. A model of effective instruction that focuses on elements that teachers can directly control. (p. 234)

Random assignment. Selection by chance into different treatment groups to try to ensure the equality of the groups. (p. 10)

Randomized field experiment. Experiments conducted under realistic conditions in which individuals are assigned by chance to receive different practical treatments or programs. (p. 11)

Readiness. The state of having skills and knowledge necessary for a given activity. (p. 63)

Recency effect. The tendency for items that appear at the end of a list to be more easily recalled than other items. (p. 146)

Reception learning. Learning that occurs when students are presented information in organized, teacher-structured lessons. (p. 194)

Reciprocal teaching. Method that teaches metacognitive skills, through instruction and teacher modeling, to improve the reading performance of students who have poor comprehension. (p. 177)

Reflectivity. The act of analyzing oneself and one's own thoughts. (p. 83)

Reflexes. Natural responses that people are born with. (p. 28)

Regrouping. A method of ability grouping in which students in mixed-ability classes are assigned to reading or math classes on the basis of their performance levels. (p. 284)

Rehearsal. Mental repetition of information, which can improve its retention. (p. 136)

Reinforcer. A pleasurable consequence that maintains or increases a behavior. (p. 104)

Relative grading standard. A system of allocating grades to students on the basis of their positions in a group or class. (p. 500)

Reliability. A measure of the consistency of test scores obtained from the same students at different times. (p. 490)

Remediation. Instruction given to students having difficulty learning that supplements whole-class instruction. (p. 304)

Retroactive facilitation. Increased comprehension of previously learned information due to the acquisition of new information. (p. 145)

Retroactive inhibition. Decreased ability to recall previously learned information caused by learning of new information. (p. 144)

Reverse chaining. Shaping process in which the final subskills of a complex task are learned before the first subskills. (p. 110)

Reversibility. The ability to perform a mental operation and then reverse one's thinking to return to the starting point. (p. 31)

Rote learning. Memorization of facts or associations. (p. 162)

Rule-example-rule. Pattern of teaching concepts by presenting a rule or definition, giving examples, and then showing how the examples illustrate the rule. (p. 179)

Schedule of reinforcement. The frequency and predictability of reinforcement. (p. 112)

Schemata. Mental networks of related concepts that influence understanding of new information. (p. 139)

Schemes. Mental patterns that guide behavior. (p. 26)

Seatwork. Work that students are assigned to do independently during class. (p. 249)

Secondary reinforcer. A consequence that people learn to value through its association with a primary reinforcer. (p. 104)

Self-actualization. A person's desire to develop to his or her full potential. (p. 321)

Self-concept. A person's perception of his or her own strengths and weaknesses. (p. 74)

Self-regulation. Rewarding or punishing one's own behavior. (p. 121)

Semantic memory. A part of long-term memory that stores facts and general knowledge. (p. 138)

Sensorimotor stage. Stage during which infants learn about their surroundings by using their senses and motor skills. (p. 28)

Sensory register. Component of the memory system where information is received and held for very short periods of time. (p. 130)

Serial learning. A task requiring recall of a list of items. (p. 149)

Shaping. Using small steps combined with feedback to help learners reach goals. (p. 109)

Short-term memory. Component of memory where limited amounts of information can be stored for a few seconds. (p. 136)

Simulation programs. Computer programs that model real-life phenomena to promote problem-solving and motivate interest in the areas concerned. (p. 307)

Single-case experiment. Study of a treatment's effect on one person or one group by contrasting behavior before, during, and after the treatment is applied. (p. 13)

Sociodramatic play. Activities in which children act out prescribed roles. (p. 67)

Socioeconomic status. A measure of prestige within a social group most often based on income and education (often abbreviated SES). (p. 449)

Software. Programs that instruct the computer to perform different applications such as CAI and word-processing. (p. 306)

Special education. Programs that address the needs of students with mental, emotional, or physical handicaps. (p. 423)

Speech disorders. Articulation problems occurring most frequently among children in the early elementary school grades. (p. 418)

SQ4R. Study strategy that directs the learner to *survey*, *question*, *read*, *reflect*, *recite*, and *review*. (p. 177)

Stage theories of development. Explanations of various aspects of development that stress the existence of series of steps or phases of growth. (p. 25)

Standard deviation. A statistical measure of the degree of dispersion in a distribution of scores. (p. 518)

Standardized tests. Tests that are usually commercially prepared for nationwide use to provide accurate and meaningful information on students' levels of performance relative to others at their age or grade levels. (p. 510)

Stanine. A type of standardized score ranging from 1 to 9, having a mean of 5 and a standard deviation of 2. (p. 521)

Stimulus. Environmental condition that activates the senses. (p. 98)

Stimulus coding. Using aspects of stimuli and mental images to promote recall. (p. 152)

Stimulus selection. Choosing aspects of stimuli on which to focus attention. (p. 152)

Student evaluations. Formal assessments of student performance using tests, written reports, and grades. (p. 479)

Summative evaluations. Assessments that follow instruction and evaluate student knowledge or skills. (p. 484)

Summative quiz. Final test of an objective. (p. 299)

Table of specifications. List of instructional objectives and expected levels of understanding that guide test development. (p. 490)

Task analysis. Breaking down tasks into fundamental subskills. (p. 221)

Taxonomy of educational objectives. Bloom's ordering of objectives from simple learning tasks to more complex ones. (p. 212)

Team-Assisted Individualization. Teaching program in which students work on individualized instruction materials in four-member mixed-ability groups. (p. 301)

Thematic Apperception Test. A test of motivational orientation that asks individuals to characterize the behaviors of characters depicted in ambiguous situations. (p. 329)

Theory. A set of principles that explains and relates certain phenomena. (p. 6)

Time out. Removing a student from a situation in which misbehavior was reinforced. (p. 386)

Tracks. Classes or curricula targeted for students of a specified achievement or ability level. (p. 277)

Trainable mentally retarded. Category of mental retardation applied to those with moderate handicaps, whose education usually focuses on self-help skills. (p. 407)

Transfer-appropriate processing. A theory which proposes that memory is stronger and lasts longer when the conditions of performance are similar to those under which learning occurred. (p. 142)

Transfer of learning. The application of knowledge acquired in one situation to new situations. (p. 181)

Transformational grammar theory. A theory that emphasizes the quality of language as dependent on its ideas or content rather than its external form. (p. 60)

Treatment. A special program that is the subject of an experiment. (p. 10)

Tutorial CAI programs. Programs that teach lessons by varying their content and pace according to student responses. (p. 307)

Unconditioned Response (UR). A behavior prompted automatically by stimuli. (p. 99)

Unconditioned Stimulus (US). A stimulus that naturally evokes a particular response. (p. 99)

Uncorrelated variables. Lack of relationship between two variables. (p. 14)

Unidimensional classroom. Classroom in which a teacher imposes a single standard by which children's success is measured. (p. 48)

Utility program. Computer programs, such as word-processors, that help people perform specified tasks. (p. 308)

Validity. A measure of the degree to which a test is appropriate for its intended use. (p. 522)

Variable. Something that can have more than one value. (p. 10)

Variable-interval schedules (VI). Dispensing reinforcement for behavior emitted following an unpredictable amount of time. (p. 114)

Variable-ratio schedule (VR). Dispensing reinforcement following an unpredictable number of correct behaviors. (p. 113)

Verbal learning. The study of how students learn lists of words or facts under controlled conditions. (p. 148)

Vicarious learning. Learning from observing the consequences of others' behavior. (p. 121)

Wait time. Length of time that a teacher allows a student to take to answer a question. (p. 248)

Within-class ability grouping. System of accommodating student differences by dividing a class of students into two or more ability groups for instruction in certain subjects. (p. 285)

Withitness. The degree to which the teacher is aware of, and responsive to, student behavior. (p. 370)

Word magic. Objectives that are too general and vague to be useful in measuring student performance. (p. 209)

Yodai mnemonics. A strategy, developed in Japan, to increase memory by use of vivid imagery, poems, and songs. (p. 152)

z-scores. Set of standardized scores having a mean of zero and a standard deviation of 1. (p. 521)

References

ABRAMI, P. C., LEVENTHAL, L., and PERRY, R. P. (1982). Educational seduction. *Review of Educational Research, 52,* 446–462.

ABT ASSOCIATES (1976). *Education as experimentation: A planned variation model,* Vol. III. Cambridge, Mass.: Abt Associates.

ABT ASSOCIATES (1977). *Education as experimentation: A planned variation model,* Vol. IV. Cambridge, Mass.: Abt Associates.

ADAMS, J. L. (1974). *Conceptual blockbusting.* San Francisco, Calif.: Freeman.

ADAMS, M. J. (1989). Thinking skills curricula: Their promise and progress. *Educational Psychologist, 24,* 25–77.

ADAMS, R. S., and BIDDLE, B. J. (1970). *Realities of teaching: Explorations with video tape.* New York: Holt, Rinehart, and Winston.

AHMANN, J. S., and GLOCK, M. D. (1981). *Evaluating student progress: Principles of tests and measures.* Boston: Allyn and Bacon.

AIKEN, L. R. (1983). Determining grade boundaries on classroom tests. *Journal of Educational and Psychological Measurement, 43,* 759–762.

ALEXANDER, C., and STRAIN, P. (1978). A review of educators' attitudes toward handicapped children and the concept of mainstreaming. *Psychology in the Schools, 15,* 390–396.

ALEXANDER, K. L., ENTWISLE, D. R., and THOMPSON, M. S. (1987). *School performance, status relations, and the structure of sentiment: Bringing the teacher back in* (Technical Report No. 9). Baltimore, Md.: Johns Hopkins University, Center for Research on Elementary and Middle Schools.

ALLEN, J. D. (1986). Classroom management: Students' perspectives, goals, and strategies. *American Educational Research Journal, 23,* 437–459.

ALLEN, J., CLARK, F., GALLAGHER, P., and SCOFIELD, F. (1982). *Classroom strategies for accommodating exceptional learners.* Minneapolis: University of Minnesota, National Support Systems Project.

ALLEN, L. E. (1969). *Equations: A game of creative mathematics.* Turtle Creek, Penn.: WFF 'n' Proof.

ALLEN, M. S. (1962). *Morphological creativity.* Englewood Cliffs, N.J.: Prentice-Hall.

ALLPORT, G. (1954). *The nature of prejudice.* Cambridge, Mass.: Addison-Wesley.

ALSCHULER, A. S. (1973). *Developing achievement motivation in adolescents.* Englewood Cliffs, N.J.: Education Technology Publications.

ALVERMANN, D. E., et al. (1985). Prior knowledge activation and the comprehension of compatible and incompatible text. *Reading Research Quarterly, 20,* 420–436.

AMERICAN INSTITUTES FOR RESEARCH (1977). *Evaluations of the impact of ESEA Title VII Spanish/English Bilingual Education Programs.* Palo Alto, Calif.: AIR.

AMERICAN PSYCHIATRIC ASSOCIATION (1982). *Diagnostic and statistical manual of mental disorders* (3rd ed.–DSM III). Washington, D.C.: American Psychiatric Association.

AMES, C. (1984). Achievement attributions and self-instructions under competitive and individualistic goal structures. *Journal of Educational Psychology, 76,* 478–487.

AMES, C. (1986). Effective motivation: The contribution of the learning environment. In R. S. Feldman (Ed.), *The social psychology of education.* Cambridge, England: Cambridge University Press.

AMES, C. (Ed.) (1987). The enhancement of student motivation. In D. A. Kleiber and M. L. Maehr, *Enhancing motivation.* Greenwich, Conn.: JAI.

AMES, C., and AMES, R. (1984). Systems of student and teacher motivation: Toward a qualitative definition. *Journal of Educational Psychology, 76,* 535–556.

AMES, C., AMES, R., and FELKER, D. W. (1977). Effects of competitive reward structure and valence of outcome on children's achievement attributions. *Journal of Educational Psychology, 69,* 1–8.

AMES, C., and ARCHER, J. (1988). Achievement goals in the classroom: students learning strategies and motivation processes. *Journal of Educational Psychology, 80,* 260–267.

AMES, R., and AMES, C. (1989). *Research on motivation in education* (Vol. 3). New York: Academic Press.

ANASTASI, A. (1958). *Differential psychology.* New York: Macmillan.

ANASTASI, A. (1981). Abilities and the measurement of achievement. In W. B. Schrader (Ed.), *New directions for testing and measurement,* Vol. 5. San Francisco: Jossey-Bass.

ANDERSON, J. R. (1985). *Cognitive psychology and its implications* (2nd ed.). San Francisco, Calif.: Freeman.

ANDERSON, J. R., and BOWER, G. (1983). *Human associative memory.* Washington, D.C.: Winston.

ANDERSON, L. M., BRUBAKER, N. L., ALLEMAN-BROOKS, J., and DUFFY, G. G. (1985). A qualitative study of seatwork in first-grade classrooms. *Elementary School Journal, 86,* 123–140.

ANDERSON, L. M., EVERTSON, L. M., and BROPHY, J. E. (1979). An experimental study of effective teaching in first-grade reading groups. *Elementary School Journal, 79,* 193–223.

ANDERSON, L. M., EVERTSON, C., and BROPHY, J. (1979). An experimental study of effective teaching in first-grade reading-groups. *Elementary School Journal, 79,* 193–223.

ANDERSON, L. M., EVERTSON, C. M., and BROPHY, J. E. (1982). Principles of small group instruction in elementary reading (Occasional Paper No. 58). Institute for Research on Teaching, Michigan State University.

ANDERSON, L. W., SCOTT, C., and HUTLOCK, N. (1976, April). The effects of a mastery learning program on selected cognitive, affective, and ecological variables in grades 1 through 6. Paper presented at the annual meeting of the American Educational Research Association, San Francisco.

ANDERSON, R. C., and HIDDE, J. L. (1971). Imagery and sentence learning. *Journal of Educational Psychology, 62,* 81–94.

ANDERSON, R. C., and PICHERT, J. W. (1978). Recall of previously unrecallable information following a shift in perspective. *Journal of Verbal Learning and Verbal Behavior, 17,* 1–12.

ANDERSON, R. C., SPIRO, R. J., and MONTAGUE, W. E. (Eds.) (1977). *Schooling and the acquisition of knowledge.* Hillsdale, N.J.: Erlbaum.

ANDERSON, T. H., and ARMBRUSTER, B. B. (1984). Studying. In P. D. Pearson (Ed.), *Handbook of reading research.* New York: Longman.

ANDRE, T. (1973). Retroactive inhibition of prose and change in physical or organizational context. *Psychological Reports, 32,* 781–782.

ANDRE, T. (1979). Does answering higher-level questions while reading facilitate productive learning? *Review of Educational Research, 49,* 280–318.

ANDRE, T. (1984). Problem-solving. In G. Phye and T. Andre (Eds.), *Cognitive instructional psychology.* New York: Academic Press.

ANDRE, T., ANDERSON, R. C., and WATTS, G. H. (1976). Item-specific interference and list discrimination in free recall. *Journal of General Psychology, 72,* 533–543.

ANDRE, T., and SOLA, J. (1976). Imagery, verbatim and paraphrased questions and retention of meaningful sentences. *Journal of Educational Psychology, 68,* 661–669.

ANDRE, T., and WOMACK, S. (1978). Verbatim and paraphrased questions and learning from prose. *Journal of Educational Psychology, 70, 796*–802.

ANDREWS, G. R., and DEBUS, R. L. (1978). Persistence and the casual perception of failure: Modifying cognitive attributions. *Journal of Educational Psychology, 70,* 154–166.

ARCHAMBAULT, F. X. (1989). Instructional setting and other design features of compensatory education programs. In R. E. Slavin, N. L. Karweit, and N. A. Madden (Eds.), *Effective programs for students at risk.* Boston: Allyn and Bacon.

ARCHIBALD, D., and NEWMANN, F. (1988). *Beyond standardized testing: Authentic academic achievement in the secondary school.* Reston, Va.: NASSP Publications.

ARIAS, M. B. (1986). The context of education for Hispanic students: An overview. *American Journal of Education, 95,* 26–57.

ARLIN, M. (1979). Teacher transitions can disrupt time flow in classrooms. *American Educational Research Journal, 16,* 42–56.

ARLIN, M. (1984a). Time, equality, and mastery learning. *Review of Educational Research, 54,* 65–86.

ARLIN, M. (1984b) Time variability in mastery learning. *American Educational Research Journal, 21,* 103–120.

ARLIN, M., and WEBSTER, J. (1983). Time costs of mastery learning. *Journal of Educational Psychology, 75,* 187–195.

ARNOLD, W. R., and BRUNGARDT, T. M. (1983). *Juvenile misconduct and delinquency.* Boston: Houghton Mifflin.

ARON, I. E. (1977). Moral philosophy and moral education: A critique of Kohlberg's theory. *School Review, 85,* 197–217.

ARONFREED, J., and REBER, A. (1965). Internal behavioral suppression and the timing of social punishment. *Journal of Personality and Social Psychology, 1,* 3–16.

ARONSON, E. (1972). *The social animal.* San Francisco: W. H. Freeman.

ARONSON, E., BLANEY, N., STEPHAN, C., SIKES, J., and SNAPP, M. (1978). *The jigsaw classroom.* Beverly Hills, Calif.: Sage.

ASH, P. (1950). The relative effectiveness of massed versus spaced film presentations. *Journal of Educational Psychology, 41,* 19–30.

ASHER, S. R., ODEN, S. L., and GOTTMAN, J. M. (1977). Children's friendships in school settings. In L. G. Katz (Ed.), *Current topics in early childhood education,* Vol. 1, pp. 33–62. Norwood, N.J.: Ablex Publishing Corp.

ASHER, S. R., RENSHAW, P. D., and HYMEL, S. (1982). Peer relations and the development of social skills. In S. G. Moore and C. R. Cooper (Eds.), *The young child: Reviews of research,* Vol. 3, pp. 137–158. Washington, D.C.: National Association for the Education of Young Children.

ATKINSON, J. W. (1958). Towards experimental analysis of human motivation in terms of motive expectancies, and incentives. In J. W. Atkinson (Ed.), *Motives in fantasy, action, and society.* Princeton, N.J.: Van Nostrand.

ATKINSON, J. W. (1964). *An introduction to motivation.* Princeton, N.J.: Van Nostrand.

ATKINSON, J. W., and BIRCH, D. (1978). *An introduction to motivation* (2nd ed.). New York: Van Nostrand.

ATKINSON, J. W., and LITWIN, G. H. (1960). Achievement motive and test anxiety as motives to approach success and avoid failure. *Journal of Abnormal and Social Psychology, 60,* 52–63.

ATKINSON, M. L. (1984). Computer-assisted instruction: Current state of the art. *Computers in the Schools, 1,* 91–99.

ATKINSON, R. C. (1968). Computerized instruction and the learning process. *American Psychologist, 12,* 225–239.

ATKINSON, R. C. (1975). Mnemonotechnics in second language learning. *American Psychologist, 30,* 821–828.

ATKINSON, R. C., and FLETCHER, J. D. (1972). Teaching children to read with a computer. *The Reading Teacher, 25,* 319–327.

ATKINSON, R. C., and RAUGH, M. R. (1975). An application of the mnemonic keyword method to the acquisition of Russian vocabulary. *Journal of Experimental Psychology: Human Learning and Memory, 104,* 126–133.

ATKINSON, R. C., and SHIFFRIN, R. M. (1968). Human memory: A proposed system and its component processes. In K. Spence and J. Spence (Eds.), *The psychology of learning and motivation,* Vol. 2. New York: Academic Press.

ATWOOD, R. (1983, April). The interacting effects of task form and activity structure on students' task involvement and teacher evaluations. Paper presented at the annual meeting of the American Educational Research Association, Montreal.

AUSUBEL, D. P. (1960). The use of advanced organizers in the learning and retention of meaningful verbal material. *Journal of Educational Psychology, 51,* 267–272.

AUSUBEL, D. P. (1961). In defense of verbal learning. *Education Theory, 11,* 15–25.

AUSUBEL, D. P. (1963). *The psychology of meaningful verbal learning.* New York: Grune and Stratton.

AUSUBEL, D. P. (1968). *Educational psychology: A cognitive view.* New York: Holt, Rinehart, and Winston.

AUSUBEL, D. P. (1978). In defense of advance organizers: A reply to the critics. *Review of Educational Research, 48,* 251–258.

AUSUBEL, D. P., and YOUSSEF, M. (1963). Role of discriminability in meaningful parallel learning. *Journal of Educational Psychology, 54,* 331–336.

AYLLON, T., GARBER, S., and PISOR, K. (1975). The elimination of discipline problems through a combined school-home motivational system. *Behavior Therapy, 1975, 6,* 616–626.

AYLLON, T., and ROBERTS, M. D. (1974). Eliminating discipline problems by strengthening academic performance. *Journal of Applied Behavior Analysis, 7,* 71–76.

BAKER, L., and BROWN, A. L. (1984). Metacognitive skills and reading. In P. D. Pearson (Ed.), *Handbook of reading research* (pp. 353–394). New York: Longman.

BALDWIN, J., and OLIVER, J. (1975). Epidemiology and family characteristics of severely abused children. *British Journal of Preventive and Social Medicine, 29,* 205–221.

BALL, S., and BOGATZ, G. A. (1970). *The first year of Sesame Street: An evaluation.* Princeton, N.J.: Educational Testing Service.

BALL, S., and BOGATZ, G. A. (1972). *Reading and television: An evaluation of the Electric Company* (PR-72-2). Princeton, N.J.: Educational Testing Service.

BALLARD, M., CORMAN, L., GOTTLIEB, J., and KAUFFMAN, M. (1977). Improving the social status of mainstreamed retarded children. *Journal of Educational Psychology, 69,* 605–611.

BALOW, I. H. (1964). The effects of homogeneous grouping in seventh grade arithmetic. *Arithmetic Teacher, 11,* 186–191.

BALTIMORE PUBLIC SCHOOLS (1972). A report of the study group on school attendance/dropouts. Baltimore, Md.

BANDURA, A. (1965). Influence of models' reinforcement contingencies on the acquisition of imitative responses. *Journal of Personality and Social Psychology, 1,* 589–595.

BANDURA, A. (1969). *Principles of behavior modification.* New York: Holt, Rinehart, and Winston.

BANDURA, A. (1977). *Social learning theory.* Englewood Cliffs, N.J.: Prentice-Hall.

BANDURA, A. (1986). *Social foundations of thought and action: A social-cognitive theory.* Englewood Cliffs, N.J.: Prentice-Hall.

BANGERT, R., KULIK, J., and KULIK, C. (1983). Individualized systems of instruction in secondary schools. *Review of Educational Research, 53,* 143–158.

BANGERT-DROWNS, R. L., KULIK, J. A., and KULIK, C.-L. (1986, April). Effects of frequent classroom testing. Paper presented at the annual convention of the American Education Research Association, San Francisco.

BARBER, R. M., and KAGEY, J. R. (1977). Modification of school attendance for an elementary population. *Journal of Applied Behavior Analysis, 10,* 41–48.

BARKER-LUNN, J. C. (1970). *Streaming in the primary school.* London: National Foundation for Educational Research in England and Wales.

BARNES, B. R., and CLAWSON, E. V. (1975). Do advance organizers facilitate learning? Recommendations for further research based on an analysis of 32 studies. *Review of Educational Research, 45,* 637–660.

BARNES, E., BERRIGAN, C., and BIKLEN, D. (1978). *What's the difference? Teaching positive attitudes toward people with disabilities.* Syracuse, N.Y.: Human Policy Press.

BARNETT, J. E., DiVESTA, F. J., and ROGOZINSKI, J. T. (1981). What is learned in note taking. *Journal of Educational Psychology, 73,* 181–192.

BARON, J. B. (1989). Performance testing in Connecticut. *Educational Leadership, 46* (7), 8.

BARON, R., TOM, D., and COOPER, H. (1985). Social class, race, and teacher expectations. In J. Duser (Ed.), *Teacher expectations.* Hillsdale, N.J.: Erlbaum.

BARR, R., and DREEBEN, R. (1983). *How schools work.* Chicago: University of Chicago Press.

BARR, R. (1987). Content coverage. In M. J. Dunkin (Ed.), *International encyclopedia of teaching and teacher education.* New York: Pergamon.

BARR, R. (in press). The social organization of literacy instruction. In S. McCormick and J. Zutell (Eds.), *Thirty-ninth yearbook of the National Reading Conference.* Chicago: National Reading Conference.

BARRINGER, C., and GHOLSON, B. (1979). Effects of type and combination of feedback upon conceptual learning by children: Implications for research in academic learning. *Review of Educational research, 49,* 459–478.

BARRISH, H. H., SAUNDERS, M., and WOLF, M. M. (1969). Good behavior game: Effects of individual contingencies for group consequences on disruptive behavior in a classroom. *Journal of Applied Behavior Analysis, 2,* 119–124.

BAR-TAL, D. (1979). Interactions of teachers and pupils. In I. H. Frieze, D. Bar-Tal, and J. S. Carroll (Eds.), *New approaches to social problems: Applications of attribution theory.* San Francisco: Jossey-Bass.

BARTH, R. (1979). Home-based reinforcement of school behavior: A review and analysis. *Review of Educational Research, 49,* 436–458.

BARTON, K. (1973). Recent data on the culture-fair scales. In *Information Bulletin 16.* Champaign, Ill.: Institute for Personality and Ability Testing.

BASKIN, B. H., and HARRIS, K. H. (1977). *Notes from a different drummer: A guide to juvenile fiction portraying the handicapped.* New York: R. R. Bowker.

BATES, J. A. (1979). Extrinsic reward and instrinsic motivation: A review with implications for the classroom. *Review of Educational Research, 19,* 557–576.

BATES, J. A. (1987). Reinforcement. In M. J. Dunkin (Ed.), *The international encyclopedia of teaching and teacher education.* New York: Pergamon.

BAUMRIND, D. (1973). The development of instrumental competence through socialization. In A. Pick (Ed.), *Minnesota symposium on child psychology,* Vol. 7, pp. 3–46. Minneapolis: University of Minnesota Press.

BAUMRIND, D. (1980). New directions in socialization research. *American Psychologist, 35,* 639–652.

BEADY, L. L., SLAVIN, R. E., and FENNESSEY, G. M. (1981). Alternative student evaluation structures and a focused schedule of instruction in an inner-city junior high school. *Journal of Educational Psychology, 73,* 518–523.

BECKER, H. J. (1983). *Microcomputers in the classroom: Dreams and realities.* Eugene, Ore.: International Council for Computers in Education.

BECKER, H. J. (1983–1984). *School uses of microcomputers.* Baltimore, Md.: Center for Social Organization of Schools, Johns Hopkins University.

BECKER, H. J. (1986). *Instructional uses of computers: Reports from the 1985 national survey* (Issue No. 1). Baltimore, Md.: Johns Hopkins University. Center for Research on Elementary and Middle Schools.

BECKER, H. J. (1990a, April). *Computer use in United States schools: 1989.* Paper presented at the annual convention of the American Educational Research Association, Boston.

BECKER, H. J. (1990b, April). *Effects of computer use on mathematics achievement: Field findings from a nationwide field experiment in grade five to eight classes.* Paper presented at the annual meeting of the American Educational Research Association, Boston.

BECKER, W., and CARNINE, D. (1980). Direct instruction: An effective approach for educational intervention with the disadvantaged and low performers. In B. Lahey and A. Kazdin (Eds.), *Advances in child clinical psychology.* New York: Plenum.

BECKER, W. C., MADSEN, C. H., ARNOLD, C. R., and THOMAS, D. R. (1967). The contingent use of teacher attention and praise in reducing classroom behavior problems. *Journal of Special Education, 1,* 287–307.

BEEZER, B. (1985). Reporting child abuse and neglect: Your responsibilities and your protections. *Phi Delta Kappan, 66,* 434–436.

BEHNKE, G. J. (1979). *Coping with classroom distractions: The formal research study* (Tech. Ref. No. 79–2). San Francisco: Far West Laboratory.

BELGARD, M., ROSENSHINE, B., and GAGE, N. L. (1971). Effectiveness in explaining: Evidence on its generality and correlation with pupil rating. In I. Westbury and A. Bellack (Eds.), *Research into classroom processes: Recent developments and next steps.* New York: Teachers College Press.

BELLEZA, F. S. (1981). Mnemonic devices classification, characteristics, and criteria. *Review of Educational Research, 51,* 247–275.

BENBOW, C. P., and STANLEY, J. C. (1980). Sex differences in mathematical ability: Fact or artifact? *Science, 210,* 1262–1264.

BEREITER, C., and ENGLEMANN, S. (1966). *Teaching disadvantaged children in the preschool.* Englewood Cliffs, N.J.: Prentice-Hall.

BEREITER, C., and SCARDAMALIA, M. (1987). *The psychology of written composition.* Hillsdale, N.J.: Erlbaum.

BERK, R. (1986). A consumer's guide to setting performance standards on criterion-referenced tests. *Review of Educational Research, 56,* 137–172.

BERK, R. A. (1980). *Criterion-referenced testing: State of the art.* Baltimore, Md.: Johns Hopkins University Press.

BERKO, J. (1958). The child's learning of English morphology. *Word, 14,* 150–177.

BERLINER, D. C. (1968). The effects of test-like events and note-taking on learning from lecture instruction. Unpublished doctoral dissertation, Stanford University.

BERLYNE, D. E. (1965). Curiosity and education. In J. D. Krumboltz (Ed.), *Learning and the educational process.* Chicago: Rand McNally.

BERNDT, T. J. (1982). The features and effects of friendship in early adolescence. *Child Development, 53,* 1447–1460.

BERRUETA-CLEMENT, J. R., SCHWEINHART, L. J., BARNETT, W. S., EPSTEIN, A. S., and WEIKART, D. P. (1984). *Changed lives.* Ypsilanti, Mich.: High/Scope.

BERSOFF, D. N. (1981). Testing and the law. *American Psychologist, 36,* 1047–1056.

BILLINGS, K. (1983). Research on school computing. In M. T. Grady and J. D. Gawronski (Eds.), *Computers in curriculum and instruction* (pp. 12–18). Alexandria, Va.: Association for Supervision and Curriculum Development.

BIRMAN, B. F., ORALAND, M. E., JUNG, R. K., ANSON, R. J., GARCIA, G. N., MOORE, M. T., FUNKHOUSER, J. E., MORRISON, D. R., TURNBULL, B. J., and REISNER, E. R. (1987). *The current operation of the Chapter 1 program.* Washington, D.C.: Office of Educational Research and Improvement, U.S. Department of Education.

BIRNBRAUER, J. S., WOLF, M. M., KIDDER, J. D., and TAGUE, C. E. (1965). Classroom behavior of retarded pupils with token reinforcement. *Journal of Experimental Child Psychology, 2,* 219–235.

BLACK, J. K. (1981). Are young children really egocentric? *Young Children, 36,* 51–55.

BLACKADAR, A. R., and NACHTIGAL, P. (1986). *Cotapaxi/Westcliffe follow-through project: Final evaluation report.* Denver: Mid-Continent Regional Educational Laboratory.

BLACKHURST, A. E., and BERDINE, W. H. (1981). *An introduction to special education.* Boston: Little, Brown.

BLOCK, J. H., and ANDERSON, L. W. (1975). *Mastery learning in classroom instruction.* New York: Macmillan.

BLOCK, J. H., and BURNS, R. B. (1976). Mastery learning. In L. S. Shulman (Ed.), *Review of research in education,* Vol. 4. Itasca, Ill.: F. E. Peacock.

BLOOM, B. S. (1964). *Stability and change in human characteristics.* New York: Wiley.

BLOOM, B. S. (1968). Learning for mastery (UCLA-CSEIP). *Evaluation Comment, 1,* 2.

BLOOM, B. S. (1976). *Human characteristics and school learning.* New York: McGraw-Hill.

BLOOM, B. S. (1984). The 2 sigma problem: The search for methods of instruction as effective as one-to-one tutoring. *Educational Researcher, 13,* 4–16.

BLOOM, B. S. (1986). Automaticity: The hands and feet of genius. *Educational Leadership, 43,* 70–77.

BLOOM, B. S., ENGLEHART, M. B., FURST, E. J., HILL, W. H., and KRATHWOHL, O. R. (1956). *Taxonomy of educational objectives: The classification of educational goals. Handbook 1: The cognitive domain.* New York: Longman.

BLOOM, B. S., HASTINGS, J. T., and MADAUS, G. F. (1971). *Handbook on formative and summative evaluation of student learning.* New York: McGraw-Hill.

BLOS, P. (1979). *The adolescent passage.* New York: International Universities Press.

BLUME, G. W. (1984, April). *A review of research on the effects of computer programming on mathematical problem solving.* Paper presented at the annual convention of the American Educational Research Association, New Orleans.

BODEN, M. A. (1980). *Jean Piaget.* New York: Viking Press.

BOOCOCK, S. S. (1980). *Sociology of education* (2nd ed.). Boston: Houghton Mifflin.

BOOKBINDER, S. R. (1978). *Mainstreaming: What every child needs to know about disabilities.* Providence: Rhode Island Easter Seal Society.

BORNSTEIN, P. H. (1985). Self-instructional training: A commentary and state-of-the-art. *Journal of Applied Behavior Analysis, 18,* 69–72.

BORSTEIN, M., and QUEVILLON, R. (1976). The effects of a self-instructional package with overactive preschool boys. *Journal of Applied Behavior Analysis, 9,* 179–188.

BOTVIN, G. (1984). Prevention of alcohol misuse through the development of personal and social competence: A pilot study. *Journal of Alcohol Studies, 45,* 37.

BOWER, G. H., CLARK, M. C., LESGOLD, A. M., and WINZENZ, D. (1969). Hierarchical retrieval schemes in recall of categorized word lists. *Journal of Verbal Learning and Verbal Behavior, 8,* 323–343.

BOWER, G. H., and KARLIN, M. B. (1974). Depth of processing pictures of faces and recognition memory. *Journal of Experimental Psychology, 103,* 751–757.

BOWERMAN, C. E., and KINCH, J. W. (1969). Changes in family and peer orientation of children between the fourth and tenth grades. In M. Gold and E. Douvan (Eds.), *Adolescent development.* Boston: Allyn and Bacon.

BOYKIN, A. W. (1986). The triple quandary and the schooling of Afro-American children. In U. Neisser (Ed.), *The school achievement of minority children.* Hillsdale, N.J.: Erlbaum.

BRADDOCK, J. H. (1985). School desegregation and black assimilation. *Journal of Social Issues, 41,* 9–22.

BRAININ, S. S. (1985). Mediated learning: Pedagogical issues in the improvement of cognitive functioning. In E. W. Gordon (Ed.), *Review of Research in Education,* Vol. 12. Washington, D.C.: American Educational Research Association.

BRANSFORD, J. D. (1979). *Human cognition: Learning, understanding, and remembering.* Belmont, Calif.: Wadsworth.

BRANSFORD, J. D., BURNS, M. S., DELCLOS, V. R., and VYE, N. J. (1986b). Teaching thinking: Evaluating evaluations and broadening the data base. *Educational Leadership, 44* (2), 68–70.

BRANSFORD, J. D., SHERWOOD, R. D., VYE, N. J., and RIESER, J. (1986a). Teaching thinking and problem solving: Research foundations. *American Psychologist, 41,* 1078–1087.

BRANSFORD, J. D., STEIN, B. S., VYE, N. J., FRANKS, J. J., AUBLE, P. M., MEZYNSKI, K. J., and PERFETTO, G. A. (1982). Differences in approaches to learning: An overview. *Journal of Experimental Psychology: General, III,* 390–398.

BRANSFORD, L. A., BACA, L., and LANE, K. (1973). *Cultural diversity and the exceptional child.* Reston, Va.: Council for Exceptional Children.

BRETZING, B. B., and KULHAVY, R. W. (1979). Note taking and depth of processing. *Contemporary Educational Psychology, 4,* 145–153.

BRETZING, B. B., and KULHAVY, R. W. (1981). Note taking and passage style. *Journal of Educational Psychology, 73,* 242–250.

BREWER, W. F., and NAKAMURA, G. V. (1984). The nature and function of schemas. In R. S. Wyer and T. K. Srull (Eds.), *Handbook of social cognition* (pp. 119–160). Hillsdale, N.J.: Erlbaum.

BRODEN, M., BRUCE, C., MITCHELL, M. A., CARTER, V., and HALL, R. V. (1970b). Effects of teacher attention on attending behavior of two boys at adjacent desks. *Journal of Applied Behavior Analysis, 3,* 199–203.

BRODEN, M., HALL, R. V., DUNLAP, A., and CLARK, R. (1970a). Effects of teacher attention and a token reinforcement system in a junior high school special education class. *Exceptional Children, 36,* 341–349.

BRODEN, M., HALL, R. V., and MITTS, B. (1971). The effects of self-recording on the classroom behavior of two eighth-grade students. *Journal of Applied Behavior Analysis, 4,* 191–199.

BROOKOVER, W., BEADY, C., FLOOD, P., SCHWEITER, J., and WISENBAKER, J. (1979). *School social systems and student achievement.* New York: Praeger.

BROOKS, B. D. (1975). Contingency management as a means of reducing school truancy. *Education, 95,* 206–211.

BROOKS, D. M. (1985). Beginning the year in junior high: The first day of school. *Educational Leadership, 42,* 76–78.

BROPHY, J. (1981). Teacher praise: A functional analysis. *Review of Educational Research, 51,* 5–32.

BROPHY, J. (1987). Synthesis of research on strategies for motivating students to learn. *Educational Leadership, 45*(2), 40–48.

BROPHY, J. E. (1979). Teacher behavior and its effects. *Journal of Educational Psychology, 71,* 733–750.

BROPHY, J. E. (1982, April). Fostering student

learning and motivation in the elementary school classroom. Occasional Paper No. 51, East Lansing, Mich.: Institute for Research on Teaching.

BROPHY, J. E. (1988). Research on teacher effects: Uses and abuses. *Elementary School Journal, 89,* 3–21.

BROPHY, J. E., and EVERTSON, C. M. (1974). Process-product correlations in the Texas teacher effectiveness study: Final report (Research Report No. 74–4). Austin: Research and Development Center for Teacher Education, University of Texas.

BROPHY, J. E., and EVERTSON, C. M. (1976). *Learning from teaching: A developmental perspective.* Boston: Allyn and Bacon.

BROPHY, J. E., and EVERTSON, C. M. (1981). *Student characteristics and teaching.* New York: Longman.

BROPHY, J. E., and GOOD, T. L. (1974). *Teacher-student relationships: Causes and consequences.* New York: Holt, Rinehart, and Winston.

BROPHY, J. E., and GOOD, T. L. (1986). Teacher behavior and student achievement. In M. C. Wittrock (Ed.), *Handbook of research on teaching* (3rd ed.). New York: Macmillan.

BROWN, A. L. (1978). Metacognitive development and reading. In R. J. Spiro, B. C. Bruce, and G. W. F. Brewer (Eds.), *Theoretical issues in reading comprehension.* Hillsdale, N.J.: Erlbaum.

BROWN, A. L. (1984, April). Learner characteristics and scientific texts. Paper presented at the Annual Meeting of the American Educational Research Association, New Orleans.

BROWN, A. L., BRANSFORD, J. D., FERRARA, R. A., and CAMPIONE, J. C. (1983). Learning, remembering, and understanding. In J. Flavell and E. M. Markman (Eds.), *Handbook of child psychology,* 4th ed, Vol. 3, pp. 515–629. New York: Wiley.

BROWN, A. L., CAMPIONE, J. C., and DAY, J. D. (1981). Learning to learn: On training students to learn from texts. *Educational Researcher, 10,* 14–21.

BROWN, A. L., SMILEY, S. S., DAY, J. D., TOWNSEND, M. A. R., and LAWSON, S. C. (1977). Intrusion of a thematic idea in children's comprehension and retention of stories. *Child Development, 48* (1), 454–466.

BROWN, J. S., COLLINS, A., and DUGUID, P. (1989). Situated cognition and the culture of learning. *Educational Researcher, 18,* 32–42.

BRUNER, J. S. (1966). *Toward a theory of instruction.* New York: Norton.

BRYAN, J. H. (1975). Children's cooperation and helping behaviors. In E. M. Hetherington (Ed.), *Review of child development research,* Vol. 5, pp. 127–181. Chicago: The University of Chicago Press.

BURNETTE, J. (1987). *Adapting instructional materials for mainstreamed students.* Reston, Va.: Council for Exceptional Children.

BURNS, M. (1986). Teaching "what to do" in arithmetic vs. teaching "what to do and why." *Educational Leadership, 43*(7), 34–38.

BURNS, R. B. (1984). How time is used in elementary schools: The activity structure of classrooms. In L. W. Anderson (Ed.), *Time and school learning: Theory, research, and practice.* London: Croom Helm.

BUROS, O. K. (1978). *The eighth mental measurement yearbook.* Highland Park, N.J.: Gryphon Press.

BURTON, F. (1983). *A study of the letter grade system and its effects on the curriculum.* ERIC No. 238143.

BURTON, N. W., and JONES, L. V. (1982). Recent trends in achievement levels of black and white youth. *Educational Researcher, 11* (4), 10–14.

BURTON, R. V. (1976). Honesty and dishonesty. In T. Lickona (Ed.), *Moral development and behavior.* New York: Holt, Rinehart, and Winston.

BURTT, H. E. (1932). The retention of early memories. *Journal of Genetic Psychology, 40,* 287–295; *50,* (1937), 187–192; *58,* (1941), 435–439. Articles abridged in W. Dennis (Ed.), Readings in child psychology. Englewood Cliffs, N.J.: Prentice-Hall, 1963.

BUTTERFIELD, E. C. (1988). On solving the problem of transfer. In M. M. Grunesberg, P. E. Morris, and R. N. Sykes (Eds.), *Practical aspects of memory* (Vol. 2, pp. 377–382). London, England: Academic Press.

CAIRNS, L. G. (1987). Behavior problems. In M. J. Dunkin (Ed.), *International encyclopedia of teaching and teacher education.* New York: Pergamon.

CALDWELL, B. (1977). Aggression and hostility in young children. *Young Children, 32,* 4–13.

CALFEE, R. C. (1976). Sources of dependency in cognitive processes. In D. Klahr (Ed.), *Cognition and instruction.* Hillsdale, N.J.: Erlbaum.

CALHOUN, G., and ELLIOTT, R. (1977). Self-concept and academic achievement of educable retarded and emotionally disturbed children. *Exceptional Children, 44,* 379–380.

CALIFORNIA STATE DEPARTMENT OF EDUCATION (1983). *Basic principles for the education of language-minority students: An overview.* Sacramento: California State Department of Education.

CALKINS, L. M. (1983). *Lessons from a child: On the teaching and learning of writing.* Exeter, N.H.: Heinemann.

CAMP, E., ISLOM, G., HERBERT, F., and VAN DOORNICK, W. (1977). "Think aloud": A program for developing self-control in young aggressive boys. *Journal of Abnormal Child Psychology, 5,* 157–169.

CAMPBELL, V. N. (1964). Self-direction and programmed instruction for five different types of learning objectives. *Psychology in the Schools, 1,* 348–359.

CANNELL, J. J. (1987). *Nationally normed elementary achievement testing in America's public schools: How all fifty states are above the national average.* Daniels, W. Va.: Friends for Education.

CANTER, L., and CANTER, M. (1976). *Assertive discipline.* Los Angeles: Lee Canter and Associates.

CANTRELL, R., and CANTRELL, M. (1976). Preventive mainstreaming: Impact of a supportive services program on pupils. *Exceptional Children, 46,* 381–386.

CAPLAN, P. J., MACPHERSON, G. M., and TOBIN, P. (1985). Do sex-related differences in spatial abilities exist? A multilevel critique with new data. *American Psychologist, 40,* 786–799.

CARBO, M., DUNN, R., and DUNN, K. (1986). *Teaching students to read through their individual learning styles.* Englewood Cliffs, N.J.: Prentice-Hall.

CARPENTER, T. P., FENNEMA, E., PETERSON, P. L., CHIANG, C.-P., and LOEF, M. (1988, April). *Using knowledge of children's mathematics thinking in classroom teaching: An experimental study.* Paper presented at the annual convention of the American Educational Research Association, New Orleans.

CARROLL, J. B. (1963). A model of school learning. *Teachers College Record, 64,* 723–733.

CARROLL, J. B. (1987). The national assessments in reading: Are we misreading the findings? *Phi Delta Kappan, 68,* 424–430.

CARROLL, J. B. (1989). The Carroll model: A 25-year retrospective and prospective view. *Educational Researcher, 18,* 26–31.

CARTER, L. F. (1984). The sustaining effects study of compensatory and elementary education. *Educational Researcher, 13,* (7), 4–13.

CARTER, T. P., and SEGURA, R. D. (1979). *Mexican Americans in school: A decade of change.* Princeton, N.J.: College Entrance Examination Board.

CARTWRIGHT, P., and DEREVENSKY, J. (1976). An attitudinal study of computer assisted testing as a learning method. *Psychology in the Schools, 13,* 317–321.

CASE, R. (1985). *Intellectual development: A systematic reinterpretation.* New York: Academic Press.

CASTO, G., and MASTROPIERI, M. A. (1986). The efficacy of early intervention programs:

A meta-analysis. *Exceptional Children, 52,* 417–424.

CATTELL, R. B. (1957). *Culture-fair intelligence test.* Champaign, Ill.: Institute for Personality and Ability Testing.

CHAMBERS, J. A., and SPRECHER, J. W. (1983). *Computer-assisted instruction.* Englewood Cliffs, N.J.: Prentice-Hall.

CHANG, T. M. (1986). Semantic memory: Facts and models. *Psychological Bulletin, 99,* 199–220.

CHANSEY, N. M. (1975). A critical examination of school report cards from K through 12. *Reading Improvement, 12,* 184–192.

CHAPMAN, J. W. (1988). Learning disabled children's self-concepts. *Review of Educational Research, 58,* 347–371.

CHOBOT, R., and GARIBALDI, A. (1982). In-school alternatives to suspension: A description of ten school district programs. *The Urban Review, 14.*

CHOMSKY, C. (1969). *The acquisition of syntax in children from 5 to 10.* M.I.T. Press Research Monogram No. 57. Cambridge, Mass.: M.I.T. Press.

CHOMSKY, N. (1968). *Language and mind.* New York: Harcourt Brace Jovanovich.

CHRISTIE, J. F. (1980). The cognitive significance of children's play: A review of selected research. *Journal of Education, 162,* 23–33.

CHRISTOPLOS, F., and RENZ, P. (1969). A critical examination of special education programs. *Journal of Special Education, 3,* 371–379.

CLARIZIO, H., and McCOY, G. (1976). *Behavior disorders in children* (2nd ed.). New York: Crowell.

CLARK, C. M. (1987). The Carroll model. In M. J. Dunkin (Ed.), *International encyclopedia of teaching and teacher education.* New York: Pergamon.

CLARK, C. M., GAGE, N. L., MARX, R. W., PETERSON, P. L., STAYROOK, N. G., and WINNE, P. H. (1979). A factorial experiment on teacher structuring, soliciting, and reacting. *Journal of Educational Psychology, 71,* 534–552.

CLARK, C. M., and PETERSON, P. L. (1986). Teachers' thought processes. In M. C. Wittrock (Ed.), *Handbook of research on teaching* (3rd ed.). New York: Macmillan.

CLARK, R. E. (1985). Evidence for confounding in computer-based instruction studies: Analyzing the meta-analyses. *Educational Communication and Technology Journal, 33,* 249–262.

CLARKE, A. M., and CLARKE, A. D. B. (Eds.) (1976). *Early experience: Myth and evidence.* New York: The Free Press.

CLEMENTS, D. H. (1986). Effects of logo and CAI environments on cognition and creativity. *Journal of Educational Psychology, 78,* 309–318.

CLEMENTS, D. H., and GULLO, D. F. (1984). Effects of computer programming on young children's cognition. *Journal of Educational Psychology, 76,* 1051–1058.

CLIFFORD, M. M. (1984). Thoughts on a theory of constructive failure. *Educational Psychologist, 19,* 108–120.

CLOWARD, R. A., and OHLIN, L. E. (1960). *Delinquency and opportunity.* New York: The Free Press.

CLOWARD, R. D. (1967). Studies in tutoring. *Journal of Experimental Education, 36,* 14–25.

COATS, W. D., and SMIDCHERS, U. (1966). Audience recall as a function of speaker dynamism. *Journal of Educational Psychology, 57,* 189–191.

COHEN, E., INTILLI, J., and ROBBINS, S. (1978). Teachers and reading specialists: Cooperation or isolation? *Reading Teacher, 32,* 281–287.

COHEN, E. G. (1984). Talking and working together: Status, interaction, and learning. In P. Peterson, L. C. Wilkinson, and M. Hallinan (Eds.), *The social context of instruction: Group organization and group processes.* New York: Academic Press.

COHEN, E. G. (1986). *Designing groupwork: Strategies for the heterogeneous classroom.* New York: Teachers College Press.

COHEN, E. G., and ANTHONY, B. (1982, March). Expectation states theory and classroom learning. Paper presented at the annual convention of the American Educational Research Association, New York.

COHEN, N. J., and SQUIRE, L. R. (1980). Preserved learning and retention of pattern analyzing skill in amnesia: Dissociation of knowing how and knowing that. *Science, 210,* 207–209.

COHEN, S., and DEBETTENCOURT, L. (1983). Teaching children to be independent learners: A step-by-step strategy. *Focus on Exceptional Children, 16*(3), 1–12.

COHEN, S. A. (1987). Instructional alignment: Searching for a magic bullet. *Educational Researcher, 16,* 16–20.

COLBY, C., and KOHLBERG, L. (1984). Invariant sequence and internal consistency in moral judgment stages. In W. Kurtines and J. Gewirts (Eds.), *Morality, moral behavior, and moral development.* New York: Wiley-Interscience.

COLE, N. S. (1981). Bias in testing. *American Psychologist, 36,* 1067–1077.

COLEMAN, J. (1961). *The adolescent society.* New York: Free Press.

COLEMAN, J. S., CAMPBELL, E. Q., HOBSON, C. L., McPARTLAND, J. M., MOOD, A. M., WEINFELD, F. D., and YORK, R. L. (1966). *Equality of educational opportunity.* Washington, D.C.: U.S. Department of Health, Education and Welfare.

COLEMAN, J. S., and HARRIS, T. R. (1969). *Economic system* (Simulation Game). Indianapolis: Bobbs-Merrill.

COLEMAN, J. S., and KARWEIT, N. L. (1972). *Information systems and performance measures in schools.* Englewood Cliffs, N.J.: Educational Technology Publications.

COLLEGE ENTRANCE EXAMINATION BOARD (1985). *Equality and excellence: The educational status of black Americans.* New York: CEEB.

COLLINS, A. M., and LOFTUS, E. I. (1975). A spreading-activation theory of semantic processing. *Psychological Review, 82,* 407–428.

COLSON, S. (1980). The evaluation of a community-based career education program for gifted and talented students. *Gifted Child Quarterly, 24,* 101–106.

COMBS, A. W. (Ed.) (1967). *Humanizing education: The person in the process.* Washington, D.C.: Association for Supervision and Curriculum Development, National Education Association.

COMBS, J., and COOLEY, W. (1968). Dropouts: In high school and after school. *American Educational Research Journal, 5,* 343–363.

COMMONS, M. L., RICHARDS, F. A., and KUHN, D. (1982). Systematic and metasystematic reasoning: A case for levels of reasoning beyond Piaget's stage of formal operations. *Child Development, 53,* 1058–1069.

CONGER, J. J., and PETERSEN, A. C. (1984). *Adolescence and youth: Psychological development in a changing world.* New York: Harper & Row.

COOLEY, W. W. (1981). Effectiveness in compensatory education. *Educational Leadership, 38,* 298–301.

COOLEY, W. W., and LEINHARDT, G. (1980). The instructional dimensions study. *Educational Evaluation and Policy Analysis, 2,* 7–26.

COOPER, H. (1989). Synthesis of research on homework. *Educational Leadership, 47* (3), 85–91.

COOPER, H. M., and GOOD, T. L. (1983). *Pygmalion grows up: Studies in the expectation communication process.* New York: Longman.

COOPER, H. M., and TOM, D. Y. H. (1984). Teacher expectation research: A review with implications for classroom instruction. *Elementary School Journal, 85,* 77–89.

COPELAND, W. D. (1983, April). Classroom management and student teachers' cognitive abilities: A relationship. Paper presented at the annual convention of the American Educational Research Association, Montreal.

CORNO, L., and ROHRKEMPER, M. (1985). The intrinsic motivation to learn in classrooms. In C. Ames and R. Ames (Eds.), *Research on motivation to learn in classrooms, Vol II: The classroom milieu.* Orlando, Fla.: Academic Press.

CORNO, L., and SNOW, R. E. (1986). Adapting teaching to individual differences among learners. In M. C. Wittrock (Ed.), *Handbook of research on teaching* (3rd ed.) New York: Macmillan.

COSTANZO, P. R., and SHAW, M. E. (1966). Conformity as a function of age level. *Child Development, 37,* 967–975.

COVINGTON, M. V. (1984). The self-worth theory of achievement motivation: Findings and implications, *Elementary School Journal, 85,* 5–20.

COVINGTON, M. V., CRUTCHFIELD, R. S., DAVIES, L., and OLTON, R. M. (1974). *The productive thinking program: A course in learning to think.* Columbus, Ohio: Merrill.

CRAIG, G. J. (1989). Human development (5th ed.). Englewood Cliffs, N.J.: Prentice-Hall.

CRAIK, F. I. M. (1979). Human memory. *Annual Review of Psychology, 30,* 63–102.

CRAIK, F. I. M., and LOCKHART, R. S. (1972). Levels of processing: A framework for memory research. *Journal of Verbal Thinking and Verbal Behavior, 11,* 671–684.

CRAIN, R., and MAHARD, R. (1978). Desegregation and black achievement: A review of the research. *Law and Contemporary Problems, 42,* 17–56.

CRAIN, R., and MAHARD, R. (1983). The effect of research methodology on desegregation-achievement studies: A meta-analysis. *American Journal of Sociology, 88,* 839–855.

CRAIN, R. L., MAHARD, R. E., and NAROT, R. E. (1982). *Making desegregation work: How schools create social climate.* Cambridge, Mass.: Ballinger.

CRAIN, W. C. (1985). *Theories of development: Concepts and applications.* Englewood Cliffs, N.J.: Prentice-Hall.

CRATTY, B. J. (1970). *Perceptual and motor development in infants and children.* New York: Macmillan.

CRATTY, B. J. (1982). Motor development in early childhood: Critical issues for researchers in the 1980's. In B. Spodek (Ed.), *Handbook of research in early childhood education,* pp. 27–46. New York: The Free Press.

CRAWFORD, J. (1983). *A study of instructional processes in Title I classes: Executive summary.* Oklahoma City: Oklahoma City Public Schools.

CRAWFORD, J. (1989). Instructional activities related to achievement gain in Chapter 1 classes. In R. E. Slavin, N. L. Karweit, and N. A. Madden (Eds.), *Effective programs for students at risk.* Boston: Allyn and Bacon.

CRAWFORD, R. P. (1954). *Techniques of creative thinking.* Englewood Cliffs, N.J.: Hawthorne.

CRESCIMBENI, J. (1965). *Arithmetic enrichment activities for elementary school children.* West Nyack, N.Y.: Parker.

CROCKER, R. K., and BROOKER, G. M. (1986). Classroom control and student outcomes in grades 2 and 5. *American Educational Research Journal, 23,* 1–11.

CROOKS, T. J. (1988). The impact of classroom evaluation practices on students. *Review of Educational Research, 58,* 438–481.

CROSS, L. H., and CROSS, G. M. (1980–1981). Teachers' evaluative comments and pupil perception of control. *Journal of Experimental Education, 49,* 68–71.

CSIKSZENTMIHALYI, M., and LARSON, R. (1984). *Being adolescent.* New York: Basic Books.

CTB/McGRAW-HILL (1982). *Examination materials: An illustrated overview of the comprehensive tests of basic skills.* Monterey, Calif.: CTB/McGraw-Hill.

CUMMINS, J. (1984). *Bilingualism and special education.* San Diego, Calif.: College Hill.

CUMMINS, J. (1986). Empowering minority students: A framework for intervention. *Harvard Educational Review, 96,* 18–36.

CURETON, L. E. (1971). The history of grading practice. *Measurement in Education, 2,* 1–8.

DAIUTE, C. (1982, March/April). Word processing: Can it make good writers better? *Electronic Learning,* pp. 29–31.

DALIS, G. T. (1970). Effect of precise objectives upon student achievement in health education. *The Journal of Experimental Education, 39,* 20–23.

DAMON, W. (1977). *The social world of the child.* San Francisco: Jossey-Bass.

DAMON, W. (1983). *Social and personality development: Infancy through adolescence.* New York: Norton.

DAMON, W. (1984). Peer education: The untapped potential. *Journal of Applied Developmental Psychology, 5,* 331–343.

DAMON, W., and HART, D. (1982). The development of self-understanding from infancy through adolescence. *Child Development, 53,* 841–864.

DANSEREAU, D. F. (1985). Learning strategy research. In J. Segal, S. Chipman, and R. Glaser (Eds.), *Thinking and learning skills: Relating instruction to basic research,* Vol. 1. Hillsdale, N.J.: Erlbaum.

DANSEREAU, D. F., McDONALD, B. A., COLLINS, K. W., GARLIND, J. C., HOLLEY, C. T., LIEKHOFF, G. M., and EVANS, S. H. (1979). Evaluation of a learning strategy system. In H. F. O'Neill, Jr., and C. D. Spielberger (Eds.), *Cognitive and affective learning strategies.* New York: Academic Press.

DAURIO, S. P. (1979). Educational enrichment versus acceleration: A review of the literature. In W. C. George, S. J. Cohn, and J. C. Stanley (Eds.), *Educating the gifted: Acceleration and enrichment.* Baltimore, Md.: Johns Hopkins University Press.

DAVIS, G. A. (1983). *Educational psychology: Theory and practice.* Reading, Mass.: Addison-Wesley.

DAVIS, H. (1970). Abnormal hearing and deafness. In H. Davis and R. Silverman (Eds.), *Hearing and deafness.* New York: Holt, Rinehart, and Winston.

DEAUX, K. (1984). From individual differences to social categories: Analysis of a decade's research on gender. *American Psychologist, 39,* 105–116.

DECHARMS, R. (1976). *Enhancing motivation.* New York: Irvington Press/Wiley.

DECHARMS, R. (1980). The origins of competence and achievement motivation in personal causation. In L. J. Fyons, Jr. (Ed.), *Achievement motivation.* New York: Plenum.

DECHARMS, R. (1984). Motivation enhancement in educational settings. In R. Ames and C. Ames (Eds.), *Research on motivation in education, Vol. 1: Student motivation.* New York: Academic Press.

DECI, E. L. (1975). *Intrinsic motivation.* New York: Plenum.

DELANDSHEERE, V. (1977). On defining educational objectives. *Evaluation in Education, 1,* 73–150.

DELIN, P. S. (1969). The learning to criterion of a serial list with and without mnemonic instructions. *Psychomatic Science, 16,* 169–170.

DELON, F. G. (1970). A field test of computer-assisted instruction in first grade mathematics. *Educational Leadership Research Supplement, 27,* 170–180.

DEMPSTER, F. N. (1987). Time and the production of classroom learning: Discerning implications from basic research. *Educational Psychologist, 22,* 1–21.

DEMPSTER, F. N. (1989). Spacing effects and their implications for theory and practice. *Educational Psychology Review, 1,* 309–330.

DEMYER, M. K. (1975). The nature of neuropsychological disability in autistic children. *Journal of Autism and Childhood Schizophrenia, 5,* 109–128.

DENO, S. L. (1985). Curriculum-based measurement: The emerging alternative. *Exceptional Children, 52,* 219–232.

DERRY, S. J., and MURPHY, D. A. (1986). Designing systems that train learning ability: From theory to practice. *Review of Educational Research, 56,* 1–39.

DEUTSCH, M. (1949). A theory of cooperation and competition. *Human Relations, 2,* 129–152.

DEVIN-SHEEHAN, L., FELDMAN, R. S., and ALLEN, V. L. (1976). Research on children tutoring children: A critical review. *Review of Educational Research, 46,* 355–385.

DEVRIES, D. L., and EDWARDS, K. J. (1974). Student teams and learning games: Their effects on cross-race and cross-sex interaction. *Journal of Educational Psychology, 66,* 741–749.

DEVRIES, D. L., and SLAVIN, R. E. (1978). Teams-Games-Tournament (TGT): Review of ten classroom experiments. *Journal of Research and Development in Education, 12,* 28–38.

DEWAR, J. (1964). Grouping for arithmetic instruction in sixth grade. *Elementary School Journal, 63,* 266–269.

DICK, W., and REISER, R. A. (1989). *Planning effective instruction.* Englewood Cliffs, N.J.: Prentice-Hall.

DICKERSON, D., SPELLMAN, C. R., LARSEN, S., and TYLER, L. (1973). Let the cards do the talking: A teacher-parent communication program: Daily report card system. *Teaching Exceptional Children, 5,* 170–178.

DIENER, C. I., and DWECK, C. S. (1978). An analysis of learned helplessness: Continuous changes in performance, strategy, and achievement cognitions following failure. *Journal of Personality and Social Psychology, 36,* 451–462.

DOCTOROW, M., MARKS, C., and WITTROCK. M. (1978). Generative processes in reading comprehension. *Journal of Educational Psychology, 70,* 109–118.

DONALDSON, M. (1978). *Children's minds.* New York: Norton.

DONOVAN, J. F., SOUSA, D. A., and WALBERG, H. J. (1987). The impact of staff development on implementation and student achievement. *Journal of Educational Research, 80,* 348–351.

DOOLING, D. J., and LACHMAN, R. (1971). Effects of comprehension on retention of prose. *Journal of Experimental Psychology, 8,* 216–222.

DORNBUSCH, S. M., CARLSMITH, J. M., BUSHWALL, S. J., RITTER, P. L., LEIDERMAN, H., HASTORF, A. H., and GROSS, R. T. (1985). Single parents, extended households, and the control of adolescents. *Child Development, 56,* 326–341.

DORR-BREMME, D. W., and HERMAN, J. (1986). *Assessing school achievement: A profile of classroom practices.* Los Angeles: Center for the Study of Evaluation, UCLA.

DORVAL, B., WALLACH, L., and WALLACH, M. A. (1978, April). Field evaluation of a tutorial reading program emphasizing phoneme identification skills. *The Reading Teacher,* 784–790.

DOTY, C. R. (1968). *The effect of practice and prior knowledge of educational objectives on performance.* Unpublished doctoral dissertation, Ohio State University.

DOUGHERTY, E., and DOUGHERTY, A. (1977). The daily report card: A simplified and flexible package for classroom behavior management. *Psychology in the Schools, 14,* 191–195.

DOWNING, J., COUGHLIN, R. M., and RICH, G. (1986). Children's invented spellings in the classroom. *Elementary School Journal, 86,* 295–303.

DOYLE, W. (1983). Academic work. *Review of Educational Research, 53,* 159–199.

DOYLE, W. (1984). How order is achieved in classrooms: An interim report. *Journal of Curriculum Studies, 16,* 259–277.

DOYLE, W. (1986). Classroom organization and management. In M. C. Wittrock (Ed.), *Handbook of research on teaching* (3rd ed.), pp. 392–431. New York: Macmillan.

DOYLE, W., and CARTER, K. (1984). Academic tasks in classrooms. *Curriculum Inquiry, 14,* 129–149.

DRABMAN, R., SPITALNIK, R., and O'LEARY, K. (1973). Teaching self-control to disruptive children. *Journal of Abnormal Psychology, 82,* 10–16.

DREYER, S. S. (1977). *The bookfinder: A guide to children's literature about the needs and problems of youth aged 2–15.* Circle Pines, Minn.: American Guidance Service.

DUBOULAY, J. B. H., and HOWE, J. A. M. (1984). Logo building blocks: Student teachers using computer-based mathematics apparatus. *Computers and Education, 6,* 93–98.

DUCHASTEL, P. C. (1977, April). Functions of instructional objectives: Organization and direction. Paper presented at the annual convention of the American Educational Research Association, New York.

DUCHASTEL, P. C., and MERRILL, P. F. (1973). The effects of behavioral objectives on learning: A review of empirical studies. *Review of Educational Research, 43,* 53–69.

DUELL, O. K. (1978). Overt and covert use of objectives of different cognitive levels. *Contemporary Educational Psychology, 3,* 239–245.

DUFFY, G. G., and ROEHLER, L. R. (1986). The subtleties of instructional mediation. *Educational Leadership, 43,*(7), 23–27.

DUKES, R., and SEIDNER, C. (1978). *Learning with simulations and games.* Beverly Hills, Calif.: Sage.

DULAY, H., and BURT, M. (1977, August). Learning and teaching research in bilingual education. Paper presented to the National Institute of Education Task Force on Teaching and Learning, San Francisco.

DUNCAN, O. D., FEATHERMAN, D. L., and DUNCAN, B. (1972). *Socioeconomic background and achievement.* New York: Seminar Press.

DUNKER, K. (1945). On problem solving. *Psychological Monographs, 58* (Whole No. 270).

DUNKIN, M. (1978). Student characteristics, classroom processes, and student achievement. *Journal of Educational Psychology, 70,* 998–1009.

DUNKIN, M. J., and BIDDLE, B. J. (1974). *A study of teaching.* New York: Holt, Rinehart, and Winston.

DUNKIN, M. J., and DOENAU, S. J. (1987). Students' ethnicity. In M. J. Dunkin (Ed.), *International encyclopedia of teaching and teacher education.* New York: Pergamon.

DUNN, K., and DUNN, R. (1987). Dispelling outmoded beliefs about student learning. *Educational Leadership, 44*(6), 55–62.

DUNN, L. M. (1968). Special education for the mentally retarded—Is it justified? *Exceptional Children, 35,* 5–22.

DUNN, R., BEAUDREY, J. S., and KLAVAS, A. (1989). Survey of research on learning styles. *Educational Leadership, 46*(6), 50–58.

DUNN, R. S., and DUNN, K. J. (1978). *Teaching students through their individual learning styles: A practical approach.* Reston, Va.: Reston.

DURAN, R. P. (1983). *Hispanics' education and background.* New York: College Entrance Examination Board.

DWECK, C. S. (1986). Motivational processes affecting learning. *American Psychologist, 41,* 1040–1048.

DWECK, C. S., and ELLIOT, E. S. (1983). Achievement motivation. In E. M. Hetherington (Ed.), *Socialization, personality, and social development.* New York: Wiley.

DWECK, C. (1975). The role of expectations and attributions in the alleviation of learned helplessness. *Journal of Personality and Social Psychology, 31,* 674–685.

DYER, H. S. (1967). The discovery and development of educational goals. *Proceedings of the 1966 Invitational Conference on Testing Problems.* Princeton, N.J.: Educational Testing Service.

DYSON, A. H. (1984). Teachers and young children: Missed connections in teaching/learning to write. *Language Arts, 59,* 674–680.

EBEL, R. L. (1972). *Essentials of educational measurement* (3rd ed.). Englewood Cliffs, N.J.: Prentice-Hall.

EBEL, R. L. (1980a). Achievement tests as measures of developed abilities. In W. B. Schrader (Ed.), *New directions for testing and measurement,* Vol. 5. San Francisco: Jossey-Bass.

EBEL, R. L. (1980b). Evaluation of students: Implications for effective teaching. *Educational Evaluation and Policy Analysis, 2,* 47–51.

EDGERTON, R. B. (1984). Mental retardation: An anthropologist's changing view. In B. Blatt and R. Morris (Eds.), *Perspectives in Special Education,* Vol. 1. Glenview, Il.: Scott, Foresman.

EDLUND, C. (1969). Rewards at home to promote desirable school behavior. *Teaching Exceptional Children, 1,* 121–127.

EDUCATIONAL RESEARCH SERVICE (1978). *Class*

size: A summary of research. Arlington, Va.: Educational Research Service.

EDWARDS, J. R. (1979). *Language and disadvantage.* London, England: Wauld.

EDWARDS, P. E., LOGUE, M. E., and RUSSELL, A. S. (1983). Talking with young children about social ideas. *Young Children, 39,* 12–20.

EDWARDS, W. (1954). The theory of decision making. *Psychology Bulletin, 51,* 380–417.

EHLY, S. W., and LARSEN, S. C. (1980). *Peer tutoring for individualized instruction.* Boston: Allyn and Bacon.

EHRLICK, D., GUTTMAN, J., SCHONBACK, P., and MILLS, J. (1957). Postdecision exposure to relevant information. *Journal of Abnormal Social Psychology, 54,* 98–102.

EIBEN, R. M., and CROCKER, A. C. (1983). Cerebral palsy within the spectrum of developmental disabilities. In G. H. Thompson, I. L. Rubin, and R. M. Bilenker (Eds.), *Comprehensive management of cerebral palsy.* New York: Grune & Stratton.

EICHORN, D. (1966). *The middle school.* New York: Center for Applied Research in Education.

EISNER, E. W. (1969). Instructional and expressive educational objectives: Their formulation and use in curriculum. In W. J. Popham, E. W. Eisner, H. J. Sullivan, and L. L. Tyler (Eds.), *Instructional objectives.* AERA. Monograph series on Curriculum Evaluation, No. 3. Chicago: Rand McNally, pp. 1–31.

EISNER, E. W. (1982). The contribution of painting to children's cognitive development. *Journal of Education, 164,* 227–237.

ELASHOFF, J. D., and SNOW, R. E. (1971). *Pygmalion reconsidered.* Worthington, Ohio: Charles A. Jones.

ELAWAR, M. C., and CORNO, L. (1985). A factorial experiment in teachers' written feedback on student homework: Changing teacher behavior a little rather than a lot. *Journal of Educational Psychology, 77,* 162–173.

ELKIND, D. (1981). *The hurried child: Growing up too fast, too soon.* Reading, Mass.: Addison-Wesley.

ELKIND, D. (1984). *All grown up and no place to go.* Boston: Addison-Wesley.

ELKIND, D. (1986a). Helping parents make healthy educational choices for their children. *Educational Leadership, 44* (3), 36–38.

ELKIND, D. (1986b, May). Formal education and preschool education: An essential difference. *Phi Delta Kappan,* 631–636.

ELLSON, D. G. (1976). Tutoring. In N. L. Gage (Ed.), *The psychology of teaching methods* (pp. 130–165). Chicago: University of Chicago Press.

ELLSON, D. G., HARRIS, P., and BARBER, L. (1968). A field test of programmed and directed tutoring. *Reading Research Quarterly, 3,* 307–367.

EMMER, E., EVERTSON, C., and ANDERSON, L. (1980). Effective classroom management at the beginning of the school year. *Elementary School Journal, 80,* 219–231.

EMMER, E. T., EVERTSON, C. M., SANFORD, J. P., CLEMENTS, B. S., and WORSHAM, M. E. (1984). *Classroom management for secondary teachers.* Englewood Cliffs, N.J.: Prentice-Hall.

EMMER, E. T., SANFORD, J., CLEMENTS, B., and MARTIN, J. (1982). *Improving classroom management and organization in junior high schools: An experimental investigation.* Austin: University of Texas, Research and Development Center for Teacher Education.

ENGEL, R. S. (1968). *An experimental study of the effect of stated behavioral objectives on achievement in a unit of instruction on negative and rational base systems of numeration.* Unpublished master's thesis, University of Maryland.

ENTWISTLE, D., and HAYDUK, L. (1981). Academic expectations and the school achievement of young children. *Sociology of Education, 54,* 34–50.

ENTWISTLE, N. (1981). *Styles of learning and teaching.* New York: Wiley.

EPSTEIN, C. (1980). Brain growth and cognitive functioning. In *The emerging adolescent: Characteristics and implications.* Columbus, Ohio: NMSA.

EPSTEIN, J. L. (1985). After the bus arrives: Resegregation in desegregated schools. *Journal of Social Issues, 41,* 23–43.

EPSTEIN, J. L. (1988). *Homework practices, achievements, and behaviors of elementary school students* (Tech. Rep. No. 26). Baltimore, Md.: Johns Hopkins University, Center for Research on Elementary and Middle Schools.

EPSTEIN, J. L., and MCPARTLAND, J. M. (1975). *The effects of open school organization on student outcomes.* Baltimore, Md.: Center for Social Organization of Schools, Johns Hopkins University.

ERIKSON, E. H. (1963). *Childhood and society* (2nd ed.). New York: Norton.

ERIKSON, E. H. (1968). *Identity, youth and crisis.* New York: Norton.

ERIKSON, E. H. (1980). *Identity and the life cycle.* (2nd ed.). New York: Norton.

ESPOSITO, D. (1973). Homogeneous and heterogeneous ability grouping: Principal findings and implications for evaluating and designing more effective educational environments. *Review of Educational Research, 43,* 163–179.

ESTES, N. K. (1982). Learning, memory, and intelligence. In R. J. Sternberg (Ed.), *Handbook of human intelligence.* New York: Cambridge University Press.

EVERTSON, C. M. (1982). Differences in instructional activities in higher- and lower-achieving junior high English and math classes. *Elementary School Journal, 82,* 329–350.

EVERTSON, C. M., and EMMER, E. T. (1982). Effective management at the beginning of the year in junior high classes. *Journal of Educational Psychology, 74,* 485–498.

EVERTSON, C. M. EMMER, E. T., and BROPHY, J. E. (1980). Predictors of effective teaching in junior high mathematics classrooms. *Journal for Research in Mathematics Education, 11,* 167–178.

EVERTSON, C. M., EMMER, E. T., CLEMENTS, B. S., SANFORD, J. P., and WORSHAM, M. E. (1984). *Classroom management for elementary teachers.* Englewood Cliffs, N.J.: Prentice-Hall.

EVERTSON, C. M., EMMER, E. T., SANFORD, J., and CLEMENTS, B. (1983). Improving classroom management: An experiment in elementary school classrooms. *Elementary School Journal, 84,* 173–188.

EVERTSON, C. M., WEADE, R., GREEN, J., and CRAWFORD, J. (1985). *Effective classroom management and instruction: An exploration of models.* Nashville, Tenn.: Vanderbilt University.

FAGAN, E. R., HASSLER, D. M., and SZABO, M. (1981). Evaluation of questioning strategies in language arts instruction. *Research in the Teaching of English, 15,* 267–273.

FAIRBROTHER, R. W. (1975). The reliability of teachers' judgments of the abilities being tested by multiple choice items. *Educational Research, 17,* 202–210.

FEATHER, N. (Ed.) (1982). *Expectations and actions.* Hillsdale, N.J.: Erlbaum.

FEDERAL REGISTER (1977, August). Washington, D.C.: U.S. Government Printing Office.

FEIN, G. G. (1979). Play and acquisition of symbols. In L. G. Katz (Ed.), *Current topics in early childhood education,* Vol. 2, pp. 195–226. Norwood, N.J.: Albex Publishing Corp.

FEIN, G. G. (1981). The physical environment: Stimulation or evocation. In R. M. Lerner and N. A. Busch-Rossnagel (Eds.), *Individuals as producers of their development: A lifespan perspective,* pp. 257–279. New York: Academic Press.

FELDHUSEN, J. F., and SOKOL, L. (1982). Extra-school programming to meet the needs of gifted youth: Super Saturday. *Gifted Child Quarterly, 21,* 450–476.

FENNEMA, E., and SHERMAN, J. (1977). Sex-related differences in mathematics achievement, spatial visualization, and affective factors. *American Educational Research Journal, 14,* 51–71.

FESTINGER, L. A. (1957). *A theory of cognitive dissonance.* Evanston, Ill.: Ron, Peterson.

FEUERSTEIN, R. (1980). *Instrumental enrichment: An intervention program for cognitive modifiability.* Baltimore: University Park Press.

FEUERSTEIN, R., and JENSEN, M. R. (1980, May). Instrumental enrichment: Theoretical basis, goals, and instruments. *Educational Forum,* 401–423.

FEUERSTEIN, R., MILLER, R., HOFFMAN, M. B., RAND, Y., MINTZKER, Y., and JENSEN, M. R. (1981). Cognitive modifiability in adolescence: Cognitive structure and the effects of intervention. *Journal of Special Education, 15,* 269–287.

FINDLEY, W. G., and BRYAN, M. (1971). *Ability grouping: 1970 status, impact, and alternatives.* Athens, Ga.: Center for Educational Improvement, University of Georgia. (ERIC Document Reproduction Service No. ED 060 595.)

FIORDALISO, R., LORDEMAN, A., FILIPCZAK, J., and FRIEDMAN, R. M. (1977). Effects of feedback in absenteeism in the junior high school. *Journal of Educational Research, 70,* 188–192.

FISHBURNE, P., ABELSON, H., and CISIN, I. (1980). *The national survey on drug abuse: Main findings, 1979.* Washington, D.C.: U.S. Government Printing Office.

FISHER, C. W., BERLINER, D. C., FILBY, N. N., MARLIAVE, R., CAHEN, L. S., DISHAW, M. M., and MOORE, J. E. (1978). *Teaching behaviors, academic learning time, and student achievement: Final report of Phase III-B, beginning teacher evaluation study.* (Tech. Report V-1.) San Francisco: Far West Laboratory for Educational Research and Development.

FISKE, E. B. (1989, July 12). The misleading concept of "average" on reading tests changes, and more students fall below it. *New York Times.*

FLANAGAN, J. C., SHANNER, W. M., ISRUDNER, H. J., and MARKER, R. W. (1975). An individualized instructional system: PLAN. In H. Talmage (Ed.), *Systems of individualized instruction.* Berkeley, Calif.: McCutchan.

FLAVELL, J. H. (1977). *Cognitive development.* Englewood Cliffs, N.J.: Prentice-Hall.

FLAVELL, J. H. (1985). *Cognitive development* (2nd ed.). Englewood Cliffs, N.J.: Prentice-Hall.

FLAVELL, J. H. (1986, January). Really and truly. *Psychology Today,* 38–44.

FLOYD, C. (1954). Meeting children's reading needs in the middle grades: A preliminary report. *Elementary School Journal, 55,* 99–103.

FOO, P. W., and FISHER, R. P. (1988). Using tests as learning opportunities. *Journal of Educational Psychology, 80,* 179–183.

FOREHAND, G., and RAGOSTA, M. (1976). *A handbook for integrated schooling.* Washington, D.C.: U.S. Department of Education.

FORMAN, G. E., and FOSNOT, C. T. (1982). The use of Piaget's constructivism in early childhood programs. In B. Spodek (Ed.), *Handbook of research in early childhood education,* pp. 185–211. New York: The Free Press.

FORSTERLING, F. (1985). Attribution retraining: A review. *Psychological Bulletin, 98,* 495–512.

FORSYTH, D. R. (1986). An attributional analysis of students' reactions to success and failure. In R. S. Feldman (Ed.), *The social psychology of education.* Cambridge: England, Cambridge Press.

FOX, L. H. (1979). Programs for the gifted and talented: An overview. In A. H. Passow (Ed.), *The gifted and talented: Their education and development.* Chicago: University of Chicago Press.

FRANKENBURG, W. K., and DODDS, J. B. (1970). *Denver Developmental Screening Test.* Denver: University of Colorado Medical Center.

FRASE, L. T. (1970). Boundary conditions for mathemagenic behaviors. *Review of Educational Research, 40,* 337–349.

FREDERICK, W., and WALBERG, H. (1980). Learning as a function of time. *Journal of Educational Research, 73,* 183–194.

FREDERIKSEN, N. (1984a). Implications of cognitive theory for instruction in problem solving. *Review of Educational Research, 54,* 363–407.

FREDERIKSEN, N. (1984b). The real test bias: Influences of testing on teaching and learning. *American Psychologist, 39,* 193–202.

FRENCH, E. G. (1956). Motivation as a variable in work partner selection. *Journal of Abnormal and Social Psychology, 55,* 96–99.

FRENCH, E. G., and THOMAS, F. (1958). The relation of achievement motivation to problem-solving effectiveness. *Journal of Abnormal and Social Psychology, 56,* 45–48.

FRIEZE, I., and WEINER, B. (1971). Cue utilization and attributional judgments for success and failure. *Journal of Personality, 39,* 91–109.

FROST, J. L., and KLEIN, B. (1979). *Children's play and playgrounds.* Boston: Allyn and Bacon.

FUCHS, D., and FUCHS, L. S. (1989). Exploring effective and efficient preferral interventions: A component analysis of behavioral consultation. *School Psychology Review, 18,* 258–281.

FUDOR, E. M. (1971). Resistance to social influence among adolescents as a function of level of moral development. *Journal of Social Psychology, 85,* 121–126.

FURMAN, W., and BIERMAN, K. L. (1984). Children's conceptions of friendship: a multi-method study of developmental changes. *Developmental Psychology, 21,* 1016–1024.

FURST, E. J. (1981). Bloom's taxonomy of educational objectives for the cognitive domain: Philosophical and educational issues. *Review of Educational Research, 51,* 441–453.

FYANS, L. J., JR., and MAEHR, M. L. (1980). Attributional style, task selection and achievement. In L. J. Fyans, Jr. (Ed.), *Achievement motivation.* New York: Plenum.

GADOW, K. (1981). Effects of stimulant drugs on attention and cognitive deficits. *Exceptional Educational Quarterly, 2,* 83–93.

GAGE, N. L. (1978). *The scientific basis of the art of teaching.* New York: Teachers College Press.

GAGE. N. L., and BERLINER, D. C. (1984). *Educational psychology* (3rd ed.). Boston: Houghton Mifflin.

GAGE, N. L., and NEEDELS, M. C. (1989). Process-product research on teaching: A review of criticisms. *Elementary School Journal, 89,* 253–300.

GAGNÉ, R. (1970). *The conditions of learning* (2nd ed.). New York: Holt, Rinehart, and Winston.

GAGNÉ, R. (1977). *The conditions of learning* (3rd ed.). New York: Holt, Rinehart, and Winston.

GAGNÉ, R., and BRIGGS, L. (1979). *Principles of instructional design* (2nd ed.). New York: Holt, Rinehart, and Winston.

GAGNÉ, R. M. (1974). *Essentials of learning for instruction.* Hinsdale, Ill.: Dryden.

GAGNÉ, R. M. (1984). Learning outcomes and their effects. *American Psychologist, 39,* 377–385.

GAGNÉ, R. M., and DRISCOLL, M. P. (1988). *Essentials of learning for instruction* (2nd ed.). Englewood Cliffs, N.J.: Prentice-Hall.

GALL, M. (1984). Synthesis of research on teachers' questioning. *Educational Leadership, 42,* 40–47.

GALL, M., WARD, B., BERLINER, D., CAHEN, L., WINNE, P., GLASHOFF, J., and STANTON, G. (1978). Effects of questioning techniques and recitation on student learning. *American Educational Research Journal, 15,* 175–199.

GALL, M. D. (1970). The use of questions in teaching. *Review of Educational Research, 40,* 707–721.

GALL, M. D. (1987). Discussion methods. In M. J. Dunkin (Ed.), *International encyclopedia of teaching and teacher education.* New York: Pergamon.

GALL, M. D., FIELDING, G., SCHALOCK, D., CHARTERS, W. W., and WILCZYNSKI, J. M. (1984). *Involving the principal in teachers' staff development: Effects on the quality of mathematics instruction in elementary schools.* Eugene, Oreg.: Center for Educational Policy and Management, University of Oregon.

GALLAGHER, J. J. (1975). *Teaching the gifted child* (2nd ed.). Boston: Allyn and Bacon.

GALLAGHER, J. J. (1979). Issues in education for the gifted. In A. H. Passow (Ed.), *The 78th yearbook of the National Society for the Study of Education. Part I: The gifted and talented: Their education and development.* Chicago: University of Chicago Press.

GALLAGHER, P. A. (1979). *Teaching students with behavior disorders: Techniques for classroom instruction.* Denver: Love.

GAMORAN, A. (1984, April). Egalitarian versus elitist use of ability grouping. Paper presented at the annual convention of the American Educational Research Association, New Orleans.

GARBER, H. L. (1988). *The Milwaukee Project: Preventing mental retardation in children at risk.* Washington, D.C.: American Association on Mental Retardation.

GARDNER, H. (1982). *Developmental psychology* (2nd ed.). Boston: Little, Brown.

GARDNER, H., and HATCH, T. (1989). Multiple intelligences go to school. *Educational Researcher, 18* (8), 4–10.

GARDNER, M. K. (1985). Cognitive psychological approaches to instructional task analysis. In E. W. Gordon (Ed.), *Review of Research in Education,* Vol. 12, pp. 157–195. Washington, D.C.: American Educational Research Association.

GARNER, R., and ALEXANDER, P. A. (1989). Metacognition: Answered and unanswered questions. *Educational Psychologist, 24,* 143–158.

GELMAN, R. (1979). Preschool thought. *American Psychologist, 34,* 900–905.

GENESEE, F. (1985). Second language learning through immersion: A review of U.S. programs. *Review of Educational Research, 55,* 541–561.

GENTER, D. (1989). The mechanisms of analogical reasoning. In S. Vosniadou and A. Ortony (Eds.), *Similarity and analogical reasoning.* Cambridge, England: Cambridge University Press.

GEOFFRION, L. D., and GOLDENBERG, E. P. (1981). Computer-based exploratory learning systems for communication-handicapped children. *Journal of Special Education, 15,* 325–331.

GERARD, H. B., and MILLER, N. (1975). *School desegregation: A long-range study.* New York: Plenum.

GERBER, M. M., and SEMMEL, M. I. (1984). Teacher as imperfect test: Reconceptualizing the referral process. *Educational Psychologist, 19,* 137–148.

GERN, T., and GERN, P. (1986). *Substance abuse prevention activities for elementary children.* Englewood Cliffs, N.J.: Prentice-Hall.

GERSTEN, R., and CARNINE, D. (1984). Direct instruction mathematics: A longitudinal evaluation of low-income elementary school students. *Elementary School Journal, 84,* 395–407.

GERSTEN, R., and KEATING, T. (1987). Long-term benefits from direct instruction. *Educational Leadership, 44* (6), 28–31.

GETSIE, R. L., LANGER, P., and GLASS, G. V. (1985). Meta-analysis of the effects of type and combination of feedback on children's discrimination learning. *Review of Education Research, 55,* 9–22.

GETTINGER, M. (1989). Effects of maximizing time spent and minimizing time needed for learning on pupil achievement. *American Educational Research Journal, 26,* 73–91.

GETZELS, J. W., and JACKSON, P. W. (1962). *Creativity and intelligence.* New York: Wiley.

GHATALA, E. S. (1986). Strategy-monitoring training enables young learners to select effective strategies. *Educational Psychologist, 21,* 43–54.

GIACONIA, R. M., and HEDGES, L. V. (1982). Identifying features of effective open education. *Review of Educational Research, 52,* 579–602.

GIBBS, J. C., ARNOLD, K. D., and BURKHART, J. F. (1984). Sex differences in the expression of moral judgment. *Child Development, 55,* 1040–1043.

GICKLING, E., and THEOBALD, J. (1975). Mainstreaming: Affect or effect. *Journal of Special Education, 9,* 317–328.

GILLES, C., BIXBY, M., CROWLEY, P., CRENSHAW, S., HENRICHS, M., REYNOLDS, F., and PYLE, D. (1988). *Whole language strategies for secondary students.* New York: Richard C. Owen.

GILLIGAN, C. (1982). *In a different voice: Sex differences in the expression of moral judgment.* Cambridge: Harvard University Press.

GILLIGAN, C. (1985). Remapping development. Paper presented at the biennial meeting of the Society for Research in Child Development, Toronto.

GILSTRAP, R. L., and MARTIN, W. R. (1975). *Current strategies for teachers: A resource for personalizing education.* Pacific Palisades, Calif.: Goodyear.

GINOTT, H. (1972). *Teacher and child.* New York: Macmillan.

GLANZER, M. (1982). Short-term memory. In C. R. Puff (Ed.), *Handbook of research methods in human memory and cognition.* New York: Academic Press.

GLASER, R. (1965). *Teaching-machines and programmed learning II: Data and directions.* Washington, D.C.: National Education Association.

GLASER, R. (1984). Education and thinking: The role of knowledge. *American Psychologist, 39,* 93–104.

GLASS, G., CAHEN, L., SMITH, M. L., and FILBY, N. (1982). *School class size.* Beverly Hills, Calif.: Sage.

GLASS, G. V., and SMITH, M. L. (1977). *Pull out in compensatory education.* Washington, D.C.: Department of Health, Education and Welfare.

GLASSER, W. L. (1969). *Schools without failure.* New York: Harper and Row.

GLAVIN, J., QUAY, H., ANNESLY, F., and WERRY, J. (1971). An experimental resource room for behavior problem children. *Exceptional Children, 38,* 131–138.

GLEASON, J. B. (1981). Code switching in children's language. In E. M. Hetherington and R. D. Parke (Eds.), *Contemporary reading in child psychology* (2nd ed.), pp. 134–138. New York: McGraw-Hill.

GOFFIN, S. G., and TULL, C. Q. (1984, March). *Encouraging possibilities for cooperative behavior with young children.* Paper presented at the annual meeting of the Southern Association for Children under Six, Lexington, Ky.

GOFFIN, S. G., and TULL, C. Q. (1985). Problem solving: Encouraging active learning. *Young Children, 40*(3), 28–32.

GOLD, M. (1970). *Delinquent behavior in an American city.* Belmont, Calif.: Brooks/Cole.

GOLD, R. M., REILLY, A., SILBERMAN, R., and LEHR, R. (1971). Academic achievement declines under pass-fail grading. *Journal of Experimental Education, 39,* 17–21.

GOLDBERG, M., PASSOW, A., and JUSTMAN, J. (1966). *The effects of ability grouping.* New York: Teacher's College Press.

GOLDHABER, D. (1979). Does the changing view of early experience imply a changing view of early development? In L. G. Katz (Ed.), *Current topics in early childhood education,* Vol. 2, pp.117–140. Norwood, N.J.: Ablex Publishing Co.

GOLDSTEIN, H., MOSS, J., and JORDAN, J. (1966). *The efficacy of special class training on the development of mentally retarded children* (Cooperative Research Project No. 619). Washington, D.C.: U.S. Office of Education.

GOOD, T. (1983a, April). Classroom research: A decade of progress. Paper presented at the annual meeting of the American Educational Research Association, Montreal.

GOOD, T. L. (1983b). Classroom research: Past and future. In F. Sykers and L. S. Shulman (Eds.), *Handbook of teaching and policy.* New York: Longman.

GOOD, T. L., and BROPHY, J. E. (1973). *Looking in classrooms.* New York: Harper and Row.

GOOD, T. L., and BROPHY, J. E. (1984). *Looking in classrooms* (3rd ed.). New York: Harper and Row.

GOOD, T. L., and BROPHY, J. E. (1989). Teaching the lesson. In R. E. Slavin (Ed.), *School and classroom organization.* Hillsdale, N.J.: Erlbaum.

GOOD, T., and FINDLEY, N. (1985). Sex role expectations and achievement. In J. Dusek

(Ed.), *Teacher expectations*. Hillsdale, N.J.: Erlbaum.

GOOD, T., and GROUWS, D. (1977). Teaching effects: A process-product study in fourth grade mathematics classes. *Journal of Teacher Education, 28,* 49–54.

GOOD, T., and GROUWS, D. (1979). The Missouri Mathematics Effectiveness Project: An experimental study in fourth-grade classrooms. *Journal of Educational Psychology, 71,* 355–362.

GOOD, T., GROUWS, D., and EBMEIER, H. (1983). *Active mathematics teaching.* New York: Longman.

GOOD, T., and MARSHALL, S. (1984). Do students learn more in heterogeneous or homogeneous groups? In P. Peterson, L. C. Wilkinson, and M. Hallinan (Eds.), *The social context of instruction: Group organization and group processes,* pp. 15–38. New York: Academic Press.

GOODLAD, J. (1960). Classroom organization. In C. Harris (Ed.), *Encyclopedia of educational research* (3rd ed.), pp. 221–225. New York: Macmillan.

GOODLAD, J. I. (1983). *A place called school.* New York: McGraw-Hill.

GOODMAN, K. S. (1986). *What's whole in whole language?* Portsmouth, N.H.: Heinemann.

GOODMAN, P. (1964). *Compulsory miseducation.* New York: Horizon Press.

GORDON, I. (1975). *Human development: A transactional perspective.* New York: Harper and Row.

GOTTFREDSON, G. D. (1984). *How schools, families, and justice agencies can reduce youth crime.* Baltimore, Md.: Center for Social Organization of Schools, Johns Hopkins Univ.

GOTTFREDSON, G. D., KARWEIT, N. L., and GOTTFREDSON, G. D. (1989). *Reducing disorderly behavior in middle schools.* Baltimore, Md.: Johns Hopkins University for Research on Elementary and Middle Schools.

GOTTFRIED, A. E. (1985). Academic intrinsic motivation in elementary and junior high school students. *Journal of Educational Psychology, 77,* 631–645.

GOTTLIEB, J., and LEYSER, Y. (1981). Friendship between mentally retarded and nonretarded children. In S. Asher and J. Gottman (Eds.), *The development of children's friendships.* Cambridge: Cambridge University Press.

GRADEN, J. L., CASEY, A., and BONSTROM, O. (1985). Implementing a preferral intervention system: Part II. The data. *Exceptional Children, 51,* 487–496.

GRAUBARD, P. S. (1969). Utilizing the group in teaching disturbed delinquents to learn. *Exceptional Children, 36,* 267–272.

GRAVES, D. (1983). *Writing: Teachers and children at work.* Exeter, N.H.: Heinemann.

GREEN, G., and OSBORNE, J. G. (1985). Does vicarious instigation provide support for observational learning theories? A critical review. *Psychological Bulletin, 97,* 3–16.

GREENBLAT, C. S. (1982). Games and simulations. In H. E. Mitzel (Ed.), *Encyclopedia of educational research,* pp. 713–716. New York: Free Press.

GREENE, D., and LEPPER, M. R. (1974). How to turn play into work. *Psychology Today, 8,* 49–54.

GREENE, R. L. (1986). Sources of recency effects in free recall. *Psychological Bulletin, 99,* 221–228.

GREENO, J. (1978). Understanding and procedural knowledge in mathematics instruction. *Educational Psychologist, 12,* 262–283.

GREGORY, I. D. (1975). A new look at the lecture method. *British Journal of Educational Technology, 6,* 55–62.

GREIF, E. B., and ULMAN, K. J. (1982). The psychological impact of menarche on early adolescent females: A review of the literature. *Child Development, 53,* 1413–1430.

GRESHAM, F. (1981). Social skills training with handicapped children: A review. *Review of Educational Research, 51,* 139–176.

GRONLUND, N. E. (1976). *Measurement and evaluation in teaching* (3rd ed.). New York: Macmillan.

GRONLUND, N. E. (1978). *Stating objectives for classroom instruction* (2nd ed.). New York: Macmillan.

GRONLUND, N. E. (1982). *Constructing achievement tests* (3rd ed.). Englewood Cliffs, N.J.: Prentice-Hall.

GROSSMAN, H. (1983). *Classification in mental retardation.* Washington, D.C.: American Association on Mental Deficiency.

GRUSEC, J., and ARNASON, L. (1982). Consideration for others: Approaches to understanding altruism. In S. G. Moore and C. P. Cooper (Eds.), *The young child: Reviews of research,* Vol. 3, pp. 159–174. Washington, D.C.: National Association for the Education of Young Children.

GUILFORD, J. P. (1939). *General psychology.* New York: Van Nostrand.

GUMP, P. V. (1982). School settings and their keeping. In D. L. Duke (Ed.), *Helping teachers manage classrooms,* pp. 98–114. Alexandria, Va.: Association for Supervision and Curriculum Development.

GUNDERSON, D. V. (1982). Bilingual education. In H. E. Mitzel (Ed.), *Encyclopedia of educational research.* New York: Free Press.

GURALNICK, M. J., and WEINHOUSE, E. (1984). Peer-related social interactions of developmentally delayed young children: Developmental characteristics. *Developmental Psychology, 20,* 815–827.

HAAN, N., SMITH, M. B., and BLOCK, J. (1968). Moral reasoning of young adults: Political-social behavior, family background, and personality correlates. *Journal of Personality and Social Psychology, 10,* 183–201.

HACKER, A. (Ed.) (1983). *U/S: A statistical portrait of the American people.* New York: Viking Press.

HAERTEL, E. (1985). Construct validity and criterion-referenced testing. *Review of Educational Research, 55,* 23–46.

HAERTEL, E. (1986, April). *Choosing and using classroom test: Teachers' perspectives on assessment.* Paper presented at the annual meeting of the American Educational Research Association, San Francisco.

HAKUTA, K., and GARCIA, E. E. (1989). Bilingualism and education. *American Psychologist, 44,* 374–379.

HAKUTA, K., and GOULD, L. J. (1987). Synthesis of research on bilingual education. *Educational Leadership, 44*(6), 38–45.

HALES, L. W., BAIN, P. T., and RAND, L. P. (1971, February). An investigation of some aspects of the pass-fail grading system. Paper presented at the annual meeting of the American Educational Research Association, New York.

HALL, R. V., AXELROD, S., FOUNDOPOULOS, M., SHELLMAN, J., CAMPBELL, R. A., and CRANSTON, S. (1971). The effective use of punishment to modify behavior in the classroom. *Educational Technology, 11,* 24–26.

HALL, R. V., LUND, D., and JACKSON, D. (1968). Effects of teacher attention on study behavior. *Journal of Applied Behavior Analysis, 1,* 1–12.

HALLAHAN, D., and KAUFFMAN, J. (1976). *An introduction to learning disabilities.* Englewood Cliffs, N.J.: Prentice-Hall.

HALLAHAN, D. P., and KAUFFMAN, J. M. (1982). *Exceptional children* (2nd ed.). Englewood Cliffs, N.J.: Prentice-Hall.

HALLAHAN, D. P., and KAUFFMAN, J. M. (1986). *Exceptional children* (3rd ed.). Englewood Cliffs, N.J.: Prentice-Hall.

HAMAKER, C. (1986). The effects of adjunct questions on prose learning. *Review of Educational Research, 56,* 212–242.

HAMBLIN, R. L., BUCKHOLDT, D., FERRITOR, D., KOZLOFF, M., and BLACKWELL, L. (1971). *The humanization processes.* New York: Wiley-Interscience.

HAMILTON, R. J. (1985). A framework for the evaluation of the effectiveness of adjunct questions and objectives. *Review of Educational Research, 55,* 47–85.

HARPRING, S. A. (1985, April). Inclass alternatives to traditional Chapter I pullout programs. Paper presented at the annual meeting of the American Educational Research Association, Chicago.

HARRIS, J. R., and LIEBERT, R. M. (1987). *The child: Development from birth through adoles-*

cence (2nd ed.). Englewood Cliffs, N.J.: Prentice-Hall.

HARRISON, G. V. (1972). *Beginning reading. I: A professional guide for the lay tutor.* Provo, Utah: Brigham Young University Press.

HARROP, A., and McCANN, C. (1983). Behavior modification and reading attainment in the comprehensive school. *Educational Research, 25,* 191–195.

HARSTE, J. C., and BURKE, C. L. (1980). Examining instructional assumptions: The child as informant. *Theory into Practice, 19,* 170–178.

HARTER, S. (1982). The perceived competence scale for children. *Child Development, 53,* 87–97.

HARTLEY, J., and DAVIES, I. K. (1976). Preinstructional strategies: The role of pretests, behavioral objectives, overviews, and advance organizers. *Review of Educational Research, 46,* 239–266.

HARTLEY, S. S. (1978). *Meta-analysis of the effects of individually paced instruction in mathematics* (doctoral dissertation, University of Colorado, 1977). *Dissertation Abstracts International, 38,* 4003A (University Microfilms No. 77–29, 926).

HARTSHORNE, H., and MAY, M. A. (1928). *Studies in the nature of character. I: Studies in deceit.* New York: Macmillan.

HASS, A. (1979). *Teenage sexuality.* New York: Macmillan.

HASTINGS, W. M. (1977). In praise of regurgitation. *Intellect, 105,* 349–350.

HAWKINS, J. D., DOUECK, H. J., and LISHNER, D. M. (1988). Changing teaching practices in mainstream classrooms to improve bonding and behavior of low achievers. *American Educational Research Journal, 25,* 31–50.

HAWLEY, W. D., CRAIN, R. L., RUSSELL, C. H., SMYLIE, M. A., FERNANDEZ, R. R., SCHOFIELD, J. W., TOMPKINS, R., TRENT, W. T., and ZLOTNIK, M. S. (1983). *Strategies for effective desegregation.* Lexington, Mass.: D. C. Heath.

HAYES, L. (1976). The use of group contingencies for behavioral control: A review. *Psychological Bulletin, 83,* 628–648.

HEMBREE, R. (1988). Correlates, causes, effects, and treatment of test anxiety. *Review of Educational Research, 58,* 47–77.

HERB, D. O. (1972). *A textbook of psychology* (3rd ed.). Philadelphia: Saunders.

HERMAN, S. H., and TRAMONTANA, J. (1971). Instructions and group versus individual reinforcement in modifying disruptive group behavior. *Journal of Applied Behavior Analysis, 4,* 113–119.

HERSEN, M. (Ed.) (1986). *Pharmacological and behavioral treatment: An integrative approach.* New York: Wiley.

HERSEN, M., and BARLOW, D. (1976). *Single-*

case experimental designs. Elmsford, N.Y.: Pergamon Press.

HESS, R. D., and SHIPMAN, V. C. (1970). Early experiences and the socialization of cognitive modes in children. In M. W. Miles and W. W. Charters, Jr. (Eds.), *Learning in social settings.* Boston: Allyn and Bacon.

HEWARD, W., and ORLANSKY, M. (1980). *Exceptional children.* Columbus, Ohio: Charles E. Merrill.

HEYNS, B. (1978). *Summer learning and the effects of schooling.* New York: Academic Press.

HIDI, S., and ANDERSON, V. (1986). Producing written summaries: Task demands, cognitive operations, and implications for instruction. *Review of Educational Research, 56,* 473–493.

HIEBERT, E. (1983). An examination of ability groupings for reading instruction. *Reading Research Quarterly, 18,* 231–255.

HIGBEE, K. L. (1978). Some pseudo-limitations of mnemonics. In M. M. Gruneberg, P. E. Morris, and R. N. Sykes (Eds.), *Practical aspects of memory.* New York: Academic Press.

HIGBEE, K. L. (1979). Recent research on visual mnemonics: Historical roots and educational fruits. *Review of Educational Research, 49,* 611–629.

HIGBEE, K. L., and KUNIHIRA, S. (1985). Cross-cultural applications of Yodai mnemonics in education. *Educational Psychologist, 20,* 57–64.

HILGARD, E. R., and BOWER, G. H. (1966). *Theories of learning.* New York: Appleton-Century-Crofts.

HILL, J. R. (1977). *Measurement and evaluation in the classroom.* Columbus, Ohio: C. E. Merrill.

HILL, K., and HORTON, M. (1985, April). *Validation of a classroom curriculum teaching elementary school students test-taking skills that optimize test performance.* Paper presented at the annual meeting of the American Educational Research Association, Chicago.

HILL, K., and WIGFIELD, A. (1984). Test anxiety: A major educational problem and what can be done about it. *Elementary School Journal, 85,* 105–126.

HIROTO, D. S., and SELIGMAN, M. E. P. (1975). Generality of learned helplessness in man. *Journal of Personality and Social Psychology, 31,* 311–327.

HIRSCH, B. J., and RAPKIN, B. D. (1987). The transition to junior high school: A longitudinal study of self-esteem, psychological symptomatology, school life, and social support. *Child Development, 58,* 1235–1243.

HIRSCHI, T. (1969). *Causes of delinquency.* Berkeley: University of California Press.

HITCHCOCK, D. (1983). *Critical thinking: A guide to evaluating information.* Toronto: Methven.

HIXON, T. J., SHRIBERG, L. D., and SAXMAN, J. H. (Eds.) (1980). *Introduction to communication disorders.* Englewood Cliffs, N.J.: Prentice-Hall.

HODGKINSON, H. L. (1985). *All one system: Demographics of education, kindergarten through graduate school.* Washington, D.C.: Institute for Educational Leadership.

HODGES, W., and SHEEHAN, R. (1978). Follow through as ten years of experimentation: What have we learned? *Young Children, 34,* 4–14.

HODGES, W., and SMITH, L. (1978, August). Retrospect and prospect in early childhood and special education. Paper presented at the annual meeting of the American Psychological Association, Toronto.

HOFFMAN, M. L. (1979). Development of moral thought, feeling and behavior. *American Psychologist, 34,* 958–966.

HOGAN, R., and EMLER, N. P. (1978). Moral development. In M. E. Lamb (Ed.), *Social and personality development,* pp. 200–233. New York: Holt, Rinehart, and Winston.

HOLT, J. (1964). *How children fail.* New York: Pitman.

HOPKINS, K. D., and BRACHT, G. H. (1975). Ten-year stability of verbal and nonverbal IQ scores. *American Educational Research Journal, 12,* 469–477.

HORN, R. E., and CLEAVES, A. (1980). *The guide to simulations/games for education and training* (4th ed.). Beverly Hills, Calif.: Sage.

HORWITZ, R. (1979). Psychological effects of the "open classroom." In H. J. Walberg (Ed.), *Educational environments and effects: Evaluation, policy and productivity.* Berkeley: McCutchen.

HOVLAND, C. I., LUMSDAINE, A. A., and SHEFFIELD, F. D. (1949). *Experiments on mass communication. Vol. 3: Studies in social psychology in World War II.* Princeton, N.J.: Princeton University Press.

HOWARD, E. R. (1978). *School discipline desk book.* West Nyack, N.Y.: Parker.

HULL, F. M., and HULL, M. E. (1973). Children with oral communication disabilities. In L. M. Dunn (Ed.), *Exceptional children in the schools: Special education in transition.* New York: Holt, Rinehart, and Winston.

HULL, F. M., MIELKE, P. W., TIMMONS, R. J., and WILLEFORD, J. A. (1971). The national speech and hearing survey: Preliminary results. *Asha, 13,* 501–509.

HUNTER, M. (1982). *Mastery teaching.* El Segundo, Calif.: TIP Publications.

HYDE, T. S., and JENKINS, J. J. (1969). Differential effects of incidental tasks on the organization of recall of a list of highly associated words. *Journal of Experimental Psychology, 82,* 472–481.

INDIVIDUALLY PRESCRIBED INSTRUCTION (1972). *Individually prescribed instruction.* New York: Appleton-Century-Crofts.

INHELDER, B., and PIAGET, J. (1958). *The growth of logical thinking from childhood to adolescence.* New York: Basic Books.

ISAACSON, R. L. (1964). Relation between achievement, test anxiety, and curricular choices. *Journal of Abnormal and Social Psychology, 64,* 447–452.

JACKLIN, C. N. (1983). Boys and girls entering school. In M. Marland (Ed.), *Sex differentiation and schooling.* London: Heinemann.

JACKSON, P., and LAHADERNE, H. (1967). Inequalities of teacher-pupil contacts. *Psychology in the Schools, 4,* 204–208.

JAMES, W. (1912). *Talks to teachers on psychology: And to students on some of life's ideals.* New York: Holt.

JENKINS, J. R., and JENKINS, L. M. (1987). Making peer tutoring work. *Educational Leadership, 44*(6), 64–68.

JENSEN, A. R. (1969). How much can we boost IQ and scholastic achievement? *Harvard Educational Review, 39,* 1–123.

JOHNSON, D., and JOHNSON, R. (1975). *Learning together and alone.* Englewood Cliffs, N.J.: Prentice-Hall.

JOHNSON, D. W., and JOHNSON, R. T. (1974). Instructional goal structure: Cooperative, competitive, or individualistic. *Review of Educational Research, 44,* 213–240.

JOHNSON, D. W., and JOHNSON, R. T. (1979). Conflict in the classroom: Controversy and learning. *Review of Educational Research, 49,* 51–70.

JOHNSON, D. W., and JOHNSON, R. T. (1987). *Learning together and alone.* Englewood Cliffs, N.J.: Prentice-Hall.

JOHNSON, G. O. (1950). A study of the social position of the mentally retarded child in the regular grades. *American Journal of Mental Deficiency, 55,* 60–89.

JOHNSON, L. C., and WAXMAN, H. C. (1985, March). *Evaluating the effects of the "Groups of Four" program.* Paper presented at the annual convention of the American Educational Research Association, Chicago.

JOHNSON, L. D., BACHMAN, J. G., and O'MALLEY, P. M. (1979). *Drugs and the class of '78: Behaviors, attitudes, and national trends.* Rockville, Md.: National Institute on Drug Abuse.

JOHNSON-LAIRD, P. N., HERRMANN, D. J., and CHAFFIN, R. (1984). Only connections: A critique of semantic networks. *Psychological Bulletin, 96,* 292–315.

JOHNSTON, P., ALLINGTON, R., and AFFLERBACH, P. (1985). The congruence of classroom and remedial instruction. *Elementary School Journal, 85,* 465–477.

JONES, J. (1961). *Blind children: degree of vision mode of reading.* Washington, D.C.: U.S. Department of Health, Education and Welfare.

JONES, L. V. (1984). White-black achievement differences: The narrowing gap. *American Psychologist, 39,* 1207–1213.

JONES, R. M. (1968). *Fantasy and feeling in education.* New York: Harper and Row.

JOYCE, B., and WEIL, M. (1980). *Models of teaching.* Englewood Cliffs, N.J.: Prentice-Hall.

KAGAN, D. (1988). Teaching as clinical problem solving: A critical examination of the analogy and its implications. *Review of Educational Research, 58,* 482–505.

KAGAN, J. (1964). Acquisition and significance of sex typing and sex-role identity. In M. L. Hoffman and L. W. Hoffman (Eds.), *Review of child development research.* New York: Sage.

KAGAN, J. (1976). Emergent themes in human development. *American Scientist, 64,* 186–196.

KAGAN, J., KLEIN, R. E., FINLEY, G. E., ROGOFF, B., and NOLAN, E. (1979). A cross-cultural study of cognitive development. *Monographs of the society for research in child development, 44,* No. 5.

KAGAN, S. (1983). Social orientation among Mexican-American children: A challenge to traditional classroom structures. In E. E. Garcia (Ed.), *The Mexican-American child: Language, cognition, and social development.* Tempe, Ariz.: Center for Bilingual Education.

KAGAN, S., ZAHN, G. L., WIDAMAN, K. F., SCHWARTZWALD, J., and TYRRELL, G. (1985). Classroom structural bias: Impact of cooperative and competitive classroom structures on cooperative and competitive individuals and groups. In R. E. Slavin et al. (Eds.), *Learning to cooperate, cooperating to learn.* New York: Plenum.

KALLISON, J. M. (1986). Effects of lesson organization on achievement. *American Educational Research Journal, 23,* 337–347.

KAMII, C., and DEVRIES, R. (1978). *Physical knowledge in preschool education: Implications of Piaget's theory.* Englewood Cliffs, N.J.: Prentice-Hall.

KAMII, C., and DEVRIES, R. (1980). *Group games in early education: Implications of Piaget's theory.* Washington, D.C.: National Association for the Education of Young Children.

KAMIN, L. J. (1975). *The science and politics of IQ.* New York: Wiley.

KAPLIN, R. M., and PASCOE, G. C. (1977). Humorous lectures and humorous examples: Some effects upon comprehension and retention. *Journal of Educational Psychology, 69,* 61–65.

KARRAKER, R. (1972). Increasing academic

performance through home managed contingency programs. *Journal of School Psychology, 10,* 173–179.

KARWEIT, N. (1976). A reanalysis of the effect of quantity of schooling on achievement. *Sociology of Education, 49,* 236–246.

KARWEIT, N. L. (1981). Time in school. *Research in Sociology of Education and Socialization, 2,* 77–110.

KARWEIT, N. L. (1989a). Effective kindergarten programs and practices for students at risk of academic failure. In R. E. Slavin, N. L. Karweit, and N. A. Madden (Eds.), *Effective programs for students at risk.* Boston: Mass.: Allyn and Bacon.

KARWEIT, N. L. (1989b). Preschool programs for students at risk of school failure. In R. E. Slavin, N. L. Karweit, and N. A. Madden (Eds.), *Effective programs for students at risk.* Boston: Mass.: Allyn and Bacon.

KARWEIT, N. L. (1989c). Time and learning: A review. In R. E. Slavin (Ed.), *School and classroom organization.* Hillsdale, N.J.: Erlbaum.

KARWEIT, N., and SLAVIN, R. E. (1981). Measurement and modeling choices in studies of time and learning. *American Educational Research Journal, 18,* 157–171.

KAUFFMAN, J. M. (1985). *Characteristics of children's behavior disorders* (3rd ed.). Columbus, Ohio: Charles E. Merrill.

KELLER, F. S. (1968). "Good-bye, teacher . . ." *Journal of Applied Behavior Analysis, 1,* 78–89.

KELLOG, R. (1967). Understanding children's art. *Psychology Today, 1,* 16–25.

KENDALL, P. C. (1981). Cognitive-behavioral interventions with children. In B. B. Lahey and A. E. Kazdin (Eds.), *Advances in clinical psychology,* Vol. 4. New York: Plenum.

KENNEDY, M. M., BIRMAN, B. F., and DEMALINE, R. E. (1986). *The effectiveness of Chapter 1 services.* Washington, D.C.: Office of Educational Research and Improvement, U.S. Department of Educational Research and Improvement, U.S. Department of Education.

KERSH, M. E. (1972). A study of mastery learning in elementary mathematics. Paper presented at the annual convention of the National Council of Teachers of Mathematics, Chicago.

KESSEN, W. (1979). The American child and other cultural inventions. *American Psychologist, 34,* 815–820.

KESTENBAUM, J. M. (1969). Achievement performance related to achievement motivation and test anxiety. *Journal of Consulting and Clinical Psychology, 34,* 343–344.

KEYSER, D. J., and SWEETLAND, R. C. (Eds.) (1984–85). *Test critiques* (Vols. 1–4). Kansas City: Test Corporation of America.

KIERSTEAD, J. (1985). Direct instruction and experiential approaches: Are they really mutually exclusive? *Educational Leadership, 42* (8), 25–30.

KIEWRA, K. A. (1983). The process of review: A levels-of-processing approach. *Contemporary Educational Psychology, 8,* 366–374.

KIEWRA, K. A. (1985a). Investigating note-taking and review: A depth of processing alternative. *Educational Psychologist, 20,* 23–32.

KIEWRA, K. A. (1985b). Providing the instructor's notes: An effective addition to student notetaking. *Educational Psychologist, 20,* 33–39.

KIEWRA, K. A. (1988). Cognitive aspects of autonomous note taking: Control processes, learning strategies, and prior knowledge. *Educational Psychologist, 23,* 39–56.

KIRBY, F. D., and SHIELDS, F. (1972). Modification of arithmetic response rate and attending behavior in a seventh-grade student. *Journal of Applied Behavior Analysis, 5,* 79–84.

KIRK, S. A. (1972). *Educating exceptional children* (2nd ed.). Boston: Houghton Mifflin.

KIRKPATRICK, C. (1926). *Intelligence and immigration.* Mental Measurement Monographs, Serial No. 2. Baltimore: The Williams and Wilkins Co.

KIRSCHENBAUM, H., SIMON, S. B., and NAPIER, R. W. (1971). *Wad-Ja-Get? The grading game in American education.* New York: Hart Publishing Co.

KLAUSMEIER, H. J., and HARRIS, C. W. (1966). *Analysis of concept learning.* New York: Academic Press.

KLAUSMEIER, H. J., JETER, J. T., QUILLING, M. R., FRAYER, D. A., and ALLEN, P. S. (1975). *Individually guided motivation.* Madison, Wisc.: Research and Development Center for Cognitive Learning.

KLEIN, S. (1985). *Handbook for achieving sex equality through education.* Baltimore, Md.: Johns Hopkins University Press.

KLIEBER, D. A., and BARNETT, L. A. (1980). Leisure in childhood. *Young Children, 35,* 47–52.

KLINE, S. (1977). *Child abuse and neglect: A primer for school personnel.* Reston, Va.: Council for Exceptional Children.

KNEEDLER, R. (1984). *Special education for today.* Englewood Cliffs, N.J.: Prentice-Hall.

KNELLER, G. F. (1965). *Educational anthropology: An introduction.* New York: John Wiley and Sons.

KOHLBERG, L. (1963). The development of children's orientations toward moral order. I: Sequence in the development of human thought. *Vita Humana, 6,* 11–33.

KOHLBERG, L. (1969). Stage and sequence: The cognitive-developmental approach to socialization. In D. A. Goslin (Ed.), *Hand-book of socialization theory and research,* pp. 347–380. Chicago: Rand McNally.

KOHLBERG, L. (1984). *Essays on moral development.* San Francisco: Harper and Row.

KOHN, M. L. (1969). *Class and conformity.* Homewood, Ill.: Dorsey.

KOHN, M. L. (1976). Social class and parental values: Another confirmation of the relationship. *American Sociological Review, 41,* 538–545.

KORNETSKY, C. (1975). Minimal brain dysfunction and drugs. In W. M. Cruickshank and D. P. Hallahan (Eds.), *Perceptual and learning disabilities in children. Vol 2: Research and theory.* Syracuse, N.Y.: Syracuse University Press.

KOUNIN, J. (1970). *Discipline and group management in classrooms.* New York: Holt, Rinehart, and Winston.

KRASNOR, L. R., and PEPLER, D. J. (1980). The study of children's play: Some suggested future directions. *New Directions for Child Development, 9,* 85–95.

KRATHWOHL, D. R., BLOOM, B. S., MASIA, B. B. (1964). *Taxonomy of educational objectives: The classification of educational goals. Handbook II: Affective domain.* New York: David McKay.

KRUEGER, W. C. F. (1929). The effect of overlearning on retention. *Journal of Experimental Psychology, 12,* 71–128.

KUKLA, A. (1972a). Attributional determinants of achievement-related behavior. *Journal of Personality and Social Psychology, 21,* 166–174.

KUKLA, A. (1972b). Foundations of an attributional theory of performance. *Psychological Review, 79,* 454–470.

KULIK, C., KULIK, J., and BANGERT-DROWNS, R. L. (1984, April). Effects of computer-based education of elementary school pupils. Paper presented at the annual convention of the American Educational Research Association, New Orleans.

KULIK, C. L., KULIK, J. A., and BANGERT-DROWNS, R. L. (1986, April). Effects of testing for mastery on student learning. Paper presented at the annual convention of the American Educational Research Association, San Francisco.

KULIK, J. A., and KULIK, C. L. (1984). Effects of accelerated instruction on students. *Review of Educational Research, 54,* 409–425.

KULIK, J. A., and KULIK, C. L. (1988). Timing of feedback and verbal learning. *Review of Educational Research, 58,* 79–97.

KULIK, J. A., KULIK, C. L., and BANGERT, R. L. (1984). Effects of practice on aptitude and achievement test scores. *American Educational Research Journal, 21,* 435–447.

KULIK, J. A., KULIK, C. L., and COHEN, P. A., (1979). A meta-analysis of outcome studies of Keller's Personalized System of Instruction. *American Psychologist, 34,* 307–318.

KUNIHIRA, S., KUZMA, R., MEADOWS, G., and LOTZ, T. (1981, April). Effects of visually aided verbal mnemonics in developing computational skills with fractional numbers. Paper presented at the annual meeting of the Western Psychological Association, Los Angeles.

LABERGE, D., and SAMUELS, S. J. (1974). Toward a theory of automatic information processing in reading. *Cognitive Psychology, 6,* 293–323.

LAHADERNE, H. (1968). Attitudinal and intellectual correlates of attention: A study of four sixth-grade classrooms. *Journal of Educational Psychology, 59,* 320–324.

LAHEY, B., GENDRICH, J., GENDRICH, S., SCHNELLE, L., GANT, D., and McNEE, P. (1977). An evaluation of daily report cards with minimal teacher and parent contacts as an efficient method of classroom intervention. *Behavior Modification, 1,* 381–394.

LAMBIE, R. A. (1980). A systematic approach for changing materials, instruction, and assignments to meet individual needs. *Focus on Exceptional Children, 6* (8), 1–14.

LAMPERT, M. (1986). Knowing, doing, and teaching multiplication. *Cognition and Instruction, 3,* 305–342.

LAND, M. L. (1987). Vagueness and clarity. In M. J. Dunkin (Ed.), *International encyclopedia of teaching and teacher education.* New York: Pergamon.

LANDY, F. J. (1984). *Psychology: The science of people.* Englewood Cliffs, N.J.: Prentice-Hall.

LARRIVEE, B. (1985). *Effective teaching behaviors for successful mainstreaming.* New York: Longman.

LAURIE, T. E., BUCHWACH, L., SILVERMAN, R., and ZIGMOND, N. (1978). Teaching secondary learning disabled students in the mainstream. *Learning Disability Quarterly, 1,* 62–72.

LAVATELLI, C. (1970). *Piaget's theory applied to an early childhood curriculum.* Cambridge, Mass.: American Science and Engineering.

LAVE, J. (1988). *Cognition in practice.* Boston: Cambridge Press.

LAWSON, G., PETERSON, J., and LAWSON, A. (1983). *Alcoholism and the family.* Rockville, Md.: Aspen Systems.

LAWTON, J. T., and WANSKA, S. K. (1977). Advance organizers as a teaching strategy: A reply to Barnes and Clawson. *Review of Educational Research, 47,* 233–244.

LAY, M. Z., and DOPYERA, J. E. (1977). *Becoming a teacher of young children.* Lexington, Mass.: Heath.

LEACH, D. M., and GRAVES, M. (1973). The effects of immediate correction on improving seventh grade language arts performance. In A. Egner (Ed.), *Individualizing junior and senior high instruction to provide special education within regular classrooms.* Burlington, Vt.: University of Vermont.

LEEPER, R. W. (1935). A study of a neglected portion of the field of learning: The development of sensory organization. *Pedagogical Seminary and Journal of Genetic Psychology, 46,* 41–75.

LEFCOURT, H. (1976). *Locus of control: Current trends in research and theory.* Hillsdale, N.J.: Erlbaum.

LEFKOWITZ, W. (1975). Communication grows in a "magic circle." In D. A. Read and S. B. Simon (Eds.), *Humanistic education sourcebook,* pp. 457–459. Englewood Cliffs, N.J.: Prentice-Hall.

LEINHARDT, G., and BICKEL, W. (1989). Instruction's the thing wherein to catch the mind that falls behind. In R. E. Slavin (Ed.), *School and classroom organization.* Hillsdale, N.J.: Erlbaum.

LEINHARDT, G., and PALLAY, A. (1982). Restrictive educational settings: Exile or haven? *Review of Educational Research, 52,* 557–578.

LEPPER, M. R. (1983). Extrinsic reward and intrinsic motivation: Implications for the classroom. In J. M. Levine and M. C. Wang (Eds.), *Teacher and student perceptions: Implications for learning,* pp. 281–317. Hillsdale, N.J.: Erlbaum.

LEPPER, M. R. (1985). Microcomputers in education: Motivational and social issues. *American Psychologist, 40,* 1–18.

LEPPER, M. R., GREENE, D., and NISBETT, R. E. (1973). Undermining children's intrinsic interest with extrinsic rewards: A test of the overjustification hypothesis. *Journal of Personality and Social Psychology, 28,* 129–137.

LERNER, B. (1981). The minimum competency testing movement: Social, scientific, and legal implications. *American Psychologist, 36,* 1057–1066.

LEVER, J. (1978). Sex differences in the complexity of children's play and games. *American Sociological Review, 43,* 471–483.

LEVIN, H. M., and MEISTER, G. (1986). Is CAI cost-effective? *Phi Delta Kappan, 68,* 745–749.

LEVIN, J. R. (1981). The mnemonic 80's: Keywords in the classroom. *Educational Psychologist, 16,* 65–82.

LEVIN, J. R. (1986). Four cognitive principles of learning-strategy instruction. *Educational Psychologist, 21,* 3–17.

LEVIN, J. R., MORRISON, C. R., McGIVERN, J. E., MASTROPIERI, M. A., and SCRUGGS, T. E. (1986). Mnemonic facilitation of text-embedded science facts. *American Educational Research Journal, 23,* 489–506.

LEVIN, J. R., SHRIBERG, L. K., MILLER, G. E., McCORMICK, C. B., and LEVIN, B. B. (1980). The keyword method as applied to elementary school children's social studies content. *Elementary School Journal, 80,* 185–191.

LEVINE, C., KOHLBERG, L., and HEWER, A. (1985). The current formulation of Kohlberg's theory and a response to critics. *Human Development, 28,* 94–100.

LEVINE, D. U. (Ed.) (1985). *Improving student achievement through mastery learning programs.* San Francisco: Jossey-Bass.

LEVINE, D. V., and HAVINGHURST, R. S. (1984). *Society and education* (6th ed.). Boston: Allyn and Bacon.

LEVINE, D. V., and STARK, J. (1982). Instructional and organizational arrangements that improve achievement in inner-city schools. *Educational Leadership, 39,* 41–46.

LEWIN, K. (1947). Group decision and social change. In T. M. Newcomb and E. L. Hartley (Eds.) *Readings in social psychology.* New York: Holt, Rinehart, and Winston.

LIEBERT, R. M., and WICKS-NELSON, R. (1981). *Developmental psychology* (3rd ed.). Englewood Cliffs, N.J.: Prentice-Hall.

LINDEMAN, R. H., and MERENDA, P. F. (1979). *Educational measurement.* Glenview, Ill.: Scott Foresman.

LITOW, L., and PUMROY, D. K. (1975). A brief review of classroom group-oriented contingencies. *Journal of Applied Behavior Analysis, 8,* 341–347.

LIVSON, N., and PESKIN, H. (1980). Perspectives on adolescence from longitudinal research. In J. Adelson (Ed.), *Handbook of adolescent psychology.* New York: Wiley.

LOCKE, E. A., CARTLEDGE, N., and KOEPPEL, J. (1968). Motivational effects of knowledge of results: A goal-setting phenomenon? *Psychological Bulletin, 70,* 474–485.

LOCKHEED, M. E. (1984). Sex segregation and male preeminence in elementary classrooms. In E. Fennema and M. J. Ayer (Eds.), *Women and education: Equity or equality?* Berkeley: McCutchan.

LOCKHEED, M. E., and HARRIS, A. M. (1982). Classroom interaction and opportunities for cross-sex peer learning in science. *Journal of Early Adolescence, 2,* 135–143.

LOCKHEED, M. E., HARRIS, A. M., and FINKELSTEIN, K. J. (1979). *Curriculum and research for equity: A training manual for promoting sex equity in the classroom.* Princeton, N.J.: Educational Testing Service.

LONG, B. (1967). Developmental changes in the self-concept during middle childhood. *Merrill Palmer Quarterly, 13.*

LONGFELLOW, C. (1979). Divorce in context: Its impact on children. In G. Levinger and O. Moles (Eds.), *Divorce and separation.* New York: Basic Books.

LUECKEMEYER, C. L., and CHIAPPETTA, E. L. (1981). An investigation into the effects of a modified mastery learning strategy on achievement in a high school human physiology unit. *Journal of Research in Science Teaching, 18,* 269–273.

MACCOBY, E. E., and JACKLIN, C. N. (1974). *The psychology of sex differences.* Stanford, Calif.: Stanford University Press.

MACHIDA, K., and CARLSON, J. (1984). Effects of a verbal mediation strategy on cognitive processes in mathematics learning. *Journal of Educational Psychologist, 76,* 1382–1385.

MacMILLAN, D. L., KEOGH, B. K., and JONES, R. L. (1986). Special educational research on mildly handicapped learners. In M. C. Wittrock (Ed.), *Handbook of research on teaching* (3rd ed.). New York: Macmillan.

MacMILLAN, D. L., MEYERS, C. E., and MORRISON, G. M. (1980). System-identification of mildly mentally retarded children: Implications for interpreting and conducting research. *American Journal of Mental Deficiency, 85,* 108–115.

MADAUS, G. F., WOODS, E. M., and NUTTALL, R. L. (1973). A causal model of Bloom's taxonomy. *American Educational Research Journal, 10,* 253–262.

MADDEN, N. A., and SLAVIN, R. E. (1983a). Effects of cooperative learning on the social acceptance of mainstreamed academically handicapped students. *Journal of Special Education, 17,* 171–182.

MADDEN, N. A., and SLAVIN, R. E. (1983b). Mainstreaming students with mild academic handicaps: Academic and social outcomes. *Review of Educational Research, 53,* 519–569.

MADDEN, N. A., SLAVIN, R. E., and STEVENS, R. J. (1986). *Cooperative integrated reading and composition: Teacher's manual.* Baltimore, Md.: Johns Hopkins University, Center for Research on Elementary and Middle Schools.

MADDOX, H., and HOOLE, E. (1975). Performance decrement in the lecture. *Educational Review, 28,* 17–30.

MADSEN, C. H., BECKER, W. C., and THOMAS, D. R. (1968). Rules, praise, and ignoring: Elements of elementary classroom control. *Journal of Applied Behavior Analysis, 1,* 139–150.

MADSEN, C. H., and MADSEN, C. R. (1968). *Teaching/discipline.* Boston: Allyn and Bacon.

MADSEN, K. (1961). *Theories of motivation: A comparative study of modern theories of motivation* (2nd ed.). Cleveland: H. Allen.

MAGER, R. F. (1975). *Preparing instructional objectives.* Belmont, Calif.: Fearon.

MAHONE, C. H. (1960). Fear of failure and unrealistic vocational aspiration. *Journal of Abnormal and Social Psychology, 60,* 253–261.

MAIER, N. R. (1930). Reasoning in humans. I. On direction. *Journal of Comparative Psychology, 10,* 115–143.

MAIER, S. F., SELIGMAN, M. E. P., and SOLOMON, R. L. (1969). Pavlovian fear conditioning and learned helplessness. In B. A. Campbell and R. M. Church (Eds.), *Punishment and adversive behavior*. New York: Appleton-Century-Crofts.

MALINA, R. M. (1982). Motor development in the early years. In S. G. Moore and C. R. Cooper (Eds.), *The young child: Reviews of research*, Vol. 3, pp. 211–230. Washington, D.C.: National Association for the Education of Young Children.

MALLERY, D. (1962). *High school students speak out*. New York: Harper and Row.

MALONE, T., and LEPPER, M. (1988). Making learning fun: A taxonomy of intrinsic motivation for learning. In R. Snow and M. Farr (Eds.), *Aptitude, learning, and instruction, Vol. III: Cognitive and affective process analysis*. Hillsdale, N.J.: Erlbaum.

MANDEVILLE, G. (1988, April). *An evaluation of PET using extant achievement test data*. Paper presented at the annual convention of the American Educational Research Association, New Orleans.

MANNING, B. H. (1988). Application of cognitive behavior modification: First and third graders' self-management of classroom behaviors. *American Educational Research Journal, 25*, 193–212.

MARLAND, M. (Ed.) (1983). *Sex differentiation and schooling*. London: Heinemann.

MARLAND, S. P. (1972). *Education of the gifted and talented*. Washington, D.C.: U.S. Government Printing Office.

MARLIAVE, R., FISHER, C., and DISHAW, M. (1978). Academic learning time and student achievement in the B–C period. Far West Laboratory for Educational Research and Development, Technical note v-29.

MARSH, H. W. (1986). Self-serving effect (bias?) in academic attributions: Its relation to academic achievement and self-concept. *Journal of Educational Psychologist, 78*, 190–200.

MARSHALL, H. (1981). Open classroom: Has the term outlived its usefulness? *Review of Educational Research, 51*, 181–192.

MARSHALL, P. M. (1982). *Homework and social facilitation theory in teaching elementary school mathematics*. Unpublished doctoral dissertation, Stanford University.

MARSHALL, S. P. (1984). Sex differences in children's mathematics achievement: Solving computations and story problems. *Journal of Educational Psychologist, 76*, 194–204.

MARTIN, J. E., RUSCH, F. R., and HEAL, L. W. (1982). Teaching community survival skills to mentally retarded adults: A review and analysis. *Journal of Special Education, 16*, 243–267.

MASLOW, A. H. (1954). *Motivation and personality*. New York: Harper and Row.

MASLOW, A. H. (1968). *Toward a psychology of being* (2nd ed.). New York: Van Nostrand Reinhold.

MASTERSON, J. F. (1967). *The psychiatric dilemma of adolescence*. Boston: Little, Brown.

MASTIN, V. E. (1963). Teacher enthusiasm. *Journal of Educational Research, 56*, 385–386.

MAYER, R. E. (1979). Can advance organizers influence meaningful learning? *Review of Educational Research, 49*, 371–383.

MAYER, R. E. (1989). Models for understanding. *Review of Educational Research, 59*, 43–64.

McALLISTER, L. W., STACHOWIAK, J. G., BAER, D. M., and CONDERMAN, L. (1969). The application of operant conditioning techniques in a secondary school classroom. *Journal of Applied Behavior Analysis, 2*, 277–285.

McCALEB, J., and WHITE, J. (1980). Critical dimensions in evaluating teacher clarity. *Journal of Classroom Interaction, 15*, 27–30.

McCLELLAND, D. C. (1969). The role of educational technology in developing achievement motivation. *Educational Technology, 9* (10), 7.

McCLELLAND, D.C., and ATKINSON, J. W. (1948). The projective expression of needs: II. The effect of different intensities of the hunger drive on thematic apperception. *Journal of Experimental Psychology, 38*, 643–658.

McCLELLAND, D. C., ATKINSON, J. W., CLARK, R. T., and LOWELL, E. L. (1953). *The achievement motive*. New York: Appleton-Century-Crofts.

McCOMBS, B. L. (1984). Processes and skills underlying continuing motivation to learn: Toward a definition of motivational skills training interventions. *Educational Psychologist, 19*, 199–218.

McCORMICK, C. B., and LEVIN, J. R. (1984). A comparison of different prose-learning variations of the mnemonic keyword method. *American Educational Research Journal, 21*, 379–398.

McDONALD, B. A., LARSON, C. D., DANSEREAU, D. I., and SPURLIN, J. E. (1985). Cooperative dyads: Impact on text learning and transfer. *Contemporary Educational Psychology, 10*, 369–377.

McKENZIE, G. (1979). Effects of questions and testlike events on achievement and on-task behavior in a classroom concept learning presentation. *Journal of Educational Research, 72*, 348–350.

McKENZIE, G. R., and HENRY, M. (1979). Effects of testlike events on on-task behavior, test anxiety, and achievement in a classroom rule-learning task. *Journal of Educational Psychologist, 71*, 370–374.

McKENZIE, M. (1977). The beginnings of literacy. *Theory into Practice, 16*, 315–324.

McKEY, R., CONDELLI, L., GANSON, H., BARRETT, B., McCONKEY, C., and PLANTZ, M. (1985). *The impact of Head Start on children, families, and communities*. Washington, D.C.: CSR, Inc.

McKINNEY, J. D., and SPEECE, D. L. (1986). Academic consequences and longitudinal stability of behavioral subtypes of learning disabled children. *Journal of Educational Psychologist, 78*, 365–372.

McPARTLAND, J. M., COLDIRON, J. R., and BRADDOCK, J. H. (1987). *School structures and classroom practices in elementary, middle, and secondary schools (Tech. Rep. No. 14)*. Baltimore, Md.: Johns Hopkins University, Center for Research on Elementary and Middle Schools.

MEDLEY, D. M. (1979). The effectiveness of teachers. In P. L. Peterson and H. Walberg (Eds.), *Research on teaching: Concepts, findings, and implications*, pp. 11–27. Berkeley: McCutchan.

MEICHENBAUM, D. (1977). *Cognitive behavior modification: An integrative approach*. New York: Plenum.

MEICHENBAUM, D., and GOODMAN, J. (1971). Training impulsive children to talk to themselves: A means of developing self-control. *Journal of Abnormal Psychology, 77*, 115–126.

MELTON, R. F. (1978). Resolution of conflicting claims concerning the effect of behavioral objectives on student learning. *Review of Educational Research, 18*, 291–302.

MENYUK, P. (1982). Language and development. In C. B. Kapp and J. B. Krakow (Eds.), *The child: Development in a social context*, pp. 282–331. Reading, Mass.: Addison-Wesley.

MERCER, J. R. (1973). *Labeling the mentally retarded*. Berkeley: University of California Press.

MESSER, S. (1972). The relation of internal-external control to academic performance. *Child Development, 43*, 1456–1462.

MESSICK, S. (1982). Issues of effectiveness and equity in the coaching controversy: Implications for educational and testing practice. *Educational Psychologist, 17*, 67–91.

MESSICK, S. (1984). The nature of cognitive styles: Problems and promise in educational practice. *Educational Psychologist, 19*, 59–74.

METFESSEL, N. S., MICHAEL, W. B., and KIRSNER, D. A. (1969). Instrumentation of Bloom's and Krathwohl's taxonomies for the writing of educational objectives. *Psychology in the Schools, 6*, 227–231.

METZ, M. H. (1978). *Classrooms and corridors: The crisis of authority in desegregated secondary schools*. Berkeley: University of California Press.

MEYER, L., GERSTEN, R. M., and GUTKIN, J. (1983). Direct instruction: A project follow-through success story in an inner-city school. *Elementary School Journal, 84*, 241–252.

MEYER, L. A. (1984). Long-term academic effects of the Direct Instruction Project

Follow-Through. *Elementary School Journal, 84,* 380–394.

MEYER, W. J., and THOMPSON, G. G. (1963). Teacher interaction with boys as contrasted with girls. In R. G. Kuhlen and G. G. Thompson (Eds.), *Psychological studies of human development.* New York: Appleton-Century-Crofts.

MIELE, F. (1979). Cultural bias in the WISC. *Intelligence, 3,* 149–164.

MICHAEL, W. B. (1977). Cognitive and affective components of creativity in mathematics and the physical sciences. In J. C. Stanley, W. C. George, and C. H. Solano (Eds.), *The gifted and the creative: A fifty year perspective.* Baltimore: Johns Hopkins Press.

MILLER, G. A. (1956). The magical number seven, plus or minus two: Some limits on our capacity for processing information. *Psychological Review, 63,* 81–97.

MILLER, G. A., GALANTER, E., and PRIBRAM, K. H. (1960). *Plans and the structure of behavior.* New York: Holt, Rinehart, and Winston.

MILLER, G. E., LEVIN, J. R., and PRESSLEY, M. (1980). An adaptation of the keyword method to children's learning of verbs. *Journal of Mental Imagery, 4,* 57–61.

MILLER, P. H. (1983). *Theories of developmental psychology.* San Francisco: W. H. Freeman.

MILLER, R. L. (1976). Individualized instruction in mathematics: A review of research. *The Mathematics Teacher, 69,* 345–351.

MILLER, T. L., and SABATINO, D. (1978). An evaluation of the teacher-consultant model as an approach to mainstreaming. *Exceptional Children, 45,* 86–91.

MITCHELL, B. M. (1984). An update on gifted/talented education in the U.S. *Roeper Review, 6,* 161–163.

MITCHELL, J. V. (Ed.) (1985). *The ninth mental measurements yearbook.* Lincoln: University of Nebraska, Buros Institute of Mental Measurement.

MITCHELL, P., and ERICKSON, D. K. (1980). The education of gifted and talented children: A status report. *Exceptional Children, 45,* 12–16.

MOLES, O. (1984, April). In-school alternatives to suspension: stability and effects. Paper presented at the annual convention of the American Educational Research Association, New Orleans.

MORELLA, J. R. (1974). Preschool education as a factor in first-grade performance of middle-class children. *Dissertation Abstracts International, 34,* 7590A (University Microfilms No. 74–12, 316).

MORGAN, M. (1984). Reward-induced decrements and increments in intrinsic motivation. *Review of Educational Research, 54,* 5–30.

MORINE-DERSHIMER, G. (1983). Instructional strategy and the "creation" of classroom status. *American Educational Research Journal, 20,* 645–661.

MORRIS, C. C., BRANSFORD, J. D., and FRANKS, J. J. (1977). Levels of processing versus transfer appropriate processing. *Journal of Verbal Learning and Verbal Behavior, 16,* 519–533.

MORRIS, L. G. (1985). *Psychology: An introduction* (5th ed.). Englewood Cliffs, N.J.: Prentice-Hall.

MORRISON, D. M. (1985). Adolescent contraceptive behavior: A review. *Psychological Bulletin, 98,* 538–568.

MORSE, J. A., and TILLMAN, M. H. (1972, April). Effects on achievement of possession of behavioral objectives and training concerning their use. Paper presented at the annual convention of the American Educational Research Association, Chicago.

MOSS, H. A. (1967). Sex, age, and state as determinants of mother-infant interaction. *Merrill-Palmer Quarterly, 13,* 19–36.

MURPHY, R. T., and APPEL, L. R. (1984). *Evaluation of the writing to read instructional system, 1982–1984.* Princeton, N.J.: Educational Testing Service.

MURRAY, F. B. (1982). Teaching through social conflict. *Contemporary Educational Psychology, 7,* 257–271.

MURRAY, H. (1983). *Explorations in personality: A clinical and experimental study of fifty men of college age.* New York: Oxford University Press.

NAFPAKTITIS, M., MAYER, G. R., and BUTTERWORTH, T. (1985). Natural rates of teacher approval and disapproval and their relation to student behavior in intermediate school classrooms. *Journal of Educational Psychology, 77,* 362–367.

NAGY, P., and GRIFFITHS, A. K. (1982). Limitations of recent research relating Piaget's theory to adolescent thought. *Review of Educational Research, 52,* 513–556.

NAKANE, M. (1981). *Yodai.* Kyoto, Japan: New Teaching Method Research Center, Ryoyo Schools.

NAREMORE, R. C. (1980). Language disorders in children. In T. J. Hixon, L. D. Shriberg, and J. H. Saxman (Eds.), *Introduction to communication disorders.* Englewood Cliffs, N. J.: Prentice-Hall.

NASH, W. R., BORMAN, C., and COLSON, S. (1980). Career education for gifted and talented students: A senior high school model. *Exceptional Children, 46,* 404–405.

NATIONAL ASSESSMENT OF EDUCATIONAL PROGRESS (1981). *Three national assessments of reading: Changes in performance, 1970–80.* Washington, D.C.: NAEP.

NATIONAL CENTER FOR EDUCATIONAL STATISTICS (1984). *The condition of education.* Washington, D.C.: NCES.

NATIONAL CENTER FOR EDUCATIONAL STATISTICS (1985). *The school-age handicapped.* Washington, D.C.: NCES.

NATIONAL CENTER FOR EDUCATIONAL STATISTICS (1988). *Digest of educational statistics.* Washington, D.C.: U.S. Department of Education, NCES.

NATIONAL CLEARINGHOUSE FOR DRUG ABUSE INFORMATION (1986). *Teen involvement for drug abuse prevention.* Rockville, Md.: NCDAI.

NATIONAL COMMISSION ON EXCELLENCE IN EDUCATION (1983). *A nation at risk.* Washington, D.C.: U.S. Department of Education.

NATIONAL INSTITUTE OF EDUCATION (1978). *Compensatory education study.* Washington, D.C.: NIE.

NATIONAL INSTITUTE ON DRUG ABUSE (1985). *Use of licit and illicit drugs by America's high school students, 1975–1984.* Washington, D.C.: U.S. Department of Health and Human Services.

NATIONAL SOCIETY FOR THE PREVENTION OF BLINDNESS (1966). *Estimated statistics on blindness and vision problems.* New York: NSPB.

NATIONAL SOCIETY FOR THE PREVENTION OF BLINDNESS (1969). Vision screening in the schools (Pub. #257). New York: National Society for the Prevention of Blindness.

NATRIELLO, G. (1989). The impact of evaluation processes on students. In R. E. Slavin (Ed.), *School and classroom organization.* Hillsdale, N.J.: Erlbaum.

NATRIELLO, G., and DORNBUSCH, S. M. (1984). *Teacher evaluative standards and student effort.* New York: Longman.

NEDELSKY, L. (1965). *Science teaching and testing.* New York: Harcourt, Brace, and World.

NEILL, A. S. (1960). *Summerhill: A radical approach to child rearing.* New York: Hart.

NEWELL, A., and SIMON, H. (1972). *Human problem solving.* Englewood Cliffs, N.J.: Prentice-Hall.

NEWMANN, F. M., and THOMPSON, J. (1987). *Effects of cooperative learning on achievement in secondary schools: A summary of research.* Madison, Wisc.: University of Wisconsin, National Center on Effective Secondary Schools.

NICHOLLS, J. G. (1984). Conceptions of ability and achievement motivation. In R. Ames and C. Ames (Eds.), *Research on motivation in education,* Vol. 1. New York: Academic Press.

NIEMIEC, R. P., and WALBERG, H. J. (1985). Computers and achievement in the elementary schools. *Journal of Educational Computing Research, 1,* 435–440.

NITSCHE, K. E. (1977). Structuring decontextualized forms of knowledge. Unpublished doctoral dissertation, Vanderbilt University.

NOLL, V. H., SCANNEL, D. P., and CRAIG, R. C. (1979). *Introduction to educational measurement* (4th ed.). Boston: Houghton Mifflin.

NORRIS, S. P. (1985). Synthesis of research on critical thinking. *Educational Leadership, 42,* 40–45.

NOWICKI, S., DUKE, M. P., and CROUCH, M. P. D. (1978). Sex differences in locus of control and performance under competitive and cooperative conditions. *Journal of Educational Psychology, 70,* 482–486.

NUCCI, L. (1987). Synthesis of research on moral development. *Educational Leadership, 44,* 86–92.

NURSS, J. R., and HODGES, W. L. (1982). Early childhood education. In H. E. Mitzel (Ed.) *Encyclopedia of Educational Research* (5th ed.), pp. 477–513. New York: Free Press.

NUTHALL, G. (1987). Reviewing and recapitulating. In M. J. Dunkin (Ed.), *International encyclopedia of teaching and teacher education.* New York: Pergamon.

OAKES, J. (1985). *Keeping track: How schools structure inequality.* New Haven, Conn.: Yale University Press.

OAKES, J. (1989). Tracking in secondary schools: A contextual perspective. In R. E. Slavin (Ed.), *School and classroom organization.* Hillsdale, N.J.: Erlbaum.

OAKLAND, T. (Ed.) (1977). *Psychological and educational assessment of minority children.* New York: Brunner/Mazel.

OAKLEY, D. A. (1981). Brain mechanisms of mammalian memory. *British Medical Bulletin, 37,* 175–180.

OAKLEY, D. A. (1983). The varieties of memory: A phylogenetic approach. In A. Mayes (Ed.), *Memory in animals and humans,* pp. 20–82. Woringham, England: Van Nostrand Reinhold.

ODEN, S. (1982). Peer relationship development in childhood. In L. G. Katz (Ed.), *Current topics in early childhood education,* Vol. 4, pp. 87–117. Norwood, N.J.: Ablex Publishing Corp.

ODLE, S. J., and GALTELLI, B. (1980). The Individualized Education Program (IEP): Foundation for appropriate and effective instruction. In J. W. Schifani, R. M. Anderson, and S. J. Odle (Eds.), *Implementing learning in the least restrictive environment.* Baltimore: University Park Press.

O'DONNELL, H. (1982). Computer literacy. II: Classroom applications. *Reading Teacher, 35,* 614–617.

OISHI, S., SLAVIN, R. E., and MADDEN, N. A. (1983, April). Effects of student teams and individualized instruction on cross-race and cross-sex friendships. Paper presented at the annual meeting of the American Educational Research Association, Montreal.

OKEY, J. R. (1974). Altering teacher and pupil behavior with mastery teaching. *School Science and Mathematics, 74,* 530–535.

OKEY, J. R. (1977). Consequences of training teachers to use a mastery learning strategy. *Journal of Teacher Education, 28,* 57–62.

O'LEARY, K. D. (1980). Pills or skills for hyperactive children. *Journal of Applied Behavior Analysis, 13,* 191–204.

O'LEARY, K. D., and BECKER, W. C. (1967). The effects of the intensity of a teacher's reprimands on children's behavior. *Journal of School Psychology, 7,* 8–11.

O'LEARY, K. D., KAUFMAN, K. F., KASS, R. E., and DRABMAN, R. S. (1970). The effects of loud and soft reprimands on the behavior of disruptive students. *Exceptional Children, 37,* 145–155.

O'LEARY, K. D., and O'LEARY, S. G. (1972). *Classroom management: The successful use of behavior modification.* New York: Pergamon.

O'LEARY, K. D., and O'LEARY, S. G. (Eds.) (1977). *Classroom management: The successful use of behavior modification* (2nd ed.). New York: Pergamon.

OLSON, D. R., and PAU, A. S. (1966). Emotionally loaded words and the acquisition of a sight vocabulary. *Journal of Educational Psychology, 57,* 174–178.

ORLICK, T. (1978). *Winning through cooperation.* Washington, D.C.: Acropolis Books.

ORMELL, C. P. (1979). The problem of analyzing understanding. *Educational Research, 22,* 32–38.

OSBORN, A. F. (1963). *Applied imagination* (3rd ed.). New York: Scribner's.

OSBORN, J. D., and OSBORN, P. K. (1983). *Cognition in early childhood.* Athens, Ga.: Education Associates.

OSGUTHORPE, R. T. (1984). Handicapped students as tutors for nonhandicapped peers. *Academic Therapy, 19,* 473–483.

OSGUTHORPE, R. T., and SCRUGGS, T. E. (1986). Special education students as tutors: A review and analysis. *Remedial and Special Education, 7* (4), 15–25.

O'SHEA, T., and SELF, J. (1983). *Learning and teaching with computers: Artificial intelligence in education.* Englewood Cliffs, N.J.: Prentice-Hall.

OSWALD, J. M., and FLETCHER, J. D. (1970). Some measured effects of specificity and cognitive level of explicit instructional objectives upon test performance among eleventh grade social science students. Paper presented at the annual meeting of the American Educational Research Association, Minneapolis.

OWEN, S. L., FROMAN, R. D., and MOSCOW, H. (1981). *Educational psychology* (2nd ed.). Boston: Little, Brown.

OTTENBACHER, K. J., and COOPER, H. M. (1983). Drug treatment of hyperactivity in children. *Developmental medicine and child neurology, 25,* 358–366.

PAGE, E. B. (1958). Teacher comments and student performance: A seventy-four classroom experiment in school motivation. *Journal of Educational Psychology, 49,* 173–181.

PAIVIO, A. (1971). *Imagery and verbal processes.* New York: Holt.

PALINCSAR, A. S. (1984, April). Reciprocal teaching: Working within the zone of proximal development. Paper presented at the annual convention of the American Educational Research Association, New Orleans.

PALINCSAR, A. S. (1986). *Reciprocal teaching teacher's manual.* East Lansing: Michigan State University, Institute for Research on Teaching.

PALINCSAR, A. S. (1987, April). Reciprocal teaching: Field evaluations in remedial and content-area reading. Paper presented at the annual convention of the American Educational Research Association, Washington, D.C.

PALINCSAR, A. S., and BROWN, A. L. (1984). Reciprocal teaching of comprehension fostering and comprehension monitoring activities. *Cognition and Instruction, 2,* 117–175.

PALINCSAR, A. S., BROWN, A. L., and MARTIN, S. M. (1987). Peer interaction in reading comprehension instruction. *Educational Psychologist, 22,* 231–253.

PAPERT, S. (1980). *Mindstorms: Children, computers, and powerful ideas.* New York: Basic Books.

PARIS, S., CROSS, D., and LIPSON, M. (1984). Informal strategies for learning: A program to improve children's reading awareness and comprehension. *Journal of Educational Psychology, 76,* 1239–1252.

PARIS, S. G., WIXSON, K. K., and PALINCSAR, A. (1986). Instructional approaches to reading comprehension. In E. Z. Rothkopf (Ed.), *Review of Research in Education,* Vol. 13, pp. 91–128. Washington, D.C.: American Educational Research Association.

PARKE, B. N. (1983). Use of self-instructional materials with gifted primary aged students. *Gifted Child Quarterly, 27,* 29–34.

PARSONS, J., ADLER, T., and KACZALA, C. (1982). Socialization of achievement attitudes and beliefs: Parental influences. *Child Development, 53,* 310–339.

PASSOW, A. H. (Ed.) (1979). *The gifted and talented: Their education and development.* Chicago: University of Chicago Press.

PATTERSON, G. R., REID, J. B., JONES, R. R., and CONGER, R. E. (1975). *A social learning approach to family intervention. Vol. 1: Families with aggressive children.* Eugene, Oreg.: Castalia.

PEA, R. D., and KURLAND, D. M. (1984). *Logo programming and the development of planning skills.* (Tech. Rep. No. 16). New York: Bank Street College of Education, Center for Children and Technology.

PECKHAM, P. D., and ROE, M. D. (1977). The effects of frequent testing. *Journal of Research and Development in Education, 10,* 40–50.

PENFIELD, W. (1969). Consciousness, memory, and man's conditioned reflexes. In K. H. Pribram (Ed.), *On the biology of learning.* New York: Harcourt Brace Jovanovich.

PEPITONE, E. A. (1980). *Children in cooperation and competition: Toward a developmental social psychology.* Lexington, Mass.: D. C. Heath.

PEPITONE, E. A. (1985). Children in cooperation and competition: Antecedents and consequences of self-orientation. In R. E. Slavin, S. Sharan, S. Kagan, R. Hertz-Lazarowitz, C. Webb, and R. Schmuck (Eds.), *Learning to cooperate, cooperating to learn.* New York: Plenum.

PERFETTI, C., and LESGOLD, A. (1977). Discourse comprehension and sources of individual differences. In M. Just and P. Carpenter (Eds.), *Cognitive processes in comprehension.* Hillsdale, N.J.: Erlbaum.

PERFETTO, G. A., BRANSFORD, J. D., and FRANKS, J. J. (1983). Constraints on access in a problem solving context. *Memory and Cognition, 11,* 24–31.

PERKINS, D. N., and SALOMON, G. (1988). Teaching for transfer. *Educational Leadership, 46* (1), 22–32.

PERKINS, D. N., and SALOMON, G. (1989). Are cognitive skills context-bound? *Educational Researcher, 18,* 16–25.

PERKINS, W. H. (1980). Disorders of speech flow. In T. J. Hixon, L. D. Shriberg, and J. H. Saxman (Eds.), *Introduction to communication disorders.* Englewood Cliffs, N.J.: Prentice-Hall.

PERL, E., and LAMBERT, W. E. (1962). The relation of bilingualism to intelligence. *Psychological Monographs, 76,* 1–23.

PESKIN, H. (1967). Pubertal onset and ego functioning. *Journal of Abnormal Psychology, 72,* 1–15.

PETERS, E. E., LEVIN, J. R., McGIVERN, J. E., and PRESSLEY, M. (1985). Further comparison of representational and transformational prose-learning imagery. *Journal of Educational Psychology, 77,* 129–136.

PETERSON, L. R., and PETERSON, M. J. (1959). Short-term retention of individual verbal items. *Journal of Experimental Psychology, 58,* 193–198.

PETERSON, P. L. (1979). Direct instruction reconsidered. In P. Peterson and H. Walberg (Eds.), *Research on teaching: Concepts, findings, and implications,* pp. 57–69. Berkeley: McCutchan.

PETERSON, P. L., and FENNEMA, E. (1985). Effective teaching, student engagement in classroom activities, and sex-related differences in learning mathematics. *American Educational Research Journal, 22,* 309–335.

PETRIE, C. R. (1963). Informative speaking: A summary and bibliography of related research. *Speech Monography, 30,* 79–91.

PETTY, M. F., and FIELD, C. J. (1980). Fluctuations in mental test scores. *Educational Research, 22,* 198–202.

PHILLIPS, B., PITCHER, G., WORSHAM, M., and MILLER, S. (1980). Test anxiety and the school environment. In I. Sarason (Ed.), *Test anxiety: Theory, research, and applications.* Hillsdale, N.J.: Erlbaum.

PHILLIPS, J. L. (1975). *The origins of intellect: Piaget's theory* (2nd ed.). San Francisco: W. H. Freeman.

PIAGET, J. (1932). *The moral judgment of the child.* Glencoe, Ill.: Free Press.

PIAGET, J. (1952a). *The language and thought of the child.* London: Routledge and Kegan-Paul.

PIAGET, J. (1952b). *The origins of intelligence in children.* New York: Basic Books.

PIAGET, J. (1962). *Play dreams and imitation in childhood.* New York: Norton.

PIAGET, J. (1964). *The moral judgment of the child.* New York: Free Press.

PIAGET, J. (1972). Intellectual evolution from adolescence to adulthood. *Human Development, 15,* 1–12.

PIAGET, J. (1973). *The psychology of intelligence.* Totowa, N.J.: Littlefield, Adams.

PIAGET, J., and INHELDER, B. (1956). *The child's conception of space.* Boston: Routledge and Kegan Paul.

PIAGET, J., and INHELDER, B. (1969). *The psychology of the child.* New York: Basic Books.

PINNELL, G. S. (1988, April). *Sustained effects of a strategy-centered early intervention program in reading.* Paper presented at the annual convention of the American Educational Research Association, New Orleans.

PINTRICH, P. R., and BLUMENFELD, P. (1985). Classroom experience and children's self-perceptions of ability, effort, and conduct. *Journal of Educational Psychology, 77,* 646–657.

PITTMAN, T. S., BOGGIANO, A. K., and RUBLE, D. N. (1983). Intrinsic and extrinsic motivational orientations: Limiting conditions on the undermining and enhancing effects of reward on intrinsic motivation. In J. M. Levine and M. C. Wang (Eds.), *Teacher and student perceptions: Implications for learning,* pp. 319–340. Hillsdale, N.J.: Erlbaum.

PLAY (1982, December). Play: Practical applications of research. Newsletter of Phi Delta Kappa's Center on Evaluation, Development and Research, Bloomington, Ill.

PLUMB, J. H. (1974). The great change in children. In S. Coopersmith and L. Feldman (Eds.), *The formative years: Principles of early childhood education,* pp. 28–37. San Francisco: Albion Publishing Co.

POLYA, G. (1957). *How to solve it* (2nd ed.). New York: Doubleday.

POPHAM, W. J. (1981). *Modern educational measurement.* Englewood Cliffs, N.J.: Prentice-Hall.

PORTER, A. C., and BROPHY, J. E. (1988). Synthesis of research on good teaching: Insights from the work of the Institute for Research on Teaching. *Educational Leadership, 45,* 74–85.

POSTMAN, L., and UNDERWOOD, B. J. (1973). Critical issues in interference theory. *Memory and Cognition, 1,* 19–40.

POSTMAN, N. (1982). *The disappearance of childhood.* New York: Delacorte Press.

POTTER, E. F. (1977, April). Children's expectancy of criticism for classroom achievement efforts. Paper presented at the annual convention of the American Educational Research Association, New York.

PREMACK, D. (1965). Reinforcement theory. In D. Levine (Ed.), *Nebraska symposium on motivation.* Lincoln, Neb.: University of Nebraska Press.

PRESSLEY, M. (1979). Increasing children's self-control through cognitive interventions. *Review of Educational Research, 49,* 319–370.

PRESSLEY, M. (1986). The relevance of the good strategy user model to the teaching of mathematics. *Educational Psychologist, 21,* 139–161.

PRESSLEY, M., GOODCHILD, F., FLEET, J., ZAJCHOWSKI, R., and EVANS, E. D. (1989). The challenges of classroom strategy instruction. *Elementary School Journal, 89,* 301–342.

PRESSLEY, M., and LEVIN, J. R. (1978). Developmental constraints associated with children's use of the keyword method of foreign language vocabulary learning. *Journal of Experimental Child Psychology, 26,* 359–372.

PRESSLEY, M., and LEVIN, J. R. (Eds.) (1983). Cognitive strategy research: Educational applications. New York: Springer-Verlag.

PRESSLEY, M., LEVIN, J. R., and DELANEY, H. (1982). The mnemonic keyword method. *Review of Educational Research, 52,* 61–92.

PRICE, G. G. (1982). Cognitive learning in early childhood education: Mathematics, science, and social studies. In B. Spodek (Ed.), *Handbook of research in early childhood education,* pp. 264–294. New York: The Free Press.

QUAY, H. (1979). Classification. In H. Quay and J. Werry (Eds.), *Psychopathological disorders of childhood* (2nd ed.). New York: Wiley.

QUAY, H., and WERRY, J. (Eds.) (1979). *Psychopathological disorders of children* (2nd ed.). New York: Wiley.

RAFFINI, J. P. (1986). Student apathy: A motivational dilemma. *Educational Leadership, 44* (1), 53–55.

RAGOSTA, M. (1983). Computer-assisted instruction and compensatory education: A longitudinal analysis. *Machine-mediated Learning, 1,* 97–127.

RAMIREZ, J. D. (1986). Comparing structured English immersion and bilingual education: First-year results of a national study. *American Journal of Education, 95,* 122–148.

RAPPAPORT, M. D., MURPHY, M. A., and BAILEY, J. E. (1982). Ritalin vs. response cost in the control of hyperactive children: A within-subject comparison. *Journal of Applied Behavior Analysis, 5,* 205–216.

RAUDENBUSH, S. W. (1984). Magnitude of teacher expectancy effects on pupil IQ as a function of the credibility of expectancy induction: A synthesis of findings from 18 experiments. *Journal of Educational Psychology, 76,* 85–97.

READ, C. (1975). Lessons to be learned from the preschool orthographer. In E. H. Lennenberg and E. Lennenberg (Eds.), *Foundations of language development,* pp. 329–346. New York: Academic Press.

REDER, L. M. (1980). The role of elaboration in the comprehension and retention of prose. *Review of Educational Research, 50,* 5–54.

REDFIELD, D. L., and ROUSSEAU, E. W. (1981). A meta-analysis of experimental research on teacher questioning behavior. *Review of Educational Research, 51,* 237–245.

REIGELUTH, C. M. (Ed.) (1983). *Instructional design theories and models: An overview of their current status.* Hillsdale, N.J.: Erlbaum.

REISS, S., and CELLERINO, M. (1983). Guiding gifted students through independent study. *Teaching Exceptional Children, 15,* 136–139.

RENZULLI, J. S. (1977). *The enrichment trial model: A guide for developing defensible programs for the gifted and talented.* Wethersfield, Conn.: Creative Learning Press.

RENZULLI, J. S. (1978). What makes giftedness? Re-examining a definition. *Phi Delta Kappan, 60* (3), 180–184, 261.

RHODES, L. K. (1977). Predictable books: An instructional resource for meaningful reading and writing. In D. Strickland (Ed.), *The affective dimension of reading,* pp. 195–202. Bloomington: Indiana University Press.

RICHARDSON, F., and WOOLFOLK, R. (1980). Mathematics anxiety. In I. Sarason (Ed.), *Test anxiety: Theory, research, and applications.* Hillsdale, N.J.: Erlbaum.

RICHER, S. (1977). *The kindergarten as a setting for sex-role socialization.* Ottawa: Carleton University, Department of Sociology, unpublished paper.

RICHMOND, B. O., and WEINER, G. P. (1973). Cooperation and competition among young children as a function of ethnic grouping, grade, sex, and reward condition. *Journal of Educational Psychology, 64,* 329–334.

RICKARDS, J. P. (1979). Adjunct postquestions in text: A critical review of methods and processes. *Review of Educational Research, 49,* 181–196.

RIST, R. (1970). Student social class and teacher expectations: The self-fulfilling prophecy in ghetto education. *Harvard Educational Review, 40,* 411–451.

RIST, R. C. (1978). *The invisible children: School integration in American society.* Cambridge, Mass.: Harvard University Press.

ROBINS, L. N. (1974). Antisocial behavior disturbances of childhood: Prevalence, prognosis, and prospects. In E. J. Anthony and C. Koupernik (Eds.), *The child in his family: Children at psychiatric risk.* New York: Wiley.

ROBINSON, F. P. (1961). *Effective study.* New York: Harper and Row.

ROBINSON, N., and ROBINSON, H. (1976). *The mentally retarded child* (2nd ed.). New York: McGraw-Hill.

ROEBER, E., and DUTCHER, P. (1989). Michigan's innovative assessment of reading. *Educational Leadership, 46* (7), 64–69.

ROGERS, C. (1969). *Freedom to learn.* Columbus, Ohio: Charles E. Merrill.

ROHRKEMPER, M. M. (1984). The influence of teacher socialization style on students' social cognition and reported interpersonal classroom behavior. *Elementary School Journal, 85,* 245–275.

ROHRKEMPER, M. M., and BERSHON, B. L. (1984). Elementary school students' reports of the causes and effects of problem difficulty in mathematics. *Elementary School Journal, 85,* 127–147.

ROSE, B. C. (1980). Child abuse and the educator. *Focus on Exceptional Children, 12* (9), 1–13.

ROSE, T. L. (1984). Current uses of corporal punishment in American public schools. *Journal of Educational Psychology, 76,* 427–441.

ROSENBAUM, J. (1980). Social implications of educational grouping. *Review of Research in Education, 8,* 361–401.

ROSENBAUM, J. E. (1976). *Making inequality: The hidden curriculum of high school tracking.* New York: Wiley.

ROSENBAUM, M. S., and DRABMAN, R. S. (1982). Self-control training in the classroom: A review and critique. *Journal of Applied Behavior Analysis, 15.*

ROSENBLATT, D. B. (1982). Play. In M. Rutter (Ed.), *Scientific foundations of developmental psychiatry.* Baltimore: University Park Press.

ROSENHOLTZ, S. J., and SIMPSON, C. (1984). The formation of ability conceptions: Developmental trend or social construction? *Review of Educational Research, 54,* 31–63.

ROSENHOLTZ, S. J., and WILSON, B. (1980). The effects of classroom structure on shared perceptions of ability. *American Educational Research Journal, 17,* 175–182.

ROSENSHINE, B. (1971). Objectively measured behavioral predictors of effectiveness in explaining. In I. D. Westburg and A. A. Bellack (Eds.), *Research in classroom processes.* New York: Teachers College Press.

ROSENSHINE, B. (1979). The third cycle of research on teacher effects: Content covered, academic engaged time, and direct instruction. In P. L. Peterson and H. J. Walberg (Eds.), *Research on teaching: Concepts, findings, and implications.* Berkeley: McCutchan.

ROSENSHINE, B. (1982, April). The master teacher and the master developer. Paper presented at the annual convention of the American Educational Research Association, New York.

ROSENSHINE, B. V. (1980). How time is spent in elementary classrooms. In C. Denham and A. Lieberman (Eds.), *Time to learn.* Washington, D.C.: National Institute of Education.

ROSENSHINE, B. V. (1986). Synthesis of research on explicit teaching. *Educational Leadership, 43* (7), 60–69.

ROSENSHINE, B. V., and STEVENS, R. J. (1986). Teaching functions. In M. C. Wittrock (Ed.), *Third handbook of research on teaching.* Chicago: Rand McNally.

ROSENTHAL, R., and JACOBSON, L. (1968). *Pygmalion in the classroom.* New York: Holt, Rinehart, and Winston.

ROSSELL, C. H. (1983). Desegregation plans, racial isolation, white flight, and community response. In C. H. Rossell and W. D. Hawley (Eds.), *The consequences of school desegregation.* Philadelphia: Temple University Press.

ROTHKOPF, E. Z. (1965). Some theoretical and experimental approaches to problems in written instruction. In J. D. Krumboltz (Ed.), *Learning and the educational process.* Chicago: Rand McNally.

ROTHKOPF, E. Z. (1970). The concept of mathemagenic activities. *Review of Educational Research, 40,* 325–326.

ROTHKOPF, E. Z., and KAPLAN, R. (1972). Exploration of the effect of density and specificity of instructional objectives on learning from text. *Journal of Educational Psychology, 63,* 295–302.

ROTHKOPF, E. Z., and KAPLAN, R. (1974). Instructional objectives as directions to learners: Effect of passage length and amount of objective-relevant content. *Journal of Educational Psychology, 66,* 448–454.

ROTHROCK, D. (1982). The rise and decline of individualized instruction. *Educational Leadership, 39,* 528–531.

ROTTER, J. (1954). *Social learning and clinical psychology.* Englewood Cliffs, N.J.: Prentice-Hall.

ROWAN, B., and MIRACLE, A. (1983). Systems of ability grouping and the stratification of achievement in elementary schools. *Sociology of Education, 56,* 133–144.

ROWE, M. B. (1974). Wait time and rewards as instructional variables, their influence on language, logic, and fate control. I: Wait time. *Journal of Research in Science Teaching, 11,* 81–94.

ROYER, J. M., and FELDMAN, R. S. (1984). *Educational psychology: Applications and theory.* New York: Alfred A. Knopf.

RUBIN, J. H., and EVERETT, B. (1982). Social perspective-taking in young children. In S. G. Moore and C. R. Cooper (Eds.), *The young child: Reviews of research,* Vol. 3, pp. 97–114. Washington, D.C.: The National Association for the Education of Young Children.

RUBIN, Z. (1980). *Children's friendships.* Cambridge, Mass.: Harvard University Press.

RUIZ, C. J. (1985). *Effects of Feuerstein instrumental enrichment program on pre-college students.* Guayana, Venezuela: University of Guayana.

RUMELHART, D. E., and ORTONY, A. (1977). The representation of knowledge in memory. In R. C. Anderson, R. J. Spiro, and W. E. Montague (Eds.), *Schooling and the acquisition of knowledge,* pp. 99–135. Hillsdale, N.J.: Erlbaum.

RUNDUS, D., and ATKINSON, R. C. (1970). Rehearsal processes in free recall: A procedure for direct observation. *Journal of Verbal Learning and Verbal Behavior, 9,* 99–105.

RUNGE, A., WALKER, J., and SHEA, T. M. (1975). A passport to positive parent-teacher communications. *Teaching Exceptional Children, 7,* 91–92.

SADKER, M., and SADKER, D. (1985, March). Sexism in the schoolroom of the '80s. *Psychology Today, 19,* 54–57.

SADKER, M. P., and SADKER, D. M. (1982). *Sex equity handbook for schools.* New York: Longman.

SADKER, M., SADKER, D., and STEINDAM, S. (1989). Gender equity and educational reform. *Educational Leadership, 46* (6), 44–47.

SAFER, D. J. (1982). *School programs for disruptive adolescents.* Baltimore, Md.: University Park Press.

SAFER, D. J., HEATON, R. C., and PARKER, F. C. (1981). A behavioral program for disruptive junior high school students: Results and follow-up. *Journal of Abnormal Child Psychology, 9,* 483–494.

SALGANIK, M. W. (1980, January 27). Teachers busy teaching make city's 16 "best" schools stand out. *Baltimore Sun,* p. A4.

SAMEROFF, A. (1975). Early influences on development: Fact or fancy. *Merrill-Palmer Quarterly, 21,* 267–294.

SAMUELS, S. J. (1981). Some essentials of decoding. *Exceptional Education Quarterly, 2,* 11–25.

SANFORD, J. P., and EVERTSON, C. M. (1981). Classroom management in a low SES junior high: Three case studies. *Journal of Teacher Education, 32,* 34–38.

SARNACKI, R. E. (1979). An examination of test-wiseness in the cognitive test domain. *Review of Educational Research, 49,* 252–279.

SAVELL, J. M., TWOHIG, P. T., and RACHFORD, D. L. (1986). Empirical status of Feuerstein's "Instrumental Enrichment" (FIE) technique as a method of teaching thinking skills. *Review of Educational Research, 56,* 381–409.

SCARR, S. (1981). *Race, social class, and individual differences in I.Q.* Hillsdale, N.J.: Erlbaum.

SCARR, S., and McCARTNEY, K. (1983). How people make their own environments: A theory of genotype-environmental effects. *Child Development, 54,* 424–435.

SCARR, S., and WEINBERG, R. A. (1976). I.Q. Test performances of black children adopted by white families. *American Psychologist, 31,* 726–739.

SCARR, S., and WEINBERG, R. A. (1986). The early childhood enterprise: Care and education of the young. *American Psychologist, 41,* 1140–1146.

SCHAFER, W. E., and OLEXA, C. (1971). *Tracking and opportunity.* Scranton, Pa.: Chandler.

SCHALLERT, D. L. (1976). Improving memory for prose: The relationship between depth of processing and context. *Journal of Verbal Learning and Verbal Behavior, 15,* 621–632.

SCHEUNEMAN, J. D. (1984). A theoretical framework for the exploration of causes and effects of bias in testing. *Educational Psychologist, 19,* 219–225.

SCHICKENDANZ, J. A. (1978). "Please read that story again!" Exploring relationships between story reading and learning to read. *Young Children, 33,* 48–55.

SCHICKENDANZ, J. A. (1981). "Hey! This book's not working right." *Young Children, 37,* 18–27.

SCHICKENDANZ, J. A. (1982). The acquisition of written language in young children. In B. Spodek (Ed.), *Handbook of research in early childhood education,* pp. 242–263. New York: Free Press.

SCHICKENDANZ, J. A., SCHICKENDANZ, D. I., and FORSYTH, P. D. (1982). *Toward understanding children.* Boston: Little, Brown.

SCHIFANI, J. W., ANDERSON, R. M., and ODLE, S. J. (Eds.) (1980). *Implementing learning in the least restrictive environment.* Baltimore, Md.: University Park Press.

SCHIFF, M., DUYMÉ, M., DUMARET, A., and TOMKIEWICZ, S. (1982). How much could we boost scholastic achievement and IQ scores? A direct answer from a French adoption study. *Cognition, 12,* 165–196.

SCHMUCK, R. A., and SCHMUCK, P. A. (1971). *Group processes in the classroom.* Dubuque, Iowa: Wm. C. Brown.

SCHOEN, H. L. (1976). Self-paced mathematics instruction: How effective has it been? *Arithmetic Teacher, 23,* 90–96.

SCHOENFELD, A. H. (1985). *Mathematical problem solving.* Orlando, Fla.: Academic Press.

SCHUNK, D. H. (1981). Modeling and attributional effects on children's achievement: A self-efficacy analysis. *Journal of Educational Psychology, 73,* 93–105.

SCHUNK, D. H. (1982). Effects of effort attributional feedback on children's perceived self-efficacy and achievement. *Journal of Educational Psychology, 74,* 548–556.

SCHUNK, D. H. (1983). Reward contingencies, and the development of children's skills and self-efficacy. *Journal of Educational Psychology, 75,* 511–518.

SCHWARTZ, J. I. (1981). Children's experiments with language. *Young Children, 36,* 16–26.

SCIENCE RESEARCH ASSOCIATES, INC. (1972). *Using test results: A teacher's guide.* Chicago: Science Research Associates, Inc.

SCRUGGS, T. E., and RICHTER, L. (1986). Tutoring learning disabled students: A critical review. *Learning Disability Quarterly, 9,* 2–14.

SEDDON, G. M. (1978). The properties of Bloom's taxonomy of educational objectives for the cognitive domain. *Review of Educational Research, 48,* 303–323.

SELIGMAN, M. E. P. (1981). A learned helplessness point of view. In L. P. Rehm (Ed.), *Behavior therapy for depression: Present status and future directions,* pp. 123–141. New York: Academic Press.

SELMAN, R. L. (1981). The child as a friendship philosopher. In S. R. Asher and J. M. Gottman (Eds.), *The development of children's friendships,* pp. 242–272. Cambridge: Cambridge University Press.

SELMAN, R. L., and SELMAN, A. P. (1979). Children's ideas about friendship: A new theory. *Psychology Today, 13,* 71–72, 74, 79–80, 114.

SHARAN, S. (1980). Cooperative learning in small groups: Recent methods and effects on achievement, attitudes, and ethnic relations. *Review of Educational Research, 50,* 241–249.

SHARAN, S., and HERTZ-LAZAROWITZ, R. (1980). The group investigation method of cooperative learning in the classroom. In S. Sharan, P. Hare, C. Webb, and R. Hertz-Lazarowitz (Eds.), *Cooperation In Education,* pp. 14–46. Provo, Utah.: Brigham Young Press.

SHARAN, S., HERTZ-LAZAROWITZ, R., and ACKERMAN, Z. (1980). Academic achievement of elementary school children in small-group vs. whole-class instruction. *Journal of Experimental Education, 48,* 125–129.

SHARAN, S., KUSSELL, P., HERTZ-LAZAROWITZ, R., BEJARANO, Y., RAVIV, S., and SHARAN, Y. (1984). *Cooperative learning in the classroom: Research in desegregated schools.* Hillsdale, N.J.: Erlbaum.

SHARAN, S., and SHARAN, Y. (1976). *Small-group teaching.* Englewood Cliffs, N.J.: Educational Technology Publications.

SHARAN, Y., and SHARAN, S. (1989/90). Group investigation expands cooperative learning. *Educational Leadership, 47* (4), 17–21.

SHAYWITZ, S. E., and SHAYWITZ, B. A. (1988). Attention deficit disorder: Current perspectives. In J. F. Kavanagh and T. J. Truss (Eds.), *Learning disabilities: Proceedings of the National Conference.* Parkton, Md.: York.

SHEPARD, L. A. (1989). Why we need better assessments. *Educational Leadership, 46* (7), 4–9.

SHEPARD, L. A., and SMITH, M. L. (1986). Synthesis of research on school readiness and kindergarten retention. *Educational Leadership, 44,* 78–86.

SHIFFRIN, R. M., and SCHNEIDER, W. (1977). Controlled and automatic human information processing: Perceptual learning, automatic attending, and a general theory. *Psychological Review, 84,* 127–190.

SHIMMERLIK, S. M. (1978). Organization theory and memory for prose: A review of the literature. *Review of Educational Research, 48,* 103–120.

SHIMMERLIK, S. M., and NOLAN, J. D. (1976). Organization and the recall of prose. *Journal of Educational Psychology, 68,* 779–786.

SHIREY, L. L., and REYNOLDS, R. E. (1988). Effect of interest on attention and learning. *Journal of Educational Psychology, 80,* 159–166.

SHRIBERG, L. D. (1980). Developmental phonological disorders. In T. J. Hixon, L. D. Shriberg, and J. H. Saxman (Eds.), *Introduction to communication disorders.* Englewood Cliffs, N.J.: Prentice-Hall.

SHUELL, T. J. (1981). Dimensions of individual differences. In F. H. Farley and N. J. Gordon (Eds.), *Psychology and education: The state of the Union.* Berkeley, Calif.: McCutchan.

SHULMAN, L., and KEISLAR, R. (Eds.) (1966). *Learning by discovery: A critical appraisal.* Chicago: Rand-McNally.

SIEGLER, R. S. (1986). *Children's thinking.* Englewood Cliffs, N.J.: Prentice-Hall.

SIKES, J. N. (1972, July). Differential behavior of male and female teachers with male and female students. *Dissertation Abstracts International, 33,* 217A.

SILVER, E. A. (1985). *Teaching and learning mathematical problem solving: Multiple research perspectives.* Hillsdale, N.J.: Erlbaum.

SILVERMAN, R. E. (1985). *Psychology* (5th ed.). Englewood Cliffs, N.J.: Prentice-Hall.

SIMMONS, R. G., BURGESON, R., CARLETON-FORD, S., and BLYTH, D. (1987). The impact of cumulative change in early adolescence. *Child Development, 58,* 1220–1234.

SIMMONS, W. (1985). Social class and ethnic differences in cognition: A cultural practice perspective. In S. F. Chipman, J. W. Segal, and R. Glaser (Eds.), *Thinking and learning skills,* Vol. 2. Hillsdale, N.J.: Erlbaum.

SIMON, S. B., and BELLANCA, J. A. (Eds.) (1976). *Degrading the grade myths: A primer of alternatives to grades and marks.* Washington, D.C.: Association for Supervision and Curriculum Development.

SIMPSON, C. (1981). Classroom structure and the organization of ability. *Sociology of Education, 54,* 120–132.

SIMPSON, E. J. (1966). *The classification of educational objectives: Psychomotor domain.* Urbana, Ill.: University of Illinois Press.

SIMPSON, R. L. (1980). Modifying the attitudes of regular class students toward the handicapped. *Focus on Exceptional Children, 13* (3), 1–11.

SINGLE PARENT (1979). *22,* 31–33.

SKINNER, B. F. (1953). *Science and human behavior.* New York: Macmillan.

SKINNER, B. F. (1968). *The technology of teaching.* New York: Appleton-Century-Crofts.

SLAVIN, R. E. (1977a, April). A new model of classroom motivation. Paper presented at the annual convention of the American Educational Research Association, New York.

SLAVIN, R. E. (1977b). Classroom reward structure: An analytic and practical review. *Review of Educational Research, 47,* 633–650.

SLAVIN, R. E. (1978a). Separating incentives, feedback, and evaluation: Toward a more effective classroom system. *Educational Psychologist, 13,* 97–100.

SLAVIN, R. E. (1978b). Student teams and achievement divisions. *Journal of Research and Development in Education, 12,* 38–49.

SLAVIN, R. E. (1979). Effects of biracial learning teams on cross-racial friendships. *Journal of Educational Psychology, 71,* 381–387.

SLAVIN, R. E. (1980). Effects of individual learning expectations on student achievement. *Journal of Educational Psychology, 72,* 520–524.

SLAVIN, R. E. (1983a). *Cooperative learning.* New York: Longman.

SLAVIN, R. E. (1983b). *Student team learning.* Washington, D.C.: National Education Association.

SLAVIN, R. E. (1984a). Component building: A strategy for research-based instructional improvement. *Elementary School Journal, 84,* 255–269.

SLAVIN, R. E. (1984b). *Research methods in education: A practical guide.* Englewood Cliffs, N.J.: Prentice-Hall.

SLAVIN, R. E. (1985a). Team Assisted Individualization: A cooperative learning solution for adaptive instruction in mathematics. In M. Wang and H. Walberg (Eds.), *Adapting instruction to individual difference.* Berkeley: McCutchan.

SLAVIN, R. E. (1985b). Team Assisted Individualization: Combining cooperative learning and individualized instruction in mathematics. In R. E. Slavin, S. Sharan, S. Kagan, R. Hertz-Lazarowitz, C. Webb, and R. Schmuck (Eds.), *Learning to cooperate, cooperating to learn,* pp. 177–209. New York: Plenum.

SLAVIN, R. E. (1985c). Cooperative learning: Applying contact theory in desegregated schools. *Journal of Social Issues, 41,* 45–62.

SLAVIN, R. E. (1986a). The Napa evaluation of Madeline Hunter's ITIP: Lessons learned. *Elementary School Journal, 87,* 165–171.

SLAVIN, R. E. (1986b). *Using student team learning* (3rd ed.). Baltimore, Md.: The Johns Hopkins University, Center for Research on Elementary and Middle Schools.

SLAVIN, R. E. (1987a). A theory of school and classroom organization. *Educational Psychologist, 22,* 89–108.

SLAVIN, R. E. (1987b). Grouping for instruction in the elementary school. *Educational Psychologist, 22,* 109–127.

SLAVIN, R. E. (1987c). Ability grouping and student achievement in elementary schools: A best-evidence synthesis. *Review of Educational Research, 57,* 293–336.

SLAVIN, R. E. (1987d). Mastery learning reconsidered. *Review of Educational Research, 57,* 175–213.

SLAVIN, R. E. (1987e). Cooperative learning: Where behavioral and humanistic approaches to classroom motivation meet. *Elementary School Journal. 88,* 29–37.

SLAVIN, R. E. (1988). Synthesis of research on grouping: In elementary and secondary schools. *Educational Leadership, 46* (1), 67–77.

SLAVIN, R. E. (1989). Achievement effects of substantial reductions in class size. In R. E. Slavin (Ed.), *School and Classroom Organization.* Hillsdale, N.J.: Erlbaum.

SLAVIN, R. E. (1990a). *Achievement effects of ability grouping in secondary schools: A best-evidence synthesis.* Baltimore, Md.: The Johns Hopkins University, Center for Research on Elementary and Middle Schools.

SLAVIN, R. E. (1990b). *Cooperative learning: Theory, research, and practice.* Englewood Cliffs, N.J.: Prentice-Hall.

SLAVIN, R. E. (in press b). Grouping for instruction: Equity and effectiveness. *Equity and Excellence*.

SLAVIN, R. E., BRADDOCK, J. H., HALL, C., and PETZA, R. J. (1989). *Alternatives to ability grouping*. Baltimore, Md.: The Johns Hopkins University, Center for Research on Effective Schooling for Disadvantaged Students.

SLAVIN, R. E., and KARWEIT, N. L. (1982a, August). School organizational vs. developmental effects on attendance among young adolescents. Paper presented at the annual convention of the American Psychological Association, Washington, D.C.

SLAVIN, R. E., and KARWEIT, N. L. (1982b). *Ability-Grouped Active Teaching (AGAT): Teacher's manual*. Baltimore, Md.: Center for Social Organization of Schools, Johns Hopkins University.

SLAVIN, R. E., and KARWEIT, N. (April 1984a). Within-class ability grouping and student achievement: Two field experiments. Paper presented at the annual convention of the American Educational Research Association, New Orleans.

SLAVIN, R. E., and KARWEIT, N. (1984b). Mastery learning and student teams: A factorial experiment in urban general mathematics classes. *American Educational Research Journal, 21*, 725–736.

SLAVIN, R. E., and KARWEIT, N. (1985). Effects of whole class, ability grouped, and individualized instruction on mathematics achievement. *American Educational Research Journal*.

SLAVIN, R. E., LEAVEY, M. B., and MADDEN, N. A. (1984). Combining cooperative learning and individualized instruction: Effects on student mathematics achievement, attitudes, and behaviors. *Elementary School Journal, 84*, 409–422.

SLAVIN, R. E., LEAVEY, M. B., and MADDEN, N. A. (1985). *Team Assisted Individualization: Mathematics*. Watertown, Mass.: Charlesbridge.

SLAVIN, R. E., and MADDEN, N. A. (1979). School practices that improve race relations. *American Educational Research Journal, 16* (2), 169–180.

SLAVIN, R. E., and MADDEN, N. A. (1987, April). Effective classroom programs for students at risk. Paper presented at the annual convention of the American Educational Research Association, Washington, D.C.

SLAVIN, R. E., MADDEN, N. A., and KARWEIT, N. L. (Eds.) (1989). *Effective programs for students at risk*. Boston: Allyn and Bacon.

SLAVIN, R. E., MADDEN, N. A., KARWEIT, N. L., LIVERMON, B. J., and DOLAN, L. (in press). Success for All: First-year outcomes of a comprehensive plan for reforming urban education. *American Educational Research Journal*.

SLAVIN, R. E., MADDEN, N. A., and LEAVEY, M. B. (1984a). Effects of cooperative learning and individualized instruction on mainstreamed students. *Exceptional Children, 84*, 409–422.

SLAVIN, R. E., MADDEN, N. A., and LEAVEY, M. B. (1984b). Effects of Team-Assisted Individualization on the mathematics achievement of academically handicapped and nonhandicapped students. *Journal of Educational Psychology, 76*, 813–819.

SLUYTER, D., and HAWKINS, R. (1972). Delayed reinforcement of classroom behavior by parents. *Journal of Learning Disabilities, 5*, 16–24.

SMITH, C., and LLOYD, B. (1978). Maternal behavior and perceived sex of infant: Revisited. *Child Development, 49*, 1263–1265.

SMITH, J. K., and KATIMS, M. (1977). Reading in the city: The Chicago Mastery Learning Reading Program. *Phi Delta Kappan, 59*, 199–202.

SMITH, L., and LAND, M. (1981). Low-inference verbal behaviors related to teacher clarity. *Journal of Classroom Interaction, 17*, 37–42.

SMITH, L. R., and COTTEN, M. L. (1980). Effect of lesson vagueness and discontinuity on student achievement and attitudes. *Journal of Educational Psychology, 72*, 670–675.

SMITH, P. K. (1978). A longitudinal study of social participation in preschool children: Solitary and parallel play re-examined. *Developmental Psychology, 14*, 517–523.

SNAREY, J. R. (1985). Cross-cultural universality of socio-moral development: A critical review of Kohlbergian research. *Psychological Bulletin, 97*, 202–232.

SNOW, R. E. (1986). Individual differences and the design of educational programs. *American Psychologist, 41*, 1029–1039.

SNOW, R. E., and LOHMAN, D. F. (1984). Toward a theory of cognitive aptitude for learning from instruction. *Journal of Educational Psychology, 76*, 347–376.

SNOWMAN, J. (1984). Learning tactics and strategies. In G. Phye and T. Andre (Eds.), *Cognitive instructional psychology*. New York: Academic Press.

SNYDERMAN, M., and ROTHMAN, S. (1987). Survey of expert opinion on intelligence and aptitude testing. *American Psychologist, 42*, 137–144.

SOLOMON, R. L., TURNER, L. H., and LESSAC, M. S. (1968). Some effects of delay of punishment on resistance to temptation in days. *Journal of Personality and Social Psychology, 8*, 233–238.

SOMMERVILLE, J. C. (1982). *The rise and fall of childhood*. Beverly Hills: Sage Publications.

SØRENSEN, A. B. (1984). The organizational differentiation of students in schools. In H. Oosthoek and P. Van Den Eeden (Eds.), *Education from the multilevel perspective*. London: Gordon and Breach.

SPENCE, E. S. (1958). Intra-class grouping of pupils for instruction in arithmetic in the intermediate grades of the elementary school. *Dissertation Abstracts International, 19*, 1682 (University Microfilms, No. 58–5635).

SPERLING, G. A. (1960). The information available in brief visual presentations. *Psychological Monographs, 74*, No. 498.

SPRIGLE, J. E., and SCHAEFER, L. (1985). Longitudinal evaluation of the effects of two compensatory preschool programs on fourth through sixth-grade students. *Developmental Psychology, 21*, 702–708.

SPURLIN, J. E., DANSEREAU, D. F., LARSON, C. O., and BROOKS, L. W. (1984). Cooperative learning strategies in processing descriptive text: Effects of role and activity level of the learner. *Cognition and Instruction, 1*, 451–463.

STAHL, S. A., and MILLER, P. D. (1989). Whole language and language experience approaches for beginning reading: A quantitative research synthesis. *Review of Educational Research, 59*, 87–116.

STALLINGS, J., and KRASAVAGE, E. M. (1986). Program implementation and student achievement in a four-year Madeline Hunter follow-through project. *Elementary School Journal, 87*, 117–138.

STALLINGS, J. A. (1979). How to change the process of teaching reading in secondary schools. *Educational Horizons, 57*, 196–201.

STALLINGS, J. A., and KASKOWITZ, D. (1974). *Follow-through classroom observation evaluation 1972–73*. Menlo Park, Calif.: Stanford Research Institute.

STALLINGS, J. A., and STIPEK, D. (1986). Research on early childhood and elementary school teaching programs. In M. C. Wittrock (Ed.), *Handbook of Research on Teaching* (3rd ed.). New York: Macmillan.

STANLEY, J. C. (1979). The study and facilitation of talent for mathematics. In A. H. Passow (Ed.), *The gifted and talented: Their education and development*. Chicago: University of Chicago Press.

STEIN, B. S., LITTLEFIELD, J., BRANSFORD, J. D., and PERSAMPIERI, M. (1984). Elaboration and knowledge acquisition. *Memory and Cognition, 12*, 522–529.

STEIN, M. K., LEINHARDT, G., and BICKEL, W. (1989). Instructional issues for teaching students at risk. In R. E. Slavin, N. L. Karweit, and N. A. Madden (Eds.), *Effective programs for students at risk*. Boston: Allyn and Bacon.

STEINBERG, L. D., and HILL, J. P. (1978). Patterns of family interaction as a function of age, the onset of puberty, and formal thinking. *Developmental Psychology, 14*, 683–684.

STERNBERG, R. J. (1982). Reasoning, problem solving, and intelligence. In R. J. Sternberg (Ed.), *Handbook of human intelligence.* New York: Cambridge University Press.

STERNBERG, R. J. (Ed.) (1986a). *Advances in the psychology of human intelligence,* Vol. 3. Hillsdale, N.J.: Erlbaum.

STERNBERG, R. J. (1986b). Intelligence, wisdom, and creativity: Three is better than one. *Educational Psychologist, 21,* 175–190.

STERNBERG, R. J., and BHANA, K. (1986). Synthesis of research on the effectiveness of intellectual skills programs: Snake-oil remedies or miracle cures? *Educational Leadership, 44* (2), 60–67.

STERNBERG, R. J., and DETTERMAN, D. K. (Eds.) (1986). *What is intelligence?* Norwood, N.J.: Ablex.

STEVENS, A., COLLINS, A., and GOLDIN, S. (1982). Misconceptions in students' understanding. In D. Sleeman and J. S. Brown (Eds.), *Intelligent tutoring systems,* pp. 13–24. London: Academic Press.

STEVENS, R. J., MADDEN, N. A., SLAVIN, R. E., and FARNISH, A. M. (1986). *Cooperative integrated reading and composition: Two field experiments* (Tech. Rep. No. 7). Baltimore, Md.: Johns Hopkins University, Center for Research on Elementary and Middle Schools.

STEWART, L. G., and WHITE, M. A. (1976). Teacher comments, letter grades, and student performance: What do we really know? *Journal of Educational Psychology, 68,* 488–500.

STIGGINS, R. J. (1985). Improving assessment where it means the most: In the classroom. *Educational Leadership, 43* (2), 69–74.

STIGGINS, R. J., and BRIDGEFORD, N. J. (1985). The ecology of classroom assessment. *Journal of Educational Measurement, 22,* 271–286.

STIGLER, S. M. (1978). Some forgotten work on memory. *Journal of experimental psychology: Human learning and memory, 4,* 1–4.

STIPEK, D. J. (1981). Children's perceptions of their own and their classmates' ability. *Journal of Educational Psychology, 73,* 404–410.

STIPEK, D. J. (1988). *Motivation to learn: From theory to practice.* Englewood Cliffs, N.J.: Prentice-Hall.

STITELMAN, L., and COPLIN, W. (1969). *American government simulation series.* Chicago: Science Research Associates.

ST. JOHN, N. H. (1975). *School desegregation: Outcomes for children.* New York: John Wiley and Sons.

STOKER, H. W., and KROPP, R. P. (1964). Measurement of cognitive processes. *Journal of Educational Measurement, 1,* 39–42.

STRAIN, P., and KERR, M. M. (1981). *Main-streaming of children in schools.* New York: Academic Press.

STRAUS, M. A., GELLES, R. J., and STEINMETZ, S. K. (1980). *Behind closed doors: Violence in the American family.* New York: Doubleday.

STRIKE, K. A. (1975). The logic of learning by discovery. *Review of Educational Research, 45,* 461–483.

STRINGFIELD, S., and HARTMAN, A. (in press). The detection of group level irregularities on standardized achievement tests. *Journal of Educational Measurement.*

SUCHMAN, J. R. (1962). *The elementary school training program in scientific inquiry.* Urbana: University of Illinois.

SUHOR, C. (1989). "English Only" movement emerging as a major controversy. *Educational Leadership, 46* (6), 80–82.

SULLIVAN, H. S. (1953). *Interpersonal theory of psychiatry.* New York: Norton.

SULZERS-AZAROFF, B., and MAYER, G. R. (1986). *Achieving educational excellence using behavioral strategies.* New York: Holt, Rinehart, and Winston.

SUND, R. (1976). *Piaget for educators.* Columbus, Ohio: Merrill.

SURANSKY, U. P. (1982). *The erosion of childhood.* Chicago: University of Chicago Press.

SURANSKY, U. P. (1983). Tale of rebellion and resistance. The landscape of early institutional life. *Journal of Education, 165,* 135–157.

SWANSON, H. L. (1980). Auditory and visual vigilance in normal and learning disabled readers. *Learning Disabilities Quarterly, 3,* 70–78.

SYLVESTER, R. (1985). Research on memory: Major discoveries, major educational challenges. *Educational Leadership, 42,* 69–75.

TABA, H. (1967). *Teacher's handbook for elementary social studies.* Reading, Mass.: Addison-Wesley.

TAFT, R. (1987). Ethnographic methods. In M. J. Dunkin (Ed.), *International encyclopedia of teaching and teacher education.* Oxford: Pergamon.

TALMAGE, H. (Ed.) (1975). *Systems of individualized education.* Berkeley: McCutcheon.

TANNER, J. M. (1978). *Foetus into man: Physical growth from conception to maturity.* Cambridge, Mass.: Harvard University Press.

TAYLOR, D. (1983). *Family literacy: Young children learning to read and write.* Exeter, N.H.: Heinemann.

TAYLOR, R. (1984). *Assessment of exceptional students: Educational and psychological procedures.* Englewood Cliffs, N.J.: Prentice-Hall.

TEDDLIE, C., and STRINGFIELD, S. (in press). The ethics of behavior for teachers in four types of schools. *Ethics in education.*

TENBRINK, T. D. (1986). Writing instructional objectives. In J. Cooper (Ed.), *Classroom teaching skills* (3rd ed.). Lexington, Mass.: D. C. Heath.

TENENBAUM, G. (1982). A method of group instruction which is as effective as one-to-one tutorial instruction (doctoral dissertation, University of Chicago, 1982). *Dissertation Abstracts International, 43,* 1822A.

TENNYSON, R. D., and PARK, O. (1980). The teaching of concepts: A review of instructional design literature. *Review of Educational Research, 50,* 55–70.

TERMAN, L. M., and MERRILL, M. A. (1960). *Stanford-Binet Intelligence Scale, Manual for the Third Revision Form L–M.* Boston: Houghton Mifflin.

TERMAN, L. (1926). *Genetic studies of genius. Vol. 1: Mental and physical traits of a thousand gifted students* (2nd ed.). Stanford, Calif.: Stanford University Press.

TERMAN, L. M., and ODEN, M. H. (1959). The gifted group in mid-life. In *Genetic studies of genius,* Vol. 5. Stanford, Calif.: Stanford University Press.

THELEN, H. A. (1967). *Classroom grouping for teachability.* New York: Wiley.

THIBAULT, J. W., and KELLEY, H. H. (1959). *The social psychology of groups.* New York: Wiley.

THIEME-BUSCH, C. A., and PROM, S. E. (1983, April). Impact of teacher use of time training on student achievement. Paper presented at the annual convention of the American Educational Research Association, Montreal.

THISTLEWAITE, D. L., DEHAAN, H., and KAMENETZKY, J. (1955). The effects of "directive" and "non-directive" communication procedures on attitudes. *Journal of Abnormal and Social Psychology, 51,* 107–118.

THOMAS, A. (1981). Current trends in developmental theory. *American Journal of Orthopsychiatry, 51,* 580–609.

THOMAS, E. J., and ROBINSON, H. A. (1972). *Improving reading in every class: A source book for teachers.* Boston: Allyn and Bacon.

THOMAS, J. W., and ROHWER, W. D. (1986). Academic studying: The role of learning strategies. *Educational Psychologist, 21,* 19–41.

THOMAS, R. M. (1979). *Comparing theories of child development.* Belmont, Calif.: Wadsworth.

THOMPSON, E. (1960). An experimental investigation of the relative effectiveness of organizational structure in oral communication. *Southern Speech Journal, 26,* 59–69.

THORNBURG, H. (1979). *The bubblegum years: Sticking with kids from 9–13.* Tucson, Ariz.: HELP Books.

THORNDIKE, E. L., and WOODWORTH, R. S. (1901). The influence of improvement in one mental function upon the efficiency of other functions. *Psychological Review, 8,* 247–261.

Thorndike, R. L., and Hagen, E. (1969). *Measurement and evaluation in psychology and education* (3rd ed.). New York: Wiley.

Timpson, W. M., and Tobin, D. N. (1982). *Teaching as performing: A guide to energizing your public presentation.* Englewood Cliffs, N.J.: Prentice-Hall.

Tobias, S. (1981). Adaptation to individual differences. In F. H. Farley and N. J. Gordon (Eds.), *Psychology and education: The state of the Union*, pp. 60–81. Berkeley, Calif.: McCutchan.

Tobias, S. (1985). Test anxiety: Interference, defective skills, and cognitive capacity. *Educational Psychologist, 20,* 135–142.

Tobin, K. (1986). Effects of teacher wait time on discourse characteristics in mathematics and language arts classes. *American Educational Research Journal, 23,* 191–200.

Tobin, K. (1987). The role of wait time in higher cognitive level learning. *Review of Educational Research, 57,* 69–95.

Tobin, K. G., and Capie, W. (1982). Relationships between classroom process variables and middle-school science achievement. *Journal of Educational Psychology, 74,* 441–454.

Toll, D. (1970). *Ghetto* (Simulation Game). Indianapolis, Ind.: Bobbs-Merrill.

Tompkins, G. E. (1981). Writing without a pencil. *Language Arts, 58,* 823–833.

Top, B. L., and Osguthorpe, R. T. (1987). Reverse-role tutoring: The effects of handicapped students tutoring regular class students. *Elementary School Journal, 87,* 413–423.

Top, F. (Ed.) (1970). *Report of the Committee on Infectious Diseases.* Evanston, Ill.: American Academy of Pediatrics.

Torrance, E. P. (1962). Developing creative thinking through school experience. In S. J. Parnes and H. P. Harding (Eds.), *A source book for creative thinking.* New York: Scribner.

Torrance, E. P. (1981). Ten ways of helping young children gifted in creative writing and speech. In J. C. Gowan, J. Khatena, and E. P. Torrance (Eds.), *Creativity: Its educational implications.* Dubuque, Iowa: Kendall/Hunt.

Torrance, E. P. (1986). Teaching creative and gifted learners. In M. C. Wittrock (Ed.), *Handbook of research on teaching* (3rd ed.). New York: Macmillan.

Towson, S. (1985). Melting pot or mosaic: Cooperative education and interethnic relations. In R. E. Slavin et al. (Eds.), *Learning to cooperate, cooperating to learn.* New York: Plenum.

Tseng, M. (1972). Comparisons of selected familial, personality, and vocational variables of high school students and dropouts. *Journal of Educational Research, 65,* 462–466.

Tulving, E. (1972). Episodic and semantic memory. In E. Tulving and W. Donaldson (Eds.), *Organization of memory.* New York: Academic Press.

Tulving, E. (1985). How many memory systems are there? *American Psychologist, 40,* 385–398.

Turnbull, A. P., and Brantley, J. C. (1982). *Mainstreaming: Developing and implementing individualized education programs* (2nd ed.). Columbus, Ohio: Charles E. Merrill.

Turnbull, A. P., and Schulz, J. B. (1979). *Mainstreaming handicapped students: A guide for the classroom teacher.* Boston: Allyn and Bacon.

Tyler, L. E. (1965). *The psychology of human differences.* New York: Appleton-Century-Crofts.

U.S. Census Bureau (1981, July). *Race of the population by states.* Washington, D.C.: U.S. Government Printing Office.

U.S. Commission on Civil Rights (1975). *A better chance to learn: Bilingual bicultural education.* Washington, D.C.: Government Printing Office.

U.S. Department of Health, Education and Welfare (1969). *The problem of mental retardation.* Washington, D.C.: U.S. Government Printing Office.

U.S. Department of Health, Education and Welfare (1975). *Sex stereotyping in children's readers.* Washington, D.C.: U.S. Government Printing Office.

U.S. Department of Health, Education and Welfare (1978). Height and Weight of Children. United States: NC for HS, Series 11 (104), Rockville, Md., September 1970. Pp. 2 and 4.

U.S. Department of Health and Human Services (1987). *Drug use among American high school students and other young adults, National trends through 1986.* Washington, D.C.: Author.

U.S. Office of Education (1970). *Manual for project applicants and grantees.* Washington, D.C.: USOE.

Valencia, S. W., Pearson, P. D., Peters, C. W., and Wixson, K. K. (1989). Theory and practice in statewide reading assessment: Closing the gap. *Educational Leadership, 46* (7), 57–63.

Vander Zanden, J. W. (1978). *Human development.* New York: Alfred A. Knopf.

Van Patten, J., Chao, C.-I., and Reigeluth, C. M. (1986). A review of strategies for sequencing and synthesizing instruction. *Review of Educational Research, 56,* 437–471.

VanSickle, R. L. (1986, April). *A quantitative review of research on instructional simulation gaming: A twenty-year perspective.* Paper presented at the annual convention of the American Educational Research Association, San Francisco.

VanTassel-Baska (1989). Appropriate curriculum for gifted learners. *Educational Leadership, 46* (6), 13–15.

Vosniadou, S., and Schommer, M. (1988). Explanatory analogies can help children acquire information from expository text. *Journal of Educational Psychology, 80,* 524–536.

Vukelich, C., and Golden, J. (1984). Early writing: Development and teaching strategies. *Young Children, 39,* 3–8.

Vygotsky, L. S. (1978). *Mind in society* (M. Cole, V. John-Steiner, S. Scribner, and E. Souberman, Eds.). Cambridge, Mass.: Harvard University Press.

Wadsworth, B. (1978). *Piaget for the classroom teacher.* New York: Longman.

Wadsworth, B. (1989). *Piaget's theory of cognitive and affective development* (4th ed.). New York: Longman.

Walberg, H. J., and Anderson, G. J. (1968). Classroom climate and individual learning. *Journal of Educational Psychology, 59,* 414–419.

Walden, E. L., and Thompson, S. A. (1981). A review of some alternative approaches to drug management of hyperactive children. *Journal of Learning Disabilities, 14,* 213–217.

Walker, J. E., and Shea, T. M. (1980). *Behavior modification: A practical approach for educators* (2nd ed.). St. Louis: C. V. Mosby.

Wallach, M. A., and Kogan, N. (1965). *Modes of thinking in young children: A study of the creativity-intelligence distinction.* New York: Holt, Rinehart, and Winston.

Wallen, N. E., and Vowles, R. O. (1960). The effect of intraclass ability grouping on arithmetic achievement in the sixth grade. *Journal of Educational Psychology, 51,* 159–163.

Waller, P., and Gaa, J. (1974). Motivation in the classroom. In R. Coop and K. White (Eds.), *Psychological concepts in the classroom.* New York: Harper and Row.

Wallerstein, J., and Ketty, J. (1980). California's children of divorce. *Psychology Today, 11,* 67–76.

Walters, R. H., Parke, R. D., and Cane, V. A. (1965). Timing of punishment and the observation of consequences to others as determinants of response inhibition. *Journal of Experimental Child Psychology, 2,* 10–30.

Wang, M. C., and Stiles, B. (1976). Effects of the self-schedule system on teacher and student behaviors. In M. C. Wang (Ed.), *The self-schedule system for instructional-learning management in adaptive school learning environments.* Pittsburgh: Learning Research and Development Center, University of Pittsburgh.

Ward, M. H., and Baker, B. L. (1968). Reinforcement therapy in the classroom.

Journal of Applied Behavior Analysis, 1, 323–328.

WATSON, D. J. (1989). Defining and describing whole language. *Elementary School Journal, 90,* 129–141.

WATT, D. (1982, June). Word processors and writing. *Popular Computing,* pp. 124–126.

WATTENBERG, W. W., and CLIFFORD, C. (1964). Relationship of self-concepts to beginning achievement in reading. *Child Development, 35,* 461–467.

WEBER, E. (1973). The function of early childhood education. *Young Children, 28,* 265–274.

WECHSLER, D. (1955). *Wechsler Adult Intelligence Scale.* New York: Psychological Corporation.

WEIKART, D. P., ROGERS, L., and ADLOCK, C. (1971). *The cognitively oriented curriculum.* Urbana, Ill.: University of Illinois Press.

WEINBERG, R. A. (1979). Early childhood education and interventions: Establishing an American tradition. *American Psychologist, 34,* 912–916.

WEINER, B. (1972). *Theories of motivation: From mechanism to cognition.* Chicago: Markham.

WEINER, B. (1979). A theory of motivation for some classroom experiences. *Journal of Educational Psychology, 71,* 3–25.

WEINER, B. (1980). *Human motivation.* New York: Holt, Rinehart, and Winston.

WEINER, B., and ROSENBAUM, R. M. (1965). Determinants of choice between achievement and nonachievement-related activities. *Journal of Experimental Research of Personality, 1,* 114–121.

WEINSTEIN, C. S. (1979). The physical environment of the school: A review of the research. *Review of Educational Research, 49,* 557–610.

WEINSTEIN, C. S. (1987). Seating Patterns. In M. J. Dunkin (Ed.), *International encyclopedia of teaching and teacher education.* New York: Pergamon.

WEINSTEIN, R. S. (1976). Reading group membership in first grade: Teacher behaviors and pupil experience over time. *Journal of Educational Psychology, 68,* 103–116.

WEIR, S. (1981, September). Logo and exceptional children. *Microcomputing,* 76–82, 84.

WEIS, J. G., and SEDERSTROM, J. (1981). *The prevention of serious delinquency: What to do?* Center for Law and Justice, University of Washington.

WEISS, S. (1989). The Ritalin controversy. *NEA Today, 8*(1), 10–11.

WEITZMAN, L. J. (1979). Sex-role socialization. In J. Freeman (Ed.), *Women: A feminist perspective* (2nd ed.), pp. 153–216. Palo Alto: Mayfield Publishing Co.

WENDT, A. W. (1955). Motivation, effort, and performance. In D. C. McClelland (Ed.), *Studies in motivation.* New York: Appleton-Century-Crofts.

WHALEN, C. K. (1983). Hyperactivity, learning problems, and attention deficit disorders. In T. H. Ollendick and M. Hersen (Eds.), *Handbook of child psychopathology,* pp. 151–199. New York: Plenum.

WHEELER, R. (1977, April). Predisposition toward cooperation and competition: Cooperative and competitive classroom effects. Paper presented at the annual convention of the American Psychological Association, San Francisco.

WHITE, S. H., and BUKA, S. L. (1987). Early education: Programs, traditions, and policies. In E. Z. Rothkopf (Ed.), *Review of research in education (Vol. 14).* Washington, D.C.: American Educational Research Association.

WHITLEY, B. E., and FRIEZE, I. H. (1985). Children's causal attributions for success and failure in achievement settings: A meta-analysis. *Journal of Educational Psychology, 77,* 608–616.

WIGGINS, G. (1989). Teaching to the (Authentic) Test. *Educational Leadership, 46*(7), 41–47.

WIIG, E. H. (1982). Communication disorders. In H. Haring (Ed.), *Exceptional children and youth.* Columbus, Ohio: Charles E. Merrill.

WILKERSON, R. M., and WHITE, K. P. (1988). Effects of the 4Mat system of instruction on students' achievement, retention, and attitudes. *Elementary School Journal, 88,* 357–368.

WILLIAMS, C. D. (1959). The elimination of tantrum behavior by extinction procedures: Case report. *Journal of Abnormal and Social Psychology, 59,* 269.

WILLIAMS, L. (1974). Black pride, academic relevance, and individual achievement. In R. W. Taylor and R. M. Wolf (Eds.), *Crucial issues in testing.* Berkeley: McCutchan.

WILLIG, A. C. (1985). A meta-analysis of selected studies on the effectiveness of bilingual education. *Review of Educational Research, 55,* 269–317.

WILLIS, D. H. (1976). *A study of the relationship between visual acuity, reading mode, and school systems for blind students—1976.* Louisville, Ky.: American Printing House for the Blind.

WILSON, B., and SCHMITS, D. (1978). What's new in ability grouping? *Phi Delta Kappan, 59,* 535–536.

WILSON, B. G. (1971). Evaluation of learning in art education. In B. S. Bloom, J. T. Hastings, and G. F. Madaus (Eds.), *Handbook on formative and summative evaluation of student learning.* New York: McGraw-Hill.

WILSON, R. (1984). A review of self-control treatments for aggressive behavior. *Behavioral Disorders, 9,* 131–140.

WINE, J. D. (1980). Cognitive-attentional theory of test anxiety. In I. Sarason (Ed.), *Test anxiety: Theory, research, and applications.* Hillsdale, N.J.: Erlbaum.

WINNETT, R. A., and VACHON, E. M. (1974). Group feedback and group contingencies in modifying behavior of fifth graders. *Psychological Reports, 34,* 1283–1292.

WINNETT, R. A., and WINKLER, R. C., Current behavior modification in the classroom: Be still, be quiet, be docile. *Journal of Applied Behavior Analysis, 5,* 499–504.

WINNE, P. H. (1979). Experiments relating teachers' use of higher cognitive questions to student achievement. *Review of Educational Research, 49,* 13–50.

WILSON, S. (1977). The use of ethnographic techniques in educational research. *Review of Educational Research, 47,* 245–265.

WITHALL, J. (1987). Teacher-centered and learner-centered teaching. In M. J. Dunkin (Ed.), *International encyclopedia of teaching and teacher education.* New York: Pergamon.

WITKIN, H. A., and GOODENOUGH, D. R. (1981). *Cognitive styles: Essence and origins.* New York: International Universities Press.

WITKIN, H. A., MOORE, C. A., GOODENOUGH, D. R., and COX, P. W. (1977). Field-dependent and field-independent cognitive styles and their educational implications. *Review of Educational Research, 47,* 1–64.

WITTROCK, M. C. (1974). Learning as a generative process. *Educational Psychologist, 11,* 87–95.

WITTROCK, M. C. (1978). The cognitive movement in instruction. *Educational Psychologist, 13,* 15–29.

WITTROCK, M. C. (1986). Students' thought processes. In M. C. Wittrock (Ed.), *Handbook of research on teaching* (3rd ed.). New York: Macmillan.

WOLF, D. P. (1989). Portfolio assessment: Sampling student work. *Educational Leadership, 46*(7), 35–40.

WOLF, M., BIRNBAUER, J. S., WILLIAMS, T., and LAWLER, J. (1965). A note on apparent extinction of vomiting behavior of a retarded child. In L. Ullmann and L. Krassner (Eds.), *Case studies in behavior modification.* New York: Holt, Rinehart, and Winston.

WOLFGANG, C. H., and GLICKMAN, C. D. (1980). Solving discipline problems: Strategies for classroom teachers.

WOLFGANG, D. C., and SANDERS, S. (1981). Defending young children's play as the ladder to literacy. *Theory into Practice, 20,* 116–120.

WOLFGANG, M. E., FIGLIO, R. M., and SELLIN, T. (1972). *Delinquency in a birth cohort.* Chicago: University of Chicago Press.

WONG, B. Y. L. (1985). Self-questioning instructional research: A review. *Review of Educational Research, 55,* 227–268.

WONG, H. D., BERNSTEIN, L., and SHEVICK, E. (1978). *Life science* (2nd ed.). Englewood Cliffs, N.J.: Prentice-Hall.

WONG-FILLMORE, L., and VALADEZ, C. (1986). Teaching bilingual learners. In M. C. Wittrock (Ed.), *Handbook of Research on Teaching* (3rd ed.). New York: Macmillan.

WOODWARD, J., CARNINE, D., and GERSTEN, R. (1988). Teaching problem solving through computer simulations. *American Educational Research Journal, 25,* 72–86.

WOOLFOLK, A. E., and BROOKS, D. (1982). Nonverbal communication in teaching. In E. Gordon (Ed.), *Review of research in education* (Vol. 10). Washington, D.C.: American Educational Research Association.

WOOLFOLK, A. E., and BROOKS, D. M. (1985). Beyond words: The influence of teachers' nonverbal behaviors on students' perceptions and performances. *Elementary School Journal, 85,* 513–528.

WOOLFOLK, A. E., and McCUNE-NICOLICH, L.

(1984). *Educational psychology for teachers* (2nd ed.). Englewood Cliffs, N.J.: Prentice-Hall.

WYCKOFF, W. L. (1973). The effect of stimulus variation on learning from lecture. *Journal of Experimental Education, 41,* 85–90.

YAWKEY, T. D. (1980). More on play as intelligence in children. *Journal of Creative Behavior, 13,* 247–258, 262.

YSSELDYKE, J., and ALGOZZINE, B. (1982). *Critical issues in special and remedial education.* Boston: Houghton Mifflin.

ZEPPERT, L. T., and CRUZ, B. R. (1977). *Bilingual education: An appraisal of empirical research.* Berkeley: Bay Area Bilingual Education League (ERIC No. Ed 153 758).

ZIEGLER, S. (1981). The effectiveness of cooperative learning teams for increasing cross-ethnic friendship: Additional evidence. *Human Organization, 40,* 264–268.

ZIGLER, E., and VALENTINE, J. (1979). *Project Head Start: A legacy of the war on poverty.* New York: Free Press.

ZIGLER, E., and SEITA, V. (1982). Head Start as a national laboratory. *Annals American*

Academy of Political and Social Science, 461, 81–90.

ZIMMERMAN, B. J., and KLEEFELD, C. F. (1977). Toward a theory of teaching: A social learning view. *Contemporary Educational Psychology, 2,* 158–171.

ZIMMERMAN, B. J., and SCHUNK, D. H. (Eds.) (1989). *Self-regulated learning and academic achievement: Theory, research, and practice.* New York: Springer.

ZIMMERMAN, E. H., and ZIMMERMAN, J. (1962). The alteration of behavior in a special classroom situation. *Journal of the Experimental Analysis of Behavior, 5,* 59–60.

ZIV, A. (1988). Teaching and learning with humor: Experiment and replication. *Journal of Experimental Education, 57,* 5–18.

ZUCKER, R. (1979). Development aspects of drinking through the young adult years. In H. Blane and M. Chafetz (Eds.), *Youth, alcohol, and social policy.* New York: Plenum.

ZUCKERMAN, M. (1979). Attribution of success and failure revisited, or: The motivational bias is alive and well in attribution theory. *Journal of Personality, 47,* 245–287.

References

Acknowledgments

PHOTOGRAPHS

Chapter 1: ii Lawrence Migdale/Photo Researchers. **xxii** Bob Daemmrich Photos/Texas. **2** Bob Daemmrich/The Image Works. **4** Elizabeth Crews. **8** Erik Anderson/Stock Boston. **9** Paul Conklin/Monkmeyer Press. **15** Spencer Grant/Monkmeyer Press. **17** Elizabeth Crews.

Chapter 2: 22 Mathew McVay/Allstock. **25** Jill Krementz. **31** Elizabeth Crews. **34** Martha W. Nichols. **37** Louie Psihoyos/Woodfin Camp & Associates. **42** Charles Gupton/Stock, Boston. **49** Martha W. Nichols.

Chapter 3: 56 Carole Silver/Courtesy Packard Collegiate Institute. **61** Ted Horowitz/The Stock Market. **63** Tom Marotta/UNICEF. **65** Lawrence Migdale/Photo Researchers. **67** Randy Matusow, Courtesy Packer Collegiate Institute. **73** Martha W. Nichols. **76** Elizabeth Crews. **78** Elizabeth Crews. **81** Randy Matusow, Courtesy Packer Collegiate Institute. **83** Martha W. Nichols. **88** Richard Hutchings/Photo Researchers.

Chapter 4: 96 Steve Firebaugh/AllStock. **103** Eliot Elisofon, LIFE Magazine. **106** Richard Hutchings/Photo Researchers. **112** Smith/Garner/The Stock Market. **113** Frank Siteman/The Picture Cube. **120** Bob Daemmrich Photos/Texas.

Chapter 5: 128 Stephen Frisch/Stock, Boston. **133** Lawrence Migdale,/Photo Researchers. **144** Deni McIntyre/Photo Researcher. **147** Library of Congress. **147** Library of Congress. **147** Library of Congress. **154** Renate Hiller/Monkmeyer Press.

Chapter 6: 160 Frank Siteman/The Picture Cube. **163** Bob Daemmrich Photos/Texas. **172** Lew Merrim/Monkmeyer Press. **177** Will & Deni McIntyre/Photo Researchers. **184** Robert Hernandez/Photo Researchers (Penguin). **184** Stephen Kraseman/Photo Researchers (Robin). **184** M. P. Kahl/Photo Researchers (Ostrich). **184** MacDonald/The Picture Cube (Mockingbird). **189** Bob Daemmrich Photos/Texas. **192** Phil Schermeister/Allstock.

Chapter 7: 204 Randy Matusow, Courtesy Packer Collegiate Institute. **208** Elizabeth Crews/Stock, Boston. **213** Bill Stanton/Rainbow. **218** Robert Frerck/Odyssey Productions.

Chapter 8: 230 Hugh Rogers/Monkmeyer Press. **232** Bill Stanton/Rainbow (left). **232** Bob Daemmrich Photos/Texas (right). **235** Christina Dittmann/Rainbow. **245** Will & Deni McIntyre/Photo Researchers. **259** David Frazier/The Stock Market. **264** Dan McCoy/Rainbow.

Chapter 9: 274 Daniel DeWilde. **282** Richard Hutchings/INFO EDIT. **285** Lew Merrim/Monkmeyer Press. **287** Lew Merrim/Monkmeyer. **293** Richard Hutchings/INFO EDIT. **302** Elizabeth Crews. **304** Bob Daemmrich/The Image Works. **309** Kindra Clineff/The Picture Cube.

Chapter 10: 316 Barbara Kirk/The Stock Market. **322** George Goodwin/Monkmeyer Press. **326** Jim Caccavo/Stock, Boston. **333** Tony Freeman/Photo Edit. **337** Richard Hutchings/INFO EDIT. **341** Blair Seitz/Photo Researchers. **345** Bob Daemmrich/Photos, Texas. **356** Suzanne Szasz/Photo Researchers.

Chapter 11: 360 Elizabeth Crews. **366** MacDonald Photography/The Picture Cube. **369** Alan Oddie/PhotoEdit. **373** Ulrike Welsch/Photo Researchers. **377** Tony Freeman/ PhotoEdit. **378** Kevin Horan/Stock, Boston. **382** Elizabeth Crews. **387** Walter Hodges/Woodfin Camp.

Chapter 12: 402 Mickey Pfleger. **406** Lew Merrim/Monkmeyer Press. **417** Tony Freeman/PhotoEdit. **421** Ed Lettau/Photo Researchers. **424** Will McIntyre/Photo Researchers. **432** Will McIntyre/Photo Researchers. **438** Lawrence Migdale/Photo Researchers. **440** Paul Conklin/PhotoEdit.

Chapter 13: 446 A. & M. Pechter/The Stock Market. **449** Julie Houck/Stock, Boston. **459** Will/Deni McIntyre/Photo Researchers. **464** Barbara Rios/Photo Researchers. **470** Lawrence Migdale.

Chapter 14: 476 Victoria Beller-Smith/The Stock Market. **480** Lawrence Migdale. **486** Bob Daemmrich Photos/Texas. **487** Mimi Forsyth/Monkmeyer Press. **499** Daniel DeWilde.

Chapter 15: 508 Stephen Collins/Photo Researchers. **512** AFL-CIO News. **524** Elizabeth Crews. **527** Bill Stanton/RAINBOW. **535** Elizabeth Crews.

FIGURES

Chapter 1: Figure 1.1: Barrish, H. H., Saunders, M., and Wolf, M. M. (1969). Good behavior game: Effects of individual contingencies for group consequences on disruptive behavior in a classroom. *Journal of Applied Behavior Analysis, 2,* 119–124.

Chapter 2: Figure 2.2: R. M. Liebert, R. Wicks-Nelson, R. V. Kail, *Developmental Psychology,* 4/e, Copyright © 1986, p. 185. Reprinted by permission of Prentice-Hall, Inc., Englewood Cliffs, New Jersey. **Figure 2.4:** Inhelder, B., and Piaget, J. (1958). *The Growth of logical thinking from childhood to adolescence.* New York: Basic Books.

Chapter 4: Figure 4.4: Hall, R. V., Lund, D., and Jackson, D. (1968). Effects of teacher attention on study behavior. *Journal of Applied Behavior Analysis, 1,* p. 3. **Figure 4.5:** Adapted from Hall et al., Punishment. *Educational Technology,* April 1971, pp. 24–26. Reproduced with permission. **Figure 4.8:** Adapted from Albert Bandura in the *Journal of Personality and Social Psychology, 1,* 589–596.

Chapter 5: Figure 5.1: Charles G. Morris, *Psychology: An introduction,* 5th ed., © 1985, p. 221. Reprinted by permission of Prentice-Hall, Inc., Englewood Cliffs, NJ.

Chapter 6: Figure 6.1: Royer, J. M., and Feldman, R. S. (1984). *Educational psychology: Applications and theory.* New York: Alfred A. Knopf, p. 255. **Figure 6.2:** Bower et al. *Hierarchical retrieval schemes in recall,* "Journal of Verbal Learning and Verbal Behavior", Academic Press. **Figure 6.3:** Feuerstein, R., and Jensen, M. R. (1980, May). *Instrumental Enrichment: Theoretical basis, goals, and instruments.* Educational Forum, 401–423. Reprinted with permission. **Figure 6.4:** Bruner, J. S., (1966). *Toward a theory of instruction.* Harvard University Press. Reprinted by permission. **Figures 6.5 and 6.6:** Gagne', Robert M. (1974). *Essentials of learning for instruction.*

Chapter 7: Figure 7.1: Mager, Robert F. (1984). *Preparing instructional objectives.* David S. Lake Publishers: Belmont, CA. **Figures 7.2 and 7.3:** Evertson, Clements, Sanford, and Worsham (1984). *Classroom management for elementary teachers,* Prentice-Hall, Inc.: Englewood Cliffs, N.J., p. 7.

Chapter 9: **Figure 9.1:** Thorndike, R. L. and Hagen, E. (1969). *Measurement and evaluation in psychology and education* (3rd ed.). John Wiley, Inc.: New York. **Figure 9.2:** Bloom, B. S. (1976). *Human characteristics and school learning*, McGraw-Hill, Inc. Reprinted with permission. **Figure 9.3:** Individual Prescribed Instruction (1972). Meredith Corp. division of Penguin USA, Inc..

Chapter 10: **Figure 10.2:** Maslow, A. H. (1954). *Motivation and personality*. New York: Harper & Row. **Figure 10.3:** From *Motives in fantasy, action, and society* by John W. Atkinson © 1958 by D. Van Nostrand Company, Inc.. Reprinted by permission of Wadsworth, Inc. **Figure 10.4:** Slavin, R. E. (1983). *Student team learning*. Washington, DC: National Education Association.

Chapter 11: **Figure 11.1:** From Karweit and Slavin, *Measurement and modeling choices in studies of time and learning*, copyright © 1981, American Educational Research Association, Washington, DC. **Figure 11.2:** Kirby, F. D., and Shields, F. (1972). Modification of arithmetic response rate and attending behavior in a seventh-grade student. *Journal of Applied Behavior Analysis, 5*, 82. **Figure 11.3:** Dougherty, E., and Dougherty A. (1977). The daily report card: A simplified and flexible package for classroom behavior management. *Psychology in the Schools, 14*, 191–195. **Figure 11.4:** The effects of the intensity of a teacher's reprimands on children's behavior by K. D. O'Leary and W. C. Becker, *Journal of School Psychology, 1*, pp. 8–11. Human Science Press, Inc., 72 Fifth Avenue, NY 10011. Copyright © 1967. **Figure 11.5:** Barrish, H. H., Saunders, M., and Wolf, M. M. (1969). Good behavior game: Effects of individual contingencies for group consequences on disruptive behavior in a classroom. *Journal of Applied Behavior Analysis, 2*, 119–124.

Chapter 12: **Figure 12.3:** From Fig. 6.1 in *Exceptional children in the schools: Special education in transition*, 2/e by Lloyd M. Dunn. Copyright © 1973 by Holt, Rinehart and Winston, Inc. Reprinted by permission of the publisher. **Figure 12.4:** Daniel P. Hallahan/James M. Kauffman, *Exceptional Children: Introduction to Special Education*, 3rd Ed., copyright © 1986, pp. 33–35. Reprinted by permission of Prentice-Hall, Inc., Englewood Cliffs, New Jersey. **Figure 12.5:** Madden, N. A., and Slavin, R. E. (1983). Effects of cooperative learning on the social acceptance of mainstreamed academically handicapped students. *Journal of Special Education, 17*, 171–182.

Chapter 13: **Figure 13.1:** Heyns, B. (1978). *Summer learning and the effects of schooling*. New york: Academic Press. **Figure 13.2:** Carter, L. F. (1984). The sustaining effects study of compensatory and elementary education. *Educational Researcher, 13* (7), 4–13. Copyright © 1984, American Educational Research Association. Washington, DC.

Chapter 15: **Figure 15.1:** Coleman, J. S., and Karweit, N. L. (1972). *Information systems and performance measures in schools*. Englewood Cliffs, NJ: Educational Technology Publications. **Figure 15.2:** Robert E. Slavin, *Research methods in education: A practical guide*, copyright © 1984, p. 165. Reprinted by permission of Prentice-Hall, Inc. Englewood Cliffs, New Jersey. **Figure 15.3:** Robert E. Slavin, *Research methods in education: A practical guide*, copyright © 1984, p. 167. Reprinted by permission of Prentice-Hall, Inc. Englewood Cliffs, New Jersey. **Figure 15.5 and 15.6:** Reproduced by permission of the publisher, CTB/McGraw-Hill, 2500 Garden Road, Monterey, CA 93940. Copyright © 1981 by McGraw-Hill, Inc.. All rights reserved. Printed in the U.S.A.

TABLES

Chapter 1: **Table 1.1:** Lahaderne, H. M., Attitudinal and intellectual correlates of attention: A study of four sixth-grade classrooms. *Journal of Educational Psychology*, 1968, 59, 320–324.

Chapter 2: **Extract pp. 26–27:** From *Piaget for the classroom teacher* by Barry J. Wadsworth, copyright © 1978 by Longman, Inc. All rights reserved. **Table 2.2:** Erikson, E. H. (1980). *Identity and the life cycle*. New York: Norton, p. 178. Copyright © 1959 by International Universities Press, Inc. Copyright renewed 1987. **Table 2.3:** Lamb, Michael E. (1978), *Social* and personality development, by Holt, Rinehart, and Winston. Reprinted by permission of the publisher.

Chapter 4: **Table 4.2:** Frank J. Landy, *Psychology: The science of people*, copyright © 1984, p. 219. Reprinted by permission of Prentice-Hall, Inc., Englewood Cliffs, New Jersey, **Figure 4.8:** Adapted from Albert Bandura in the *Journal of Personality and Social Psychology, 1*, 589–595.

Chapter 5: **Table 5.2:** Craik and Lockhart (1972). *Level of processing*, "Journal of Verbal Learning and Verbal Behavior", Academic Press, pp. 671–684.

Chapter 7: **Table 7.3:** Gagné, Robert, M. (1974). *Essentials of learning for instruction*, Dryden Press. Reprinted by permission of CBS College Publishing.

Chapter 8: **Table 8.1:** Good, Grouws, and Ebmeier (1983). *Educator's active mathematics teaching*, Longman Publishing Group. Reprinted by permission. **Table 8.3:** Davis, G. A. (1983). *Values encouraged in humanistic education*, McGraw-Hill, Inc.. **Table 8.4:** Giaconia, R. M. and Hedges, L. V. (1982). "Identifying features of effective open education", *Review of Educational Research, 52*, American Educational Research Association: Washington, D.C., pp. 579–602.

Chapter 9: **Table 9.1:** Gardiner and Hatch (1989). "Multiple Intelligences Go to School", *Educational Researcher, Vol. 18, No. 8*, p. 6. American Educational Research Association: Washington D.C.. **Table 9.3:** Anderson, L. M., Evertson, C. M., and Brophy, J. E. (1982). *Principles of small-group instruction in elementary reading*. East Lansing: Institute for Research on Teaching, Mighican State University. **Table 9.4:** Harrison, G. V. (1972). *Beginning reading. I: A professional guide for the tutor*. Provo, Utah: Brigham Young University Press. **Table 9.5:** Stevens, A., Collins, A., Goldin, S. (1982). Misconceptions in students' understanding. In D. Sleeman and J. S. Brown (Eds.), *Intelligent tutoring systems*, pp. 13–24. London: Academic Press.

Chapter 10: **Table 10.1:** Weiner, B. (1979). A theory of motivation for some classroom experiences. *Journal of Educational Psychology, 71*, 3–25. **Table 10.2:** From "Achievement goals in the classroom: Students learning classroom strategies and motivation processes", by Ames and Archer in the *Journal of Educational Psychology*, 1988, Vol. 80, p. 261. Copyright © 1988 by the American Psychological Association. Reprinted by permission. **Table 10.3:** From "Test anxiety: A major educational problem and what can be done about it" by Hill and Wigfield in *Elementary School Journal*, 1984, Vol. 85, p. 123. Published by the University of Chicago Press.

Chapter 12: **Table 12.2:** Daniel P. Hallahan and James M. Kauffman, *Exceptional children: An introduction to special education*, copyright © 1982, p. 43. Reprinted by permission of Prentice-Hall, Inc. **Table 12.4:** From *An Introduction to Special Education*, 2/E by William H. Berdine and A. Edward Blackhurst. Copyright © 1985 by William H. Berdine and A. Edward Blackhurst/Reprinted by permission of Scott Foresman and Company. **Table 12.5:** From *Hearing and Deafness*, 3/E by Hollowell Davis and S. Richard Silverman, copyright © 1970, p. 322 by Holt, Rinehart, and Winston, Inc.. Reprinted by permission of the publisher.

Chapter 13: **Table 13.2:** From Daniel U. Levine and Robert J. Havighurst, *Society and education*, 7/E, copyright © 1989, by Boston: Allyn & Bacon, Inc. Reprinted with permission.

Chapter 14: **Table 14.2:** Norman E. Gronlund, *Constructing achievement tests*, copyright © 1982, p. 15. Reprinted by Permission of Prentice-Hall, Inc. Englewood Cliffs, New Jersey. **Table 14.4:** Bloom, B. S., Hastings, J. T., and Madaus, G. F. (1971). *Handbook on formative and summative evaluation of student learning*. New York: McGraw-Hill. Copyright © 1971 by McGraw-Hill. Reprinted by permission. **Table 14.5:** Normal E. Gronlund, *Constructing achievement tests*, copyright © 1982. p. 26. Reprinted by permission of Prentice-Hall, Inc., Englewood Cliffs, New Jersey.

Chapter 15: **Table 15.1:** Ahmann, J. S., and Glock M. D. (1981). *Evaluating student progress: Principles of tests and measures*. Boston: Allyn & Bacon. **Table 15.2:** Science Research Associates, Inc. (1972). *Using test results: A teacheer's guide*. Chicago: Science Research Associates., Inc. **Table 15.3:** From *Modern educational measurement* by W. J. Popham (1981). Prentice Hall, Inc.: Englewood Cliffs, New Jersey.

Name Index

Brown, A. L., 173, 175, 177, 178, 194, 302
Brown, D. S., 224
Brown, J. S., 192, 268
Brubaker, N. L., 287
Bruce, C., 121
Bruner, J. S., 191, 192
Brungardt, T. M., 416
Bryan, J. H., 66
Bryan, M., 283
Buchwach, L., 442
Buckholdt, D., 379
Buka, S. L., 62, 63
Burgeson, R., 91
Burke, C. L., 69
Burkhart, J. F., 52
Burnett, J., 436
Burns, M. S., 191, 268
Burns, R. B., 193, 292, 293, 368
Burt, M., 465
Burton, F., 499, 503
Burton, N. W., 458
Burton, R. V., 52
Bushwall, S. J., 91
Butterfield, E. C., 181
Butterworth, T., 348

Cahen, L., 248, 299
Cahen, L. S., 249
Cairns, L. G., 375
Caldwell, B., 66
Calfee, R. C., 135
Calhoun, G., 396, 434, 435
California State Department of Education, 466, 474
Calkins, L. M., 62, 268
Callison, W. L., 315
Campbell, D. T., 21
Campbell, E. Q., 277
Campbell, R. A., 106, 107, 386
Campbell, V. N., 264
Cannell, J. J., 518
Canter, L., 377, 393, 401
Canter, M., 377, 393, 401
Cantrell, M., 427
Cantrell, R., 427
Capie, W., 248
Caplan, P. J., 467
Carleton-Ford, S., 91
Carlsmith, J. M., 91
Carlson, J., 151
Carmody, D., 33
Carnine, D., 248, 257, 258, 259, 307, 438
Carpenter, T. P., 268
Carroll, J. B., 233, 273, 293, 458
Carter, B., 237
Carter, K., 372
Carter, L. F., 455
Carter, T. P., 462, 465, 474
Carter, V., 121
Cartledge, N., 352
Cartwright, P., 438
Case, R., 130
Casey, A., 427
Casto, G., 408

Cellerino, M., 411
Chaffin, R., 139
Chambers, J. A., 309
Chang, T. M., 139
Chansky, N. M., 479, 503
Chao, C.-L., 168, 173, 245
Chapman, J. W., 410
Charters, W. W., 248, 253
Chen, M., 302
Chiang, C.-P., 268
Chiappetta, E. L., 298
Chira, S., 7
Chobot, R., 397
Chomsky, C., 60
Chomsky, N., 60, 95
Chopman, J. W., 426
Christie, J. F., 67
Christoplos, F., 424
Chull, J. J., 450
Clarizio, H., 394
Clark, C. M., 206, 233, 244, 248, 309
Clark, M. C., 168, 169
Clark, R., 121, 329, 390
Clarke, A. D. B., 641
Clarke, A. M., 641
Clawson, E. V., 167
Cleaves, A., 341
Clements, B. S., 224, 225, 238, 239, 290, 366, 401
Clements, D. H., 312
Clifford, C., 48
Clifford, M. M., 343
Cloward, R. A., 381, 394
Cloward, R. D., 302
Coats, W. D., 245
Cohen, E. G., 79, 286, 331, 454
Cohen, S. A., 48, 533
Colby, C., 50
Coldiron, J. R., 283, 285, 482
Cole, N. S., 539
Coleman, J. S., 277, 341, 353, 518, 519
College Entrance Examination Board, 458
Collins, A., 140, 192, 268, 308
Collins, K. W., 173, 174
Collins, W. A., 95
Colson, S., 411
Combs, A. W., 265
Combs, J., 374
Commins, N. L., 464
Commons, M. L., 37
Condelli, L., 63
Conderman, L., 390
Conger, J. J., 91
Conger, R. E., 414
Cook, T. D., 21
Cooley, W. W., 211, 220, 374, 455, 456, 474
Cooper, H. M., 252, 280, 335, 336, 358, 415
Copeland, W. D., 372
Coplin, W., 341
Coppola, M. A., 415
Corman, I., 436
Cornell, N., 368
Corno, L., 252, 339, 281, 315

Costa, A. L., 511
Costanzo, P. R., 86
Cotten, M. L., 244
Cotten, N. J., 138
Coughlin, R. M., 62
Covington, M. V., 188, 323, 324
Cox, P. W., 281
Cox, W. F., 301
Craig, G. J., 58
Craik, F. I. M., 138, 141
Crain, R. L., 141, 460, 461, 474
Crain, W. C., 28, 53
Cranston, S., 106, 107, 386
Cratty, B. J., 59
Crawford, J., 253, 366, 456
Crawford, R. P., 188
Crescimbeni, J., 342
Crocker, A. C., 422
Crocker, R. K., 245, 375
Crooks, T. J., 169, 479, 486, 506
Cross, D., 177, 178
Cross, G. M., 481
Cross, L. H., 481
Crouch, M. P. D., 326
Crutchfield, R. S., 188
Cruz, B. R., 465
Csikszentimihalyi, M., 95
CTB/McGraw-Hill, 528, 529
Cummins, J., 465
Cureton, L. E., 500

Dahl, T., 170
Daiute, C., 309
Dalis, G. T., 218
Damon, W., 38, 66, 68, 69, 74, 95
Daniels, L. A., 182, 327
Dansereau, D. F., 153, 173, 174, 175
Dansereau, D. I., 173
Darch, C. B., 259
Daurio, S. P., 411
Davies, I. K., 167
Davies, L., 188
Davis, H., 265, 421
Deaux, K., 468
DeCharms, R., 332
Deci, E. L., 339
DeLandsheere, V., 214
Delaney, H., 151
Delclos, V. R., 191
Delin, P. S., 151
Delon, F. G., 309
Dempster, F. N., 252, 490
Demyer, M. K., 279
Deno, S. L., 524
Derevensky, J., 438
Derry, S. J., 191
Detterman, D. K., 277, 513
Devin-Sheehan, L., 301, 302
DeVries, D. L., 342, 469
DeVries, R., 39, 69, 95
Dewar, J., 286
Dickerson, D., 389
Diener, C. I., 331
Digest of Education Statistics, 458

Dillon, J. T., 248
Dishaw, M., 363
Dishaw, M. M., 249
Doctorow, M., 173
Doenau, S. J., 460
Dolan, L., 304, 454
Donaldson, M., 38
Donovan, J. F., 253
Dooling, D. J., 166
Dopyera, J. E., 95
Dornbusch, S. M., 91, 479, 480, 482, 507
Dorr-Bremme, D. W., 487
Dorval, B., 304
Doty, C. R., 218
Doueck, H. J., 396
Dougherty, A., 387, 389
Dougherty, E., 387, 389
Downing, J., 62
Doyle, W., 363, 366, 368, 370, 372, 373, 376, 401
Drabman, R. S., 122, 127, 386
Dreeben, R., 245, 273
Dreyer, S. S., 442
DuBoulay, J. B. H., 312
Duchastel, P. C., 218, 220, 229
Duell, O. K., 173
Duffy, G. G., 193, 287
Duguid, P., 192, 268
Duke, D. L., 401
Duke, M. P., 326
Dukes, R., 342, 358
Dulay, H., 465
Dumaret, A., 280
Duncan, B., 449
Duncan, O. D., 449
Duncker, K., 186
Dunkin, J. J., 247
Dunkin, M. J. 460
Dunlap, A., 121, 390
Dunn, K. J., 281
Dunn, L. M., 424
Dunn, R., 281
Dunn, T. G., 301
Duran, R. P., 462
Dutcher, P., 538
Duyme, M., 280
Dweck, C. S., 330, 331, 332
Dyer, H. S., 209
Dyson, A. H., 69

Ebel, R. L., 478, 507, 513, 534
Ebmeier, H., 10, 238, 245, 249, 253, 255, 273, 367
Eccles, J., 336
Edgerton, R. B., 404
Edlund, C., 389
Educational Research Service, 6, 95
Edwards, K. J., 469
Edwards, W., 61, 332
Efthim, H., 273
Ehly, S. W., 302
Ehrlick, D., 324
Eiben, R. M., 422
Eichorn, D., 70
Eisner, E. W., 68, 217
Elashoff, J. D., 335

Elawar, M. C., 252
Elkind, D., 38, 64, 69, 84, 90, 95
Elliot, E. S., 330, 331
Elliott, R., 396, 434, 435
Ellson, D. G., 302, 315
Ellwein, M. C., 534
Emler, N. P., 45, 51, 52, 55
Emmer, E. T., 224, 225, 238,
        239, 249, 290, 366, 370,
        372, 373, 376, 401
Engel, R. S., 218
Englehart, M. B., 213, 229
Entwistle, D., 48
Entwistle, D. R., 452
Entwistle, N., 72, 281
Epstein, A. S., 63, 95
Epstein, C., 72, 401
Epstein, J. G., 252
Epstein, J. L., 266, 461
Erikson, E. H., 25, 40, 41, 42, 43,
        48, 49, 55, 72, 74, 84, 90
Esposito, D., 283
Estes, N. K., 513
Evans, S. H., 173, 174
Evertson, C. M., 224, 225, 238,
        239, 248, 249, 251, 253,
        290, 291, 315, 363, 365,
        366, 367, 368, 370, 372,
        373, 374, 376, 401, 468
Evertson, L. M., 248

Fagan, E. R., 248
Fairbrother, R. W., 214
Fallow, D., 62
Farnish, A. M., 175, 292, 355
Feather, N., 332
Featherman, D. L., 449
Federal Register, 409
Fein, G. G., 67
Feldhusen, J. F., 411
Feldman, R. S., 165, 301, 302
Felker, D. W., 331, 500
Fennema, E., 268, 467
Fennessey, G. M., 353
Ferguson, D. L., 432
Ferguson, P. M. 432
Fernandez, R. R., 474
Ferritor, D., 379
Festinger, L. A., 323
Feuerstein, R., 189, 190
Field, C. J., 280
Fielding, G., 248, 253
Filby, N., 249, 299
Filipczak, J., 396
Findley, N., 336
Findley, W. G., 283
Finkelstein, F. J., 474
Finley, G. E., 64
Fiordaliso, R., 396
Fisher, C., 490
Fisher, C. W., 249
Fiske, E. B., 7, 85, 210, 502,
        517, 518
Flanagan, J. C., 300
Flavell, J. H., 34, 35, 55, 173
Fletcher, J. D., 220, 306
Flood, P., 326
Floyd, C., 284

Fodor, E. M., 52
Foos, P. W., 490
Forehand, G., 460, 474
Forsterling, F., 332, 359
Forsyth, D. R., 325
Forsyth, P. D., 58, 60, 61, 95
Foundopoulos, M., 106, 107, 386
Fox, C., 3
Fox, L. H., 411
Franks, J. J., 142, 164
Frayer, D. A., 342
Frederiksen, N., 187, 488
French, E. G., 329
Fresko, B., 302
Friedman, R. M., 396
Frieze, I. H., 325
Froman, R. D., 26, 32
Frost, J. L., 59
Fuchs, D., 427
Fuchs, L. S., 427
Funkhouser, J. E., 454
Furman, W., 66
Furst, E. J., 213, 214, 229
Furth, H. G., 55

Gaa, J., 352
Gadow, K., 415
Gage, N. L., 153, 215, 244, 248,
        253, 273, 318
Gagné, R. M., 191, 195, 196,
        215, 216, 221, 238, 245,
        257, 273
Galdwin, J. I., 127
Gall, M., 248, 258
Gall, M. D., 21, 248, 253, 258
Gallagher, J. J., 411
Gallagher, P. A., 411, 437, 444
Galtelli, B., 428
Gamoran, A., 331, 336
Ganson, H., 63
Gant, D., 389
Garber, H. L., 408
Garber, S., 387, 389
Garcia, E. E., 465
Garcia, G. N., 454
Gardner, H., 38, 277, 278
Gardner, M. K., 221
Garibaldi, A., 397
Garlind, J. C., 173, 174
Garner, R., 173
Gartner, A., 423
Gelman, R., 38, 55
Gendrich, J., 389
Gendrich, S., 389
Genesee, F., 464
Genter, D., 168
Gerard, H. B., 461
Gerber, M. M., 405
Gern, P., 416
Gern, T., 416
Gersten, R., 258, 307, 438
Getsie, R. L., 118
Getzels, J. W., 186
Ghatala, E. S., 178
Gholson, B., 118, 251
Giaconia, R. M., 266, 267, 268
Gibbs, J. C., 52
Gickling, E., 434

Gilligan, C., 52
Gilstrap, R. L., 192
Ginott, H., 377
Ginsburg, H. P., 72
Glanzer, M., 136
Glaser, R., 191, 300
Glashoff, J., 248
Glass, G. V., 118, 299, 454, 534
Glasser, W. L., 74, 265
Glavin, J., 414, 435
Gleason, J. B., 60
Glickman, C. D., 395, 401
Glock, M. D., 515
Goetz, E. T., 164
Goffin, S. G., 68, 69
Gold, M., 396
Gold, R. M., 265, 352, 498
Golden, J., 68
Goldhaber, D., 64
Goldini, S., 308
Goleman, D., 463
Golem and Leinhardt, 245, 299
Good, T., 10, 11–12, 226, 238,
        245, 249, 253, 255, 257,
        273, 283, 336, 367
Good, T. L., 238, 248, 250, 252,
        273, 280, 335, 358, 377
Goodenough, D. R., 281
Goodlad, J. I., 283, 284, 285
Goodman, J., 122
Goodman, K. S., 268
Goodman, P., 264
Goodman, W., 237
Gordon, I., 74
Gotfredson, G. D., 395
Gottfried, A. E., 239
Gottlieb, J., 414, 434, 435, 436,
        444
Gottman, J. M., 66
Gould, L. J., 465
Graden, J. L., 427
Graubard, P. S., 397
Graves, D., 194, 268
Graves, M., 108, 109
Green, B. F., 539
Green, J., 253, 366
Green, M., 55
Greenblat, C. S., 341
Greene, D., 10, 11, 12, 339
Greene, R. L., 146
Greeno, J., 143
Gregory, I. D., 239
Greif, E. B., 81
Gresham, F., 66, 414
Griffiths, A. K., 38
Gronlund, N. E., 207, 229, 484,
        485, 487, 490, 491, 492,
        507, 539
Gross, R. T., 91
Grossman, H., 406
Grouws, D., 10, 11–12, 238,
        245, 249, 253, 255, 257,
        273, 367
Grusec, J., 66
Guilford, J. P.
Gullo, D. F., 312
Gump, P. V., 369
Gunderson, D. V., 465

Guralnick, M. J., 67
Gutkin, J., 258
Guttman, J., 324

Haan, N., 52
Haertel, E., 487, 525
Hakuta, K., 465
Hales, L. W., 498
Hall, C., 284
Hall, R. V., 105, 106, 107, 121,
        122, 390, 386
Hall, W. S., 178
Hallahan, D. P., 404, 407, 409,
        421, 445
Hallinan, 315
Hamaker, C., 170, 248
Hamblin, R. L., 379
Hamilton, R. J., 170, 208, 326
Harpring, S. A., 454
Harris, A. M., 469, 474
Harris, J. R., 87, 95
Harris, K. H., 442
Harris, P., 302
Harris, T. R., 341
Harrison, G. V., 303
Harste, J. C., 69
Hart, D., 74
Harter, S., 74
Hartley, J., 167
Hartshorne, H., 52
Hass, A., 80
Hassler, D. M., 248
Hastings, J. T., 481, 490, 491,
        506
Hastings, W. M., 214
Hastorf, A. H., 91
Hatch, T., 277, 278
Hathaway, D., 273
Havinghurst, R. S., 456, 457,
        474
Hawkins, J. D., 396
Hawsins, R., 387
Hawley, W. D., 474
Hayduk, L., 48
Hayes, L., 391
Hays et al., 122
Hechinger, F. M., 7, 33
Hedges, L. V., 266, 267, 268
Hembree, R., 480
Henry, M., 249
Herman, J., 487
Herrmann, D. J., 139
Hersen, M., 13, 21, 415
Hertz-Lazarowitz, R., 264
Hess, R. D., 449
Heward, W., 422
Hewer, A., 52
Heyns, B., 450
Hidde, J. L., 150
Hidi, S., 172, 178
Hiebert, E., 286
Higbee, K. L., 148, 150, 151
Hilgard, E. R., 101
Hill, J. P., 81
Hill, J. R., 493
Hill, K., 336, 337, 338, 359, 480
Hill, W. F., 127
Hill, W. H., 213, 229

Hillard, A. G. III, 461
Hillocks, 268
Hiroto, D. S., 331
Hirsch, B. J., 91
Hirschi, T., 91
Hitchcock, D., 191
Hixon, T. J., 445
Hodges, W. L., 63, 64, 95
Hodgkinson, H. L., 456
Hoffman, M. B., 190
Hoffman, M. L., 66
Hogan, R., 45, 51, 52, 55
Holley, C. T., 173, 174
Holmes, S. A., 182
Holt, J., 264
Hoole, E., 244
Hopkins, K. D., 280, 539
Horn, R. E., 341
Horson, C. L., 277
Horton, M., 337, 338
Horwitz, R., 267
Hovland, C. I., 242
Howard, E. R., 396, 401
Howe, J. A. M., 312
Hull, F. M., 419
Hull, M. E., 419
Hunter, M., 238, 246, 249, 254,
    257, 273, 324, 328, 359
Hutlock, N., 298
Hyde, J. S., 468
Hyde, T. S., 141
Hymel, S., 66, 69

Inhelder, B., 26, 27, 32, 35, 36,
    37, 55, 81
Intilli, J., 454
Isaacson, R. L., 330
Isenberger, J., 67
Isrudner, H. J., 300

Jacklin, C. N., 467, 468, 475
Jackson, D., 105
Jackson, P., 469
Jackson, P. W., 186
Jacobson, L., 335
James, W., 163
Jenkins, J. J., 141
Jenkins, J. R., 302
Jenkins, L. M., 302
Jensen, A. R., 280
Jensen, M. R., 189, 190
Jenson, W. R., 107, 211
Jeter, J. T., 342
Johnson, D. W., 259, 353, 434
Johnson, G. O., 435
Johnson, R. T., 259, 353, 434
Johnson-Laird, P. N., 139
Johnston, P., 91, 454 (Allington,
    R., Afflerbach, P.)
Jones, L. V., 458
Jones, R. M., 265
Jones, R. R., 414
Joyce, B., 39, 166, 168, 180, 181,
    260, 273
Jung, R. K., 454

Kaczala, C., 337
Kagan, D., 4

Kagan, J., 62, 64, 451, 466, 468
Kagan, S., 451, 466
Kagey, J. R., 396
Kallison, J. M., 243
Kameenui, E. L., 259
Kamii, C., 39, 69, 95
Kamin, L. J., 280
Kaplan, R., 220
Kaplan, R. M., 245
Karlin, M. B., 141
Karraker, R., 389
Karthwohl, O. R., 213, 229
Karweit, N., 253, 286, 289, 298,
    301, 363, 364, 435, 436
Karweit, N. L., 63, 64, 236, 284,
    287, 288, 304, 363, 454,
    475, 518, 519
Kaskowitz, D., 248, 257, 304,
    375
Kass, R. E., 386
Kauffman, D. P., 404
Kauffman, J. M., 404, 407, 409,
    413, 415, 417, 420, 421,
    445
Kauffman, M., 436
Kaufman, K. F., 386
Kearsley, R., 62
Keating, T., 258
Keith, T. Z., et al., 252
Keller, F. S., 293, 295
Kelley, H. H., 318
Kendall, P. C., 122
Kennedy, M., 455
Kerr, M. M., 414
Kessler, J., 154
Kestenbaum, J. M., 329
Ketty, J., 417
Keyser, D. J., 531
Kidder, J. D., 386
Kierstead, J., 269
Kiewra, K. A., 172, 242
Kilborn, P. T., 439
Kinch, J. W., 86, 87
Kirby, F. D., 384
Kirkpatrick, C., 459
Kirschenbaum, H., 265, 498
Kirsner, D. A., 215
Kjur, 345
Klausmeier, H. J., 342
Klavas, A., 281
Kleefeld, C. F., 121
Klein, B., 59
Klein, R. E., 64
Klein, S., 470, 474
Klieber, D. A., 70
Kline, S., 418
Kneedler, R., 413, 415
Kneller, G. F., 451
Koeppel, J., 352
Kogan, N., 188
Kohlberg, L., 25, 44, 47, 50, 51,
    52, 55
Kohlerberg, L., 52
Kohn, M. L., 452, 471
Kounin, J., 367, 369, 370, 372,
    375, 376, 401
Kozloff, M., 379
Krasavage, E. M., 253, 372

Krasnor, L. R., 66
Krathwohl, D. R., 217, 229
Kropp, R. P., 214
Krueger, W. C. F., 154
Kuhn, D., 37
Kukla, A., 334
Kulhavy, R. W., 172
Kulik, C., 300, 485, 533
Kulik, C. L., 309, 411
Kulik, C.-L., 108, 251, 294, 343,
    352
Kulik, J., 300, 485, 533
Kulik, J. A., 108, 251, 294, 309,
    343, 352, 411
Kunihira, S., 151
Kurland, D. M., 312
Kussell, P., 264
Kuzma, R., 151

LaBerge, D., 143
Lachman, R., 166
Lahaderne, H., 14–16, 469
Lahey, B., 389
Lambert, W. E., 465
Lambie, R. A., 436
Lampert, M., 192, 268
Land, M., 244
Land, M. L., 244
Landy, F. J., 116
Lane, K., 163
Langer, P., 118
Larrivee, B., 248, 410, 436, 445
Larsen, S. C., 302, 389
Larson, C. D., 173
Larson, C. O., 173, 175
Larson, R., 95
Laurie, T. E., 442
Lavatelli, C., 39
Lave, J., 181
Lawson, A. 416
Lawson, G., 416
Lawton, J. T., 167
Lay, M. Z., 95
Leach, D. M., 108, 109
Leavey, M. B., 301, 454
Lee, V. E., 470
Leeper, R. W., 134
Lefcourt, H., 326, 359
Lefkowitz, W., 265
Lehr, R., 265, 352, 498
Leiderman, H., 91
Leinhardt, G., 170, 211, 220,
    410, 437, 442, 445, 455,
    456
Lepper, M., 339
Lepper, M. R., 10, 11, 12, 339,
    341, 359
Lerner, B., 534, 539
Lesgold, A., 143
Lesgold, A. M., 168, 169
Lessac, M. S., 378
Leventhal, L., 245
Levin, B. B., 151
Levin, H. M., 310
Levin, J. R., 151, 154, 159, 178
Levine, C., 52
Levine, D. V., 315, 456, 457,
    474

Lewin, K., 259
Leyser, Y., 414, 434, 435, 444
Lezotte, L., 273
Liebert, R. M., 29, 87, 95
Liekhoff, G. M., 173, 174
Lindeman, R. H., 492, 493, 495,
    507
Linn, M. C., 468
Lipsky, D. K., 423
Lipson, M., 177, 178
Lishner, D. M., 396
Litow, L., 388
Litwin, G. H., 330
Livermon, B. J., 304, 454
Livson, N., 81
Lloyd, B., 468
Locke, E. A., 352
Lockhart, R. S., 138, 141
Lockheed, M. E., 469, 474
Loef, M., 268
Loftus, E. I., 140, 159
Longfellow, C., 417
Lordeman, A., 396
Lotz, T., 151
Lowell, E. L., 329
Lueckemeyer, C. L., 293
Lumsdaine, A. A., 242
Lund, D., 105

McAllister, L. W., 390
McCaleb, J., 244
McClelland, D. C., 329
McCombs, B. L., 332
McConkey, C., 63
McCormick, C. B., 151, 154
Maccoby, E. E., 467, 468, 475
McCoy, G., 394
McCune-Nicolich, L. R., 337
McDaniel, T. R., 394
McDonald, B. A., 173, 174
McGivern, J. E., 151
Machida, S., 151
McKean, K., 159
McKenzie, G. R., 249
McKenzie, M., 61, 68, 69
McKey, R., 63
McKinney, J. D., 410
MacMillan, D. L., 434, 445
McNee, P., 389
McPartland, J. M., 266, 277, 283,
    285, 482
MacPherson, G. M., 467
Madaus, G. F., 214, 481, 490,
    491, 506
Madden, N. A., 63, 175, 287,
    292, 301, 304, 315, 355,
    396, 414, 426, 434, 435,
    445, 454, 455, 461, 468,
    475
Maddox, H., 244
Madsen, C. H., 349, 381, 384,
    386
Madsen, C. R., 386
Madsen, K., 320
Mager, R. F., 206, 207, 209,
    211, 218, 221, 229
Mahard, R., 141
Mahard, R. E., 460, 461, 474

Mahone, C. H., 330
Maier, N. R., 186
Maier, S. F., 331
Malina, R. M., 59
Mallery, D., 283
Mandeville, G., 253
Manning, B. H., 122
Marker, R. W., 300
Marks, C., 173
Marland, M., 475
Marliave, R., 249
Marsh, H. W., 325, 468
Marshall, H., 266
Marshall, P. M., 252
Marshall, S. P., 283, 467
Martin, J., 366
Martin, S. M., 302
Martin, W. R., 192
Marx, R. W., 244, 248
Maryland State Board of
    Education, 425
Marzano, B. J., 511
Masia, B. B., 217, 229
Maslow, A. H., 320, 321, 322
Masterson, J. F., 91
Mastropieri, M. A., 151, 408
Matson, J. L., 445
May, M. A., 52
Mayer, G. R., 127, 348, 383,
    385, 401
Mayer, R. E., 167, 170
Meadows, G., 151
Meckel, A. M., 401
Medland, M., 382, 401
Medley, D. M., 250
Meece, J. I., 336
Meichenbaum, D., 122
Meichenbaum, D. H., 122, 127,
    281
Meister, G., 310
Melton, R. F., 220, 229
Menyuk, P., 60
Mercer, J. R., 280, 404
Merenda, P. F., 492, 493, 495,
    507
Merrill, M. A., 406
Merrill, P. F., 218, 220, 229
Messer, S., 326
Messick, S., 278, 281, 533
Metfessel, N. S., 215
Metz, M. H., 16–17
Metzger, M. T., 3
Meyer, L. A., 250, 257, 258
Meyer, W. J., 468
Meyers, C. E., 434, 445
Mezynski, K. J., 142
Michael, W. B., 188, 215
Miele, F., 280
Miller, G. A., 38, 136
Miller, G. E., 151, 154
Miller, N., 461
Miller, P. D., 268
Miller, P. H., 40, 55
Miller, R., 190
Miller, R. L., 300
Miller, S., 273, 337
Mills, J., 324
Mintzker, Y., 190

Miracle, A., 286
Miramontes, O. B., 464
Mitchell, J. V., 329, 531
Mitchell, M. A., 121
Mitts, B., 122
Moely, B. E., 152
Moles, O., 397
Montague, W. E., 159, 298
Mood, A. M., 277
Moore, C. A., 281
Moore, J. E., 249
Moore, M. T., 454
Morella, J. R., 63
Morgan, M., 339, 359
Morine-Dershimer, G., 374
Morrison, C. R., 151
Morrison, D. M., 91
Morrison, D. R., 454
Morrison, G. M., 434, 445
Morse, J. A., 220
Moscow, H., 26, 32
Mulich, J. A., 445
Murphy, D. A., 191
Murphy, M. A., 415
Murray, F. B., 39
Murray, H., 244, 320, 329
Muuss, R. E., 52

Nachtigal, P., 372
Nafpaktitis, M., 348
Nagy, P., 38
Nakamura, G. V., 139
Nakane, M., 151
Napier, R. W., 265, 498
Narot, R. E., 460, 474
Nash, W. R., 411
National Center for Educational
    Statistics, 405, 410, 411,
    413, 426
National Clearinghouse for Drug
    Abuse Information, 416
National Commission on
    Excellence in Education,
    465
National Institute of Education
    (NIE), 454
National Institute on Drug Abuse,
    91, 416
National Society for the
    Prevention of Blindness,
    421
Natriello, G., 479, 480, 482, 507
Nedelsky, L., 214
Needels, M. C., 253, 273
Neergaard, L., 143
Neill, A. S., 185, 264
Newell, A., 185
Newmann, F., 498, 539
Newmann, F. M., 355
Nicholls, J. G., 330
Niemiec, R. P., 309
Nimmer, D. M., 522
Nisbett, R. E., 10, 11, 12, 339
Nitsche, K. E., 182, 183
Nolan, E., 64
Norris, S. P., 191
Northcutt, L., 465
Nowicki, S., 326

Nucci, L., 52
Nurss, J. R., 63, 64, 95
Nuthall, G., 252
Nuttal, R. L., 214

Oakes, J., 283, 284, 315
Oakland, T., 539
Oakley, D. A., 138
Oden, S. L., 66
Odle, S. J., 428
O'Donnell, H., 309
Ohlin, I. E., 381, 394
Oishi, S., 461, 468
O'Leary, K. D., 107, 348, 385,
    386, 388, 390, 415
O'Leary, S. G., 107, 348, 385
O'Leary and Dubey (1979), 122
Olexa, C., 283, 284
Oliver, J., 417
Olson, D. R., 135
Olton, R. M., 188
Oraland, M. E., 454
Orlansky, M., 422
Ormell, C. P., 214
Ortony, A., 164
Osborn, A. F., 188
Osborn, J. D., 71, 95
Osborn, P. K., 71, 95
Osguthorpe, R. T., 302, 439, 440
Oswald, J. M., 220
Ottenbacher, K. J., 415
Owen, S. L., 26, 32

Page, E. B., 481
Paivio, A., 141
Palincsar, A. S., 175, 176, 177,
    194, 302, 437
Pallay, A., 445
Papert, S., 312
Paris, S., 177, 178
Park, O., 179
Parke, B. N., 411
Parsons, J., 337
Pascoe, G. C., 245
Passalacqua, J., 273
Passow, A. H., 414
Patterson, G. R., 414
Pau, A. S., 135
Pea, R. D., 312
Pearson, P. D., 538
Peckham, P. D., 345, 481
Penfield, W., 146
Pepitone, E. A., 451
Pepler, D. J., 66
Perfetti, C., 143
Perfetto, G. A., 142, 164
Perkins, D. N., 183, 184, 191
Perkins, W. H., 419
Perl, E., 465
Perry, R. P., 245
Peskin, H., 80, 81
Peters, C. W., 538
Peters, E. E., 151
Petersen, A. C., 91
Peterson, J., 416
Peterson, L. R., 144
Peterson, M. J., 144

Peterson, P. L., 206, 244, 248,
    252, 267, 268, 273, 315,
    467
Petrie, C. R., 244
Petty, M. F., 280
Petza, R. J., 284
Phillips, B., 337
Phillips, J. L., 31, 32
Piaget, J., 17, 26, 27, 32, 33, 35,
    36, 37, 38, 46, 55, 67, 69,
    81, 83
Pichert, J. W., 147, 150, 159,
    164, 298
Pinnell, G. S., 304
Pintrich, P. R., 281, 326
Pisor, K., 387, 389
Pitcher, G., 337
Pittman, T. S., 339
Plantz, M., 63
Polya, G., 184
Popham, W. J., 220, 522, 525,
    531, 539
Porter, A. C., 238
Postman, L., 144
Postman, N., 68, 69, 95
Potter, E. F., 369
Premack, D., 106
Pressley, M., 151, 154, 159, 127,
    178
Pressley, M. S., 127
Price, G. G., 38, 69
Prom, S. E., 253
Pumroy, D. K., 388

Quay, H., 413, 414, 435
Quilling, M. R., 342
Quisenberry, Nancy L., 67

Rachford, D. L., 189
Raffini, J. P., 328
Ragosta, M., 310, 460, 474
Ramirez, J. D., 465
Rand, L. P., 498
Rand, Y., 190
Rapkin, B., 91
Rappaport, M. D., 415
Rather, J., 85
Raudenbush, S. W., 335
Raugh, M. R., 150, 151
Raviv, S., 264
Reber, A., 377, 378
Redfield, D. L., 248
Reid, J. B., 414
Reigeluth, C. M., 168, 170, 173,
    245
Reilly, A., 265, 352, 498
Reiss, S., 411
Renshaw, P. D., 66, 69
Renz, P., 424
Renzulli, J. S., 411, 445
Restak, R., 143
Reynolds, R. E., 164, 341
Rhodes, L. K., 69
Rich, G., 62
Rich, H. L., 427
Richards, F. A., 37
Richardson, F., 337
Richmond, B. O., 451

Richter, L., 440
Rickards, J. P., 169
Ridley, D. S., 170
Rieser, J., 191
Reisner, E. R., 454
Rist, R. C., 452
Ritter, P. L., 91
Roberts, M. D., 390
Roberts, S. V., 33
Robbins, S., 454
Robins, L. N., 414
Robinson, F. P., 174
Robinson, H. A., 178, 407
Robinson, N., 407
Rocklin, T., 99
Roe, M. D., 345, 481
Roeber, E., 538
Roehler, L. R., 193
Roethlisberger and Dickson, 11
Rogers, C., 265, 269
Rogers, L., 39
Rogoff, B., 64
Rohrkemper, M., 339
Rohrkemper, M. M., 79
Rohwer, W. D., 172
Rose, B. C., 418
Rose, T. L., 385
Rosenbaum, J. E. (1976), 283, 461
Rosenbaum, M. S., 122
Rosenbaum, R. M., 330
Rosenblatt, D. B., 66
Rosenholtz, S. J., 48, 331, 336
Rosenshine, B. V., 238, 244, 245, 246, 248, 249, 251, 252, 253, 258, 273
Ross, J. A., 353
Ross, S. M., 427
Rossell, C. H., 461
Rothkopf, E. Z., 139, 169, 220
Rothman, S., 277, 513
Rothrock, D., 300
Rotter, J., 325
Rousseau, E. W., 248
Rowan, B., 286
Rowe, 248, 336
Royer, J. M., 165
Rubin, Z., 76
Ruble, D. N., 339
Ruiz, C. J., 190
Rumelhart, D. E., 164
Rundus, D., 146
Runge, A., 389
Russell, C. H., 474
Rydell, L., 465

Sadker, D., 469, 471, 475
Sadker, M., 469, 471, 475
Safer, D. J., 396, 401
St. John, N. H., 461
Salganik, M. W., 362, 364
Salomon, G., 183, 184, 191
Samuels, S. J., 143
Sanders, S., 394
Sanford, J. P., 224, 225, 238, 239, 290, 366, 373, 401
Sarnacki, R. E., 533
Saunders, M., 13, 14, 391, 392

Savell, J. M., 189
Saxman, J. H., 445
Scardamalia, M., 194
Scarr, S., 62, 280
Schafer, W. E., 283, 284
Schallert, D. L., 164
Schalock, D., 248, 253
Scheuneman, J. D., 530
Schickedanz, D. I., 58, 60, 61, 95
Schickedanz, J. A., 58, 60, 61, 68, 69, 95
Schiff, M., 280
Schmits, D., 283
Schneider, W., 143
Schnelle, L., 389
Schoen, H. L., 300
Schoenfeld, A. H., 193
Schofield, J. W., 474
Schommer, M., 168
Schonback, P., 324
Schulz, J. B., 440
Schunk, D. H., 177, 332, 480
Schwartz, J. I., 60
Schwartzwald, J., 451, 466
Schweinhart, L. J., 63, 95
Schweiter, J., 326
Scott, C., 298
Scriberg, L. K., 151
Scruggs, T. E., 151, 440, 534
Seddon, G. M., 214, 229
Sederstrom, J., 395
Segura, R. D., 462, 465, 474
Seidner, C., 342, 358
Seitz, V., 64
Seligman, M. E. P., 331
Selman, A. P., 66
Selman, R. L., 66
Semmel, M. I., 405
Shanner, W. M., 300
Sharan, S., 264, 354, 356
Sharan, Y., 264, 354
Shaw, M. E., 86
Shaywitz, B. A., 415
Shaywitz, S. E., 415
Shea, T. M., 127, 389, 401
Sheffield, F. D., 242
Shellman, J., 106, 107, 386
Shepard, L. A., 64, 537
Sherman, J., 467
Sherwood, R. D., 191
Shevick, E., 223
Shields, F., 384
Shiffrin, R. M., 130, 141, 143
Shimmerlik, M. M., 169
Shipman, V. C., 449
Shirey, L. L., 341
Shriberg, L. D., 419, 445
Shuell, T. J., 281
Siegler, R. S., 130, 159
Sikes, J. N., 354, 469
Silberman, R., 265, 352, 498
Silver, E. A., 184
Silverman, R., 442
Silverman, R. E., 91
Simmons, R. G., 91
Simmons, W., 280
Simon, H., 185
Simon, S. B., 265, 478, 498

Simpson, C., 48, 336
Simpson, E. J., 218
Simpson, R. L., 442, 503
Sizer (1984), 498
Skinner, B. F., 17, 123, 127, 319, 384
Slavin, R. E., 6, 21, 63, 66, 175, 234, 253, 256, 257, 273, 282, 283, 284, 286, 287, 288, 289, 292, 293, 298, 301, 304, 315, 333, 334, 342, 350, 352, 353, 354, 355, 356, 359, 363, 364, 372, 391, 396, 414, 426, 434, 435, 436, 445, 454, 455, 461, 466, 468, 475, 479, 481, 485, 486, 519, 520, 539
Sloane, H. N., 107, 211
Sluyter, D., 387
Smidchens, U., 245
Smith, C., 468
Smith, L., 244
Smith, L. R., 244
Smith, M. B., 52
Smith, M. L., 64, 299, 454, 534
Smith, S. M., 152
Smylie, M. A., 474
Snapp, M., 354
Snarey, J. R., 52
Snellgrove, L., 345
Snow, C. E., 450
Snow, R. E., 281, 315, 335
Snowman, J., 171, 172, 173
Snyderman, M., 277, 513
Sola, J., 170
Solomon, R. L., 331, 378
Sommerville, J. C., 69
Sousa, D. A., 253
Speece, D. L., 410
Spellman, C. R., 389
Spence, E. S., 286
Sperling, G. A., 131, 132
Spiro, R. J., 159, 298
Spitalnick, R., 122
Sprecher, J. W., 309
Spurlin, J. E., 173, 175
Squire, L. R., 138
Stachowiak, J. G., 390
Stahl, S. A., 268
Stallings, J. A., 63, 248, 253, 257, 304, 372, 375
Stanley, J. C., 21, 411, 471, 539
Stanton, G., 248
Stayrook, N. G., 244, 248
Stein, B. S., 142
Stein, M. K., 170, 259, 456
Steinberg, L. D., 81
Stephan, C., 354
Sternberg, R. I., 410
Sternberg, R. J., 190, 277, 513
Stevens, A., 308
Stevens, R. J., 175, 238, 246, 248, 273, 292, 315, 355
Stewart, L. G., 481
Stiggins, R. J., 507
Stigler, S. M., 146
Stiles, B., 264

Stipek, D., 63
Stipek, D. J., 340, 374
Stitelman, L., 314
Stoker, H. W., 214
Strain, P., 414, 434
Stringfield, S., 533
Suchman, J. R., 260
Suhor, C., 462
Sullivan, H. S., 86
Sulzer-Azaroff, B., 127, 383, 385, 401
Sund, R., 55, 72
Suransky, U. P., 69, 70
Swanson, H. L., 410
Sweetland, R. C., 531
Sylvester, R., 139, 159
Szabo, M., 248

Taft, R., 16
Tague, C. E., 386
Talmage, H., 300
Tanner, J. M., 80
Taylor, D., 61
Taylor, R., 413, 445
Teddlie, C., 533
TenBrink, T. D., 209, 229
Tenenbaum, G., 294
Tennyson, R. D., 179
Terman, L. M., 406, 411
Theobald, J., 434
Thibault, J. W., 318
Thieme-Busch, C. A., 253
Thomas, A., 64
Thomas, D. R., 349, 381, 384
Thomas, E. J., 178
Thomas, J. W., 172
Thomas, R. M., 41, 55
Thompson, E., 243
Thompson, G. G., 468
Thompson, J., 355
Thompson, M. S., 452
Thompson, S. A., 415
Thornburg, H., 77, 95
Thorndike, E. L., 181
Tiedemann, J., 278
Tillman, M. H., 220
Timpson, W. M., 245
Tobias, S., 280, 281, 336
Tobin, D. N., 245
Tobin, K., 248, 336
Tobin, P., 467
Toll, D., 341
Tom, D. Y. H., 336
Tomkiewicz, S., 280
Tompkins, G. E., 68
Tompkins, R., 474
Top, B. L., 302, 439
Tornatsky, L., 273
Torrance, E. P., 412, 445, 469
Towson, S., 466
Trelease, J., 60
Trent, W. T., 474
Trollip, S. R., 315
Trost, C., 395
Tseng, M., 374
Tull, C. Q., 68, 69
Tulving, E., 138

Turnbull, A. P., 428, 440, 445
Turnbull, B. J., 454
Turner, L. H., 378
Twohig, P. T., 189
Tyler, L., 389
Tyrrell, G., 451, 466

Ulman, K. J., 81
Underwood, B. J., 144
U.S. Census Bureau, 457
U.S. Commission on Civil Rights, 464
U.S. Department of Health, Education, and Welfare, 70, 408, 469
U.S. Department of Health and Human Services, 415
U.S. Government, Bureau of Labor Statistics, 62
U.S. Office of Education, 464

Vachon, E. M., 391
Valencia, S. W., 538
Valentine, J., 63, 95
Van Patten, J., 168, 173, 245
Van Sickle, R. L., 341–42
Van Tassel-Baska, 411
Vitale, M., 382, 401
Vosniadou, S., 168
Vowles, R. O., 286
Vukelich, C., 68
Vye, N. J., 142, 191
Vygotsky, L. S., 39, 55

Wadsworth, B., 26, 29, 31, 55
Wagner, R. K., 410
Walberg, H., 363

Walberg, H. J., 244, 253, 273, 309, 315, 363
Walden, E. L., 415
Walker, J., 389
Walker, J. E., 127, 389, 401
Wallach, L., 304
Wallach, M. A., 188, 304
Wallen, N. E., 286
Waller, P., 332
Wallerstein, J., 417
Wang, M. C., 264, 315
Wanska, S. K., 167
Ward, B., 248
Ware, N. C., 470
Watson, D. J., 268, 465
Watt, D., 309
Wattenberg, W. W., 48
Watts, G. H., 147
Waxman, H. C., 268
Weade, R., 253, 366
Weber, E. S., 170
Webster, J., 295
Wechsler, D., 278
Weikart, D. P., 39, 63, 95
Weil, M., 39, 166, 168, 180, 181, 260, 273
Weinberg, R. A., 62, 64
Weiner, B., 324, 329, 330, 359, 486
Weiner, G. P., 451
Weinfeld, F. D., 277
Weinhouse, E., 67
Weinstein, C. S., 170, 224, 226, 229
Weinstein, R. R., 286
Weis, J. G., 395
Weiss, S., 210, 415
Weitzman, L. J., 471

Werry, J., 414, 435
Whalen, C. K., 410
Wheeler, R., 451
White, J., 244
White, K. R., 88, 534
White, M. A., 481
White, S. H., 62, 63
Whitener, 281
Whitley, B. E., 325
Wicks-Nelson, R., 29
Wigfield, A., 336, 359, 480
Wiggins, G., 498, 537, 538
Wilcox, R. T., 194
Wilkerson, I., 117
Wilkerson, R. M., 88
Wilkinson, L. C., 315
Williams, C. D., 111
Willig, A. C., 465
Willis, D. H., 420
Wilson, B., 283, 331
Wilson, B. G., 16
Wilson, K. K., 538
Wilson, R., 122
Wilszynski, J. M., 248, 253
Wine, J. D., 337
Winett, R. A., 391
Winkler, R. C., 393
Winn, M., 67
Winne, P. H., 244, 248
Winnett, R. A., 393
Winzenz, D., 168, 169
Wisenbaker, J., 326
Withall, J., 264
Witkin, H. A., 281
Wittrock, M. C., 166, 173
Wolf, D. P., 498, 538
Wolf, M. M., 13, 14, 386, 391, 392

Wolfgang, C. H., 395, 401
Wolfgang, D. C., 394
Womack, S., 170
Wong, B. Y. L., 173
Wong, H. D., 223
Wong-Fillmore, L., Valadez, C., 465, 475
Woods, E. M., 214
Woodword, J., 307, 438
Woodworth, R. S., 181
Woolfolk, A. E., 226, 337, 376
Worsham, M. E., 224, 225, 238, 239, 290, 337, 401
Wyckoff, W. L., 245

Yawkey, T. D., 67
York, R. L., 6, 277
Young, K. R., 107, 211
Youssef, M., 167
Ysseldyke, J., 405, 445

Zahn, G. L., 451, 466
Zelazo, P., 62
Zeppert, L. T., 465
Ziegler, S., 461
Zigler, E., 63, 64, 95
Zigmond, N., 442
Zimlin, L., 177
Zimmerman, B. J., 121, 177
Zimmerman, E. H., 111, 384
Zimmerman, J., 111, 384
Ziv, A., 238
Zlotnik, M. S., 474
Zucker, R., 416
Zuckerman, M., 325

Subject Index

Ability grouping, 282–89, 374
  Ability-Grouped Active
    Teaching (AGAT), 288–89
    outline of activities for, 289
  between-class, 282–85
    compared to within-class
      ability grouping, 286–87
    and Joplin plan, 284
    regrouping for reading and
      mathematics, 284
    research on, 283–84
    special education and
      programs for the gifted,
      285
  general principles of, 287–88
  within class, 288–89, 313
    applicability of, 287
    compared to between-class
      ability grouping, 286–87
    definition, 285
    and reading, 289–90
    research on, 285–87
  See also Between-class ability
    grouping; Within-class
    ability grouping
Absolute grading standards, 500
Academic achievement:
  and desegregation, 461–62
  and ethnicity/race, 456–59
  gender differences in, 470–71
  social-class differences in, 450
Acceleration programs for the
  gifted, 411
Accountability programs, 511,
  534–35
Achievement motivation, 329–31
  and attribution training, 331–
    32
  and failure avoidance, 330
  learning vs. performance goals,
    330–31
  See also Motivation
Achievement tests, 487–98, 514–
  16
  achievement batteries, 514
  basic principles, 487–90
  criterion-referenced tests, 512–
    13, 515–16, 534
    reliability, 530
  evaluating, 495–98
    problem-solving, 496–98
    short essay, 495–96

norm-referenced, 512–13
standardized, See Standardized
  tests
tables of specifications for, 490–
  91
writing test items, 492–98
  fill-in-the-blank items, 494
  matching items, 494–95
  multiple-choice items, 492–
    94
  problem-solving items, 496–
    98
  short essay items, 495
  true-false items, 494
  See also Aptitude tests
Acquisition phase, as event of
  learning, 196–97
ACT, See American College
  Testing (ACT) program
Adapting instruction, 436–37
  communication mode
    adaptations, 437
  content adaptations, 436–37
  format adaptations for written
    assignments, 436
  teaching of learning strategies,
    437
Adolescent development, 78–92,
  94
  and classroom management,
    372–75
  cognitive, 81–83
    combinational systems,
      82–83
    hypothetical conditions, 83
    Piagetian theory, 81–82
  education, 85
  emotional conflicts, 90–91
  physical, 79–81
  problems of adolescence, 90–
    92
  socioemotional, 83–90
    autonomy, 86
    conformity, 86
    dating, 90
    friendships, 86, 89
    identity, 84–86
    interpersonal development,
      86
    intimacy, 86–90
    reflectivity, 83
Adult tutoring, 303–4

Advance organizers, 166–68, 195,
  201
Affective objectives, 217–18
  and discussions, 259
Aggressive behavior, 414, 443
  gender differences in, 468
  in middle childhood, 78
  See also Misbehavior; Serious
    misbehavior/delinquency
Alcohol abuse, 91, 415–16, 443
Allocated time for instruction,
  365–66
  avoiding interruptions, 365–66
  avoiding late starts/early
    finishes, 365
  handling routine procedures,
    366
  minimizing discipline time, 366
Allocation of mental resources,
  142–44
American College Testing (ACT)
  program, 510, 511, 532
"American Government
  Simulation Series," 341
Antecedent stimuli, 117–18
*Anti-intellectualism in American
  Culture* (Hofstadter), 182
Anxiety, 336–37
  and stuttering, 419
Applied behavior analysis, See
  Behavior analysis
Apprehending phase, as event of
  learning, 195–96
Aptitude tests, 512, 513–14
  general intelligence tests, 513
  multifactor aptitude tests, 513–
    14
  See also Achievement tests;
    Standardized tests; Tests
Aptitude-treatment interactions,
  281
Assessment:
  frequency of, 345
  and Individualized Education
    Programs (IEPs), 428
  and instructional objectives,
    210–12
  and lessons, 250–51
  and quizzes, 345, 357
  See also Achievement tests;
    Student evaluations; Tests
Assimilation, 26

Attention, 133–35
  directing, 198
  maintaining, 135
  and new material presentations,
    245
Attentional phase, modeling, 120
Attention deficit, 410
Attribution theory, 324–28, 356–
  57
  definition, 324–25
  importance to education, 326–
    28
  locus of control, 325–26
Authoritarian parents, 65
Authoritative parents, 65
Autism, 415
Automatization, 143–44
Autonomous reality, 45, 47
Autonomy:
  in adolescence, 86
  vs. doubt, 41
Aversive stimuli, 106

Backward planning process, 222
Behavioral disorders, 415–18
  alcohol abuse, 415–16
  child abuse and neglect, 417–18
  delinquency, 416
  drug abuse, 415–16
  and family issues, 416–17
Behavioral learning theories, 97–
  127
  applications, 123
  classical conditioning, 99–101
  law of effect, 101–2
  learning:
    definition, 98–99
    theories of, 99
  operant conditioning, 102–3
  principles of, 104–19
    antecedent stimuli, 117–18
    consequences, immediacy of,
      107–9
    discrimination, 118
    extinction, 111–12
    generalization, 118–19
    maintenance, 115–17
    punishers, 106–7
    reinforcers, 104–6
    schedules of reinforcement,
      112–15
    shaping, 109–10

Reinforcement schedules, *See*
  Schedules of reinforcement
Reinforcers, 104–6, 117
  definition, 104
  and misbehavior, 379–80
  and motivation, 319
  negative, 104–6
  positive, 104–6
  and Premack Principle, 106
  primary, 104
  secondary, 104
  See also Feedback; Punishers;
    Rewards
Reintegration, following serious
  misbehavior, 397
Relative grading standards, 500–
  502
Reliability:
  tests, 525–30, 532
    adequacy of, 525–30
    criterion-referenced tests,
      530
  See also Validity
Remediation, 304
Remembering, 157–58
Report card grades, 503–4
  See also Student evaluation
Reproduction phase, modeling,
  120
Research:
  on between-class ability
    grouping, 283–84
  on bilingual education, 465–66
  on compensatory education,
    454–56
  on computer-assisted instruction
    (CAI), 309–11
  descriptive, 16–17
  on educational psychology, 6–7
  on feedback, 352
  on instructional objectives,
    218–19
  on mainstreaming, 434–38
  on mastery learning, 298
  on open education, 267–68
  on peer tutoring, 303–4
  on programmed instruction,
    300–301
  on small-group discussions,
    262–64
  on team-assisted
    individualization (TAI),
    301
  on within-class ability grouping,
    285–87
Research methods, 10–20
  correlation studies, 13–16
  descriptive research, 16–17
  experiments, 10–13
Restricted test format, 535–36
Retention phase:
  as event of instruction, 198
  as event of learning, 197
  modeling, 120
Retroactive facilitation, 145
Retroactive inhibition, 144
  reducing, 147
Reversability, 31

Reverse chaining, 110
Review:
  prerequisites, 242–43, 271
  providing, 252
  See also Lessons
Rewards:
  availability of, 346–47
  for effort/improvement, 352–56
    behavior modification/home-
      based reinforcement
      strategies, 353
    cooperation and competition,
      353
    cooperative learning methods,
      354–56
  as extrinsic motivator, 348, 357
  frequency of, 345
  value of, 345–46
  See also Punishers; Reinforcers
Rhyming, 153
Role confusion:
  and identity foreclosure, 85
  vs. identity, 41–42
Rote learning:
  definition, 162
  and meaningful learning, 162–
    64
Routine misbehavior, *See*
  Misbehavior
Routine procedures, handling,
  366
Rule-example-rule, 179, 202

SATs, *See* Scholastic Achievement
  Tests (SATs)
Schedules of reinforcement, 112–
  15
  fixed interval (FI), 114, 115
  fixed ratio (FR), 113, 114, 115
  variable interval (VI), 114–15
  variable ratio (VR), 113, 114,
    115
Schemata, definition, 139
Schemata theory, 164–69
  advance organizers, 166–68
  generative learning, 166
  hierarchical organization, 168–
    69
  and meaningful learning, 164–
    65
Schemes, definition, 26
Scholastic Achievement Tests
  (SATs), 458, 510, 511,
  532, 538
  transforming into IQ scores,
    521
School desegregation, *See*
  Desegregation
Scores, tests, *See* Test scores
Screening, and Individualized
  Education Programs
  (IEPs), 428
Seatwork, 249
Secondary reinforcers, 104
Seizure disorders, 422–23
Self-absorption vs. generativity, 43
Self-actualization, 321–22
Self-concept, 74, 84

Self-esteem, of learning-disabled
  students, 410
Self-regulation, 121–23
Semantic memory, 138, 139–41
Sensorimotor stage, 28–29
  and intentional behavior, 28–29
  and trial-and-error learning, 29
Sensory register, 130–35
  attention, 133–35
  Gestalt psychology, 132–33
  perception, 131–32
Serial learning, 149, 152, 153
Serious emotional disturbance,
  413–15, 443
  aggressive behavior, 414
  autism, 415
  characteristics of students with,
    413–14
  childhood schizophrenia, 415
  definition, 413
  hyperactivity, 414–15
  immature behavior, 414
  psychotic disorders, 415
  withdrawn behavior, 414
  See also Aggressive behavior;
    Behavior disorders
Serious misbehavior/delinquency,
  91, 378–82, 394–98, 416,
  443
  managing, 378–79
  preventing, 394–98
  and reinforcers, 379–82
  See also Discipline; Misbehavior
Sex bias, in curriculum materials,
  469–70
Sex-role stereotyping, avoiding,
  469–70
Sexual activity, in adolescence, 80,
  91
Sexual intimacy, 88–89
Shaping, 109–10, 126
  reverse chaining, 110
Short essay items:
  evaluating responses, 495–96
  writing, 495, 506
Short-term memory, 136–37
  and rehearsal, 136
Simulation programs, 307
Simulations, 341–42
Single-case experiments, 13
Skinner box, 102, 103, 115
Skinner's learning theories, 17
Small-group discussions, 262–64,
  272
Smoothness of instruction,
  maintaining, 367–68
Social class, 449–56, 473
  compensatory education, 452–
    56
  and future time orientation, 451
  implications for teachers, 451–
    52
  and individuality, 451
  schools as middle-class
    institutions, 451–52
  socioeconomic status (SES),
    defined, 449
Social-class differences, 471–73

in academic achievement, 450
in child-rearing practices, 449–
  50
Social learning theory, 119–23
  modeling, 119–21
    attentional phase, 120
    motivational phase, 120–21
    reproduction phase, 120
    retention phase, 120
    vicarious learning, 121
  self-regulation, 121–23
Sociodramatic play, 67
Socioemotional development:
  in adolescence, 83–90
    autonomy, 86
    conformity, 86
    dating, 90
    friendships, 86, 89
    identity, 84–86
    interpersonal development,
      86
    intimacy, 86–90
    reflectivity, 83
  in early childhood, 64–66
    friendships, 66
    parenting, 65
    peer relationships, 65–66
    psychosocial development,
      64–65
    encouraging, 88
  in middle childhood, 74–78
    emotions, 78
    parents, 74
    peers, 74–76
    self-concept, 74
  See also Piaget's theory of
    cognitive development;
    Psychosocial development
Software, 306–7
Soundly based evaluations,
  definition, 480
"Spanish detention," 462
Special education, 423–32
  continuum of services, 425–32,
    443
    consultation and itinerant
      services, 427
    homebound instruction, 432
    regular classroom placement,
      426
    resource room placement,
      427
    self-contained special
      education, 427–28
    special class placement with
      part-time mainstreaming,
      427
  definition, 423
  Public Law 94–142, 423–25
    Individualized Education
      Program (IEP), 424–25
    least restrictive environment,
      424
  See also Exceptional students;
    Mainstreaming
Specific instructional objectives,
  208–9
Specificity, studying and, 178

Notes

Notes

Notes

Notes

Notes

Notes

Notes

Notes